AF828123

THE FUTURE OF IP: STIMULATING CREATIVITY AND INCLUSIVITY

Photographer: Rob Stevens

THE FUTURE OF IP: STIMULATING CREATIVITY AND INCLUSIVITY

Liber Amicorum Geertrui Van Overwalle

Edited by
Amandine LÉONARD
Arina GORBATYUK
Esther VAN ZIMMEREN

INTERSENTIA
LEFEBVRE GROUP

Intersentia
Lefebvre Belgium SA
Avenue Jean Monnet 4
1348 Louvain-la-Neuve
Belgium
Email: contact@larcier-intersentia.com

Distribution for the UK, Ireland and
Rest of the World (excl. France, Belgium and Luxembourg)
Ingram Publisher Services UK
1 Deltic Avenue, Rooksley
Milton Keynes MK13 8LD
United Kingdom
Tel: +44 1752 202 301 | Fax: +44 1752 202 331
Email: ipsuk.customercare@ingramcontent.com

Distribution for France and Rest of the World (excl. Ireland and the UK)
Interforum Editis
Avenue de France 92
75013 Paris
France

Distribution for Belgium and Luxembourg
Larcier-Intersentia
Avenue Jean Monnet 4
1348 Louvain-la-Neuve
Belgium

The Future of IP: Stimulating Creativity and Inclusivity. Liber Amicorum Geertrui Van Overwalle

© The editors and contributors severally 2025

The editors and contributors have asserted the right under the Copyright, Designs and Patents Act 1988, to be identified as authors of this work.

No part of this book may be reproduced, stored in a retrieval system, or transmitted, in any form, or by any means, without prior written permission from Intersentia, or as expressly permitted by law or under the terms agreed with the appropriate reprographic rights organisation. Enquiries concerning reproduction which may not be covered by the above should be addressed to Intersentia at the address above.

Cover design by Danny Juchtmans / www.dsigngraphics.be
Illustrations: Jacques Carelman, Catalog of Fantastic Things (Ballantine Books, New York 1971)
© SABAM Belgium 2025

ISBN 978-1-83970-595-3
D/2025/06040/0517
NUR 820

British Library Cataloguing in Publication Data. A catalogue record for this book is available from the British Library.

BIOGRAPHY OF GEERTRUI VAN OVERWALLE

Geertrui Van Overwalle (°1958) has been one of the leading voices of the European intellectual property (IP) law scholarship for nearly four decades. After earning her Master of Laws *magna cum laude* from KU Leuven in 1985, she went on to complete her PhD in 1995 on 'the Patentability of Plants'.

She joined the Centre for Intellectual Property Rights in 1991 and later became part of the Centre for IT and IP Law (CiTiP) where she served until her retirement as a full professor in 2023. Alongside her work at KU Leuven, she held professorships at Tilburg University, the University of Liège, and SciencesPo, and was a visiting scholar at universities across Europe, Asia, and Australia.

Her research explores patent law at national, European, and international levels, focusing on the balance between exclusivity and inclusivity, and the tension between individual and public interest. Initially centred on biotechnology and genetics, her work expanded to ICT, 3D printing, sharing platforms, the circular economy, and AI. In addition, she extensively contributed to advancing legal research methodology and introducing empirical approaches such as case studies, surveys, and interviews into IP scholarship.

As an educator, Geertrui taught graduate and postgraduate courses on IP law, patent law, life sciences, and plant breeder's law, and inspired students to pursue careers in these fields, whether in practice, policy, or academia. As a scholar, she supervised and collaborated with numerous PhD, postdoctoral, and master's students, advancing European IP scholarship, including in such challenging areas as biotechnology, genetics, and public health.

Her expertise was sought by leading research, policy, and ethics bodies worldwide. She was an active member of the International Association of the Advancement of Teaching and Research in IP (ATRIP), the International Association for the Study of the Commons, and the European Policy for IP (EPIP). She also served on the Scientific Advisory Board of the Max Planck Institute for Innovation and Competition and the European Patent Office's (EPO) Economic and Scientific Advisory Board. Geertrui played an influential role in the Board of Appeal of the Community Plant Variety Office and the Belgian High Council for Intellectual Property. The European Commission sought her advice on biotechnological inventions, and she contributed her expertise to the Unitaid Medicines Patent Pool, policy reports for the European Parliament, and the Expert Group on Ethics in Science and New Technologies. In Belgium, she actively advised the Federal Council for Sustainable Development and the Belgian Advisory Committee on Bioethics.

Throughout her career, she combined academic leadership with impactful contributions to policy, ethics, and access to innovation.

PUBLICATIONS OF GEERTRUI VAN OVERWALLE

ARTICLES IN INTERNATIONAL JOURNALS

Van Overwalle, Geertrui (2020), 'Will Covid Patents Save the World?', Gewerblicher Rechtsschutz und Urheberrecht – Internationaler Teil (GRUR-Int), Vol. 69 (9), pp. 883–884

Nicol, Dianne; Dreyfuss, Rochelle; Gold, E Richard; Li, Wei; Liddicoat, John and **Van Overwalle, Geertrui** (2019), 'International Divergence in Gene Patenting', Annual Review of Genomics and Human Genetics, Vol. 20, pp. 519–541

Van Dycke, Lodewijk and **Van Overwalle, Geertrui** (2017), 'Genetically Modified Crops and Intellectual Property Law: Interpreting Indian Patents on Bt Cotton in View of the Socio-Political Background', Journal of Intellectual Property, Information Technology and Electronic Commerce Law (JIPITEC), Vol. 8(2), pp. 151–165

Van Overwalle, Geertrui and Leys, Reinout (2017), '3D Printing and Patent Law: A Disruptive Technology Disrupting Patent Law?', International Review of Intellectual Property and Competition Law (IIC), Vol. 48(5), pp. 504–537

Gorbatyuk, Arina; **Van Overwalle, Geertrui** and van Zimmeren, Esther (2016), 'Intellectual Property Ownership in Coupled Open Innovation Processes', International Review of Intellectual Property and Competition Law (IIC), Vol. 47(3), pp. 262–302

Lamping, Matthias; Hilty, Reto; Burk, Dan L.; Correa, Carlos M.; Drahos, Peter; Gopalakrishnan, N.S.; Grosse Ruse-Khan, Henning; Kur, Annette; **Van Overwalle, Geertrui**; Reichman, Jerome H. and Ullrich, Hanns (2014), Declaration on Patent Protection – Regulatory Sovereignty under TRIPS, International Review of Intellectual Property and Competition Law (IIC), Vol. 45(6), pp. 679–698

Stevens, Hilde; **Van Overwalle, Geertrui**; Van Looy, Bart and Huys, Isabelle (2016), 'Intellectual property policies in early-phase research in public–private partnerships', Nature Biotechnology, Vol. 34(5), pp. 504–510

Stevens, Hilde; **Van Overwalle, Geertrui**; Van Looy, Bart and Huys, Isabelle (2015), 'Innovative Medicines Initiative (IMI) Case Study Analysis Reveals the True Added Value of Early-Phase Public-Private Partnerships (PPPs)', Biotechnology Law Report, Vol. 34(4), pp. 153–165

Van Overwalle, Geertrui (2015), 'Inventing Inclusive Patents. From Old to New Open Innovation', in: Drahos, Peter; Ghidini Gustavo and Ullrich, Hanns Kritika, Vol. 1(1), pp. 206–277

Matthijs, Gert; Huys, Isabelle; **Van Overwalle, Geertrui** and Stoppa-Lyonnet, Dominique (2013), 'The European BRCA Patent Oppositions and Appeals: Coloring inside the Lines', Nature Biotechnology, Vol. 31(8), pp. 704–710

Stevens, Hilde; **Van Overwalle, Geertrui**; Van Looy, Bart and Huys, Isabelle (2013), 'Perspectives and Opportunities for Precompetitive Public-Private Partnerships in the Biomedical Sector', Biotechnology Law Report, Vol. 32, pp. 131–139

Van Overwalle, Geertrui (2013), 'Exclusive Property versus Open Commons. The Case of Gene Patents', The WIPO Journal: Analysis and Debate of Intellectual Property Issues, Vol. 13, pp. 139–158

Huys, Isabelle; Matthijs, Gert and **Van Overwalle, Geertrui** (2012), 'The Fate and Future of Patents on Human Genes and Genetic Diagnostic Methods', Vol. 13(6) Nature Reviews Genetics, Vol. 13(6), pp. 441–448

Van Overwalle, Geertrui (2011), 'Policy Levers Tailoring Patent Law to Biotechnology. Comparing U.S. and European Approaches', University of California (UC) Irvine Law Review, pp. 435–517

Huys, Isabelle; Du Plessis, Mariette; Waer, Christophe; **Van Overwalle, Geertrui** and Van Looy, Bart. (2011), 'The Impact of Legislative Framework Conditions on the Development of Stem Cell Technology: Assessment of National Innovation Systems', Biotechnology Law Report, Vol. 30, pp. 191–196

Van Zimmeren, Esther; Vanneste, Sven; Matthijs, Gert; Vanhaverbeke, Wim and **Van Overwalle, Geertrui** (2011), 'Patent Pools and Clearinghouses in the Life Sciences', Trends in Biotechnology, Vol. 29(11), pp. 569–576

Huys, Isabelle; Matthijs, Gert and **Van Overwalle, Geertrui** (2011), 'Gene and Genetic Diagnostic Method Patent Claims. A Comparison under current European and US Patent Law', European Journal of Human Genetics (EJHG), Vol. 19(10), pp. 1104–1107

Berthels, Nele; Matthijs, Gert and **Van Overwalle, Geertrui** (2011), 'Impact of gene patents on diagnostic testing: a new patent landscaping method applied to spinocerebellar ataxia', European Journal of Human Genetics (EJHG), Vol. 19(10), pp. 1114–1121 van Zimmeren, Esther and **Van Overwalle, Geertrui** (2011), 'A Paper Tiger? Compulsory License Regimes for Public Health in Europe', International Review of Intellectual Property and Competition Law (IIC), Vol. 42(1), pp. 4–40

Van Overwalle, Geertrui (2011), 'The CJEU Monsanto Soybean Decision and Patent Scope: As Clear As Mud', International Review of Intellectual Property and Competition Law (IIC), Vol. 42(1), pp. 1–3

Van Overwalle, Geertrui (2010), 'Turning Patent Swords into Shares', Science, Vol. 330 (issue 6011), pp. 1630–1631

Huys, Isabelle; Berthels, Nele; Matthijs, Gert and **Van Overwalle, Geertrui** (2009), 'Legal Uncertainty in the Area of Genetic Diagnostic Testing', Nature Biotechnology, Vol. 27, pp. 903–909

Van Overwalle, Geertrui and Schovsbo, Jens (2007), 'Policy Options for the Improvement of the European Patent System', International Review of Intellectual Property and Competition Law (IIC), Vol. 38, pp. 834–838

Van Overwalle, Geertrui; Van Zimmeren, Esther; Verbeure, Birgit and Matthijs, Gert (2007), 'Dealing with Patent Fragmentation in ICT and Genetics: Patent Pools and Clearing Houses', First Monday, May 2007

Van Overwalle, Geertrui (2007), 'Patent Law in Crisis? Functions and Limits of the Patent System in a Globalised World', Revue de la Faculté de Droit de l'Université de Liège, pp. 317–322

Van Overwalle, Geertrui (2006), 'The Implementation of the Biotechnology Directive in Belgium and its Aftereffects. The Introduction of a New Research Exemption and a Compulsory License for Public Health', International Review of Intellectual Property and Competition Law (IIC), Vol. 37, pp. 889–920

Van Zimmeren, Esther; Verbeure, Birgit; Matthijs, Gert and **Van Overwalle, Geertrui** (2006), 'A Clearinghouse for Diagnostic Testing: the Solution to Ensure Access to and Use of Patented Genetic Inventions?', Bulletin of the World Health Organization, Vol. 84(5), pp. 352–359.

Verbeure, Birgit; Van Zimmeren, Esther; Matthijs, Gert and **Van Overwalle, Geertrui** (2006), 'Patent pools and diagnostic testing', Trends in Biotechnology (TIB), Vol. 24(3), pp. 115–120

Van Overwalle, Geertrui; Van Zimmeren, Esther; Verbeure, Birgit and Matthijs, Gert (2006), 'Models for facilitating access to patents on genetic inventions', Nature Review Genetics, Vol. 7, pp. 143–148

Verbeure, Birgit; Matthijs, Gert and **Van Overwalle, Geertrui** (2006), 'Analysing DNA patents in relation with diagnostic genetic testing', European Journal of Human Genetics (EJHG), Vol. 14(1), pp. 26–33

Van Overwalle, Geertrui (2005), 'Protecting and Sharing Biodiversity and Traditional Knowledge: Holder and User Tools', Ecological Economics, Vol. 53(4), pp. 585–607

Van Overwalle, Geertrui (2006), 'Reconciling Patent Policies and University Mission', Ethical Perspectives, Vol. 13, pp. 231–247

Van Overwalle, Geertrui and van Zimmeren, Esther (2006), 'Reshaping Belgian Patent Law: The Revision of the Research Exemption and the Introduction of a Compulsory License for Public Health', IIP Forum (Japan), pp. 42–49, available at: www.iip.or.jp/e/index.html

Van Overwalle, Geertrui (2003), 'Bio-Patents, Law and Ethics. Critical Analysis of the EU Biotechnology Directive', Revista de Derecho y Genoma Humano – Law and the Human Genome Review, Vol. 19, pp. 187–203, available at: http://ssrn.com/abstract=1718674

Van Overwalle, Geertrui (2002), 'Belgium Goes Its Own Way on Biodiversity and Patents', European Intellectual Property Review (EIPR), pp. 233–236

Jacobs, Philippe and **Van Overwalle, Geertrui** (2001), 'Gene Patents: A Different Approach', European Intellectual Property Review (EIPR), pp. 505–506

Van Overwalle, Geertrui (2000), 'The Legal Protection of Biological Material in Belgium', International Review of Industrial Property and Copyright Law (IIC), Vol. 31(3), pp. 259–284

Van Overwalle, Geertrui (1999), 'Patent Protection for Plants: a Comparison of American and European Approaches', IDEA-Journal of Law and Technology, Vol. 39, pp. 143–194

ARTICLES IN NATIONAL JOURNALS

Van Overwalle, Geertrui (2017), 'Plant Patents: From Exclusivity to Inclusivity', Berichten industriële eigendom (BIE) – Special – Afscheidsnummer Paul van der Kooij, maart 2017, pp. 29–32

Van Overwalle, Geertrui and Schellekens, Maurice (2011), 'Test je rijk: genoctrooien en gezondheid', Ars Aequi, Bijzonder nummer Gezondheidsrecht, Vol. 60, pp. 519–525

Van Overwalle, Geertrui (2006), 'De implementatie van de EU-Biotechnologierichtlijn: de Belgische octrooiwet in spreidstand', Tijdschrift voor Belgisch Handelsrecht (TBH), pp. 571–576

Van Overwalle, Geertrui (2005), 'Zonder trommels en trompetten. De definitieve omzetting van de EU-Biotechnologierichtlijn in het Belgisch recht', Intellectuele Rechten – Droits Intellectuels (IRDI), pp. 349–378

Van Overwalle, Geertrui (2003), 'Over kwekers, boeren en trieerders: driehoeksverhoudingen in het kwekersrecht onder de loep', noot bij Rechtbank van Koophandel Hoei, 14 mei 2003 en 18 mei 2004, Intellectuele Rechten – Droits Intellectuels (IRDI), pp. 168–169

Van Overwalle, Geertrui (2004), 'Van groene muizen met rode oortjes: de EU-Biotechnologierichtlijn en het Belgisch wetsontwerp van 21 september 2004', Intellectuele Rechten – Droits Intellectuels (IRDI), pp. 357–386

Van Overwalle, Geertrui (2004), 'Landbouwersvoorrecht en informatieplicht', noot bij Arrest Hof van Justitie, 10 april 2003 (Prejudiciële vraag vanwege Oberlandesgericht Frankfurt am Main, gerezen in een geding tussen C. Schulin, landbouwer, en Saatgut-Treuhandverwaltungsgesellschaft mbH, een Duitse maatschappij voor het beheer van teeltmateriaal), Intellectuele Rechten – Droits Intellectuels (IRDI), pp. 262–264

Van Overwalle, Geertrui (2003), 'Academische kennis, octrooirecht en ethiek: een netelige verkenning', Ethische Perspectieven, Vol. 13, pp. 8–20

Van Overwalle, Geertrui (2003), 'De Belgische implementatie van de Biotechnologierichtlijn: het parlement is aan zet', Tijdschrift voor Europees en Economisch Recht (SEW), pp. 311–313

Van Overwalle, Geertrui (2002–2003), 'Van muizen en mensen. De EU-Biotechnologierichtlijn van 6 juli 1998 en de omzetting in het Belgisch octrooirecht', Rechtskundig Weekblad (RW), pp. 401–415

Van Overwalle, Geertrui (2001), 'Traditional Medicinal Knowledge, Patents and the Convention on Biological Diversity', Revue de droit intellectuel – l'Ingénieur Conseil, pp. 161–182

Jacobs, Philippe and **Van Overwalle, Geertrui** (2001), 'Octrooien op genen. Naschrift', Bijblad bij de Industriële Eigendom, pp. 221–222

Jacobs, Philippe and **Van Overwalle, Geertrui** (2001), 'Octrooien op genen: een alternatieve benadering', Bijblad bij de Industriële Eigendom, pp. 113–116

Van Overwalle, Geertrui (2000), 'Klinische proeven en volksgezondheid. Naar een herijking van het algemeen belang in het octrooirecht', Tijdschrift voor Privaatrecht (TPR), pp. 899–968

Van Overwalle, Geertrui (1999), 'Octrooien voor planten onder de EG-Biotechnologierichtlijn van 6 juli 1998', Agrarisch recht (NL), pp. 111–127; Tijdschrift voor Agrarisch Recht (BE), pp. 1–15

Van Overwalle, Geertrui (1998), 'Europese harmonisatie in het octrooirecht, het kwekersrecht en het gebruiksmodellenrecht: van wiel naar mens naar wieltje', Intellectuele Rechten – Droits Intellectuels (IRDI), pp. 149–168

Van Overwalle, Geertrui (1997), 'TRIPs en het octrooirecht', Intellectuele Rechten - Droits Intellectuels (IRDI), pp. 222–244

Van Overwalle, Geertrui (1993), 'Biotechnologie en milieuwetgeving', Milieurecht-Info, Afl. 8, pp. 1–9

Van Overwalle, Geertrui (1993), 'Recht op zoek naar Nederlandstalige terminologie', Vlaams Jurist Vandaag, pp. 26–29

Van Overwalle, Geertrui (1988), 'Het Nederlandstalig juridisch tijdschrift in België: een analyse', Vlaams Jurist Vandaag, pp. 12–27

BOOKS

Van Zimmeren, Esther; Vanneste, Sven and **Van Overwalle, Geertrui** (2011), Patent Licensing in Medical Biotechnology in Europe: A Role for Collaborative Licensing Strategies?, 145 p. (Leuven, Academic Cooperative Publishers (ACCO)

Van Overwalle, Geertrui (2002), Study on the patenting of inventions related to human stem cell research, European Communities, Luxembourg, 218 p., available at: http://ec.europa.eu/european_group_ethics/publications/docs/stud_vanoverw_en.pdf

Van Overwalle, Geertrui (1997), The Legal Protection of Biotechnological Inventions in Europe and in the United States. Current Framework and Future Developments, in Leuven Law Series, 78 p. (Leuven, University Press)

Van Overwalle, Geertrui (1996), Octrooieerbaarheid van plantenbiotechnologische uitvindingen. Een rechtsvergelijkend onderzoek naar een rechtvaardiging van een uitbreiding van het octrooirecht tot planten – Patentability of Plant Biotechnological Inventions. A Comparative Study towards a Justification of Extending Patent Law to Plants, 739 p. (Brussels, Bruylant)

Herboth, Jacques and **Van Overwalle, Geertrui** (1986), Juridische heuristiek en juridische vaardigheden, 213 p. (Leuven, ACCO)

(CO-)EDITED BOOKS

Godt, Christine; **Van Overwalle, Geertrui**; Guibault, Lucie and Beyleveld, Deryck (eds.) (2022), Boundaries to Information Property (Cambridge, Intersentia)

De Weyer, Jessie; Janssens, Marie-Christine; Leonard, Amandine and **Van Overwalle, Geertrui** (eds.) (2016), IP Intellectuele Eigendom/Propriété Intellectuelle. Wetboek/Code 2016–2017 (Brussels, Larcier)

De Weyer, Jessie; Janssens, Marie-Christine; Leonard, Amandine and **Van Overwalle, Geertrui** (eds.) (2015), IP Intellectuele Eigendom/Propriété Intellectuelle. Wetboek/Code 2015–2016 (Brussels, Larcier)

Janssens, Marie-Christine and **Van Overwalle, Geertrui** (eds.) (2012), Harmonisation of European IP Law. From European Rules to Belgian Law and Practice. Contributions in honour of Frank Gotzen, (CIR-Reeks 23), 334 p. (Brussels, Bruylant-Larcier)

Gotzen, Frank; Janssens, Marie-Christine and **Van Overwalle, Geertrui** (eds.) (2011), Intellectuele Rechten, 96 p. (Bruges, Die Keure)

Van Overwalle, Geertrui (ed.) (2009), Gene Patents and Collaborative Licensing Models. Patent Pools, Clearinghouses, Open Source Models and Liability Regimes, 477 p. (Cambridge, Cambridge University Press)

Van Overwalle, Geertrui (ed.) (2007), Gene Patents and Public Health, 241 p. (Brussels, Bruylant)

Pattyn, Bart and **Van Overwalle, Geertrui** (eds.) (2006), Tussen Markt en Agora. Over het statuut van universitaire kennis, 216 p. (Leuven, Peeters)

Van Overwalle, Geertrui (ed.) (2001), Naar een nieuw Europees octrooirecht – Vers un nouveau droit europeén des brevets – Towards a new European patent law' (Proceedings of the Symposium organised by the Centre for Intellectual Property Rights, Leuven, 18.05.2001), Intellectuele Rechten – Droits Intellectuels (IRDI) (Gent, Mys & Breesch)

Van Overwalle, Geertrui (ed.) (2000), Octrooirecht en geneesmiddelen, (CIR-Reeks 16), 166 p. (Brussels, Bruylant)

Van Overwalle, Geertrui (ed.) (1998), Octrooirecht, ethiek en biotechnologie – Patent Law, Ethics and Biotechnology – Droit des brevets, éthique et biotechnologie, (CIR-Reeks 13), 182 p. (Brussels, Bruylant)

CHAPTERS IN BOOKS

Van Overwalle, Geertrui and Van Dycke, Lodewijk (2024), 'It Takes Two to Tango. Patents and Markets in the Periphery and the Centre. Prebisch Dancing with Hilty', in: Kreation Innovation Märkte – Creation Innovation Markets' Festschrift Reto M. Hilty, pp. 807–832 (Berlin, Springer)

Van Overwalle, Geertrui and Granata, Sam (2023), 'Recente ontwikkelingen in het octrooirecht', in: Themis IP- en ICT-Recht, Vol. 125, pp. 57–80 (Antwerp, Intersentia)

Van Overwalle, Geertrui (2023), 'Food Security, Food Crisis and Boundaries to Intellectual Property', in: Frankel, Susy; Chon, Margaret; Dinwoodie, Graeme B.; Lauriat, Barbara and Schovsbo, Jens (eds.), Improving Intellectual Property. A Global Project, pp. 75–86 (Cheltenham, Edward Elgar)

Van Overwalle, Geertrui (2023), 'Voedselzekerheid, voedselcrisis en grenzen aan intellectuele eigendom', in: Recht in beweging, Verslagboek 30e VRG-Alumnidag, pp. 215–226 (Antwerp, Gompel & Svacina)

Van Overwalle, Geertrui and Léonard, Amandine (2023), 'The Public Interest in Compulsory Licensing: Examining the Complementarity Between IP and Competition Law', in: Godt, Christine and Lamping, Matthias (eds.), A Critical Mind, Hanns Ullrich's Footprint in Internal Market Law, Antitrust and Intellectual Property, Vol. 30, pp. 331–365 (Berlin, Springer)

Van Overwalle, Geertrui (2022), 'Regulation Theory and Intellectual Property Law', in: Godt, Christine; Van Overwalle, Geertrui; Guibault, Lucie and Beyleveld, Deryck (eds.), Boundaries to Information Property, pp. 33–56 (Cambridge, Intersentia)

Van Overwalle, Geertrui (2022), 'Comparative Remarks on Farmer's Rights', in: Godt, Christine; Van Overwalle, Geertrui; Guibault, Lucie and Beyleveld, Deryck (eds.), Boundaries to Information Property, pp. 520–528 (Cambridge, Intersentia)

Van Overwalle, Geertrui (2021), 'Heisa rond COVID-octrooien. Staan octrooien een brede toegang tot gezondheidszorg in de weg', in: Recht in beweging, Verslagboek 28e VRG-Alumnidag, pp. 245–258 (Antwerp, Gompel & Svacina)

Van Overwalle, Geertrui (2021), 'Rethinking IP Protection for Plants? Revisiting the Exclusivity-Access Balance through the Type-Token Ontology', in: Sikorski, Rafał and Zemła Pacud, Żaneta (eds.), Patents as an Incentive for Innovation, pp. 145–159 (Alphen aan de Rijn, Kluwer Law International)

Van Overwalle, Geertrui (2020), 'Gene Patents and Human Rights', in: Torremans, Paul L. C. (ed.), Intellectual Property Law and Human Rights, pp. 101–1062 (Alphen aan de Rijn, Kluwer Law International)

Van Overwalle, Geertrui and Kestemont, Lina (2021), 'Multidisciplinary Legal Research: Science and Technology as an Object of Study in IP Research', in: Calboli, Irene and Montagnani, Lila, Maria (eds.), Approaches and Methodologies in Intellectual Property Research, pp. 434–452 (Cambridge, Cambridge University Press)

Van Overwalle, Geertrui (2018), 'Beslag inzake namaak in het octrooirecht: recente ontwikkelingen vanuit Belgisch en Europees perspectief', in: IP- & ICT-recht, pp. 77–103 (Bruges, Die Keure)

Van Overwalle, Geertrui (2018), 'Creating universal and sustainable access to plants and seeds: the role of clearinghouses, open source licenses and inclusive patents', in: Girard, Fabien and Frison, Christine (eds.), Commons, Plant Breeding and Agricultural Research: Challenges for Food Security and Agrobiodiversity, pp. 88–106 (Earthscan/Routledge, Abingdon/New York)

Van Overwalle, Geertrui (2017), 'Patent Pools and Clearinghouses in the Life Sciences: Back to the Future', in: Matthews, Duncan and Zech, Herbert, Research Handbook on Intellectual Property and the Life Sciences, pp. 304–334 (Cheltenham, Edward Elgar)

Van Overwalle, Geertrui (2016), 'Innovation without Property?', in: Achten, Veerle; Bouckaert, Geert and Schokkaert, Erik (eds.), 'A Truly Golden Handbook': The Scholarly Quest for Utopia, pp. 300–314 (Leuven, Leuven University Press)

Larouche, Pierre and **Van Overwalle, Geertrui** (2015), 'Interoperability Standards, Patents and Competition Policy', in: Delimatsis, Panagiotis (ed.),The Law, Economics and Politics of International Standardization, pp. 367–393 (Cambridge, Cambridge University Press)

Van Overwalle, Geertrui (2015), 'Gene Patents and Human Rights', in: Torremans, Paul L. C. (ed.), Intellectual Property Law and Human Rights, pp. 87–914 (Alphen aan de Rijn, Kluwer Law International)

Van Overwalle, Geertrui (2014), 'Fair Use – A Workable Concept in European Patent Law?' in: Hilty, Reto and Liu, Kung-Chung (eds.), Compulsory Licensing, pp. 421–435 (Berlin, Springer)

Van Overwalle, Geertrui (2014), 'Governing Genomic Data: Plea for an 'Open Commons' in: Frischmann, Brett M.; Madison, Michael J. and Strandburg, Katherine J. (eds.) Governing the Knowledge Commons, pp. 137–153 (Oxford, Oxford University Press)

Van Zimmeren, Esther and **Van Overwalle, Geertrui** (2014), 'A False Sense of Security Offered by Zero-Price Liability Rules? Research Exceptions in the United States, Europe and Japan in an Open Innovation Context', in: Okediji, Ruth and Bagley, Margo A. (eds.), Patent Law in Global Perspective, pp. 379–417 (Oxford, Oxford University Press)

Van Overwalle, Geertrui (2013), 'The Impact of Emerging Market Patent Systems on Europe: Awaiting 'The Rape Of Europa'?, in: Abbott, Frederick M. and Correa, Carlos M. and Drahos, Peter (Eds.), Emerging Markets and the World Patent Order, pp. 355–368 (Cheltenham, Edward Elgar)

Van Overwalle, Geertrui (2013), 'Smart Innovation and Inclusive Patents for Sustainable Food and Health Care: Redefining the Europe 2020 Objectives', in: Geiger, Christophe (ed.), Constructing European Intellectual Property. Achievements and New Perspectives, pp. 231–254 (Cheltenham, Edward Elgar)

Van Overwalle, Geertrui (2012), 'Individualism, Collectivism and Openness in Patent Law: from Exclusion to Inclusion Through Licensing, in: Rósen, Jan (ed.), Individualism and Collectiveness in Intellectual Property Law, pp. 71–114 (Cheltenham, Edward Elgar)

Van Overwalle, Geertrui (2012), 'Wet 10 januari 2011 ter bescherming van kweekproducten' in: Brison, Fabienne; Janssens, Marie-Christine and Vanhees, Hendrik (eds.), Wet en Duiding Economisch Recht – Deel 1. Intellectuele Eigendom, pp. 532–560 (Brussels, Larcier)

Van Overwalle, Geertrui and van Zimmeren, Esther (2011), 'Recente ontwikkelingen in het octrooirecht', in: Gotzen, Frank and Janssen, Marie-Christine (eds.), Intellectuele Rechten, 53–75 (Bruges, Die Keure)

Van Overwalle, Geertrui (2011), 'Open innovatie en intellectuele eigendom', in: Pattyn, Bart en Raymaekers, Bart (eds.), Lessen voor de eenentwintigste eeuw 2011 - XXI. Europa, interdisciplinariteit en wetenschap, pp. 287-308 (Leuven, Universitaire Pers)

Van Overwalle, Geertrui (2011), 'Uncorking Trade Secrets: Sparking the Interaction Between Trade Secrecy and Open Biotechnology', in: Dreyfuss, Rochelle C. and Strandberg, Katherine (eds.), The Law and Theory of Trade Secrecy: A Handbook of Contemporary Research, pp. 246–268 (Cheltenham, Edward Elgar)

Van Overwalle, Geertrui (2010), 'De uitvinding van het algemeen belang. Over volksgezondheid, duurzame ontwikkeling en octrooirecht', in: Liber Amicorum Ludovic De Gryse, pp. 321–330 (Brussels, Larcier)

Van Overwalle, Geertrui (2010), 'IPR Issues and High Quality Genetic Testing', in: Kristoffersson, Ulf, Schmidtke, Jörg and Cassiman, Jean-Jacques (eds.), Quality Issues in Clinical Genetic Services, (eds.), pp. 251–265 (Berlin-Heidelberg, Springer)

Van Overwalle, Geertrui (2010), 'Human Rights' Limitations in Patent Law', in: Grosheide, Willem (ed.), Intellectual Property and Human Rights. A Paradox, pp. 236–271 (Cheltenham, Edward Elgar)

Van Overwalle, Geertrui (2010), 'Differential Pricing: Piercing or Fostering the IP Incentive for Public Health?', in: Godt, Christine (ed.), Differential Pricing of Pharmaceuticals inside Europe. Exploring Compulsory Licenses and Exhaustion for Access to Patented Essential Medicines, Schriftenreihe des Zentrums für Europäische Rechtspolitik (ZERP), No. 58, pp. 113–124 (Baden-Baden, Nomos)

Van Overwalle, Geertrui (2010), 'Designing Models to Clear Patent Thickets in Genetics', in: Dreyfuss, Rochelle C.; First, Harry and Zimmerman, Diane L. (eds.), Working within the Boundaries of Intellectual Property, pp. 305–324 (Oxford, Oxford University Press)

Van Overwalle, Geertrui (2009), 'Of Thickets, Blocks and Gaps: Designing Tools to Resolve Obstacles in the Gene Patents Landscape', in: **Van Overwalle, Geertrui** (ed.), Gene Patents and Collaborative Licensing Models. Patent Pools, Clearing Houses, Open Source Models and Liability Regimes, pp. 381–463 (Cambridge, Cambridge University Press)

Van Overwalle, Geertrui and van Zimmeren, Esther (2009), 'Functions and Limits of Patent Law', in: Claes, Erik; Devroe, Wouter and Keirsbilck, Bert (eds.), Facing the Limits of the Law, pp. 415–442 (Berlin-Heidelberg, Springer)

Van Overwalle, Geertrui (2009), 'A Man of Flowers. A Reflection on Plant Patents, the Right to Food and Competition Law', in: Drexl, Jozef (ed.), Technology and Competition – Technologie et concurrence. Contributions in honour of Hanns Ullrich Mélanges en l'honneur de Hanns Ullrich, pp. 355–372 (Brussels, Larcier)

Van Overwalle, Geertrui (2008), 'L' intérêt général, le domaine public, les commons et le droit des brevets d'invention', in: Buydens, Mireille and Dusollier, Severine (eds.), L'intérêt général et l'accès à l'information en propriété intellectuelle, pp. 149–175 (Brussels, Bruylant)

Van Overwalle, Geertrui (2008), 'Biotechnology and Patents: Global Standards, European Approaches and National Accents', in: Wuger, Daniel and Cottier, Thomas (eds.), Genetic Engineering and the World Trade System, pp. 77–108 (Cambridge, Cambridge University Press)

Van Overwalle, Geertrui and van Zimmeren, Esther (2008), 'Reshaping Belgian Patent Law: The Revision of the Research Exemption and the Introduction of a Compulsory License for Public Health', in: Reddy, Jayanthi P.L. (ed.), Compulsory Licensing: Developing Economies, pp. 168–181 (Hyderabad, Icfai University Press)

Van Overwalle, Geertrui and Berthels, Nele (2007), 'Patents and Venus. About oocytes and human embryonic stem cells', in Stem Cells and Women's Health – Cellules souches et santé des femmes – Stamcellen en vrouwengezondheid, pp. 148–178 (Louvain-la-Neuve, Anthemis-Intersentia)

Van Overwalle, Geertrui (2007), 'Regulating Protection, Preservation and Technology Transfer of Biodiversity-Based Drugs. Patents, Contracts and Local Working Requirements under the Microscope', in: Govaere, Inge and Ullrich, Hanns (eds.), Intellectual Property, Public Policy and International Trade, pp. 113–141 (Bruxelles-Bern-Berlin-Frankfurt am Main-New York-Oxford-Wien, Peter Lang)

Van Overwalle, Geertrui (2007), 'Gene Patents and Public Health. Setting the Scene', in: **Van Overwalle, Geertrui** (ed.), Gene Patents and Public Health, pp. 11–24 (Brussels, Bruylant)

Van Overwalle, Geertrui (2007), 'The Belgian Compulsory License for Public Health', in: **Van Overwalle, Geertrui** (ed.), Gene Patents and Public Health, pp. 199–209 (Brussels, Bruylant)

Van Overwalle, Geertrui (2007), 'Holder and User Perspectives in the Traditional Knowledge Debate: a European View', in: McManis, Charles R. (ed.), Biodiversity & the Law, pp. 355–370 (London-Sterling, EarthScan)

Van Overwalle, Geertrui (2007), 'Reshaping Bio-Patents: Measures to Restore Trust in the Patent System', in: Somsen, Han (ed.), The Regulatory Challenge of Biotechnology. Human Genetics, Food and Patents, pp. 238–256 (Cheltenham, Edward Elgar)

Van Overwalle, Geertrui (2006), 'IP Protection for Medicinal and Aromatic Plants', in: Bogers, Robert J., Craker, Lyle E. and Lange, Dagmar (eds.), Medicinal and Aromatic Plants. Agricultural, Commercial, Ecological, Legal, Pharmacological and Social Aspects, pp. 121–128 (Wageningen, Springer)

Van Overwalle, Geertrui (2006), 'Universitaire octrooien op maat? Naar een evenwicht tussen publieke opdracht en privaat goed', in: Pattyn, Bart and **Van Overwalle, Geertrui** (eds.), Tussen Markt en Agora. Over het statuut van universitaire kennis, pp.181–214 (Leuven, Peeters)

Van Overwalle, Geertrui (2005), 'Legal and Ethical Aspects of Bio-Patenting: Critical Analysis of the EU Biotechnology Directive', in: Drahos, Peter (ed.), Death of Patents, pp. 212–227 (Oxon, Lawtext Publishing)

Van Overwalle, Geertrui (2005), 'Patenting Stem Cell Research in Europe and in the United States', in: Bender, Wolfgang; Hauskeller, Christine and Manzei, Alexandra (eds.), Crossing Borders. Cultural, Religious and Political Differences Concerning Stem Cell Research, pp. 519–546 (Münster, agenda Verlag)

Van Overwalle, Geertrui (2003), 'Legal and Ethical Aspects of Bio-Patenting. A Critical Analysis of the EU Biotechnology Directive', in: Baumgartner, Christoph and Mieth, Dietmar (eds.), Patente am Leben? Ethische rechtliche und politische Aspekte der Biopatentierung, pp. 145–158 (Paderborn, Mentis)

Van Overwalle, Geertrui (2003), 'Juridische bescherming van biotechnologische uitvindingen', in: Repertorium Procestechnieken en – Engineering (Kluwer)

Van Overwalle, Geertrui (2002), 'Legal Protection of Traditional Knowledge. A Critical Synthesis', in: Grosheid, Willem and Brinkhof, Jan (eds.), Articles on Cultural Expressions and Indigenous Knowledge, Intellectual Property Law – Molengrafica Series, pp. 251–268 (Antwerp, Intersentia)

Van Overwalle, Geertrui (2002), 'La directive européenne en matière de biotechnologie et la transposition en droit belge', in: Droits intellectuels: à la rencontre d'une stratégie pour l'entreprise, pp. 119–172 (Brussels, Bruylant)

Van Overwalle, Geertrui (2001), 'Octrooien en producttoelating', in: Schellekens, Huub et al. (eds.), Medische biotechnologie, pp. 81–97 (Amsterdam, Elsevier)

Van Overwalle, Geertrui (2000), 'Biotechnology Patents in Europe. From Law to Ethics', in: Sterckx, Sigrid (ed.), Biotechnology, Patents and Morality, pp. 197–206 (Aldershot, Ashgate)

Van Overwalle, Geertrui (2000), 'Proeven met geneesmiddelen. De situatie in België in het licht van de recente rechtspraak en rechtsleer in Nederland en Duitsland', in: **Van Overwalle, Geertrui** (ed.), Octrooirecht en geneesmiddelen, CIR-Reeks 16, pp. 65–91 (Brussels, Bruylant)

Van Overwalle, Geertrui (2000), 'De ontwikkeling van een geneesmiddel', in: **Van Overwalle, Geertrui** (ed.), Octrooirecht en geneesmiddelen, CIR-Reeks 16, pp. 3–11 (Brussels, Bruylant)

Van Overwalle, Geertrui (1998), 'Octrooieerbaarheid van biotechnologische uitvindingen', in: **Van Overwalle, Geertrui** (ed.), Octrooirecht, ethiek en biotechnologie – Patent Law, Ethics and Biotechnology – Droit des brevets, éthique et biotechnologie, CIR-Reeks 13, 33–63 (Brussels, Bruylant)

Van Overwalle, Geertrui (1997), 'Biotechnology Patents in Europe. From Law to Ethics', in: Sterckx, Sigrid (ed.), Biotechnology, Patents and Morality, pp. 139–148 (Aldershot, Ashgate)

Van Overwalle, Geertrui (1995), 'Kwekersrecht', in: Descheemaeker, Koen; Oleo, Michele and Raspoet, Daniëlle (eds.), Valorisatie van onderzoek, pp. 295–309 (Leuven, Garant)

Van Overwalle, Geertrui (1995), 'Juridische bescherming van biotechnologische uitvindingen' in: Descheemaeker, Koen; Oleo, Michele and Raspoet, Daniëlle (eds.), Valorisatie van onderzoek, pp. 310–320 (Leuven, Garant)

Van Overwalle, Geertrui (1994), 'The Protection of Plants and Animals in the Russian Federation', in: Elst, Michiel and Malfliet, Karlijn (eds.), Intellectual Property in the Russian Federation. A System in Transition, CIR-Reeks 8, pp. 99–126 (Brussels, Bruylant)

Van Overwalle, Geertrui (1982), 'Rechtstreekse Vordering', in: Dillemans, Rogier (ed.), Rechtsgids (Ghent, Story-Scientia)

Van Zimmeren, Esther and **Van Overwalle, Geertrui**, 'Compulsory License Regimes for Public Health in Europe', in: Doelle, Horst Werner and Rokem, J. Stefan (eds.), Encyclopedia for Life Support Systems (EOLSS) (Theme Biotechnology – Topic Medical Biotechnology), see /www.eolss.net

REPORTS

Keulemans, Wannes; Avermaete, Tessa; De Coninck, Barbara; De Tavernier, Johan; Elsen, Annemie; Govers, Gerard; Honnay, Olivier; Janssens, Charlotte; Rolland, Filip; Saeys, Wouter and **Van Overwalle, Geertrui** (2024), Duurzame landbouwproductie en de maatschappelijke uitdagingen (Werkgroep Metaforum KU Leuven)

OTHER

Van Overwalle, Geertrui (2021), 'Haal alles uit de kast, ook de dwanglicentie', De Standaard, 1 maart 2021

Van Overwalle, Geertrui (2020), 'Zullen Covid-patenten ons redden?' De Tijd May 2020, p. 9

CONTENTS

INTRODUCTION

The Future of IP, Liber Amicorum Geertrui Van Overwalle

Arina GORBATYUK, Amandine LÉONARD and Esther VAN ZIMMEREN

'[...] I want to unfold.
I don't want to stay folded nowhere,
because where I am folded, there I am a lie.
And I want my grasp of things
true before you. I want to describe myself
like a painting that I observed
closely for a long time,
like a saying that I finally understood,
like the pitcher I use every day,
like the face of my mother,
like a ship
that took me safely
through the wildest storm of all.'[1]

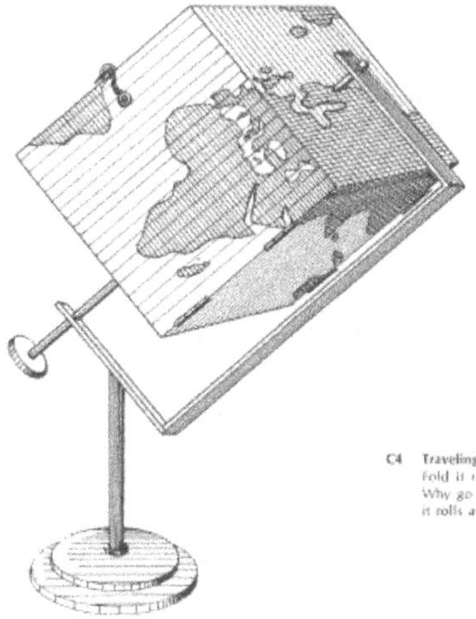

C4 Traveling Globe
Fold it neatly and transport it easily. Why go on chasing a round globe as it rolls away from you?

1 Rainer Maria Rilke, *Rilke's Book of Hours: Love Poems to God, trans Anita Barrows and Joanna Macy* (Riverhead Books 2005).

1. UNFOLDING GEERTRUI – IP SCHOLAR, SUPERVISOR, MENTOR, COLLEAGUE, INSPIRATOR, AND CREATOR

Every academic has that one person who opens the mysterious door to the scholarly world. For us, that person is Prof. dr. Geertrui Van Overwalle. This book is our way of saying thank you to our dear Geertrui for opening that academic door and holding the torch for as long as needed until we were able to find our own way.

We are pleased to dedicate this book to our PhD supervisor, mentor and the person who launched our academic journeys. Journeys that were closely intertwined for a formative chapter of our professional development. For the three of us, this book project was also an opportunity to reconnect and create something meaningful together. It is, in many ways, a tribute that commemorates both our relationship with Geertrui and our own academic journeys under her careful guidance. After all, it is only when looking back that one can truly appreciate how far one has come and thank the people who helped shape the way.

Geertrui always rigorously reviewed our work, often dissecting our methodologies to ensure our research was robust and bulletproof, generally with the help of some visual support, figures and tables that helped us see things clearer. She also guided us through the ups and downs of our PhD journeys with patience, insight, and genuine care. Most importantly, she encouraged us to pursue research that inspired us and to do so in a way that reflected our individual personalities.

In Geertrui's view, the PhD is a journey and not a destination, a precious time granted to researchers to explore their academic path, develop their own style, and embrace creativity. She trusted us and, from the very first weeks of our PhD journeys, encouraged us to participate in conferences, seminars, and workshops, introducing us to her international network. To the greatest extent possible, she shielded us from overburdening faculty tasks, giving us time and space to grow. She patiently waited for us to find our own voice in academic research, never imposing her own. And for that, we are truly grateful.

Geertrui is leading by example, choosing to pursue only research she truly cares about, regardless of what might be considered 'trendy' at any given moment. For those unfamiliar with the realities of academic life, this is not obvious as trending topics often come with greater visibility and access to funding. Yet, academic integrity, the lasting value of her legacy and the strength of her academic voice have remained her guiding forces, never swayed by fleeting academic hypes.

Similarly, she also resisted the creeping 'consultancy' model of academia, where funding often trumps substance. Although that type of research projects may bring in considerable funding, in her view, many of such projects are not advancing the critical, fundamental thinking. In particular, the latter is, according to Geertrui, entrusted on academics. Geertrui fought this battle on her own terms, by never folding. She protected her PhD researchers from the pressures of externally driven projects and only applied for funding that aligned with her intellectual values and satisfied her high academic standards.

Considering Geertrui's research focused on what truly mattered to her, it perfectly reflects her personality and values which are acknowledged and celebrated by the contributors to this book. Over the years, she has critically engaged with the foundations of patent law, exploring questions of inclusivity and exclusivity, the role of openness in the patent system, and mechanisms that may make knowledge more accessible. Her work on biotech and plant patents, in particular, has consistently raised fundamental questions about distributive justice, fairness, the balance between protection and access, public interest in general, public health, access to food and the broader tension between patenting and global well-being. She has done so using a variety of conceptualisations while building theoretical frameworks and proposing new typologies that could be used to better understand the implication of the theory.

Geertrui's strong and persistent focus on using law to promote public interest and societal well-being is part of what makes her such a respected academic. Many contributors to this book describe her as a forward-looking and critical scholar, uncompromising in her pursuit of academic quality and deeply committed to thinking outside of the box. They also highlight her generosity, her intellectual curiosity, and her ability to elevate and encourage young researchers with thoughtful mentorship and genuine support. Considering that another core value and commitment of Geertrui is empowering women, it is only fitting that her *Liber Amicorum* is co-edited by three of her female PhD researchers.

Considering the central role Geertrui has played in our academic journeys, collecting all the contributions for a retirement book for her feels almost surreal. Time passed so quickly that we barely noticed and yet, here we are, celebrating an academic career that spans 40 years. Although Geertrui had her formal Emeritus Celebration in December 2023 with her Valedictory Lecture, several speeches and a workshop with authors in this volume, a book project of this scale takes time to fully materialise. In a beautiful twist of timing, the book publication and launch happen to coincide with another milestone. It is 40 years since she earned her law degree cum laude from KU Leuven in 1985 and began her career at the university as a teaching assistant at the Centre for Heuristics and Methodology of Law.

In 1991 Geertrui joined the Centre for Intellectual Property Rights (the CIR at the time), and in 1995 she obtained her PhD with a dissertation on the 'Patentability of Plants'. Plants, seeds, biodiversity, GMOs, remained a core line of research in her work. In 2015 she joined the Centre for IT & IP Law (the current CiTiP) until her retirement as a full professor in 2023. She taught various IP courses at graduate and at postgraduate level relating to amongst others patent law, patent law and life sciences, and plant breeder's rights. She authored multiple academic works that were published by the various prestigious publishers which have served and will continue to serve as a basis for many academic works yet to be written.

Even though her main base throughout her academic career remained KU Leuven, her career transcended the national borders on her pursuit of becoming an international scholar on patent law, with a special focus on biotechnology and plant varieties. Even at a time when pursuing an international career was much more challenging than today, Geertrui made it her mission to reach beyond national borders, explore diversity in legal perspectives, and connect with like-minded, passionate scholars around the world. Many of whom have generously contributed to this *Liber Amicorum*.

She was also an active member of various international IP communities and was the first one to pack her bag to join an international conference or to leave for a research stay. She encouraged her students and PhD researchers enthusiastically to follow her path. She highlighted the importance of going beyond one jurisdiction exploring and learning from different legal cultures, different disciplines, schools of thought, stakeholders, and communities.

Beyond KU Leuven, Geertrui held part-time and visiting professorships at renowned institutions, including Sciences Po Law School in Paris, Tilburg University, and the University of Liège, as well as visiting lectureships in Melbourne, Essex, Amsterdam and more recently China and Japan. Her international perspective and collaborative approach made her a valuable voice in expert circles, including advisory roles at the European Patent Office, the European Commission, the Community of Plant Variety Office, and the Medicines Patent Pool.

As a long-standing member and former president of the European Policy for Intellectual Property (EPIP) association, she helped shape the scholarly IP community in Europe and beyond. Therefore, it is a pleasure to launch this book at the occasion of yet another milestone: the 20th anniversary of the EPIP conference hosted in Antwerp in September 2025. EPIP has always been one of her most treasured academic communities as it brings together scholars from various disciplines, policymakers and practitioners sharing the same passion for IP. EPIP conferences offer a great platform to share and get feedback on interdisciplinary research on the intersection of IP, innovation, and society. The theme of the EPIP 2025 conference, 'Turning IP Ambitions into Action: Creating Connections, Collaborations and Communities', could not be more fitting. These are some of the core values that Geertrui embodies and promotes through her scholarship and mentorship.

Family, friends and close colleagues of Geertrui understand that retirement is merely a formality for her. True academic minds like Geertrui do not simply stop exploring, wondering, questioning, challenging, testing, developing concepts and theories and creating. Over the past 40 years, Geertrui has not only made a lasting contribution to academic thinking in IP law but also challenged those around her to push conventional research boundaries, explore alternative approaches, and open up to experimentation. Those who know her personally understand that, for Geertrui, academic work should both be creative and accessible. She is known for her memorable speeches inspired by art and music at conferences and PhD defences. She is also a tireless advocate for making complex ideas clear, relatable, and meaningful. That is why we wanted this *Liber Amicorum* to reflect this spirit.

The three of us are immensely grateful to have been mentored by Geertrui. She taught us to explore without fear, to embrace our own voices in life and research. Without the courage to do so, we would remain 'folded' (see opening poem to this introduction). And as long as we are folded, we are not fully engaging and investing in developing ourselves. To unfold is both about an act of courage and of clarity. It is an act of refusing to remain hidden or confined. It is also an act of vulnerability, of showing the world who you truly are. Geertrui never hides behind 'safe' approaches, neither in her academic work, nor in her personal life. She has always been the one to ask deeper, challenging, and important questions, even, and especially, when they were difficult or uncomfortable. Those who know Geertrui would never describe her as conventional. Some see her as a true inspiration or as a brilliant academic mind that transcends boundaries. Others may see Geertrui as somewhat bold, uncompromising, or to some her approach may have been intimidating. But regardless of how Geertrui is perceived, she never folds herself into the convenient narratives of institutional expectations, hierarchical structures, or the need to 'fit' into shifting academic trends.

She dissected methodologies without hesitation, challenged assumptions, and raised the bar for doctoral research. As a long-time member of the Faculty Doctoral Committee, she did not approve research proposals unless she was convinced of their methodological soundness. This earned her both deep respect and, at times, a fair share of fear and frustration from those whose proposals she scrutinised. Her goal was never to please, but to ensure that PhD research at the KU Leuven Faculty of Law met the highest academic standards.

From the beginning of this book project, she asked us to develop something personal, creative, and (not surprising) academically unconventional. We gently tried to suggest a more traditional format, arguing that 'everyone is busy' and that 'the simpler the task, the more likely scholars will find the time to contribute'. However, Geertrui would not fold. We wanted a book that she would genuinely enjoy reading from first page to the last and for it to be special. Specially tailored for her. We encouraged the authors to go beyond producing a carefully reasoned legal text complete with footnotes, exceptions, and caveats, and to add a creative touch. Some authors were even genuinely poetic in their approach.

Moreover, in close collaboration with Geertrui, we found inspiration in Jacques Carelman's 'Catalog of Fantastic Things', published in New York in 1971. The book features a range of peculiar inventions; some are truly fantastic and others perhaps questionable in utility (we leave that up for you to judge). Authors were invited to select one or more inventions from the special book and to integrate them in a meaningful way into their chapters. In our view, the result of all this creativity is not only a collection of intellectually rich contributions, but also an innovative and personal reflection of the legacy of the scholar.

2. UNFOLDING THE BOOK – LOOKING BACK AT THE PAST, REFLECTING ON THE PRESENT AND HELPING SHAPE THE FUTURE OF IP

The contributors engaged with Geertrui's legacy, reflecting on how their own scholarship intersected with hers. This alignment allowed us to shape the book into six thematic parts, each echoing the purpose of this celebratory book: to look back at the past, reflect on the present and help shape the future:

Part I. Back to the Future: Inclusivity and Openness
Part II. Unfolding the Future: Sustainability and IP
Part III. Editing the Future: Biotech and Agriculture
Part IV. Unlocking the Future: Science, Knowledge and Biological Materials
Part V. Interpreting the Future: Patent Language, Policy and Procedure
Part VI. Digitising the Future: Copyright, Labor, and Digital Technologies

This book begins by going **back to the future (Part I)**. Much like the time-travelling characters in the iconic film, our authors in this section turn to foundational concepts and justifications of IP, not out of nostalgia, but to revisit, question and to reimagine its future potential. They challenge the conventional understanding of IP as a right to exclude and invite us to reconsider the very essence of ownership in pursuit of openness, access, and fairness.

This journey opens with a powerful **Chapter 1** by **Séverine Dussolier 'Inclusive (Intellectual) Properties'** that sets the tone for the entire volume. Her contribution dives deep into the concept and various meanings of 'inclusive property', which challenges the dominance of exclusivity in both property and IP regimes. She explores inclusivity as a normative and narrative tool and invites us to rethink how we view property and its function in society. In particular, she suggests that we should be able to embrace a 'pluralist model of property' and 'welcome new forms of inclusive property and give them normative force'. Séverine Dusollier engages directly with Geertrui's idea of the 'inclusive patent' and offers a rich and personal dialogue between two scholars who have long searched for ways to unlock doors of (intellectual) property and make space for fairness, openness, and shared innovation.

In **Chapter 2, '"The Inclusive Patent" (Invented by Geertrui Van Overwalle): Is it the Opposite of an Exclusive Patent?', Reto M. Hilty and Gregor Rauch** trace the conceptual development of the inclusive patents. This contribution is rooted in discussion between Geertrui and Reto Hilty during the ATRIP 2012 Conference. ATRIP, the International Association for the Advancement of Teaching and Research in Intellectual Property is another association of IP scholars dear to Geertrui. The authors critically engage with the concept introduced and refined by Geertrui, assessing its strengths and critiques its boundaries and limitations. Whereas the authors acknowledge its 'imperfections', they affirm Geertrui's lasting influence on how we understand openness in the patent system. Their message is clear: no single legal mechanism will achieve 'perfect' openness, but a multifaceted approach and scholarly dialogue, which Geertrui truly enjoys and contributes to, is essential to building more inclusive IP frameworks.

Chapter 3, 'Open Innovation and Intellectual property: How Open Are "Open Innovation" Agreements?', is authored by co-editor **Arina Gorbatyuk**. This piece reflects her own PhD journey, supervised by Geertrui and Esther van Zimmeren, and revisits a chapter initially drafted during her PhD research. That early version sparked lengthy, inspiring, and sometimes heated discussions among the three scholars. In that sense, this contribution is truly a return back to the future. With the benefit of years of additional insights, Arina Gorbatyuk now pushes the debate further, offering Geertrui yet another opportunity to critically engage with the topic. Her contribution reveals that the concept of open innovation (OI) is often contradictory for legal scholars. Despite its name, it does not necessarily imply broad openness of knowledge. Rather, the degree of 'openness' in OI varies and is often defined and limited by contractual arrangements. These agreements may restrict broader access to knowledge and follow-on innovation. The chapter ultimately suggests that the kind of openness aimed at enabling knowledge sharing for public good and bettering the future, for which Geertrui has consistently advocated, often lies beyond the boundaries of the current OI framework.

Amandine Léonard, another former PhD researcher of Geertrui and co-editor of this volume authored **Chapter 4, 'Use and Disclosure of Marine Genetic Resources of Areas Beyond National Jurisdiction: A Role for the "Inclusive Patent"'**. Her chapter is dedicated to her mentor, who inspired her to take a plunge in the High Seas and explore the relationship between patenting activities and marine genetic resources. In her contribution, Amandine Léonard considers various mechanisms envisaged by two new international treaties in order to promote transparency, sustainability, and the conservation of biodiversity in areas of the world which have not been regulated before, i.e. areas beyond national jurisdiction. She considers how the 'inclusive patent' may respond to some of the risks associated with (unregulated) privatization of resources meant to be used for the benefit of all humanity.

Part I concludes with **Chapter 5** and the contribution of **Pascale Chapdelaine** on **'Relational Aspects of IP and Inclusivity in Academia'**. This chapter starts with a review of the role of inclusivity in IP scholarship and Geertrui's contribution to the debate through her work on the inclusive patent. Pascale Chapdelaine then contrasts inclusivity in IP with inclusivity in the legal IP academe. In this second part of her contribution, she highlights the key role that Geertrui played in her academic journey. In particular, she emphasises Geertrui's ability to include others (colleagues, PhD students, researchers) and how such inclusivity has led to academic success and a strong legacy in the IP academy.

Part II unfolds new pathways and invites us to consider how IP can play a role in addressing one of the greatest societal challenges: **sustainability**.

It opens with **Chapter 6, 'Write-A-Bike: Intellectual Property and the Sustainable Development Goals'** authored by **Margaret Chon**. The contribution focuses on the UN Agenda for Sustainable Development and its Sustainable Development Goals (SDG). Margaret Chon examines the interaction between SDG 9, i.e. 'industry, innovation and infrastructure', and the issue of food security. She questions whether more could be done in order to bridge IP and innovation with inclusivity and sustainability. After exploring various mechanisms aimed at this bridging exercise and their shortcomings, she ponders that the debate should 'continue to move away from equating development primarily with industrial and economic development' and that there is a myriad of ways in which IP can encourage the production of global public goods. In her conclusive section, Margaret Chon turns to Geertrui's work and the 'typology of licences and access mechanisms for patent law' which may be of help. She concludes that, in line with Geertrui's work, 'a better balance' could be achieved in order to reach this goal.

This contribution is followed by **Chapter 7, 'A "Right to Repair" in European Patent Law?'**, authored by **Ansgar Ohly**. This chapter raises a simple but complex question: Is there, or should there be, a 'right to repair' in European patent law? Through the humorous metaphor of a 'recirculating faucet', Ansgar Ohly analyses the desirability of a right to repair in patent law and its potential role in the circular economy. He identifies and reviews three 'tests' which have been elaborated by courts on the basis of the principle of patent exhaustion and which have allowed for a 'repair' to take place. Next to exhaustion, he also reviews other mechanisms of patent law which may already hold some of the keys to achieve the objective of sustainability. Ansgar Ohly concludes that the creation of a right to repair is not the answer and that 'patent law, contract law, competition law and general principles of abuse of rights constitute a toolbox that can largely satisfy the public interest in allowing repair.'

The right to repair also inspired the following contribution. In **Chapter 8** entitled **'The Right to Repair and to Reuse Patented Products in a Circular Economy – It's Time to Get Exhausted'**, explore how patent law intersects with sustainability by examining how current exhaustion rules under Nordic and German patent law may hinder the right to repair and resell patented products. The authors call for a shift in perspective. Rather than assuming products have a limited lifespan, the law should support broader repair rights unless the patent holder has legitimate ground for objection. In essence, they invite us to reimagine patent exhaustion as a legal tool for promoting environmental sustainability.

In **Chapter 9 Esther van Zimmeren** engages with the growing number of reports regarding scenarios for the future of IP and she shares some ideas as to how this could contribute to **'Unfolding Scenarios for the Future(s) of Intellectual Property Systems'**. In her chapter, she starts by discussing the relevance of such projects and then describes three scenario studies that have been carried out in different decades, different jurisdictions, and for different purposes. Some of these studies represent a fascinating foresight as to the societal challenges we are facing today and the corresponding pressures on IP systems. The author argues in favour of a revival of the memorable Scenarios for the Future by the European Patent Office (2007), a major study providing critical and key suggestions still valuable today. Interestingly, the most recent foresight study for the European Commission on 'The Futures of Innovation and Intellectual Property Regulation in 2040' suggests in scenario 4 of this report 'Global and balanced IP for open innovation' that the 'EU should take a lead in the design of balanced, global transparent, solid and inclusive IP institutions for open innovation.' It will not surprise the reader that this suggestion was inspired – amongst others – by the work of Geertrui. The author applauds the fact that key actors in patent systems have invested in such scenario studies. They create a forum to challenge traditional assumptions and rationales of IP systems. Moreover, it allows for a consideration of the type of difficult and fundamental question, beloved by Geertrui, such as 'How might IP regimes evolve by 2025', 'Does the patent system benefit society' and 'Can the patent system adapt to the changing nature and pace of technology'?

If Part II aimed at unfolding new paths, **Part III** pauses to revise the map. In this section, we enter the realm of **life sciences**, a field where Geertrui's scholarly impact is particularly profound. In this Part, authors explore how innovation in biotech and agriculture challenges legal boundaries and ethical frameworks. They question which paths should be preserved, which require revision, and which must be laid anew.

Saurav Ghimire and Christine Frison describe in **Chapter 10 'Accommodating Farmers-breeders' Access to Breeding Materials in IP and ABS regime for Inclusive Innovation'** farmers' breeding practices and discuss various regulatory obstacles that hinder their access to breeding materials, including IP rights and the international access and benefit-sharing regime.

Christine Frison is a former PhD researcher of Geertrui as well and her PhD focused on access and benefit sharing (ABS) for food and agriculture. The authors show in the chapter that from revival of landraces to breeding with modern cultivar, farmers are involved in a wide range of plant innovation activities. They explain how IP rights and the multilateral system for the International Treaty on Plant Genetic Resources for Food and Agriculture (PGRFA) affect farmers' access to PGRFA for further breeding. However, no explicit and clear answer can be given to the question whether farmers can continue the process of selection and breeding with the materials provided by CGIAR centres as they used to. They conclude by indicating that more legal certainty for farmers is needed accommodating the right of farmer-breeders in both IP law and the ABS mechanism and offering farmers a wide range of diverse varieties for further improvement.

Christine Godt also focuses on green biotech and in particular on plant gene editing in **Chapter 11 'Genome Editing: Biotech at a New Legal Crossroads'**. The author provides a commentary related to some developments regarding plant gene editing triggered by recent experiences in various working and expert groups. The chapter starts by providing an overview of regulatory challenges raised by gene-editing. It then discusses two far-reaching proposals from the perspective of the governance and interface between IP rights and marketing authorisation. The final section builds on the literature on regulation theory and explores how legal change comes about and which role academic expertise may play in this process. She concludes with a call for Geertrui to continue to be involved in regulatory processes despite her retirement. According to Godt, 'it requires individuals who withstand the pressure, and trust in the mixture of factors which determine an argument to prevail' and 'it would be a loss if [Geertrui] turned her back to the legislative processes only because of a given retirement time thresholds' as her 'thoughtful input is dearly needed.'

In **Chapter 12 'Protecting Swiss Knives and Plant Varieties', Niels Louwaars** offers some practical reflections on patent law's protection of incremental and cumulative innovation as well as fundamental elements of the plant breeder's rights (PBR) framework. He advocates for a careful approach with regards to a cumulative regime of patentability and PBR protection for plant varieties as this may lead to counterproductive blocking scenarios. His professional experience leads to the conclusion that research led by independent IP-specialists such as Geertrui is essential to challenge and provide creative thinking in the field and that such research is key to 'secure the future of food and a healthy green environment'.

Part IV focuses on the simple (but extremely challenging) task of **unlocking knowledge for the future**. The contributors investigate the delicate balance between protecting innovation and ensuring the circulation of knowledge, scientific discoveries, and biological materials. In doing so, they celebrate

Geertrui's long-standing effort to unlock IP systems for broader societal benefit.

In his thought-provoking **Chapter 13 'Science in the Garden of Midnight'**, **Peter Drahos** encourages us to reflect on how IP and contracts have been 'integral to the construction of a framing paradigm of militarised science for the institution of science' and how they have placed University science – and universities more generally – in an 'iron cage'. Peter Drahos explores the historical developments and current challenges posed by ownership of military inventions which have been developed through publicly funded research. He identifies a dense web – also referred to as an iron cage – of contractual relationships between government branches, universities, and private contractors. It is argued that this dense web should be revisited in order to free 'the knowledge-creation infrastructure of universities from the military-industrial system.' Peter Drahos then puts forward avenues for universities to explore in order to break from this cage. One of the suggestions discussed in his contribution is the 'inclusive patent' as suggested by Geertrui.

Rochelle C. Dreyfuss explores how reverse engineering functions as a lawful and essential tool for technological progress in **Chapter 14**, titled **'Reverse Engineering and its Limits: Lessons from the Nostalgia Clock'**. In her contribution, she distinguishes between disclosed knowledge, trade secrets, and what she terms deep trade secrets, forms of knowledge that are particularly difficult to access and replicate, especially in the age shaped by AI and sophisticated technologies. Her voice is loud and clear. In order to innovate, we must be able to look backward, to build upon existing knowledge, including that which may be hidden or heavily protected. However, this access must be balanced with the need to preserve incentives to innovate. Rochelle Dreyfuss suggests that a development of new frameworks that could allow certain secrets to be revealed only for specific uses or to designated users. This way we will provide for responsible access without erasing the foundations of protections and significantly harm incentives to innovate.

Chapter 15 'Patenting Humans' is contributed by **Dianne Nicol**. In continuation with her groundbreaking work on the topic, Dianne Nicol reviews in her chapter the approach taken in Europe, the US and Australia regarding the existence, origin, nature, and scope of the morality-based exclusion of patenting humans. She presents to us key court cases and discussion points on the interpretation of the exclusion and brings to light some new challenges connected to emerging reproductive technologies as well as new ethical and legal concerns. She concludes by sharing some insights on the Australian approach and how this approach may serve as a model in other jurisdictions.

Enrique Santamaria Echeverria and Tine de Moor analyse in **Chapter 16, 'Unlocking Our Common Body? Biological Materials, Data and Knowledge Commons for Research and Development'** how the interplay of different principles and rules in EU legislation facilitates the commodification of human biological materials, data, and knowledge. They revisit the connections between Open Access Goods (OAG) and Common Pool Resources Commons (CPRC) and propose an alternative commons-based model for the governance of these resources, with a particular focus on their application in research and development (R&D), such as knowledge commons, medical knowledge commons, and genomic commons. In this chapter, the authors link to the work of Geertrui and her team on patent thickets and anticommons.

In **Chapter 17 'What if Invention Already Happened? Reactionary vs Ingenuity Bike'**, **Lodewijk Vandycke**, another former PhD researcher of Geertrui, shares his thoughts on a cycling revolution. It is argued in this contribution that bikes might represent a better and greener alternative to electric cars and that we, as society, should push in the direction of 'more bikes and less cars' if we truly aspire at meeting our green objectives. Lodewijk Vandycke notes, however, that contemporary innovation-driven motivations are lacking and that since patent law is naturally entrenched in the 'market-based innovation, profit-oriented entrepreneurs and growth-oriented states' framework, it most likely will not award the bicycle the priority it deserves.

Part V examines how we interpret the map that leads to the future. This part delves into how patent law is navigated through its **languages, procedures and evolving regulatory frameworks**. The authors in these chapters show that interpreting the future of IP also means challenging and addressing how the system operates.

It opens with **Chapter 18 'Semiotic Translation in Patent Claims'** by **Dan L. Burk**. In this captivating contribution, Dan Burk introduces us to the role of semiotics, i.e. the study of signs and their meaning, in patent claim construction. He firstly presents that, under a semiotic approach, translation and interpretation can have a 'connotative meaning' (considering nuances and alternatives) and a 'denotative meaning' (more usual, common, or ordinary definition). Dan Burk skilfully demonstrates that while we traditionally see literal claim interpretation as being entirely modern and denotative, this might not be entirely true, and some nuanced interpretation should be considered more carefully. In conclusion, Dan Burk suggests that we should recognise that, with regard to patent claim construction, the society or community which may influence the interpretation is the specialised and insular community of patent practice and not society as a whole. Therefore, he concludes that, literal claim interpretation is more a connotative exercise than one might think.

Chapter 19 continues to explore the transformative role of key actors involved in the patent system. In her contribution **'(Ir)rationality in Patent Law'**, **Daria Kim** reviews the mainstream justification of patent law: its connection with rational choice theory. She argues that we have a tendency to consider right holders as rational actors who weigh the costs and benefits of alternatives before making any decision regarding the exploitation of their rights. However, she argues that this approach makes us blind to some of the shortcomings of this ideal model. She concludes that, in order to have a stronger regime which supports the 'incentive to innovate' justification, the patent system might want to reflect further on the tenets of the rational choice theory and the linkage that may exist between individual and collective utility maximisation.

Chapter 20 describes key procedural aspects of the patent system. In **'Double Patenting: A Sensible Approach or Abuse of Proceedings?'**, **Liesbet Paemen** reviews the opportunity to engage in 'double patenting' under the Unitary Patent (UP) regime. She first provides a nuanced commentary on the differences between double patenting, evergreening and portfolio development. She then presents three scenarios of 'true' double patenting and the strategic opportunities left for right holders under the UP system. She links her work with that of Geertrui by observing that the patent system must be fair and that the possibility of abuse should be prevented.

In **Chapter 21 'Protective Letters – To Be or Not to Be?'**, **Carina Gommers** examines the role of protective letters within the evolving landscape of IP enforcement under the Unified Patent Court (UPC) framework. She poses a provoking question: are protective letters a shield for infringers, or a safeguard of procedural fairness? After examining the limited and inconsistent approaches to protective letters in Belgian IP litigations, she contracts this fragmented framework with the codified structure introduced by the UPC. In her view, within a system where a preliminary injunction can apply across 18 Member States, protective letters can serve an important function. They can help prevent the misuse of enforcement tools by powerful rights holders and offer more procedure balance for alleged infringers.

Catalina Martinez reflects on a shared vision of the patent system as a dynamic, ever growing evolving and challengeable system in her chapter **Chapter 22 'Reinventing Patents'**. According to Catalina Martinez, the status quo of patent systems can be, and should be challenged if there is room for improving its impact on social welfare. In fact, a large and growing interdisciplinary academic community does so. In this respect, fostering dialogue and collaboration between economists, legal scholars, policymakers, practitioners, patent attorneys and business is essential, and this is one of the key objectives for EPIP, the forum where Catalina Martinez and Geertrui got to know and appreciate each other's work.

Part VI confronts the **digital terrain** that is already reshaping our present and that promises to be even more challenging in the future. We have long accepted that the future is digital. However, how we shape it remains a pressing question of law, regulation, and ethics. In this final part, contributors examine the shifting role of IP in a digital economy defined by platforms, data, artificial intelligence (AI) and new forms of labour.

In **Chapter 23 'Flexibilisation and Digitalisation of Work: Finding a New Income Paradigm for the Financing of Social Security'**, **Paul Schoukens and Eleni De Becker** focus on one of the systems heavily affected by the digital transformation: social security. As digital platforms, AI and shifting work models disrupt traditional labour structure, they observe that it becomes increasingly difficult to ensure financial protections when there is no longer a clear and overarching definition of 'work', let alone a way to effectively regulate and tax the wide variety of new income streams. The authors examine how emerging income-generative activities, such as self-employment or platform-based 'gigs', complicate and challenge frameworks traditionally tied to stable employment and wage labour. They advocate for rethinking the way social security systems are financed and propose a set of forward-looking reforms to adapt to this new reality.

Jozefien Vanherpe questions whether copyright law fairly values the creative contributions of performing artists in **Chapter 24 'Be Your Own String Quartet? A Plea for the Legal Revaluation of Musical Performances'**. She points out that composers traditionally receive strong legal recognition, whereas performers, sadly, remain under protected, despite being the ones who bring a composition to life. Jozefien Vanherpe argues that when performers enjoy creative freedom and their interpretative choices reflect personal expression, their contributions may meet the threshold of originality and deserve stronger copyright protection. She calls for rethinking the strict divide between composers and performers in copyright law and suggests that a more inclusive legal framework would better support the creative and collaborative nature of music-making and ensure a fairer future for music industry.

In our final **Chapter 25 'Regulating IP Exclusion/Inclusion on a Global Scale: The Example of Copyright vs. AI Training'**, **Alexander Peukert** applies the concepts of exclusion and inclusion to one of the most pressing issues in current copyright law, namely the use of protected works to train AI. By comparing the EU, US, Chinese and Japanese legal frameworks, he explores how different legal systems respond to the tension between AI and copyright law. Alexander Peukert highlights that AI training (global in its nature) is significantly complicated by fragmented and territorially bound copyright regimes. However, rather than calling for harmonisation, he points to contract law as the most promising path forward. He reaffirms the value of contracts, describing them 'as a flexible "golden oldie" of resource allocation and inclusion.'

3. UNFOLDING THE FUTURE OF IP – PROMOTING OPENNESS, COLLABORATION, AND INCLUSIVITY

Together, these six parts offer a multidimensional perspective on what the future of IP might hold. This book embraces the uncertainty of what lies ahead, points to lessons that can be learnt from the past and affirms the values that should guide society, and more specifically academic thinking, forward. In line with Geertrui's academic aspirations, the authors reflect on how IP can and must evolve to safeguard and promote openness, accessibility, inclusivity, sustainability, fairness, and the public good. For decades, IP has centred around exclusion; perhaps it is now time to focus on inclusion.

With the support of 25 generous contributors, we hope we have made that vision a reality. We are extremely pleased and deeply grateful that so many great academic minds, Geertrui's dear colleagues, collaborators, and friends, contributed to this celebratory volume. This book could not have come to life without their open-mindedness and willingness to dedicate their precious time to this project.

While collecting the contributions for this volume, we were painfully reminded of just how precious time truly is. On February 4, 2024, the academic IP community was shaken by the unexpected passing of Dan Burk. Despite his depleting health, he took his truly precious time to prepare his contribution to this book. He sent it to us less than a month before his passing. We cannot express how deeply grateful we are for this very special gift. Dan Burk was an extraordinary scholar. One who not only shaped academic thought in the United States but also engaged deeply and generously with the European IP community. Dan Burk and Geertrui met at many academic fora for great discussions and contributed to many of each other's projects. They inspired each other in dissecting and rebuilding notions related to policy levers and property and liability rules with implications in their respective jurisdictions. Dan Burk's presence in this volume reminds us that scholarly communities continue to thrive though the ideas and passions that transcend borders, generations, and lifetimes.

We worked on this *Liber Amicorum* with great pleasure, enthusiasm and commitment inspired by Geertrui's spirit of inclusivity and collaboration. In our respective academic careers, we are transferring the many valuable PhD lessons that she taught us, to junior colleagues. Moreover, we put those lessons in practice by working closely together on this book and with the aim of further strengthening academic bonds in Flanders, Belgium, Europe, and beyond. This book is a celebration of those connections that are continuing to unfold, the many academic challenges and 'wild storms' and of a shared commitment to shaping a meaningful future for IP. A future that challenges convention, crosses borders, spans generations, and builds connections, communities, and collaborations.

And finally, we refer you to the Traveling Globe from the book of Jacques Carelman represented at the beginning of this introduction. It depicts a world that folds neatly into a box, easy to carry, contained. The caption asks: 'Why go on chasing a round globe as it rolls away from you?' Certainly, there is comfort in conformity. But the square shape also creates limitations, it narrows the mind and suggests there is a right and a wrong way to understand the world. In our view, like any world, the world of IP is not meant to be folded away into a fixed, four-cornered form. It is meant to roll, to unfold, to be explored, questioned, opened to new possibilities, even when the path ahead is uncertain. The future of IP is indeed uncertain and full of challenges, but it is also full of discoveries, inspiring debates, and unexpected turns that invite us to rethink the system built on exclusivity and control. Let us delve into this book and imagine a more open and inclusive future for IP.

PART I

BACK TO THE FUTURE: INCLUSIVITY AND OPENNESS

CHAPTER 1
INCLUSIVE (INTELLECTUAL) PROPERTIES

Séverine Dusollier
Professor, Sciences Po Paris

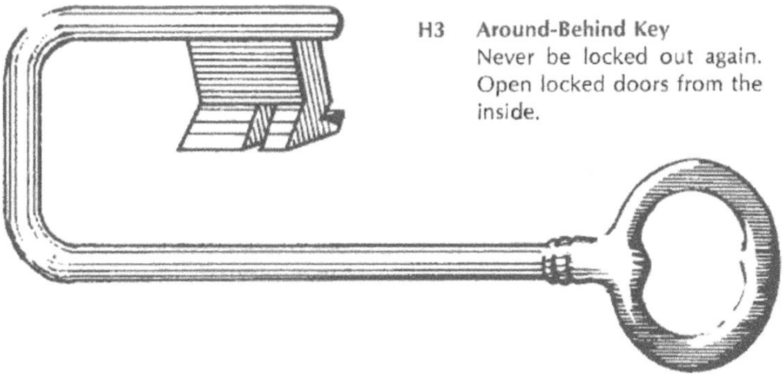

1. INTRODUCTION

Geertrui Van Overwalle has been one of the first scholars to challenge the exclusivity of intellectual property. Not that she denied that IP rights, particularly patents, her field of expertise, were aimed and designed to exclude others from the exploitation of the protected work, invention or sign, but she intuitively perceived that a more complex picture emerged beyond the traditional narrative of individual and exclusionary rights and exercise of such rights, granted by patent law. In the mid-2000's, Geertrui wrote a series of papers on 'protecting and sharing' biotechnology and traditional knowledge,[1] a combination of verbs that would sound antithetical at the time for most IP scholars, and on diverse

[1] Geertrui Van Overwalle, 'Protecting and Sharing Biodiversity and Traditional Knowledge: Holder and user Tools' (2005) 53(4) Ecological Economics: The Journal of the International Society for Ecological Economics, 585.

collaborative models such as pooling patents and clearing houses, focusing first on genetic inventions.[2]

In the next decade, her research looked at open innovation,[3] commons in patents[4] and she started to use the terminology of inclusivity to attenuate or subvert the exclusive model of intellectual property,[5] turning, in her own words, 'patent swords into shares.'[6]

All her endeavours purported to enhance innovation and fairness and to reverse the dominant course towards strengthened rights and tight enforcement, insisting instead on collective solutions, openness, and 'promoting access through exclusion.'[7] This is where our paths crossed, and our friendship started. We were both busy, with other intellectual locksmiths all over the world, bending the keys to open what we both conceived as excessive locks, in copyright or patent laws and exploring diverse options from leaving the door unlocked to devising around-behind keys as illustrated above.

We sought not only to defeat exclusive protection but to imagine alternative and complementary modes of governing creations and innovations, centred on sharing over reserving, on collectiveness and collaboration over individuality, on inclusion over exclusion. The final destination of our respective journeys is not the demise of intellectual property and its exclusivity, that both Geertrui and I recognise as an important feature in protection of works and inventions. Our explorations of forgotten places, that have been increasingly covered and hidden by the profuse foliage of invasive and intensified IP protection, is rather a discovery of a richer ecology in the patent and copyright landscape, where protection and openness co-exist, an ecology that we both consider as more promising for a thriving innovation and culture than what a commodified and extractive property model, with no breathing spaces, fallow lands or weeds, could develop.

---

2 Geertrui Van Overwalle, Esther van Zimmeren, Birgit Verbeure, Gert Matthijs, 'Models for facilitating access to patents on genetic inventions' (2006) 7(2) Nature Reviews – Genetics, 143; Geertrui Van Overwalle, 'Of Thickets, Blocks and Gaps: Designing Tools to Resolve Obstacles in the Gene Patents Landscape' in Geertrui Van Overwalle (ed), *Gene Patents and Collaborative Licensing Models. Patent Pools, Clearing Houses, Open Source Models and Liability Regimes* (Cambridge University Press, 2009) 383.

3 Geertrui Van Overwalle, 'Innovation without Property?' in Veerle Achten, Geert Bouckaert, Erik Schokkaert (eds), *A Truly Golden Handbook: The Scholarly Quest for Utopia* (Leuven University Press 2016) 300.

4 Geertrui Van Overwalle, 'Governing Genomic Data: Plea for an 'Open Commons'' in Brett M. Frischmann, Michael J. Madison & Katherine Strandburg (eds), *Governing the Knowledge Commons* (Oxford University Press 2014) 137; Geertrui Van Overwalle, 'Exclusive Property versus Open Commons. The Case of Gene Patents' (2013) 4(2) WIPO Journal, 139.

5 Geertrui Van Overwalle, 'Inventing Inclusive Patents. From Old to New Open Innovation' in Peter Drahos, Gustavo Ghidini, Hanns Ullrich (eds), *Kritika – Essays on Intellectual Property* (Edward Elgar Publishing, vol. 1 2015) 206.

6 Geertrui Van Overwalle, 'Turning Patent Swords into Shares' (2010) 330(6011) Science, 1630.

7 Geertrui Van Overwalle, 'Individualism, Collectivism and Openness in Patent Law. Promoting Access through Exclusion' in Jan Rosen (ed), *Individualism and Collectiveness in Intellectual Property Law* ATRIP Conference Proceedings (Edward Elgar Publishing 2012) 135.

Though both of us have applied a concept of inclusion and inclusivity to refer to some opening of the intellectual property regimes. I think our understanding of what is 'inclusive', while it is similarly associated with related notions of openness and commons, differs to some extent and is nourished by distinct thinking. This paper aims at explaining what I mean by inclusive, inclusion and inclusivity, and how I developed it from property theory before applying it to intellectual property.[8]

It starts from retracing the central role the notions of exclusion and exclusivity historically took in property discourse and model, which explained why commons, sharing and collective ownership were forcefully and theoretically expelled from the property construction (2). I then develop an alternative narrative of property, visiting the places where these inclusive properties are devised and practiced (3). Finally, I explain how the notions of inclusion and inclusivity have been used by property and intellectual property scholars before coming to what I mean by a regime of inclusive properties (4).

2. THE EXCLUSIVE PROPERTY AS A MODEL AND NARRATIVE

2.1. EXCLUSIVITY AS INDIVIDUALISM AND EXCLUSION

At the heart of the proprietary dogma of French civil law lies Pothier's assertion that 'own and common are contradictory.'[9] What Pothier meant, and what has been translated into the modern imaginary of property, is that what one owns cannot be encumbered by others; ownership is selfish and solitary. Such aloneness transpires both internally and externally in property: the internal face of the property is the 'solely me', the *individual* relationship between the subject and his property; the external face of the property is also the 'only me', to the *exclusion of* others.

These are the two dimensions of exclusive property rights: the individuality of the right of ownership and the right to exclude. Exclusive ownership means being alone in one's property. What is my own does not belong to others and loathes shared use. A similar solitary and exclusionary vision dominates the concept of property in common law system, often related to the famous quotation of William Blackstone who defines it as 'that sole and despotic dominion which one man claims and exercises over the external things of the world, in total exclusion of the right of any other individual in the universe.'[10] The pompous

---

8 This paper is a very incomplete summary of a book, still in writing, entitled *Inclusive Properties* (forthcoming in Cambridge University Press), that is the outcome of a research (having received funding from the European Research Council under European Community's Seventh Framework Programme (FP7/2007-2013) Grant Agreement no. 616103).

9 Robert-Joseph Pothier, *Traité du droit de domaine de propriété. Œuvres de Pothier*, t. X (M. Siffrein Paris 1821) 10.

10 William Blackstone, *Commentaries on the Laws of England* (1765) bk.2, ch1.

and emphatic declaration of Blackstone sounds greatly exaggerated today[11] and has been regularly 'ridiculed as a caricature of reality.'[12] Yet, his 'sole and despotic dominion' words, whether hyperbolic or not,[13] have endured as a metaphor and a canon talk[14] that informs our thinking about property.[15] Under the exclusive dominium paradigm, or the 'Exclusivity Axiom', as Carol Rose dubs it,[16] property is omnipotent, absolute, unitary, monolithic, exclusive and prominent. It encompasses all utilities of the resource owned and reserves them to the owner, who enjoys all the prerogatives to use the thing in discrete ways. Property is thus the epitome of legal entitlements in an asset and, as we know it in our western liberal legal regimes, is the triumph of modern possessive individualism.

2.2. EXCLUSIVITY IN INTELLECTUAL PROPERTY

Intellectual property is generally considered as being one form of property,[17] despite some scholarly challenges to the 'property' label.[18] First, the *theory* of property, notably rooted in Locke, helps justify the exclusive control granted on creations and innovations, the labour and individual act of creation legitimising the legal appropriation.[19] Second, the *legal category* of property[20] contributes to

---

11 See also the critique of M. Xifaras, of an impossible exclusion of others from all utilities of things. Mikhail Xifaras, *La propriété – Etude de philosophie du droit* (PUF 2004) 136.

12 Thomas W. Merrill, 'Property and the Right to Exclude' (1998) 77 Nebraska L Rev 753.

13 *Ibid.*

14 Carol M. Rose, 'Canons of Property Talk, or Blackstone's Anxiety' (1998) 108 Yale LJ, 601, 603.

15 *Ibid.* 602.

16 *Ibid.* 603.

17 See Robert Merges, 'What kind of rights are intellectual property rights' in Rochelle C. Dreyfuss & Justine Pila (eds), *The Oxford Handbook of Intellectual Property Law* (OUP 2018) 59: '[IP] walks like property, talks like property, and acts like property. And so it is.' For a more comprehensive analysis of the role of the narrative and concept property in intellectual property, but mostly in copyright, see Séverine Dusollier, 'Intellectual property and the bundle-of-rights metaphor' in Hanns Ullrich, Peter Drahos and Gustavo Ghidini (eds), *Kritika – Essays on Intellectual Property* (Edward Elgar Publishing, vol.3, 2020) 146.

18 On those challenges and a different vision of what property label could mean for intellectual property. See Dusollier (n 17).

19 Peter Drahos, *A Philosophy of Intellectual Property* (Routledge 1996) 41; William Fisher, 'Theories of Intellectual Property' in Stephen Munzer (ed) *New essays in the legal and political theory of property* (CUP 2001) 184. Other justifications of intellectual property have emerged, mostly in copyright where Kantian communicational theories have detached the right vested in literary and artistic works from its Lockean appropriation root. See for instance Anne Barron, 'Kant, Copyright and Communicative freedom' (2012) 31 Law and Philosophy, 1; Laura Biron, 'Public Reason, Communication and Intellectual Property', in Annabelle Lever (ed), *New Frontiers in the Philosophy of Intellectual Property* (CUP 2012) 225; Paul E. Geller, 'Copyright history and the future: what's culture got to do with it' (2000) 47 Journal of the Copyright Society of the USA, 223.

20 Civil law scholars have particularly questioned the qualification of intellectual property rights as 'property', considering that they should be considered rather as a specific category of subjective rights. On those debates, see Alain Strowel, *Droit d'auteur et*

an extensive protection of copyright and patent right, to which both a nature of fundamental right and a broad scope of rights are attached, or are, at least, pleaded for. The tool of property was strategically adopted by the 18th century defenders of a right in literary publications, notably by Diderot, for it could justify its transferability from authors to publishers.[21] In civil law countries, the qualification of copyright or patent right as property enables to endow those legal reservations with an absolute scope, potentially extending the economic rights they confer to any use of the work or invention not explicitly excluded by a rule of limitation or exception. The breadth of the 'property' category in common law maybe explains the less contested belonging of intellectual property to this category, for it seems more flexible to welcome a broader range of relationships to resources.

The characterisation of intellectual property as 'property' brings as a consequence, that the right to exclude and the exclusivity would feature amongst the key elements of its regime, if not being its core. However, exclusion does not sound completely right to the ears of an intellectual property expert. True, an intellectual property owner is entitled to exclude anyone from the enjoyment of her work or invention. Such exclusion conveys the no-trespass message that one usually associates with the property in land that serves as the paradigmatic case of property. However, exclusive rights in copyright or patent are more about exclusivity than about exclusion for two reasons. The first one pertains to the essentially non-rival nature and ubiquity of intangible assets: a work or an invention can be enjoyed by many without depriving anyone else from its benefit. This is the very reason why intellectual property rights create an artificial rivalry and exclusivity to remedy the impossible exclusive 'possession' and mastering over works or inventions. More fundamentally, the process of creation or invention is not one of appropriation and individual possession, but one of *depropriation*, divulgation and distribution.[22] To say it differently, intellectual property has an extroverted purpose, to the contrary of the introverted finality of property that is generally conveyed by the notion of possessive individualism.

A second reason lies in the necessity to include others in the use of the creation or innovation to reap its full benefit. Compared to a property in a piece of land, the typical example of a Blackstonian depiction of property, excluding everyone from the benefit of the asset would not make much sense in intellectual property. The exclusivity attached to intellectual property rights

---

Copyright – Divergences et Convergences (Bruylant 1993), 102 seq; Séverine Dusollier, *Droit d'auteur et protection des oeuvres dans l'univers numérique – Droits et exceptions à la lumière des dispositifs de verrouillage des œuvres* (Bruxelles Larcier 2005) 309 et seq.

21 See for a vibrant pleading in favor of publishers, Denis Diderot, *Lettre historique et politique adressée à un magistrat sur le commerce de la librairie* (1763) but also in the discussions leading to the UK Statute of Anne, the petition in *Journal of the House of* Commons (1706).

22 Xifaras (n 11) 367.

is not only a right to exclude others from exploiting the protected intangible asset but also represents a means of managing this exploitation. Through their exclusive right, the holders of a copyright or patent organise the circulation of the work or invention on the market, reserve a share of it for themselves, or obtain remuneration by authorising others to exploit its value.[23] With the exception of a few specific cases,[24] intangible property needs to circulate, to be shared and used by many people, if the right holder is to extract its full economic value. Intellectual property rights, combined with contractual tools, achieve this circulation by authorising the use of the good by others.

Therefore, one could say that intellectual property seeks to include others in the use of the asset. Its exclusive rights serve as means to manage the exploitation of the intangible resource, substituting the 'keep out' message of *ius excludendi* by an invitation to be authorised to enjoy the resource. The exclusivity in intellectual property has the effect to grant owners a broad and individual freedom to decide how to exploit the subject-matter of their right. More than an exclusive reservation of the thing itself, the copyright or patent holder controls the economic utilities of the work or invention through an exploitation exclusivity, all other utilities, and particularly the intellectual enjoyment of the work or the technical effect of the invention being shared with the public.[25]

That exclusivity in intellectual property is about managing the resource and decide what could be done with it, rejoices some major critiques of exclusivity in property, such as Larissa Katz who depicts exclusivity as the power of owners to decide without interference of others,[26] or Hanoch Dagan that equates exclusivity as a governance tool which highlights the 'internal life of property, which is often structured by sophisticated mechanisms aiming to facilitate various forms of interpersonal relationships in ways that no contractual arrangement can.'[27] The examples of inclusivity in intellectual property that will be developed below would illustrate how inclusive arrangements can indeed consist in an exercise or governance of exclusivity, rather than in its denial. Besides, this inadaptation of intellectual *property* to a robust right and narratives of exclusion and individual dominion might explain that it hosts or induces many inclusive regimes of relations to creations and inventions.

---

23 On the special role of exclusivity in intellectual property law, see Dusollier (n 17).

24 A trademark, e.g., is reserved for the exclusive and individual use of its owners to designate their products and services alone; certain patents, notably those relating to medicines, will generally only be exploited by the company that developed the invention.

25 André Lucas, 'Droits des biens et biens spéciaux: l'exemple de la propriété intellectuelle' in Faculté de droit et des sciences sociales de Poitiers (ed), *Les modèles* propriétaires (LGDJ 2012) 21; see also Alexandra Abello, 'La propriété intellectuelle, une propriété de marché' in Marie-Anne Frison-Roche et Alexandra Abello (eds), *Droit et économie de la propriété intellectuelle* (LGDJ 2005) 341.

26 Larissa Katz, 'Exclusion and Exclusivity in Property Law' (2008) 58 Univ of Toronto LJ, 275.

27 Hanoch Dagan, 'Inside Property' (2013) 63 Univ Toronto L Rev, 1.

3. TOWARDS INCLUSIVE PROPERTIES

3.1. INCLUSIVITY AS ANOTHER NARRATIVE

In a western liberal system that equates property with exclusivity and exclusion, is it impossible then to imagine properties that are non-exclusive, that are devoid of the right to exclude, or that turn their backs on individuality to embrace others and become common property? Is it impossible in our law to have non-exclusive properties? According to Mikhail Xifaras, what is at stake in Pothier's statement about the antinomy between proper and common, 'lies entirely in the ways in which we refuse to make room for the concept of non-exclusive properties: are they pure logical and semantic voids? Do they have an essence devoid of existence (the common property as a thinkable but unattainable ideal)? Do they have an essence that includes existence, but no reality in positive law (common property as a thinkable, realisable, but unrealised ideal)?'[28]

Non-exclusive property regimes do, however, exist in our contemporary realities, and are undoubtedly tending to multiply and reinvent themselves, as a new, non-selfish solution to the scarcity of things and their unequal distribution. These non-exclusive properties are neither unthinkable nor unattainable, yet they largely remain unthought of in law.

One of my research projects is to think about these non-exclusive properties, that oxymoron according to Pothier, by reconciling the proper and the common, by making the common re-emerge within properties against the pretended uniqueness of the exclusive property model.

I use the term inclusive properties to designate those situations where several people share the use of a resource without the possibility of totally excluding others. Rather than speaking of non-exclusive properties, the term 'inclusive' denotes a positive approach: communality of use and non-exclusion is not a lack, a defect, but a fullness. It is not the absence of exclusion that defines it, but the presence of inclusion, the flip side of exclusivity, characterised by (1) the inclusion of others in the use of the resource ('me and others'), and (2) the necessarily common use of the resource ('me with others'). Moreover, 'me' can be transformed into 'we' from the outset, i.e. 'we and others' and 'we with others'.

In these inclusive properties, the proper and the common are accommodated: property can be owned or used in common, without this being an anomaly or an exception to the principle of individual ownership, but a variation on property that can oscillate between individual and common, exclusive and inclusive. It is not so much a question of replacing exclusive property with inclusive, common property as of dethroning the former as the sole, monolithic model of legal thinking on property, and bringing back the common in our imaginaries.

---

28 Xifaras (n 11) 138.

Moreover, inclusive property is necessarily plural. Merely juxtaposing some inclusive property to exclusive property would simply create a binary model, whereas the plural ('properties') dissolves proprietary dogma into continuums, degrees of exclusivity/inclusivity and individuality/commonality, along which various arrangements of rights over property would be situated, like so many modalities of entitlements over things, whether tangible or intangible.

The exercise is not just conceptual and semantic. It is narrative and normative. The notion of inclusive properties implies – and this is a founding step – the development of new stories of property. For property is not just a legal organisation but also operates as an idea and as an institution that follows a recurring narrative.

Here, I mean narration in the *storytelling* sense of Carol Rose, the eminent American property specialist. In her book *Property and Persuasion*,[29] Carol Rose turns her attention to the ways in which property is narrated, and how these explain and justify elements of its regime that could not be determined solely by theoretical or functional justifications. This narrative of property is the way in which the legal regime reconstructs a concept after it has been established in law, through repetition, along Walter Benjamin's definition of *storytelling* as the art of repeating stories.

The story of the exclusivity of property has been repeated, asserted and reiterated over and over again, from Pothier and Blackstone to contemporary property law textbooks, with little regard for what property can really be, or how much reality can deny of this tale. This paradigm of property as necessarily exclusive and excluding is even confirmed by its most resolute opponents, like Proudhon who wrote: 'the most exact notion of property is the absolute, exclusive, autocratic domain of man over his thing.'[30] The narrative is thus unanimously shared by property's defenders and detractors alike, demonstrating its persuasive force. It is both performative, as it aims to enforce ownership around this paradigm of exclusivity, and suffocating, as it evacuates other ways of enjoying things.

Yet, this 'sadly jealous and solitary way of enjoying property'[31] is neither essential nor real. Paolo Grossi writes that unitary property is merely an accident of modernity,[32] and it is only through the affirmation of the Civil Code and systematic doctrinal construction that it has replaced the older forms of simultaneous ownership and shared enjoyment.

---

29 Carol M. Rose, *Property and Persuasion: Essays on the History, Theory, and Rhetoric of Ownership* (1st edn Westview Press 1994).

30 Pierre-Joseph Proudhon, 'Deuxième mémoire sur la propriété' in *Oeuvres complètes* (Paris Rivière 1935 [1840]) t. XI, 80.

31 Sarah Vanuxem, *La propriété de la terre* (Wildproject 2018) 36.

32 Paolo Grossi, *Il mondo delle terre collettive – Itinerari giuridici tra ieri e domani* (Quodlibet 2020).

Thinking about inclusive property would aim to replace, or rather enrich and diversify, the history/story of property fabricated by modernity to support possessive individualism as a necessary instrument of capitalism and liberalism. Telling another story means going beyond exclusive property as the only narrative, deconstructing and undoing it, because our contemporary period marked by resource scarcity and the ecological impact of extractive and individualist property calls for other models of rights that are less destructive of resources and more shared. Such renewed story can easily find its key characters and events in diverse plots of property unfolding today.

3.2. CASES OF INCLUSIVE PROPERTIES

There is no shortage of examples of more inclusive ways of enjoying the use of property, whether it applies to tangible or intangible resources. Such inclusivity might flow from the absence of exclusive entitlements, their subverted or reverted exercise, or their combination into an inclusive commons.

3.2.1. The Absence of Exclusivity or Open Access Commons

When no exclusive property vests in a resource, the lack of any exclusionary power can result in an unregulated space with no rights to use and no proper governance of the benefit of the resource. On the contrary, it can also give birth to multiple legal entitlements or privileges to use the resource that are equally shared amongst the members of the public without anyone having a right to appropriate the good and to exclude others from its benefit. This symmetrical enjoyment of a resource is found in the public domain in copyright or patent, encompassing intellectual assets that are not protected by an exclusive property right: anyone can use ideas or works or inventions whose legal protection has lapsed. Public domain, in most IP laws is not granted any positive status against exclusive claims and only finds some precarious protection as a legal defence. In addition, the obsession with the exclusive property model in our legal regimes makes it difficult to understand or give normative force to situations in which subjects share a non-exclusive right to use works. As a result, these uses are relegated to the status of tolerances, always subaltern derogations to the dominant model of exclusive ownership, and their intrinsic value is not acknowledged.[33]

Instead, recognising that the privilege of anyone to use the resource is necessarily accommodating the privileges of others and should be preserved could lead to a regime of normative inclusivity, where such entitlements,

[33] Séverine Dusollier, 'Unlimiting Limitations in Intellectual Property' in Gustavo Ghidini & Valeria Falce (eds), *Reforming Intellectual Property* (Edward Elgar Publishing 2022) 64.

devoid of any exclusivity, would be protected and secured for their essential communality.[34] In some countries, this could take the form of a *res communes*, a regime of goods inherited from roman law where no ownership applies and a right to use is granted to anyone.[35] Courts have sometimes taken a step further to give a positive status to such open access commons by recognising the legal standing of any user to claim the unfettered enjoyment of the resource and to enjoin anyone who would curtail such common use for his sole benefit from exercising any factual or legal exclusivity over the resource.[36]

3.2.2. Exclusivity Subverted into Inclusion of Others

In addition, a regime of inclusive intellectual property may be constituted by free and open-source licenses, also called copyleft licenses, by which the holder of the intellectual property right, generally a copyright,[37] opts to exercise her exclusive right in reverse, to include others in the use of the work. Free licenses create a double absence of exclusivity. Firstly, the copyright or patent owner relinquishes her exclusivity in order to include others, barring any reconstitution of an exclusive reservation on the copyleft work of invention, through the viral effect of the license that imposes derivative works or improvements to inventions to be distributed under the same permissive licensing regime.[38] Secondly, the 'licensees' of these particular licenses are granted an inclusive right of use, which, unlike traditional licenses, is characterised by the symmetrical entitlement shared by all users. No single user enjoys this freedom of use alone, but in parallel with all other users of the work. This shared freedom is also essential in the construction of a commons or 'free work'[39] through modifications and alterations to the work: additions or derivations of the work find their legitimacy in this inclusive license, but must themselves allow the same freedom, to avoid breaking the chain of

---

34 Séverine Dusollier, 'The Future of Public Domain' in Enrico Bonadio & Caterina Sganga (eds), *A Research Agenda for EU Copyright Law* (Edward Elgar Publishing 2025) 173.

35 Judith Rochfeld, 'Chose commune (approche juridique)' in Marie Cornu, Fabienne Orsi and Judith Rochfeld (eds), *Dictionnaire des biens communs* (PUF 2017) 176.

36 See for an analysis of Belgian case law granting a positive and protective status to res communes, Benoit Jadot, 'L'article 714 du Code civil et la protection de l'environnement', in Actualités du droit de l'environnement – Actes du colloque des 17 et 18 novembre 1994 (Bruxelles Bruylant 1995) 53. A French bill of 2015 proposed to organise a positive protection of the public domain in copyright, renamed the 'informational common domain'. See Séverine Dusollier, 'Domaine public (propriété intellectuelle)' in Marie Cornu, Fabienne Orsi and Judith Rochfeld (eds), *Dictionnaire des biens communs* (PUF 2017) 377.

37 But copyleft licensing has also been experimented with patented inventions, see Esther van Zimmeren, *Towards a new patent paradigm in the biomedical sector? Facilitating access, open innovation and social responsibility in patent law in the US, Europe and Japan* (2011) Thesis, KU Leuven; Séverine Dusollier, 'Sharing Access to Intellectual Property through Private Ordering' (2007) 82 Chicago-Kent Law Review (2007) 1391.

38 Dusollier (n 37).

39 Mélanie Clément-Fontaine, *L'œuvre libre* (Larcier 2014).

shared and inclusive uses. Consequently, the work itself incorporates the terms of the license that governs it, so that the inclusivity created by the contract becomes an *in-rem* characteristic of the work.[40]

Copyleft licenses create non-exclusivity by exercising exclusivity, in a subversive move. This is not the law that declares the absence of exclusivity as it is the case of public domain and intellectual property exceptions. The assertion of the exclusive right is paradoxically the founding rule of the licensing process and the strategy to trump the void of the public domain. Copyleft licenses retain the control on the creation and condition the granting of freedoms to some obligations, including the further prohibition to prohibit. Conversely, when a creation is in the public domain, the complete absence of exclusivity makes it impossible to restrain its free use and prevent reconstitution of exclusivity on derivative works or inventions. Some authors have described such method by explaining that free licences create 'a self-binding commons rather than an unrestricted public domain,'[41] or a 'modernist kind of property.'[42]

Following the example of intellectual property, individual properties can be opened up to collective use projects, transforming them into inclusive properties dedicated to sharing and the absence of exclusion. This is the case, for example, with collective gardens or other collective spaces organised around a community of users, at the will of the owner, whether public or private, with legal arrangements that aim at securing this dedication to the commons.

3.2.3. *The Exclusivity Dissolved in an Inclusive Commons*

Open licenses are particularly well-suited to the creation of collaborative and incremental online content, such as Wikipedia, which requires that each new contributor to the work has the right to modify it. But beyond the rights that these licenses grant to successive contributors, the very process of open online collaborative creation creates a particular copyright whose exclusivity is paralyzed.[43] Indeed, when a Wikipedia page, or any similar type of content, is made up of the successive additions and modifications of hundreds of contributors (not all of whom can be qualified as co-authors, in the absence of an original contribution within the meaning of copyright law), the copyright in the work at any stage of its development is necessarily shared between too many

40 Margaret J. Radin, 'Humans, Computers, and Binding Commitment' (2000) 75(4) Indiana LJ, 1125.

41 Amy Kapczynski, Samantha Chaifetz, Zachary Katz and Yochai Benkler, 'Addressing Global Health Inequities: An Open Licensing Approach for University Innovations' (2005) 20 Berkeley Tech LJ, 1032.

42 Carol M. Rose, 'Ostrom and the lawyers: the impact of Governing the Commons on the American legal academy' (2011) 5(1) International Journal of the Commons (2011) 28, 42.

43 Sunimal Mendis, 'Public open collaborative creation (POCC): A new archetype of authorship?' (2019) 22(1-2) The Journal of World Intellectual Property Law, 59.

co-authors for each or all of them to be able to exercise their exclusive rights. In a way, this incapacity of copyright law to address multiple authorship creation conveys the attachment that copyright law has to exclusivity and individuality (the normal model of creation being an individual, concentrating on her person the exclusivity of property) and the reluctance of this legal regime to envisage a more inclusive approach. Existing legal regimes of co-authorship generally require that all co-authors of a collaborative creation join forces in order to exercise their rights, in line with the exclusive logic of ownership, necessarily re-constituting a unitary right with all contributions.

A more adapted framing of such multiple and open creation would be to recognise a more inclusive form of copyright, based on a community of contributors to the creation, who also undertake not to exclude new contributors nor to exercise their right exclusively.

3.2.4. Exclusive Rights Gathered in an Inclusive Commons

While intangible goods are by nature more open to sharing and common use, tangible property is not to be outdone. Despite the rivalry that characterises tangible goods, common ownership and use organisations have also developed. Admittedly, ownership is sometimes divided between various owners, but doctrine generally sees cases of co-ownership as anomalies that are not destined to prosper,[44] and the estate can always be dissolved and divided, which ensures a possible return to exclusive individual ownership, which remains the norm.[45]

In some cases, though, co-ownership cannot be dissolved because it is accessory to individual properties that share certain things in common, as in the case of co-ownership of commons in condominiums. Here, individual private property (the 'propre') is backed up by an undivided property that provides the goods essential to the whole (the commons).[46] This exclusive logic also explains the rules governing the governance of this type of co-ownership, with voting rights and shares in charges determined by the relative surface area of the individual dwellings, the strength of each individual property thus organising the collective.

In a sense, co-ownership is nothing more than a competition between individual properties, in 'a very impoverished model of collective ownership,'[47] which aims above

---

44 Florent Masson, *La propriété commune* (Thesis Université Panthéon-Sorbonne Paris I 2016) 3; See also Geraldine Salord, 'Propriété collective et exclusivité: proposition d'une conciliation des contraires' in Faculté de droit et des sciences sociales de Poitiers, *Les modèles propriétaires* (LGDJ 2012) 195.

45 Xifaras (n 11) 148.

46 Aurore Chaigneau, 'Copropriété' in Marie Cornu, Fabienne Orsi and Judith Rochfeld (eds), *Dictionnaire des biens communs* (PUF 2017) 317.

47 Geraldine Salord, *La propriété collective des œuvres – Contribution du modèle du droit d'auteur au droit commun* (Thesis Université Panthéon-Assas Paris II 2007) 6.

all 'to manage this competition'[48] of individual rights whose exclusivity remains, but only comes up against the rights of others, which limit their usefulness.

However, there are cases of genuine, non-exclusive property sharing that escape this competitive and conflictual apprehension of co-ownership. Participatory housing in its various forms, such as *habitats groupés* in Belgium or *baux réels solidaires* in France,[49] and in a different way, community land trusts,[50] can be an opportunity for real collective and inclusive ownership, as it is rooted in a desire to cooperate on a common project and share spaces and living experiences. Whereas co-ownership of the common areas in a building with individual apartments is incidental and compulsory, as it is imposed on the various owners of individual units who cannot get rid of it, a collective and participative housing project voluntarily associates the common area with the autonomy of individual spaces. In this type of housing, households decide to bring their living spaces together in a collective project that is neither accessory nor inevitable, but central and chosen. Such new forms of home ownership in collective projects aimed at making housing more accessible, can to some extent also be described as inclusive, as they replace exclusive and autonomous property rights with an inseparable link to a community of inhabitants that limits, for example, the possibility of reselling the property under normal market conditions and binds instead any new acquirer to the common project.

Here too, the inclusive model of shared ownership or use is not immediately recognised by the law, which persists in a logic of exclusive, individual ownership either by applying thereto exclusivity-inspired and unequal voting rules, or by requiring the constitution of a legal entity that absorbs collective ownership into the appearance of individual ownership.[51]

4. FROM A RIGHT TO INCLUDE TO INCLUSIVITY

These cases of shared use of tangible goods or intellectual creations provide other stories and realities. But the difficulties of understanding them through the law, whose grammar remains predominantly and by default exclusive, show that it is time to diversify our ownership regime and integrate inclusive ownership.

Several scholars in property or intellectual property, including Geertrui Van Overwalle, have defended some idea of inclusion in law (4.1.). I myself follow that path by proposing to develop a regime of inclusive properties within the property model (4.2.).

---

48 Masson (n 44) 9.

49 Marie-Alice Chardeaux, 'Repenser la propriété pour promouvoir la solidarité -À propos du bail réel solidaire' (2020) 10(2) *Délibérée*, 38.

50 Vincent Le Rouzic, 'Community Land Trust' in Marie Cornu, Fabienne Orsi and Judith Rochfeld (eds), *Dictionnaire des biens communs* (PUF 2017) 263.

51 Salord (n 44) 242.

4.1. THE MANY SCHOLARS OF INCLUSION

The notion of inclusion is not new in property scholarship. Already in 1978, Crawford MacPherson, in its overall critique of possessive individualism, argued that: 'Property (…) need not be confined, as liberal theory has confined it, to a right to exclude others from the use or benefit of some thing, but may equally be an individual right not to be excluded by others from the use or benefit of some thing.'[52] If the possessive individualism was the necessary offspring of 18th century liberalism, freeing the subjects from the feudal system, MacPherson wonders whether a renewed liberalism at the end of the 20th century, grounded in a social state and the fulfilment of fundamental needs and freedoms of its citizens, should not lead to a revised model of property in which the interests of non-owners to get access to basic resources and notably to means of labour, would weigh more than those of the owner of the property right.[53]

MacPherson's call for a property that would guarantee the non-exclusion of others in the enjoyment of resources has spread in legal scholarship on both sides of the Atlantic, following two modalities, a *voluntary* inclusion of others in the enjoyment of the owned resource or an *involuntary* or imposed inclusion in the form of a right of non-owners to be included or not to be excluded.[54] The first mode of a right to include logically follows the exercise of exclusivity: if the owner benefits from a right to exclude, she is equally free not to exercise it, hence tolerating uses of her ownership by others, or to turn its exercise into an inclusion of others, which has been underlined both by scholars attenuating the exclusionary feature of property such as Katz or Dagan,[55] and by scholars strongly attached to the exclusion in property, who provide examples of such division of property rights by contract or easements.[56]

Other property scholars have gone a step further by conceptualising a right to include in property and by detaching it from the right to exclude, in one way

---

52 Crawford Brough MacPherson, 'Liberal Democracy and Property' in Crawford Brough MacPherson (ed), *Property. Mainstream and Critical Positions* (University of Toronto Press 1978) 201; See also, Crawford Brough MacPherson, *The Political Theory of Possessive Individualism. Hobbes to Locke* (OUP 1962). For an interesting analysis of MacPherson critique from a political philosophical perspective, see Etienne Balibar, 'Le renversement de l'individualisme possessif' in *La proposition de l'égaliberté. Essais politiques 1989–2009* (PUF 2010) 91.

53 Stefano Rodotà, *Il terribile diritto – Studi sulla proprietà privata e i beni communi* (3rd edn Il Mulino 2013) 450. See also for a right to be included modelled on the transformation of economy from property to access, Jeremy Rifkin, *The Age of Access* (Penguin Publishing Group 2001) who argues to recognise an individual right of access to productive resources.

54 On this distinction see Daniel B. Kelly, 'The right to include' (2014) 68(4) Emory LJ, 857, 868–869.

55 Katz (n 26); Dagan (n 27).

56 Thomas W. Merrill and Henry E. Smith, *Property: Principles and Policies* (2nd edn Foundation Press 2012) 449; Robert C. Ellickson, 'Two Cheers for the Bundle of Sticks Metaphor, Three Cheers for Merrill and Smith' (2011) 8(3) Econ J Watch, 215, 218.

or another. In *The right to include*,[57] Daniel B. Kelly stands in contrast with the accent put by the US doctrine on the right to exclude and contends instead that the ability of owners to include others in their property is a central attribute of property and a critical mode of organising economic and social activities and relationships. Such inclusion, he writes, can proceed 'by waiving exclusion rights, dividing existing rights by contract or recognised forms of property, or creating new rights and forms.'[58]

In Kelly's perspective, inclusion is socially beneficial 'because human beings depend upon each other, not only to survive but also to flourish,'[59] which leads him to analyse at length the benefits and costs of inclusion, including coordination difficulties, strategic behaviour, and conflicts over use. This 'exchange function of inclusion' is actually the exploitation of property to extract its value by sharing, leasing or exchanging the asset.[60] Use of property to include is conceived not as a wall but as a gate.[61]

Another part of scholarship on property develops the involuntary inclusion, i.e. a nonowner's right to be included, either based on limitations of property that create in counterpart a right to get access to the resource or grounded by fundamental needs that justify access to key resources. Hanoch Dagan in *Property, Values and Institutions*,[62] finds in discrete limitations of property, such as public accommodations law or fair use in copyright, a right to be included, that would prevail over the principle of the owner's right to exclude.[63] Such a right to be included is not a negation of the right to exclude, but the consequence of the many limitations imposed to property. In a more recent book, *A Liberal Theory of Property*, Dagan develops this right of non-owners to be included on the ground of his model of property's relational justice, that imposes a reciprocal respect for self-determination and equality.[64]

Italian legal scholars have been particularly active in the last years to look for an inclusive property, by which they refer to a property regime that would have to include others in the access to the resource.[65] Limitations of property are hence transformed into an inclusive property, i.e. in their conception, into a regime of property that requires including others in the benefit of the thing. The Italian legal system provides a fertile ground, for the notion of property is

57 Kelly (n 54) 857–924.
58 *Ibid.* 859.
59 *Ibid.* 871.
60 *Ibid.* 922.
61 *Ibid.* 923.
62 Not exactly a US scholar but Hanoch Dagan, though a Tel Aviv Law professor, is largely engaged in US doctrinal discussions on property.
63 Hanoch Dagan, *Property: Values and Institutions* (OUP 2011) 37–56.
64 Hanoch Dagan, *A Liberal Theory of Property* (CUP 2021) see particularly chapter 5, 126.
65 See Rodotà (n 53); Matteo Ferrari, 'Proprietà e diritto ad essere inclusi' (2016) 34(4) Rivista critica del diritto privato, 525.

there given a specific role in the Constitution whose Article 42, adopted after the second world war, recognises and guarantees the protection of private property but simultaneously posits that the law determines its limits in order to ensure its social function and to make it accessible to all.[66] Informed by this specific constitutional function of property, the Italian Court of Cassation has regularly acknowledged some public access to private property where necessary to fundamental rights or social needs.[67]

With such a background, it is unsurprising that prominent Italian property scholars have regularly insisted on a right to get access to others' possessions in the form of a right to be included[68] or a right not to be excluded.[69] Stefano Rodotà, an influential law professor in Italy, was certainly a pioneer in the conceptualisation of such an inclusion in property. His book, *Il Terribile Diritto*,[70] is an attempt to reconsider the theory of property in a social perspective in order to reconcile the private and individual property with the fulfilment of fundamental rights and needs of non-owners. Standing against the strict model of possessive individualism, Rodotà introduces the social function of property and the obligation to satisfy fundamental rights of people and pleads for a right not to be excluded that would transform property into an inclusive regime.[71] As the chair of the commission nominated by the Italian government to revise the civil code and the categories of property, Rodotà took its proposal for inclusion rights a step further by calling for the legal recognition of commons in each case where the access to a resource would be crucial to the fulfilment of fundamental rights.[72] Private owners would not only be forced to grant a right to access to the resource in such cases, so a right not to be excluded, but the regime of property itself would turn to a commons, where collective access would be organised.

In an article dedicated to the right to be included,[73] Matteo Ferrari contends that the right to exclude in property necessarily coexists with an *obligation* to include, whereas Alessandra Quarta has developed a figure of 'non-property'

---

66 Article 42: '*La proprietà è pubblica o privata. I beni economici appartengono allo Stato, ad enti o a privati. La proprietà privata è riconosciuta e garantita dalla legge, che ne determina i modi di acquisto, di godimento e i limiti allo scopo di assicurarne la funzione sociale e di renderla accessibile a tutti*' (The property is public or private. The economic goods belong to the State, to institutions or to private individuals. Private property is recognized and guaranteed by law, which determines the methods of acquisition, enjoyment and limits in order to ensure its social function and make it accessible to all).

67 Maria Rosaria Marella, 'The Commons as a Legal Concept' (2017) 28 Law & Critique, 61.

68 Ferrari (n 65) 550.

69 Rodotà (n 53).

70 The title can be translated as *The Terrible Right*, which refers to property as the subtitle (Studies on private property and commons) clearly indicates.

71 Rodotà (n 53) 40; see also Marella (n 67) 14 (equally insisting on a gradual opposition between a right to exclude, on one side, and the right of not being excluded on the other).

72 On the *Beni communi* commission in Italy, see Marella (n 67) 67.

73 Ferrari (n 65).

(*non-proprietà* in Italian[74]) to characterise cases where non-owners enjoy an access right to some utilities of the thing, where access and 'non-owning' are considered as counter-principles to rethink the paradigm of property.[75] However, in the opposition Quarta draws between to-have and to-have-not, access right is coupled with the absence of property which typically reasserts the position that property inevitably comports the right to exclude, only limited at the margins by an obligation to grant some access to non-owners.

The notions of 'inclusivity' and 'inclusive' also appear in intellectual property scholarship.[76] Robert Merges has been one of the first to attach to the exclusive right of property discrete forms of inclusion, which he equates to the lack of enforcement or to a waiver of IP rights.[77] That many individuals choose collaboration and surrender their IP rights for sharing, proves in his view the flexibility of intellectual property, as well as the very autonomy and freedom of choices given by the institution of property.[78] Merges recommends that property regimes implement a *right to include* that would be coextensive with the traditional right to exclude,[79] for 'the ability to easily include is an important flip side to the grant of property rights – one that is obscured by an overemphasis on the muscular rights that accompany a grant of property.'[80]

The research of Geertrui Van Overwalle is not unrelated to Merges' work, both on collective institutions for licensing and the flexibility of property to grant a right to include. One of her recent research proposals works out a notion of inclusive patent as a tool to overcome intricate transactions costs in some technology sectors plagued with numerous overlapping patents, the infamous patent thicket, and the desire, for some patent owners, to include others in the use of their inventions.[81]

After thoroughly reviewing different licensing schemes, copyleft or not, and identifying their shortcomings in achieving low-cost and sustainable openness,[82] Van Overwalle pleads for the creation of a new intellectual property entitlement that could be added to traditional exclusionary patent. This so-called inclusive patent would aim at providing a new form of open innovation less centred

---

74 Alessandra Quarta, *Non-Proprietà. Teoria e prassi dell'accesso ai beni* (Edizioni Scientifiche Italiane 2016).

75 *Ibid.* 11–12.

76 Peter Drahos, 'A defence of intellectual commons' (2006) 16(3) Consumer Policy Rev, 101 (referring to the dichotomy between exclusive and inclusive to organise a typology of commons).

77 Robert Merges, *Justifying Intellectual Property* (Harvard university Press 2011) 295.

78 *Ibid.* 227.

79 *Ibid.* 290.

80 *Ibid.* 296.

81 Van Overwalle, (n 5); Toshiko Takenaka, 'Inclusive Patents for Open Innovation' (2020) 29 Tex Intell Prop LJ, 187.

82 Van Overwalle, (n 5).

on firms, but also more technology-oriented than community-centred open innovation. In a nutshell, an inclusive patent could be alternatively filed for by innovators who want to commit to open innovation. Its regime, obtained at a lower cost than a traditional patent, would only encompass a right to include and to conclude licenses aiming at sharing the invention.[83] Inclusive patent owners would not get the right to exclude further uses of the technology, but could enforce the sharing attribute of the patent by taking non-sharing users to court, which would ensure the sustainability and continuity of the sharing feature.

In a close model and based on a similar identification of patent flaws to incentivise technology sharing, Toshiko Takenaka proposes instead to apply an incentive-to-share theory by granting anyone a right to make, sell and use the protected innovation.[84] Her proposal differs from Van Overwalle's model in two ways. Firstly, the inclusive patent would be granted without substantive examination, being hence closer to a utility model.[85] Secondly, the inclusive patent owners would benefit from a compulsory license on prior inventions defending them against blocking injunctions on one side,[86] and of a remaining exclusive right that inclusive patent owners can enforce against patent infringement assertions, on the other side, which could also help achieving cross-licensing.

Both Van Overwalle and Takenaka suggest creating a patent with reduced exclusion, to which a general right to use the technology would be associated, through some form of compulsory licensing. The unitary patent enacted by most EU Member States,[87] and recently entered into force and granted by the EPO, contains a form of open and non-exclusive patent: Article 8 of the 2012 Unitary Patent Regulation offers indeed the possibility for a patent owner to file a statement to allow any person to use the invention against some remuneration, which has to effect to grant a contractual license in an inclusive way to all potential users of the invention. Such license, that results in a small reduction of renewal fees, as suggested by Van Overwalle in her inclusive patent model, is incompatible with existing or eventual exclusive licences, which to some extent transforms the patent itself into an open object.[88]

---

83 *Ibid.*

84 Takenaka (n 81) 221.

85 *Ibid.* 216.

86 This side of her proposal is mostly aimed at the US legal framework as such a compulsory license already exists in some EU countries.

87 Regulation (Eu) No 1257/2012 of the European Parliament and of the Council of 17 December 2012 implementing enhanced cooperation in the area of the creation of unitary patent protection.

88 Rule 12, Rules relating to Unitary Patent Protection as adopted by decision of the Select Committee of the Administrative Council of the European Patent Organisation of 15 December 2015 and as last amended by decision of the Select Committee of the Administrative Council of 23 March 2022, OJ EPO, 2016, A39.

4.2. FROM A RIGHT TO BE INCLUDED TO INCLUSIVE PROPERTIES

The right to include or to be included developed by these discrete doctrinal trends is actually not the radical demise of the model of property as a right to exclude, that it pretends. Most proposals elaborated by property scholars essentially introduce a right to include as a modulation of the exercise of the right to exclude, hence centering its determination on the head of the owner, still considered as the individual deciding voice. Inclusion here is only one declination of the right to exclude, granted to the owner, without undermining the centrality or operation of the exclusion right in property.

By revealing how much plural property forms already organise discrete inclusion of others, by non-enforcing or waiving the right to exclude, by contractually distributing the use of the thing or by dividing the property through legal instruments, a less exclusionary or individualistic conception of property is suggested. But such a right to include does not change fundamentally the principle of exclusion, it only transforms it into an exclusive power: the owner remains the only one who is entitled to decide to exclude or include others in her property. Obviously, a despotic exercise of property, where all possessions are hoarded and secluded from external eyes beyond gates, is a metaphor of exclusionary property that rarely finds a reality. Actually, a myriad of ways of including others exists within property regime. Insisting that property also leads to inclusion is only putting light on the merely theoretical concept of a complete exclusion of others.

The scholars who have alternatively found a right to be included (or a right not to be excluded) in the many limitations the property right is subject to, do not really endanger either the right to exclude whose scope of application is merely confined to the boundaries of property itself. The access right that such limitations confer to non-owners, empowers third parties to get a glimpse at the property, to be entitled to benefit from some of its utilities under certain conditions. Opening access to the resource as an exception or derogation to the rule[89] could here also be said as reinforcing the principle of exclusion itself, only eroded at its margins. What better way to affirm a principle than to organise its exceptions! When access to the resource is presented as a force contrary to property, it bears the risk to strengthen the very principle of exclusion that defines the latter.

My concept of inclusive property goes beyond a right to include or a right to be included that would modulate the core principle of exclusivity. As such,

---

[89] Ugo Mattei and Alessandra Quarta, *The Turning Point in Private Law. Ecology, Technology and the Commons* (Edward Elgar Publishing 2019), 42 'Property Law' ('exclusion represents the rule, while the opposite power, which is the right to be included or the power of access recognized for non-owners, is only an exception to the rule').

it overcomes the individualisation of the right not to be excluded or to be included,[90] for inclusivity would rather characterise entitlements to benefit from a resource that would necessarily be shared by many legal subjects. Benefiting from an inclusive property would not consist only in being included by the owner or by a legal mechanism of limitation of property, though it could be one source of the inclusivity, but would result from the very organisation of property regime, inclusivity being its essential or primary feature. When property can be characterised as inclusive, its intrinsic hallmark and objective, and not its accident or possibility, is to share the use of the object owned amongst several individuals, none of them prevailing over others or being entitled to some residual exclusionary power.

A regime of relations to things can be described, in my view, as inclusive on two conditions: (1) the absence of power to exclude others from use of the property, and (2) the impossibility of individual exercise of one's right due to common use. Those two criteria stand in opposition to what prevails in our predominant model of property, marked by exclusion and individuality.

This notion of inclusivity also rejoices Yochai Benkler's definition of the commons as 'the freedom to operate under symmetrical conditions, offered to an open or undefined group of users',[91] which he contrasts with exclusive ownership, itself characterised by the asymmetrical power of one or more specific persons to decide on the use and disposition of the thing.[92] The element of symmetry on which Benkler insists could be equated with inclusivity that would then serve to legally characterise the commons, a notion that is not, in itself, strictly legal. Indeed, all commons are based on the organisation of relations to things, material or immaterial, whose use is common and shared within an inclusive community. Depending on the type of commons, the power to exclude disappears, or applies only to third parties. No beneficiary of a 'right' to use the resource has asymmetrical power *vis-à-vis* others but enjoys a prerogative symmetrical to that of other users or owners.

This criterion of symmetrical use makes it possible to extend inclusivity to uses of goods that are not subject to a system of ownership or governance organised by the community that shares this use, two features that tend to be associated with the commons.[93] For example, the public domain in copyright law, or *common resources* such as water or the environment, i.e. the open access

90 Balibar (n 52).

91 Yochai Benkler, 'Between Spanish Huertas and the Open Road: A Tale of Two Commons?', in Brett M. Frischmann, Michael J. Madison & K. Strandburg (eds), *Governing the Knowledge Commons* (OUP 2014) 69, 71.

92 *Ibid.*

93 Benjamin Coriat, 'Communs fonciers, communs intellectuels. Comment définir un Commun ?' in Benjamin Coriat (dir) *Le retour des communs: La crise de l'idéologie propriétaire* (Paris Les Liens qui Libèrent 2015) 30. As such, Benjamin Coriat refuses to include common or open-access things in the notion of the commons. Yochai Benkler, on the other hand, considers

commons referred to by Benkler, escape ownership but remain non-appropriable resources whose common use must be guaranteed. An inclusive regime of non-proprietary uses, establishing entitlements of shared use for all, could form the legal protection necessary to preserve such openness and commonality.

Detaching a concept of inclusivity from the recognition of individual rights to be included or not excluded also entails that the regime of inclusivity would move from individual legal subjects and subjective rights to properties of the resource itself and the relations it entertains with all its beneficiaries. This re-imagination of property is here in dialogue with two other doctrinal propositions: Sarah Vanuxem's notion of property as a faculty of habitation and Sarah Keenan's characterisation of property as belonging rather than control.

In her thesis on property, Sarah Vanuxem suggests to envisage things as environments, as a *milieu*, and rights as faculties of inhabitation, of living in, with legal subjects being merely inhabitants of the thing, not masters over it.[94] Things would always be in common use, and the rights relating to them would grant faculties to inhabit them: 'Since property does not relate to things themselves, but only to rights or places in them, the owner would be the one to whom a right, or a place, is assigned, attributed or reserved. She would be the one who benefits from a place in the thing.'[95] These resources, considered as *milieux*, would not be 'appropriated' by individual ownership, but would host within them a community which would no longer be antinomic to the idea of ownership, and which would be made up of 'inhabitants', holders of various rights or titles, not in a competitive relationship against each other, but in coexistence, in cohabitation.[96]

This redefinition of property as a place in a thing transforms 'having' into 'having a place', and inverts the relationship between property and community, between the subject and the object. This is in line with the writings of Sarah Keenan, in her book *Subjective Properties*, who conceives of property as belonging rather than as a relationship of domination over the thing.[97] She takes up a distinction made by Davina Cooper in a study of the property and community regime of a school,[98] between property as *owning*, i.e. possession and control of a thing, and property as *belonging*, i.e. belonging to a thing or to an organised community in connection with that thing.[99]

---

that open-access goods that do not require ownership should also qualify as commons. See Benkler (n 91).

94 Sarah Vanuxem, *Les choses saisies par la propriété* (Paris IRJS Editions 2012).

95 Vanuxem (n 31) 67.

96 *Ibid.* 71–72.

97 Sarah Keenan, *Subversive Property: Law and the Production of Spaces of Belonging* (Routledge 2015).

98 Davina Cooper, 'Opening up Ownership: Community Belonging, Belongings, and the Productive Life of Property' (2007) 32(3) Law & Social Inquiry, 625.

99 Keenan (n 97) 65.

The thing no longer belongs to us, but we belong to it, and this grammatical reversion leads to a relational vision of ownership, as in Sarah Vanuxem. In its original sense, belonging is to be understood as 'having a share' in the thing, as a bond of *membership*. With both authors, we move from a right to the thing to a thing linked to people, from a subjective approach to an objective one in which the resource, the good, is the starting point for rights, and obligations. It is also a relational approach to ownership.[100] The owner is no longer the subject who dominates the object, but is part of a whole made up of the thing and the community of inhabitants or subjects who are members of it.[101] The owner-subject is *embedded* in a network of relations, which 'decenters or reverses her domination over the thing.'[102] This integration is not fixed, however, but remains dynamic, in line with the social processes and structures that underpin these networks and memberships.[103]

While exclusion remains possible, it is less an extension of the subject – characteristic of modern property seen as a mode of subject autonomy and an external translation of possessive individualism – than a relationship between subjects. As such, property is more a practice, a performance, as Nicholas Blomley writes.[104] This relational approach forms a third meaning to inclusive, beyond the absence of exclusion and the collective use. This performative and relational dimension of property also moves away from the commodification of the object of property and its extractive purpose. If the resource is no longer the dominated object of ownership, but the place we inhabit, to which we belong with others, then we must take care of it, and not just exploit or exhaust it. This is necessarily an ecological perspective on property,[105] where the sustainability and generativity of things matter. The granting of biocultural rights, or even legal personality, to nature[106] is another way, outside the strict framework of property, of inscribing the community in the environments it inhabits, and of making the

100 *Ibid.* 73.

101 *Ibid.* 12–13 (who distinguishes two types of relationship that can be constitutive of ownership and that intertwine: 'part-whole' and 'subject-object').

102 Cooper (n 98) 636.

103 Keenan (n 97) 72.

104 Nicholas Blomley, 'Performing Property: Making the World' (2013) 26(1) Canadian Journal of Law and Jurisprudence, 23.

105 Ugo Mattei and Fritjof Capra, *The Ecology of Law: Toward a Legal System in Tune with Nature and Community* (1st edn Berrett-Koehler Publishers 2015) who call for an ecology of law and property to replace possessive individualism.

106 On these rights of nature, see Christopher Stone's seminal article, 'Should Trees Have Standing? – Toward Legal Rights for Natural Objects' (1972) 45 Southern California Law Review, 450; but also the notion of biocultural rights developed by Sanjay Kabir Bavikatte, *Stewarding the Earth – Rethinking Property and the Emergence of Biocultural Rights* (1st edn OUP 2014). These doctrinal conceptions, but above all their concretization by judicial institutions or legislators in Latin America, India or New Zealand, participate in the same legal re-imagining that challenges a dominant approach of the subject over the object, and precisely nature, and an extractivist vision of property.

relationship with things, environments and nature, not a bond of domination, but a relationship, an obligation, a care.

Beyond renewing the narration and narrative of property, and overcoming the modern possessive individualism, what concrete consequences do such inclusive properties entail?

First and foremost, it renews the narrative of property as a monolithic regime of exclusion and individuality and installs in property law, a variation of diverse regimes of relationships to things, more or less inclusive/exclusive, more or less individual/collective. Inclusive property does not substitute to exclusive property but adds many nuances to it.

Situations of inclusive ties to things, whether created by law or by contractual organisations, could then be given some normative force and be recognised by law and the courts, not as a situation subaltern or derogatory to exclusive ownership, but as a model of ownership that produces effects other than individuality and the right to exclude. Judges could interpret rules marked by an exclusive vision of property and bend them when necessary to apply to cases of inclusive properties. For example, inclusive housing organisations mixing collective ownership with individual dwellings will be able to derogate from the strict rules of co-ownership law, still marked by the relative importance of private units, to take account of the participative and inclusive project. The specific rules and limitations on resale, which organises a partial collective appropriation of the realised added-value, as well as the indispensable inclusion of the acquirer in the community of inhabitants and the common project, may be validated and justified by the vision of ownership as belonging to this collective project, and not as the acquisition of an asset over which one would have control as a subject isolated from its environment.

In copyright law, replacing the exclusivist approach with a relational and inclusive one would organise the multiple uses of creation within a cultural ecosystem, making creation the place where authors' rights and users' uses of works cohabit, not equally, but symmetrically.[107] More specifically, multi-authored collaborative works could carry with them this community of authors and contributors, without necessarily having to deal with an addition of individual and exclusive links of authorship that end up paralyzed by this multiplicity. Similarly, a work disseminated under free and copyleft licenses could be one in which authors and users have chosen to exercise their copyright in this inclusive way, without having to resort to a complex and fragile contractual construction in which each part of the common work must be duly authorised and shared by its sole and exclusive author. Outside the realm of property,[108]

107 See Dusollier (n 33).

108 The public domain remains a situation of rights or legal links to a good, which justifies its inclusion in the reorganization of models of relations to things, as part of an option for pluralism of 'proprietary' models.

the public domain in copyright, a legal situation in which the freedom to use the work, enjoyed by any member of an indefinite public, replaces the author's individual and exclusive entitlement, would be recognised as a system of parallel and symmetric entitlements, devoid of any exclusivity, but not of legal value, which would make it possible to resist re-appropriations or exclusive claims on elements of the public domain.[109]

5. CONCLUSION

We are deluding ourselves into thinking that all property regimes are linked to a strong rule of exclusion and individuality, as the sole mould and ultimate horizon of our relationship with things. Exclusive ownership is a historically and socially situated technique for shaping relationships and exploiting resources. Today, other constructions and experiments are flourishing, pursuing goals of sharing, living together and reducing our extractive and consumptive footprints on resources. A pluralist model of property could embrace these diverse uses, practices and relations to goods, breaking free from the paradigm of possessive and exclusive individualism to welcome new forms of inclusive property and give them normative force. Such rethought properties have to be unearthed in the interstices of the law, those interstices into which, to follow Serge Gutwirth, we have 'inserted legal crowbars [to] push, open, evolve, yes "twist" the law in the hope of meeting judges and other lawyers inclined to participate in this movement of reattaching the law (not the legislation!) to what concerns life in the earth's atmosphere.'[110] In order to meet contemporary needs for the preservation and sharing of resources, it is urgent to acknowledge that the forms of ownership that the law recognises and to which it gives force are multiple and plastic.

In intellectual property, reimagining the notion of exclusivity and adding thereto a plurality of inclusive modes of use, creation, and sharing, enables, as Geertrui Van Overwalle early understood and tested, an expansion of the possibilities of exercising rights in a work or invention, to enhance cooperation, innovation, collective creation, community-building, distribution and re-use as well as to transform practices to new legal forms beyond old and sometimes stifling paradigms.

109 Dusollier (n 34).

110 Serge Gutwirth, 'Les Communs: Avec, malgré ou contre le droit?' (2022) 33(6913) Journal des Tribunaux, 592.

CHAPTER 2

THE 'INCLUSIVE PATENT' (INVENTED BY GEERTRUI VAN OVERWALLE)

Is it the Opposite of an Exclusive Patent?

Reto M. Hilty
Director Emeritus, Max Planck Institute for Innovation and Competition, Munich
Professor Emeritus, University of Zurich

Gregor Rauch
Doctoral candidate, University of Zurich
Former research fellow, Max Planck Institute for Innovation and Competition, Munich

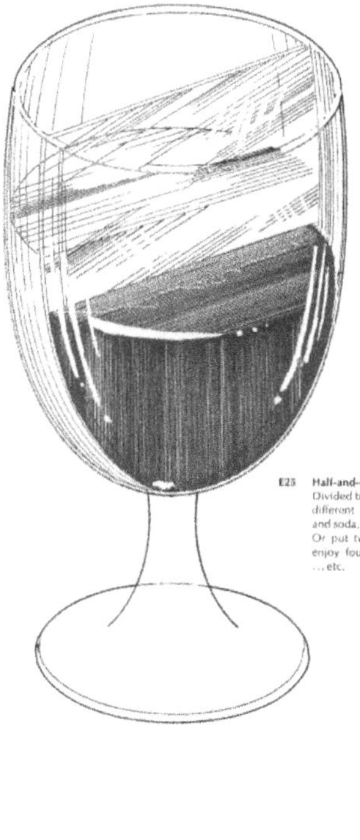

E25 **Half-and-Half Glass**
Divided by a glass partition. Enjoy two different drinks at once, e.g., scotch and soda, rum and coke, gin and tonic. Or put two drinks in each side and enjoy four at once. Or four in each ...etc.

Geertrui Van Overwalle's pioneering work in the life sciences has placed her at the forefront of one of the most pressing debates in intellectual property law. The seemingly never-ending expansion of patentable subject matter, coupled with the ever-increasing number of patents, has fundamentally challenged her main areas of research, particularly in biotechnology and (human) genetics. Van Overwalle has played a significant role in shaping the discourse to better balance the demands of innovation with broader societal interests.

The idea of the 'inclusive patent' that Van Overwalle developed in her later work can be seen as a culmination of her extensive research into various strategies for promoting openness in patent law and addressing the drawbacks of granting excessive exclusivity in the patent system. For roughly two decades, Van Overwalle has systematically explored a broad range of licensing mechanisms and legal remedies to address the challenges posed by patent thickets, fragmented ownership, and restrictive patent practices, particularly in the field of life sciences.

An overarching theme in Van Overwalle's work has been her consistent emphasis on the need to recalibrate the 'social contract' of patent law, particularly in the post-grant phase of a patent's life cycle, where it is crucial to ensure that the exercise of the exclusive rights granted by patents does not overshadow the public benefits of innovation. This trajectory naturally led her to consider how the patent system itself could be restructured to better align with the principles of openness and accessibility, drawing particular inspiration from the open-innovation and open-source movements. The inclusive patent, with its emphasis on sharing, collaboration, ethical and social responsibility and the underlying principle of voluntariness clearly mirrors these foundational ideas.

Our reflections on the solutions proposed by Van Overwalle are rooted in intensive debates between her and the first author, in particular on the occasion of the ATRIP conference in Chicago in 2012.[1] These discussions at the time were inspired by copyright law, the advantage of which is that it operates under the principle of 'automatic protection', granting rights at the moment of creation without the need for formal registration and at no cost. This favours openness because the right holder is not only able to exclude others; he may also permit free use of his work, while the exclusivity allows him to further enforce openness in subsequent creations in terms of derivative works. We concluded that there should be some kind of a similar, low-cost tool within patent law to maintain openness for subsequent inventions.

---

1 Kindly mentioned in the acknowledgments at the beginning of her article Geertrui Van Overwalle, 'Inventing inclusive patents: From old to new open innovation' in Peter Drahos, Gustavo Ghidini and Hanns Ullrich (eds), *Kritika: Essays on Intellectual Property Vol. 1* (Edward Elgar 2015).

In this light, exclusivity serves two distinct functions. One could imagine it as the 'half and half glass' – a quirky design where the glass itself is split down the middle, letting you, for example, enjoy scotch on one side and soda on the other. Just as the glass offers two different drinks depending on which side he chooses, exclusivity allows the right holder to decide whether to keep things strictly exclusive or to foster openness.

Van Overwalle developed this – still very abstract – idea further in a refreshingly creative way, which is our major focus here. Our article is structured in three main sections. The first one explores Van Overwalle's early work, examining the intellectual path that led her to the development of the inclusive patent. It traces her exploration of various remedies within patent law, including narrowing patentability, promoting open innovation, and the dynamic interplay between public and private ordering mechanisms. The second section delves into the inclusive patent itself, providing a detailed explanation of what Van Overwalle envisions with this approach and how it seeks to integrate principles of openness, collaboration, and ethical responsibility into the patent system. Finally, the article offers a critical evaluation of the inclusive patent from the authors' perspective, assessing its strengths, potential challenges, and implications for the future of patent law.

1. NARROWING EXCLUSIVITY

Van Overwalle's academic journey toward the idea of the inclusive patent is rooted in her early focus on the question of patentability, particularly in ethically sensitive areas like plant biotechnology[2] and human genetics.[3] While patents in the former field have always been contentious, often sparking public debate,[4] the controversy over their eligibility for patent protection in the latter largely subsided with the introduction of the EU Biotechnology Directive in 1998.[5] Consequently, Van Overwalle early on shifted her focus away from the question

---

2 Geertrui Van Overwalle, *Patentability of Plant Biotechnological Inventions. A Comparative Study towards a Justification of Extending Patent Law to Plants* (Bruylant 1996).

3 Geertrui Van Overwalle, *Study on the patenting of inventions related to human stem cell research* (European Communities 2002); see also Geertrui Van Overwalle, 'Biotechnology and patents: global standards, European approaches and national accents' in Daniel Wüger and Thomas Cottier (eds), *Genetic Engineering and the World Trade System* (Cambridge University Press 2008).

4 Geertrui Van Overwalle and Esther van Zimmeren, 'Functions and Limits of Patent Law' in Erik Claes, Wouter Devroe and Bert Keirsblick (eds), *Facing the Limits of the Law* (Springer 2009).

5 Directive 98/44/EC of 6 July 1998 on the legal protection of biotechnological inventions [1998] OJ L 213/13.

of patentability, acknowledging that it was simply too dynamic to be effectively managed within the existing legal framework.[6]

Van Overwalle's research increasingly centred on mechanisms and remedies aimed at mitigating the negative effects of excessive exclusion. She examined a range of strategies, from targeted research[7] and diagnostic use exemptions[8] to more innovative approaches like applying the U.S. fair use doctrine to European patent law.[9] Although these measures offered potential to alleviate some of the negative effects of exclusivity, Van Overwalle found that their effectiveness was often limited by varying legal interpretations and inconsistent application across jurisdictions.[10] In light of the 2010 Monsanto decision of the ECJ,[11] Van Overwalle also touched upon the possibility of limiting the scope of patent protection by introducing a purpose-bound protection regime – especially for gene patents. Under this regime, a patent for a DNA sequence would no longer encompass all possible future applications but would be restricted to the specific use described in the patent application.[12]

In 2011, Van Overwalle, together with van Zimmeren, dealt extensively with compulsory licences in the field of public health. In their analysis, they recognise the potential advantages of compulsory licences, particularly their ability to ensure public access to essential medicines during health emergencies and to balance the interests of patent holders with broader societal needs.[13] However, they also saw potential shortcomings, most notably the often cumbersome and complex legal frameworks that make it challenging to issue compulsory licences efficiently in the first place.[14] While Van Overwalle and van Zimmeren acknowledged the value of compulsory licences as a case-by-case remedy, she ultimately argued for broader, systemic changes in

---

6 Geertrui Van Overwalle, 'Patent Law in Crisis? Functions and Limits of the Patent System in a Globalised World' (2007) Rev. Dr. ULg 320.

7 Geertrui Van Overwalle and others, 'Models for facilitating access to patents on genetic inventions' (2006) Nature Reviews. Genetics 143; Geertrui Van Overwalle, 'The Implementation of the Biotechnology Directive in Belgium and its After-Effects. The Introduction of a New Research Exemption and a Compulsory Licence for Public Health' (2006) IIC 905.

8 Geertrui Van Overwalle, 'Turning Patent Swords into Shares' (2010) Science 1630.

9 Geertrui Van Overwalle, 'Fair use – a workable concept in European patent law?' in Kung-Chung Liu and Reto M. Hilty (eds), *Compulsory Licensing* (Springer 2015). She explored this as part of the fifth conference on European and Asian Intellectual property, held on 3–5 December 2012 in Taipei under the auspices of the Max Planck Institute for Innovation and Competition, Institutum Iurisprudentiae and Academia Sinica.

10 Van Overwalle and others (n 7) 143ff.; Esther van Zimmeren and Geertrui Van Overwalle, 'A False Sense of Security Offered by Zero-Price Liability Rules?' in Ruth L. Okediji and Margo A. Bagley (eds), *Patent Law in Global Perspective* (OUP 2014).

11 Case C-428/08 *Monsanto Technology v Cafetra and others* [2010] ECR I-6765.

12 Van Overwalle (n 8) 1630.

13 Esther van Zimmeren and Geertrui Van Overwalle, 'A Paper Tiger? Compulsory License Regimes for Public Health in Europe' (2011) IIC 4.

14 *Ibid.* 38.

patent law to promote openness, rather than relying on compulsory licences as a general solution.

It was thus only natural that Van Overwalle's research increasingly gravitated towards more collective and open approaches as a remedy for the negative effects that patents can lead to, particularly in the field of life sciences, where the growing number of patents has led to patent thickets and fragmented ownership.[15] Her theory was that innovation can be fostered, sustained and made more open through a dynamic interplay between public ordering (property rights) and private ordering (contracts).[16] The latter can come in form of (individual) licensing schemes, such as licences of right[17] or open-source licences,[18] and collaborative/collective structures, like patent pools,[19] standardised clearinghouses,[20] or royalty-collecting clearinghouses.[21]

These types of licensing models obviously are of voluntary nature. When patent holders enter into collaborative agreements, they decide to limit their exclusive rights in exchange for the benefits of collective action. This voluntary limitation means that the exclusivity granted by the patent is no longer unlimited; it is shared and managed within the collective framework, thereby facilitating access to the patented technology. Especially in the field of life sciences, Van Overwalle observed that 'through the shaping of license policies, exclusive or proprietary rights are used to leverage access, to promote dissemination, and to safeguard downstream use rights. [...] The notion of promoting access through rights that exclude is indeed the underlying paradox of IP law and policy.'[22]

---

15 Geertrui Van Overwalle, 'Designing Models to Clear Patent Thickets in Genetics' in Rochelle C. Dreyfuss, Harry First and Diane L. Zimmerman (eds), *Working Within the Boundaries of Intellectual Property* (OUP 2010), 306.

16 Geertrui Van Overwalle, 'Individualism, Collectivism and Openness in Patent Law: from exclusion to inclusion through licensing' in Jan Rósen (ed), *Individualism and Collectiveness in Intellectual Property Law*, (Edward Elgar 2011), 112.

17 Geertrui Van Overwalle, 'Exclusive Property Versus Open Commons. The Case of Gene Patents' (2013) The WIPO Journal 143.

18 *Ibid.*

19 'A patent pool consists of a set of agreements, where licenses are bundled into one package and licensed out by the pool to third party licensees, allowing interested parties to gain access to all patents to use an invention with one single package license, sometimes called a "one-stop-license", rather than obtaining licenses from each patent owner individually,' see Esther van Zimmeren and others, "Patent pools and clearinghouses in the life sciences" (2011) Trends in Biotechnology 570. Patent pools are hardly a new concept; the first known patent pool was established in 1856 by three sewing machine manufacturers. The idea to 'pool patents' was brought up by U.S. lawyer Orlando B. Potter in order to 'enable the production of complicated machines without legal battles over patent rights,' see Elisabeth Eppinger, *Patent Pools* (Springer 2015), 53ff.

20 Clearinghouses are platforms that operate as a neutral intermediary or platform for a wide variety of licensable technologies with substantial expertise in licensing, see Van Overwalle (n 15) 312.

21 Van Overwalle (n 16) 112.

22 *Ibid.*

This apparent 'paradox' was the decisive steppingstone of her academic path towards creating the inclusive patent, and the hypothesis of whether it should indeed be considered paradoxical will be explored in the third section of this chapter. However, closer analysis of her research shows that the conceptual idea of the inclusive patent started to develop even earlier. For instance, already in a 2010 article she subtly called for a reconceptualisation of patent law toward its conclusion.[23] In that article, she emphasised that a patent should 'no longer be viewed as a title giving (almost) complete freedom to exclude others from use, but rather as a temporary permit to exploit monopoly rights under fair and reasonable conditions, investing technology owners with the authority to invent and share, in other words, as a "duty bearing privilege"'.[24]

She then uses the term 'inclusive' patent for the first time in the title of the article 'Smart Innovation and Inclusive Patents for Sustainable Food and Health Care: Redefining the Europe 2020 Objectives' from 2013.[25] Interestingly, in that article Van Overwalle references the broader policy goals outlined in the 'Europe 2020 Strategy', which itself was published in 2010, emphasising the need for the European Union to move 'Towards a smarter, greener, and more inclusive EU economy', setting out a vision for 'sustainable growth' that is both 'socially inclusive' and innovation driven.[26] This linguistic and temporal alignment might suggest that Van Overwalle's inclusive patent, at least in its terminology, has been inspired by the broader European policy goals.

2. THE INCLUSIVE PATENT

Van Overwalle unfolds her inclusive patent idea in 2015 in an article titled 'Inventing Inclusive Patents: From Old to New Open Innovation', published in the inaugural volume of a new periodical named 'Kritika'.[27] While editor Hanns Ullrich envisioned the periodical as 'an island of tranquillity'[28] for

---

23 Van Overwalle (n 8) 1630.

24 *Ibid.* 1631.

25 Geertrui Van Overwalle, 'Smart Innovation and Inclusive Patents for Sustainable Food and Health Care: Redefining the Europe 2020 Objectives' in Christophe Geiger (ed), *Constructing European Intellectual Property. Achievements and New Perspectives* (Edward Elgar 2013). In the introduction, she also juxtaposes the concept of 'inclusivity' with 'exclusivity', noting that 'patents may also have some unintended, over-exclusive ("under inclusive") consequences and hinder access and further research and development in the area of biotechnology.'

26 European Commission, 'EUROPE 2020. A strategy for smart, sustainable and inclusive growth' COM (2010) 2020 final, 10.

27 Van Overwalle (n 1) 206ff. She published the same framework in a slightly shortened version one year later, see Geertrui Van Overwalle, 'Innovation without Property?' in Veerle Achten, Geert Bouckaert and Erik Schokkaert (eds), *A Truly Golden Handbook. The Scholarly Quest for Utopia* (Leuven University Press 2016).

28 See the editorial of Kritika: Volume 1 (n 1) at xiii.

the analysis of intellectual property law – where authors could freely explore principles, assumptions, and goals – Van Overwalle did not hesitate to stir the pot. She issued bold calls for essential reform to patent law, setting in motion a process of emergent critical scholarship with her vision for a more accessible, collaborative, and sustainably open innovation ecosystem. In doing so, she perfectly embodied the periodical's mission to 'set in train a process of emergent critical scholarship.'[29]

Van Overwalle envisioned the inclusive patent as a groundbreaking mechanism designed to cultivate an innovation ecosystem that is not only more accessible and collaborative but also deeply aligned with the principles of universal and sustainable openness. To fully grasp the significance and potential of the inclusive patent, it is essential to first explore the intricacies of the 'new open innovation' approach that underpins it.

Van Overwalle's conceptualisation of new open innovation rests on three essential criteria. First, it must embrace both for-profit and not-for-profit innovation and motivation, since she critiques the traditional concept of 'open innovation' for being predominantly firm-centred, heavily focused on for-profit motives within an IP dominated system.[30] In much of the existing literature, open innovation is framed around the strategies and interests of large firms, where the primary goal is commercial gain.[31] According to Van Overwalle, this traditional view neglects user and community-centred innovation movements, which prioritise accessibility and collaboration over profit. She emphasises that this form of open innovation, despite its potential to foster a more inclusive and widespread innovation ecosystem, has been underrepresented in the literature for a long time.[32] Therefore, new open innovation should accommodate both for-profit and not-for-profit motivations.

Second, Van Overwalle argues that new open innovation should strive for universal and sustainable openness. While she criticised the binary classification of openness (open vs. closed) in the past, suggesting instead that openness exists on a continuum,[33] she emphasises that new open innovation should foster a regime where technology and inventions are freely accessible to all, allowing everyone to use and improve the invention without the need for prior

---

29 *Ibid.* xiii.

30 Van Overwalle (n 1) 226ff.

31 The concept of 'open innovation', that was coined 2003 by Henry Chesbrough, indeed mainly focuses on firm-centred innovation; see Henry Chesbrough, *Open Innovation: The New Imperative for Creating and Profiting from Technology* (Harvard Business School Press 2003); Henry Chesbrough, 'Open Innovation: A New Paradigm for Understanding Industrial Innovation' in Henry Chesbrough, Wim Vanhaverbeke and Joel West (eds), *Open Innovation* (Oxford University Press 2006).

32 Van Overwalle (n 1) 209ff.

33 Van Overwalle (n 16) 105.

permission.[34] More crucially, she underscores the importance of sustainability – ensuring that this openness is perpetuated over time, so that the benefits of innovation are continually passed from one inventor to the next, fostering a 'chain of openness among follow-on innovators.'[35]

Third, Van Overwalle asserts that new open innovation must be established at a low cost, in contrast to the cost-intensive nature of 'old' open innovation models. She emphasises that innovation should be made open and kept open through the dynamic interplay between property rights and contracts – what she terms the 'marriage of public and private ordering.'[36] However, as her previous research showed, this interplay is often too expensive to be widely adopted, which undermines its attractiveness as a strategy for fostering openness.[37]

This is where the inclusive patent should come into play. Van Overwalle proposes this idea as a solution to achieving this new form of open innovation. It shall be a credible, low-cost, and easy-to-obtain property right that encourages sharing and collaboration rather than exclusion. The inclusive patent does not aim to replace or alter the traditional patent system, which is centred on exclusivity. Instead, it introduces a voluntary, one-sided right that 'encompasses the right to include' others. In other words, this right should entitle the owner to conclude licences that establish and enforce sharing behaviour, thereby supporting further downstream innovation in a sustainable manner.[38] 'The inclusive patent owner is free to request pecuniary compensation or not. When he acts in a for-profit motivation, he may well ask a fee. However, when he operates under a not-for-profit mind set, he may not charge any remuneration.'[39] The inclusive patent does not allow the rightsholder to exclude a third party from the use of his patent – even if the rightsholder later on were to change his mind.[40] It only allows him to enforce his patent against 'non-willing or non-sharing' users and put an end to their right of use and invalidate the licence.[41]

Conceptually, the inclusive patent, like the traditional patent, would be a high-threshold patent, meaning it would need to meet the same stringent protection requirements. The inclusive patent is envisioned as an 'at your fingertips' registration patent, where substantive examination would occur

---

34 Van Overwalle (n 1) 227.

35 In her previous works, she criticised that most 'totally open regimes – created through licenses of right, compulsory licenses, patent pools or clearinghouses – only establish "fist generation", "one shot" or "relative" openness: openness is established towards a first subsequent user, after which openness comes to an end', see Van Overwalle (n 16) 113.

36 Van Overwalle (n 1) 249.

37 *Ibid.* 248.

38 *Ibid.* 250; Van Overwalle (n 27) 308.

39 Van Overwalle (n 1) 255.

40 *Ibid.* 253.

41 *Ibid.* 253ff; Van Overwalle (n 27) 309.

only if requested by the patent owner, a third party, or the patent office after the grant.[42] It would be protected for the same duration as a traditional patent, but significantly lower in cost to promote the underlying ethos of sharing; however, Van Overwalle notes that further research is needed to determine the exact cost structure.[43]

To implement an inclusive patent regime, Van Overwalle suggests two potential modes of action. The first is a hybrid, public-private, semi-codified regime where the inclusive patent entitlement is established by law, while the specific licensing terms are determined by private parties. The second option is a fully codified regime, where the sharing ethos is not left to private actors but is fully legislated, with the law serving as the sole driving force behind inclusivity.[44]

To sum it up, Van Overwalle envisions the inclusive patent as a desirable legal tool designed to foster collaborative innovation by prioritising inclusion over exclusion. While a traditional patent grants the holder an exclusive right to exclude others from using the patented product without consent, it also implicitly includes the right to include others through licensing. The inclusive patent, in contrast, is to be constructed as a 'one sided' legal tool that is specifically targeted at including others. In other words, the inclusive patent – only – provides a legal entitlement 'empowering the right holder to control licensing conditions and establish and enforce open source type licenses.'[45]

3. EXCLUSIVITY DOES NOT EXCLUDE INCLUSIVITY – EXCLUSIVITY JUST NEEDS TO BE CONFINED

Following her detailed exploration of the inclusive patent, Van Overwalle underscores that 'the ultimate goal of both the patent narrative and the sharing ethos is the achievement of welfare,' clarifying that 'sharing is *not* a value in itself, but rather an instrument to achieve something else.'[46] In other words, openness should not be ends in themselves but should be evaluated based on their contribution to broader objectives, including economic efficiency, access to essential technologies, and public health. Thus, Van Overwalle's emphasis on inclusion cannot be viewed just for its own sake but because it can lead to a more dynamic, equitable, and socially beneficial innovation ecosystem. This careful balancing act underscores her nuanced approach to intellectual property.

---

42 Van Overwalle (n 1) 259ff; Van Overwalle (n 27) 309.
43 Van Overwalle (n 1) 262; Van Overwalle (n 27) 310.
44 Van Overwalle (n 1) 255; Van Overwalle (n 27) 309.
45 Van Overwalle (n 27) 308.
46 Van Overwalle (n 1) 262.

A cornerstone of Van Overwalle's vision for the inclusive patent is its ability to formalise and facilitate the enforcement of follow-up sharing behaviour through its design as a one-sided right. As such, the inclusive patent is specifically aimed at institutionalising sharing behaviour, ensuring that improvements and follow-up inventions are consistently shared and integrated within the innovation ecosystem. This approach prevents any single participant from monopolising the benefits of shared innovation and guarantees that the advantages of innovation are perpetually shared, reinforcing the collective nature of progress.

Particularly compelling is her nuanced recognition of the diverse nature of innovation ecosystems, where the drivers of innovation can vary across sectors and communities. Her research shows that alternative systems can flourish under the right conditions, especially when there is a strong community ethos. Her purpose-driven perspective is further evidenced by the fact that Van Overwalle's research was never merely theoretical; it is deeply grounded in the practical examples and realities of how open innovation initiatives have been successfully implemented across various industries. She delved into real-world examples where collaborative efforts have effectively navigated and, in some cases, overcome the limitations of traditional, exclusionary patent systems. The examples that her research provides are numerous, but to name a few: The DVD and MPEG-2 patent pools,[47] the Golden Rice[48] and Medicines patent pools (MPP),[49] Pool for neglected tropical diseases,[50] the SARS Patent Pool,[51] and

47 DVD patent pools emerged as the industry developed standards for DVD technology. Two distinct pools were formed: the DVD4C pool and the DVD6C pool, involving major players in the industry. Similarly, the MPEG-2 patent pool was created to manage the patents essential to the MPEG-2 digital video compression standard. This pool allowed multiple patent holders to combine their patents, offering a single license to users, thereby simplifying access to essential technology for manufacturers and fostering the global spread of the standard, see Van Overwalle (n 16) 94.

48 The Golden Rice patent pool was established to facilitate access to patents for genetically enriched rice. This pool allowed key patent holders to grant licences free of charge to developing countries, enabling the transfer of technology to improve nutrition in these regions, see Van Overwalle (n 15) 311; Geertrui Van Overwalle, 'Patent pools and clearinghouses in the life sciences: back to the future' in Duncan Matthews and Herbert Zech (eds), *Research Handbook on Intellectual Property and the Life Sciences* (Edward Elgar 2016).

49 Established by UNITAID and supported by the WHO, the is a United Nations-backed public health organisation working to increase access to and facilitate the development of life-saving medicines for low- and middle-income countries (https://medicinespatentpool.org/ accessed 04 March 2025), see van Zimmeren and others (n 19) 570.

50 Proposed by GlaxoSmithKline, this pool aims to encourage research and development for treatments of neglected tropical diseases. By pooling patents and related know-how, the initiative seeks to overcome the lack of market incentives that typically hinders innovation in this area, see van Zimmeren and others (n 19) 570.

51 The SARS patent pool, supported by the WHO, showcased how patent pooling could mobilise resources during a health crisis. Though the pool itself became inactive, see Van Overwalle (n 16) 96. Similar ideas emerged during COVID-19 pandemic with initiatives like C-TAP (www.who.int/initiatives/covid-19-technology-access-pool, accessed 04 March 2025) and the Open COVID Pledge (https://opencovidpledge.org/ accessed 04 March 2025).

more recently the Syngenta e-Licensing Platform and ILP Vegetable platform,[52] or the Open Source Seed Initiative (OSSI).[53]

However, while these examples may demonstrate that openness is sought and achieved in various circumstances, they have all been developed within the framework of the 'traditional' exclusive patent system. This naturally raises a central question: If open innovation can indeed flourish under the current system, what particular gaps might the inclusive patent be designed to fill? To explore this, we must closely examine the legal nature of the widely embraced term 'inclusion'. Understanding how inclusion operates within the framework of patent law is crucial, not just to determine if it stands in opposition to exclusion, but to uncover the extent to which these concepts are intertwined. Can the inclusive patent, with its design as a 'one-sided right', truly be considered 'only' one side of the 'half and half glass', or does it suggest that inclusion and exclusion are not as distinct as they might seem?

What quickly becomes evident is that the inclusive patent inherently relies on a certain degree of exclusion. Inclusion requires patent holders to enforce specific obligations, particularly the requirement to maintain openness for follow-up innovations. This setup means that patent holders retain the right to enforce such conditions, and if others fail to comply, they may still be excluded from using the patented technology. What may initially seem paradoxical – using exclusivity to enforce openness – is, in fact, not a paradox at all. Exclusivity remains the cornerstone of IP law and policy, providing the rightsholder with the freedom to decide how and for what purpose his granted rights are used. Therefore, the inclusive patent, which ostensibly seeks to reduce the exclusionary nature of traditional patents, cannot fully escape the need to exclude those who do not adhere to the set conditions.

This inherent reliance on exclusion becomes even more pronounced when considering the costs associated with enforcing inclusivity. Even though Van Overwalle envisions the inclusive patent as a low-cost tool within the patent system, the financial burden of enforcing inclusion would remain significant. Litigation costs in patent law usually are substantial, typically justified by the

---

52 The SGC is a public-private partnership that offers breeders and research institutes guaranteed access to a wide portfolio of patented native traits and enabling technologies present in their commercial vegetable varieties. ILP Vegetable was launched by a group of breeding companies to guarantee worldwide access to patents covering crucial vegetable plant traits. The aim is to guarantee worldwide access to patents that cover crucial vegetable plant traits that are currently covered by patent claims by ILP Vegetable member companies, see Geertrui Van Overwalle, 'Creating universal and sustainable access to plants and seeds' in Fabien Girard and Christine Frison (eds), *The Commons, Plant Breeding and Agricultural Research*, (Routledge 2018) 91.

53 OSSI is dedicated to maintaining fair and open access to plant genetic resources worldwide. Inspired by the free and open-source software movement, it aims to ensure that any distributed seeds or new varieties bred from them remain accessible under the same open terms, see Van Overwalle (n 52) 95.

potential for profit or market advantage. Enforcing inclusion, particularly the principles of universal and sustainable openness, will involve similar expenses but would not operate within the same framework of economic self-interest. That is because there normally will be no immediate financial gain from enforcing compliance by third parties. Instead of financial gains, the primary rewards for ensuring inclusivity lie in fostering collaboration, facilitating knowledge sharing to the benefit of third parties, thereby contributing to broader societal or communal benefits. While these goals certainly are valuable from a public good perspective, they lack the immediate and personal financial incentives that drive enforcement in traditional patent contexts, making it more challenging for patent holders to justify the high costs of litigation in such circumstances – potentially weakening the inclusive patent's ability to achieve its intended impact.

Moreover, the traditional patent system, while fundamentally centred on the principle of exclusivity, is already designed with a built-in versatility that allows patent holders to exercise both exclusion and inclusion as they see fit. This adaptability allows patent holders to shape and balance their strategies – whether focusing on protecting a competitive advantage, generating revenue through licensing, or fostering collaboration – depending on what best serves their interests at any given time. Therefore, at its core, what Van Overwalle describes as (voluntary) inclusion might be more accurately understood as willingness of patent holders accept 'less exclusion'. From this perspective, inclusion is not an independent principle but rather a way of how exclusivity can be used, more concretely: to temper the exclusionary power of patents.

This leads to the crucial question: Are the incentives that are provided within the current patent system sufficient to achieve the level of openness envisioned by Van Overwalle on a voluntary basis?

One way in which the right holder can opt for collaboration in the current system are mechanisms like the licence of right, which essentially means a declaration to a patent office to the effect that 'the proprietor is prepared to allow any person to use the invention as a licensee in return for appropriate consideration.'[54] While this concept has longstanding roots – Germany, for instance, has incorporated the licence of right since 1936,[55] and similar ideas can be traced back even further[56] – it is worth examining whether such a mechanism effectively promotes the level of openness and collaborative innovation envisioned by proposals like the inclusive patent.

---

54 Article 8(1) of the Regulation (EU) 1257/2012 of 17 December 2012 implementing enhanced cooperation in the area of the creation of unitary patent protection [2012] OJ L 361/1.

55 §14 of the German Patent Act (1936), now regulated in §23 of the German Patent Act.

56 See Daniel Krauspenhaar, *Liability Rules in Patent Law* (Springer 2015) 104, according to whom the first licences of right provisions were introduced in 1903 in Canada, which was at that time a British Crown Colony, and subsequently in 1919 in England.

A key distinction between the inclusive patent and the licences of right lies in the timing of the commitment to openness. The inclusive patent, as envisioned by Van Overwalle, requires such a commitment from the outset – a one-way street where the patent holder decides, at the very beginning, to prioritise inclusion and collaboration over exclusivity. This decision cannot be reversed, meaning the patent holder must embrace the potential benefits and risks of openness without the option to revert to exclusivity later on.[57] In contrast, licence of right offer more flexibility. Patent holders can opt for openness at a later stage, after evaluating the technology's market impact and potential value. This allows them to retain full exclusivity initially, securing their competitive advantage, and only later deciding to open up access if and when it aligns with their strategic goals. From the perspective of commercially driven and profit-oriented actor, this raises the question of why one would choose to file for an inclusive patent when licence of right offers greater flexibility.

That being said, empirical research suggests that licence of right is used primarily 'by large firms with large patent portfolios for less valuable and/or older patents in order to save costs' and 'predominantly in the area of complex technologies and less likely in fields where a firm directly competes with others.'[58] It becomes clear that although the licence of right mechanism has gained certain traction, it will not be the final solution to opening up the system if it is mainly used for cost-saving in older patents. On the contrary, firms are highly unlikely to renounce exclusivity for patents that hold significant commercial value. Therefore, alternative incentives and mechanisms must be explored to encourage more widespread and early sharing of valuable technologies – incentives that go beyond mere cost reductions and simplifying registration or other administrative processes.

One idea would be to directly incentivise the licensing process by having the state double the licensing fees at least for specific, strategically important technologies.[59] The advantage of this approach is that it would directly encourage patent holders to consider licensing as a financially attractive option, potentially increasing the availability of valuable technologies in the market. By offering a significant financial incentive, the state could make sharing these technologies more appealing, even for patents that hold substantial commercial value. However, the effectiveness of this approach may vary significantly across different industries. In highly competitive sectors like pharmaceuticals or high-tech, where patents are often the core of a company's competitive advantage, patent holders may resist licensing despite direct financial incentives. It could also lead to unintended market distortions: By offering financial incentives for

---

57 Van Overwalle (n 1) 253.

58 Krauspenhaar (n 56) 125.

59 This idea was suggested by Prof. Dietmar Harhoff, Director at the Max Planck Institute for Innovation and Competition, during a discussion with the first author.

specific licensing, the state could inadvertently distort the market, encouraging the licensing of technologies that might not otherwise be considered viable or strategic. This distortion could lead to a misallocation of resources within the innovation ecosystem.

Ultimately, the question remains whether a truly optimal balance between openness and exclusivity within the patent system can ever be achieved solely through voluntary actions by patent holders. What seems to be clear is that no single tool or legal mechanism will be sufficient to untangle that 'Gordian knot'. Van Overwalle's inclusive patent makes a compelling case for institutionalising inclusivity within the patent system, but it is not a silver bullet for resolving the system's inherent challenges. To ensure that third parties have sufficient access to critical technologies, despite the exclusivity granted by patents, a coordinated and multifaceted approach will be required. While creating incentives to encourage patent holders to voluntarily forego exclusivity is certainly one avenue, though its intricacies cannot be fully explored here, it is also important to recognise the limits of this approach. In many cases, mandatory measures such as targeted statutory rights of use and compulsory licences – measures that are already in place but potentially insufficient – may be necessary to overcome barriers to access. As mentioned above, Van Overwalle has also done pioneering work in this area, and it remains to be hoped that she will continue to accompany the development of patent law with her scientific acumen, particularly from this perspective.

CHAPTER 3

OPEN INNOVATION AND INTELLECTUAL PROPERTY

How Open are 'Open Innovation' Agreements?

Arina Gorbatyuk
Researcher Fellow, KU Leuven Centre for IT & IP Law
IP Legal Consultant, Sirius Legal Business Law Firm (Belgium)

H4 AC-DC Key
With this key, you can open a door from both sides at the same time.

1. INTRODUCTION

The concept 'open innovation' (OI), initially introduced by Henry Chesbrough in his book of 2003,[1] became so popular that it naturally turned into a 'buzzword'.[2] Over time, the meaning of the term broadened to cover nearly any form of inter-organisational knowledge exchanges, especially those related to innovation processes and collaborative research and development (R&D) initiatives.[3] The concept was not only the subject of numerous academic

---

1 Henry William Chesbrough, *Open Innovation: The New Imperative for Creating and Profiting from Technology* (Harvard Business Press 2003).

2 Helmut Traitler, Heribert J Watzke and I Sam Saguy, 'Reinventing R&D in an Open Innovation Ecosystem' (2011) 76 Journal of Food Science R62, R62.

3 Originally, Chesbrough defined OI as 'a paradigm that assumes firms can and should use external ideas as well as internal ideas, and internal and external paths to market, as the firms look to advance their technology' (Chesbrough (n 1) xxiv), already in 2006 the term was redefined as 'the use of purposive inflows and outflows of knowledge to accelerate internal innovation, and expand the markets for external use of innovation, respectively' (Henry Chesbrough, 'Open Innovation: A New Paradigm for Understanding Industrial Innovation' in Henry Chesbrough, Vanhaverbeke Wim and Joel West (eds), *Open Innovation: Researching*

articles[4] but was also embraced by the industry, which proudly stated that they engaged in OI activities.[5] Moreover, policymakers, including the European Commission, referenced OI to justify the importance of their legislative initiatives.[6] Like-minded researchers even established a strong international community that continues to actively study the concept and gathers annually at the OI conference to share their latest findings.[7]

Even though the concept of OI is not as widely referenced today, back in 2012, the year when my path crossed with my PhD supervisors Prof. Dr. Geertrui Van Overwalle and Prof. Dr. Esther van Zimmeren, exploring OI was without doubt a major focus for many scholars, particularly those in management and economics. Since the concept was primarily studied by these disciplines, translating it for a legal audience proved to be a challenging task. Within the legal community, the term 'open' is often associated with something that is shared freely, accessible to everyone, or not significantly burdened by legal barriers, conditions that are not central to engaging in OI activities. In fact, in line with the OI philosophy, the innovation process can be considered open when relevant actors are willing to open the boundaries of their internal R&D processes, cooperate with external partners, make use of external knowledge, and share their own knowledge in the pursuit of advancing knowledge and technologies. These opening up processes can be restrictive, done on a bilateral and pecuniary basis. Providing access to all interested parties or offering access free of charge can be a way to open up the innovation process, but it is not a core requirement for being considered a pro-OI entity.

---

a New Paradigm (Oxford University Press 2006) 1) and in 2014 the concept was further nuanced: 'we define open innovation as a distributed innovation process based on purposively managed knowledge flows across organizational boundaries, using pecuniary and non-pecuniary mechanisms in line with the organization's business model' (Henry Chesbrough and Marcel Bogers, 'Explicating Open Innovation: Clarifying an Emerging Paradigm for Understanding Innovation' in Henry Chesbrough, Wim Vanhaverbeke and Joel West (eds), *New Frontiers in Open Innovation* (Oxford University Press 2014) 17).

4 To keep pace with the rapid developments on OI scholarship, the scholarly community has frequently produced literature review papers, see, for instance, Adrián Kovács, Bart Van Looy and Bruno Cassiman, 'Exploring the Scope of Open Innovation: A Bibliometric Review of a Decade of Research' (2015) 104 Scientometrics 951; Barbara Bigliardi and others, 'The Past, Present and Future of Open Innovation' (2021) 24 European Journal of Innovation Management 1130.

5 See, for instance, Ruchon (2014) 'For Philips, Open Innovation is Vital to Stay Ahead of Competition' Innovation Management https://innovationmanagement.se/2014/06/25/for-philips-open-innovation-is-vital-to-stay-ahead-of-competition/; GE (2014) 'Open Innovation and Advanced Technology Empowers Energy Revolution' Press Release www.ge.com/news/press-releases/open-innovation-and-advanced-technology-empowers-energy-revolution; Michael Idelchik and Sam Kogan, 'GE's Open Collaboration Model' (2012) 55 Research-Technology Management 28; Luke Collins, 'Netherlands "Technopole" Takes Open Innovation To Next Stage' (2006) 49 Research Technology Management 2.

6 See, for instance, the preamble of the Directive (EU) 2016/943 of the European Parliament and of the Council of 8 June 2016 on the protection of undisclosed know-how and business information (trade secrets) against their unlawful acquisition, use and disclosure.

7 http://openinnovation.net.

Prof. Van Overwalle, Prof. van Zimmeren, and I spent numerous hours exploring how to, on the one hand, overcome the professional bias of our core audience (legal scholars) and, on the other hand, how best to translate OI strategies to legal architecture and the field of intellectual property (IP) law. This book provides a wonderful opportunity to commemorate our cooperation on this challenging, yet rewarding, academic journey.

After reviewing multiple managerial and economic scholarships, which were summarised by another invaluable member of our KU Leuven OI research team, Dr. Adrián Kovács,[8] it soon became apparent that what the existing scholarship lacked was a deep understanding of how OI activities were shaped from a legal perspective. More specifically, OI scholars often viewed IP predominantly as an object of exchange, without considering the dynamic nature of IP legislation and the flexibilities offered by contract law. However, this very dynamism plays a significant role in determining how 'open' a given OI activity truly is.

As explained in Section 2 of this contribution, economic and managerial scholars quickly realised that the dichotomy of closed versus open innovation, as initially introduced by Chesbrough, was not functional in practice as it was too black-and-white and did not represent the realities of knowledge exchange.[9] To address this shortcoming, some scholars turned to exploring the degree of openness of OI activities, focusing more specifically on three core aspects: the openness of OI processes, the openness of shared knowledge, and the openness of innovation outcomes.

Whereas the managerial and economic literature on the openness of OI provides a solid understanding that some OI activities are more open than others depending on the explored criteria, it does not examine the dynamics provided by legal instruments, such as flexibilities offered by IP contracts (Section 3). As legal scholars, we found it surprising that this aspect was overlooked, as IP contracts are, from our professional perspective, the core mechanisms for determining the conditions under which knowledge is exchanged and the level of access granted.

Contracts are, in essence, keys to otherwise locked IP. IP, in turn, are believed (until proven otherwise) to be a valuable driver of innovation. In other words, contractual arrangements are the actual tools that unlock IP-protected knowledge and are primary enablers of OI activities.

If we take this analogy further, a standard house key typically allows one to open and close a door and have access to what lies behind it. A homeowner is generally free to decide whom to give a key to their property.

8 Kovács, Van Looy and Cassiman (n 4).

9 Paul Trott and Dap Hartmann, 'Why "open Innovation" Is Old Wine in New Bottles' (2009) 13 International Journal of Innovation Management 715, 716.

Similarly, contracts act as intangible keys to unlock IP and provide access to it to interested parties. However, whereas standard tangible keys allow one to either open or close a door, contracts may provide varying degrees of openness. For instance, some contracts grant a sophisticated key that ensures that the keyholder can never be locked out (H3). Others allow 'smaller' actors (parties with lower bargaining power) to enter the room, thus, overcoming barriers established by more dominant parties (H1). Still others permit the door to be unlocked from both sides, providing a higher level of accessibility and ensuring reciprocal, equal rights to what lies behind the door (H4). Not every key to IP allows the property owner to close the door again or invite others in. The keyholder may also not be permitted to open the door widely. In other words, keys to IP come in different shapes and forms, offering different degrees of openness (Section 4).

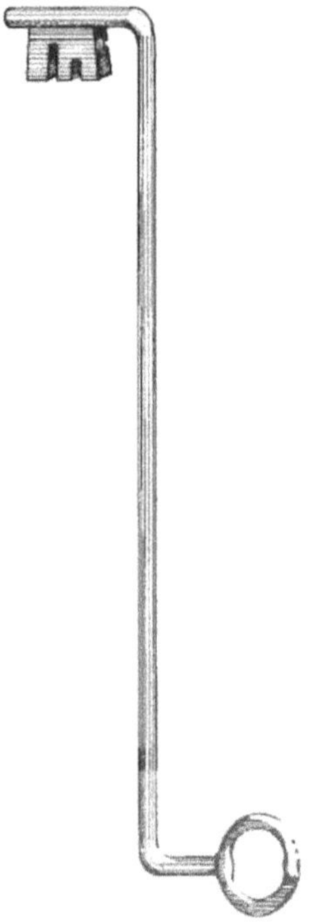

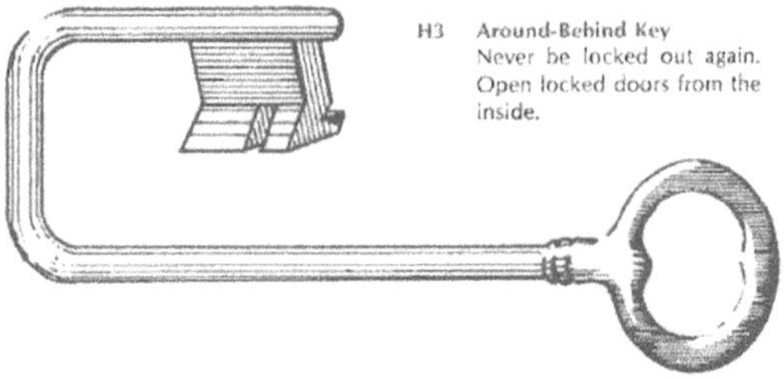

H3 Around-Behind Key
Never be locked out again. Open locked doors from the inside.

H1 Tiny Tim Key
For short people with high locks on doors or tall people with low locks. Please indicate your height, and the height of your lock.

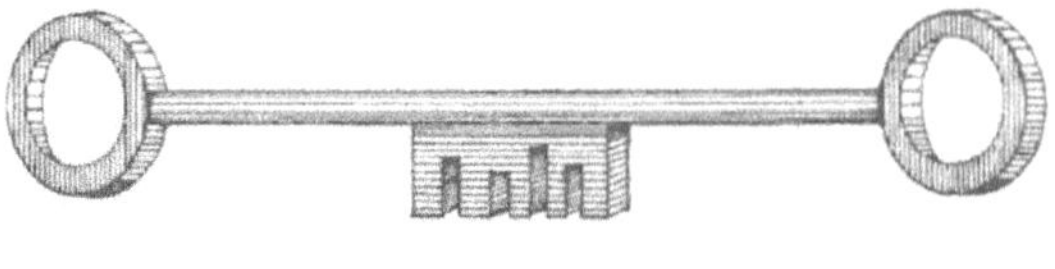

H4 AC-DC Key
With this key, you can open a door from both sides at the same time.

2. OPENNESS OF OI: AN ECONOMIC AND MANAGERIAL PERSPECTIVE

As explained in the introduction, the word 'open' in OI created a high level of confusion as it may inaccurately suggest that such innovation is 'open' because the underlying shared knowledge is open for everyone for free and without (legal) constraints. However, according to the definition put forward by Chesbrough, OI is not primarily centred on making knowledge available to all interested parties, contrary to such concepts as open science, open access, or open source.[10] Some scholars even refer to the concept developed by Chesbrough as 'OI à la Chesbrough' to distinguish it from the mentioned concepts as well as works of other renowned scholars such as Eric von Hippel (open user innovation)[11] and Robert Allen (collective innovation).[12,13]

To add nuance to the concept and counter this misconception, economic and managerial scholars have dedicated significant attention to exploring what makes innovation 'open', and numerous scholarly works have been dedicated to examining the degrees of openness of OI from various perspectives.[14] As with any complex matter, there is no universal understanding or definition of what constitutes 'openness' in the context OI. Nor does this contribution aim to provide an exhaustive overview of the existing scholarship on openness in OI. The economic and managerial literature on this topic is extensive and approaches the subject from various angles.[15] However, not all of these angles are

---

10 Even these mechanisms do not provide for 'unlimited' and 'uncontrolled' openness. Depending on the type of open access license (e.g. Creative Commons licenses) or open source license (e.g. MIT, GPL) applied, the use of shared knowledge may still be subject to legal conditions, such as attribution requirements, non-commercial use limitations, or share-alike obligations. For more information, see Amanda Brock, *Open Source Law, Policy, and Practice* (Second edition, Oxford University Press 2022); Zachary Katz, 'Pitfalls of Open Licensing: An Analysis of Creative Commons Licensing' (2005) 46 IDEA: The Intellectual Property Law Review 391.

11 Eric von Hippel, 'Open User Innovation' in Bronwyn H Hall and Nathan Rosenberg (eds), *Handbook of the Economics of Innovation*, vol 1 (North-Holland 2010).

12 Robert C Allen, 'Collective Invention' (1983) 4 Journal of Economic Behavior & Organization 1.

13 Julien Pénin, 'More Open than Open Innovation? Rethinking the Concept of Openness in Innovation Studies' [2008] Working Papers of BETA https://ideas.repec.org//p/ulp/sbbeta/2008-18.html, accessed 27 September 2023.

14 Eelko KRE Huizingh, 'Open Innovation: State of the Art and Future Perspectives' (2011) 31 Technovation 2; Linus Dahlander and David M Gann, 'How Open Is Innovation?' (2010) 39 Research Policy 699; Linus Dahlander, David M Gann and Martin W Wallin, 'How Open Is Innovation? A Retrospective and Ideas Forward' (2021) 50 Research Policy 104218; Keld Laursen and Ammon Salter, 'Open for Innovation: The Role of Openness in Explaining Innovation Performance among U.K. Manufacturing Firms' (2006) 27 Strategic Management Journal 131; Keld Laursen and Ammon J Salter, 'The Paradox of Openness: Appropriability, External Search and Collaboration' (2014) 43 Open Innovation: New Insights and Evidence 867.

15 See, for instance, Christina Öberg and Allen T Alexander, 'The Openness of Open Innovation in Ecosystems – Integrating Innovation and Management Literature on Knowledge Linkages' (2019) 4 Journal of Innovation & Knowledge 211; Moulay Othman Idrissi Fakhreddine,

relevant to the core focus of this chapter, namely assessing the openness of OI activities based on the contingencies established in the underlying contractual relationships.

In this contribution, I focus only on the core scholarly works that originally shaped our understanding of how open OI is by assessing the openness of OI processes, the openness of shared knowledge, and the openness of innovation outcomes. More specifically, this section reviews academic contributions that examine the dimension of openness by focusing on how the innovation processes are organised, how openly the underlying IP and knowledge are shared, and how open/accessible outcomes of OI activities are to third parties. However, as explained in Section 2.4, these approaches have limitations as they do not delve into the contractual technicalities that shape the degree of openness of access to knowledge.

2.1. OPENNESS OF INNOVATION PROCESSES

Henry Chesbrough, in his original book, claimed that since approximately 1980, public and private entities gradually shifted from the so-called 'closed innovation' (CI) model to an OI model by increasingly relying on external partners and using external knowledge throughout the innovation process.[16] Chesbrough relies on the term 'open' to signify the phenomenon of opening up organisations' boundaries during the innovation process.[17] The proposed definition suggests that any type of knowledge exchange aimed at advancing knowledge and technologies and transcending the boundaries of an entity should be considered an OI activity. On the contrary, if a company does not rely on external knowledge and expertise, its innovation processes should be considered closed.

Scholars have defined specific modes of OI ('OI activities') that describe how entities engage in knowledge exchange and co-development, namely inbound and outbound processes[18] (also known as inside-out and outside-in processes), and coupled processes.[19] The outside-in/inbound process involves an entity enhancing its knowledge base by acquiring necessary external technology. By engaging in inside-out/outbound processes, an entity can generate revenue

Nabil Amaraa and Réjean Landrya, 'SMEs' Degree of Openness: The Case of Manufacturing Industries' (2012) 7 Journal of Technology Management & Innovation 186; Laursen and Salter, 'Open for Innovation' (n 14); Valentina Lazzarotti and Raffaella Manzini, 'Different Modes Of Open Innovation: A Theoretical Framework And An Empirical Study' (2009) 13 International Journal of Innovation Management 615; Dahlander, Gann and Wallin (n 14).

16 Chesbrough (n 1) xxiv.

17 *Ibid.*

18 Henry Chesbrough and Adrienne Kardon Crowther, 'Beyond High Tech: Early Adopters of Open Innovation in Other Industries' (2006) 36 R&D Management 229.

19 Oliver Gassmann and Ellen Enkel, 'Towards a Theory of Open Innovation: Three Core Process Archetypes'.

by selling or licensing its technologies to external partners. Entities can also combine inside-out and outside-in OI activities and engage in a coupled OI process with complementary partners by establishing R&D partnerships. Coupled OI generally involves a mutual exchange of existing knowledge (background IP) and aims to jointly improve this exchanged background IP and/or co-develop new knowledge (foreground IP), which makes it a more sophisticated form of OI.[20]

In his early works, Chesbrough applied a somewhat black-and-white approach to openness. Chesbrough did not distinguish between the scale or intensity of OI activities to measure the degree of openness of innovation processes. Following the logic of his book, it seemed sufficient for a company to grant or obtain a single license (in other words, engaging in inside-out/outbound process) to proclaim itself as an OI-spirited entity. Furthermore, the critics shortly pointed out that the dichotomy of closed versus open is inherently false as no industry in the 21st century can continue engaging in R&D in an old-fashioned (closed) way – due to various internal and external factors, such as technology complexity, patent thickets, governmental stimuli to engage in OI – and entities are naturally 'forced' to explore more open approaches to innovation.[21]

Considering these obvious imperfections in the narrative of Chesbrough, managerial and economic scholars questioned whether it is sufficient to apply such a narrow binary dichotomy to identify whether organisation's innovation processes are open or closed and suggested that, in reality, OI incorporates variable degrees of openness.[22] They denoted that some innovation activities may be less open depending on particular factors, e.g. openness of shared and/or co-developed knowledge and their accessibility to third parties.

2.2. OPENNESS OF SHARED KNOWLEDGE

Chesbrough's broad definition of openness fails to capture the complexities and nuances of engaging in knowledge exchange with external parties. To address this limitation, Dahlander and Gann assert that, in practice, organisations adopt different forms of openness when opening up their

20 Arina Gorbatyuk, Geertrui Van Overwalle and Esther van Zimmeren, 'Intellectual Property Ownership in Coupled Open Innovation Processes' (2016) 47 IIC – International Review of Intellectual Property and Competition Law 262, 264.

21 Trott and Hartmann (n 9) 728. In addition, Trott and Hartmann go as far as to question the originality of the concept, suggesting that it is little more than old wine in new bottles claiming that 'this paradigm represents little more than the repackaging and representation of concepts and findings presented over the past forty years within the literature on innovation management' (*ibid.* 715).

22 Huizingh (n 14) 3; Dahlander and Gann (n 14) 670.

innovation processes and sharing their knowledge.[23] In their renowned article 'How open is open innovation?' – the title that clearly inspired the title of this contribution – the authors developed an analytical framework for assessing the degree of openness of OI by distinguishing inbound and outbound innovation and pecuniary and non-pecuniary modes of knowledge exchange. By applying this dichotomy, they identified four types of openness: (1) acquiring (pecuniary inbound innovation); (2) selling (pecuniary outbound innovation; (3) sourcing (non-pecuniary inbound innovation); and revealing (non-pecuniary outbound innovation).[24]

When evaluating the degree of openness of shared knowledge based on their typology, they explain that each mode has its advantages and disadvantages when shaping the extent of openness.[25] In principle, the non-pecuniary innovation permits access to a wide spectrum of knowledge and fosters incremental and cumulative innovation[26] as the knowledge is shared in a more 'open' form.

More specifically, by engaging in outbound innovation on a non-pecuniary basis, organisations engage in knowledge 'revealing' activity.[27] The process of 'revealing' is based either on the decision not to protect knowledge by IP or to open up IP through such mechanisms as open source licenses.[28] Opening up knowledge and moving away from a classic focus on tightly controlling ownership (the so-called use of IP as a shield) makes OI activities significantly more open, as any interested third party can potentially obtain access to the knowledge at stake. Thus, one can conclude that revealing knowledge to others and allowing them to use it with minimal proprietary constraints demonstrates a higher level of openness and encourages follow-on innovation. The process of 'revealing' is connected to such concepts as open science, open access, and open source.

By contrast, engaging in outbound/inbound innovation on a pecuniary basis requires a higher level of constraints as a 'buyer' and a 'seller' need to reach an agreement tailored to their specific purposes. To ensure that a 'buyer' is incentivised to engage in this transaction, it is important that underlying shared knowledge and technologies are protected by IP rights. Thus, this transaction is contingent on whether the parties reach a suitable agreement, which makes this transaction, in comparison to the act of 'revealing', less open as underlying knowledge is shared on an individual basis.

---

23 Dahlander and Gann (n 14).
24 *Ibid.* 702.
25 See Table 5 in *ibid.* 716.
26 *Ibid.* 706.
27 The counterparty in this scenario is engaging in the process of inbound innovation and the act of 'sourcing'.
28 Dahlander and Gann (n 14) 703.

However, the authors do not necessarily advocate for more openness as a higher level of openness to innovation activities comes at a cost and may entail negative consequences that may not be in line with corporate interests, such as unwanted disclosure of internal knowledge to competitors or difficulty in managing a high number of cooperation partners.[29] In this context, some scholars even attempted to investigate the 'optimal degree of openness in OI'.[30]

2.3. THE OPENNESS OF INNOVATION OUTCOMES

Huizingh offers yet another perspective on how the openness of innovation can be assessed by focusing on how accessible the innovation outcomes to third parties are. As a starting point, he revisits the original closed versus open innovation typology introduced by Chesbrough and adds another analytical layer to it. Huizingh's work advances the somewhat black-and-white approach of Chesbrough and asserts that to assess the level of openness of an organisation's innovation practices it is not sufficient to only assess whether the innovation process is closed or open, it is also important to consider whether the innovation outcome is accessible to external parties.[31]

Whereas Dahlander and Gann conduct their review of openness of the output differentiating between two types of OI processes and pecuniary and non-pecuniary modes of knowledge exchange, Huizingh invites the reader to take a step back. He demonstrates that a CI process can lead to OI outcomes and vice versa. Thus, when evaluating the openness of innovation, it is important to look at the broader framework to come to accurate and nuanced conclusions.

More specifically, according to Huizingh, both the process and the outcome of innovation can either be closed or open. Based on this starting point, he developed a typology that describes four ways of innovation based on the openness of both the process and the outcome of innovation: (1) closed innovation (CI process and CI outcome); (2) private OI (OI process and CI outcome); (3) public innovation (CI process and OI outcome); and (4) open source innovation (OI process and OI outcome).[32]

---

29 *Ibid.* 706.

30 Haizhen Wu, Zhao'an Han and Yong Zhou, 'Optimal Degree of Openness in Open Innovation: A Perspective from Knowledge Acquisition & Knowledge Leakage' (2021) 67 Technology in Society 101756.

31 Huizingh (n 14).

32 *Ibid.* 3. Even though it is not precisely accurate to combine different typologies, as important nuances put forward by the scholars are not taken into account – and in general it is impossible to put specific innovation processes into 'boxes' – one can suggest that the process of 'revealing' of Huizingh to some extent fits into the dimension of open source innovation and the process of 'selling' into private OI.

When assessing the overall degree of openness, according to Huizingh, the highest level is exercised in the case of 'open source innovation'. The most notable example of such innovation is open source software.[33] Whereas under the 'private OI' innovation process is open, as it is also the case for open source innovation, the outcomes of private OI are closed and can only be accessed by selected parties and generally on specified conditions. Under 'public innovation', the process of innovating is not open, but the innovation outcomes are accessible to any external party, for instance, through a standard setting, where the original innovators do not exclude others from using their technology. However, such openness can still be strategically motivated. Establishing a standard allows a company to position its technology as the default choice across the industry, which can maximise revenue opportunities, increase market control, and secure long-term influence. Finally, the lowest degree of openness is exercised in 'closed innovation' as under this mode the innovation process is conducted in-house, and the outcomes of such innovation process are not accessible to third parties unless the authorisation is granted by the rightsholder.[34]

2.4. OPENNESS OF ACCESS TO KNOWLEDGE

Typologies of openness developed by Dahlander and Gann and by Huizingh provide important nuances regarding the degree of openness of innovation processes and review the underlying access modes based on the selected parameters. Dahlander and Gann emphasise the pecuniarity/non-pecuniarity of knowledge exchange, whereas Huizingh focuses on the general openness of innovation outcomes. However, they do not delve into the contractual technicalities that shape the degree of openness of access to knowledge. Nor do they examine the specific conditions under which the knowledge is shared or how these conditions can affect follow-on innovation.

More specifically, their typologies are two-by-two dimensional which does not reflect the continuum of openness. In fact, the openness of OI activities depends on various parameters that cannot be functionally placed into a two-by-two table. To provide a nuanced evaluation of the degree of openness, in my view, one must consider a variety of factors. These include whether the knowledge is IP protected (and by which mechanism), whether access is granted on a pecuniary/non-pecuniary basis, and whether access is provided through bilateral contractual arrangements, under standard conditions, or without any contractual constraints. In addition, it is important to examine whether any

33 See Section 2.4 for more details.

34 Huizingh (n 14) 4.

limitations apply to reuse of the accessed knowledge for follow-on innovation. Depending on these parameters, the degree of openness of OI activity varies significantly. The 'most open' inside-out OI activities should provide access to any interested external party without any restrictive conditions and free of charge (Figure 1).

Figure 1. Degree of openness of inside-out/outside in OI activities based on access to knowledge modes

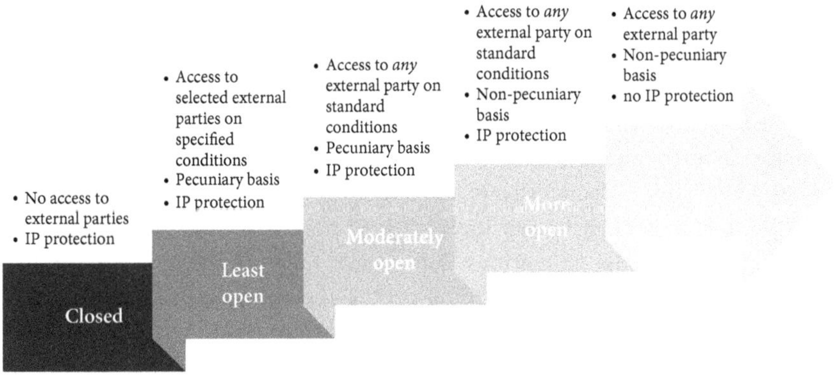

The 'closed' approach is self-explanatory and suggests that developed knowledge is inaccessible to third parties, as its holder chooses to rely on the CI model (develop knowledge internally and keep it within the boundaries of the firm).

The 'least open' degree of openness corresponds to the most common form of knowledge exchange in OI: granting a license to a selected interested external party on specific contractual conditions (e.g. time, territory, exclusivity, remuneration).[35] That type of inside-out OI activity is the least open because the IP owner retains full discretion to select which external parties may access the knowledge and under what terms. Access can only be granted if the external party is 'approved' by the IP owner and accepts the negotiated contractual conditions.

It should be noted, however, that access to knowledge is not always granted on a pecuniary basis. The negotiated access may be granted free of charge or alternative forms of remuneration may be explored. For instance, organisations may negotiate royalty-free cross-licenses, particularly in the context of R&D partnerships where parties exchange pre-existing knowledge (background IP) necessary for the joint project. Nevertheless, if a collaborating party wishes to

[35] The conditions are discussed in further detail in Section 3.2.

continue using background knowledge shared by another party beyond the duration of collaboration, an additional license is generally required.[36]

The 'moderately open' degree of openness differs from the 'least open' model in that access to knowledge is granted to any interested party under pre-defined standard terms, including a uniform fee structure and identical access conditions for all parties. An example of such a 'moderately open' activity is a patent pool or any other type of collective IPR licensing.[37] To ensure that access to knowledge remains controlled, it must be protected by IP rights.

Moving further along the openness spectrum, the 'more open' inside-out OI activities are those in which the owner grants access to any interested external party on standard conditions, without requiring any financial remuneration and even without clear oversight of who receives access. A typical example of such an activity is the use of open source licenses. Even in such cases, shared knowledge is generally protected by IP rights to maintain a basic level of legal control. It is also important to note that open source licenses come with contractual obligations that govern how others may use, modify, or distribute the software. Depending on the specific type of license applied (e.g. GNU General Public License (GPL), Affero GPL (AGPL), or MIT licenses), licensees are required to comply with conditions such as preserving license notices, disclosing source code, or applying the same license to derivative works.[38]

Finally, the 'most open' approach refers to the decision of a knowledge creator not to seek IP protection or to abandon it, choosing not to exercise control or capture any financial benefits in favor of making it freely available to the public. This may be done with the explicit intention of making the knowledge accessible to all, for instance, when openness and accessibility are seen as core values. However, such 'opening up' can also be driven by more pragmatic reasons, such as business strategy, budgetary constraints, or legal limitations, for example, when the subject matter is not eligible for IP protection, does not meet patentability requirements, or cannot be kept sufficiently secret to qualify for trade secret protection. Once placed in the public domain, such knowledge can be accessed by any external party free of charge and without the need to satisfy any additional conditions.

In sum, typologies addressed in Sections 2.1–2.3 have their limits, as they primarily focus on more standard managerial parameters and do not fully explore the more nuanced legal flexibilities arising from IP rights and contractual

---

[36] Arina Gorbatyuk, 'The Allocation of Patent Ownership in R&D Partnerships: Default Rules v. Contractual Practices' (2020) 17 SCRIPT-ed 4.

[37] Robert P Merges, 'Institutions for Intellectual Property Transactions: The Case of Patent Pools', *Expanding the Boundaries of Intellectual Property* (Oxford University Press 2001).

[38] Brock (n 10); Tal, 'Open Source Licenses: Types and Comparison' (*Snyk*) https://snyk.io/articles/open-source-licenses/, accessed 14 May 2025.

arrangements. More specifically, in Section 2.4 I emphasise that it is important to recognise that 'least open', 'moderately open' and 'more open' OI activities are cantered around IP and that specific terms of underlying contractual arrangements add further complexity to the definition of openness in a particular knowledge exchange activity. The dimensions of openness shaped by contractual terms cannot be captured within a 2x2 framework, as each contractual provision can independently affect the level of openness of access to shared knowledge. In Section 3, I further explore the spectrum of openness influenced by the type of IP protection chosen and by the structure of contractual arrangements, as they provide additional nuances that go beyond the 'openness' modes illustrated in Figure 1.

3. OPENNESS OF OI: A LEGAL PERSPECTIVE

When assessing the level of openness of innovation activities, the abovementioned managerial studies do not profoundly consider either the role of IP rights, underlying IP contracts or, in general, dynamics of law and flexibilities of legal instruments. Economic and managerial scholars generally acknowledge the important role IP rights play when shaping the openness of innovation and acknowledge that IP rights 'are the basis for open innovation and enable markets for technologies to function efficiently'.[39] Some scholars even engaged in discussions which led to diverging opinions on whether IP is a barrier or enabler of OI.[40]

Overall, IP protection is viewed by OI scholars as an important enabling mechanism of OI.[41] Organisations are more willing to share their knowledge with others when it is safeguarding by IP rights[42] as IP enables them to control who has access to protected knowledge and under which conditions, and to request financial remuneration. If the knowledge is not efficiently protected, there is a risk it falls into the public domain. In addition, IP can serve as a signal that an organisation takes its business seriously and is a trustworthy collaboration

39 Dahlander, Gann and Wallin (n 14).

40 *Ibid.*; Oliver Alexy, Paola Criscuolo and Ammon Salter, 'Does IP Strategy Have to Cripple Open Innovation?' (2009) 51 MIT Sloan Management Review 71; Davide Aloini and others, 'IP, Openness, and Innovation Performance: An Empirical Study' (2017) 55 Management Decision 1307.

41 David Kline, 'Sharing the Corporate Crown Jewels' (2003) 44 MIT Sloan Management Review 89; Henry Chesbrough and Roya Ghafele, 'Open Innovation and Intellectual Property: A Two-Sided Market Perspective' in Henry Chesbrough, Wim Vanhaverbeke and Joel West (eds), *New Frontiers in Open Innovation* (Oxford University Press 2014) https://doi.org/10.1093/acprof:oso/9780199682461.003.0010, accessed 27 September 2023.

42 John Hagedoorn and Ann-Kristin Zobel, 'The Role of Contracts and Intellectual Property Rights in Open Innovation' (2015) 27 Technology Analysis & Strategic Management 1050, 1056.

partner. Not to mention, IP assets are often essential for demonstrating the value of a business, for instance, in the context of market valuation, securing investments, or preparing for acquisition.[43] Not every organisation is willing to apply the 'most open' degree of openness as illustrated in Figure 1, as it does not allow them to recoup their R&D investments.

Whereas the importance of IP in shaping OI activities is generally recognised, existing managerial and economic studies often do not differentiate between different types of IP. Instead, they use IP as a broader term to indicate that underlying knowledge is protected, overlooking the deeper implications of specific IP regimes. IP rights give their owners the power to decide how their intangible assets may be exploited (or not) by others. In turn, contractual arrangements allow tailoring the scope of granted exploitation rights and play an essential role in facilitating or hindering further engagement in OI.

Thus, to truly assess the level of openness of OI activities one must take into consideration both the underlying IP protection mechanisms (Section 3.1) and contractually established scope of granted exploitation rights (Section 3.2).

3.1. OPENNESS OF OI ACTIVITIES BASED ON SELECTED IP PROTECTION MECHANISM

Since OI typically focuses on technological innovation, developed knowledge is often safeguarded through patents or trade secrets.[44] Patent protection provides the patent owner with an exclusive right to 'prevent third parties not having the owner's consent from the acts of making, using, offering for sale, selling, or importing' and with 'the right to assign, or transfer by succession, the patent and to conclude licensing contracts'.[45] On the contrary, a trade secret holder does not receive any exclusive rights preventing third parties from using a trade secret. The only way for a trade secret holder to retain the protection of its knowledge is by maintaining its secrecy,[46] either by keeping it secret from external parties or sharing it under strict confidentiality conditions. Thus, a trade secret holder can either rely on a 'closed' approach or engage in the 'least open' inside-out OI activities[47] and under very strict confidentiality conditions. Other suggested degrees of openness are unlikely to be applied since a more open approach may normally harm secrecy and, hence, lead to the loss of the trade secret. Consequently, knowledge protected under trade

43 'Why Intellectual Property Is Essential for Your Business' (*WIPO*) www.wipo.int/web/business, accessed 14 May 2025.
44 Hagedoorn and Zobel (n 42) 1055.
45 Article 28 TRIPS.
46 Article 39(2) TRIPS.
47 See Figure 1.

secret protection is by default less open than patent-protected knowledge as trade secret protection is a much more 'fragile' protection mechanism that may demotivate trade secret holders from sharing their trade secrets with others.

Another important aspect to consider is whether IP subject to OI activities is solely or jointly owned. The co-ownership regime may add another level of complexity when it comes to sharing co-owned knowledge with external parties to engage in further OI activities. The co-ownership regime may entail a requirement to obtain consent from other co-owners when granting access to the co-owned knowledge to an external party. Such a requirement may affect the level of openness of an OI activity generated by one of the co-owners.[48]

In the context of patents, for example, the sole owner of a patent owner generally exercises the right to assign the patent and to conclude licensing contracts independently, whereas the exploitation of co-owned patents is subject to additional complications. Depending on the jurisdiction, co-owners of a patent use the right to assign that patent and to conclude licensing contracts independently or jointly.[49] Joint exploitation generally means that co-owners should in some cases ask for the consent of other co-owners to give access to a patent to external parties. Consequently, such a consent requirement may negatively affect the degree of openness of OI activities since an interested external party would need to obtain consent not only from one co-owner but from all co-owners. The exploitation rights of co-owned patents can be contractually tailored which allows co-owners to contract out of the default rules[50] specified by the legislator and establish their own.[51] In principle, independent exploitation of co-owned patents is regarded as more 'open' as each co-owner can independently engage in OI activities and share the co-owned inventions with others.

IP owners can typically choose freely to apply any of the degrees of openness identified in Figure 1 when engaging in inside-out OI activities. However, one should not forget that any type of IP has its legislative limits. Within these limits, third parties can generally obtain access to patents and trade secrets without the need to obtain prior consent of the rightsholder.

For instance, patent protection is subject to exceptions and limitations, such as research exemption, bolar exception, or prior use rights, all of which

48 Gorbatyuk, Van Overwalle and van Zimmeren (n 20); Gorbatyuk (n 36); Arina Gorbatyuk, 'Rethinking Intellectual Property Ownership in the Context of Open Innovation' (KU Leuven Faculteit Rechtsgeleerdheid 2019).

49 Gorbatyuk (n 36).

50 In legal theory, default rules are provisions of law that apply unless the parties agree otherwise. They are contrasted with mandatory rules, which apply regardless of the parties' intentions and cannot be contractually altered.

51 Gorbatyuk (n 36).

are defined by applicable national laws.[52] Access to patents can also be granted through a compulsory license, without the authorisation of the patent owner. Compulsory licenses are governed by national legislation and are generally issued by public authorities under specific circumstances, such as national emergencies or public health needs.[53] Although such licenses are not granted voluntarily, patent owners are usually entitled to compensation.

In general, the functionality of compulsory licenses as a viable mechanism for enabling access to technologies is highly criticised. Compulsory licensing remains a limited, case-specific instrument that is invoked only in exceptional situations, which results in few compulsory licenses being granted in practice.[54] It does not offer a functional mechanism for truly opening up innovation processes, as it runs counter to the spirit of voluntary cooperation that is central to the OI philosophy. In addition, when a compulsory license is granted, it generally covers the patent rights and not the associated trade secrets, which are often essential for practical implementation. Despite various proposals to require the disclosure of related trade secrets in such situations these initiatives have not progressed beyond the discussion stage.[55]

When it comes to trade secret protection, one needs to consider that the scope of trade secret protection is limited. Unlike patents, trade secrets do not confer exclusive rights but rely entirely on maintaining strict confidentiality.[56]

---

52 WIPO, 'Research Exception' (2018) www.wipo.int/edocs/mdocs/scp/en/scp_29/scp_29_3.pdf.

53 WIPO, 'Exceptions and Limitations to Patent Rights: Compulsory Licenses and/or Government Use (Part I)' (2014) www.wipo.int/edocs/mdocs/scp/en/scp_21/scp_21_4_rev.pdf; WIPO, 'Exceptions and Limitations to Patent Rights: Compulsory Licenses and/or Government Use (Part II)' (2014) www.wipo.int/edocs/mdocs/scp/en/scp_21/scp_21_5_rev.pdf; WIPO, 'Overview of National Law Privisions on Compulsory Licenses' www.wipo.int/edocs/mdocs/mdocs/en/cdip_5/cdip_5_4_rev-annex1.pdf; Carlos M Correa, 'Guide for the Granting of Compulsory Licenses and Government Use of Pharmaceutical Patents' (South Center 2020) www.southcentre.int/wp-content/uploads/2020/04/RP-107.pdf>; EPO, 'Compulsory Licensing in Europe' (2018) www.epo.org/en/learning/learning-resources-profile/judges-lawyers-and-prosecutors/compulsory-licensing-europe, accessed 18 November 2023.

54 Lindor Qunaj, Anna Kaltenboeck and Peter B Bach, 'Compulsory Licensing of Pharmaceuticals in High-Income Countries: A Comparative Analysis' (2022) 100 The Milbank Quarterly 284.

55 Olga Gurgula and Luke McDonagh, 'On Compulsory Licensing of Trade Secrets to Safeguard Public Health' (Social Science Research Network, 25 March 2024) https://papers.ssrn.com/abstract=4771745, accessed 14 May 2025; Olga Gurgula and John Hull, 'Compulsory Licensing of Trade Secrets: Ensuring Access to COVID-19 Vaccines via Involuntary Technology Transfer' (2021) 16 Journal of Intellectual Property Law & Practice 1242.

56 Sharon K Sandeen, 'The Limits of Trade Secret Law: Article 39 of the TRIPS Agreement and the Uniform Trade Secrets Act on Which It Is Based' in Rochelle Dreyfuss and Katherine Strandburg, *The Law and Theory of Trade Secrecy* (2011); Elizabeth A. Rowe and Sharon K Sandeen, *Trade Secrecy and International Transactions: Law and Practice* (Edward Elgar 2015); Andrew Beckerman-Rodau, 'The Choice between Patent Protection and Trade Secret Protection: A Legal and Business Decision' (2002) 84 Journal of the Patent and Trademark Office Society 371.

As a result, trade secret holders cannot prevent third parties from independently developing the technology or reverse engineering it. Furthermore, if a trade secret is disclosed, regardless of whether the disclosure is done intentionally or non-intentionally, the underlying know-how becomes part of the public domain, and the original holder can no longer restrict access to it. It is this fragility that makes trade secrets not as strong IP as patents when it comes to enforcement. Given this fragility, it is logical to question whether trade secret protection even fits within the OI framework as it revolves around sharing knowledge with other, whereas secrecy can only be preserved under a highly controlled environment. In principle, trade secrets can be shared with others and licensing models are applicable to trade secrets. However, it is essential to carefully consider to how many actors the access is granted and under which conditions. 'Oversharing' or relying on vague confidentiality obligations may not only increase the risk of disclosure but may also undermine the ability to prove that reasonable steps were taken to maintain secrecy, which is an essential requirement for safeguarding trade secret protection as provided by Article 39 TRIPS of the TRIPS Agreement. The broader debate about whether trade secrets act as a bottleneck to the advancement of knowledge and technology is also highly relevant in this context.[57]

3.2. OPENNESS OF OI ACTIVITIES BASED ON SELECTED CONTRACTUAL ARRANGEMENTS

Contractual freedom – the basic principle of contract law – allows parties to negotiate contractual provisions according to their goals and interests. However, mandatory rules, for instance, contract law, IP law, competition law, or labour law can at times overrule contractual freedom.[58] Since contracting parties can, in principle, freely influence the conditions for knowledge sharing, the openness of an OI activity can be assessed by analysing the scope of exploitation rights granted by negotiated contractual provisions. Presumably, the clauses with stricter and narrower exploitation rights should be considered less open than the ones that give contracting parties (e.g. licensees) more flexibility and allow them to engage in further OI activities.

The owner of the knowledge subject to an OI activity has the right to decide under which conditions they are willing to provide access to it to an interested party.[59] Typically, in the context of OI the most common forms of

57 Andrea Contigiani and David H Hsu, 'How Trade Secrets Hurt Innovation' *Harvard Business Review* https://hbr.org/2019/01/how-trade-secrets-hurt-innovation, accessed 14 May 2025.

58 Gorbatyuk (n 49) 267.

59 The strength of negotiation position of the owner, however, may depend on his bargaining power.

knowledge exchange (which fall under inside-out/outside-in OI activities) are conducted via licensing or assignment agreements. Coupled OI activities are established through various R&D partnership agreements, such as contract research, collaboration, and consortia agreements.[60] As explained in Section 2.4, it is generally the IP owner that decides which type of openness mode they wish to apply and how restrictive their underlying agreements should be. More specifically, following the spectrum depicted in Figure 1, the contractual arrangements are relevant in the context of 'least open', 'moderately open' and 'more open' modes. Whereas (pecuniary or non-pecuniary) open licenses or other modes of access on standard terms are well accepted in certain industries, such as ICT, the majority of OI activities are still positioned in the 'least open' spectrum. In other words, contractually tailored case specific access to certain IP still is the default mode of obtaining access to IP protected knowledge and technologies.

However, even within the context of the 'least open' mode, one could further differentiate between various degree of openness. In general, labelling or mapping certain agreements as more or less open is challenging as the actual degree of openness provided in each specific agreement depends on multiple factors that must be considered as a whole. Every contractual clause potentially influences the overall degree of openness of a contract. Thus, the degree of openness applied in each agreement should be interpreted on a case-by-case basis depending on how individual components (e.g. scope, territory, duration, exclusivity, sublicensing, transferability) affect overall openness. For generalisation purposes, one can assert that an OI contract is more open if it permits broader exploitation rights and facilitates further engagement in OI activities, such as by allowing the grant of sublicenses by a licensee or granting additional licenses to other interested parties by a licensor.

When evaluating the openness of a license agreement, several essential factors must be considered.[61] First, the scope of granted rights can either be broad or narrow. An agreement is more open if it allows the licensee to exploit the patented technology for various purposes. Second, the restrictions on the field of application, such as a specific industry sector, territory, or duration also influence openness. Narrower fields of application and territories and shorter durations make an underlying OI activity, in principle, less open. In this context, it is also important to assess whether the granted rights are revocable or non-revocable. Third, the nature of a license can also impact openness. More specifically, exclusive licenses generally limit the licensor's ability to give similar licenses to other interested third parties, which may lead to the technology being 'locked' by the exclusive licensee and restrict follow-on OI activities. On

---

60 Gorbatyuk (n 36); Gorbatyuk (n 49).

61 Donna Bobrowicz, 'A Checklist for Negotiating License Agreements', *Intellectual Property Management in Health and Agricultural Innovation* (MIHR and PIPRA 2007) 1136.

the contrary, non-exclusive licenses are more open as they allow various parties to exploit a patent simultaneously. Fourth, the openness is further enhanced by the permission for the licensee to sublicense the shared technology. Fifth, the way improvements to the licensed technologies are handled also influences the overall openness of an OI contract and underlying OI activity. More 'open' licensing arrangements allow the licensee to exploit any improvements made to the licensed technology. The allocation of ownership of improved licensed technology (background IP) by the licensee can also influence the openness of OI activity. For instance, if the licensor contractually requires the licensee to assign all the improvements back to them, it may hinder follow-on innovation by limiting the licensee's ability to further exploit and share the improved technology.

From the perspective of openness, the analysis of contractual arrangements conducted in coupled OI adds another level of complexity. Within various types of R&D partnerships, collaborating parties generally grant access to each other's background IP for the duration of their cooperation. However, if access to background IP is needed beyond the joint R&D project or after its completion, collaborating parties are often required to negotiate separate licenses, in line with factors discussed in the previous paragraph, which may limit access to knowledge and hinder follow-on innovation.

Not only should collaborating parties define terms of access to their background IP, but the collaborating parties must decide which protection mechanism to apply to protect their (jointly) developed inventions and know-how (foreground IP) and how the ownership and allocation rights for foreground IP will be allocated.[62] The choices and technicalities of openness of selected IP protection mechanisms were discussed in Section 3.1. When it comes to the allocation of ownership and exploitation rights, contractually assigning ownership to only one of the collaborating parties may be viewed as less open because only one of the parties generally has control over the developed IP and can decide upon its further exploitation. On the contrary, both co-owners can exploit the co-owned patents within the boundaries specified by law or their contractual arrangements. In principle, contractual arrangements that allow collaboration parties to become co-owners of jointly developed patents and to exploit them without strict consent requirements are more open and permit those co-owners to engage in further OI activities without internal barriers. However, in practice, co-owners are rarely comfortable granting such broad (consent-free) exploitation rights to their partners.[63] Furthermore, many organisations, particularly multinational enterprises (MNEs), prefer to avoid co-ownership, and opt for other allocation strategies, suggesting that even

62 Gorbatyuk, Van Overwalle and van Zimmeren (n 20); Gorbatyuk (n 36).

63 Gorbatyuk (n 36).

though these arrangements may be perceived as more open, in practice, they entail a high administrative burden (the need to acquire the consent of the other co-owner when exploiting co-owned patents) which in turn may impose barriers to follow-on innovation.[64]

Thus, it is evident that the true level of openness of OI activities can be only fully grasped when also examining the selected IP protection mechanism and carefully analysing the scope of rights granted under contracts underling certain OI activity. Without delving into the legal technicalities, one risks overlooking an essential layer that fundamentally shapes the degree of openness of a given OI activity.

4. CONCLUDING REMARKS: HOW OPEN ARE OI CONTRACTS AFTER ALL?

The concept of OI is not synonymous with unrestricted or barrier-free access to knowledge and technologies. It is not about sharing knowledge without restrictions. Rather, it is about the willingness of organisations to open up innovation processes and engage in knowledge exchanges, while more often than not maintaining a sufficient level of control over the underlying knowledge assets. Thus, OI activities cover a range of different levels of openness, where some initiatives are more open than others.

In this contribution, I claim that the degree of openness in OI activities heavily depends on the legal frameworks organisations choose to adopt. From a legal (often overlooked) perspective, openness is influenced by two intertwined dimensions: the selected IP protection mechanisms that safeguard the knowledge and technologies subject to OI exchanges, and the specific contractual arrangements that govern access, exploitation, and follow-on innovation opportunities.

Thus, even though organisations may label all their external knowledge exchange activities as 'open innovation', the reality behind their contractual and IP arrangements often reveals a more nuanced picture. Every OI activity occupies its own place on the openness spectrum. In practice, many OI contracts are positioned in the 'least open' end of this spectrum when analysed through the lens of broader access to knowledge and the context of enabling follow-on innovation that extends beyond the scope of a single OI activity. Such 'least open' OI activities allow organisations to balance their aspiration to collaborate and share knowledge with the necessity to manage risks, maintain control over IP, and protect competitive advantage.

---

64 See more information on the allocation strategies of foreground IP in *ibid.*

Organisations that embrace OI activities (regardless of the exact spectrum of openness) have already taken an important step towards moving away from the traditional 'IP as a shield' business strategy. Even when operating under the 'least open' degree of openness, they demonstrate a willingness to share knowledge without overindulging themselves to the negative consequences of letting others benefit from their knowledge and IP.

However, the majority of OI activities are far from being 'open' in the sense of broader public access to knowledge and technologies, a context particularly dear to Prof. Van Overwalle, whose academic legacy is largely dedicated to opening up technologies for the public good. If broader access and a higher level of openness are socially desirable, it becomes the responsibility of the legislators and policymakers to intervene.

Just as contracts act as intangible keys to unlock IP, legislators and policymakers have a role in shaping the lock itself. By regulating the lock, they can determine how easily that door can be opened and by whom and help shift the system toward a higher level of openness, when such openness is justifiable and socially desirable. This can be done by further defining the limitations that could restrict the exclusive rights granted to IP rightsholders and by developing clear and viable incentives that would outweigh the advantages organisations gain from maintaining strict control over their IP as means of preserving their competitive edge. Such measures could stimulate organisations to engage in more 'open' OI activities and to negotiate OI agreements that allow broader access, impose fewer constraints on knowledge use, and provide greater opportunities for follow-on innovation.

CHAPTER 4

USE AND DISCLOSURE OF MARINE GENETIC RESOURCES OF AREAS BEYOND NATIONAL JURISDICTION

A Role for the 'Inclusive Patent'?

Amandine Léonard
Lecturer, Assistant Professor in Intellectual Property Law,
University of Edinburgh, Law School
Senior Affiliated Researcher, Centre for IT&IP Law, KU Leuven

J3 **Ocean Wiper**
Particularly useful when skin-diving in polluted waters or in heavy fish traffic.

1. INTRODUCTION

In June 2023, the United Nations adopted an international agreement to conserve and sustainably use marine biodiversity of areas beyond national jurisdiction. This agreement is known as the BBNJ Agreement or the Treaty of the

High Seas.[1] It has been signed by more than 80 countries and will enter into force once it receives 60 ratifications.[2] It is part of the 2030 UN Agenda for Sustainable Development and materialises parts of the sustainable development goal (SDG) number 14: Life Below Water.[3] In October of the same year, the European Commission submitted a proposal to the Council to approve the conclusion of the BBNJ Agreement on behalf of the EU. This was then adopted in June 2024 and is expected to be ratified before the UN Ocean conference of June 2025.[4] The agreement still has a long way to go before its entry into force but carries many opportunities and promises.

The role of intellectual property (IP) within the BBNJ Agreement has been debated at length during its development and drafting process. While some IP-related provisions were included in the first drafts of the agreement, it was ultimately considered that these provisions should be governed by its specialised IP agency, i.e. the World Intellectual Property Office (WIPO). These drafted provisions were therefore removed from the final version of the text and what remains is a 'light touch' approach to regulating IP.[5]

In parallel to the discussions that were taking place at the UN – and even for quite some time before that – work had been carried at WIPO, within its Intergovernmental Committee on Intellectual Property and Genetic Resources, Traditional Knowledge and Folklore, for a new international agreement on

---

1 Agreement under the United Nations Convention on the Law of the Sea on the Conservation and Sustainable Use of Marine Biological Diversity of Areas Beyond National Jurisdiction (2023) available at www.un.org/bbnjagreement/en/bbnj-agreement/text-bbnj-agreement, accessed 23 April 2025.

2 At the time of writing (April 2025) only 21 countries had ratified the Agreement. See https://highseasalliance.org/treaty-ratification/, accessed 09 April 2025.

3 The United Nations. Department of Economic and Social Affairs. Sustainable Development. 'Goal 14. Life Below Water'. Conserve and sustainably use the oceans, seas and marine resources for sustainable development, see www.globalgoals.org/goals/14-life-below-water/, accessed 09 April 2025.

4 Council Decision on the conclusion, on behalf of the European Union, of the Agreement under the United Nations Convention on the Law of the Sea on the conservation and sustainable use of marine biological diversity of areas beyond national jurisdiction. 19 March 2024. 7577/24 available at https://data.consilium.europa.eu/doc/document/ST-7577–2024-INIT/en/pdf/, accessed 09 April 2025.

5 The words 'intellectual property' are totally absent from the final version of the text and 'patents' are only mentioned once in reference to the notification of activities with respect to MGRs of ABNJ – discussed *infra*. Overall, it can be said that the BBNJ Agreement has a light touch approach to IP as it focuses on fair-benefit sharing from the use of MGRs without imposing strict IP requirements, therefore leaving the regulation of patents to national, regional or international IP laws and systems. Conference papers, statements and versions of draft Treaty text are available at www.un.org/bbnj/, accessed 23 April 2025. See also: Siva Thambisetty, 'Marine Genetic Resources Beyond National Jurisdictions: Components of an Informed, Fair and Progressive Internationally Binding Legal Instrument' (2018). Available at https://ssrn.com/abstract=3215356, accessed 23 April 2025.

disclosure of Genetic Resources.[6] And in May 2024, WIPO adopted its Treaty on Intellectual Property, Genetic Resources and Traditional Knowledge Associated with Genetic Resources. In essence, the WIPO Treaty establishes a new international disclosure requirement for genetic resources (GRs) and traditional knowledge (TK) associated with GRs.[7]

Both treaties envisage some obligations in terms of either notifying (under the BBNJ Agreement) or disclosing (under the WIPO Treaty) the use of marine genetic resources (MGR) of areas beyond national jurisdiction (ABNJ) in relation to IP and patent applications more specifically. How these obligations may materialise at the regional and/or national level once (and if) the treaties come into force remains a question mark. However, one question that may be worth exploring is the following: In light of the (potential) new obligations provided for in the two treaties, what are the challenges linked to the use of MGR of ABNJ in patent applications, and what consequences might there be in case of failure to disclose such use?

To see more clearly in these murky waters, one might try to wear the 'Ocean Wiper' mask as advertised by Carelman in his book of 'fantastic things'.[8] It is described as being particularly useful for waters with heavy fish traffic – arguably an appropriate metaphor for the combination of a UN Agreement and a WIPO Treaty as well as their regional and national ramifications on this question of MGR of ABNJ. However, this method might not be the most legalistic one. Therefore, I suggest exploring whether the inclusive patent, as developed by Prof. Geertrui Van Overwalle,[9] could serve as our ocean wiper mask in this debate. More specifically, this contribution turns to the role an inclusive patent could play and considers whether it offers some food for thought in the scenario where, applicants who have used MGR of ABNJ did not disclose this use in their patent application.

As Geertrui will know, with this theme, I am exploring new depths and take-ing a plunge in the legal high seas, but, over the years, she has consistently provided me with the courage and determination to engage with challenging subjects. It is my hope that this contribution, made in her honour, will serve to continue along this path.

---

6 For information on the WIPO IGC see www.wipo.int/en/web/igc, accessed 09 April 2025.

7 WIPO Treaty on Intellectual Property, Genetic Resources and Associated Traditional Knowledge. TRT/GRSTK/001. Available at www.wipo.int/wipolex/en/text/593055, accessed 09 April 2025.

8 Jacques Carelman, *Catalog of Fantastic Things* (Ballantine Books New York 1971) 60.

9 Geertrui Van Overwalle, 'Inventing Inclusive Patents. From Old to New Open Innovation', in Peter Drahos, Gustavo Ghidini and Hanns Ullrich (eds) *Kritika: Essays on Intellectual Property* (Edward Elgar, Vol. 1 2015) 206–277.

2. THE BBNJ AGREEMENT AND THE USE OF MGR

Areas beyond national jurisdiction (ABNJ) cover 64% of the ocean's surface and 95% of its volume. They contain ecological, economic, social, cultural, scientific and food-security benefits to humanity. However, they are highly vulnerable to pollution and the impact of climate change is greatly felt in these parts of the world. In addition to these environmental risks, there are also some risks related to overexploitation, or unregulated usage, of the resources available in these areas. As technology and human needs evolve, there is a growing demand for MGR in the pharmaceutical, cosmetic, biotechnological, and food industries.[10] In the pharmaceutical industry specifically, this demand may drive innovation and lead to the development of new lifesaving drugs.[11] However, extraction and use of MGR of ABNJ has to be conducted in light of the conservation and sustainability objectives of the BBNJ Agreement.

The BBNJ Agreement is made of four main parts. A part on MGR and fair and equitable sharing of benefits (Part II). A part on area-based management tools (Part III). A part on environmental impact assessments (Part IV), and, finally, a part on capacity building and the transfer of technology (Part V). The most relevant provisions of the BBNJ Agreement for a discussion on disclosure and patent law (as connected to the new WIPO Treaty) reside in the second part of the text. In particular, Part II of the agreement envisages the establishment of an information-exchange system which would ultimately lead to the sharing of benefits which are issued from the use of MGR.

2.1. THE LEGAL NATURE OF MGR OF ABNJ

One key issue regarding the legal nature of MGR of ABNJ is whether these resources should be considered as part of the 'common heritage of mankind' or subject to the 'freedom of the high seas' principle.[12] Historically, the ocean has been considered as the epitome of a commons or a *res communis*. Its resources should not belong to anyone and any benefits which can be extracted from it

---

10 For an overview of the challenges and promises of the high seas, see: Helen Scales, *The Brilliant Abyss* (Grove Press 2022); Helen Scales, *What the Wild Sea Can Be: The Future of the World's Ocean* (Atlantic Monthly Press 2024); Ilaria Perissi and Ugo Bardi, *The empty sea. The future of the Blue Economy* (Springer 2021); Olive Heffernan, *The High Seas: Greed, Power and the Battle for the Unclaimed Ocean* (Greystone Books 2024); Guy Standing, *The Blue Commons. Rescuing the Economy of the Sea* (Pelican 2022).

11 Scales 2022 (n 10) 130.

12 See e.g. Charles Lawson, Susan Downing, 'It's patently absurd – benefit sharing genetic resources from the sea under UNCLOS, the CBD and TRIPs' (2002) 5(3) Journal of international wildlife law and policy, 211; Siva Thambisetty, The Unfree Commons: Freedom of Marine Scientific Research and the Status of Genetic Resources Beyond National Jurisdiction (2025) 88(2) Modern Law Review, 302.

should be shared, equally, among everyone. However, the UN Convention of the Law of the Sea (UNCLOS)[13] states in Article 136 that 'The Area and its resources are the common heritage of mankind.' In its Preamble, UNCLOS also indicates that 'the area of the seabed and ocean floor and the subsoil thereof, beyond the limits of national jurisdiction, as well as its resources, are the common heritage of mankind' and that 'the exploration and exploitation [of such resources] shall be carried out for the benefit of mankind as a whole, irrespective of the geographical location of States.' However, it is understood that, under UNCLOS, the resources in the Area, ocean floor or subsoil refer to mineral resources but do not include MGR since they belong to natural *living* resources.[14] Additionally, the waters above the Area, ocean floor or subsoil, where we might also find MGR discussed in this chapter, are equally not captured by the Convention.

On the other hand, the principle of the freedom of the high seas,[15] which is also a core element of UNCLOS, suggests that the resources to be found in the ocean may equally be treated as *res nullius*. While, indeed, not belonging to anyone, the resources held in the ocean are nonetheless 'up for grabs' by everyone and may be captured and appropriated for exclusive proprietary use. UNCLOS does stipulate that this freedom 'shall be exercised [...] with due regard for the rights under this Convention with respect to activities in the Area' and could therefore require some consideration for the principle of the common heritage of mankind. However, this, as explained in the previous paragraph, does not concern MGR of ABNJ as they are not covered by the Convention. One may wonder if the Convention on Biological Diversity (CBD) may settle this debate, but it does not regulate access (and extraction) of components of biodiversity to be found in ABNJ – as it is only concerned with resources from areas within national jurisdiction.[16]

Article 7 of the BBNJ Agreement recognises that the conservation and sustainable use of these resources, i.e. the ultimate objective of the agreement, are to be achieved through the 'Common Heritage of Humankind' as a guiding principle.[17] Additionally, Article 11.4 stipulates that 'no State shall claim or exercise sovereignty or sovereign rights over marine genetic resources of areas beyond national jurisdiction' and that 'activities with respect to marine genetic resources and digital sequence information on marine genetic resources of areas beyond national jurisdiction are in the interests of all States *and for the benefit of all humanity* [...]' (Article 11.6, emphasis added). The agreement therefore does

---

13 Convention on the Law of the Sea (adopted 10 December 1982, entered into force 16 November 1994) 1833 UNTS 397.

14 Bevis Fedder, *Marine Genetic Resources, Access and Benefit Sharing. Legal and Biological Perspectives* (Routledge, 2013) 60.

15 Article 87 UNCLOS.

16 Fedder (n 14) 61.

17 Zakieh Taghizadeh, 'Marine genetic resources as common heritage of mankind under the BBNJ Agreement; the international community toward a pragmatic benefit-sharing approach?' (2025) 34 Biodiversity and Conservation, 131.

not explicitly recognise that MGR of ABNJ are to be treated as *res communis* but it is clear that the use of these resources (including when relevant to patenting activities) should be consistent with the principle of common heritage as well as leading to a fair and equitable sharing of benefits. In order to do so, the agreement notably envisages an information and benefit-sharing system.

2.2. INFORMATION AND BENEFIT SHARING

More specifically, the agreement stipulates that where MGR of ABNJ are subject to utilisation, including commercialisation, some information shall be notified to the newly created clearing-house.[18] The clearing-house mechanism envisaged by the agreement would be a centralised, open-access, platform to enable Parties to access, provide and disseminate information such as links to relevant databases, repositories and gene banks.[19] Relevant for this contribution is the sharing of information which relates to 'patents granted'.[20] In brief, the agreement envisages that, when patent holders use or commercialise products and processes which include MGR of ABNJ, a reporting mechanism should be in place to notify the clearing-house.

But how would this reporting mechanism work? The idea is relatively (or maybe illusorily) simple: for each MGR collected in an ABNJ, the collector should inform the clearinghouse, which, in turn would allocate a BBNJ standardised batch identifier[21] which would then be used to trace further uses of this MGR. With this tracing, any potential benefits which would derive from the use of MGR could also be identified and shared appropriately. Additionally, the collector should also inform the clearinghouse of the repository and/or database where the MGR (or digital sequence information – DSI – on this MGR) might be deposited.[22] In case of failure to notify, the agreement does not provide for punitive sanctions such as fines or trade restrictions. However, failure to notify may be considered as an act of non-compliance and the Compliance Committee may make recommendations to the entity (or State) in order to restore the notification. Moreover, it is possible for the Committee to issue a publication of non-compliance.

The uses of MGR envisaged by the agreement notably include patent applications and further commercialisation. Therefore, in order to have a 'full circle' approach and heightened traceability, patent holders should also notify the clearinghouse of any use or commercialisation of patented products or processes. Much of this information-sharing system rest on the shoulders of collectors and

---

18 Article 12.8 BBNJ Agreement. The governance of the clearing house mechanism is to be shared between the Conference of the Parties and the Secretariat. Article 51(2) BBNJ Agreement.

19 *Ibid.*, Article 51.

20 *Ibid.*, Article 12.8(a). We are leaving out of this contribution any discussion on Digital Sequence Information (or DSI) as this would go beyond the scope of this chapter.

21 *Ibid.*, Article 12.3.

22 *Ibid.*, Article 12.5(a).

users. The ultimate objective of this reporting mechanism is to ensure that the extraction of MGR is closely monitored but also to make sure that the use of these resources lead to fair and equitable sharing of benefits.

Figure 1. Notification mechanism as envisaged under the BBNJ Agreement and connection with patenting activities

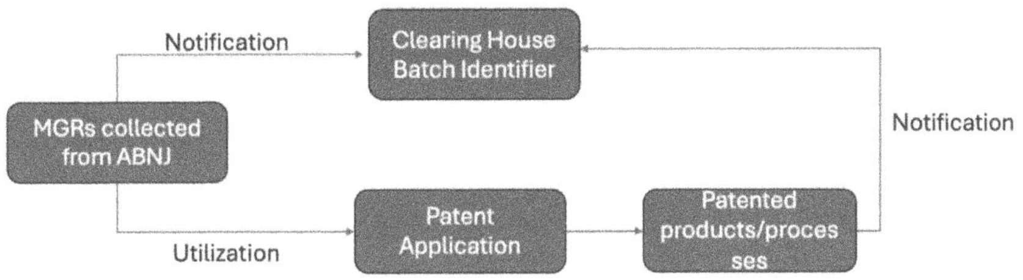

The question explored in this chapter is whether and how patent law can help in attaining this objective, through similar mechanisms of traceability and transparency. This is where the WIPO Treaty comes into play.

3. THE WIPO TREATY AND THE DISCLOSURE OF MGR

As mentioned in the introduction, in parallel to the development of the BBNJ Agreement, WIPO was conducting, since the early 2000s, its own 'Special Session[s] of the Intergovernmental Committee on Intellectual Property and Genetic Resources, Traditional Knowledge and Folklore (ICG).'[23] The work undertaken by the committee ultimately led to adoption of the WIPO Treaty on Intellectual Property, Genetic Resources and Traditional Knowledge Associated with Genetic Resources.[24]

The objective of the treaty is to have an international disclosure requirement for GRs and TK associated with GRs.[25] This should support 'efficacy, transparency

---

[23] WIPO IGC (n 6). For the various sessions see www.wipo.int/meetings/en/topic.jsp?group_id=110, accessed 23 April 2025.

[24] First, a 'proposal for an international legal instrument relating to intellectual property, genetic resources and traditional knowledge associated with genetic resources' was discussed in Geneva on May 13 to 24 2024. The final version of the international agreement was then adopted on 24.05.2024. 1200 delegates were present at the conference. See: GRATK/DC/7, Diplomatic Conference to Conclude an International Legal Instrument Relating to Intellectual Property, Genetic Resources and Traditional Knowledge Associated with Genetic Resources (www.wipo.int/edocs/mdocs/tk/en/gratk_dc/gratk_dc_7.pdf, accessed 23 April 2025).

[25] The treaty is not without opposition. There is, e.g., a strong opposition from the US as well as Japan and Korea. One of the main criticisms being that the treaty creates unnecessary additional obligations on applicants. Such burden being considered counterproductive and risking dis-incentivising patenting activities. Additionally, some commentators also argue that the new disclosure will encourage more patent applications based on GRs and therefore

and quality of the patent system in relation to genetic resources and traditional knowledge associated with genetic resources,'[26] but also, 'prevent patents from being granted erroneously for inventions that are not novel or inventive.'[27] Arguably, this new treaty could help in avoiding misappropriation of resources and fits in the general narrative of 'access and benefit sharing' mechanisms already included in the CBD as well as the Nagoya Protocol.[28] It is considered that the treaty could contribute to increased legal certainty and consistency and better distribution of benefits between providers and users of such resources and knowledge.

From a bird's eye view, there is no explicit relation between the BBNJ Agreement and the WIPO Treaty. However, we can find the conventional wording that 'this instrument and other international instruments should be mutually supportive.'[29] Moreover, it is clear that they share the objectives of avoiding misappropriation of resources as well as enhancing the current mechanisms of access, use, and benefit-sharing of genetic resources. If we turn to the text of the WIPO Treaty, we can see from the working documents and various drafts, that MGR of ABNJ were not initially intended to be included in the text.[30] This was notably due to the parallel negotiations that were taking place and the IP-related provisions which had been envisaged under the BBNJ Agreement. However, once these were removed from the final draft of the Agreement, MGR of ABNJ

---

enhance bioprospecting and potential for biopiracy. The treaty is also not without a long historical background. Propositions to have a new Article 29bis in the TRIPS Agreement have been made in the past. See e.g. Communication from Brazil, China, Colombia, Cuba, India, Pakistan, Peru, Thailand and Tanzania. Doha Work Programme – The Outstanding Implementation Issue on the Relationship Between the TRIPS Agreement and the Convention on Biological Diversity, WTO Doc. WT/GC/W/564/Rev.2 (July 5, 2006). Also proposed by Switzerland at WIPO in 2003. See: WIPO, Working Group on Reform of the Patent Cooperation Treaty, Proposals by Switzerland Regarding the Declaration of the Source of Genetic Resources and Traditional Knowledge in Patent Applications, at 1, U.N. Doc. PCT/R/WG/5/11 Rev. (Nov. 19, 2003). See also: Secretariat of the Convention on Biological Diversity, Bonn Guidelines on Access to Genetic Resources and Fair and Equitable Sharing of the Benefits Arising Out of Their Utilization, 16(d)(2) (2002). Available at www.cbd.int/doc/publications/cbd-bonn-gdls-en.pdf, accessed 09 April 2025.

26 Article 1(a) WIPO Treaty.

27 *Ibid.*, Article 1(b).

28 See: Frederic Perron-Welch, Bio-Based Innovation and the Global Patent System: Exploring the WIPO Treaty on Intellectual Property, Genetic Resources and Associated Traditional Knowledge (2024) GRUR Int. 1; Robert Blasiak et al., Scientists Should Disclose Origin in Marine Gene Patents (2019) 34(5) Trends in Ecology & Evolution 392.

29 Article 7 WIPO Treaty: this treaty shall be implemented in a mutually supportive matter with other international agreements relevant to this treaty.

30 See Consolidated Document Relating to Intellectual Property and Genetic Resources, March 2022, WIPO/GRTKF/43/4. Draft Article 5.1 'exceptions and limitations' stipulated that: A [IP][patent] disclosure requirement related to genetic resources and [traditional knowledge associated with genetic resources][shall]/[should] not apply to the following: [...] (e) [Genetic resources from areas beyond national jurisdictions [and economic zones]]; [...]. www.wipo.int/edocs/mdocs/tk/en/wipo_grtkf_ic_43/wipo_grtkf_ic_43_4.pdf, accessed 23 April 2025.

made a 'comeback' in the WIPO Treaty. It is clear from the final version of the text that these resources are now covered by the treaty.[31]

But what is this new international disclosure requirement envisaged in the WIPO Treaty? In essence, the treaty stipulates that where a claimed invention in a patent application is *based on* GRs (including MGR), each Contracting Party shall require applicants to disclose (a) the *country of origin* of the genetic resources or, (b) in case where this information is not known to the applicant or where the principle of 'the country of origin' does not apply, the *source of the genetic resources* (emphasis added).[32]

Article 2 provides some clarifications on the terms relevant for the treaty. In particular it stipulates that if 'the country of origin' of GRs may not exist or be identified, then one must be able to disclose the 'source of GRs'. This is particularly relevant for our discussion on MGR from areas *beyond* national jurisdiction, since these cannot, per se, have a *country* of origin since they are, by definition, from areas beyond any country's jurisdiction. Therefore, for these specific MGR, another method for identifying the source must then be used. There seems to be some agreement that, in this case, the source can be *any* source such as a research centre, a gene bank, indigenous people and local communities, a multilateral system of international treaty (such as the Treaty on Plant Genetic Resources for Food and Agriculture[33]), or any other ex situ collection or depository of genetic resources.[34] The list is not exhaustive. Therefore, when we think of MGR of ABNJ, the BBNJ standardised batch identifier provided by the clearinghouse (mentioned *supra*) may be particularly helpful in order to identify the right source.[35,36]

---

31 The draft Article 5.1 mentioned in (n 30) has been removed from the final version of the text. There are no more 'exceptions and limitations' included. Moreover, Article 2 defines 'genetic resources' as 'genetic material of actual or potential value.' There is no specific mention of GRs from areas beyond national jurisdictions which would lead us to believe that these are excluded from the scope of the treaty.

32 Article 3 WIPO Treaty.

33 Food and Agriculture Organization of the United Nations (2001) International Treaty on Plant Genetic Resources for Food and Agriculture (ITPGRFA). www.fao.org/plant-treaty/overview/texts/en/, accessed 13 May 2025.

34 Notes to the Text of a Draft International Legal Instrument Relating to Intellectual Property, Genetic Resources and Traditional Knowledge Associated with Genetic Resources (GRATK/DC/INF/4). Available at www.wipo.int/meetings/en/doc_details.jsp?doc_id=625832, accessed 23 April 2025.

35 This is also envisaged in the Notes (n 34) 4. Under 'Notes on Article 3' – 'Content of Disclosure', it is indicated (at 6(b)) that: 'Sub paragraphs 3.1(b) and/or 3.2(b) apply in those cases where the information in sub paragraph 3.1(a) and/or 3.2(a) is not available or these sub-paragraphs do not apply, and thus it is not possible for the patent applicant to disclose this information. *For example, GRs in areas beyond national jurisdiction such as the high seas*' (emphasis added).

36 If no country or source can be identified, the applicant can give 'any source' wherefrom they have obtained the relevant resource or knowledge. And if that is not available, they can make a declaration that the content of the application is true and correct to their 'best knowledge' (Article 3.3). This might trigger some issues in terms of reliance on good faith from applicants, but this goes beyond the scope of this contribution.

Figure 2. Notification mechanism as envisaged under the BBNJ Agreement and relation with the WIPO Treaty

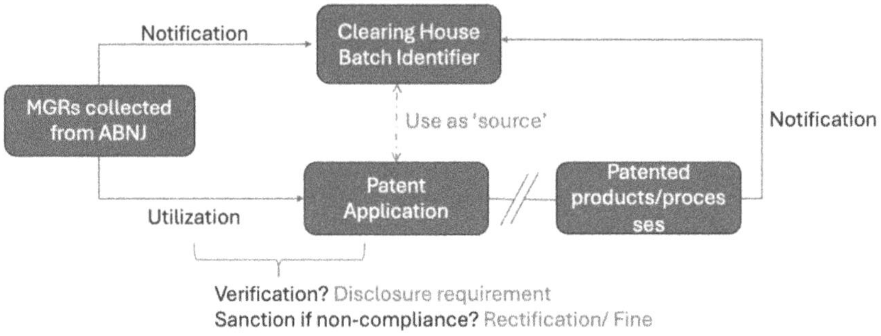

3.1. CHALLENGES FOR THE NEW TREATY?

Four points of potential contention require some attention. First, is the meaning of an invention which would be 'based on' GRs. In the previous iterations of the treaty, the mandatory disclosure requirement was envisaged for application which were 'materially' or 'directly' based on GRs. Arguably, 'materially/directly' aimed at amplifying and specifying when a disclosure should take place. This nuance, which may not have been easier to interpret, has been removed from the final version of the text. Article 2 nonetheless stipulates that 'based on' means that the resources 'must have been necessary for the claimed invention, and the claimed invention must depend on the specific properties of the genetic resources [...]'.[37] It is unclear if 'necessary for the claimed invention' is not going to prove difficult to interpret coherently across jurisdictions.

Second, while the WIPO Treaty might impose a new international requirement on Contracting States, this 'enhanced' disclosure for GRs already exists in various jurisdictions. Countries such as Brazil, China, India, South Africa, Colombia, Germany, France, Belgium, Spain, Sweden, Norway, Italy, Switzerland, Denmark, The Philippines, Costa Rica, Venezuela, and the Andean Community already consider that applications 'based on GRs' (and/or TK and associated with GRs) should disclose their source. Overall, around 30 regimes are in place across the globe.[38] There are nonetheless some significant variations in the current national texts and practices in terms of scope, content, relationship with access and benefit-sharing regimes, and sanctions.[39] Some adaptation of these national provisions may have to

37 Article 2 WIPO Treaty.

38 See www.wipo.int/export/sites/www/tk/en/docs/genetic_resources_disclosure.pdf, accessed 23 April 2025.

39 In terms of textual differences, provisions refer to: directly based on, based on, based on or derived from, is the basis of, used in an invention, invention concerns, relates to or makes

be reviewed in light of the new treaty and the definition provided under Article 2 as well as Article 5 and the sanctions and remedies envisaged.

Third, another challenge lies in Article 3 and the requirement to disclose the *source* of GRs but not the type of information (or the extent of that information) that should be disclosed. The text stipulates that it is 'up for Offices to provide guidance to applicants' on this matter but that Contracting States 'shall not place an obligation on Offices to verify the authenticity of the disclosure.'[40] While this is meant to minimise the disclosure regime's transaction cost and burden on patent offices,[41] this may lead to significant disparities between offices and some common practices should be identified for more legal certainty.

Finally, and beyond this risk of disparities between contracting states and offices, one may wonder if this caveat may not be difficult to reconcile with other provisions of the agreement – or even the ultimate objective of the treaty to enhance transparency and reliability in disclosure. In particular, how would one reconcile Article 3 with Article 5 (discussed in the following section) which posits that offices will have to determine if an application has been made 'fraudulently'. If offices do not have any obligation to verify the authenticity of the disclosure, how will they be able to determine if there has been a fraudulent application? The system relies extensively on third parties to challenge the authenticity of the disclosure as well as to identify the true motives of applicants. It may also be difficult to reconcile with the preamble of the treaty which states that it is particularly important for offices to have access to appropriate information on GRs in order to prevent erroneous grants. If the requirement relies exclusively on listing 'a' source but that offices do not verify this source, it may turn out to

---

use, an invention-creation accomplished by relying on genetic resources. In terms of content and sanctions: Article 3 of the D.A. 486 (Colombia) provides that: the granting of patents on inventions that have been developed on the basis of material derived from that heritage or knowledge shall be subject to that material having been acquired in accordance with international, community and national legal provisions. Therefore, allowing for the refusal to grant and potential revocation of patents not respecting these provisions. In Brazil, Federal Law No. 13,123/2015 mandates patent applicants to disclose (i) the origin of genetic material and associated traditional knowledge, if applicable, along with (ii) the authorisation number for access to such assets. Until this authorisation is provided, the application process is suspended. An electronic registration of the source before the patent application is therefore required. However, there is no revocation envisaged in case a patent ends up being granted without having complied with this obligation. Margo A. Bagley (2016) 'Of Disclosure "Straws" and IP System "Camels": Patents, Innovation, and the Disclosure of Origin Requirement', Virgina Public Law and Legal Theory Research Paper No. 2016-40 https://ssrn.com/abstract=2802186, accessed 13 May 2025. For an overview of the relationship between genetic resources, including the disclosure of origin, and access and benefit-sharing mechanism, see the extensive work of Christine Frison such as: Fabien Girard and Christine Frison (eds) *The Commons, Plant Breeding and Agricultural Research* (Routledge 2023), Fabien Girard, Ingrid Hall and Christine Frison (eds) *Biocultural Rights, Indigenous Peoples and Local Communities* (Routledge 2022).

40 Article 3.4 and 3.5 WIPO Treaty.

41 See The Notes (n 34) 4.

be a 'tick-boxing' exercise rather than a true disclosure requirement aimed at strengthening access and benefit-sharing mechanisms.

3.2. FAILURE TO DISCLOSE: SANCTIONS AND REMEDIES

We now turn to the core provision of the WIPO Treaty which might be connected to the 'inclusive patent' as suggested by Prof. Van Overwalle. Article 5 specifies the 'sanctions and remedies' that shall be put in place in case of failure to disclose. Much rests on the shoulders of Contracting States as the main guidance from the treaty are twofold. First, it is up to Contracting States to put in place 'appropriate, effective and proportionate legal, administrative and/or policy measures to address a failure to provide the information required.'[42] Second, 'no contracting party shall revoke or render unenforceable a patent *solely* on the basis of an applicant's failure to disclose'[43] (emphasis added). The redress mechanism is therefore adopting a two-staged approach. First, applicants are given the opportunity to rectify their application and then, if they fail to rectify their mistake, sanctions or remedies will kick in. One carve-out in this approach is that, in case of 'fraudulent conduct' or 'intent'[44] (terms which will have to be defined and/or interpreted by the relevant authorities of contracting states), applicants will not be offered the possibility to rectify their application.

As previously mentioned, one of the challenges of this two-staged approach is that PO should not be under any monitoring obligations. Therefore, the possibility to rectify an application (or identify a fraudulent one) would only be triggered if a third party challenges the completeness of the application. There are no *ex officio* powers for POs to review the application and potentially refuse it if it does not abide by the enhanced disclosure requirement.[45] The Notes suggest that, as pre-grant sanctions, the application process could be suspended until a complete disclosure or the refusal to disclose could lead to the withdrawal or lapse of the application.[46]

Regarding the second stage, i.e. sanctions and remedies, the treaty clearly stipulates that the failure to disclose the source of GRs upon which patent applications are based, shall not, in itself, be sufficient to lead to the revocation or unenforceability of a patent. Contracting States will therefore be able to provide for sanctions and remedies, but revocation and unenforceability are off the table. Here again, the Notes suggest that, as post-grant sanctions, fines could

42 Article 5.1 WIPO Treaty.

43 *Ibid.*, Article 5.3.

44 *Ibid.*, Article 5.4.

45 See also Peter K. Yu, 'WIPO Negotiations on Intellectual Property, Genetic Resources and Associated Traditional Knowledge' (2024) Texas A&M University, School of Law, Legal Studies Research Paper Series, Research Paper No. 23-71, 13-14. Bagley (n 39).

46 The Notes (n 34) 6.

be imposed and the 'publication of judicial rulings' could serve as a publicity measure.[47] While the former is fairly straightforward (although its strength may depend on the amount of the fine to be imposed), the latter remains vague and may be considered as rather weak.[48] The incentive to comply with the enhanced disclosure requirement under the threat of 'publication' may be of limited effect as this would not create limits on the exploitation of the underlying patent. The actual strengths and weaknesses of these sanctions may nonetheless vary and should be considered with flexibility.[49]

Two additional comments are warranted on this point. First, as emphasised supra, the failure cannot *solely* lead to revocation or enforceability. Therefore, it could be argued that, in the eventuality where the failure to disclose the source of a MGR also equates to an *insufficient* disclosure as envisaged in many patent laws as a ground for revocation, there might still be a possible to revoke a patent which did not respect the enhanced disclosure. Second, the fact that revocation cannot be a sanction in case of failure to disclose, is not without criticism. The absence of revocation option is considered by some to be insufficiently dissuasive or 'disappointingly weak'.[50] It is also quite problematic for countries (mentioned under 2.1.) which already have a provision providing for revocation as a sanction.[51] The argument behind a 'no revocation' rule is that such revocation would destroy the basis for benefits sharing. If an application were to fall into the public domain (or potentially re-enters some world of secrecy) because of a failure to disclose, this would not be in line with the objective of the treaty to provide an 'effective and balanced protection of GRs,' nor would it be in line with other relevant treaties such as the CBD or the Nagoya Protocol. Without a trace in patent registers, benefits generated from the exploitation of GRs might be more difficult to identify and, in turn, more difficult, if not impossible, to share with relevant third parties. When one think of the objectives of sustainable use and benefit-sharing of the BBNJ Agreement, it could be argued that a revocation rule would also run counter the objective of the UN Agreement. This is where the inclusive patent, as developed by Prof. Van Overwalle, can provide some interesting food for thoughts.

---

47 *Ibid.*

48 *A contrario*, see also Bagley (n 39) 5 observing that this sanction already exists in Switzerland and that the mechanism based on a fine and a publication is 'perceived as functioning well by the Swiss Industrial Property Office' she nonetheless observes that 'their sample size is small: only eleven disclosures as of 2014, two objections, which were corrected, and no criminal sanctions.'

49 For an early discussion on the issue of sanctions, see Joshua D. Sarnoff & Carlos M. Correa, (2006) 'Analysis of Options for Implementing Disclosure of Origin Requirements in Intellectual Property Applications – A Contribution to UNCTAD's Response to the Invitation of the Seventh Conference of the Parties of the Convention on Biological Diversity'. Doc. UNCTAD/DITC/TED/2004/14.

50 Yu (n 45) 10.

51 E.g. India Patents Act – Section 25(1)(j) for pre-grant opposition and 64(1)(p) for post-grant revocation.

4. A ROLE FOR THE INCLUSIVE PATENT?

In her piece 'inventive Inclusive Patents. From Old to New Open Innovation',[52] Prof. Van Overwalle proposes to reconsider the exclusive nature of patents and to introduce 'a new, alternative patent: the inclusive patent.' This new right would encompass 'as an attribute the right to enforce sharing behaviour and take non-sharing users to court.'[53] It would not replace traditional *exclusive* patents but would be an alternative regime which would empower its owner to 'include others, to control licensing conditions and to enforce alignment with the open source like commitments.'[54] While the suggestion to have an inclusive patent was made in the context of open innovation and with 'community inventors' in mind as primary beneficiaries,[55] this new right presents interesting characteristics which could be considered within the framework of MGR of ABNJ and the WIPO Treaty.

In particular, one such characteristics being that the inclusive patent may offer 'a powerful property entitlement *to enforce the sharing ethos*' (emphasis added).[56] Such sharing objective being key under the BBNJ Agreement and the benefit-sharing mechanisms envisaged (see supra and Article 12). This sharing ethos would also align with the idea that the use of MGR of ABNJ should take place within the guiding principle of the 'common heritage of mankind' (as stipulated under Article 7). Prof. Van Overwalle envisages two regimes for the legal effect of such new patent. First, it could be a 'semi-codified regime where the inclusive patent entitlement is provided by law and the open source copyleft type license is built on top by private parties.'[57] Second, it may be 'a fully-codified regime where the legislature imposes universal and sustainable access and use *ex ante*.'[58] In this contribution we envisage the inclusive patent under the second option, i.e. a fully-codified regime. A distinctive feature in our proposal would be that the inclusive patent is not something right holders may opt for at the stage of applying for a patent but rather would have to embrace in case of inaction. More specifically, the triggering requirement for this regime to apply would be when right holders fail to disclose the use of MGR of ABNJ. This trigger presents similarities with other mechanisms which may already exist in patent law such as compulsory licensing, or FRAND licensing. The changing nature of

52 Van Overwalle (n 9).
53 *Ibid.* 206.
54 *Ibid.* 209.
55 *Ibid.* 220, observing that 'the starting point of the present paper is the belief that there is an increasing group of users/inventors who want to expand access to and use of their work under less restrictive terms than the conditions applied under firm-centered open innovation regimes.'
56 *Ibid.* 209.
57 *Ibid.*, 239.
58 *Ibid.*, 209. See also her reference to Severine Dusollier (2007) 'Sharing Access to Intellectual Property through Private Ordering', 82 Chicago-Kent Law Review, 1391.

an MGR-related patent would be determined by the action (or rather inaction) of right holders. Under compulsory licensing rules, it is the refusal of right holders to license which triggers the mechanism under which a third party may be granted a license. Under FRAND licensing, it is the declaration of essentiality, or the inclusion of a patented technology deemed essential in a standard, which generates FRAND licensing terms. However, instead of imposing contractual or licensing conditions on the exploitation of one's patent, the proposed mechanism would go one step further and would actually alter the nature of the right itself and transform the obligations originating from this right. As such, the inclusive patent suggested by Prof. Van Overwalle would remain a right in itself and a real alternative to the exclusive patent and would not simply represent an additional exception or limitation.

Traditional mechanisms for openness and inclusivity in patent law are usually concerned with contract law. Right holders may decide to 'open' or 'share' their exclusive rights with others via the use of licenses. The ABS mechanism is similar to this as it also relies on contract law for its enforceability. However, this system presents some shortcomings. It has been demonstrated that to rely on negotiations (both in order to obtain prior informed consent and mutually agreed terms – the PIC and MAT rules of ABS) where different parties may have different bargaining powers and tools may be particularly difficult, especially in the context of GRs and TK. Shortcomings of ABS mechanisms can be seen in cases where indigenous communities struggled to have the terms and spirit of the agreements respected.[59] When we think of MGR the problem crystallises even more as there is, de facto, no *human* community which may have any type of bargaining power. Therefore, to rely on licensing agreements and contract to ensure an element of 'openness' or a 'sharing ethos' may hold some difficulties.

Alternatively, if the sanction to a lack of proper disclosure of MGR is to transform an exclusive right into an inclusive patent, therefore changing the nature of the right itself and to connect it with access and use conditions established *ex ante* by the legislator, one could potentially avoid having to rely on these licensing mechanisms to create a certain degree of inclusivity. Additionally, this proposal could fall within the sphere of discretion left to Contracting States under the WIPO Treaty to put in place 'appropriate, effective and proportionate legal, administrative and/or policy measures to address a failure to provide the information required.'[60] This suggestion would also not violate the prohibition of revocation or unenforceability as sanction to a failure to disclose.

---

[59] For a general overview see Evanson Chege Kamau (ed) *Global Transformations in the Use of Biodiversity for Research and Development* (Springer 2022). See also Christine Frison, Elsa Tsioumani, 'Access and Benefit Sharing and Digital Sequence Information' in Charles Lawson, Michelle Rourke and Fran Humphries (eds) *Access and Benefit Sharing of Genetic Resources, Information and Traditional Knowledge* (Routledge 2013) 123.

[60] Article 5.1WIPO Treat.

5. CONCLUSION

The inclusive patent may not be the panacea, and further reflections in order to have a fully functioning system need to be developed. Models for what the inclusive patent would look like under various Contracting States laws would have to be elaborated and procedural avenues would need to be envisaged. For example, the attributes of the 'right to enforce sharing behaviour' and to 'take non-sharing users to court', identified by Prof. Van Overwalle as key for the inclusive patent, would have to be translated to the particular needs of MGR of ABNJ and the benefit-sharing mechanism provided for under the BBNJ Agreement. Moreover, mechanisms to detect when an applicant has failed to disclose the source of MGR of ABNJ, and who might have legal standing to raise this failure and trigger the transformative nature of the inclusive patent, would also have to be elaborated. Finally, it might also be worth considering that the inclusive patent could serve in other instances than simply the failure to disclose the origin of MGR of ABNJ. It is possible to envisage this option as something right holders might voluntarily opt for.

Despite these shortcomings of this contribution, we wanted to highlight that, at a conceptual level, the parameters of the inclusive patent offer an opportunity to rethink traditional models of exclusivity and inclusivity in the particular context of MGR of ABNJ. This requires a shift in thinking and in regulating patenting activities within the commons' framework. A topic dear to Geertrui's research. In some ways, the novelty of the BBNJ Agreement and the WIPO Treaty provide a great opportunity to finally infuse some of that inclusivity in patent law. While this re-thinking opportunity may traditionally be more difficult as the resources used in IP are more easily captured by private property rules, in the case of MGR of ABNJ, privatisation is (and should be) more challenging due to the guiding principles of the common heritage of humankind. While this may very well be wishful thinking, it does not take away from the fact that, with the development and adoption of these two international treaties, we are at a moment in time where we can avoid some of the mistakes of the past when it comes to regulating the use of GRs (and associated TK).

Thinking outside the box and to consider old problems, such as issues of openness and inclusivity within the exclusivity regime of patent law, with new lenses such as the Ocean Wiper' mask, or the inclusive patent in this case, has always been a cherished exercise for Geertrui and I hope this contribution continues her work and carries her ideas a little further down the path she helped shape.

CHAPTER 5

INCLUSIVITY, INTELLECTUAL PROPERTY, AND THE IP ACADEMY*

Pascale CHAPDELAINE
Associate Professor at the Faculty of Law, University of Windsor
Chair in Law, Intellectual Poperty, and the Digital Marketplace

T4 **Flexible Pocket Watch**
Gives you a choice of three times. Pick your favorite.

1. INTRODUCTION

To many, inclusivity in Intellectual property (IP), an exclusionary tool, is an oxymoron. But likely not so for Geertrui Van Overwalle, who has spent a large part of her prolific academic career studying the benefits of various collaboration

* Thank you to the organizsrs and participants at the Festschrift Workshop held on December 15, 2023 at the Faculty of Law of the KU Leuven in honour of Dr. Geertrui Van Overwalle coinciding with her celebration as emeritus professor. In particular thank you to Esther Van Zimmeren, Amandine Léonard and Arina Gorbatyuk for inviting me to contribute to this *Liber Amicorum*.

and sharing models of IP: patent pools, creative commons, and other IP licencing arrangements. Dr. Van Overwalle's inclination toward inclusivity is not only reflected in her scholarship. She exemplifies the openness, collaboration, and collegiality of the best kind.

In this short piece, I begin with a discussion on the relationship between inclusivity and IP, one of the main themes of this *liber amicorum*. In doing so, I will refer to Geertrui's original contribution to this discussion published in 2015: 'Inventing Inclusive Patents. From Old to New Open Innovation.'[1] I then consider inclusivity in the IP Law Academy as a way to highlight some of Geertrui's distinct contributions as a professor and colleague.

2. INCLUSIVITY AND IP

Some definitions and context are needed to situate how I envision the relationship between inclusivity and IP, based on my own experience as a legal practitioner, researcher and teacher. Etymologically, 'inclusivity' requires a deliberate act of involving others rather than a passive state of being.[2] The act of inclusion is desirable when exerted by a person or entity with power and something valuable to offer to another, and meaningful if such other person acts upon it as well. Inclusivity is often associated with openness in innovation, some industries, and communities. However, 'openness' refers to something else. The state of something accessible, not enclosed, not restricted to a particular category of people or institutions.[3] Inclusiveness requires a concerted act, while openness is a state that may or may not be the result of a preceding action. In other words, inclusivity usually requires some degree of openness toward others, but openness does not necessarily involve a concerted act of incorporating others and their contributions in research and development endeavours. These definitions and distinctions are important when looking at IP, its exclusionary powers, and its connection with inclusivity.

---

1 Geertrui Van Overwalle, 'Inventing Inclusive Patents. From Old to New Open Innovation' in Peter Drahos, Gustavo Ghidini & Hanns Ullrich (eds) *Kritika: Essays on Intellectual Property* (Edward Elgar, vol. 1, 2015) https://papers.ssrn.com/sol3/papers.cfm?abstract_id=2705109, accessed 12 May 2025. [Inventing Inclusive Patents].

2 The Oxford Dictionary defines 'inclusion' as 'the action or an act of including something or someone'. And 'to include' as 'to have, put in, or incorporate as part of a whole' comprise or reckon in as part of a whole' as well as 'to invite, welcome, or encourage the involvement of (a person) in an activity, conversation, etc'. 'Inclusion' and 'to include' in Oxford English Dictionary, www.oed.com/, accessed 12 May 2025.

3 The Merriam-Webster dictionary defines 'openness' as 'having no enclosing or confining barrier: accessible on all or nearly all sides'; 'not restricted to a particular group or category of participants'. 'Openness' in Merriam-Webster, https://www.merriam-webster.com/dictionary/openness, accessed 12 May 2025. The list of meanings for 'openness' is relatively long; however, these two definitions are the most relevant definitions of openness for the purpose of our discussion relating to IP.

IP, whether patents, copyright, trademarks, or plant breeders' rights, confers on its right holder powers to exclude e.g.: from using a confusingly similar trademark with respect to similar goods, from making a device covered by a registered patent claim, or from reproducing a substantial part of a copyrighted work, and so on.

The tension between exclusivity and access to IP is embedded within human rights law,[4] and well-illustrated by the passionate debates on the theoretical justifications underpinning the protection of IP, whether right-based theories (e.g. desert-based or personhood theories), or utilitarian, instrumentalist theories.[5]

What is the relationship between having the power to exclude through IP rights and inclusivity? This does not require looking into how for instance, statutory or judge-made law exceptions and limitations to IP exclusive rights (e.g. fair dealing, interoperability purposes, right to repair, etc ...) may stimulate inclusivity. Exceptions and limitations create a space where IP exclusive rights do not apply and thus are out of scope when examining the correlation between IP and inclusivity.

For most IP rights, the power to exclude also entails the privilege not to do so, a critical feature to understanding IP and other proprietary rights. Except perhaps with respect to trademarks, whereby the right holder must enforce their trademark at the risk of losing their rights through dilution of the trademark, IP most often confers the power and flexibility for the right holder to not enforce their IP rights, without running the risk of losing such rights. There may be as many good reasons not to enforce IP rights as there are to do so. This includes: preserving good business relations with business partners, suppliers, or customers; the time, cost, and uncertainty involved in litigation; and the fear that poking the competitor-infringer may come and bite the IP right holder, who may not be entirely in the clear regarding the competitor-infringer's IP rights either. These are all good reasons why IP right holders may choose to not enforce their exclusive rights at any given point in time. Short of inclusiveness, the rationales to do nothing set intrinsic limits to the power to exclude. This is not to suggest that such inherent restraints on the exercise of those IP rights are optimal in the greater IP ecosystem of reward, use, and reuse. IP exclusionary rights confer strong powers that can be used at the right holder's leisure. The use of someone's IP without proper authorization entails risks and legal uncertainty for anyone in that situation.

---

4 United Nations General Assembly, Universal Declaration of Human Rights (adopted 10 December 1948 UNGA Res 217 A(III)), Articles 27 and 26 (about the right to the protection of authors' scientific, literary or artistic productions, as well as the right to education and to participate in cultural life, enjoy the arts and share in scientific advancement).

5 See e.g. Edwin C. Hettinger, 'Justifying Intellectual Property' (1989)18 Philosophy & Public Affairs, 31; Jeremy Waldron, 'From Authors to Copiers: Individual Rights & Social Values in Intellectual Property' (1993) 69 Chicago-Kent Law Review 841.

More overt than the privilege not to enforce one's IP rights is the right holder privilege to make one's IP accessible through open licence models such as Creative Commons.[6] Under such models, right holders of copyright works voluntarily and explicitly make their works available to others, whether to individuals or organisations, as long as they agree to respect a list of conditions in how such works are used and further disseminated.[7] Here, the right holder takes more of an active step by making their works available through such licence model, than choosing to not enforce their rights in a specific instance. At the other end of IP sharing models are statutory compulsory licences whereby the right holder`s privilege to share their IP with or without compensation, is converted into an obligation to do so in specific circumstances, and is subject to the licensee respecting strict conditions that usually include monetary compensation to the right holder.[8]

For its part, inclusion connotes something more active and concerted on the part of the right holder than letting their IP rights be by not enforcing them or making them accessible through open sharing models.[9] Inclusion is also more subject to the other party(ies)' willingness to act on the right holders' invitation to be included. Unlike statutory compulsory licences, inclusion occurs with the volition of the right holder. Cross-licencing agreements and patent pools are good examples where IP and inclusivity not only co-exist but also define the relationships between the selected parties. The ability to include others by sharing existing or developing future IP depends on others' agreement to be included and share in return. Meanwhile, the power to exclude remains an integral part of those frameworks against anyone outside the patent pool or cross-licencing circle, or against parties within the circle breaching the terms of IP sharing. This state of IP inclusivity goes only so far as that specific group is concerned.

In 'Inventing Inclusive Patents', Dr. Van Overwalle skillfully examines the vast literature on various sharing models of IP.[10] She correctly emphasizes how IP's defining power to exclude underlies those sharing models and is often a condition *sine qua none* to the existence of such models. Dr. Van Overwalle and many other commentators refer to this as the paradox of *excluding to include* when it comes to IP and openness.[11] Rather than a paradox, one may on the contrary view inclusivity as the corollary of IP and other proprietary interests which generally confer powers to exclude. This is a hard truth for Dr. Van Overwalle

---

6 Creative Commons, 'Share your Work', https://creativecommons.org/share-your-work/, accessed 22 May 2025.

7 Van Overwalle (n 1) 26–27.

8 *Ibid.*, 16, 34.

9 See (n 2).

10 Van Overwalle (n 1).

11 *Ibid.* at 18: 'A large set of legal scholarship has recognized for quite some time now, that stepping into the property logic may be an essential prerequisite to maintain openness. Excluding to include is one of the major paradoxes in contemporary thinking on openness.'

and the many others in search of sustainable IP openness or inclusivity models, the ones that cannot be easily dismantled through the right holder re-exercising their power to exclude, or by another party having accessed the openly shared IP downstream and fencing it off through further IP protection.

Geertrui Van Overwalle's bold proposal to develop a new system of 'inclusive patents' seeks to offer a more lasting alternative to IP sharing models relying on traditional patent exclusionary frameworks. With inclusive patents, openness and accessibility rather than exclusion become the baseline. Geertrui invokes a strong culture or ethos of collaboration in innovative communities, as the backdrop justification for developing this new inclusive patents' stream. At the same time, she recognizes that open innovation models are not necessarily always more desirable in terms of increasing overall welfare, and that more empirical evidence and economic analysis are required to identify when openness is effectively more beneficial.[12] As someone who practiced IP law for several years, I witnessed firsthand the negative connotation that engineers and software developers sometimes attach to IP exclusionary powers, seen as counterproductive in the greater scheme of innovation and product development. I also saw how such collaboration culture could sometimes clash with business management objectives under which patent portfolios were viewed as assets to be grown and enforced against infringers.

Through her proposed 'inclusive patent' system, an inventor could opt to file through the 'inclusive patent' stream for any given invention, an option co-existing with the traditional exclusionary patent system. Such 'inclusive patent' would confer a power to include with enforcement rights being limited against those who use these patent rights to exclude others.[13] In the spirit of accessibility and longevity, the 'inclusive patent' would be available at a lower cost than traditional patents, favouring a registration system over an examination-based process, with low registration fees, and a twenty-year period grant.[14] It is unclear whether the proposed system would be more of an 'open patent' system requiring little active involvement of the patent holder toward the patent user than an 'inclusive patent' requiring a more active approach toward some collaboration on both sides.

What would be the real incentives to file for 'inclusive patents' and how they would co-exist with traditional patents are important questions that require further development. Without clear incentives for choosing the 'inclusive patent' stream, it seems that its co-existence with traditional patents would exacerbate rather than alleviate the *exclude to include* paradox or corollary embedded within IP. In other words, the traditional patent system offering the incentive of exclusivity in exchange for invention disclosure would remain the more attractive base for IP sharing models than the 'inclusive patent' stream.

---

12 *Ibid.* at 42.

13 *Ibid.* at 29–32.

14 *Ibid.* at 35–37.

In short, sharing, openness, and inclusivity towards one's IP are privileges that derive from the right holder's exclusionary powers. Such privileges may be exercised by choice or by necessity. Unlike sharing and openness, inclusivity requires more concerted actions both from the right holder and the beneficiary to be meaningful. In other words, the exercise of the privilege of inclusion requires more than the sole will of the right holder. Dr. Van Overwalle's valuable scholarly contributions shed more light on how inextricably imbricated exclusionary powers, openness and inclusivity are when it comes to IP.

3. INCLUSIVITY IN ACADEMIA

There are obvious parallels to be drawn between IP and academia (more specifically the IP Law Academy) as it relates to inclusivity. Academia is a highly competitive environment. For students of all levels and for faculty, and at various stages: the selection and admission or hiring process, assessment, ranking and promotions. Administrative decisions effectively give universities the power to exclude. There is a stark contrast between those who are appointed as faculty and those who are not, in terms of the opportunities such appointments offer for teaching and scholarship. *Ditto* regarding students being admitted to one university and not another, in education systems with a competitive selection process.[15]

The comparisons may well stop here. Academic institutions have many distinct features and responsibilities as it relates to inclusivity that IP systems don't share. For instance, in Canada's post-secondary institutions and other parts of the world, *inclusion* is closely associated with diversity. At the institutional level, initiatives are put in place to address inequality (based on socio-economic, gender, ethnic, race, disability, gender identity, and other factors) and to prevent various forms of discrimination for students, faculty, and staff regarding determinant administrative decisions (admissions, hiring, promotions, etc.). This includes '*Equity, Diversity, and Inclusion (EDI)*' offices or task forces. Whether these initiatives are always successful is another matter. The objectives are laudable and ambitious, and the effective means to achieve them open for debate. They give

---

15 A variety of scholarly works explore issues of diversity and inclusion in law schools and in the IP Law academy. See: Irene Calboli and Srividhya Ragavan, *Diversity in Intellectual Property: Interests, Identities and Intersections* (Cambridge University Press, 2015); James Lindgren, 'Measuring diversity: law faculties in 1997 and 2013' (2016) 39(1) Harvard Journal of Law and Public Policy, 89; Shontavia Johnson et al, 'Diversifying Intellectual Property Law: Why Women of Color Remain "Invisible" and How to Provide More Seats at the Table' (2018) 10(4) Landslide 14 Meera E Dao, *Unequal Profession Race and Gender in Legal Academia* (Stanford University Press, 2019); Kenneth Oldfield, 'Structural Nepotism: On the Reluctance of Law Schools to Include Social Class Origins among their Faculty Diversity Goals' (2020) 69(2) Journal of Legal Education, 239.

rise to forums for discussion and processes whereby improvement can be tracked and measures for ameliorations put in place. Unfortunately, the very existence of these programs and the objectives they promote are increasingly under threat and have become highly politicized in the US and other parts of the world.

A university's type of governance and management style is a highly determinant factor that directly impacts on inclusivity. Whether consultation frequently takes place before key decisions are made. Whether faculty council includes various constituents of a department. And whether important decisions, e.g. faculty appointments, promotions, course offerings, student experience, etc., require the approval (or majority vote) of those various parties, etc. In that sense, and in contrast to our previous discussion about IP exclusionary powers and IP systems, universities, academia bear significant powers to create an inclusive environment … or not.

At the individual level, the concerted effort of a faculty member to include others in research projects, events, or any opportunity of exposure that can help their students or colleagues on their academic or professional path can make a world of difference. Especially to junior faculty or students in a supervision relationship, or at various other stages of their academic journey. As such, the act of inclusion can be very powerful and positively impact a colleague or (graduate) student's academic life. This brings me to the subject of this *liber amicorum* and to my personal encounter with Dr. Geertrui Van Overwalle.

I have known Dr. Van Overwalle, Geertrui since 2006. Thanks to Professor Franz Gotzen, who was at the time Director of the KU Leuven Centre for IP Rights, I was welcomed as a visiting scholar for the academic year 2006–2007. Geertrui was also affiliated to this Centre. I had and still have a special connection to the KU Leuven, having worked there in the nineties as a Research and Teaching Assistant for Professor Hans Van Houtte, and as alumna of their LL.M. program in European Union Law. And most importantly, the KU Leuven is where I met my husband, Trudo Lemmens, as we were two Research Assistants in the same department back then.

Professionally, the year I first met Geertrui was a year of transition for me, taking distance from a successful law practice career toward something else, the contours of which were not entirely clear at that point. I did not fit the traditional mold of an academic: no Ph.D., next to no publications, and no fixed position at a reputable University. Professor Van Overwalle was one of my first windows into the world of academia. Geertrui, as well as others at the Centre for IP Rights, welcomed me and my family with open arms, as if I already belonged. Geertrui attended to our needs, making sure we had everything we needed as temporary transplants from Canada to Belgium.

This inclusiveness was also palpable in the way Professor Van Overwalle worked with her doctoral students. I saw a scholar in action collaborating with a dynamic team of researchers and doctoral students whose ideas and contributions mattered. They were made to feel that they belonged through

Geertrui's words and actions. They have gone on to very successful academic careers afterward. This is a testimony of Geertrui's mentorship and ability to nurture academic success, ensuring a strong legacy in the IP Academy. The fact that many if not most of her former doctoral students and researchers were involved one way or the other in the organisation of the celebration to honour Geertrui in December 2023 also speaks for itself. The collaborative environment that she nurtured has led to lasting professional bonds and friendships. On the theme of diversity and inclusion, I note the large number of women who have benefited from Geertrui's doctoral supervision and mentorship over the years. This is something for which Professor Van Overwalle is and should be particularly proud of.

I feel very fortunate to have encountered Geertrui on my academic path. She was an inspiration as I embarked on my academic journey and continues to be to many others in the IP Law Academy. While I have some reservations about the extent to which IP systems can effectively be a fertile ground for inclusivity, I have none when it comes to Geertrui's commitment and success at actively creating nurturing learning environments for students and colleagues. Environments where others' opinions and contributions matter, in the true fashion of inclusion and academic collaboration. Dank u Geertrui, en hartelijk gefeliciteerd!

The 'Flexible Pocket Watch' (reproduced at the beginning of this chapter) is the dream watch for the professor, scholar, and mother of four … I selected this image thinking of Geertrui's conscientiousness and dedication as a mother (and now grandmother), professor, scholar, colleague, and mentor. This is a woman with a great heart, always willing to help others around her.

PART II

UNFOLDING THE FUTURE: SUSTAINABILITY AND IP

CHAPTER 6

WRITE-A-BIKE

Intellectual Property and the Sustainable Development Goals

Margaret Chon
Donald & Lynda Endowed Chair for the Pursuit of Justice
Faculty Director, Technology, Innovation Law, and Ethics Program,
Seattle University School of Law

K14 Write-A-Bike
Write while riding. Lovely oak tabletop can also carry fairly flat children.

1. INTRODUCTION

Had the imaginary Write-A-Bike been invented, it would have been a perfect vehicle for Geertrui. A prodigious scholar as well as avid bicyclist, she could have combined two of her favorite activities at once. Furthermore, its writing table would double as a place to carry children (or grandchildren), which then would allow Geertrui to introduce younger people to the joys of exploration, whether of her favorite ideas or places.

When I was a visiting professor at Katholieke Universiteit Leuven (KU Leuven) in March 2019, I glimpsed a life that was parallel to but very different from my own as a U.S.-based academic. Geertrui had invited me to her home institution to teach a short course as part of a Global Law Professors program. When I received her invitation, I was very honored as well as surprised (perhaps because of a lingering case of imposter syndrome). But of course, I accepted her invitation immediately and enthusiastically because it presented a very welcome opportunity to spend time with a respected intellectual property (IP) scholar who had already honored and surprised me once by visiting me in my hometown of Seattle, Washington.

During my visit, Geertrui took me on a memorable bicycle tour of Leuven and its outskirts. We stopped several times so that she could explain to me what we were seeing and its significance to her. At one of those pauses on the KU Leuven campus, I took a photo of her wearing a bright blue jacket highlighted against a huge bed of yellow daffodils, a reminder of that enjoyable albeit chilly afternoon.

During our tour, we also briefly discussed the history of the medieval beguinages (which, by coincidence, were the exotic setting for a murder mystery that I had read some months before Geertrui's invitation). We also explored a wooded area that was still remarkably undeveloped and obviously very familiar to Geertrui from her many bicycle outings. Throughout my visit, Geertrui's deep affection both for biking and for KU Leuven as a center of global knowledge production was very evident.

My KU Leuven course focused on the relationship of global IP to the United Nations (UN) 2030 Agenda for Sustainable Development, along with its Sustainable Development Goals (SDGs),[1] which were then at the start of their 15-year trajectory. As will be explored further below, both Geertrui's personal and scholarly choices align and resonate with the UN SDGs. For example, on that same bike (note: not car!) ride, she took me to a local organic food producer, Biogroenten van de Wikke, because of her interest in and commitment to sustainable agriculture and other activities that strengthen local communities and minimize negative impact on the planet. Not coincidentally, her scholarly themes include the uneasy fit between IP and food security[2] as well as the many tensions between IP and biodiversity.[3]

Geertrui's personal and academic attention to sustainable food production demonstrates the importance of connecting local initiatives to lofty global IP frameworks. IP can be used to further SDG 9, which centers on '[i]ndustry, *innovation*, and infrastructure,'[4] seeking to '[b]uild resilient infrastructure, promote inclusive and sustainable industrialization and *foster innovation*.'[5] The term 'innovation' in SDG 9 evokes the primary public policy goal of IP – that is, to foster and encourage innovation through the balance between exclusive rights and public access while encouraging fair competition within a market-based economic framework.

Yet SDG 9 includes the concept of 'inclusive and sustainable industrialization' in addition to 'innovation'. This in turn raises the critically important question of what *kind* of innovation IP should encourage. In other words, is it possible to have an inclusive and sustainable *innovation* in addition to inclusive and

---

1 United Nations, Department of Economic and Social Affairs. Sustainable Development, 'THE 17 GOALS'. https://sdgs.un.org/goals, accessed 28 February 2025.

2 See, e.g. Geertrui Van Overwalle, 'Food security, food crisis and boundaries to intellectual property' in Susy Frankel, Margaret Chon, Graeme B. Dinwoodie, Barbara Lauriat and Jens Schovsbo (eds) *Improving Intellectual Property: A Global Project* (Edward Elgar Publishing 2023) 75.

3 See, e.g. Geertrui Van Overwalle, 'Protecting and sharing biodiversity and traditional knowledge: Holder and user tools' (2005) 53 Ecological Economics 53, 585–607.

4 United Nations, Sustainable Development Goals, 'Goal 9: Build resilient infrastructure, promote sustainable industrialization and foster innovation'. www.un.org/sustainabledevelopment/infrastructure-industrialization/, accessed 28 February 2025 (emphasis added).

5 United Nations, Department of Economic and Social Affairs. Sustainable Development, '9. Build resilient infrastructure, promote inclusive and sustainable industrialization and foster innovation'. https://sdgs.un.org/goals/goal9, accessed 28 February 2025 (emphasis added). See also *ibid.* ('In the face of a rapidly changing global economic landscape and increasing inequalities, sustained growth must include industrialization that first of all, makes opportunities accessible to all people, and second, is supported by innovation and resilient infrastructure').

sustainable industrialization? The remainder of this brief chapter will try, at least partially, to answer this question.

Section 1 explores the various ways in which IP and innovation intersect with the SDGs. It makes the case that IP can and should impact and promote sustainable development, by contributing to the production of various global public goods including but not limited to innovation. This potential of IP is still under-recognized and under-realized, nine years after the adoption of the SDGs. Section 2 identifies conflicts between strong IP protection and the encouragement of inclusive and sustainable innovation, including the other global public goods represented by the SDGs, such as food security. The chapter concludes with some observations about the links between Geertrui's work and these two points.

2. IP AND SDGS: WHAT ARE THE CONNECTIONS?

How does IP intersect with the SDGs? The World Intellectual Property Organization (WIPO) acknowledges that as a UN agency, it has the responsibility to incorporate and implement the SDGs within its work program.[6] In addition to SDG 9, WIPO states that IP can promote the economic and social development of all countries via the following other goals: 2 – zero hunger, 3 – good health and well-being, 6 – clear water and sanitation, 7 – affordable and clear energy, 8 – decent work and economic growth, 11 – sustainable cities and communities and 13 – climate action.[7]

WIPO also states that innovation can assist with SDGs 1 – no poverty, 8 – decent work and economic growth, 14 – life below water and 15 – life on land.[8] And it notes that 'certain SDGs are relevant to the settings of an innovation policy framework', notably SDG 5 – gender equality, SDG 8 – decent work and economic growth, SDG 10 – reduced inequalities and SDG 12 – responsible consumption and production.[9] It is interesting to note that SDG 8 – decent work and economic growth – appears on all three of these lists.

Furthermore, WIPO provides three in-depth case studies of how its current work program is encouraging the realization of three goals: SDG 3 – good health

---

6 WIPO, 'The Impact of Innovation: WIPO and the Sustainable Development Goals' (2021) (hereinafter: 'The Impact of Innovation'). www.wipo.int/sdgs/en/story.html#:~:text=As%20a%20specialized%20agency%20of%20the%20United%20Nations%2C,competitiveness%20and%20creativity%20needed%20to%20achieve%20these%20goals, accessed 28 February 2025.

7 *Ibid.* 12. ('WIPO's work enables innovation for the economic, social and cultural development of all countries. As such, innovation is key to achieving the SDGs. It is not only central to SDG 9, but also has a direct impact on SDG 2, SDG 3, SDG 6, SDG 7, SDG 8, SDG 11 and SDG 13.').

8 *Ibid.* ('As a policy setting, innovation can assist in achieving SDG 1, SDG 8, SDG 14 and SDG 15.)

9 *Ibid.*

and well-being, 4 – quality education, and 13 – climate action.[10] In each of its three case studies, WIPO emphasizes its work through public-private partnerships (PPPs), which are highlighted as a primary means of implementation through SDG 17 (Partnership through the goals).[11] PPPs consist of partners that span the public and private sectors, involving intergovernmental organizations such as WIPO, but also private for-profit and not-for-profit institutions, for purposes of collaboratively reaching shared goals. Significantly, the relationship of the partners to each other is largely governed by contract law.

The PPPs highlighted by WIPO include WIPO Re:Search, a Seattle-based PPP that facilitates collaborative partnerships for research on neglected diseases,[12] WIPO Accessible Books Consortium (ABC), a Geneva-based PPP that promotes accessibility of books to visually impaired persons through 'born-accessible publishing' and other initiatives,[13] and WIPO Green, also based in Geneva, which is a PPP that provides a networking platform for the voluntary diffusion of climate change technologies.[14] WIPO's involvement with or sponsorship of PPPs such as these signals a commitment to the realization of the SDGs. And they provide a departure point for consideration of what truly sustainable and inclusive innovation might look like.

These current partnerships and others[15] represent considerable institutional evolution from an earlier era (the early 2000s) when WIPO did not include development goals or programs as part of its core mandate.[16] It now appears that WIPO embraces its development mandate as part of the on-going WIPO Development Agenda adopted in 2007,[17] and moreover has assumed a role in fostering development that does not over-rely on the ability of economic growth by itself to deliver, as had been previously advocated by some voices at WIPO.[18]

---

10 *Ibid.* 14–25.

11 See generally, Margaret Chon, Pedro Roffe and Ahmed Abdel-Latif (eds) *The Cambridge Handbook of Public-Private Partnerships, Intellectual Property Governance, and Sustainable Development* (CUP 2018).

12 The Impact of Innovation (n 6) 15–17; see also Katy M. Graef, Jennifer Dent et al., 'Creating, Managing, and Advancing Collaborations: The Road to Successful Partnerships' in Chon, Roffe, and Abdel-Latif (eds) (n 11) 72–92.

13 The Impact of Innovation (n 6) 19–21; see also Susan Isiko Štrba, 'The Marrakesh Treaty, Public–Private Partnerships, and Access to Copyrighted Works by Visually Impaired Persons' in Chon, Roffe, and Abdel-Latif (eds) (n 11) 176–198.

14 The Impact of Innovation (n 6) 23–25; see also Ahmed Abdel-Latif, 'The Rise of Public–Private Partnerships in Green Technologies and the Role of Intellectual Property Rights' in Chon, Roffe, and Abdel-Latif (eds) (n 11) 223–244.

15 The Impact of Innovation (n 6) 12–13.

16 See generally, Margaret Chon, 'Intellectual Property and the Development Divide' (2006) 27 Cardozo L. Rev. 2821.

17 The Impact of Innovation (n 6).

18 See, e.g., Kamil Idris and Hisamitsu Aral, 'The Intellectual Property-Conscious Nation: Mapping the Path from Developing to Developed' (2006) WIPO Publication Number 988(E).

Despite this good news, WIPO could do much more to deploy global IP systems to promote sustainable development. I have called this challenge the 'triple interface' of PPPs, IP, and SDGs – a challenge that presents complex global governance questions regarding the balance of private and public interests in furtherance of innovation.[19] In 2018, along with many expert colleagues, I evaluated whether and to what extent these and other PPPs 'encourage innovation, build innovation capacity, engage in technology transfer or sharing, or otherwise ensure wide dissemination and diffusion of innovation results across borders to advance the progress of the SDGs.'[20] Unfortunately, some of the very PPPs being touted by WIPO were found to have significant gaps and drawbacks at that time.

With regard to the specific challenge of ensuring accountability, inclusivity, and transparency in IP licensing and other knowledge dissemination activities, for example, PPPs are all over the map. Based on Ahmed Abdel-Latif's in-depth case study of WIPO Green, I concluded that its 'licensing agreements are entirely left to the individual technology providers and seekers.'[21] This raises significant concerns about WIPO's oversight of IP management policies, which are in the realm of private contract law and can often result in IP overreach to the detriment of the overall public interest. By contrast, the WIPO Re:Search Guiding Principles, as well as its collaboration guidelines for partners, also governed by contracts, seemed to be steps in the right direction.[22] With regards to WIPO ABC, Susan Strka's excellent case study formed the basis for observing 'very real challenges in providing digital works in accessible formats, which require accompanying and compatible software, hardware, and/or technical know-how.'[23] Thus, potential dissemination of knowledge via accessibility to the public (in this case of visually impaired persons) can be impeded by technical constraints and capacities – which then raise the question of the need for capacity-building in various global sectors.

After surveying various PPPs (including the three highlighted by WIPO and discussed briefly above), I made over a dozen recommendations to address gaps in the deployment of PPPs and IP to further the goals of the SDGs.[24] It is unclear whether and how WIPO and its PPP partners are undertaking evaluation of their on-going development activities pursuant to these and other critiques and insights. Therefore, it is important to reiterate the many unanswered questions that are raised by this triple interface of global knowledge governance. Arguably, WIPO's over-reliance on SDG 9 and on PPPs as the primary institutional mechanisms to promote development falls short of truly inclusive and sustainable development.

---

19 Margaret Chon, 'The Triple Interface: Findings and Future Directions' in Margaret Chon, Pedro Roffe, and Ahmed Abdel-Latif (eds) (n 11) 425–438.

20 *Ibid.* 425.

21 *Ibid.* 426 (citations omitted).

22 *Ibid.* 431.

23 *Ibid.* 429.

24 *Ibid.* 436.

3. IP AND SDGS: WHAT ARE THE CONFLICTS?

Recently, an international group of scholars has critically examined how IP does (or mostly does not) promote inclusive and sustainable development.[25] Addressing all the SDGs (not just the ones that WIPO has highlighted) though multiple disciplines (including but not limited to law), these scholars contend that WIPO's overly-strong protection of IP can be detrimental to the realization of the SDGs. Strong IP rights benefit private (primarily corporate) stakeholders, but do not adequately account for the public interest of access and dissemination of knowledge even within standard IP policy frameworks, not to mention with respect to the many global public goods represented by the SDGs.

For example, in an excellent chapter, 'SDG 2: zero hunger, food and plant-related intellectual property, and access to plant genetic resources,'[26] S. Ali Malik details the ways in which food security and farmers' traditional right to save seed are threatened by strong IP protection in the area of plant genetic resources. As he writes, expanding multilateral IP rights through UPOV[27] and TRIPS[28] have

> 'solidified the rights of plant breeders (typically commercial scientists with the backing of large-scale institutions such as corporations, universities, and/or state institutions) over the varieties they develop. At the same time, they restrict the ability of farmers to save and reuse their seed towards crop diversification, which has been deemed integral to increasing biodiversity and mitigating the effects of climate change. Critics have argued that these developments neglect the customary rights of traditional breeders (typically farming and/or Indigenous communities) to their genetic resources and traditional knowledge, promote an ecologically destructive industrial agricultural model reliant upon chemical fertilizers and pesticides for hybrid seeds, have furthered the consolidation of the seed and agrochemical industry, and fail to recognize the historical contributions of farmers to plant breeding which pre-date the invention of IPRs.'[29]

Despite these conflicts between strong IP protection and food security, he points to one example of an IP regime that partially reconciles the competing public and private interests at stake: India's *sui generis* legislation over plant variety

25 Bita Amani, Caroline B. Ncube and Matthew Rimmer (eds) *The Elgar Companion to Intellectual Property and the Sustainable Development Goals* (Edward Elgar Publishing 2024).

26 S. Ali Malik, 'SDG 2: Zero hunger, food and plant-related intellectual property, and access to plant genetic resources' in Amani, Ncube and Rimmer (eds) (n 25) 53–70.

27 International Union for the Protection of New Varieties of Plants 1961, opened for signature 2 December 1961, UPOV 293(E) (entered into force 10 August 1968).

28 Agreement on Trade-Related Aspects of Intellectual Property Rights, in the Marrakesh Agreement Establishing the World Trade Organization 1994, WTO Treaty Series 1, adopted on 15 April 1994 (entered into force 1 January 1995).

29 Malik (n 26) 60.

protection, the Protection of Plant Varieties and Farmers' Rights Act 2001.[30] Although this local legal framework does not completely level the playing field between small holders and the agrochemical industry, it is notable for eschewing the strong utility patent protection of genetically modified plants available in the United States[31] as well as preserving the farmers' right to 'use, save, exchange, share, or sell seed of a protected variety.'[32] This approach makes use of the flexibilities within multilateral frameworks, to fashion more limited scope of IP protection and/or strengthening exceptions and limitations to IP protection.

It is far beyond the scope of this chapter to review and summarize the other important observations of Malik and the numerous other scholars who, along with him, have analyzed IP's current contribution towards and re-imagined IP's future impacts on each of the seventeen SDGs. But briefly, as another contributor, Faith Majekolagbe notes, a truly inclusive and sustainable development facilitated by IP should continue to move away from equating development primarily with industrial and economic development,[33] and towards addressing the needs of other stakeholders, including the most vulnerable. This more capacious and outward looking IP should prioritize the myriad ways IP can encourage the production of other global public goods, whether food security, good health, adequate education, gender equality, or the many other SDGs that have yet to be satisfactorily met.

While Geertrui's work has not focused on inclusive and sustainable development *per se*, it certainly resonates with and amplifies these efforts to thread the needle between private incentives and the many public interests in and affected by IP. For instance, she has clearly set forth a typology of licenses and access mechanisms for patent law.[34] As she found:

> 'The alleged detrimental impact of individual and multiple ownership may be mitigated by the use of creative individual licensing regimes and the establishment of collaborative and collective platforms facilitating the fluid exchange of patents from patent holders to third party users [...]. Through the shaping of license policies, exclusive or proprietary rights are used to leverage access, to promote dissemination, and to safeguard downstream use rights. Imaginative and solid IP license management is a powerful tool for advancing both private and public interest.'[35]

---

30 The Protection of Plant Varieties and Farmers' Rights Act 2001 (India).

31 *Bowman v. Monsanto*, 569 U.S. 278 (2013).

32 Malik (n 26) 71.

33 Faith Majekolagbe, 'The role of the World Intellectual Property Organization in the United Nations' Sustainable Development Agenda' in Amani, Ncube and Rimmer (eds) (n 25) 481, 489.

34 See, e.g. Geertrui Van Overwalle, 'Individualism, collectivism and openness in patent law: from exclusion to inclusion through licensing' in Jan Rósen (ed), *Individualism and Collectiveness in Intellectual Property Law* (Edward Elgar Publishing 2012) 71–114.

35 *Ibid.*

Geertrui's robust analysis of the array of available patent licensing mechanisms to promote access provides strong evidence for implementing careful IP management, which can be deployed towards inclusive and sustainable development. For example, this potential licensing flexibility reinforces the recommendations my collaborators and I made in the context of evaluating the impacts of PPPs on the SDGs, as discussed above. Furthermore, she has suggested that the global IP system must seek a better balance through different boundaries of IP protection than currently exist. For example, she recently advocated in favor of 'IP measures for safeguarding access to sufficient and healthy food, such as crop exemptions and compulsory licenses for food in both plant breeder's rights law and patent law.'[36] This stance buttresses the more recent work of those such as Malik (and the Indian peasants whose advocacy he amplifies) who have raised legitimate but often disregarded concerns about the harmful impacts of strong IP regimes on the production of important global public goods such as food security.

4. CONCLUSION

When I arrived in Leuven that spring of 2019, I found a lovely university town with many qualities that Americans dream about when they think about visiting Europe: amazing architecture, complex layers of history, and of course, wonderful, locally prepared food. And I also discovered that I was one of the few women and non-Europeans in this select group of 'global' law professors. It was then that I realized that Geertrui had deliberately reached out to me to make the program more inclusive. In retrospect, Geertrui's pro-active sponsorship of me speaks to one of her many values that she revealed to me during that all-too-brief visit. She took good care of me, making sure that I was able to find the correct classrooms and she even attended a couple of my classes to signal to my students that she fully supported me. Her level of attention was far above and beyond anything I had experienced in my numerous other international teaching experiences, where I was often left to navigate situations on my own. And it ultimately resulted in a very successful and enjoyable course in which my students and I formed a solid connection, despite the cross-cultural differences. One of my students was so inspired by the course that he even decided to pursue an IP LL.M. in the United States and is now a successful IP practitioner.

As an IP colleague, Geertrui's personal instincts and fundamental values are deeply embedded within her scholarly work. They also align with the multilateral impetus behind the SDGs, which is to promote innovation for the benefit of all via the many avenues to promote human flourishing rather than innovation

[36] Van Overwalle (n 2) 86.

that benefits only a few at the expense of many. Geertrui's generosity as an IP colleague and her careful and voluminous creative scholarly legacy has already given us, and will continue to provide, many tools to imagine and implement the optimal conditions for inclusive and sustainable development, both locally and globally. In closing, this chapter is a way for me to 'Write-A-Bike' again with Geertrui, despite the geographical distance now between us.

CHAPTER 7

A 'RIGHT TO REPAIR' IN EUROPEAN PATENT LAW?

Ansgar Ohly
Professor of Private Law, Intellectual Property and Competition Law, Ludwig Maximilian University Munich
Visiting Professor, University of Oxford

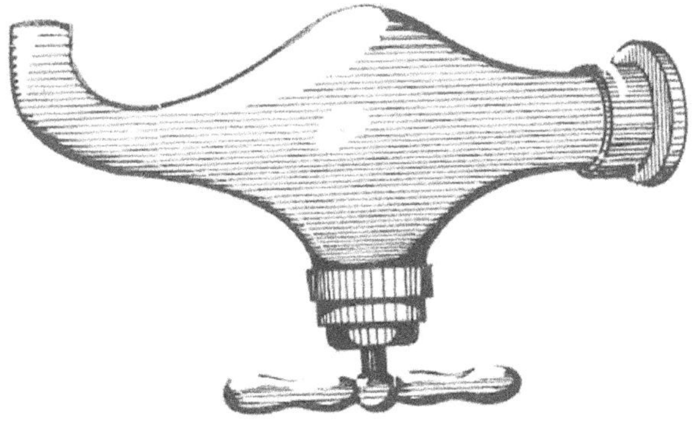

G2 Recirculating Faucet
Leaky faucets are no longer a nuisance.

1. INTRODUCTION: EXTRAORDINARY AND ORDINARY FAUCETS, AND THE RIGHT TO REPAIR

One of the extraordinary inventions presented in Jacques Carelman's hilarious book '*Catalog of Fantastic Things*' is a 'recirculating faucet'. It is turned upwards, thus solving the problem of leaky faucets. It is inventive because it overcomes the prejudice generally held among persons skilled in the art that water faucets would have to point downwards.

Our faucet also has an inner life. If we cut it open, it will look like this:

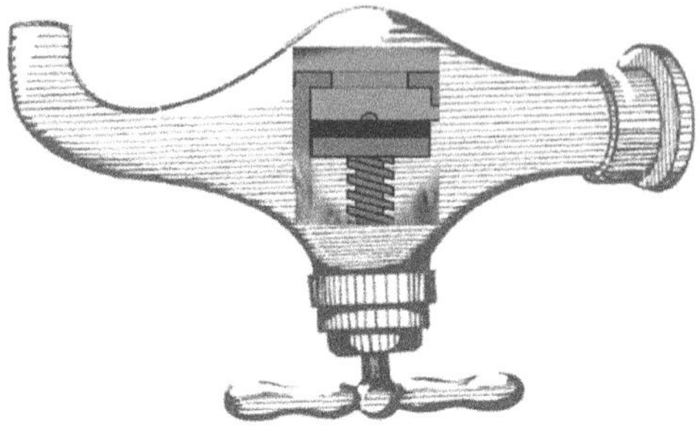

The handle is connected to a screw and a stopping device. Let us turn the 'recirculating faucet' around and transform it into a more ordinary invention, say a patented 'water-saving faucet' with a particular water-saving stopper. The stopper will need to be replaced from time to time.

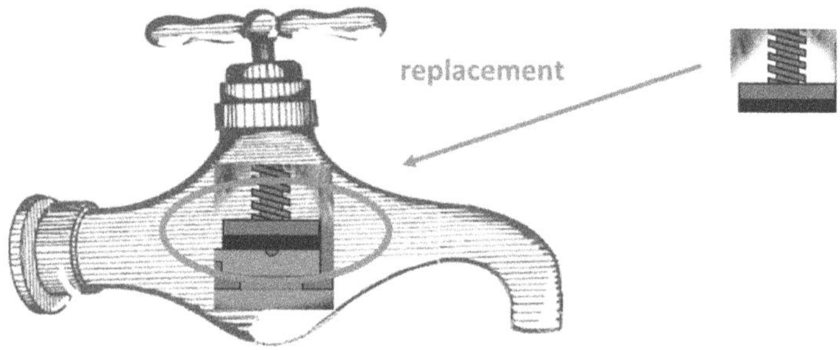

If our water-saving faucet is patented, the question arises whether the replacement of the stopper will amount to direct patent infringement by making the patented faucet and whether a third person will commit indirect infringement by selling the stopper to a user of the faucet.

In this respect, our water-saving faucet is strongly reminiscent of one of the leading German cases on patent law and repair, namely the '*Flügelradzähler*' ('impeller flow meter') case.[1] The patent read on a flow meter consisting of a housing and a measuring unit with a conical section, allowing a specific water inflow, which had several technical advantages over the state of the art. The defendant marketed measuring units which were compatible with the flow meter. Since this unit was only one component of the patented invention, there was no direct infringement. The patent owner therefore sued the seller for indirect patent infringement. The crucial question was whether the unit was supplied

1 German Federal Supreme Court (Bundesgerichtshof, hereinafter: 'BGH') GRUR 2004, 758 – *Flügelradzähler* – [2005] IIC 963 – *Impeller Flow Meter*.

to a 'person other than a party entitled to exploit the patented invention.'[2] If the user of the water meter could rely on the principle of exhaustion, he or she was entitled to use the invention,[3] but he or she was not if the exchange of the measuring unit amounted to a new manufacture. Doctrinally, this case concerns the limits of the principle of exhaustion. But the policy issue is to what extent the law allows a patented product to be repaired.

The 'right to repair' is high on the political agenda, both in the EU and in many countries. One of the building blocks of the Commissions 'Green Deal' is the Circular Economy Action Plan of 2020.[4] It sets out measures to encourage the design of sustainable products and to prevent waste. In pursuit of this goal, the EU has adopted several legal instruments. The 'Right to Repair' Directive[5] provides for obligations on manufacturers to repair goods, to keep spare parts in supply and to provide certain information. The Ecodesign for Sustainable Products Regulation[6] aims to improve the circularity, recyclability and durability of products. Also, new duties of information and bans on certain misleading practices concerning repair and obsolescence were added to the Unfair Commercial Practices Directive. Intellectual property law, however, was not addressed in any detail in the Commission's 'Green Deal'.[7]

Should it have been? Or is it sufficient to rely on the tacit wisdom of intellectual property law? Although there is no explicit 'right to repair' in patent law, or, indeed, in trade mark and copyright law,[8] the principle of exhaustion provides that 'the rights conferred by a European patent shall not extend to acts concerning a product covered by that patent after that product has been placed on the market in the European Union by, or with the consent of, the patent proprietor.'[9] While patent law does not recognise an affirmative right, the freedom to repair is often guaranteed by the principle of exhaustion.

From a patent law perspective, then, the question to be discussed is whether the present patent law system meets the requirements of a circular economy. In this respect, this chapter seeks to contribute to the growing body of scholarship

---

2 §10(1) German Patents Act; Article 26 UPCA.

3 A private user can also rely on the private use defence (Article 27(a) UPCA), but an indirect infringer cannot, see Article 26(3) UPCA.

4 Communication from the Commission, A new Circular Economy Action Plan. For a cleaner and more competitive Europe COM(2020) 98 final.

5 Directive (EU) 2024/1799 of the European Parliament and of the Council of 13 June 2024 on common rules promoting the repair of goods OJ L 2024/1799.

6 Regulation (EU) 2024/1781 of the European Parliament and of the Council of 13 June 2024 establishing a framework for the setting of ecodesign requirements for sustainable products OJ L 2024/1781.

7 The Circular Economy Action Plan (n 4) is largely silent on intellectual property issues but promises (at 6.3) that 'The Commission will propose an Intellectual Property Strategy to ensure that intellectual property remains a key enabling factor for the circular economy and the emergence of new business models.'

8 On the repair clause in design law, see (n 66).

9 Article 29 UPCA.

on IP and sustainability.[10] The argument will proceed in four steps. First, the status quo will be analysed: how have patent courts drawn the line between repair and re-manufacture? The second section will focus on a counter-exception recently added to the principle of exhaustion in the UPC Agreement and in the Regulation on the Unitary Patent according to which the owner can resist exhaustion if he or she has legitimate reasons for doing so. Thirdly, the potential for contractual rights to repair based on explicit stipulations or implied licences will be explored, before the final question is reached: is there a 'right to repair' in European patent law and, if not, should it be introduced?

The result may seem disappointing at first sight: there is no affirmative 'right to repair' in European patent law, nor should there be. But patent law, contract law, competition law and general principles of abuse of rights constitute a toolbox that can largely satisfy the public interest in allowing repair. In reaching this conclusion, I felt encouraged by Geertrui Van Overwalle's plea for a nuanced approach to patents relevant in the context of the recent COVID-19 pandemic. She pointed out that while claims for 'open source' models or patent waivers 'strike a sympathetic chord,' they could be 'detrimental to incentivising downstream development of drugs and therapies.'[11] Consequently she argued for a mix of incentives for voluntary collaboration and compulsory licences. My solution for the tension between patent protection and the public interest in allowing repair is similar. While the plea for a general 'right of repair' strikes a sympathetic chord, it seems too blunt an instrument, compared to the combined effect of exhaustion, contract law, competition law and the proportionality principle.

I dedicate this chapter to Geertrui Van Overwalle. I have always admired her innovative ways of balancing patent protection with the public interest, her intellectual rigour, her clear eye for academic quality and her encouragement of young scholars. But she has also influenced me in one respect that may seem incidental and anecdotal, but which means a lot to me. In one of her presentations, she illustrated her line of argument with photographs of signposts taken on a hike, some pointing forward, some pointing up, some pointing to dead ends. Since then, I have got into the habit of taking photos along the way that might be useful as illustrations in future presentations. For example, during a walk in the

---

10 See Aaron Perzanowski, *The Right to Repair* (CUP 2021); Irene Calboli, 'Pushing a Square Pin into a Round Hole? Intellectual Property Challenges to a Sustainable and Circular Economy, and What to Do About It' (2024) IIC 237; Christopher Heath, 'A Three-Step Test for Determining Patent Infringement Related to Repair' (2024) IIC 762; Pranvera Këllezi, Pierre Kobel and Bruce Kilpatrick (eds), *Sustainability Objectives in Competition and Intellectual Property Law* (Springer 2024); Annette Kur, 'As Good as New' – Sale of Repaired or Refurbished Goods: Commendable Practice or Trade Mark Infringement?' (2021) 70(3) GRUR Int 228; Ole-Andreas Rognstad and Inger B. Ørstavik, *Intellectual Property and Sustainable Markets* (Edward Elgar 2021); Martin Senftleben, 'Developing Defences for Fashion Upcycling in EU Trademark Law' (2024) 73(2) GRUR Int 99; Anna Tischner and Katarzyna Stasiuk, 'Spare Parts, Repairs, Trade Marks and Consumer Understanding' [2023] IIC 26.

11 Geertrui Van Overwalle, 'Will Covid Patents Save the World?' (2020) 69(9) GRUR Int 883.

Norwegian Fjordlands, much to the surprise of my family, I had to stop to take a picture of this pallet container by the side of our path.

The reason why will become apparent in the next section.

2. THE STATUS QUO: REPAIRING VERSUS MAKING

According to a well-known Greek myth, the Athenians preserved the ship on which Theseus had sailed back from Crete after slaying the Minotaur. From time to time, rotten planks had to be replaced with new ones. Over time, all the planks had thus been replaced. Was the ship still identical to the original one? Since ancient times, the Paradox of Theseus has represented the ontological problem of when change affects the identity of a thing. But it also illustrates the core issue of exhaustion,[12] which is object-specific. Once a product has been placed on the market by the patent owner, that particular object can be freely resold, used and also repaired. But the making of a new product without the owner's permission infringes the patent. So, when does replacing a component change the identity of the product?

Courts in all major patent jurisdictions have wrestled with this issue. Typical cases involve consumables such as toner cartridges[13] and coffee capsules[14] or spare parts such as brake pads.[15] In one truly European case, the patent protected

---

12 I cannot claim to be the first author referring to the Ship of Theseus in the context of exhaustion, see Perzanowski (n 10) 124; Michael Kobler, *Instandhaltung und Umbau patentgeschützter Vorrichtungen* (Carl Heymanns 2015) 200.

13 See US Supreme Court, *Impression Products v Lexmark* 581 US 360 (2017); High Court of Australia *Calidad v Seiko Epson* [2020] HCA 41; Japanese Supreme Court, *Canon v Recycle Assist* [2008] IIC 982; BGH GRUR 2018, 170 – *Trommeleinheit* = [2018] IIC 972 – *Drum Unit.*

14 See Hoge Raad, *Sara Lee v Vomar Voordeelmarkt*, ECLI:NL:PHR:2003:AI0346; Rechtbank Antwerpen, *Fort Koffiebranderij v Sara Lee*, case note by Fernand De Visscher (2004) 26 EIPR N105; High Court of England and Wales, *Nestec v Dualit* [2013] EWHC (Pat) 923; Oberlandesgericht Düsseldorf (Düsseldorf Court of Appeal), GRUR-RR 2013, 185.

15 BGH GRUR 2023, 47 – *Scheibenbremse II.*

a pallet container (the one I saw in Norway) consisting of a pallet, a metal cage mounted on the pallet and a plastic bottle for liquids which fitted into the cage. Since the pallet and the cage outlived the plastic bottle, the question arose whether the latter could be replaced and whether compatible containers could be sold without infringing the patent. The case was truly European because it involved a European patent and because it was decided by both the UK[16] and the German Supreme Courts.[17] The courts in both jurisdictions allowed the container to be repaired.[18]

The German Bundesgerichtshof took a two-step approach. First it asked whether, from the consumers' point of view, the replacement of the plastic bottle was to be regarded as remanufacture or repair.[19] This was the case if the bottles were normally replaced during the lifetime of the appliance and if the pallet and cage retained some of their economic value once the plastic container was broken.[20] Secondly, even if consumers viewed the replacement of the component as a repair rather than a manufacture, patent infringement was still possible if the replacement part or the connection between the part and the other components implemented the inventive concept.[21] In this case, the Bundesgerichtshof found that it was the mounted cage rather than the plastic bottle that embodied the inventive concept, which was therefore not implemented by replacing bottle.

The UK Supreme Court held that whether an activity involved 'making' was a question of fact and degree.[22] In this case, the bottle was a freestanding interchangeable component, it could not be described as the main component, it had a significantly shorter lifespan than the cage, it did not contain any aspect of the inventive concept and it could not be described as the main component of the article.[23] On this basis, the UK Supreme Court reached the same result as the Bundesgerichtshof, whose judgment the Court took into account.[24] However, unlike its German counterpart, the UK Supreme Court did not rely on the consumer's perspective or on the opinion of trade. And while the German court had juxtaposed re-manufacturing and repair, Lord Neuberger, while acknowledging that this distinction could sometimes be helpful, cautioned that it should not obscure the central issue of whether the alleged infringer was 'making' the article.[25]

---

16 *Schutz v Werit* [2013] UKSC 16 [78].

17 BGH GRUR 2012, 1118 – *Palettenbehälter II* = [2013] IIC 351 – *Pallet Container II.*

18 To be precise, the BGH referred the case back to the Munich Court of Appeal, which then gave judgment for the defendants, OLG München BeckRS 2014, 20361.

19 BGH GRUR 2012, 1118 [29].

20 *Ibid.* [28]–[31].

21 *Ibid.* [43]–[46].

22 *Schutz v Werit* [2013] UKSC 16.

23 *Ibid.*

24 *Ibid.* [37]–[47].

25 *Ibid.* [49] referring to *United Wire v Screen Repair Services* [2001] RPC 24 [71] per Lord Hoffman.

This is not the place for a broader analysis of European or even international case law on exhaustion and repair.[26] At the risk of oversimplification, it can be said that patent courts have applied three sets of criteria: *invention-related*, *product-related* and *consumer-related*. The invention-related test is whether the replacement part or the combination embodies the inventive concept. Possible product-related criteria are whether the replacement constitutes a substantial change, whether it concerns an essential or a separable part and whether the lifespan of the replaced part is shorter than that of the remaining product.[27] A consumer-related test is whether the act is considered by consumers to be repair or remanufacture and whether consumers expect to be entitled to the replacement. Courts tend to combine these criteria. In the pallet container case,[28] they were all in favour of allowing the replacement. In other cases, they may point in different directions. In a case recently decided by the Bundesgerichtshof,[29] the patent was for a disc brake that was easier to install and repair than those which were part of the prior art. A key component was an anchor plate, which wore out and which therefore needed to be replaced regularly, but which could be replaced more easily and cheaply than the corresponding parts used in the prior art. The Bundesgerichtshof held that the anchor plate embodied the inventive concept.[30] However, from the consumer's point of view, the replacement amounted to repair rather than to remanufacture. The court held that if the sole purpose of a component was to wear out, its replacement could be regarded as repair, even if it did embody the inventive concept.[31] The court may have been influenced by the fact that the patent was weak and revoked shortly afterwards,[32] although it did not explicitly mention this aspect.

This brief analysis shows that while there is no explicit right to repair in patent law, the principle of exhaustion usually works in favour of allowing repair and of

---

26 I have tried to do this elsewhere, see Ansgar Ohly, 'Reparatur, Neuherstellung und der Erschöpfungsgrundsatz im europäischen Patentrecht' in Christian Harmsen and Axel Verhauwen (eds), *Festschrift für Thomas Kühnen* (Carl Heymanns 2024) 779–792; see also Christopher Heath, 'Exhaustion and Patent Rights' in Ruth L Okediji and Margo A Bagley (eds), *Patent Law in Global Perspective* (OUP 2014) 419; Mineko Mohri, 'Patents, Repair and Recycling from a Comparative Perspective' (2010) IIC 779; Taina Pihlajarinne, 'Repairing and re-using from an exclusive rights perspective: towards sustainable lifespan as part of a new normal?' in Rognstad and Ørstavik (n 10) 81–100.

27 This does not mean that any extension of a product's normal lifespan would amount to remanufacture and therefore to infringement, see Pihlajarinne (n 26) 87–92. In the pallet container cases, the UK and German Courts rather referred to the lifespan of the pallet container in a relative way by comparing the lifespan of the replacement part with that of the entire product and concluded on this basis that the replacement of the shorter-lived component amounted to repair.

28 (n 17) and (n 22).

29 BGH GRUR 2023, 47 – *Scheibenbremse II*.

30 *Ibid.* [32]–[34].

31 *Ibid.* [54]–[58].

32 BGH GRUR 2024, 1790 – *Scheibenbremse III*.

the replacement of broken or worn components. It remains to be seen whether the UPC will follow the approach adopted by English, German and French courts,[33] but it would not be surprising if it did. Of course, exhaustion reaches its limits when the component itself is patented. In that case, the spare part must be purchased from the patent owner or from a supplier who has manufactured it with the patent owner's consent. Also, courts will tend against repair and in favour of new manufacture if the component embodies the inventive concept.[34]

But in many cases, the principle of exhaustion allows patent law to achieve results that are consistent with the requirements of a circular economy. Patent law, however, does so tacitly. Patent courts focus on patent law. They do not always make the policy reasons for allowing repair explicit. According to the UK courts, the crucial question is not whether the article has been 'repaired' but whether the patented product has been 'made'.[35] The Bundesgerichtshof does mention the consumer's interest in the unhindered use of the product, including repair,[36] but so far it has never explicitly mentioned the public interest in sustainability. Arguably the analysis of exhaustion cases would be richer if courts were prepared to factor the 'green' interest in facilitating a circular economy into their considerations. This could be done by adding a fourth category of criteria to the remanufacture/repair distinction, namely ecological criteria. These would be just one part of a related set of criteria and would, as such, not necessarily trump the patent owner's interests. But they could sometimes tip the scales in favour of repair.

3. THE NEW COUNTER-EXCEPTION: 'LEGITIMATE GROUNDS'

In EU trade mark law, the principle of exhaustion does not apply 'where there exist legitimate reasons for the proprietor to oppose further commercialisation of the goods, especially where the condition of the goods is changed or impaired after they have been put on the market.'[37] Since trade marks indicate the origin

33 See the report of the French AIPPI Section [2008] Rapport Q 205, 4.

34 See (n 21) and (n 22) but see (n 31). This brings the infringement test in copyright law to mind: in the case of a partial reproduction, infringement depends on whether the reproduced part by itself expresses the author's own intellectual creation, see CJEU, case 5/08 *Infopaq International*. Of course, there are important differences between patent in copyright law in this respect: there is no doctrine of partial reproduction in patent law, and at least in the bifurcated German system the infringement courts have only limited competence to assess inventive step.

35 *United Wire v Screen Repair Services* [2001] RPC 24 [71]; see also *Schutz v Werit* [2013] UKSC 16 [48].

36 BGH GRUR 2023, 47 [45] – *Scheibenbremse II*; BGH GRUR 2007, 769 [27] – *Pipettensystem*.

37 Article 15 EU TM Regulation; Article 15 TM Directive.

of goods, this exception makes sense. Trade marks constitute channels of communication through which the owner of the mark can convey information. If the goods are altered after they have been put on the market, the owner's promise of quality or prestige may be compromised.

Until recently, there was no common European doctrine of exhaustion in patent law. The CJEU had established the doctrine of EU-wide exhaustion at an early stage,[38] but apart from this aspect, exhaustion was governed by the national laws of the EU member states. This has changed with the entry into force of the UPC Agreement and the Unitary Patent Regulation. Unlike the doctrine in most (or all) national patent laws before 2024, exhaustion is now subject to an exception which is reminiscent of trade mark law.[39] Under the newly introduced exception, exhaustion applies only 'unless there are legitimate grounds for the patent proprietor to oppose further commercialisation of the product.' So far, it is entirely unclear which interests could be considered 'legitimate' in this sense. For example, could a patent owner claim that the spare parts offered by a third party are of inferior quality? Or could the owner of a patent claiming the combination of a coffee machine and coffee pods even argue that the sale of pods by third parties would undermine his or her business model and thus the optimal exploitation of the patent?

At first sight, it seems tempting to look to trade mark law for orientation, and to allow the patent owner to resist exhaustion when the reputation of his or her product is at risk.[40] One could even go a step further and allow the patent owner to resist exhaustion whenever his or her economic interest in the exploitation of the invention is affected.

However, there are two reasons for interpreting the new counter-exception very narrowly. First, the owner can only oppose 'further commercialisation' of the product. While the English text could be understood to cover to all commercial uses of the invention, other language versions show that 'commercialisation' means nothing more than 'resale' ('*den weiteren Vertrieb*', '*de latere verhandeling*'). This is significant because most repair cases do not involve resale. Typically, the patent owner seeks to prevent the sale of spare parts or consumables by arguing that they amount to indirect patent infringement. In these cases, the direct infringing act is the use, not the resale.

Secondly, the counter-exception is not, as it may appear at first sight, a 'legal transplant' from trade mark law. It was already there, albeit in a slightly

---

38 Case 187/80, *Merck v Stephar* [1981] ECR 2063.

39 Article 29 UPCA; Article 6 Unitary Patent Regulation.

40 As argued by Jan Busche in Winfried Tilmann and Clemens Plassmann, *Unified Patent Protection in Europe* (OUP 2018) Article 6 EPVO para 27; see also Constantin Blanke-Roeser, *Die Erschöpfung von Patenten und ihre Grenzen* (Mohr Siebeck 2024) 390–393, 411–412.

different wording,[41] in the failed Community Patent Convention of 1975.[42] The negotiation history shows that the exception was a compromise on the controversial question of whether a first sale in an EU Member State where the invention was not protected by a patent should trigger exhaustion.[43] The drafters decided to simply refer to the then existing case law of the ECJ in this respect. Consequently, the exception was intended to be narrow and to be limited to cases of cross-border trade. Later drafts of the CPC and the proposal for a Community Patent Regulation retained this provision. In the EPCA, the wording was aligned with trade mark law, but the drafters apparently did not intend this change to be substantial, as the Commission proposal does not give any reasons for the changed wording. Meanwhile, the exhaustion provisions of the French and Dutch Patent Acts have been amended; the motives to the amendment in the Netherlands state that the change was purely 'editorial',[44] compared to the previous state of the law without a counter exception.

Thirdly, the functions of trade mark law and of patent law are different.[45] Trade marks are indications of origin. They create channels of communication and protect brand reputation. Patents do not. They are simply exclusive rights to use the invention. Protection of reputation is outside the scope of patent law. If a potential infringer offers inferior spare parts for a patented machine, everything depends on whether the patent owner markets the machine under his own trade mark. If so, the potential damage to the brand's reputation may give rise to a claim for trade mark infringement. If this is not the case, it is difficult to see how the patent owner's reputation can be affected, since his or her identity does not influence the consumer's purchase decision.

4. IMPLIED CONSENT

Historically, implied consent and exhaustion competed as doctrinal models to justify the 'first sale doctrine'. While English courts implied the right owner's

---

41 Article 32 CPC provided that exhaustion only applied 'unless there are grounds which, under Community law, would justify the extension to such acts of the rights conferred by the patent.'

42 [1976] OJ L 17/1.

43 See the report by Albrecht Krieger, 'Die Luxemburger Konferenz über das Gemeinschaftspatent – Bericht der deutschen Delegation – Die sogenannten Wirtschaftsklauseln' (1976) GRUR Int 208, 209–212; Markus Gollrad, 'Die neue Ausnahmeregelung der Erschöpfung – Was sind berechtigte Gründe?' (2023) 6 GRUR Patent 242–249.

44 Wijziging van de Rijksoctrooiwet 1995 in verband met de Overeenkomst betreffende een eengemaakt octrooigerecht en Verordening (EU) nr 1257/2012, Doc 35 187 (R2124) of 9/4/2019, 19, www.eerstekamer.nl/behandeling/20190409/memorie_van_toelichting/info, accessed 06 March 2025.

45 See also UPC (LD Munich) UPC_CFI_9/2023, *Huawei v Netgear* at 120: distinguishing the effect of contractual use restrictions in patent licences from those in trade mark licences under Article 29 UPC.

consent to resale,[46] the father of German IP scholarship, Josef Kohler, rejected this subjective approach and argued for exhaustion as an objective exception to patent law.[47] Indeed, the weakness of an implied consent approach is that it leaves the patent owner free to exclude resale by explicit stipulation. Recently, both the US Supreme Court and the High Court of Australia have adopted the doctrine of exhaustion and rejected the implied consent approach, thereby preventing manufacturers of patented toner cartridges from excluding their refilling by purchasers.[48] So there seems to be a growing international consensus that exhaustion takes precedence over contractual restraints.[49] But can implied consent also go further than exhaustion? In particular, can consent be implied where consumers expect to be free to modify the product, even if this amounts to remanufacturing? As often in law, the answer is that it depends.

First, consent may be implied where the doctrine of exhaustion is inapplicable for reasons unrelated to of the making/repairing dichotomy. Process patents, for example, are not subject to exhaustion as such. In contrast to the US Supreme Court,[50] the German Bundesgerichtshof applies this principle strictly and does not allow exhaustion even with respect to products embodying the patented process. However, when the product is sold, the court is prepared to imply a licence allowing the purchaser to use the product, even if this involves the use of a patented process.[51] Furthermore, some copyright and trade mark judgments handed down by the CJEU suggest that exhaustion in patent law is also triggered only when the product is sold, not when it is rented.[52] Again, courts will have to imply a licence in favour of the lessee if the ordinary use of the product requires the use of a patented invention.

---

46 *Betts v Willmott* (1871) LR 6 Ch App 239, 245.

47 Josef Kohler *Handbuch des Deutschen Patentrechts* (J Bensheimer Verlag 1900) 452–459.

48 (n 13).

49 For this reason, some authors consider a recourse to implied licences in the context of repair unnecessary, see Klaus Haft et al, 'Die Erschöpfung von Rechten des Geistigen Eigentums in Fällen des Recyclings oder der Reparatur von Waren (Q 205)' (2008) GRUR Int 944, 951; Thomas Hoeren, Tabea Ansorge and Oliver Lampe, 'Sustainability and Intellectual Property in Germany' in Këllezi et al (n 11) 271, 298.

50 *Quanta Computer v LG Electronics* 553 US 617, 628 (2008).

51 BGH GRUR 1980, 38, 39 – *Fullplastverfahren*. This approach is criticised by some authors, see Konstellation Wolfgang von Meibohm and Matthias F Meyer, 'Erschöpfung von Sach- und Verfahrenspatenten bei Teillieferung – Die erweiterte Erschöpfungslehre' in Michael Bergermann, Gereon Rother and Axel Verhauwen (eds), *Festschrift für Peter Mes zum 65 Geburtstag* (Beck 2009) 255; Klaus Haft and Friedrich R von Samson-Himmelstjerna, 'Kerntheorie bei der Erschöpfung von Patenten' in *Patentrecht. Festschrift für Thomas Reimann: zum 65. Geburtstag* (Heymanns 2009) 175, 183.

52 See for trade mark law CJEU case C-16/03 *Peak Holding* [42]; for copyright law case C-456/06, *Peek & Cloppenburg v Cassina* [36]; for US patent law, *Impression Prods v Lexmark* 137 SCt 1523, 1534 (2017). For European patent law, this issue is still moot, see, on the one hand, Busche (n 40) Article 6 EPUE Reg, on the other hand Uwe Scharen in Klaus Bacher (ed) *Benkard, Patentgesetz* (12th ed, Beck 2023) § 9, para 17, Heath (n 10) 770.

Secondly, public statements by a patent owner permitting certain acts of repair or reconditioning may be construed as consent or can at least give rise to estoppel.[53] Indeed, sustainability is increasingly becoming a selling point, with more and more companies making public commitments to repair their products themselves or to allow repair. In the latter case, this statement can have legal significance. A case in point is the German 'Drum Unit' case.[54] A manufacturer of laser printers and toner cartridges had made a commitment to the EU Commission not to design its cartridges in a way that would prevent recycling and not to prevent the use of non-OEM cartridges. The manufacturer later tried to enforce its patent on certain aspects of the cartridge against a company that had refilled the claimant's cartridges. The defendant pleaded exhaustion and was eventually successful on this ground,[55] but also argued that the claimant was estopped from enforcing its patent by virtue of the undertaking given to the Commission. The Düsseldorf Court of Appeal rejected this argument with regard to the specific circumstances of the case,[56] but this interpretation has been criticised as unduly narrow.[57] Indeed, the statement made by the patent owner is reminiscent of a FRAND commitment. In FRAND cases, it depends on the applicable law whether a declaration made to a public authority or to a standard-setting organisation can be construed as a contract in favour of third parties.[58] Even if this is not the case, subsequent attempts to enforce the patent in cases of repair can amount to an abuse of a dominant position under antitrust law or give rise to estoppel under the doctrine of abuse of right.[59] Consent to repair differs from the FRAND scenario because consent, if valid, justifies the defendant's conduct without the need to conclude a licencing contract. But like a commitment to grant a FRAND licence, consent given to one person can benefit third parties. And as in the FRAND context, it may make sense from a public policy perspective to encourage public statements that allow repair. Possible incentives for legislators to consider are, for example, advantages in the process of obtaining 'green' labels.

However, consent should only be implied where the right owner's conduct gives rise to such an implication. Implying consent whenever consumers expect to be able to remanufacture or even in all cases where there are environmental

53 I owe this idea to Heath (n 10) 770–772.

54 BGH GRUR 2018, 170 – *Trommeleinheit* = [2018] IIC 972 – *Drum Unit*.

55 The Düsseldorf Court of Appeal had found against exhaustion and given judgment for the claimant. The BGH overruled the Court of Appeal's finding in exhaustion and the appeal was therefore successful.

56 OLG Düsseldorf GRUR-RS 2016, 11301 [63]–[82].

57 Heath (n 10) 767.

58 See the discussion in *Unwired Planet v Huawei* [2017] EWHC 711 (Pat) [98]–[146], applying French law.

59 See below in section 5 and Heath (n 10) 772, advocating a 'three-step test' consisting of exhaustion, implied consent and abuse of right.

reasons to allow repair would be tantamount to introducing a right of repair by the back door. Whether the introduction of such a right is justified from a public policy perspective will be discussed in the following section. However, such an objective limitation of the patent right should be introduced openly and should not be based on the hypothetical and, indeed, fictitious intention of the contracting parties.

5. TOWARDS AN AFFIRMATIVE 'RIGHT TO REPAIR'?

So, is there today a 'right to repair' in EU patent law? Certainly, unlike in design law,[60] there is no explicit provision in patent law allowing the sale of patented products for repair purposes. Nor does the repair clause in design law apply by analogy to patent law.[61] However, as seen above, the principle of exhaustion often has the effect that acts of repair do not infringe the patent in the first place. Would it make sense to conceptualise the principle of exhaustion as a 'user's right', reminiscent of the copyright law debate as to whether copyright exceptions such as quotation or parody give rise to users' rights?[62]

At least under UK law as interpreted by the House of Lords in *United Wire v Screen Repair Services* and by the Supreme Court in *Schutz v Werit*, the question must be answered in the negative. In *United Wire*, Lord Hoffmann expressly rejected the notion of a 'right to repair':

> 'The owner's right to repair is not an independent right conferred upon him by licence, express or implied. It is residual right, forming part of the right to do whatever does not amount to making the product.'[63]

More generally, in the terminology of Wesley Newcomb Hohfeld,[64] there is a conceptual difference between a 'right' and a 'privilege'. Whereas a right gives rise to claims against others, the term 'privilege' denotes the situation where an act is permitted simply because no one else has a claim to prevent it. In this sense, exhaustion is a privilege, not an affirmative right. Conversely, the consumer's

---

60 See (n 66).

61 The CJEU has held in case C-500/14 *Ford/Wheeltrims* [39]–[45] that the design law repair clause is not applicable to trade mark law by analogy. The same considerations apply to patent law.

62 For a recent perspective on this discussion see Christophe Geiger and Justin Jütte, 'Copyright as an Access Right: Concretizing Positive Obligations for Rightholders to Ensure the Exercise of User Rights' (2024) 73(11) GRUR Int 1019.

63 *United Wire v Screen Repair Services* [2001] RPC 24 [71]; see also *Schutz v Werit* [2013] UKSC 16 [48].

64 Wesley Newcomb Hohfeld, 'Some fundamental legal conceptions as applied in judicial reasoning' (1913) 23 Yale L J 16, 29, 32.

'right to repair' as established by the recent EU Directive is a 'right' in the Hohfeldian sense because it gives rise to a claim against the manufacturer.

US courts have sometimes referred to a 'right to repair' in exhaustion cases.[65] However, it appears that the difference from UK and European law is mainly one of terminology rather than substance, as the criteria applied by US courts in repair cases are largely the same as those that can be identified in European judgments. So, while there are good reasons for making the users' and the public interest in repair more explicit than has been done in many cases, the interest in repair is not more than a criterion. It is an interpretive tool rather than a right.

This could be changed, of course. Article 20a(1) of the EU Design Regulation[66] provides that

> '[p]rotection shall not be conferred on an EU design which constitutes a component part of a complex product upon whose appearance the design of the component part is dependent, and which is used within the meaning of Article 19(1) for the sole purpose of the repair of that complex product so as to restore its original appearance.'

As a matter of policy, the introduction of a similar provision in patent law could be considered. However, design law differs from patent law in important respects. In some industry sectors, notably the automotive industry, manufacturers can protect the external appearances of the original product through a design right, but they can also easily secure design protection for the spare parts themselves. The right owner can recoup his or her investment in the primary market, for example in the car market. But without a repair clause, he or she could also monopolise the spare parts market, i.e. the secondary market, although there are sound economic reasons for allowing competition in the spare parts market.

In patent law, on the other hand, the principle of exhaustion usually allows the replacement of non-inventive spare parts. The plastic bottle in the pallet container case, the coffee pods or the brake pads are not new or at least not inventive. The bar for patenting spare parts is high. But if, exceptionally, a component itself – such as the measuring capsule of the flow meter[67] or the powder mixture for a toner – is indeed both new and inventive, there is a public interest in protecting the inventor. A 'right to repair' would undermine the patent incentive in these cases. It would be simplistic to assume that the public interest in sustainability

65 *Aro Manufacturing Co v Convertible Top Co*, 365 US 336, 357 (1961); see also Leah Chan Grinvald and Ofer Tur-Sinai, 'Intellectual Property Law and the Right to Repair' (2019) 88 Fordham Law Review 63, 83, 100: 'Fortunately, patent law recognizes a right to repair to a considerable extent.'

66 Regulation (EU) 2024/2822 of the European Parliament and of the Council of 23 October 2024 amending Council Regulation (EC) No 6/2002 on Community designs and repealing Commission Regulation (EC) No 2246/2002, OJ L 2024/2822.

67 See (n 1).

should always outweigh not only the inventor's interest in protection, but also the public interest in providing incentives to invent and to innovate.

For similar reasons, compulsory licensing plays a more limited role in this field than in the area of drugs and other medicinal products, where patents are not only used to block the market entry of generics, but where they can also prevent competing products with better therapeutical qualities. So far, the grant of compulsory licences has mainly been considered when patients' interests in the availability of life-saving drugs were at stake.[68] Repair cases are less dramatic. Most disputes about repair in patent law concern the offer of spare parts by independent manufacturers. The patent owner is usually prepared to satisfy the market demand, and the only issue is whether he or she can claim monopoly prices. The EU-wide compulsory licensing scheme proposed by the Commission[69] will, if it enters into force at all, only be available in situations of crisis.[70] And national courts will be reluctant to grant compulsory licences for the sole reason of reducing the price of repair when the applicant intends to produce products similar to those of the patent owner.

Furthermore, a patent owner's refusal to allow repair in cases of non-exhaustion is not abusive as such. In antitrust law,[71] it may amount to an abuse of a dominant position, but only if there are additional factors such as a FRAND commitment, discrimination,[72] the foreclosure of a secondary market under the Magill criteria[73] or the attempt to prevent intra-EU trade. Therefore,

68 On compulsory licensing during pandemics see Van Overwalle (n 11) 884; Martin Stierle, 'Ausschließlichkeit in der (Corona-)Krise – Über Alternativen und Zugangslösungen im pandemierelevanten Innovationsermöglichungsrecht' (2021) 76(2) JuristenZeitung 71–80. For an example of a compulsory licence granted in order to allow the production of an anti-HIV drug which was better tolerated by children and pregnant women than the patented product, see BGH GRUR 2017, 1017 = [2018] IIC 94 – *Raltegravir*.

69 Proposal for a regulation of the European Parliament and of the Council on compulsory licensing for crisis management and amending Regulation (EC) 816/2006, COM(2023) 224 final.

70 This limitation is open to criticism, see Matthias Lamping et al, 'Revisiting the Framework for Compulsory Licensing of Patents in the European Union' (2023) Max Planck Institute for Innovation & Competition Research Paper No. 23-07, [6]–[13].

71 In Japanese law, antitrust law has played a role in repair cases, see Tokyo District Court – Tying as an Unfair Trade Practice – *Color Cration & Elecom v Brother* (2023) 72(11) GRUR Int, 1099; Atsuhiro Furuta and Christopher Heath, 'The Right to Repair, Refill and Recycle by Way of an Anti-trust Defence – Comment on the Japanese Decisions *Ricoh I, Ricoh II* and *Brother*' (2023) 72(11) GRUR Int, 1053, 1057–1062. The authors, however, note that there are significant differences between Japanese and European antitrust law in this regard.

72 See BGH GRUR 2009, 696 [20]–[36] – *Orange Book Standard*.

73 CJEU, joined cases C-241/91 P and 242/91 P *RTE and ITP v Commission* [1995] ECR I-743 [50]–[56]. The criteria, as summarised in C-418/01, *IMS Health* [2004] I-5039 [38] are 'that that refusal is preventing the emergence of a new product for which there is a potential consumer demand, that it is unjustified and such as to exclude any competition on a secondary market.' In the repair scenario, the patent owner, at least at first glance, does not prevent the emergence of a new product. But it is open to debate to what extent the 'new product' condition has been modified in later cases.

the CJEU did not find the denial of automobile manufacturers to grant licences to independent manufacturers of spare parts to be an abuse of a dominant position,[74] which made the introduction of a statutory right to repair into design law necessary. Unfair competition law, although still largely unharmonised outside the field of consumer protection law, in most jurisdictions recognises a tort of obstruction of a competitor's business.[75] Again, however, the obstruction caused by the enforcement of an intellectual property right is not as such unfair. Additional factors, which at least partly resemble those relevant in antitrust law, must be established. Finally, the general private law doctrine of abuse of right is common to at least the jurisdictions of all EU Member States and also rooted in EU IP enforcement law.[76] Some of its categories may apply to repair cases, depending on the circumstances. The enforcement of a patent despite earlier public statements in favour of allowing repair may amount to contradictory behaviour, as discussed above. There seems to be a growing consensus that claims for injunctive relief may be excluded if they are disproportionate.[77] But, again, these doctrines only apply under specific circumstances. They do not give rise to a general 'right of repair'.

6. CONCLUSION: A TOOLBOX CONTAINING ORDINARY AND EXTRAORDINARY LEGAL INSTRUMENTS

There is no affirmative 'right to repair' in patent law. In most cases, however, the patent owner cannot prevent repair because of the principle of exhaustion. As with the Ship of Theseus, courts may struggle to distinguish between repair and remanufacture. But there is a set of applicable criteria – consumer, product and invention-related – that allow this distinction to be made in a largely rational and predictable way. Therefore, the tacit logic of patent law will often lead to outcomes that are consistent with the idea of a circular economy. However, the public interest in sustainability should be addressed more openly. It should be

74 Case 238/87 *Volvo v Veng* [1988] ECR I-6211.

75 For German law, see §4 No 4 Act against Unfair Competition; for French law see Frauke Henning Bodewig, *Unfair Competition Law: European Union and Member States* (Kluwer 2006) 124.

76 CJEU, case C-597/19 *Mircom/Telenet* [94]; Amandine Léonard, *Abuse of Rights in European Patent Law* (2019) PhD Thesis KU Leuven, 22–77; Axel Metzger, 'Abuse of Law in EU Private Law: A (Re-)Construction from Fragments' in Rita de la Feria and Stefan Vogenauer, *Prohibition of Abuse of Law* (Hart 2011) 235 –251; Martin Stierle, *Das nicht-praktizierte Patent* (Mohr Siebeck 2018) 365–370.

77 See §139(1)(3) of the German Patents Act and Léon Dijkman, *The Proportionality Test in European Patent Law: Patent Injunctions Before EU Courts and the UPC* (Hart Publishing 2023); Ansgar Ohly, 'Injunctions in the UPC and the principle of proportionality' (2022) Stockholm Intellectual Property Law Review, 58–65.

factored into the exhaustion analysis not as a trump card, but as one of several criteria. If exhaustion fails, the patent owner's representations can still give rise to implied consent, to estoppel or to defences based on antitrust law or the general concepts of disproportionality or abuse of right. From a public policy perspective, it may be wise to create incentives for patent owners to allow repair beyond the confines of exhaustion.

In result, the 'right to repair' is not an affirmative right in the Hohfeldian sense. It is not a hammer that smashes the logic of IP in favour of sustainability. Rather, it should be seen as a shorthand for a toolbox of several instruments,[78] some of them ordinary and well-established ones, some of them extraordinary ones, redesigned in the light of sustainability.

[78] Authors elaboration, combining items A 2 'Twin-Handled Hair Splitter', A 3 'Sandwich Saw' and A 4 'Pacifier Hammer' from Carelman's *Catalog*.

CHAPTER 8

THE RIGHT TO REPAIR AND TO REUSE PATENTED PRODUCTS IN A CIRCULAR ECONOMY

'It's Time to Get Exhausted'[1]

Jens Schovsbo
Centre for Information and Innovation Law (CIIR), University of Copenhagen

Thomas Riis
Centre for Information and Innovation Law (CIIR), University of Copenhagen

Timo Minssen
Centre for Advanced Studies in Bioscience Innovation Law (CEBIL),
University of Copenhagen

K5 Bach Mobile
A busy organist can practice on his way to work.

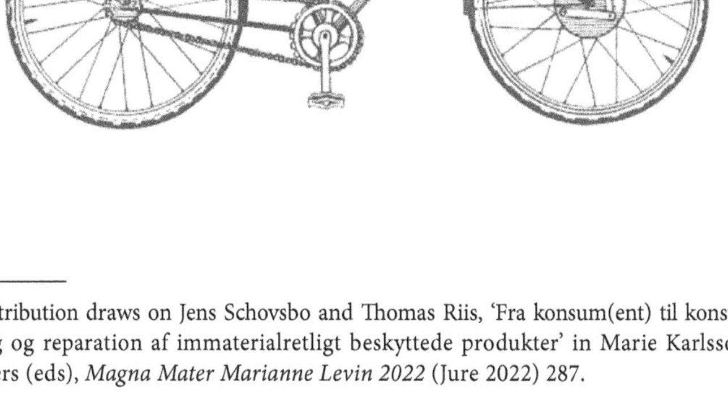

1 This contribution draws on Jens Schovsbo and Thomas Riis, 'Fra konsum(ent) til konsumption: Genbrug og reparation af immaterialretligt beskyttede produkter' in Marie Karlsson-Tuula and others (eds), *Magna Mater Marianne Levin 2022* (Jure 2022) 287.

1. SETTING THE SCENE

In her significant and influential body of scholarship, Professor Geertrui Van Overwalle has consistently demonstrated a remarkable ability to navigate between the individual interests of rights holders and users, and the broader societal concerns that shape and are shaped by patent law. Her work is characterised by a distinctive sensitivity to context, balance, and the larger implications of legal doctrine. In this contribution – offered in tribute to Geertrui and in appreciation of our longstanding friendship and collegiality – we take inspiration from this legacy. Following her example, we begin with a seemingly narrow legal issue – exhaustion in patent law – and explore how it connects to some of the most pressing global challenges of our time. Specifically, we consider how the structure and application of patent law intersect with the climate crisis and the broader consequences of an economic model driven by relentless consumption and the continual demand for new products. Through this lens, we aim to reflect not only on the intricacies of intellectual property law, but also on its role in addressing what is arguably humanity's greatest existential challenge: the sustainability of life on our planet.[2]

Before we get to this – and in keeping with the instructions for this Festschrift – we begin with a mall tale which sets the scene for our analyses and discussions. The tale involves a fantasy patent (The Bach Mobile) and three law professors from Copenhagen on their way to Leuven.

On one of the first sunny days in April just outside of Copenhagen in the small town of X, three Bach Mobiles broke down. On one of the bikes, the universal joint in the link that transfers the energy from the wheel and to the organ snapped. On the other two bikes the organ simply stopped working. This was very surprising. As it can be seen from the picture below in the catalogue, the Bach Mobiles were of the newest (and most expensive) models.

To get the bikes fixed, the three travellers made their way to a Bach Mobil-shop. However, this is where all the trouble began. To the travellers' immense surprise, the Bach Mobil-shop owner told them that because of 'pending patent disputes' she was unable to repair the bikes as this would require her to manufacture a new joint to replace the broken one. Instead, she was prepared to sell them new bikes and to dispose of the old ones on the spot. To the latter effect she had brought a sledge hammer.

The whole business made the already exhausted travellers sick and tired of Bach Mobiles, and they asked if the dealer was interested in buying the Bach

---

2 For a recent and much more general discussion about patent law and climate change see Reto M Hilty and Pedro Henrique D Batista, 'Potential and Limits of Patent Law to Address Climate Change' (2023) 72 (9) GRUR International, 821–839, https://doi.org/10.1093/grurint/ikad066, accessed 16 May 2025.

Mobiles to sell them to somebody else. The shop owner informed them that she was only authorised to sell bikes she received directly from Bach Mobil Ltd. and not to resell used bikes. This too, she said, would be in violation of the Danish Patent Act, unless she disconnected the patented method that provides for the transfer of energy from the front wheel to the organ.

2. FRAMING THE ISSUE: THE CIRCULAR ECONOMY AND THE PRINCIPLE OF EXHAUSTION

As seen from the perspective of the *Green Agenda* and *sustainability*, the practices of the Bach Mobile Company are clearly problematic. As stated in the recently adopted Directive on promoting the repair of goods, a right to repair broken products is part and parcel of the Green Agenda as it reduces premature disposal of viable goods purchased by consumers and encourages consumers to use their goods longer.[3] In this way, repair (together with other practices such as re-use and refurbishment) promotes sustainable consumption, since it is likely to generate less waste, less demand for resources as well as less greenhouse gas emissions.[4] Even though this Directive does not include amendments of the EU rules on IP, it is evidence of the importance at the level of EU policy to promote the *Green Agenda* as this has been epitomised by *the European Green Deal.*[5]

Legally speaking, the right of owners of patented products to repair or resell is determined by the principle of *exhaustion*: Unless the (patent) right is exhausted, the patent holder may prevent any third party not having the proprietor's consent from, for example, offering, placing on the market or using a product which is the subject-matter of the patent, or importing or storing the product for those purposes; or using a process which is the subject-matter of the patent.[6]

---

3 Directive (EU) 2024/1799 of the European Parliament and of the Council of 13 June 2024 on common rules promoting the repair of goods and amending Regulation (EU) 2017/2394 and Directives (EU) 2019/771 and (EU) 2020/1828 OJ L, 2024/1799, 10.7.2024, preamble point 33. Following Article 22, Member States shall bring into force the laws, regulations and administrative provisions necessary to comply with this Directive by 31 July 2026 at the latest.

4 *Ibid.* Following Article 15(6) manufacturers shall not use any contractual clauses, hardware or software techniques that impede the repair of goods covered by Union legal acts listed in Annex II to the Directive 'unless justified by legitimate and objective factors including the protection of intellectual property rights under Union and national law.'

5 Communication from the Commission to the European Parliament, the European Council, the Council, the European Economic and Social Committee and the Committee of the Regions, The European Green Deal, COM/2019/640 final.

6 See for the EU Agreement on a Unified Patent Court [2013] OJ C175/1, Article 25. Similar wording is found in patent legislations throughout the world, see TRIPS, Article 28.

2.1. EXHAUSTION: THE HISTORICAL BACKGROUND

The exhaustion principle originates from German law. Here it was first proposed in theory and later used by courts to make sure that contract terms for the sale of an IP protected product (such as mandatory resale prices) could not be enforced via intellectual property law against *bona fide* third parties.[7] The 'principle' initially had the character of a rule of presumption limiting the scope of the assignment agreement. Later, however, it became embedded in the Intellectual Property (IP) legislation as a means of counterbalancing the rights in IP to control products *post* sale. Exhaustion thus became part of the overall legal package offered by the law to rightholders, consisting of a broad 'distribution right' (to use copyright's terminology) and an internal and statutory based limitation of that right in the form of a mandatory exhaustion rule which limits rightholders' control via IP after the first sale. Or in other words, the principle is devised by the legislator to strike a balance between, on the one hand, the legitimate interests on the part of the IP rights holder in receiving a reasonable remuneration in setting the conditions for the first sale, the legitimate interests of purchasers of protected items in enjoying the benefits of ownership, and the general interests for instance in maintaining undistorted competition, the free movement of goods, or (as we will argue in the following) in promoting sustainability.

It is this principle that has been adopted by EU law. In the first wave of harmonisation of national IP legislation during the 1970's the EU Court of Justice relied on the provisions in the EC Treaty on free movement of goods and undistorted competition to develop a principle of exhaustion to safeguard the right to parallel imports of goods which had first been put on the EC market by the rightholder itself or with its consent. This harmonisation was 'negative' in the sense that the Court just struck down on national legal system which did *not* limit the right of distribution in accordance with the principle of EC-wide (regional) exhaustion. Such lack of limitation of the right of distribution could not be justified under (what is now) TFEU Article 36.[8]

In the next decades, positive and detailed provisions on exhaustion emerged in directives and regulations across most areas of IP. For patent law, which until the UPC was the least harmonised IP-area, Article 10 of the Biotech-Directive[9] provides the following.

---

7 The central figure is Josef Kohler, see in particular Josef Kohler, *Handbuch des Deutschen Patentrechts – in rechtvergleichender Darstellung* (Bensheimer 1900) 452 ff. and from early German case law on patents RGZ 51, 139 ff, 140 f – *Guajakol-Karbonat*.

8 Case C-15/74 *Centrafarm BV and Adriaan De Peijper v Sterling Drug Inc.* ECLI:EU:C:1974:114 (on patents) and Case C-16/74 *Centrafarm B.V. and Adriaan De Peijper v Winthrop BV.* ECLI:EU:C:1974:115 (on trade marks).

9 Directive 98/44/EC of the European Parliament and of the Council of 6 July 1998 on the legal protection of biotechnological inventions [1998] OJ L213/13-21.

The protection referred to in Articles 8 and 9 shall not extend to 'biological material obtained from the propagation or multiplication of biological material placed on the market in the territory of a Member State by the holder of the patent or with his consent, where the multiplication or propagation necessarily results from the application for which the biological material was marketed, provided that the material obtained is not subsequently used for other propagation or multiplication' (*cf.* Article 10).

This rule differs from the traditional rules of exhaustion in other IP areas by allowing for the *reproduction* ('multiplication or propagation') of the product ('biological material') which has been placed on the market by the patent holder or with its consent. In this way, the rule illustrates the dynamic nature and function of exhaustion as a legal principle rather than as fixed rule. As we will explain below, these traits make 'exhaustion' very well suited to address even the values of sustainability. Before we get to that, however, a few examples from case law from the CJEU and national courts from trade marks and copyright that illustrate the flexibilities and multifaceted functions of the principles of exhaustion.

2.2. EXHAUSTION IN TRADE MARK LAW AND COPYRIGHT LAW

Similarly to the provision in the Biotech-Directive, the CJEU has relied on an extended and teleological interpretation of exhaustion in trade mark law and copyright law. By way of example, in *Dior v Evora*[10] the CJEU held that exhaustion of the trade mark rights includes a right to resell and market goods with the trade marks affixed in the usual manner.[11] In this specific case, the trade mark was used for a perfume contained in a copyright protected flacon. Under such circumstances, exhaustion of the trade mark rights entitled the legitimate parallel importer to make a copy of the copyright protected flacon by depicting it and include it in an advertising brochure that was distributed extensively. The Court explained that any *copyright* protection of the perfume flacons could not lead to a different result. The judgment thus in effect implies an exhaustion of copyright's reproduction right (in this case, reproducing a copyrighted perfume flacon in an advertisement) as long as this is within the scope of normal commercial usage. This right was not derived from copyright proper but from the Treaty rules on the free movement of goods.

---

10 Case C-337/95 *Parfums Christian Dior SA and Parfums Christian Dior BV v Evora* BV. ECLI:EU:C:1997:517.

11 See in the same vein e.g. C-46/10, *Viking Gas A/S v Kosan Gas A/S, tidligere BP Gas A/S*. ECLI:EU:C:2011:485, para 31.

In the same vein, the German Federal Court of Justice (BGH) in a judgment of 4.5.2000 (Parfumflakon)[12] confirmed that copyright's exhaustion rule is usually restricted to the distribution right and would normally not extend to reproduction rights. However, the BGH then further explained that the exhaustion rule is based on a general principle according to which copyright, as well as other protective (intellectual property) rights, 'must recede' to safeguard the 'free movement capacity' of products put on the market by the rightholder itself or with its consent:

> 'Mit Recht weist die Revision allerdings darauf hin, daß sich die Beklagte ohne Erfolg auf den Erschöpfungseinwand nach §17 Abs. 2 UrhG beruft. Denn eine Erschöpfung kann im Urheberrecht grundsätzlich nur hinsichtlich des Verbreitungsrechts, nicht dagegen hinsichtlich des hier ebenfalls in Rede stehenden Vervielfältigungsrechts eintreten [internal citation omitted]. Die gesetzliche Regelung in §17 Abs. 2 UrhG ist jedoch Ausdruck des allgemeinen Grundsatzes, daß das Urheberrecht ebenso wie andere Schutzrechte gegenüber dem Interesse an der Verkehrsfähigkeit der mit Zustimmung des Berechtigten in Verkehr gesetzten Waren zurücktreten muß [internal citation omitted].'[13]

Thus, even though 'in general' exhaustion is limited to the right of distribution, this limitation is not inherent but may be waived if justified by important considerations, such as the interest of 'free movement for products and services'.

The perception of exhaustion as a legal principle or a balancing rule rather than as a 'fixed rule' can be further illustrated by the CJEU judgments in cases C-128/11, UsedSoft[14] and C-263/18, Tom Kabinet.[15] Both cases concerned digital exhaustion of copyright protected works which covers the situation where a buyer/user downloads a copy of the protected work from the copyright owner's website with the consent of the copyright owner and the question is then whether the distribution right in that digital copy is exhausted which would entitle the buyer to resell the digital copy; otherwise not. Statements in the Agreed Statements to the WIPO Copyright Treaty,[16] and in the preamble of the Infosoc Directive[17] would seem to clearly suggest that rights in digital copies

---

12 German Federal Court of Justice (BGH), Judgment of 4 May 2000 – I ZR 256/97 – *Parfumflakon I*.

13 Above n 8, section 4(a).

14 Case C-128/11 *UsedSoft GmbH v Oracle International Corp.* ECLI:EU:C:2012:407.

15 Case C-263/18 *Nederlands Uitgeversverbond, Groep Algemene Uitgevers v Tom Kabinet Internet BV*. ECLI:EU:C:2019:1111.

16 WIPO Copyright Treaty, Agreed statements concerning Articles 6 and 7: '[T]he expressions "copies" and "original and copies," being subject to the right of distribution and the right of rental under the said Articles, refer exclusively to fixed copies that can be put into circulation as tangible objects.' The statements are available at www.wipo.int/wipolex/en/text/295456, accessed 16 May 2025.

17 Directive 2001/29/EC of the European Parliament and of the Council of 22 May 2001 on the harmonisation of certain aspects of copyright and related rights in the information society

are not exhausted. Nevertheless, in UsedSoft the CJEU held that the distribution right to a digital copy is exhausted according to Article 4(2) of the Computer Programs Directive.[18] One of the arguments in reaching its decision is that, from an economic point of view, the sale of a computer program stored on a physical medium and the sale of a computer program by downloading from the internet are similar, since online transfer is functionally equivalent to storage on a physical medium.[19] The Court further states that limiting the application of the principle of exhaustion to copies of computer programs sold by means of storage on a physical medium would enable the rightholder to control the resale of copies downloaded from the internet and to claim a new remuneration for each sale, even if the first sale of that copy had already enabled the copy-rightholder to obtain an adequate remuneration.[20] Accordingly, the Court balanced the interest of the buyer in being entitled to resell the digital copy against the interest of the rightholder in obtaining an adequate remuneration, which in this case turned out in favour of the buyer.

In the later Tom Kabinet, the Court should answer the same question. This time, however, the digital copy was an e-book, and the question should be answered under the exhaustion rule in Article 4(2) of the Infosoc Directive which content-wise is similar to Article 4(2) of the Computer Programs Directive. The Court held that the distribution right in the e-book was not exhausted. In reaching that decision, the Court finds that it cannot be assumed that the supply of a book on a physical medium and the supply of an e-book are identical from an economic and functional point of view, as the case is with regard to computer programs. The Court's argument for this is that, unlike books on a physical medium, digital copies of books do not deteriorate with use, therefore second-hand copies are perfect substitutes for new copies, and that trade in such copies can take place without any additional measures or costs, and a parallel second-hand market can thus have a far greater impact on the rightholders' interest in obtaining adequate remuneration for their works than the second-hand market for physical books. The CJEU could be understood to mean that a second-hand market for digital copies is of greater economic importance for authors of books than for authors of computer programs, arguably, because books are usually read only once, whereas computer programs are usually used continuously and replaced or resold when an upgraded version is available, after which the original copy is not quite as attractive anymore. The Court used the same method as in UsedSoft by balancing the interest of the buyer in being entitled to resell the digital copy against the interest of the rightholder in

[2001] OJ L167/10. Recital 29: 'The question of exhaustion does not arise in the case of services and on-line services in particular.'

18 Directive 2009/24/EC of the European Parliament and of the Council of 23 April 2009 on the legal protection of computer programs (codified version) [2009] OJ L111/16.

19 Directive 2009/24/EC [2009] OJ L111/16, recital 61.

20 Directive 2009/24/EC [2009] OJ L111/16, recital 63.

obtaining an adequate remuneration. However, it reached the opposite conclusion despite the similarities of the two exhaustion rules.

2.3. EXHAUSTION AND SUSTAINABILITY

The examples above illustrate how the principle of exhaustion is not perceived as a dogma by either the legislator or the courts. Instead, the exact legal effects of 'exhaustion' which result from a first marketing depends on an impact analysis of the specific circumstance. The term 'exhaustion' itself gives little guidance as to exactly where to draw the lines.[21] This means that the principle is very well suited for internalising general concerns and values. So far, these concerns have mostly come from the TFEU rules which protect the internal market and safeguard parallel importation.[22]

We argue, that because of its nature and legal design the exhaustion principles are excellently well suited for internalising other values and strong public interests, such as *sustainability* and the overall Green Agenda as we described above as being on the top of the EU's policy agenda.[23]

Importantly, an obligation to include the values of the Green Agenda would seem to already exist *de lege lata*. Article 11 TFEU states that 'environmental protection requirements must be integrated into the definition and implementation of the Union's policies and activities, in particular with a view to promoting sustainable development.' On the same note Article 37 of the Charter of Fundamental Rights of the European Union (EUC) on 'Environmental protection' prescribes that 'A high level of environmental protection and the improvement of the quality of the environment must be integrated into the policies of the Union and ensured in accordance with the principle of sustainable development.'[24] Because of these norms which are found at the highest level of the EU legal hierarchy national courts are bound to include the values of 'environmental protection' and 'sustainability' when they interpret EU-harmonised IP law even if no EU IP-provision addresses sustainability expressly.[25]

---

21 For this reason, it may be described as functioning merely as a 'terminological prop', see Schovsbo and Riis (n 1), with references to Nordic sources.

22 Ole-Andreas Rognstad, 'Legally Flawed but Politically Sound? Digital Exhaustion of Copyright in Europe after UsedSoft' (2014) 1 Oslo Law Review 1, 14, http://dx.doi.org/10.5617/oslaw977, accessed 16 May 2025.

23 See also Irene Calboli, 'Pushing a Square Pin into a Round Hole? Intellectual Property Challenges to a Sustainable and Circular Economy, and What to Do About It' (2024) International Review of Intellectual Property and Competition Law (IIC) 55, 237–248, https://doi.org/10.1007/s40319-024-01431-1, accessed 16 May 2025.

24 Charter of Fundamental Rights of the European Union [2012] OJ C326/391-407.

25 This is about to change. According to Directive (EU) 2024/2823 of the European Parliament and of the Council of 23 October 2024 on the legal protection of designs, OJ L, 2024/2823,

Turning next to the specific issue of patents, in the following, we will identify two situations in traditional Nordic and German patent law where patent law's exhaustion rules may limit the right to repair and resell patented products in ways that are problematic in the light of a goal of sustainability. Next, we will argue how the new patent regime concerning patents with unitary effects based on i.a. regulation No 1257/2012[26] might provide the flexibility needed to find a balanced solution, i.e. one which reflects the legitimate interests of patent holders in receiving adequate compensation and the overall interests in sustainability and circularity.

3. EXHAUSTION AND SUSTAINABILITY IN NORDIC AND GERMAN PATENT LAW

In the following, we will use the Bach-bike tale to provide a comparative analysis of how the current exhaustion rules in Nordic and German patent law would treat relevant product and method/process patent claims that might stand in conflict with the wish to repair and resell specific products.

3.1. PRODUCT PATENT CLAIMS

In Nordic patent law, a general rule of exhaustion is found in the national (and very similar) Patent Acts.[27] The patent law exhaustion rule covers 'normal' *repair* including, where appropriate, the replacement of individual parts, as long as the identity of the product is preserved. However, actual 'construction' ('manufacturing') is not legal.

The line between (non-infringing) repair and (infringing) construction can be difficult to draw. For Nordic law, there is no case law directly to the point, but

18.11.2024, recital 33 'The repairability of products is at the core of a sustainable economy, as highlighted in the Commission communication of 11 December 2019 on "The European Green Deal"'.

26 Regulation (EU) No 1257/2012 of the European Parliament and of the Council of 17 December 2012 implementing enhanced cooperation in the area of the creation of unitary patent protection [2012] OJ L361/1.

27 For Denmark Legislative Decree No 90 of 29 January 2019, §3(3)(ii): "The exclusive right shall not extend to acts concerning products put on the market in this country or in another country within the European Economic Area (EEA) by the proprietor of the patent or with his consent". The Acts also contain specific rules which reflect Article 10 of the Directive 98/44/EC of the European Parliament and of the Council of 6 July 1998 on the legal protection of biotechnological inventions [1998] OJ L213/13, see §§3a and 3b. The Act is available at www.wipo.int/wipolex/en/legislation/details/18698, accessed 16 May 2025.

based on the joint Nordic Report from 1963,[28] it is assumed that the owner may go 'quite far' in making repairs.[29] In other jurisdictions, such as Germany, the issue has been addressed in a rich body of case law. A seminal and quite recent Federal Court of Justice (Bundesgerichtshof (BGH) – sometimes also referred to as the Federal Supreme Court) decision in this context is the *Scheibenbremse* (Disc Brake) II decision.[30] Here, the BGH developed a 2-step test to distinguish between – non-infringing – repair and – infringing – new construction.

The 1st step focuses on the question of whether the so-called 'common understanding' classifies the remanufacturing process as intended use or as new manufacture. If this 'common understanding' arrives at the conclusion that the product in question is equivalent to new manufacture because the activities under examination extend the 'normal service life' of the product, the examination comes already to an end with the likely consequence that the remanufacturing might be considered to be a patent infringement.[31] The result might be different, however, if the 'common understanding' considers reprocessing to be a normal maintenance activity, since such repairing or replacing activities are usually expected during the natural life of the product. Then, the 'intended use' condition is usually regarded to be met, and it is likely that there is no patent infringement due to patent exhaustion.[32]

This brings us to the second step of the examination developed by the BGH. Here, the Court inquires whether the public's opinion may be 'wrong' because the relevant activity is actually so invasive that the central and essential inventive idea disclosed in the claims and specifications protected by the patent is once again carried out. Where this is the case, the 'originally intended use' can go so far that it amounts again to a new manufacture, which could potentially infringe the patent law.[33]

The determination of whether the technical or economic benefits of the invention are realised through the reprocessing process involves balancing various interests. Specifically, this involves assessing whether the technical effects of the invention are evident in the replaced part, thereby indicating a patent infringement. This specific issue forms the 'core patent law examination', where many detailed questions remain unresolved and require careful evaluation, such

---

28 Nordisk utredningsserie 1963:6, Nordisk patentlovgivning (NU 1963:6), Available at https://jura.ku.dk/jurabog/pdf/offentlige-udredninger/Betaenkning_angaaende_Nordisk_Patentlovgivning_1964.pdf, accessed 16 May 2025.

29 *Ibid.* p. 149 f. (in Swedish).

30 BGH, Judgment of 8 November 2022 – X ZR 10/20 – *Scheibenbremse II.*

31 *Ibid.* See also Christoph Y Pitzer, Konstantin Sitte and Stephan Reisner, 'Remanufacturing: Wie behindern gewerbliche Schutzrechte die Wiederaufbereitung von Produkten?' (Osborne Clarke, 28 May 2024) www.osborneclarke.com/de/insights/remanufacturing-wie-behindern-gewerbliche-schutzrechte-die-wiederaufbereitung-von accessed 28 May 2024 (in German).

32 *Ibid.*

33 *Ibid.*

as: what is the key innovation of the invention? Does the part being replaced play a crucial (new) role in this innovation, or is it simply a passive component?[34]

Even though many of such questions would still have to be resolved on a case-by-case basis and much legal uncertainty remains, the Disc Brake II decision at least establishes that the replacement of mere wearing parts – i.e. parts that, according to the patent teaching, have no other effect than to wear out – is generally classified as intended use.[35]

This was also confirmed in another German judgment concerning the production, assembly and marketing of replacement containers sold by the patentee as part of a patented 'pallet' containing a replaceable container placed in a metal cage (for use, for example, on a car for transporting water). In its judgment, the German Supreme Court (BGH) emphasised in particular that, as a result of the principle of exhaustion, the owner of the pallet has the right to maintain and repair it in order to preserve its function, including the right to replace parts.

As explained in the above, German case law sets the limit of the lawful repair in particular by asking whether a replacement can be assumed to be normal within the normal lifetime of the product. If this is the case, it would be permissible for the owner to insert a new container, since even with this insertion the product would, so to speak, retain its *identity*: it is the 'same' product which the patent proprietor marketed and which the owner has acquired the right to use in the normal way by virtue of the rule of exhaustion. As a reflection of this, the manufacture and supply of the parts do not constitute indirect infringement either.[36]

It follows from the German view that if the repair is *beyond the 'foreseeable'*, e.g. because the replacement of the container extends the life of the product beyond the usual, there will typically be a patent infringement.[37] The product is then no longer the same as the one the patent holder put on the market, and the patent holder has not been able to factor the value of the unexpected life extension into its price, thereby eroding the patent holder's monopoly profit and damaging innovation. However, not all case scenarios are covered by these legal doctrines and approaches, which leads to considerable uncertainty in practice.[38] In our view – and from a 'sustainability' and 'legal certainty' perspective – it remains in particular questionable if the very ambiguous terms of 'common

34 *Ibid.*

35 *Ibid.*

36 BGH, *Palettenbehälter II*, Judgment of 17 July 2012 – X ZR 97/11, GRUR 2012, 1118; English version in (2013) 44(3) International Review of Intellectual Property and Competition Law (IIC) 351.

37 The same applies if the part is part of the technical effect of the invention, see BGH, *Trommeleinheit*, Judgment of 24 October 2017 – X ZR 55/16, GRUR 2018, 170 (where this was found not to be the case for a 'drum' which was part of a patented printer cartridge).

38 See also Pitzer, Sitte and Reisner (n 31).

understanding' and 'natural service life' are appropriate in such cases. This has also been pointed out by other commentators, who stress that this German approach with the two steps test is inappropriate from a sustainability point of view, as linking exhaustion to the normal expected life of the product removes the incentive for owners and third parties to extend the life of products beyond this point.[39] It could also be said that the German model gives too much weight to the private interests and expectations of the parties, whereas the consideration of ensuring that the product is 'kept alive' as long as possible is not of independent importance.[40]

3.2. METHOD PATENTS

In Denmark, the explicit exhaustion rule was introduced in 1978 and the *travaux préparatoires* state, *inter alia*, that it is irrelevant for the purposes of exhaustion whether the product in question relates to 'an article, a process or a particular use'. However, it is normally assumed that this refers only to the right to dispose of the physical copy of the 'product' by resale, etc. and *not* to the right to use it in a manner which falls within the exclusive rights of the process patent.[41]

If processes and applications are not exhausted, then the use of a device or product in connection with a patented process or the like would require the authorisation of the process patentee. This might be implicit (if the product was marketed by the holder of the process patent) and would arguably normally be assumed to be the case where the process is 'embodied' in a product, e.g. a computer program, or a machine which functions in such a way that it necessarily makes use of a patented process. The risk of relying on a contractual model however is in particular that the patentee could agree with the buyer that exhaustion would not occur with the consequence that the buyer would, for example, be prevented from reselling the product 'with' the function. Such a legal effect could lead to strange results, in particular *vis-à-vis* third parties (against whom a patent limitation could in principle be enforced): it would, for example, appear perverse if the holder of a patent on a method for optimising the

---

39 See also Tiana Pihlajarinne, 'Repairing and re-using from an exclusive rights perspective: towards sustainable lifespan as part of a new normal?' in Ole-Andreas Rognstad and Inger B Ørstavik (eds), *Intellectual Property and Sustainable Markets* (Edward Elgar Publishing 2021) 81–100; Rosa Maria Ballardini, Jukka Kaisto and Jukka Similä, 'Developing novel property concepts in private law to foster the circular economy' (2021) Journal of Cleaner Production, 6 f; and Calboli (n 23) 241 f.

40 And similarly, Pihlajarinne *ibid.* and Ballardini, Kaisto and Similä, *ibid.* See also Christopher Heath, 'A Three-Step Test for Determining Patent Infringement Related to Repair' (2024) 55 International Review of Intellectual Property and Competition Law (IIC) 762, https://doi.org/10.1007/s40319-024-01458-4, accessed 16 May 2025.

41 See Peter Blok, *Patentrettens konsumtionsprincip* (Kopenhamn 1974) 38.

fuel consumption of a car were to be able to prevent the resale of cars using the method. In such cases, therefore, sound policy considerations clearly suggest that it should not be ruled out on formal grounds that exhaustion has occurred. In other cases, on the other hand, it would be more obvious to conclude that there has been no exhaustion. By way of example, if the assignor of an apparatus using a patented process enabling it to be used for chemical analysis charges a fee for each analysis, it would not be obvious to consider the right to be exhausted, since the assignor would then lose its claim to the fee from any subsequent purchaser of the apparatus. This is therefore a difficult area and ideally the assessment of whether or not a transaction has given rise to exhaustion may have to be made on a case-by-case basis.[42]

But how does this rather strict Nordic approach compare to other jurisdictions? In *Germany*, the courts would also carry out case-by-case assessments of this complicated issue with varying results and a great variety of differing scholarly opinions. In 1980, the BGH held in its seminal decision in 'Fullplastverfahren' that '(t)he sale of a device with the aid of which a process protected by a patent can be carried out does not result in the exhaustion of the process patent, even if the seller is also the owner of the process patent.'[43] Hence, the right to a patented process is generally not lost if the device required for the process is sold with the patent owner's approval. In other words, German case law acknowledges that selling the device required for a process does not equate to selling the process itself, nor does it represent an immediate act of utilising the process patent.[44] This is like in the Nordic countries. However, notwithstanding this acknowledgment, and referring to the 'Fullplastverfahren' decision, the BGH subsequently held in 'Rohrschweißverfahren' (2007) that anyone who has obtained a device needed to perform a patented process from the patent holder may use it as intended, as long as there are no specific agreements stating otherwise.[45] *Moreover*, the LG Düsseldorf held in 2012, that the patent rights of the Nespresso machine, which uses a special method to produce coffee by means of capsules which are pushed into place in a machine, were exhausted by the sale of the machine to the final consumer. This meant

---

42 See Jens Schovsbo et al. *Immaterialret* (7th edn, 2024) 395 ff.; see also Are Stenvik, *Patentrett* (4th edn, 2020) 328.

43 BGH, *Fullplastverfahren*, Judgment of 24 September 1979 – KZR 14/78; see also BGH, GRUR 1980, 38; and *cf.* Gerhard Schricker, 'Das patentrechtliche Erschöpfungsprinzip und seine Auswirkungen auf die Lizenzverträge' (1980) *Mitteilungen der deutschen Patentanwälte* (Mitt) 31; see further BGH, *Bodenwaschanlage*, GRUR 2001, 223 (224); LG Düsseldorf, Judgment of 12 December 2013–4b O 87/12.

44 See also: Benkard/Scharen, *Patentgesetz: Kommentar* (10th edn, 2014) §9, para 25; LG Düsseldorf, Decision of 7 October 2008–4a O 93/07.

45 BGH, *Rohrschweißverfahren*, Decision of 27 February 2007 – X ZR 113/04, with reference to §§133, 157, 242 BGB; see also BGH, *Fullplastverfahren*, Decision of 24 September 1979 – KZR 14/78, GRUR 1980, 38.

that a company supplying copies of capsules (which did not in itself constitute patent infringement, as the capsules were known) was not infringing under the rules of indirect patent infringement. Thus, the court recognised exhaustion of the process.[46]

Differing opinions exist in German case law and literature regarding whether the rights from a *product patent and a process patent* are exhausted when a *patented device* capable of *executing a patented process* is sold by the patent holder or with their consent.[47] Obviously, these debates create some legal uncertainty and need to be decided on a case-by-case basis. But in terms of timeframes, it appears to be at least a 'rule of thumb' under German law that in cases where both the process and the device for performing the process are covered by the same patent, exhaustion may occur simultaneously.[48] Where the process and the device for performing the process are covered by separate patents, however, exhaustion does not necessarily occur simultaneously. According to the established case law, the latter situation especially applies if the product claim includes additional features.[49]

In light of recent data indicating that climate change is picking up rapidly in speed and intensity,[50] realising the green agenda and the increasing demand for a circular economy has become more important than ever. For these reasons, we believe that courts should generally favour exhaustion of products to include patented methods. However, as the discussion above indicates in some instances there might be good reasons to reject the idea that a sale would also exhaust the method. While we advocate for a broader application of the exhaustion doctrine, we also believe that a too strict and unconditional enforcement of this doctrine would under certain circumstances risk to erode the patent premium in a disproportional way. This could in particular be the cases where exhaustion would deprive the patent holder from her right to claim licensing fees from subsequent buyers of the product and where this would lead to unreasonable results. Hence, we believe that a case-by-case assessment and the consideration of proportionality principles would still be necessary in such situations.

---

46 LG Düsseldorf, Judgments of 16 August 2012–4b O 81/12 and 4b O 82/12.

47 Martin Meggle-Freund, 'Erschöpfung bei Verfahrenspatenten', www.ipwiki.de/patentrecht:erschoepfung_bei_verfahrenspatentenn accessed 10 June 2024, referring to Benkard/Scharen, *Patentgesetz: Kommentar* (10th edn, 2014) §9, para 25; see also LG Düsseldorf – 4a O 93/07; BGH, *Handhabungsgerät*, GRUR 1998, 130; BGH, *Bauschuttsortieranlage*, GRUR 2001, 407, 409; LG Düsseldorf, *Levitationsmaschine*, GRUR 1998, 115; LG Hamburg, Judgment of 27 July 2000–315 O 645/99; dissenting: Friedrich-Karl Kraßer, *Patentrecht* (5th edn, 2004) 829 with further references.

48 Martin Meggle-Freund, *ibid.*

49 *Ibid.*

50 World Meteorological Organization (WMO), State of the Global Climate 2024, https://library.wmo.int/records/item/69455-state-of-the-global-climate-2024 (2025).

4. LOOKING FORWARD: THE UNITARY PATENT AND THE UPC

The following rule on exhaustion of the rights conferred by a European patent with unitary effect is found in Article 6 of the Regulation on unitary patent protection:

'The rights conferred by a European patent with unitary effect shall not extend to acts concerning a product covered by that patent which are carried out within the participating Member States in which that patent has unitary effect after that product has been placed on the market in the Union by, or with the consent of, the patent proprietor, *unless* there are legitimate grounds for the patent proprietor to oppose further commercialisation of the product' (emphasis added).[51]

The wording in the Regulation on unitary patent protection 'acts concerning a product covered by that patent' allows for repair (which is an 'act') to be covered. This is not surprising, see above. However, the rule also provides for the possibility of limiting exhaustion ('*unless*'). Such a combination of a *starting point* with the possibility of derogation in specific cases of, for example, obvious prejudice to the patent holder's ability to obtain a reasonable economic return from the sale of the product, could open the way to the inclusion of re-use and sustainability considerations *if* the exhaustion option is interpreted broadly. In this way, the desirability of extending the life of products beyond the usual could be taken into account, while at the same time due account could be taken of the patent holder if, for example, it is not possible for her to price her product in such a way as to respect the objective of patent law to promote innovation.

As far as we can see, there are no firm guidelines in the *travaux préparatoires* for interpreting the provision in the Regulation, but a possible scope could be the just mentioned cases of process patents, where the rule might provide the desired flexibility. In support of this, it could also be pointed out that the wording 'acts *relating to a product covered by the patent*', as far as the language is concerned, also allows for processes and applications (which can be said to 'relate to' the product) to be included. The legal position would thus be one of broader exhaustion than the Danish approach, with the possibility of limitation in specific cases.

Importantly, even though neither the Regulation nor the rule of exhaustion contains explicit references to the value of sustainability, it follows from the

51 For European patents an (almost) corresponding rules is found in the Agreement on a Unified Patent Court, Article 29: 'The rights conferred by a European patent shall not extend to acts concerning a product covered by that patent after that product has been placed on the market in the European Union by, or with the consent of, the patent proprietor, unless there are legitimate grounds for the patent proprietor to oppose further commercialisation of the product'.

general principles of EU law that a court which interpret Article 6 takes account of the values associated with 'a right to repair and reuse of patented products.' Following this reasoning, in determining whether or not there are 'legitimate reasons' for the patent holder to oppose further commercialisation of the product, courts should *also* take due account of the interests of owners and repairers in reusing and repairing the product in question. In other words, deciding whether exhaustion has occurred or not cannot be assessed solely through the lens of the affected interests of the patent holder. The so-called Principle of Proportionality, which has been developed by German and other European courts, and which is by now accepted as a general principle of European Law, could be particularly helpful in this regard.

Under this principle, substantive legitimacy of the relevant action or decision depends on whether it (1) pursued a 'legitimate objective'; (2) was 'suitable' to achieve that goal; and (3) was 'necessary' to achieve the objectives legitimately pursued by the law in question. Where there is a choice between several suitable measures, the least burdensome measure to achieve the identified objective (here: sustainability) must be pursued. Finally, the measure must also be (4) 'reasonable and proportionate to the end' (i.e. any disadvantage caused must not be disproportionate to the aims pursued).[52]

This assessment is necessary to ensure that any impact on conflicting rights is mitigated while preserving the efficiency of the decision. This also implies that the balancing process to be carried out by courts and legislators will have to be based on case-by-case assessment, which – for example – could distinguish between mass market goods and custom-made products. In some cases, this might also entail that colliding fundamental rights, such as the right to life, the right to property or the freedom of profession, will have to be weighed against each other, for example in line with the principle of practical concordance in German constitutional law.[53]

---

52 *Cf.* the discussion in a different context in: Hrefna D Gunnarsdóttir, Michael S Sinha, Sara Gerke and Timo Minssen, 'Applying the Proportionality Principle to COVID-19 Antibody Testing' (2020) 7(1) Journal of Law and the Biosciences lsaa058, https://doi.org/10.1093/jlb/lsaa058 (internal citations omitted).

53 *Ibid.* stating further in fn. 14 'In Europe, the differences in national approaches are particularly well-illustrated by the discussions unfolding after the German Federal Constitutional Court's PSPP judgment' (BVerfG, Judgment of the Second Senate of 5 May 2020– 2 BvR 859/15, paras 1–237, www.bverfg.de/e/rs20200505_2bvr085915en.html accessed 4 July 2020. The German Federal Constitutional Court's PSPP Judgment: Proportionality Review Par Excellence, European Law Blog (2020), https://europeanlawblog.eu/2020/06/02/the-german-federal-constitutional-courts-pspp-judgment-proportionality-review-par-excellence/, accessed 4 July 2020. Regarding the historical developments after World War II and the differences and similarities between the German and US, see Moshe Cohen-Eliya and Iddo Porat, 'American Balancing and German Proportionality: The Historical Origins' (2010) 8 International Journal of Constitutional Law 263.

5. CONCLUSIONS AND RECOMMENDATIONS

But where does this detour in IP theory leave the three professors in the real world? They surely did not want to buy an utterly expensive new bike from the Bach shop. Moreover, the Bach bikes are infamous for being the worst in all other aspects of biking, notwithstanding the wonderfully unique and patented organ-bike connection. Hence, they were not interested in Bach bikes without the 'sound of music', and the bike-shop owner had no illusions that other customers would buy any Bach bikes without this feature. Consequently, they left their Bach bikes in the shop where they were immediately destroyed by the shop-owner with the bespoken sledgehammer.

Against this frustrating background and considering our analysis, we find that legally speaking there are good and sound arguments for internalising sustainability concerns into the exhaustion rules. In fact, the exhaustion principle as it was conceived in German law many years ago is remarkably well suited for this purpose, as it aims to balance private and public interests involved in trade in patent protected goods. Moreover, with the 'enrolment' of patent law under the EU law umbrella with the UPC system in place the duty to take sustainability into account arguably already follows from the general principles of interpretation of EU law, which require that the reference in Article 11 TFEU and the EUC Article 37 to 'sustainable development' are taken seriously and into account in the interpretation of the rules on exhaustion in the same way as considerations of competition, free movement of goods, cultural policy, etc. Balancing these interests will primarily be up to Unified Patent Court in collaboration with the CJEU.

More specifically, this leads us to suggest that courts should follow Irene Calboli's advise and interpret 'exhaustion' broadly to promote a more sustainable and circular economy.[54] By this token, for patent law the starting point for the interpretation of the exhaustion rules should be that *the owner of a product should normally be able to repair it and third parties should be allowed to contribute to this.* The limits on exhaustion should not be dogmatic and the possibility of producing copies/parts in appropriate circumstances should not be precluded *a priori, unless* the rightholder has concrete, overriding reasons for opposing this, such as a risk of erosion of the patent premium. Such a starting point would reflect the overall interests in sustainability and the circular economy and at the same time provide for a high degree of legal certainty.[55] In particular, access to

---

54 Calboli (n 23).

55 For these combined reasons we also agree with Heath (n 40) who has recently proposed a new test for assessing such questions. After describing the great variety of different approaches by national courts on this matter, the author stresses that to 'achieve a more circular economy, companies that engage in the business of repair, refill or recycle need legal certainty to operate.' He further suggests that companies that 'try to use their patents as leverage to block access to adjacent markets need to be given the clear message that such a business model is not only undesirable, but also not enforceable.'

repair should not be based on the premise that products have a limited lifetime. Instead, emphasis should be placed on the real economy and use the possibility offered by the new rule to establish a starting point of wide repair access, *unless* the patent holder has reasonable grounds to oppose further commercial exploitation of the product. In determining such reasonable grounds, the values associated with sustainability must be included in their own right alongside the legitimate interests of patent holders. The principle of proportionality could become a valuable tool in achieving reasonable results, when such interests will have to be weighed against each other.

CHAPTER 9

UNFOLDING SCENARIOS FOR THE FUTURE(S) OF INTELLECTUAL PROPERTY SYSTEMS

Esther van Zimmeren
Professor Intellectual Property Law and Governance, University of Antwerp
Research Groups Government & Law and Business & Law
Coordinator GOVTRUST Centre of Excellence

Facing uncertainty

Change is the only certainty in an uncertain world. These changes can be either radical discontinuities or gradual shifts in context – either way, they will force a reaction. In the face of constant change, there is a choice between reacting to circumstances or proactively planning for possible future outcomes.[1]

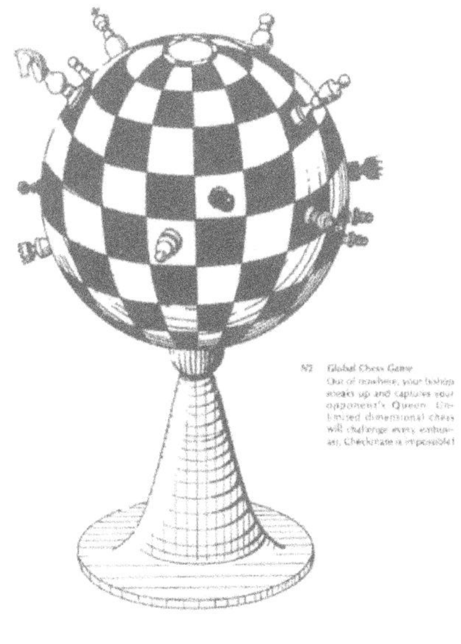

[1] European Patent Office (EPO), 'Scenarios for the Future' (EPO, 2007), available at: https://link.epo.org/web/EPO_scenarios_bookmarked.pdf, 110.

1. ADDRESSING WICKED PROBLEMS, IP AND UNFOLDING FUTURES

Governments and policymakers at different governance levels are struggling to address major societal challenges that are unfolding, such as climate change, migration, global health and inequality. Many of these challenges are also considered 'wicked problems'.[2] Wicked problems are complex, multifaceted issues that are difficult or impossible to solve definitively due to their generally incomplete, contradictory, and changing requirements. They typically involve many stakeholders with competing interests and no clear criteria for success, making traditional linear problem-solving approaches ineffective. This complex, multifaceted nature often results in stalemates in decision-making processes.

The wickedness of these problems is reflected by the image of the 'Global Chess Game' from the Carelman Catalogue of Fantastic Things (see image above). Problems occur in unexpected ways and addressing these problems requires a dynamic adaptive approach that challenges assumptions and explores a wider variety of multidimensional solutions. Unlimited dimensional chess, where anytime a 'bishop' may sneak up and capture the 'Queen' is generally not a 'game' that most governments and policymakers feel comfortable playing. Yet, current geopolitics show that the EU needs to prepare for such a 'Global Chess Game', where the rules of the game are constantly changing and unexpected moves are made. Studying different 'scenarios for the future' might be an effective way to prepare.

Interestingly, over time several IP Offices and policymakers have been using scenarios as a research tool and, as we will see below, the above-mentioned wicked problems often feature prominently in such scenarios. In my opinion, these types of studies are essential to signal to the IP community and the general public that IP systems, IP Offices and IP policymakers are not operating in a vacuum or an ivory tower. Such studies enable IP Offices and IP policymakers to consider the wider implications of decisions, practices and policies, to open up to dialogue and constructive criticism. Moreover, they create a forum to challenge key underlying assumptions of IP law, policy and systems and adopt a forward-looking approach to deal with the uncertainties IP Offices and policymakers are confronted with. In other words, 'IP exceptionalism is out and IP Realism[3] is in'.[4]

---

2 Horst W.J. Rittel and Melvin M. Webber, 'Dilemmas in a General Theory of Planning' (1973) 4 Policy Sciences 155.

3 Intellectual Property Realism encourages a more nuanced understanding of IP law, recognising that legal decisions are not made in a vacuum but are influenced by a multitude of factors. This perspective calls for ongoing empirical research to evaluate the real-world impact of IP laws and to inform policy reforms that balance the interests of a wide variety of stakeholders.

4 In another context, but a similar direction that challenges IP or patent exceptionalism and its implications, see e.g. Peter Lee, 'The Supreme Assimilation of Patent Law' (2016) 114

Innovation can contribute to solving wicked problems by introducing novel approaches, technologies, and solutions that address the complexity and interconnectedness of these problems. By fostering interdisciplinary collaboration and adaptive strategies, innovation enables stakeholders to explore multiple perspectives and identify potential interventions. Furthermore, innovative solutions can offer scalable and flexible models that evolve with changing circumstances and needs and could be applied in different contexts. However, solving wicked problems also requires continuous learning and iteration, as traditional, linear solutions often fail to account for the dynamic nature of these issues. Ultimately, innovation allows for creative problem-solving and the development of tools that enhance resilience in the face of uncertainty.

In the midst of the uncertainty linked to addressing wicked problems, the role and future of IP systems are under pressure. For instance, Artificial Intelligence (AI) is profoundly challenging the traditional framework of IP law, raising complex questions about authorship, inventorship, ownership and the use of IP protected works as training data and enforcement.[5] As AI systems increasingly generate creative works and inventions without direct human intervention, existing legal structures are being tested. Obviously, this is not

Michigan Law Review 1413 and Matthew Sag, Tonja Jacobi and Maxim Sytch 'Ideology and Exceptionalism in Intellectual Property: An Empirical Study' (2009) 97(3) California Law Review 801.

5 See e.g. European Union Intellectual Property Office (EUIPO) 'The development of Generative Artificial Intelligence from a Copyright perspective', 12 May 2025, available at: https://euipo.europa.eu/tunnel-web/secure/webdav/guest/document_library/observatory/documents/reports/2025_GenAI_from_copyright_perspective/2025_GenAI_from_copyright_perspective_FullR_en.pdf; US Copyright Office, 'Report on Copyright and Artificial Intelligence' (2024–2025), Published in Three Parts – Part 3 prepublication published May 2025, available at: www.copyright.gov/ai/; Kalpana Tyagi, 'Copyright, text & data mining and the innovation dimension of generative AI' (2024) 19(7) Journal of Intellectual Property Law & Practice 557; World Intellectual Property Organization, 'Generative AI: Navigating intellectual property' (2024), available at: www.wipo.int/edocs/pubdocs/en/wipo-pub-rn2024-8-en-generative-ai-navigating-intellectual-property.pdf; Christian E. Mammen, 'Creativity, Artificial Intelligence, and the Requirement of Human Authors and Inventors in Copyright and Patent Law' White Paper University of Oxford July 2024, available at: www.law.berkeley.edu/wp-content/uploads/2025/01/2024-07-05-Mammen-et-al-AI-Creativity-white-paper-FINAL-1.pdf; Pamela Samuelson, 'Generative AI meets copyright: Ongoing lawsuits could affect everyone who uses generative AI' (2023) 381(6654) Science 158; Thomas Margoni and Martin Kretschmer, 'A Deeper Look into the EU Text and Data Mining Exceptions: Harmonisation, Data Ownership, and the Future of Technology' (2022) 71(8) GRUR International 685; Christian Hartmann *et al.*, 'Trends and Developments in Artificial Intelligence Challenges to the Intellectual Property Rights Framework' (2020) European Commission, available at: https://op.europa.eu/en/publication-detail/-/publication/394345a1-2ecf-11eb-b27b-01aa75ed71a1/language-en, and Daryl Lim, 'AI & IP Innovation & Creativity in an Age of Accelerated Change' (2018) 52 Akron Law Review 813.

new – the rationale and justifications for the existence of IP systems have always been challenged.[6] New technologies and innovations, such as biotechnology[7] and AI, create momentum for reconsidering these age-old fundamental questions.

The future success of any system or organisation in addressing these wicked problems will depend on the robustness of the decisions taken today.[8] Choices and decisions made will depend on assumptions one starts off from. Therefore, it is essential to do more than try to predict the future in such scenario studies; a wide group of diverse stakeholders needs to be involved to identify our pre-conceptions and assumptions, challenge those assumptions and test our understanding of how the future may unfold.[9]

Different terms are being used for this type of research. Foresighting is an umbrella term for a research methodology and a way of thinking about and exploring the future according to several core principles.[10] Foresight researchers do not believe there is only one future, as the future can take different forms and shapes depending on many different factors; some of those factors are known, others are unknown. One tries to understand the different possible futures that might unfold and understand why certain trends and factors may drive the future in one direction *versus* another equally plausible direction.[11] Whereas fore*casting* was based on linear cause and effects relationships, fore*sighting* goes beyond that. Foresight, including scenario research, is a powerful tool and method, which has become quite popular in the fields of management and futures studies. Interestingly, after the Royal Dutch Shell Company popularised

---

6 See e.g. Fritz Machlup in 1958, who famously considered: 'If one does not know whether a system "as a whole" (in contrast to certain features of it) is good or bad, the safest "policy conclusion" is to "muddle through-either with it, if one has long lived with it, or without it, if one has lived without it. If we did not have a patent system, it would be irresponsible, on the basis of our present knowledge of its economic consequences, to recommend instituting one. But since we have had a patent system for a long time, it would be irresponsible, on the basis of our present knowledge, to recommend abolishing it.' Fritz Machlup, 'An Economic Review of the Patent System', Study of the Subcommittee on Patents, Trademarks, and Copyrights of the Committee on the Judiciary, US Senate, 85th Congress, 2nd Session (1958), 80.

7 See e.g. Margo A. Bagley, 'Patent First, Ask Questions Later: Morality and Biotechnology in Patent Law' (2003–2004) William & Mary Law Review 469; Geertrui Van Overwalle, 'Biotechnology patents in Europe: from law to ethics', in: Sigrid Sterckx (ed) *Biotechnology, Patents and Morality* (Routledge 2002); Drahos, 'Biotechnology Patents, Markets and Morality' (1999) 21(9) E.I.P.R. 441.

8 EPO (n 1) 110.

9 Jeremy de Beer, Alexandra Mogyoros and Sean Sidwell 'Present Thinking about the Future of Intellectual Property: A Literature Review' (2014) 11(1) Scripted 69, 70.

10 *Ibid.*, 71.

11 *Ibid.*, 71.

foresight in the 1970s, companies, governments and international organisations have become important users in recent years.[12]

Therefore, it is noteworthy that over time various IP Offices and policymakers have engaged in carrying out or supporting foresight reports and/or scenario research highlighting the influence of various driving forces such as business interests, geopolitics, societal values, and technological advancements.[13] Such studies provide a comprehensive analysis of potential futures for IP regulation and governance and offers valuable insights for policymakers, researchers, and industry leaders aiming to navigate the complexities of innovation in the coming decades.

Geertrui Van Overwalle is one of those IP scholars, who has never shied away from asking fundamental questions challenging long-held assumptions about the rationale, functions and boundaries of IP and in particular patent law[14] and expressing concerns about access to patented inventions.[15] Moreover, in her work she has explored different research methodologies, always eager to learn about new methodologies or methodologies used in other disciplines. In addition, as a PhD supervisor, member of the faculty research council and professor in research methodology she always focused on and challenged the choice for a particular methodology, triggering interesting discussions and learning moments. Even though, as far as I know, she has not engaged in scenario planning as a research method herself, she always adopts a critical and forward looking approach proposing solutions that require a thorough rethinking of already existing legal

12 EPO (n 1) 110 and De Beer, Mogyoros and Stidwill (n 9) 71.

13 For instance, the World Intellectual Property Organization (WIPO) has extensive experience publishing foresight reports regarding specific technologies, for a recent example, see WIPO, *The Future of Transportation in the Air* (WIPO, 2025), available at: www.wipo.int/publications/en/details.jsp?id=4780. The European Commission launched the foresight platform futures4europe to support engagement with strategic foresight activities for Horizon Europe. It brings together foresight experts and R&I policy-makers from across the EU, collecting national and European foresight projects and promoting futures literacy through educational material and relevant newsletters. The platform provided 8 foresight policy briefs that have been published by the Commission, including *Futures of innovation and intellectual property regulation in 2040 – Scenarios and policy implications* (European Commission, 2024). The EPO published its very extensive *Scenarios for the Future* report in 2007 and IP Australia in 2017, *IP Australia and the Future of Intellectual Property Megatrends, scenarios and their strategic implications* (IP Australia, 2017).

14 Christine Godt, Geertrui Van Overwalle, Lucie Guibault and Deryck Beyleveld, *Boundaries of Information Property* (Intersentia 2022); Geertrui Van Overwalle and Esther van Zimmeren, 'Functions and Limits of Patent Law', in: Bert Keirsbilck, Wouter Devroe, Eric Claes (eds), *Facing the Limits of the Law* (Springer, Berlin, Heidelberg 2009) and Geertrui Van Overwalle, 'Patent Law in Crisis? Functions and Limits of the Patent System in a Globalised World', (2007) Revue de la Faculté de Droit 317.

15 Geertrui Van Overwalle *et al.*, 'Models for facilitating access to patents on genetic inventions', (2005) 7(2) Nature Reviews Genetics 143.

mechanisms[16] or by presenting the need for a fundamentally different approach towards patents with her proposal regarding inclusive patents.[17] In a line of co-authored publications, Geertrui and her co-authors carried out a meticulous and detailed empirical analysis regarding the patent landscape in genetic diagnostics in Europe.[18] Whereas others were content repeating the perceived existence of patent thickets in the field, Geertrui accepted the challenge and applied for research funding that allowed her and 'her partner in crime', Gert Matthijs, to test those assumptions and explore various future solutions with a team of researchers.[19] Some of Geertrui's publications have also played a role in scenario studies, in particular her work on inclusive patents, which is also extensively discussed by authors in this book.

In 2014 De Beer, Mogyoros and Stidwill[20] published a systematic literature review and analysis of the way 'the future' is addressed in the IP literature. They found that the present thinking on the future of IP is characterised by the following four characteristics. First, in the majority of the papers they identified, the future is ancillary to another analysis and it is rarely the primary focus of IP scholarship. Second, the future is often addressed in the context of discrete events or singular incidents, such as a new technology or an important case. Third, while IP scholars and practitioners often consider what will affect or drive the future of IP, they tend to adopt, what I refer to above as a more 'IP exceptionalism' approach and rarely look at the effect of forces outside IP on IP. Fourth, despite these findings, a growing group of studies creates stories, or scenarios, as a means of understanding different alternate futures and the factors that will create them. One of the studies particularly appreciated by De Beer, Mogyoros and Stidwill, is the EPO 'Scenarios for the Future' report published in 2007.

16 Esther van Zimmeren and Geertrui Van Overwalle, 'A paper tiger? Compulsory license regimes for public health in Europe' (2011) 42 International Review of Intellectual Property and Competition Law 4.

17 Geertrui Van Overwalle, 'Inventing Inclusive Patents: From Old to New Open Innovation', in: Peter Drahos, Gustavo Ghidini and Hanns Ullrich (eds), 1 *Kritika: Essays on Intellectual Property* (Edward Elgar 2015), 206.

18 The method for this empirical study was developed in Birgit Verbeure, Gert Matthijs and Geertrui Van Overwalle, 'Analysing DNA patents in relation with diagnostic genetic testing' (2006) 14(1) European Journal of Human Genetics 26, later followed by Isabelle Huys, Gert Matthijs and Geertrui Van Overwalle, 'Legal uncertainty in the area of genetic diagnostic testing' (2009) 27(10) Nature Biotechnology, 903 and Nele Berthels, Gert Matthijs and Geertrui Van Overwalle, Impact of gene patents on diagnostic testing: a new patent landscaping method applied to spinocerebellar ataxia' (2011) 19(11) European Journal of Hulan Genetics 1114.

19 Geertrui Van Overwalle, Esther van Zimmeren, Birgit Verbeure and Gert Matthijs, 'Models for facilitating access to patents on genetic inventions' (2006) 7 Nature Reviews Genetics 143.

20 De Beer, Mogyoros and Stidwill (n 9).

For this chapter, the EPO report (2007)[21] is also one of the key studies that I have analysed, next to the report by IP Australia (2017)[22] and a study carried out by Blind *et al.* (2024)[23] for the European Commission. When the EPO published this report, I was still working on my PhD with Geertrui. The report was an eye-opener for me, and I have been hoping for a follow-up to this study. As the EPO report explores 'how IP regimes might evolve by 2025', it would be particularly timely for the EPO to carry out a similar study for the next decade. In the following sections, I will first explore the added value of foresighting and, in particular of scenario research, for IP in the context of wicked problems followed by some basic information on different methods. Then I will describe these three studies followed by an analysis of some of the key features of these reports and I end with some final thoughts about the opportunities and relevance of scenario research for shaping the future of IP.

2. RATIONALE FOR SCENARIO RESEARCH AND SCENARIO METHODOLOGY

When the context in which an organisation or system is operating is rapidly changing or the questions relating to a particular issue are too complex or uncertain, foresighting and, in particular scenarios, can play an important role. Instead of analysing a problem in isolation, scenarios look at the system as a whole seeking to understand interconnections, complexity and making sure that a holistic approach to these matters is taken.[24] This is obviously also very well aligned with the challenges related to examining wicked problems in view of their interconnected features. Scenario research is a strategic foresight methodology that can help organisations in navigating uncertainty by exploring multiple plausible futures. In order to show the variety of foresight methods used, De Beer, Mogyoros and Stidwill adapted a figure from Popper[25] referred to as the foresight diamond.[26] Each method offers a different lens through which to explore and prepare for future uncertainties.

---

21 EPO (n 1).

22 IP Australia, *IP Australia and the Future of Intellectual Property Megatrends, scenarios and their strategic implications*, CSIRO, July 2017.

23 Knut Blind *et al.*, Futures of Innovation and Intellectual Property Regulation in 2040 Scenarios and policy implications Futures of Innovation and Intellectual Property Regulation in 2040: Scenarios and Policy Implications, European Commission, May 2024, available at: www.futures4europe.eu/post/futures-of-innovation-and-intellectual-property-regulatio n-in-2040-w7l13.

24 EPO (n 1) 110.

25 Rafael Popper, 'How Are Foresight Methods Selected?' (2008) 10(6) Foresight 62.

26 De Beer, Mogyoros and Stidwill (n 9) 72.

Figure 1. Foresight Diamond adapted from Popper (2008)

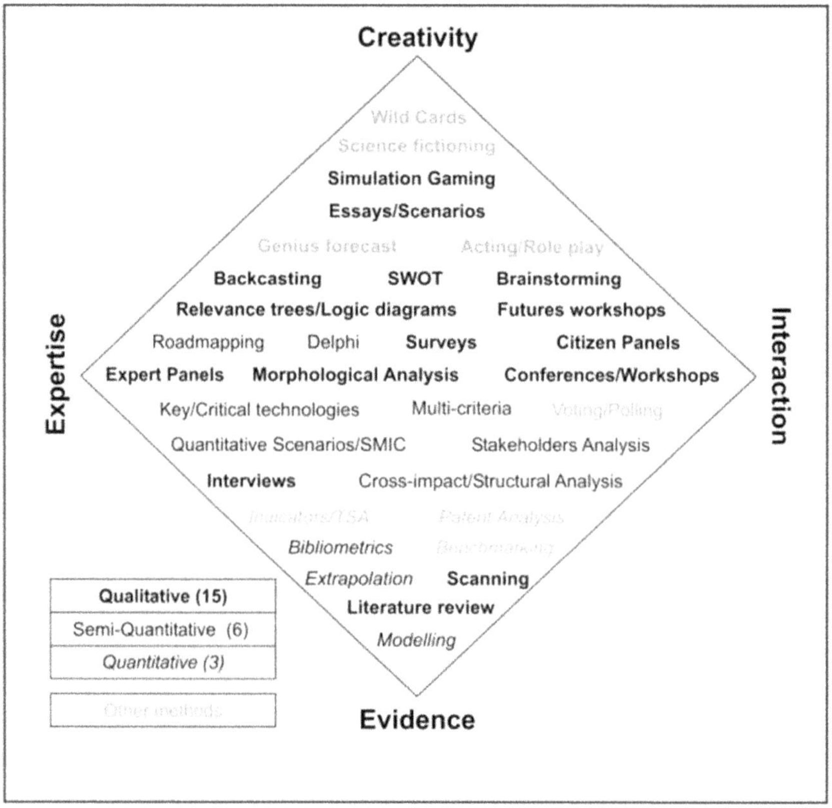

Source: Adapted from Popper (2008)

Developed by the Royal Dutch/Shell Group in the 1970s, the Intuitive Logics method[27] is one of the most widely recognised approaches to scenario planning. It emphasises the identification and analysis of critical uncertainties that could impact the future. The process typically involves: (1) identifying driving forces: recognising the key factors influencing the focal issue; (2) determining critical uncertainties: highlighting the most uncertain and impactful elements; (3) developing scenarios: crafting narratives that explore different combinations

[27] A key article regarding scenario methodology is the introduction to a special issue on scenario research and methodology, see: George Wright, George Bradfield and Ron Cairns, 'Scenario methodology: new developments in theory and practice' (2013) 80(3) Technological Forecasting and Social Change, 561. For interesting articles that further develop and explore the methodology, see e.g. Camelia Ram, 'Scenario presentation and scenario generation in multi-criteria assessments: An exploratory study' (2020) 151 Technological Forecasting and Social Change 119850 and Marwan Batrouni, Aurélie Bertaux and Christophe Nicoll, 'Scenario analysis, from Big Data to black swan' (2018) 28 Computer Science Review 131.

of these uncertainties; and (4) analysing implications: assessing the potential outcomes and strategic options. This method is particularly useful for organisations aiming to prepare for a range of possible futures by understanding the interplay of various uncertainties. A second popular method for scenarios is based on the Delphi Method.[28] The Delphi method is a structured communication technique that gathers expert opinions through multiple rounds of questionnaires. After each round, a facilitator provides a summary of the experts' forecasts and reasons, allowing participants to revise their earlier answers. This iterative process continues until a consensus is reached. The Delphi method is particularly effective in areas where expert judgment is crucial, such as forecasting technological developments or policy impacts.

Causal Layered Analysis (CLA)[29] is a futures research method that seeks to understand the multiple layers that may be influencing an issue. It involves four levels of analysis: (1) litany: the surface level of visible events and trends; (2) systemic causes: underlying structures and systems that produce the litany; (3) worldview: the deeper beliefs and values shaping the systems and, finally (4) myth/metaphor: the unconscious stories and metaphors that underpin the worldview. By examining these layers, CLA helps uncover the deeper narratives and assumptions that influence perceptions of the future, facilitating more transformative and inclusive scenario planning. Even though this poststructuralist method may be regarded as more challenging than the two other methods described here, it offers opportunities to expand the range and richness of scenarios. In addition, it allows for attention to different ways of knowing among participants and it can be used by a wider range of individuals as it incorporates non-textual and poetic/artistic expression in the futures process. Finally, this method allows for the layering of participant's positions (conflicting and harmonious ones), it moves the debate/ discussion beyond the superficial and it allows for a range of transformative actions.[30]

Organisations often choose the method or a combination of elements from different methods that best align(s) with their strategic objectives, the nature of the uncertainties they face, and the resources available for the scenario planning process.

---

28 Olaf Helmer & Nicholas Rescher, 'On the epistemology of the inexact sciences' (1959) 6(1) Management Science 25 and Adriano Bernardo Renzi and Sydney Freitas, 'The Delphi Method for Future Scenarios Construction' (2015) 3 Procedia Manufacturing 5785.

29 Sohail Inayatullah, 'Causal layered analysis: Poststructuralism as method' (1998) 30(8) Futures 815.

30 Sohail Inayatullah, 'Causal layered analysis: An Integrative and Transformative Theory and Method' in: Jerome Glenn and Theodore Gordon, Futures Research Methodology, Version 3.0., Washington D.C, The Millennium Project (2009), available at: www.metafuture.org/wp-content/uploads/2016/01/Causal-Layered-Analysis-FRM-version-3-2009.pdf.

3. THREE KEY IP SCENARIO STUDIES

For this section, three key reports were identified which have developed scenarios focusing on the future(s) of IP: the EPO (2007), IP Australia (2017) and Blind *et al.* for the European Commission DG Research and Innovation (2024). This selection is arbitrary and non-exhaustive[31] and included here for illustrative purposes only. The reports are selected to show differences and similarities between different scenario projects related to innovation and IP as developed by several IP offices and policy makers (e.g. different objectives, scopes, process and outcomes).

Table 1. Comparative Overview Key Features of the Selected Scenario Reports

	EPO Scenarios 2007	IP Australia 2017	Blind et al. for European Commission 2024
Objective	Making sure the patent system remains "fit for purpose" and is legitimate[32]	Informing IP Australia's strategic choices in areas such as core business, long-term investment and workforce planning	Exploring how changes in innovation may influence IP regimes and developing policy implications for EU research and innovation policy
Geographical Scope	Global[33]	Mainly Australia (but considering global developments)	Mainly EU (but considering global developments)
Temporal Scope (window)	2025	2030	2040

(continued)

31 For instance, the World Intellectual Property Organization (WIPO) has undertaken several initiatives to explore the future of IP through scenario planning and strategic foresight. Key initiatives include: WIPO Pulse Global intellectual property perception survey 2023 studying global attitudes towards IP, available at: www.wipo.int/publications/en/details.jsp?id=4681, WIPO Pathfinders, a global network of thought leaders that analyses the driving forces that will shape the operating and policy landscape of the IP system and WIPO Catalyst, which provides a window into the skills and roles of the IP office of the future and enables them to evolve into agencies of innovation and creativity within their economy (see www.wipo.int/en/web/future-of-ip). Moreover, while not scenario-based, WIPO's biennial World Intellectual Property Report series offers in-depth analyses of various aspects of the IP landscape, providing valuable insights for anticipating future developments and highlighting how policymakers can drive innovation in directions that best respond to societal needs to address grand challenges like climate change and health (e.g. WIPO Report 2024, 'Making Innovation Policy Work for Development', available at: www.wipo.int/publications/en/details.jsp?id=4724).

32 EPO (n 1) 1.

33 'The scenario stories in this compendium are global ones, intended to increase understanding of the different dimensions and nature of uncertainty in the world of patents and intellectual property.' EPO (n 1) 12 ('using the scenarios').

Table 1 *continued*

	EPO Scenarios 2007	IP Australia 2017	Blind et al. for European Commission 2024
Material Scope	IPRs, but focus on patents	IPRs	IPRs
Process	Started in 2005 EPO project team – support by consultants Method: over 100 formal interviews with interviewees from a wide spectrum of disciplines ranging from industry to society, from small businesses to multinationals, from politics to academia. Scenario-building process took place within the EPO with individuals drawn from all subject areas and all four EPO locations Data: interviews available on CD-ROM	Conducted by CSIRO's Data61 in close collaboration with IP Australia Method: nearly 150 people internal and external to IP Australia have been involved in one or more of five workshops, three focus groups, 28 interviews and three working groups	Started in autumn 2023 by a team of eight experts as part of the Deep Dive Foresight Studies funded by Horizon Europe Method: four workshops with the expert team and eleven external experts who also provided feedback. Close collaboration with the European Commission and its Internal Horizon Europe Foresight Network
Outcomes	4 scenarios No specific implications for EPO[34]	3 scenarios Strategic implications for IP Australia	5 scenarios Policy implications and recommendations for EU research and innovation policy

3.1. EPO SCENARIOS FOR THE FUTURE 2007

De Beer, Mogyoros and Stidwill (2014) identified the EPO report as one of the best scenario publications in their literature review.[35] The EPO employed the intuitive logics method. With the study the EPO aimed to explore how IP and patenting might evolve by 2025. It involved interviews with more than 100 key

---

[34] EPO (n 1): 'These four scenarios [...] have been developed by the EPO scenario builders, but as far as possible they reflect the many and disparate perspectives encapsulated in the interviews which we undertook as part of the initial exploration phase. They do not represent the views of the EPO on the patent system or its future.'

[35] De Beer, Mogyoros and Stidwill (n 9) 90.

stakeholders with a wide spectrum of disciplines. The interview data were also made available as part of the report with a CD-ROM, which was a valuable feature of the study in terms of the transparency of the process. The report provides a comprehensive exploration of potential futures for the patent system, highlighting the influence of various driving forces such as business interests, geopolitics, societal values, and technological advancements. Based on these insights, four distinct scenarios were developed to envision plausible futures for the patent system. Below, each of these scenarios are summarised and briefly described to illustrate the type of findings and insights derived from such scenario projects. However, it goes beyond the objective and scope of this chapter to critically and systematically assess the results of these studies.

According to the first scenario, '**Market Rules: Business-Driven IP**',[36] the patent system becomes predominantly influenced by corporate interests. Patents are viewed primarily as business assets, leading to increased filings, licensing, and monetisation through financial instruments. Multinational corporations dominate, consolidating patent portfolios and shaping regulations to protect their dominance. The system becomes highly efficient but intensely commercialised, prioritising economic power over broader societal or technological concerns.

This scenario, '**Whose Game?: Geopolitics-Driven IP**',[37] envisions a shift in global power dynamics, with emerging economies gaining influence in the IP landscape. Developed nations struggle to maintain technological superiority, while new entrants use IP to establish economic advantage. The IP system becomes regionally fragmented as enforcement becomes increasingly difficult, and attempts are made to address issues of development and technology transfer.

In the scenario, '**Trees of Knowledge: Society-Driven IP**'[38] shows how societal trust in the IP system diminishes, leading to its gradual erosion. Popular movements, often coalitions of civil society, businesses, concerned governments, and individuals, seek to challenge existing norms. The focus shifts to ensuring that knowledge remains a common good while acknowledging the legitimacy of rewarding innovation. This scenario reflects a societal push towards more equitable and accessible knowledge dissemination.

The scenario '**Blue Skies: Technology-Driven IP**'[39] anticipates a split in the patent system due to the rapid advancement of complex technologies. Technocrats and politicians respond to global crises, such as climate change, by adapting the IP system to accommodate interdisciplinary and cumulative innovation processes. The traditional patent regime applies to classic technologies, while new technologies utilise alternative forms of IP protection, such as license of rights. The system becomes more flexible and tailored to the needs of emerging technologies.

---

36 EPO (n 1) 30–47.

37 *Ibid.*, 48–65.

38 *Ibid.*, 66–83.

39 *Ibid.*, 84–101.

Table 2. Key findings from the EPO report (2007) (original table from report adapted from colour to grey scale)

How might IP regimes evolve by 2025?			
Market Rutes	**Whose Came?**	**Trees of Knowledge**	**Blue Skies**
Business as dominant driver.	Geopolitics as dominant driver	Society as dominant driver.	Technology as dominant driver
The story of consolidation in the face of a system that has been so successful that it is collapsing under its own weight.	The story of conflict in the face of a boomerang effect that strikes the dominant players as geopolitical balances shift and competing ambitions emerge.	The story of erosion in the face of diminishing societal trust and growing criticism of the patent system.	The story of differentiation of the patent system in the face of global crises, societal reliance on technology and the threat of systemic risks.
Key questions			
Could ever-increasing volumes overwhelm the patent system?	What are the main drivers for future geopolitical change? How might they steer globalisation?	How can public and private interest in IP be reconciled for the benefit of society?	How can technical expertise be identified and measured? By whom?
Will the desire for patent rights continue to increase, or will there be new forms of IP protection?	What impact might this have on existing structures and institutions?	How are the ethical and moral dilemmas raised by technology reflected by the patent system?	How can valuable knowledge be protected in emerging and complex technological fields?
How might isssues of enforcement impact the further development of patent rights as a financial asset?	How might this impact the IP system globally and regionally?	Where should the limits to patentability be drawn? By whom?	Should the 'one size fits all' system be abolished to meet the needs of different technological sectors, where will the boundaries be drawn? By whom?
Does the patent system offer buisness protection in the face of ever-increasing competition?	**Does the patent system serve the global world fairly?**	**Does the patent system benefit society?**	**Can the patent system adapt to the changing nature and pace of technology?**
… and a way to test this is to see whether business maintains its use of patent protection in the era of globalisation.	… and a way to test this is to look at LDCs and other developing countries.	… and a way to test this is to see whether it achieves a balance between rewarding innovation and providing goods and knowledge to the public	… and a way to test this is to check whether a bifurcated system can better respond to the needs of technology and society.
What legitimacy might such a regime or regimes have?			
Business says "yes" to IP; other views are irrelevant.	No global legitimacy; competing national and regional IP systems.	No legitimacy for classic monopoly rights; legitimacy for open and collaborative innovation.	IP reform restores global legitimacy.

Source: EPO report (2007), p. 103

Despite the major investment by the EPO, it explicitly stated that the four scenarios 'do not represent the views of the EPO on the patent system or its future.' Moreover, whereas the scenarios window was up to 2025, for now no publicly available follow-up seems to be given to the report. I have inquired with several EPO staff members whether any follow-up could be expected in the coming years, but it does not appear to be on the EPO's agenda. In my opinion, this is a missed opportunity as studies like these offer important signals to the public beyond the traditional IP epistemic community that the EPO is engaging in a critical and constructive dialogue about the future of the IP system. This may contribute to the democratic accountability and legitimacy of the system. So, I truly hope that the Scenario project of the EPO will receive some more traction and a follow-up that addresses the uncertain times we are in and the role of IP in dealing with complex, societal challenges. Those challenges were well considered in the report of 2007 and they have only become more urgent since 2007. In my opinion, a follow-up of the report would not necessarily require a full-scale new examination, but researchers may build on the earlier data and assessment and evaluate it in the light of new developments.

3.2. IP AUSTRALIA AND THE FUTURE OF INTELLECTUAL PROPERTY (2017)

IP Australia commissioned the Data61 Insight Team[40] to conduct a strategic foresight study aimed at exploring potential future scenarios for Australia's IP landscape. The report employs scenario planning to anticipate how several megatrends might influence IP systems and to guide IP Australia's long-term strategic decisions (e.g. core business, workforce planning, accommodation, technology, value-added services, revenue, enforcement, customer engagement, organisational structure, policy direction and the international approach). For this purpose, workshops, focus groups, interviews and working groups were organised involving nearly 150 persons internal and external to IP Australia. The process is very nicely outlined in the report with Figure 1.

---

40 Commonwealth Scientific and Industrial Research Organisation's (CSIRO) Data61 is the data and digital team of Australia's national science agency. This team has considerable experience with such foresight studies, see: www.csiro.au/en/research/technology-space/data/Data-driven-insights.

Figure 2. Overview of the strategic foresight process

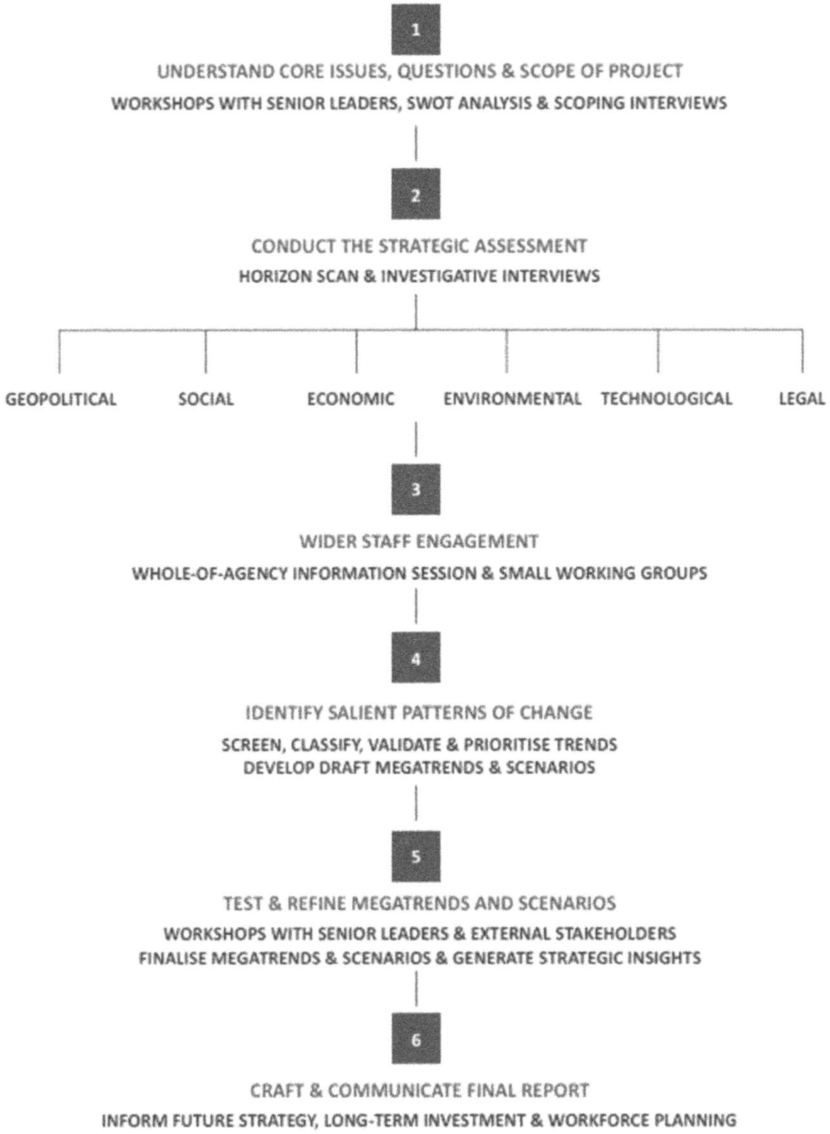

Source: IP Australia (2017), p. 67

The report[41] identifies five global megatrends that could significantly impact the IP environment: (a) tangible intangibles: the increasing economic value of intangible assets, such as data and software, over traditional physical goods (compare also EPO scenario 1 'market rules'); (b) a small world: the growing interconnectedness

41 IP Australia (n 22).

of global markets, a shift from closed to open collaborations and open source and the challenges this poses for national IP systems in terms of harmonisation; (c) building a wall: the rise of protectionist policies and their potential to disrupt international IP agreements and cooperation (compare also EPO scenario 2 'whose game'); (d) an era of skepticism: public questioning of the effectiveness and fairness of IP systems, particularly concerning access to knowledge and innovation; and (e) digital transformation: the rapid advancement of digital technologies, including AI, Internet of Things, 3D printing and blockchain, and their implications for IP creation, management, and enforcement.

Based on these megatrends, the report develops three distinct scenarios to illustrate possible futures for IP Australia.[42] The report also outlines several strategic implications for IP Australia in each scenario, which are briefly discussed as well. The first scenario '**Home Advantage**' describes a scenario where Australia strengthens its domestic IP system, focusing on local innovation and protectionist policies. This implies an emphasis on strengthening national IP laws, increasing domestic enforcement, and fostering local innovation ecosystems. The second scenario foresees a '**Renaissance**', a future characterised by a global resurgence in the value of IP, leading to enhanced international collaboration and stronger IP protection. This requires a focus on enhancing international IP agreements, improving global enforcement mechanisms, and supporting Australian entities in global markets. Finally, according to the '**Engaged**' scenario Australia adopts a more open and collaborative approach to IP, emphasising international cooperation and the sharing of knowledge. This involves a prioritisation of international collaboration, open access to knowledge, and adaptation of IP systems to facilitate global innovation networks.

Based on these scenarios, the report provides a detailed overview of the strategic implications and concrete recommendations on the short and the long-term and guides IP Australia's long-term strategic decisions on core business, long-term investment and workforce planning. The set-up and level of detail in the report may also be interesting for other IP Offices as a source of inspiration and may trigger them to consider carrying out such a study tailored to their particular circumstances to consider policy and operational implications in such study.

3.3. FORESIGHT REPORT FUTURES OF INNOVATION AND INTELLECTUAL PROPERTY REGULATION IN 2040: SCENARIOS AND POLICY IMPLICATIONS (2024)[43]

This report was conducted by a team of experts for the European Commission DG Research and Innovation in the context of the European R&I Foresight

[42] *Ibid.*
[43] Knut Blind *et al.* (n 23).

and Public Engagement for Horizon Europe. It employs scenario planning to examine how various factors – technological, societal, economic, environmental, and political – may influence IP systems by 2040. The aim is to inform EU policy-making and to ensure that the EU's IP framework remains robust and adaptive in the face of emerging challenges and opportunities. The report starts off from underscoring the importance of IP as a cornerstone of the EU's innovation ecosystem. However, it acknowledges that the traditional IP model faces increasing pressures due to a wide variety of societal, technological, environmental, economic and political drivers. Such drivers are described briefly, but systematically in the report for each of the scenarios. The report presents five scenarios that illustrate possible futures for IP regulation.

The first scenario is called '**The End of IP as We Know It**'.[44] In this scenario, traditional IP rights become obsolete due to the proliferation of open-source models and decentralised innovation platforms. Advancements in technologies like blockchain facilitate the sharing of knowledge and resources without the need for formal IP protections. This shift leads to a democratisation of innovation but also raises concerns about the sustainability of business models that rely on IP for revenue generation.

In the second scenario '**Creative Destruction' of the IP Regime**',[45] the existing IP system undergoes significant transformation driven by disruptive technologies and changing market dynamics. While IP rights remain central, their scope and enforcement mechanisms are radically redefined (e.g. rethink incentive function) to accommodate new forms of innovation and collaboration. This scenario highlights the need for a flexible and responsive IP legal framework that can adapt to rapid technological changes and (national) IP Offices that are ready to redefine their roles. Finally, more space would exist for alternative dispute resolution.

In the third scenario '**IP as a Battlefield of Geopolitics**'[46] (compare also EPO scenario 2 'whose game' and IP Australia 'building a wall') IP becomes a strategic tool in global power struggles. Nations leverage IP laws to assert dominance in critical technologies, leading to fragmented and competitive IP regimes. The EU faces challenges in maintaining a unified IP strategy amidst geopolitical tensions and competing national interests. In this scenario also special proposals are foreseen to address standardisation issues and the authors recommend that the European Commission encourages patent pools.

This scenario, '**Global and Balanced IP for Open Innovation**'[47] (compare also EPO scenario's 3 'trees of knowledge' and 4 'blue skies', and Australia 'Engaged' scenario) envisions a future where international cooperation leads to

44 Knut Blind *et al.* (n 23) 11.
45 *Ibid.*, 14.
46 *Ibid.*, 18.
47 *Ibid.*, 21.

a harmonised IP system that balances protection with access. Global standards and agreements facilitate open innovation, enabling the sharing of knowledge while ensuring fair compensation for creators. According to the authors, the EU can play a pivotal role in shaping this inclusive and balanced IP landscape.

In this scenario, **'Open-Source Collaboration Globalised Innovation'**,[48] open-source collaboration becomes the dominant model for innovation. IP rights are minimal, and innovation thrives through collective efforts and shared resources. The EU supports this model by fostering environments that encourage collaboration and knowledge sharing, while also addressing challenges related to equity and access.

Interestingly, this foresight report includes scenarios and policy implications, which would point to stimulating more open, innovative and collaborative models and mechanisms. This approach is very much in line with several works authored by Geertrui and in particular with her work on inclusive patents[49] and collaborative licensing mechanisms.[50]

It goes beyond the objective to make a systematic comparison of the various scenarios generated by these three studies. Moreover, the studies were developed in different contexts, different timespans and for different purposes, using different methodologies and involving different stakeholders. This is important to keep in mind in making such a comparison and trying to identify differences and/or similarities. Therefore, I prefer not to do so, apart from adding several comments above to show some parallels between the scenario studies. The three studies are a useful illustration of how scenario research can be brought to life in the IP context and how IP offices and policymakers can facilitate and drive such processes and studies. In the following section, I highlight some limitations and challenges of scenario research in general.

4. LIMITATIONS AND CHALLENGES OF SCENARIO RESEARCH

Scenario planning is increasingly used as a research method by academic researchers, by companies, by national, European and international policymakers and regulatory agencies for exploring and preparing for future uncertainties in

48 *Ibid.*, 25.

49 Geertrui Van Overwalle, 'Inventing Inclusive Patents: From Old to New Open Innovation', in: Peter Drahos, Gustavo Ghidini & Hanns Ullrich (eds), 1 *Kritika: Essays on Intellectual Property* (Edward Elgar 2015), 206.

50 See e.g.: Geertrui Van Overwalle (ed), *Gene Patents and Collaborative Licensing Models: Patent Pools, Clearinghouses, Open Source Models and Liability Regimes* (Cambridge University Press, 2009) and Esther van Zimmeren, Sven Vanneste, Gert Matthijs, Wim Vanhaverbeke, Geertrui Van Overwalle, 'Patent pools and clearinghouses in the life sciences' (2011) 29(11) Trends in Biotechnology 569.

IP law and beyond. However, scholars have identified several limitations and criticisms of this research method, which should also be considered in carrying out such studies in the future in IP law.[51]

One significant criticism of scenario planning is its insufficient theoretical grounding. While the methodology has been widely adopted in practice, it often lacks a robust theoretical framework to support its application and interpretation. This gap can lead to inconsistencies in how scenarios are developed and utilised, potentially limiting their effectiveness and credibility in academic research and policy and hindering the development of a coherent and standardised approach to the methodology.[52] Therefore, it would be desirable to include a chapter in every scenario study to describe both the process (see Figure 2 above IP Australia (2017)) and the theoretical framework and methodologies used. This will help readers and stakeholders to interpret the results. Moreover, effective follow-up to such scenario studies is very valuable to learn from past studies and to engage in effective feedback loops to ensure due impact on IP practice and policymaking.

Scenario studies tend to employ a diverse range of methods and techniques, leading to conceptual confusion and methodological inconsistencies. The lack of a uniform framework makes it challenging to compare and synthesise findings across different studies.[53] This confirms the need for transparency regarding the methods and techniques used in every scenario report. In addition, despite its widespread use, scenario research often lacks empirical validation. Many studies rely on qualitative methods and expert opinions, which may introduce biases depending on the selection of experts and may limit the generalisability of findings.[54] This is especially important if the available resources do not allow for a large number of experts involved. Therefore, it is essential to provide transparency about the process and selection of experts in the study. These criticisms underscore the need for a rigorous and theoretically grounded approach to scenario planning. Addressing these limitations can further enhance the power, credibility and utility of scenario planning as a tool for exploring future uncertainties in IP systems and beyond.

---

51 Kathya Cordova-Pozo and Etiënne Rouwette, 'Types of scenario planning and their effectiveness: A review of reviews' 149 Futures 103153.

52 For instance Phadnis *et al.* aim to fill this gap by articulating a set of axioms characterising the nature of human knowledge about the business environment and scenarios as depictions of that environment and by devising a structured process for developing scenarios. See: Shardul Phadnis *et al.*, 'Axiomatic foundation and a structured process for developing firm-specific Intuitive Logics scenarios Technological Forecasting and Social Change' (2014) 88 Technological Forecasting and Social Change 122–139 or Tomas J. Chermack, 'A Theoretical Model of Scenario Planning' (2004) 3(4) Human Resource Development Review 301–325.

53 For an interesting overview of the relevance, key principles and a proposal for a framework, see for instance: Mats Lindgren and Hans Bandhold, *Scenario Planning: The link between future and strategy* (Palgrave MacMillan, 2003).

54 Thomas J. Chermack and Laura M. Coons, 'Integrating scenario planning and design thinking: Learnings from the 2014 Oxford Futures Forum' (2015) 74 Futures 71.

5. FINAL THOUGHTS: LESSONS TO BE LEARNT FROM THE OPEN A.I.R. NETWORK

The literature review carried out by De Beer, Mogyoros and Stidwill (2014)[55] showed that systematic scenario planning for IP was quite uncommon when they carried out their review. They identified a limited number of academic publications and the EPO Scenario project. This essay shows that gradually foresighting studies have started to get more attention from national, regional and international IP offices and also the European Commission is heavily investing in foresight studies through Horizon Europe. In my opinion, the emergence of wicked problems and the associated uncertainty described above justify such investments and – even more so – are a reason to stimulate IP offices and policymakers to carry out such studies and to monitor and follow-up when the set time window is about to end. Foresighting studies and in particular scenario studies create a forum to challenge traditional assumptions and rationales of IP systems and open a platform for dialogue and discussion. They also allow us to connect topics that are highly complex and interrelated and require a multidisciplinary perspective.

Yet, this essay is not meant to just call for action by IP offices and policymakers – the IP scholarly community could also step up. In fact, this has already happened with the **Open A.I.R. network**. De Beer, Mogyoros and Stidwill are part of that research community-based scenarios project. Open A.I.R. is a pan-African network of nearly 60 experts from multiple academic disciplines, national and international government organisations, civil society advocates and private sector leaders. Following three years of research, 10 workshops involving dozens of participants, hundreds of interviews, and thousands of survey responses and pages of literature reviewed, they constructed three scenarios for the future of African innovation reported in the book 'Knowledge & Innovation in Africa: Scenarios for the Future'.[56] This large-scale mixed method scenario-based study was carried out with the aid of a grant from the International Development Research Centre (IDRC), Ottawa, Canada, and with financial support from the German Federal Ministry for Economic Cooperation and Development (BMZ), in cooperation with Deutsche Gesellschaft für Internationale Zusammenarbeit (GIZ).

The relevance of the Open A.I.R. scenarios goes far beyond the implications for the IP system[57] and is also directly connected to key wicked problems. The

[55] De Beer, Mogyoros and Stidwill (n 9).

[56] Shirin Elahi and Jeremy de Beer, with Dick Kawooya, Chidi Oguamanam, Nagla Rizk and the Open AIR network, 'Knowledge & Innovation in Africa: Scenarios for the Future' (Open A.I.R. 2013), available at: https://openair.africa/wp-content/uploads/2013/01/Knowledge-Innovation-Africa-Scenarios-for-Future.pdf.

[57] See for instance the scope of the questions that were addressed: 'How do we understand progress? What role does innovation play? How is knowledge governed? How are answers to these questions shaped by the political, economic, legal, social, cultural, technological and environmental contexts of time?'

first scenario, entitled '**Wireless Engagement**', suggests a world where formal African enterprises are widely interconnected with the global service economy and IP protections are largely standardised. This standardisation preserves existing forms of business relationships based on the protection of IP rights, and maintenance of an environment attractive to foreign direct investment. While this scenario allows for innovation and economic growth in African settings, it requires access to technology and education, and those who lack access will likely be unable to enter, compete in, and benefit from, the increasingly formal, globalised economy.

The second scenario, '**Informal – the New Normal**', is one in which improvisational, small-scale enterprises in Africa thrive through informal knowledge governance based on informal IP mechanisms such as trust, interpersonal networks, customer loyalty and first-mover advantage. Nonetheless, the formal economy is not eliminated in this scenario; formal business structures cooperate and support structures for their informal partners. Finally, the third scenario, '**Sincerely Africa**', emphasises how African innovators increasingly tap into traditional knowledge (TK) and inter-generational cultural practices. In this scenario, innovators increasingly employ culturally grounded IP structures, such as TK commons arrangements. Such arrangements respond to the need for sustainable resource management in the face of growing wicked environmental problems, to guard against misappropriation of their TK and undermining biodiversity.

In my opinion, this community-based initiative is marvelous and has not attracted the scholarly attention it deserves. It clearly illustrates how such studies can be tailored well to the regional and local needs. The network employed different methods, involved so many experts and stakeholders and managed to bring all their insights from various angles and disciplines together in one clear and systematic report. This scenarios project goes far beyond what IP communities have delivered at other occasions. Moreover, on a network to carry out scenario studies also allows for regular follow-up and feedback loops to the study and support from the wider multidisciplinary community. Finally, the network is an excellent basis to take due account of the 'wicked', multifaceted, interconnected nature of the phenomena and problems that are studied.

The EPO report questioned 'How might IP regimes evolve by 2025', 'Does the patent system benefit society' and 'Can the patent system adapt to the changing nature and pace of technology'? and last but not least 'What global legitimacy might IP regimes have?'. Whereas scenario studies are not meant to prescribe one particular future or point of direction, these questions and the results of the studies described here clearly show that addressing wicked problems in the IP system requires a resilient IP system that is open to *legal* innovation beyond technological innovation. Legislators have actually explored novel ways to legally enable real-world experiments.[58] Moreover, the Council of the EU emphasised how important such legal tools could be, highlighting that 'flexibility and experimentation can be important elements for an agile, innovation-friendly, future-proof, evidence-based and resilient regulatory framework which fosters competitiveness, growth, sustainability, regulatory learning as well as European technological sovereignty and leadership, and which helps to master systemic shocks and disruptive as well as long-term future challenges.'[59] For instance, regulatory sandboxes are increasingly used in a range of sectors, such as finance, health, legal services, aviation, transport and logistics as well as energy.[60] Often these initiatives include the use of new technologies or the innovative use of existing technologies. The EU AI Act is a prominent example in this respect.[61] This chapter is a call for action for IP Offices, policymakers and scholars to, first, include scenario studies in their methodological toolbox. Second, we need to make sure that results from legal experiments and regulatory sandboxes are assessed, embedded and grounded in holistic and systematic scenario studies. This may enable policymakers to better respond to the wicked problems that urgently need to be addressed. In this way well-grounded and theoretically embedded scenario studies may support IP Offices and policymakers to prepare for their "Global Chess Game' (see image at the start of this chapter).

58 See e.g. European Commission, 'Communication from the Commission to the European Parliament, the European Council, the Council, the European Economic and Social Committee and the Committee of the Regions: Coordinated Plan Artificial Intelligence', COM (2018) 795 final 4.

59 Council of the EU, 'Conclusions on Regulatory Sandboxes and Experimentation Clauses as Tools for an
Innovation-Friendly, Future-Proof and Resilient Regulatory Framework That Masters Disruptive Challenges in the Digital Age' [2020] OJ C447/1, para. 4.

60 *Ibid.*, para. 5.

61 Thomas Buocz, Sebastian Pfotenhauer and Iris Eisenberger, 'Regulatory sandboxes in the AI Act: reconciling innovation and safety?' (2023) 15(2) Law, Innovation and Technology 357.

PART III

EDITING THE FUTURE: BIOTECH AND AGRICULTURE

CHAPTER 10

ACCOMMODATING FARMERS-BREEDERS' ACCESS TO BREEDING MATERIALS IN IP AND ABS REGIME FOR INCLUSIVE INNOVATION*

Saurav GHIMIRE
Doctoral Researcher, Centre for Private and Economic Law,
Vrije Universiteit Brussel
EcoLAWgy Research Group, University of Liège

Christine FRISON
Associate Research Professor of International Environmental and Sustainable
Development Law, University of Liège

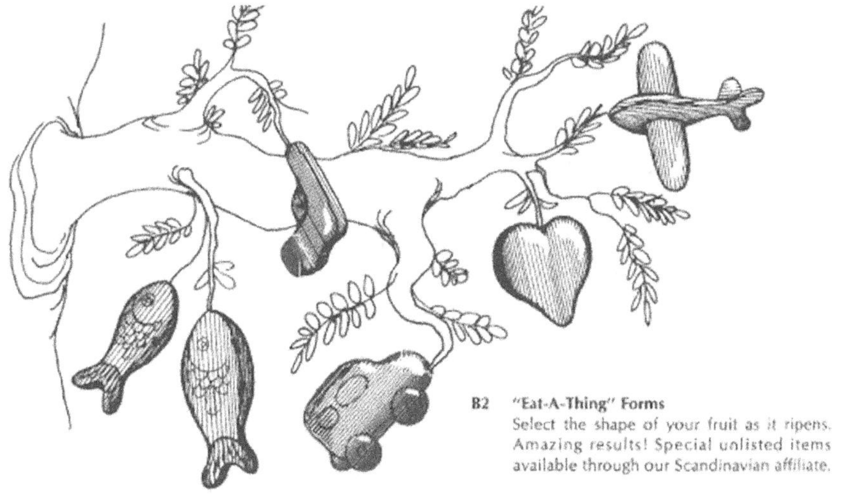

* This research was carried out within the framework of a research project funded by the Research Foundation – Flanders (FWO).

1. FARMERS IN PLANT BREEDING

The invention 'Eat-A-Thing' Forms allows to select the shape of your fruit as it ripens. However, unlike a heart-shaped, or an aeroplane-shaped fruit, farmers in West Africa have been traditionally shaping 'cultivated-like' yams by exposing tubers of wild yam species to different types of stress. Through this process, known as ennoblement, farmers obtain changes in morphological characteristics of yam tuber, and introduce them in a variety with similar tuber morphology or create a new variety.[1] Farmers evaluate different criteria such as the range of seed yam sizes, culinary capacities, resistance to diseases etc, and select tubers for reseeding.[2] This is one of the various ways farmers contribute to shaping plant breeding and creating diversity.[3]

Plant breeding was almost exclusively carried out by farmers themselves until the late nineteenth century.[4] Modern scientific breeding only began with the development of a new science of genetics based on rediscovery of Mendel's publication in 1900.[5] The establishment of the plant breeding industry soon followed, shifting the focus of plant innovation from farmers to corporations. Subsequently, legal and technological measures were developed to secure a repeated purchase of seeds by farmers.[6] The current laws, therefore consider farmers as passive users of 'genetic material' that is developed outside the communities and then made available to them primarily through sale.[7]

The formal breeding sector, which focuses on professional breeding by trained specialists, has long overlooked the contributions of farmers in plant breeding. However, despite the rise of professional formal breeding, farmer-led breeding has persisted, continuously generating new crop diversity in areas neglected by both

---

1 N. Scarcelli and others, 'Does Agriculture Conflict with In Situ Conservation? A Case Study on the Use of Wild Relatives by Yam Farmers in Benin' in N. Maxted (ed), *Crop Wild Relative Conservation and Use* (CABI 2008).

2 H. Chair and others, 'Impact of Farmer Selection on Yam Genetic Diversity' (2010) 11 Conservation Genetics 2255–2265, 2263.

3 C. Fadda, 'The Farmer's Role in Creating New Genetic Diversity' in M Halewood (ed), *Farmers' Crop Varieties and Farmers' Rights: Challenges in Taxonomy and Law* (Routledge 2016).

4 J. Sanderson, *Plants, People and Practices: The Nature and History of the UPOV Convention* (Cambridge University Press 2017) 22.

5 R.J. Pistorius and J.C.A.C. van Wijk, *The Exploitation of Plant Genetic Information: Political Strategies in Crop Development* (UA Amsterdam 1999), 36; P.J. Bowler, *Evolution: The History of Idea* (3rd edn, University of California Press 2003), 260–273; E. Mayr, *The Growth of Biological Thought: Diversity, Evolution, and Inheritance* (Harvard University Press 1982), 710–744.

6 M. Blakeney, *Intellectual Property Rights and Food Security* (CABI 2009), 79–122.

7 C. Frison, *Redesigning the Global Seed Commons – Law and Policy for Agrobiodiversity and Food Security* (Routledge 2018); D. Desclaux, 'Organic Seeds of the Future: Simple Material?' (2020) 10(1) Organic Agriculture 23–26; GNRtFN, 'Business Profits or Diverse Food Systems? Threats to Peasant Seeds and Implications in West Africa' (GNRtFN, FIAN 2018); T. Wattnem, 'Seed Laws, Certification and Standardization: Outlawing Informal Seed Systems in the Global South' (2016) 43 The Journal of Peasant Studies 850–867.

public and commercial plant breeding sectors.[8] Farmers' role in plant breeding had not received adequate attention even from the international scientific community and civil society organisations till the 1980s, and they considered farmers as strictly seed users and savers.[9] Only by the 1990s, through the seed sovereignty movement, farmers' organisations highlighted the role of farmers as plant breeders who continue to breed new varieties.[10] Farmers, therefore, are still involved in domesticating crops and developing new varieties or populations, selecting not just from landraces and local varieties but also from modern cultivars.[11] Such knowledge of farmers has been recognised in Participatory Plant Breeding (PPB) programmes. And farmers also learn breeding techniques through such PPB programmes. However, unfavourable laws may still prevent them from independently engaging in plant breeding activities.[12]

As genetic diversity constitutes the cornerstone of plant breeding, access to such diversity is of major importance for any plant breeder.[13] Although the IP regime is designed to balance exclusivity and access, in recent decades it has increasingly tilted towards exclusivity due to the expansion of the patent system, both in terms of the scope of patentable subject matter and the number of patents granted.[14] The exclusion trend is also evident in plant breeders' rights which have been progressively strengthened through successive revisions of the International Convention for the Protection of New Varieties of Plants (UPOV Convention) in 1972, 1978 and 1991, reflecting a shift toward more 'patent-like' protection of plant varieties.[15] In the case of farmers-breeders, the legal landscape becomes

---

8 R. Salazar, N.P. Louwaars, and B. Visser, 'Protecting Farmers' New Varieties: New Approaches to Rights on Collective Innovations in Plant Genetic Resources' (2007) 35(9) World Development 1515.

9 P. Mooney, 'Commentary: Recommendations: A Way Forward For Agricultural Biodiversity' in *The Future of Food: Seeds of Resilience – A Compendium of Perspectives on Agricultural Biodiversity From Around The World* (Global Alliance for the Future of Food 2016),103.

10 *Ibid.*

11 W.R. Pelegrina and R. Salazar, 'Farmers' Communities: A Reflection on the Treaty from Small Farmers' Perspectives' in C. Frison, F. López, and J. T. Esquinas-Alcázar (eds), *Plant Genetic Resources and Food Security: Stakeholder Perspectives on the International Treaty on Plant Genetic Resources for Food and Agriculture* (Earthscan 2011), 178.

12 E.g. farmers facing charges of PVP infringement were those who participated in PPB and decided to continue breeding, See S. Ghimire and others, 'Plant Variety Protection Law and Farmers' Rights to Save, Exchange and Breed Seeds: The Case of Indonesia' (2021) 16 Journal of Intellectual Property Law & Practice (JIPLP) 1013–1025.

13 N. Louwaars, and others, *Breeding Business. The Future of Plant Breeding in the Light of Developments in Patent Rights and Plant Breeder's Rights* (Centre for Genetic Resources, Wageningen University: Report 2009-14), 50.

14 G. Van Overwalle, 'Rethinking IP Protection for plants? Revisiting the Exclusivity-Access Balance Through the Type-Token Ontology' in R. Sikorski, and Z. Zemla-Pacud (eds), *Patents as an Incentive for Innovation* (Kluwer Law International 2021); G. Van Overwalle and E Van Zimmeren. 'Functions and Limits of Patent Law' in E Claes, W. Devroe and B. Keirsblick (eds), *Facing the Limits of the Law* (Springer Berlin-Heidelberg 2009).

15 H.M. Haugen, The UN Declaration on Peasants' Rights (UNDROP): Is Article 19 on Seed Rights Adequately Balancing Intellectual Property Rights and the Right to Food? (2020) Journal of World Intellectual Property, 6.

even more complex. The law does not always recognise their practices as formal breeding activities, raising uncertainty about whether they can invoke breeder exemptions provided under intellectual property regimes. While access to protected material is already contested, the challenges faced by farmer-breeders are further amplified by their marginal position and the limited recognition of their breeding practices within existing legal frameworks.

While multiple regulations influence farmers' participation in plant breeding, this chapter specifically examines the laws governing their access to breeding materials. It begins by exploring farmers' breeding practices from the standpoint of the origin of breeding materials, arguing that farmers do not only engage in improving landraces or traditional varieties but may also seek to breed using varieties protected under intellectual property (IP) regimes. The chapter then analyses how IP laws, particularly patent law and plant variety protection (PVP) regimes can restrict their access to breeding materials. Then, the chapter discusses the limitations of international Access and Benefit-Sharing (ABS) mechanisms, which, although designed to facilitate access to genetic materials, does not recognise farmer-breeders as intended users. The chapter concludes by underscoring the need to accommodate farmer-breeders' access to breeding material within both the IP and ABS regimes, in order to support and harness their innovation ensuring their freedom to operate.

2. SPECTRUM OF FARMERS' PLANT INNOVATION

Farmers actively engage in breeding their own varieties and contributing to the diversity and resilience of agricultural systems. Farmers' involvement in plant breeding and selection encompasses a wide array of activities, ranging from conserving landraces to engaging in deliberate cross breeding and seed production. The activities comprising farmers' plant innovation can be viewed in terms of a spectrum (see Figure 1). At one end of the spectrum, farmers' plant innovation involves activities like maintenance and the revival of landraces and traditional varieties using their traditional knowledge.[16] Usually farmers are in possession of the starting material, which implies comparatively less interaction with laws and formal seed systems. Similarly, they also actively engage in the domestication of crops and development of new varieties from crop wild relatives. In some countries, such collection of wild germplasm may be regulated.

Farmers also carry out deliberate breeding[17] with different varieties including modern cultivars. An illustrative case of organised farmer-led breeding can be seen

16 N. Maxted (ed) *Crop Wild Relative Conservation and Use* (CABI 2008); M. Halewood (ed) *Farmers' Crop Varieties and Farmers' Rights: Challenges in Taxonomy and Law* (Routledge 2016). H. Chair and others (n 2).

17 The term 'deliberate breeding' means intentional breeding, where conscious efforts are made to guide the selection process, in contrast to random selection.

in Vietnam, where farmers have established self-managed seed clubs that have developed over 350 rice varieties, showcasing the effectiveness of farmer-driven breeding initiatives. These clubs independently produce and supply high-quality seeds characterised by high purity, strong germination rates, uniform growth, and increased yields.[18] The formation of these seed clubs has transformed the traditional farmers' seed system in Vietnam, offering a structured alternative source of seeds for communities.[19] Even in Europe, there are farmers who improve local varieties, sometimes collaborating with researchers and agricultural extensionists.[20] Notable examples include farmers breeding vegetable and wheat in France, vegetable-breeders in Germany, etc.[21] Similarly, in the potato breeding sector in the Netherlands, specialised farmers are closely involved in the selection process, working alongside potato seed companies and trained breeders. These farmers carry out much of the hands-on selection work, making them essential to the breeding process and the success of the potato industry.[22]

Figure 1. The spectrum of farmers' innovation according to the (legal) origin of the breeding material

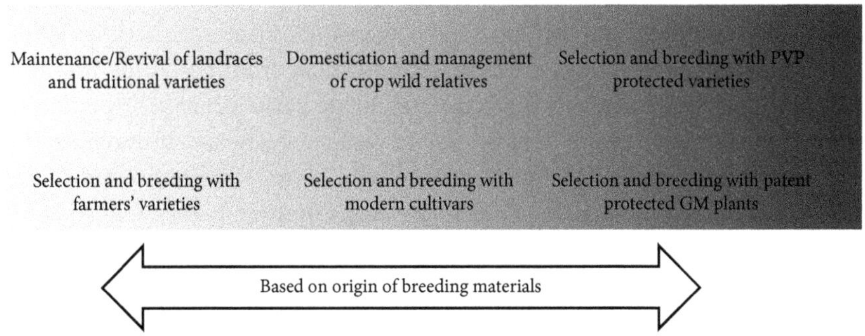

On the other side of the spectrum of farmers' plant innovation, we can see farmers experimenting and breeding even with intellectual property-protected

18 H.Q. Tin and others, 'Impacts of Seed Clubs in Ensuring Local Seed Systems in the Mekong Delta, Vietnam' (2011) 35 Journal of Sustainable Agriculture 840–854; H.Q. Tin and others, *Securing the Local Seed Systems: The Journey of Farmers' Seed Clubs in Vietnam* (SEARICE 2019) 10.

19 H.Q. Tin and others, '*Prospects for Scaling Up Crop Breeding Capacities of Seed Clubs in Vietnam*' (SEARICE, October 2020).

20 An agricultural extensionist is a professional who provides educational support or technical advice to farmers and gardeners.

21 See A. Osman and V. Chable, 'Inventory of Initiatives on Seeds of Landraces in Europe' (2009) 103(1/2) Journal of Agriculture and Environment for International Development 95–130.

22 C.J.M. Almekinders, L. Mertens, J.P. van Loon, and E.T. Lammerts van Bueren, 'Potato Breeding in the Netherlands: A Successful Participatory Model with Collaboration Between Farmers and Commercial Breeders' (2014) 6 Food Security 515–524; see also N.P. Louwaars, 'Chapter 4. Potato in the Netherlands – a Remarkable Story' in P.C. Struik and others, *Impact of Hybrid Potato: The Future of Hybrid Potato from a Systems Perspective* (Wageningen Academic Publishers 2023) 45–58, 51.

commercial varieties. Farmers' breeding with such varieties could lead to several legal challenges including infringement lawsuits, for instance, in Indonesia where farmers were prosecuted for violation of plant variety protection laws.[23] Besides, farmers' breeding may also sometimes involve patent-protected genetically modified seeds. A well-documented case in this regard is that of smallholder farmers in the Philippines who deliberately and successfully incorporated a genetically modified (GM), patent-protected trait into popular open-pollinated maize varieties, creating several distinct new varieties.[24] This has led to the widespread dissemination of glyphosate-tolerant open-pollinated farmers' varieties. Farmers breeding with GM varieties is a complex issue involving biosafety considerations and falls beyond the scope of this chapter. Nevertheless, it is important to note that smallholder farmers possess both the capacity and the willingness to develop new varieties. Whether by improving or restoring traditional varieties, selecting lines from varieties provided by breeding institutions, or crossing local varieties with public or private sector varieties to combine desired traits, farmer-breeders have been developing crops and varieties suited to local conditions.

Despite the noteworthy capacity of farmers to breed new varieties, the laws promoting plant innovations tend to overlook farmers' breeding. While the UPOV Convention does not restrict individuals from becoming breeders, its requirements for distinct, uniform, and stable varieties make it practically difficult for farmers, whose varieties are often heterogeneous, to mobilise this legal tool to protect their varieties. Additionally, farmers' collective and shared innovation poses challenges in identifying a single breeder. Rather, UPOV-based laws have been shown to negatively impact not only breeding but also farmers' rights of saving and exchanging seeds.[25] The International Treaty on Plant Genetic Resources for Food and Agriculture (ITPGRFA), on the other hand, acknowledges farmers' contributions for the conservation and development of plant genetic resources, which constitute the basis of food and agriculture production throughout the world (Article 9). However, the Treaty still tends to view farmers as providers of raw materials for breeders or as passive end users of genetic resources developed outside the farm. While the ITPGRFA mentions farmers' role in conservation and sustainable use of plant genetic resources for food and agriculture (PGRFA) and promotes farmers' participation in breeding (Article 5, 6), no substantive rights flow in relation to farmers' access to breeding materials. More recently, the UN Declaration on the Rights of Peasants

---

23 See Ghimire and others (n 12).

24 See B. De Jonge, R. Salazar, and B. Visser, 'How Regulatory Issues Surrounding New Breeding Technologies Can Impact Smallholder Farmer Breeding: A Case Study from the Philippines' (2021) 4 Plants, People, Planet 96–105.

25 A. Christinck and M.W. Tvedt, *The UPOV Convention, Farmers Rights and Human Rights: An Integrated Assessment of Potentially Conflicting Legal Frameworks* (GIZ 2015); Wattnem (n 7); Ghimire and others (n 12).

(UNDROP), however, marks significant progress by recognising farmers' rights to maintain, control, protect, and develop their seeds and traditional knowledge, and obliges states to promote and protect peasant innovations and practices.[26]

3. FARMERS' ACCESS TO BREEDING MATERIAL

Farmers in many parts of the world treat all genetic diversity as raw materials for direct use and further improvement.[27] As discussed above, farmers use a wide range of materials for a wide range of activities while engaging in plant innovation. However, different laws create difficulties for farmers to access new materials for further breeding and adaptation. Increasing intellectual property rights (IPRs), including patents and plant variety protection (PVP) on cultivars,[28] pose significant barriers. This constraint on the gene pool available to third parties impedes breeders as well as farmers in obtaining the seeds and breeding material,[29] and limits their Freedom to Operate.[30]

Additionally, international access and benefit-sharing (ABS) regimes, such as those under the Nagoya Protocol to the Convention on Biological Diversity (CBD) and the Multilateral System (MLS) of the International Treaty on Plant Genetic Resources for Food and Agriculture (ITPGRFA), are not designed to facilitate farmers' direct access to PGRFA, and do not necessarily promote the breeding role of farmers. Moreover, seed marketing laws can affect the availability of breeding materials by prohibiting the sale of farmers' varieties that do not meet stringent marketing requirements. Plant health regulations also impose requirements which might affect farmers' ability to use material for further breeding. The following sections will explain how IPRs and the MLS of ITPGRFA affect farmers' access to PGRFA for further breeding.

3.1. INTELLECTUAL PROPERTY RIGHTS

3.1.1. Patent Laws

An increasing number of countries are implementing IPRs, namely patent and PVP law covering plant varieties, plants, or their parts. According to Correa et al., around 60% of the 126 countries in the Global South allow for the patenting

[26] Articles 11(3), 19(2), 19(8), 20(2) UNDROP.

[27] Salazar, Louwaars, and Visser (n 8) 1520.

[28] WIPO, *World Intellectual Property Report: Making Innovation Policy Work for Development* (World Intellectual Property Organization 2024).

[29] C.M. Correa, J.I. Correa, and B. De Jonge, 'The Status of Patenting Plants in the Global South' (2020) 23 The Journal of World Intellectual Property 121-146; De Jonge, and others (n 24).

[30] WIPO, *Identifying Inventions in the Public Domain: A Guide for Inventors and Entrepreneurs* (WIPO 2020), 24; *ibid.*

of plants or parts thereof.[31] In 43% of these countries that allow plant patenting following the European model, plant varieties and biological processes to obtain them are excluded from patentability; however, laws would still permit the patenting of genetic material, plant parts such as cells and DNA sequences, and biotechnological processes to produce plants.[32] The patent holder's right would, therefore, extend over the further use of a whole plant, or any plant variety containing the patent component or to any variety that was obtained by use of the patented process. Consequently, patent holders can control the production and commercialisation of such plant varieties and their derivatives, even though the plant varieties themselves are not patentable as such.[33] The remaining 17% of these countries do not explicitly exclude plant varieties from patentability.[34]

Even in the countries where there is exclusion of plants from patentability, the interpretation of the scope of laws by the patent office or the courts has in practice led to patenting of isolated genes, for instance in India, and methods for producing a transgenic plant, for instance in Brazil.[35] Due to the lack of a breeder's exemption in many patent regimes, or its narrow scope where it does exist, the increasing number of patents on plant-related innovation is limiting third parties' access to breeding materials.[36] Patented varieties could often be GM varieties and whether farmers need access to these varieties is a complex issue as it involves the question of both patent infringement and biosafety. Nevertheless, since farmer-breeders may entangle themselves with patent protected varieties whether consciously or unconsciously, it is important to ensure that such laws do not unjustly shrink farmers' sphere of innovation. As New Genomic Techniques (NGTs) become more prevalent on plant breeding, such complications are likely to increase because a patentable gene edited plant can be phenotypically and genotypically indistinguishable from a naturally occurring mutant plant or a plant obtained through conventional breeding.[37] Thus, farmers as well as conventional breeders are likely to be pulled into patent infringement disputes if they develop and market a new plant variety whose main traits resemble those of a patented gene-edited plant due to congruent mutations.[38] Considering that national patent laws in most countries permit the patenting of NGTs and the plants or plant genetic material developed using these technologies, it

31 Correa and others (n 29).

32 *Ibid.*

33 *Ibid.*

34 *Ibid.*

35 *Ibid.*; De Jonge, and others (n 24).

36 In some European countries, a limited breeder's exemption has been included in patent law. For breeding exemption in patent see Viola Prifti, *The Breeder's Exception to Patent Rights* (Springer 2015).

37 H. Dederer, 'Patentability of Genome-Edited Plants: A Convoluted Debate' (2020) 51(6) IIC-International Review of Intellectual Property and Competition Law 681–684.

38 De Jonge, and others (n 24) 99.

is anticipated that the number of patents will continue to increase.[39] A study mapping the global patent landscape for synthetic biology already shows that synthetic biology patents are most prevalent in plant biotechnology after the pharmaceutical and medical sector.[40] Thus, adequate attention should be given to how these laws affect farmer-breeders and their access to genetic material, ensuring they are protected from legal suits for infringement, guaranteeing their space for innovation.

3.1.2. Plant Variety Protection Laws

The Plant Variety Protection (PVP) right based on UPOV Convention grants breeders exclusive rights over their plant varieties, provided these are distinct, uniform, stable, and (commercially) novel.[41] This right entitles the holder to exclusively produce and sell reproductive material of the protected variety within a specific territory and timeframe. While authorisation from the breeder is required for any acts concerning the propagating material of the protected variety, PVP laws have mandatory breeders' exemption, under which the PVP right does not extend to acts carried out for breeding new varieties. Plant Variety Protection law is designed with an inherent breeders' exemption that ensures access to protected varieties for further breeding and commercialisation.[42] While the right holder can exclude others from reproducing propagating material, they cannot prevent others from using the protected variety to develop new ones. Thus, the provision of a breeders' exemptions a major feature that sets the PVP system apart from patents.

Furthermore, countries may choose to provide a farmers' exemption, which permits the use of farm-saved seeds from protected varieties for planting on the farmer's own holding.[43] Ideally, farmers should also be permitted to breed using PVP-protected varieties. However, the expansion of plant breeders' rights under the UPOV Convention 1991 introduced the concept of 'Essentially Derived Varieties (EDV)', to include varieties that are derived directly or indirectly from a protected initial variety.[44] Thus, along with the protected varieties, the breeders' right covers (i) the varieties that cannot be clearly distinguished from

---

39 D. Kim and others, 'New Genomic Techniques and Intellectual Property Law: Challenges and Solutions for the Plant Breeding Sector' (Research Paper No. 23-16, 2023); In the EU, the patentability of gene edited plants has not been decided yet, www.euractiv.com/section/agriculture-food/news/eu-commission-takes-more-time-on-patentability-of-gene-edited-plants/, (Accessed 01 Sept 2024).

40 PO and S. Hall, 'Synthetic biology-mapping the patent landscape' (2018) *bioRxiv*, 12.

41 UPOV Convention 1991, Article 5(1).

42 See Van Overwalle (n 14).

43 UPOV Convention 1991, Article 51(2).

44 UPOV, (2017) *Explanatory Notes on Essentially Derived Varieties Under The 1991 Act of The UPOV Convention.*

the protected variety and also (ii) the varieties that are EDV.[45] The EDVs are the first-or-second-generation derivatives of the protected varieties.[46]

The degree of similarity between the protected variety with other varieties and the issue of EDVs remains a concerning issue for the farmers. There could be situations where material used by farmers is quite similar to a protected variety, for instance, traditional varieties might be similar to a protected variety.[47] Unlike other areas of IPRs where the question of infringement is determined by accessing similarities between the claimed subject matter and the process or product applied by the accused, in the case of PVP, this becomes a question of whether the characteristics that define a protected variety are present in the propagating material used by farmers. Therefore, difficulties arise when varieties used by farmers cannot be distinguished clearly enough from protected varieties.[48] In order to answer whether a variety is an EDV of an initial variety, the genetic distance estimate between two varieties should be compared to threshold distances. Yet, these threshold values are not statistical questions, rather they are subjective value judgements.[49] Along with the practical technical difficulties in establishing when a variety qualifies as an EDV, the concept of EDV introduces limitations preventing farmers from freely using protected varieties for further breeding.[50] In some countries, farmers have been prosecuted for such infringements.[51] However, it must be stressed that the principle of independence of variety, allowing the breeder's exemption is one of the main principles in the PVP system.[52]

A crucial aspect of securing farmers' rights to freely engage in breeding activities is the formal recognition of farmers as breeders. The explanatory note adopted by the UPOV Council clarifies that the UPOV Convention imposes no restrictions regarding the methods or techniques used to breed a new variety, nor does it restrict who can become a breeder.[53] However, a significant concern within

---

45 UPOV Convention 1991, Article 14(5)(a).

46 S. Ragavan and J.M. O'Shields, 'Has India Addressed Its Farmers' Woes: A Story of Plant Protection Issues' (2007) 20(1) Georgetown International Environmental Law Review, 4.

47 Christinck and Tvedt (n 25) 64.

48 *Ibid.*

49 See V. Lombard and others, 'Genetic Distance Estimators Based on Molecular Data for Plant Registration and Protection: A Review' (2001) 451 Acta Horticulturae 55, 61; M.D. Janis and S. Smith, 'Technological Change and the Design of Plant Variety Protection Regimes' (2007) 82 Chicago-Kent Law Review 1557, 1599.

50 C.M. Correa, *Plant Variety Protection in Developing Countries: A Tool for Designing a Sui Generis Plant Variety Protection System: An Alternative to UPOV 1991* (APBREBES 2015) 27, 30.

51 C. Antons, Y.T. Winarto, and A.F. Prihandiani, 'Farmer-Plant-Breeders and the Law on Java, Indonesia' (2020) 52(4) Critical Asian Studies 589; Ghimire and others (n 12).

52 G. Wurtenberger, 'Legal Perspectives on Essentially Derived Varieties' (2013) 8 Revista Eletronica do IBPI 200, 201; J.M.A. Blokland, 'Can We Still Take the Breeders Exemption for Granted?' (2010) 855 Acta Horticulturae 31.

53 UPOV, *Explanatory Notes on The Definition of Breeder Under The 1991 Act of The UPOV Convention* (Adopted by the Council at its forty-seventh ordinary session on October 24, 2013, UPOV/EXN/BRD/1).

the UPOV framework is that informal groups of farmers or communities do not qualify as breeders unless they have obtained legal personhood status.[54] Sanderson suggests that there are several practical challenges for farmers claiming to be breeders under UPOV-based plant variety rights schemes. These challenges arise from the collective and collaborative nature of farmers' plant breeding, which is excluded by a narrow definition of a breeder.[55] Furthermore, the UPOV based laws require the varieties to be Distinct Uniform and Stable, while farmers varieties are often heterogenous, making it difficult to qualify for any protection. As a counter example, the recognition of collective ownership exists in India, where a group of farmers is included under the definition of a breeder.[56] The law allows any farmer, group of farmers, or community of farmers to apply for variety registration, with over 1500 certificates issued to individual farmers or farming communities.[57]

Furthermore, it is important to note that several studies have documented that the UPOV based laws create difficulties in saving and exchanging seeds by farmers.[58] These activities of saving and exchanging seeds are foundational to farmers' breeding, which are often shared and collective.

3.2. INTERNATIONAL ACCESS AND BENEFIT SHARING REGIME

Farmers are also accessing materials from international gene banks. A study suggests that farmers, farmer organisations, and NGOs comprise a considerable user group of gene bank material, receiving at least 8% of the seed samples distributed from international gene banks in 2015, on par with the proportion distributed to the commercial seed sector.[59] However, it is not clear whether and to what extent the material were used by farmers for breeding.[60]

---

54 *Ibid.*

55 Sanderson (n 4) 112.

56 Section 2(c) of the Protection of Plant Varieties and Farmers' Rights (PPVFR) Act, 2001; Also see Sections 14, 16(d), 39(1).

57 PPVFRA (2018) '*Compendium of Registered Varieties under PPV&FR Act*, 2001 (Department of Agriculture and Co-operation, Ministry of Agriculture, New Delhi).

58 The cumulative analysis in academic literature is unequivocal in proving that the PVP laws based on UPOV Convention 1991 are not suitable for developing countries that rely on informal seed systems. Several studies show the negative impact of the strong IPR regime in plant varieties on farmers' access to seeds human rights, especially the right to food. See T. Braunschweig, M. François, C. Pionetti, and S. Shashikant, *Owning Seeds, Accessing Food – A Human Rights Impact Assessment of UPOV 1991* (October 2014); Christinck and Tvedt (n 25); H.M. Haugen, *The Right to Food and the TRIPS Agreement* (Martinus Nijhoff Publishers 2007); N. Louwaars, *Seeds of Confusion: The Impact of Policies on Seed Systems* (Wageningen University and Research 2007).

59 While both farmers and the commercial sector received 8% of the samples, 10% was received by 'individuals, unknown and other users,' and 74% was received by agricultural research institutes, universities, national agricultural research organisation and other gene banks. See O.T. Westengen, K. Skarbø, T.H. Mulesa, and T. Berg, 'Access to Genes: Linkages Between Genebanks and Farmers' Seed Systems' (2018) 10 *Food Security* 9–25.

60 *Ibid.*

When it comes to accessing plant genetic resources for breeding, two international mechanisms coexist: (i) the Nagoya Protocol to the CBD and (ii) the MLS under the ITPGRFA. PGRFAs are accessed more frequently under the ITPGRFA. While the ITPGRFA recognises the role of farmers in conserving and developing PGRFA diversity for millennia (Article 9), no actual de jure rights of farmers stem from this recognition at the level of international law.[61] Rather, the treaty perpetuates the imbalance of rights in international laws. Indeed, technological innovation is considered the ultimate solution for the global problem of hunger and biodiversity erosion, while farmers' innovations are side-lined by relegating to the national level the practical implementation of the recognition of farmers' rights.

One of the key features of the treaty is to provide a facilitated access to PGRFA in accordance with its Article 12.3, for which the Governing Body of the Treaty adopted the SMTA in its Resolution 1/2006 in 2006. However, the treaty limits the facilitated access to PGRFA through the SMTA for research, breeding and training for food and agriculture purposes.[62] Hence, access for activities other than research, breeding or training, falls out of the scope of the Treaty.[63] Thus, farmers do not have a right to 'claim' a facilitated access to PGRFA under the MLS and use them directly, although this question has been discussed by the GB and there is an understanding that farmers may access MLS-PGRFA for direct use.

Historically, the Consultative Group for International Agricultural Research (CGIAR) centres have been providing for PGRFA to farmers for different purposes. Therefore, the question of whether CGIAR centres have the right to provide such materials to farmers for 'direct use' was raised before the Ad Hoc Technical Advisory Committee on the SMTA and the MLS in 2010. It is noteworthy that the committee's primary question was whether CGIAR centres have the right to provide PGRFA to farmers, rather than whether farmers have the right to access them. The committee concluded that the agreement between the CGIAR and the governing body of the Treaty does not restrict CGIAR centres to make PGRFA available to farmers for direct use.[64] The committee categorised the PGRFA held by the CGIAR into different categories and recognised the legality of transferring such PGRFA to farmers for direct use. First, the material developed (or under development) by the CGIAR from PGRFA acquired under the MLS, can be distributed to farmers for direct use as a prerogative of the CGIAR.[65] The second category deals with PGRFA that are in their original form, meaning, the ones have not been improved by the CGIAR. These PGRFA

61 Frison (n 7), 197.
62 Article 12.3(a); SMTA, Article 6.1 ITPGRFA.
63 IT/AC-SMTA-MLS 2/10/7, para. 11.
64 *Ibid.* para. 13.
65 IT/AC-SMTA-MLS 2/10/Report, para. 55; IT- AC-SMTA-MLS 3-12-Report, appendix 3.

are further categorised based on their origin.[66] One sub-category of PGRFA is those that are held 'in-trust' by the CGIAR centres in their collection, which can be provided to farmers for direct use.[67] The second sub-category are those received by CGIAR under the SMTA – this material can be provided to farmers as unimproved material for direct use for cultivation only with a separate express permission from the provider allowing for such distribution.[68] This right of CGIAR centres to provide PGRFA for direct use by farmers was extended to other recipient institutions receiving PGRFA via the MLS.[69]

Table 1. Types of PGRFA held by CGIAR and their right to provide those to farmers for direct use

Type of PGRFA		Right of the CGIAR to provide PGRFA to farmers for direct use
Improved by the CGIAR/ or under development		Yes
Not improved by CGIAR	Held in trust by the CGIAR	Yes
	Received under an SMTA by the CGIAR	Yes, but only with the permission of the provider

Regarding whether farmers' access for direct use would require an SMTA, the committee opined that a key issue to consider is the intended purpose of the transfer and suggested that an SMTA is not required in cases where the purpose of the transfer is not utilisation and conservation for research, breeding and training for food and agriculture.[70] Thus, PGRFA distributed to farmers for direct use for cultivation should not be transferred with the SMTA, as it would not be an appropriate instrument.[71] Rather, a statement that the material can be used directly for cultivation would suffice.[72] However, when PGRFA are transferred for both research and breeding and for direct use for cultivation, or where it is unclear whether the transfer is for one or the other purposes, then both the SMTA and the statement giving express permission for direct use for cultivation should be used.[73]

There is no explicit answer on whether farmers can continue the process of selection and breeding with the materials provided by CGIAR centres as they

66 IT/AC-SMTA-MLS 2/10/7, para. 9.

67 IT/AC-SMTA-MLS 2/10/Report, Appendix 7.

68 *Ibid.*

69 IT- AC-SMTA-MLS 3-12-Report.

70 IT/AC-SMTA-MLS 3/12/3, para. 4–5.

71 IT/AC-SMTA-MLS 2/10/Report, para. 59.

72 The following is a suggested wording for the statement: 'This material can be used by the recipient directly for cultivation, and can be passed on to others for direct cultivation.' (IT/AC-SMTA-MLS 2/10/Report, Appendix 7).

73 IT/AC-SMTA-MLS 2/10/Report, Appendix 7.

used to.[74] While the committee points out that in the case of participatory breeding activities, the distribution is clearly predominantly for the purpose of research and breeding, it does not explicitly state whether selection and evaluation by farmers, without collaboration with formal sector like in PPB would still be considered research and breeding. While the distribution of PGRFA to farmers for restoration is explicitly exempted from using an SMTA or express permission,[75] the farmers' involvement in breeding and selection appears to require accessing the germplasm through an SMTA.

Thus, two important points emerge from the above discussion. First, farmers do not have substantive rights to access PGRFA from the MLS, even for their direct use. It is left to the prerogative of the PGRFA holding institutions like CGIAR centres. Second, although the material can be claimed as right for breeding purposes, farmers' access to PGRFA for breeding can be complicated due to several factors. Acknowledging the complexity of the SMTA in case of farmers' access to PGRFA for direct use, the committee recommended that the SMTA is not suitable for farmers' access for direct use. It was noted that in practice the SMTA could hinder farmers' access to PGRFA due to the complexity of the agreement and their possible reluctance to accept obligations they do not fully understand.[76] Besides, the material transferred under an SMTA requires to sign an SMTA in subsequent transfers, making it impractical for farmers where the seed exchange is highly informal.[77] However, these complexities are not diminished when the purpose of farmers' access is breeding. Thus, if the SMTA is complicated for farmers access for direct use, it is equally complicated for farmers' access when the purpose is breeding.

One of the reasons cited for exempting farmers' access for direct use under the SMTA was the minimal risk of farmers claiming intellectual property rights over the materials received.[78] It was also noted, albeit in a footnote, that this risk would remain low even when farmers engage in breeding, research, or training.[79] Since farmer breeders do not usually seek IPR protection over the materials they receive, it should be acceptable to provide PGRFA without using a SMTA, as they can already access for direct use. Another alternative could be establishing a mechanism to assist farmers in accessing PGRFA through gene banks or community seed banks, both nationally and internationally.

---

74 IT/AC-SMTA-MLS 3/12/3 para. 16.

75 IT/AC-SMTA-MLS 2/10/Report, Appendix 7.

76 *Ibid.*, para. 22.

77 *Ibid.*, para. 22.

78 'Though, it may also be argued that these considerations would only apply to small farmers, since industrial farmers or farmers' organizations may benefit from legal advice and possess the resources to implement the SMTA and that, in the absence thereof, they might seek or assert intellectual property rights which might be in contradiction to the provisions of the Treaty' (IT/AC-SMTA-MLS 3/12/3, para. 22).

79 IT/AC-SMTA-MLS 3/12/3, para. 22, footnote 12.

To make the international exchange of seeds between farmers easy, Mooney suggests establishing an Office for Farmer Seed Exchanges within the ITPGRFA Secretariat in Rome, which should receive requests from farmers' organisations (including individual farmers) and forwarding these to appropriate national or international gene banks.[80]

Furthermore, in order to protect farmers' varieties from misappropriation, the biodiversity-rich countries may implement restrictive laws in collecting and accessing PGRFA, which can also limit local farmers' access to plant genetic resources for breeding, as seen in Indonesia, where a license is required for genetic resource collection. For instance, in Indonesia farmers were exempted from such licence requirements only after the intervention of the constitutional court in 2013.[81] Thus, lawmakers should take caution that the laws aimed to protect farmers' varieties from misappropriation does not limit their right to collect germplasms and to improve them.

4. CONCLUSIONS

Farmers continue to demonstrate a remarkable capacity to generate crop diversity, despite receiving limited formal recognition. From the revival of landraces to breeding with modern cultivars, they engage in a wide range of plant innovation activities. Farmers' breeding even with IP protected commercial varieties and risking litigation indicates that farmer-breeders are eager to utilise new and beneficial genetic diversity. While the plant breeding industry has led to various kinds of innovation, with adequate support, farmers could also contribute to plant improvement in different yet important ways. The law should therefore open spaces for farmers' access to breeding material in order to fully harness the breeding capacity of farmers. However, as discussed above, different laws regulating PGRFA do not take into account farmers' roles and needs in breeding activities and do not view them as breeders. Thus, there is a need to accommodate farmer-breeders in the regime of IPR, as well as of international access to PGRFA to ensure farmers' access to new breeding materials.

Intellectual property regimes, particularly patents and plant variety protection laws, increasingly constrain farmers' freedom to operate, while international access and benefit-sharing mechanisms do not guarantee their direct access to genetic resources for breeding.

In this context, legal certainty is essential to prevent farmers from unintentionally becoming entangled in infringement claims and to enable their continued engagement in breeding activities. This would require clear

80 Mooney (n 9).
81 Ghimire and others (n 12).

articulation of their rights to access, use, and improve plant genetic resources, including those under protection, and formally recognising their contributions as plant breeding. Legal certainty not only protects farmers from legal risks but also empowers them to continue innovating within their own terms, ensuring a more equitable, diverse, and resilient food system. To this end, the rights of farmer-breeders must be accommodated within both IP regimes and ABS frameworks, ensuring access to a broad range of genetic resources for further improvement.

CHAPTER 11

GENOME EDITING

Biotech at a New Legal Crossroads

Christine GODT
Professor of law, Carl-von-Ossietzky University Oldenburg

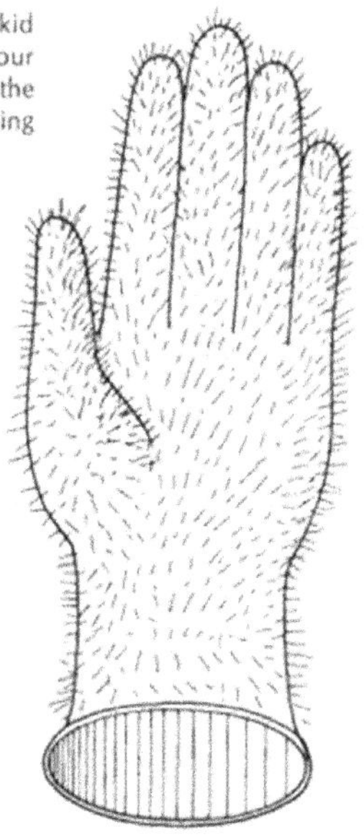

B4 Cactus Glove
When you take the kid gloves off, make your opponent really feel the difference by donning our cactus glove.

PREFACE

This article honours Geertrui Van Overwalle's sense of humour in which she finds inspiration in contradictory thought games, as mirrored in 'her' term 'inclusive patents'.[1] Carelman's 'Cactus Glove' is an example and triggers similar

---

[1] Geertrui Van Overwalle, 'Inventing Inclusive Patents. From Old to New Open Innovation' in Peter Drahos, Gustavo Ghidini and Hanns Ullrich (eds.) *Kritika*: *Essays on Intellectual*

associations. Some might be caught by the rather unpleasant anticipation of a forthcoming invitation to shake hands. Others may take the oxymoron as in invitation to enter into Geertrui's world of thoughts – interested in technological and societal change: can innovative garden gloves with spacers help gardeners to handle plants with thorns? This novel tool might be a solution for rose lovers and breeders since thorn-free roses have left the world of gardeners with twisted feelings … With this thought in mind, we enter into Geertrui's world of plant inventions, novel breeding methods, patents, breeders' rights and alike ….

1. INTRODUCTION

Biotechnology has attracted Geertrui's attention since her PhD,[2] and this fascination lasts until today – both for 'green' and 'red' biotech (notwithstanding that she became interested in all other types of technological development[3]). She entered the debate when classical genetic engineering was at its heights, and followed the evolving technology ever since, reaching from stem cell research to gen-editing, synthetic biology and COVID-19-vaccines. The licensing conundrum[4] around CRISPR-Cas as leading technique of gene-editing[5] suggests itself to become a splendid practise exercise for Geertrui's most influential academic idea, the patent clearinghouse[6] (thus expanding existing sharing platforms such as Addgene[7]) and

Property (vol. 1 Edward Elgar 2015) 206–277; Geertrui Van Overwalle, 'Plant Patents: From Exclusivity to Inclusivity' (2017) 85 De Industriële Eigendom 29–32.

2 Geertrui Van Overwalle, *The Legal Protection of Biotechnological Inventions in Europe and the United States* (Leuven University Press 1997). I had read this piece on a greyhound ride through Maryland in 1998, prior to meeting her in person at a conference in Tübingen in October 2002.

3 Including 3D-printing, Geertrui Van Overwalle and Reinout Leys, '3D Printing and Patent Law: A Disruptive Technology Disrupting Patent Law?' (2017) 48 International Review of Intellectual Property and Competition Law (IIC) 504–537.

4 Jorge L. Contreras and Jacob S. Sherkow, 'CRISP, surrogate licensing, and scientific discovery' (2017) 355 Science, 698, 699; see also Daria Kim, Reto M. Hilty, Elisabeth Hofmeister, Peter R. Slowinski, Miriam Steinhart, CRISPR/Cas Technology and Innovation: Mapping patent law issues, Max Planck Institute for Innovation and Competition Research Paper No. 22-06 (2022) 21 et seq.

5 Agnes Ricroch, 'CRISPR Processes Patents in Green Biotechnology: Collaborative Licensing Models', in Agnes Ricroch et al. (eds.) *A Roadmap for Plant Genome Editing* (Springer 2024) 453-470; Ulrich Storz, 'The CRISPR Cas patent files, part 1: Cas9 – Where to we stand at the 10 year half-time?' (2024) 379 Journal of Biotechnology 46–52; Christine Godt, 'Technology, Patents and Markets: The Implied Lessons of the EU Commission`s Intervention in the Broccoli/ Tomatoes Case of 2016 for Modern (Plant) Genome Editing' (2018) 49 IIC 512–535.

6 Geertrui Van Overwalle (ed.) *Gene Patents and Collaborative Licensing Mechanisms. Patent Pools, Clearinghouses, Open Source Models and Liability Regimes* (Cambridge University Press 2009).

7 www.addgene.org, accessed 18 May 2025. See also Ricroch 2024 (n 5) 460.

statutory use rights.[8] These publications stem from her particular double, mutually reinforcing interest in theory and practise. The theory interest is best mirrored by her article in the final publication of the project 'Boundaries of Information Property' in 2022.[9] Her interest in practise is expressed by numerous practical proposals,[10] her support to legislators,[11] and her engagement in numerous expert groups, inter alia the European Commission's expert groups on stem cells,[12] the European Parliament's export report on how the European patent system can be improved,[13] the Council's initiative to improve sustainable plant protection.[14]

This present article picks up her interest in regulation theory and will focus on plant gene-editing (thus leaves the field of 'red biotech' out). It addresses the debate which aspires to consolidate the regulatory landscape. Some are limited to propose the merging of plant patents and breeders rights,[15] others reach further to also integrate the assignment of IP rights (patents and breeder rights), market authorisation and access and benefit sharing (ABS).[16] Due to digitalisation and high through-put genome sequencing, databank protection[17] and trade secrets[18] have recently joined the debate, propelling the urge of CBD-ABS reforms.[19]

---

8 Geertrui Van Overwalle, 'Turning patent swords into shares' (2010) 330 Science 1630.

9 Geertrui Van Overwalle, 'Regulation Theory and Intellectual Property Law' in Christine Godt, Geertrui Van Overwalle, Lucie Guibault, Deryck Beyleveld (eds.) *Boundaries of Information Property* (Intersentia 2022).

10 The author's favourite: Van Overwalle 2010 (n 8).

11 Central language for amendments of the Belgium Patent Act can be traced back to Geertrui Van Overwalle.

12 Geertrui Van Overwalle, *Study on the Patenting of Inventions Related to Human Stem Cell Research* (2002) European Communities, available at SSRN, https://ssrn.com/abstract=1720002, accessed 18 May 2025.

13 EP-STOA, *Policy options for the improvement of the European patent system* (2007) Doc. No. IP/A/STOA/FWC/2005-28/SC16.

14 Launched by the Dutch Presidency of the European Council in 2016, https://web.archive.org/web/20160701100619/http://english.eu2016.nl/latest/news/2016/06/28/eu-to-accelerat e-sustainable-plant-protection, accessed 18 May 2025.

15 Axel Metzger and Herbert Zech, 'A Comprehensive Approach to Plant Variety Rights and Patents in the Field of Innovative Plants' in Christine Godt and Matthias Lamping (eds) *A Critical Mind* (Springer 2023), 619.

16 Michael Kock, *Intellectual Property Protection for Plant Related Innovation-Fit for Future?* (Springer 2022) 348 et seq.

17 Martin R. F. Senftleben, *Study on EU copyright and related rights and access and reuse of data*, Independent Expert Report commissioned by the European Commission, DG Research and Innovation, 2022. https://data.europa.eu/doi/10.2777/78973, accessed 29 May 2024.

18 Jacob S. Sherkow, 'The Myth of DNA Trade Secrets' (2024) 75 University of California Law Journal 1047–1096.

19 The COP15-CBD decided (in Montreal/Kunming) on Dec. 18, 2022 to open negotiations about a multilateral benefit sharing fund on digital sequence data (a 'placeholder terms') CBD/COP/15/30. With its decision CBD/COP/DEC/15/9, the COP clearly stated that DSI is within the scope of the Nagoya-Protocol and put an end to the debate *if* DSI is covered (see only Matthias Spranger, Expert opinion on the applicability of the Convention on Biological

Even the European Parliament jumped onto the bandwagon with its proposal to link the schemes of patents and market authorization. On 7 February 2024, the Parliament conditioned its approval to alleviate market access of gene edited plants by requiring the exclusion of patentability.[20]

This contribution is limited to a comment, triggered by some recent experiences.[21] The article proceeds as follows. It first outlines the regulatory challenges raised by gen-editing (2). It then discusses two far-reaching proposals (3), which are subsequently reflected under three arguments which ponder about the interrelations of the IP-system and approval regulations (4). The final chapter (5) asks how legal change comes about – and which role academic expertise plays in this process.

2. REGULATORY CHALLENGES OF GENE EDITING

In contrast to classical 'genetic engineering', gene-editing techniques such as CRISPR-Cas[22] purport to not introduce 'foreign' DNA into a cell,[23] but being limited to cutting out or duplicating existing DNA frames – thus mimicking

Diversity and the Nagoya Protocol to digital sequence information, submitted on behalf of the German Federal Ministry of Education and Research, Berlin 2017). On the international debate see Chris H.C. Lyal, 'Digital Sequence Information on Genetic Resources and the Convention on Biological Diversity' in Evanson Chege Kamau (ed.) *Global Transformations in the Use of Biodiversity for Research and Development* (Springer 2022) 589-619. Under this new umbrella old questions – familiar to Geertrui – re-emerge, such as the material-information distinction in genetic material (see Irma Klünker, 'Die genetische Ressource als Immateralgut' (2023) Zeitschrift für Geistiges Eigentum 121). As to Geertrui's interest in the Nagoya-System: Geertrui Van Overwalle, 'Protecting and sharing traditional knowledge: holder and user tools. Governance of Biodiversity as a Global public Good: Bioprospection' (2004) 53 Intellectual Property Rights and Traditional Knowledge 585–607; Geertrui Van Overwalle, 'Protecting and Sharing Biodiversity and Traditional Knowledge: Holder and user Tools' (2005) 53 Ecological Economics 585–607.

20 Decision adopted by the European Parliament on 7 February 2024, Doc. P9_TA (2024) 0067.

21 The author served as member of the ALLEA Working Group: ALLEA, ALLEA Statement on Measures to Ease the Impact of the IP System on New Genomic Techniques for Crop Development (2024) DOI 10.26356/IP-NGT, and was member of an expert group advising the Federal German Ministry of Justice on the implementation of the EPO-EBA- decision in G 3/19 into the EPO examination guidelines.

22 Along other techniques such as zinc finger nucleases (ZFN), transcription activator-like effector nucleases (TALENS) and grafting.

23 Which appeared until recently grossly simplifying. Critics have insisted that process material remains in the cell and reported non-target changes to the DNA (see Christoph Then, NGT plants of the future: EFSA overlooked most powerful and risky applications, Webinar slides 24.4.2024, www.no-patents-on-seeds.org/sites/default/files/2024-04/2024-04-19_presentation_Dr-Christoph-Then.pdf, accessed 31 May 2024). Recent scientific publication purport that transgene-free genome editing be possible, see: Yang, L. et al., Heritable transgene-free genome editing in plants by grafting of wild-type shoots to transgenic donor rootstocks (2023) 41 Nature Biotechnology 958–967.

natural meiosis processes.[24] These methods are characterised as specific and time-efficient.[25] For the reason that 'no foreign' DNA is brought into the cell, pressure arose as to facilitate the regulatory procedures. At the same time, the claim for re-designing the relationship of the patent and breeders' rights system emerged (infra III.). While a conceptual distinction between random and targeted mutagenesis remains disputed,[26] it is unquestioned that targeted gene editing meets the basic patentability requirements. Yet, the current problem is to distinguish products emerging from targeted mutagenesis (which may include product claims) and products which emerged from essentially biological processes (which are caught by the process patent exclusion as clarified by EPO-EBA in G 3/19).[27] The practical solution, as suggested by the EPO-EBA, is a disclaimer added to the claim aimed to eliminate doubts.[28] As explained earlier,[29] the procedural implication is that the burden to prove a non-violation rests with the defendant. This is not in line with basic principles of civil procedure.[30]

Intellectual property and regulatory law are equally challenged by these developments. The patent landscape around genome-editing[31] is highly dynamic

---

24 'Targeted mutagenesis' is usually described as a set of techniques, which includes CRISP-Cas, cisgenesis (a modification of the genetic material of an organism with a sequence from the same species or one closely related) and intragenesis (a modification of the genetic material of an organism with a combination of different sequences from the same species or one closely related) and their food and feed. Targeted mutagenesis is usually distinguished from 'transgenesis' describing techniques that introduce genetic material from a non-crossable species.

25 See only: ALLEA 2024 (n 21) 1. Breeding process are expected to be brought down from 15 years with conventional techniques to one or three years.

26 Are rather old-style techniques of 'random mutagenesis' (chemical treatment, UV-rays, x-rays) 'technical' and therefore patentable? Despite academic criticism (Godt 2018 (n 5)), Part G-II, No. 5.4 EPO Guidelines (March 2024) still list 'random mutagenesis such as UV-induced mutation' as 'technical'.

27 G3/19, EBA-EPO of 14. Mai 2020, OJ EPO 2020, A119 – *Pepper*.

28 Part G-II-Nos. 5.2.ii and 5.4 EPO Examination Guidelines (March 2024). The open question is whether or not the disclaimers solution is functional. Doubts are raised by NGOS and industry alike, see on the NGO side: Ruth Tippe, Anne-Charlotte Moy, Johanna Eckhardt, Andreas Bauer-Panskus and Christoph Then, *Zukunft der europäischen Pflanzenzucht in Gefahr*, www.no-patents-on-seeds.org,(Juli 2023) accessed 29 May 2024, on the industry side: Natalie Kirchhofer, Julia Sauerwald and Jan Desomer (Bayer) Patenting plant inventions via the EPO after G 3/19, Cohausz-florack (July 2021), www.cohausz-florack.de/en/blog/article/patenting-plant-inventions-via-the-epo-after-g-3-19/,accessed 29 May 2024. Where doubts remain, a claim is to be refused (see No. 5.4 EPO Examination guidelines March 2024).

29 Christine Godt, 'The Appropriate Scope of IP rights in the Area of Genome Editing' in Tade Spranger (ed.) *Genome Editing under Gene Technology Law* (Lexxion 2021) 44, 51, 58. The author discusses the problem of shifting substantiation duties in violation procedures involving genome editing due to indistinct material. The paper was written for a conference in 2018, thus prior to the EPO-EBA decision in G3/19.

30 These concerns are shared by Michel Kock. At an expert meeting organised by the Federal ministry of Justice on 30.9.2021, he therefore proposed the following language: 'with the proviso that the plant is not exclusively obtained by means of an "essentially biological process"' (thus securing the normal distribution of substantiation duties).

31 Position Statement of the Max-Planck Institute for Innovation and Competition, authors: Daria Kim, Michael A. Kock, Matthias Lamping, Pedro H.D. Batista, Reto M. Hilty, Peter

and complex, not only since the founding patents were opposed, and litigation will take years.[32] There is consensus about the related problems.[33] As to patents, practical problems are predictable when license agreements turn out to be built on sand. Competition related problems are programmed where area specific exclusive licenses foster market dominance. Classical concerns of patent law have re-emerged: patent thickets raise costs, un-ease users, and risk to undermine the system. The under-utilisation of promising techniques prompts innovation concerns. Royalty stacking not only raises costs but also concerns that the patent holder exerts his or her power far 'through' the chain.[34] More specific are concerns of smaller breeders which fear to lose access to breeding material, of biological breeders who either fear the loss of their business model or deliberately refrain from using gen-editing techniques. Last but not least do consumers fear to lose their freedom of choice because of the lack of transparency.

As to the regulatory level, two distinct discussions have emerged. The first involves classical market approvals. Disputes have emerged whether or not gene edited plants pose a similar risk to the environment or to public health as genetically engineered plants. In 2018, the CJEU upheld[35] that also gene edited plants are 'genetically modified organisms' (GMOs) in the sense of the EU directive on deliberate release.[36] The Commission's proposal responded to this dispute.[37] It proposed the distinction of two categories: 'Category 1 NGT plants', defined as '[differing] from the parent plant by no more than 20 genetic modifications', should be 'considered equivalent to conventional plants' and be exempt from the market authorization requirement.[38] 'Category 2 NGT plants' include all other plants obtained through NGTs – for which the GMO-rules on the deliberate release into the environment persist. While the European Parliament supported the Commission's bifurcation, it substantially deviates

R. Slowinski, Miriam Steinhart, New Genomic Techniques and Intellectual Property Law: Challenges and Solutions for the Plant Breeding Sector, Max Planck Institute for Innovation and Competition Research Paper No. 23-16 (2023) 6 et seq.; Kim et al 2022 (n 4) 6 et seq.

32 Heidi Ledford, 'Major CRISPR Patent Decision Won't End Tangled Dispute' (2022) 603 Science 373; also Kim et al 2023 (n 31).

33 Kim et al 2023 (n 31).

34 Christine Godt, 'The Role of Patents in Scientific Competition, A Closer Look at the Phenomenon of Royalty Staking' in: Max Albert, Dieter Schmidtchen and Stefan Voigt (eds) Scientific Competition, 25 *Conferences on New Political Economy* (successor of *Jahrbuch für Neue Politische Ökonomie*) (Mohr Siebeck 2008) 151–171.

35 Case C-528/16, *Confédération paysanne v Premier ministre* [2018], ECLI:EU:C:2018:583.

36 Directive 2001/18/EC of the European Parliament and of the Council of 12 March 2001 on the deliberate release into the environment of genetically modified organisms [2001] OJ L 106/1.

37 European Commission, Proposal for a regulation on plants obtained by certain new genomic techniques and their food and feed, and amending Regulation (EU) 2017/625, COM(2023) 411 final.

38 This delineation is criticised for two reasons. (1) The number of '20' is said to be arbitrary. (2) The number as such is not indicative for risk. NGT plants that are substantially different to conventionally bred plants can become qualified as 'conventional'; many powerful NGT-applications would be exempt from risk regulation, Then 2024 (n 23).

from the Commission's proposal in that it favours a full ban on patents for all NGT plants, plant material, parts thereof, genetic information and process characteristics contained therein, 'in order to avoid legal uncertainty, increased costs and new dependencies for farmers and breeders'.[39] The Parliament calls on the Commission to draft a report on the impact of patents on farmers' and breeders' access to plant reproductive material, and for a legislative proposal to update EU rules on intellectual property rights accordingly. The Parliament upheld the February standpoint in its parliamentary reading on 24 April 2024. On 6 May 2025, trilogue negotiations started.

The second debate relates to the modern digitalisation of genomes which threatens the functioning of the Nagoya-Protocol on access and benefit sharing of 2010. This mechanism was originally envisioned by the founders of the Convention on Biological Diversity (CBD) of 1992 as a bilateral *do-ut-des* exchange between a 'provider' and a 'user' (Articles 1 and 15 CBD). The mechanism never functioned well. However, with wide-spread sequencing and expanding databases, this mechanism is inoperable. While the Kunming-COP 15 clarified that DSI lies *within* the CBD-scope;[40] the CBD-COP 16 decision 16/2 clarified that the utilization of DSI gives rise to benefit sharing obligations, yet voluntarily to a multilateral fund.[41]

While it is common to distinguish IP law and regulation on the descriptive level, Geertrui would not separate these legal areas on the theoretic level. She follows an understanding of regulation as a mechanism of 'altering the behaviour with the intention of a particular interest'.[42] In this sense, IP law *is* regulation because it provides 'property rights granted for a purpose',[43] aimed at fostering innovation (sic 'remedying market failures'[44]), implemented by those to who the right is immediately assigned, those who follow on,[45] and the addressees of exemptions,[46] linked to horizontal (competition law) and vertical (command and control) regulation.[47] Gene editing has evidenced the complexity of the regulatory regime and gave rise to several reform proposals.

39 EP decision of 7 Febr. 2024 (n 20).
40 Doc. No. CBD/COP/DEC/15/9 of 19.12.2022 (n 19).
41 Doc. No. CBD/COP/DEC/16/2 of 1.11.2024.
42 Abbreviated definition provided by Julia Black as cited by Van Overwalle 2022 (n 9) 34.
43 A term attributed to Hanns Ullrich, see Matthias Lamping, 'Exclusive Rights for a Purpose', in Godt and Lamping 2023 (n 15) 219.
44 Van Overwalle 2022 (n 9) 40.
45 Seminal: Suzanne Scotchmer, 'Standing on the Sholders of Giants: Cumulative Research and the Patent Law' (1991) 5 J. Econ. Persp. 29.
46 Two examples shall suffice: Out of the realm of patents: Van Overwalle 2010 (n 7); out of the realm of copyright: Senftleben 2022 (n 17).
47 Van Overwalle 2022 (n 9) 50 et seq.

3. PROPOSALS FOR REGULATORY REFORM

Among the many thoughtful reform proposals prompted by the conundrum of gene editing,[48] two proposals stand out.

Axel Metzger and Herbert Zech advocate a unified regime for patents and breeders' rights.[49] They identify the availability of a gene-type description of traits as the cause for overlapping protection of patents and breeders' rights which potentially undermine limitations.[50] They argue that phenotype and genotype descriptions need to be linked. At the heart of their proposal is the ambitious rehaul of both systems *de lege ferenda*. Their proposal is spurred by several observations; one is that hybrid varieties can enjoy stronger protection than patents if the applicant applies for the non-disclosure of the deposited parental lines.[51] They urge for the deletion of this type of secrecy opt-in. *De lege lata*, they advocate a broad interpretation of Article, 12 Biotech-Directive.[52] More recently, Axel Metzger finetuned his conception and advocated a limitation of the protective scope of plant related patents.[53]

Michael Kock goes one step further. He calls for an integration of three pillars, namely intellectual property rights (plants and plants varieties), market authorization, and benefit sharing under a single system of 'plant innovation'.[54] His analysis of the current system is threefold. First, he holds the parallel systems of patents and breeders' rights to be inefficient. Second, he considers (possible) IP protection, but (unlikely) market authorisation contradictory. Third, he criticises access barriers caused by the Nagoya scheme. Kock conceptualises the sovereign rights on genetic resources as acknowledged by the CBD as similar to IP rights.[55] His assessment would be probably even more critical had he known at the time of writing that the parties to the CBD acknowledged in December 2022 that also digitalised gene sequences are covered by the ABS-regime.[56] At the time

48 Most noteworthy Kim et al.2023 (n 31); ALLEA 2024 (n 21).

49 Metzger and Zech 2023 (n 15) 648, providing for a 'Type 1 right' with pheno-type description and (alternatively, but not cumulatively) a 'Type 2 right' for a geno-type description.

50 *Ibid.* 631.

51 Based on Article, 88 section 3 Council Regulation (EC) 2100/94 of 27 July 2024 on Community Plant Variety Rights [1994] OJ L 227/1, Metzger and Zech 2023 (n 15) 637.

52 Metzger and Zech 2023 (n 15) 646.

53 Axel Metzger, Rechtliche Möglichkeiten zur Änderung des Patentschutzes von Pflanzen in Deutschland, Europa und im internationalen Recht, Rechtsgutachten im Auftrag der Bundestagsfraktion Bündnis 90/Die Grünen of 3 Dec. 2024, www.gruene-bundestag.de/unsere-politik/fachtexte/patente-auf-pflanzen-koennen-begrenzt-werden/, accessed 18 May 2025.

54 Kock 2022 (n 16).

55 Michael A. Kock, Einf. D, in: Axel Metzger and Herbert Zech (eds.) *Sortenschutzrecht* (Beck 2016), para. 8 '*Faktisch wird damit die Möglichkeit zur Schaffung eines geistigen Eigentumsrechts an biologischen Ressourcen geschaffen, das in der Verfügungsgewalt der Ursprungsländer liegt*'.

56 CBD/COP/15/L.30 (n 19).

when Kock wrote his book, he considered digital sequences not to be covered by the scope of the ABS-regime. Thus, he not only advocates the integration of patents and breeders' rights but also proposes the integration of upstream access to (natural) genetic information and downstream access to markets. With regard to the integration of IP and Market authorisation, his evident model is seeds law and an earlier proposal of Miguel Rapela.[57] He envisions a 'holistic system', meaning that protection lacunae shall be remedied by general rules (envisioned as rules of the patent system) in order to 'avoid falling through the cracks'.[58] He projects his system as 'expanding' the protection for plant innovations.[59]

Metzger, Zech and Kock concur, inter alia, in the substitution of patent description by deposit or a sequence protocol, a joint abbreviated protection period of 10 years for market protection and market authorization, the acceptance of pbp-claims and extensions for product protection ('Article, 64.2-extension'), EDV declarations (including administrative dispute settlement), limitation of exhaustion, transformation of 'essentially biological process' from a patentability exclusion to an estoppel rule, the substitution of injunctive relief by a clear cut compensation regime for licenses as of right.

4. APPRAISAL

While I acknowledge the thought-provoking intention, I submit that both proposals go too far. I do concur on the *descriptive* level that patents and plant breeders right have converged.[60] I also understand IP law and regulation as interlinked systems.[61] I give Rebecca Eisenberg the credit for having first described patents and regulation as two mutually re-enforcing systems,[62] long before modern instruments of legislative market exclusivity and test data protection became discussed.[63] This description is confirmed by the results of the BIP-project which shed light on how exactly regulations shape the content

57 Miguel Rapela, *Fostering innovation for Agriculture 4.0* (Springer 2019).

58 Kock 2022 (n 16) 217.

59 *Ibid.*, 219.

60 Christine Godt, *Eigentum an Information* (Mohr Siebeck 2007) 69.

61 On the interface of IP and command-and control regulation, Godt et al. 'Introduction: Background, Methodology and Results of the Boundaries of Information Property Project' in Godt et al. 2022 (n 9) 13-16.

62 Rebecca S. Eisenberg, 'Patents, Product Exclusivity, and Information Dissemination: How Law Directs Biopharmaceutical Research and Development' (2003) 72 Fordham L. Rev. 477–491.

63 Bertram Häussler, 'Arzneimittelpreise zwischen ökonomischen Partikularinteressen und gerechter globaler Verteilung' (2022) Zeitschrift für medizinische Ethik 68; Carlos M. Correa, 'Test Data Protection: Rights Conferred Under the TRIPS Agreement and Some Effects of TRIPS-plus Standards' in: Rochelle C. Dreyfuss and Katherine J. Strandburg (eds) *The Law and Theory of Trade Secrecy* (Edward Elgar 2011) 568.

of IP rights,[64] thus rebuffing the contention that regulation and IP law are two disconnected areas of law. Yet, I draw inverse conclusions from these insights of interconnectedness. As far as inefficiencies are identified, these must be alleviated by complementary reform. The system as a whole is better served with a thorough analysis of the protective intents of the sub-systems. I therefore support any legislative proposal which enhances access,[65] corrects the too broad scope of patents,[66] and eases bureaucratic burden.[67] However, the consequence of these observations is not the merger of systems. Even if exemptions were integrated, as proposed, a merged system would strengthen even further the protection for proprietary interests and side-line the protection of counter interests, be they private or public.

My central argument is that a coalescence of distinct legal systems of law is under-complex. It is well understood that differentiation is the expression of modern complex societies.[68] Simplification is no end in itself, even if it were more efficient. As to the patent-breeders rights interface, one could equally inquire if the abolition of the double protection prohibition in the 1980s was the beginning of the systemic conversion.[69] For the alignment of IP laws and market authorisation, the different legislative goals are to be contemplated. For this reason, I also oppose the linkage between patent rights and market authorisations as bargaining position in political negotiations (as presumably being the case in the European Parliament). A quid-pro-quo strategy where property rights are bartered against safety interests do not meet the standards of

---

64 On the conceptual reflections of the BIP-project results see the individual appraisals of Lucie Guibault, Christine Godt, Geertrui Van Overwalle, Mike Adcock and Deryck Beyleveld, in Godt et al. 2022 (n 9) 33–147.

65 For this reason, full support deserves the proposals of Rapela 2019 (n 57), Kock 2022 (n 16) and Kim et al. 2023 (n 31) that essentially derived varieties have to disclose the parent lines in order to enhance transparency, both for the sake of further breeding but also for the sake of keeping the ITPGRFA systemically functional.

66 Most important remedying the unfunctional current disclaimer practise; the 'enabling' patentability requirement demands the disclosure and deposit of cell-lines (as legislated under Swiss patent law), see Kim et al. 2023 (n 31) and Kim at al. 2022 (n 4) 13 et seq. See also the reform proposals as to the patent's scope submitted by Metzger 2024 (n 53).

67 I therefore criticised the build-up of parallel (independent) and non-connected enforcement structures for the ABS-system, patent filing and market authorizations, Godt 2007 (n 60) 610 f; Christine Godt, Davor Šušnjar and Franziska Wolff, *Umsetzung des Nagoya Protokolls in EU- und nationales Recht/Transposition of the Nagoya Protocol into EU and National Law* (Nomos 2020).

68 Niklas Luhmann, 'Differentiation of Society' (1977) Canadian Journal of Sociology 29–53; the connected problem of (over-)bureaucratisation has remained a pressing problem. On the different theories of 'policy growth': Xavier Fernández-i-Marín, Markus Hinterleitner, Christoph Knill and Yves Steinebach, 'Testing theories of policy growth: public demands, interest group politics, electoral competition, and institutional fragmentation' (2024) Journal of European Public Policy 1–26, https://doi.org/10.1080/13501763.2024.2317358, accessed 31 May 2024.

69 On the historic development, first the revision of UPOV 1991, later the EPO-decision in *Novartis* 1999 see Godt 2007 (n 60) 66, 67.

a learned democratic discourse. What is necessary is a substantial argumentation about which rules protect which interests (and why a protective measure fails). I will restrict this brief comment to three arguments which support this approach.

First, against a central argument of Kock, there is no contradiction between opposing decisions which emerge from regimes with different legislative goals, in this case a system of proprietary incentives and a regulatory system of safety control. As Marvin Bartels explains, only where ethical concerns are involved, non-exclusion would send 'wrong signals' to potential innovators.[70] Otherwise, patentability and marketability are two different issues. Decisions about safety and risks depend on a peculiar mixture of scientific expertise and (fragile, temporary) majoritarian decision making.[71] The market approval system which by default prohibits marketisation is not legally contradicting the availability of a patent; it is a different legal instrument with different technicalities. Different policy goals justify different outcomes in single decisions. In addition, further exemptions under IP laws protect third party liberties and rights. Yet, where interests turn out be illegitimate or have come to an end, then legislation is to be discarded. But to my understanding, this is not the case here. Deliberations in expert groups such as ALLEA's Working group on NBTs and IP have unearthed societal interests to uphold parallel distinct systems.

Second, the first argument is not to say that parallel regulatory procedures cannot be streamlined. The 'concentration of procedures' is a practised technique in administrative law. The central question is not *if* procedures can be linked, but *which procedures, for what reason* and *how*. Rapela and Kock want to streamline the diverse procedures for the reasons of *congruence of result*. This argument is only sound for decisions which result in *one* decision. Where decisions are based on different decision programmes (sic: patentability requirements vs. market authorisation prerequisites), the result does not necessarily need to be congruent (infra). However, different procedures may very well be linked in cases where the responsivity of the sub-system can be enhanced by information transfer, in other words where the functioning of a sub-system can be improved. This reason was the driving argument for the proposal to link the ABS-system to the patent application system.[72] Yet, the EU eventually rejected the connection of 'ABS-user checks' with other administrative decisions as policy instrument

70 This is different for ethical concerns as explained by Marvin Bartels, *Ethik und Patentrecht* (Mohr Siebeck 2020) at 150.

71 A unanimous answer whether or not CRISPR-Cas is safe is impossible, Hank Greely, Why the Panic over Designer Babies in the wrong worry (LeapsMag, 30 October 2017), https://upworthyscience.com/much-ado-about-nothing-much-crispr-for-human-embryo-editing/particle-6, accessed 31 May 2024; this is in line with common risk theories.

72 This applies to those proposals which do not make the patent approval as such dependent on the disclosure of origin. See: Godt 2007 (n 60) 316; Godt, Šušnjar and Wolff 2020 (n 67); Thomas R. Eimer and Favia Donadelli, 'Paradoxes of Ratification: The Nagoya Protocol and Brazilian State Transformations' (2021) Journal of Environment and Development, 1, 10.

when it transposed the Nagoya-Protocol.[73] A rudimentary idea survived as 'Due Diligence declaration' at two 'check points': the funding application with the Federal state and market approval application (Article, 7 Regulation 511/2014[74]). Yet, non-submission or false submission is qualified as merely procedural, not materially linked to the approval, and only submitted to the sanctions foreseen by Article, 11 Regulation 511/2014.

Third, instead of 'integrating' breeders' rights and patents into one regime (labelled as 'liability regime'), a profound and sincere implementation of privileges is needed, inspired by farmers and breeders' liberties under the plant varieties protection. I therefore concur on a practical level that a language revision of Article 12 Directive 98/44/EC should be set on the legislative agenda. On the conceptual level, the widely used term 'liability regime' deserves a qualification. What is envisioned by the three authors is rather a property based FRAND-regime in specific cases, in contrast to a 'liability regime' as projected by Calabresi and Melamed (1972)[75] or by Reichman for the microbial commons (2011).[76] A 'liability model' deserves this name when the conditions of access are designed in advance by third parties or by regulation.[77] The 'integration' model, however, builds on the discretion of the owner and holds on to the proprietary model. Yet, a sincere conceptual shift to a liability regime has several implications. It reverses rule and exception. As carved out in our 'BIP-book' (2022),[78] the general rule *lex specialis derogat lex generalis* becomes the guiding interpretation rule, and property gets perceived as embedded in regulation.[79] Protective exemptions absorb more weight and have to be interpreted widely. Proprietary limitations (as e.g. envisioned by the European legislator for the mandatory disclosure of

---

73 In contrast to many 'provider states', see e.g. Brazilian Law 13,123/2015. Eimer and Donadelli 2021 (n 72).

74 Regulation (EU) No 511/2014 of the European Parliament and of the Council of 16 April 2014 on compliance measures for users from the Nagoya Protocol on Access to Genetic Resources and the Fair and Equitable Sharing of Benefits Arising from their Utilization in the Union, O. J. L 150/59 of 20.5.2014.

75 Guido Calabresi and A. Douglas Melamed, 'Property Rules, Liability Rules, and Inalienability: One View of the Cathedral', (1972) 85(6) Harvard Law Review 1089–1128.

76 Jerome H. Reichman, 'A Compensatory Liability Regime to Promote the Exchange of Microbial Genetic Resources for Research and Benefit Sharing' in Paul F. Uhlir (ed.) *Designing the Microbial Research Commons: Proceedings of an International Symposium* (National Academies Press 2011) 43–53.

77 Metzger and Zech (in contrast to Kock) envision conditions of access set by the legislator (dubbed 'compulsory' or 'access as of right').

78 Godt et al. 2022 (n 9).

79 Elsabé van der Sijde, *Reconsidering the relationship between property and regulation: A systemic constitutional approach*, PhD thesis (Stellenbosch University 2015); Josef Drexl, 'Legal Challenges of the Changing Role of Personal and Non-Personal Data in the Data Economy' (2018) Max Planck Institute for Innovation and Competition Research Paper No 18-23, at 5–19, https://papers.ssrn.com/sol3/papers.cfm?abstract_id=3274519, printed in: Alberto De Franceschi und Reiner Schulze (eds.) *Digital Revolution – New Challenges for Law* (Beck/ Nomos 2019).

the function in recitals 23 and 24 Biotech Directive 44/98, but technically not implemented in the regulatory part of the Biotech directive) gain more weight.[80] Contractual deviations from protective exemptions are invalid.

5. LEGAL EXPERTS IN POLITICAL PROCESSES

The tabled proposals do not only raise the question whether they are desirable. They also bring up the more general question of how legislative change is achieved in general. Who decides which rules require change? Which role does the law play in relation to science, technology and politics?[81] Geertrui made herself experiencing various ways of law making, ranging from classical formal party proposals submitted to national parliaments to modern policy development in the European multi-level system: a topic may be put on to the European Council agenda by the Council presidency, expert committees are set up to advise the European Commission to foster or to prevent legal change. She saw legislative proposals submitted by committed individuals which found a majority in parliaments without further ado. She experienced governmental proposals aimed at fostering science but lacking scientific language.[82] All these processes are initiated, supported, commented, informed, or obstructed by an array of professionals, academics, public and private (research) organisations and interest groups for profit and for non-profit.

From the bird eye's perspective, these discourses are multifaced; their outcome is seldom predictable.[83] Organised interests ('political parties') coerced in highly regulated procedures[84] meet rather un-organised influences of lobbyists and the expression of opinions from academics. All these fora obey different rationales.[85] Political strategies (driven by interest, not arguments) play an important role. External observers are astonished by institutional arrangements (procrastinated or flexible?) which allow the conversion of the meaning of a text through the web of layers of 'concretising' regulations (sic. in patent law from the text of

---

80 Article, 5 section 3 Directive 44/98 deserves a re-formulation, see Godt 2007 (n 60) 620, 631 et seq., Ingrid Schneider, *Das Europäische Patentsystem* (Campus 2010) 426 et seq.

81 As reflected by Geertrui in her contribution (Van Overwalle 2022 (n 9) 37 et seq.) in using the typology of Morgan and Yeung for the analysis of our case studies (B. Morgan and K. Yeung, *An Introduction to Law and Regulation*, [Cambridge 2007]).

82 See Van Overwalle 2022 (n 9) 41, at fn. 41.

83 The analysis of these processes (factors, relational weight) is one of the major fields of political science research which cannot be subject of this paper, see Xavier Fernández-i-Marín, Markus Hinterleitner, Christoph Knill and Yves Steinebach 2024 (n 68).

84 See only the ordinary procedure of EU law making as stipulated in Articles 289, 294 TFEU.

85 For a critique of mixing expert opinions with majoritarian decision procedures Christine Godt, 'Experts and Politics in Patent Policy: The Final Report of the Expert Group on the Development and Implications of Patent Law in the Field of Biotechnology and Genetic Engineering of the European Commission, 17 May 2016' (2016) 47 IIC 960, 976 et seq.

the intergovernmental treaty of the EPC/and interpreting EU-language down to Examination Guidelines).[86] At the end, the process can be described through various lenses. One is to describe these processes as collective streams of thought, coerced by legislative and executive procedures, manipulated by interests, sometimes based on convincing arguments, sometimes influenced by individuals who bring enthusiasm to a particular question and thereby change the course. For those who participate, these exercises provide a learning process which – as Geertrui experienced – can be a rewarding or frustrating experience. In most of these cases, they are time-consuming, often manipulated. Personal assaults can camouflage a political argument. Positions may be intentionally overheard, twisted or instrumentalised. Yet, however frustrating those exercises can be, there is no way around it: civilised politics which strive for legitimacy require to take in as many perspectives as possible. It requires individuals who withstand the pressure, and trust in the mixture of factors which determine an argument to prevail. As active individual, Geertrui experienced that every participation opens (new) doors and provides unexpected insights. It would be a loss if she turned her back to the legislative processes only because of a given retirement time thresholds. Her thoughtful input is dearly needed.

---

86 Examples are numerous for various legal terms stipulated in Article 53 EPC ('plant' and 'animals', 'essentially biological' etc.), broken down in EPC-rules 26–28, and Examination guidelines Part G-II.

CHAPTER 12

PROTECTING SWISS KNIVES AND PLANT VARIETIES

Niels LOUWAARS
Fellow, Law Group, Wageningen University
Former director, Plantum, association of seed companies in The Netherlands

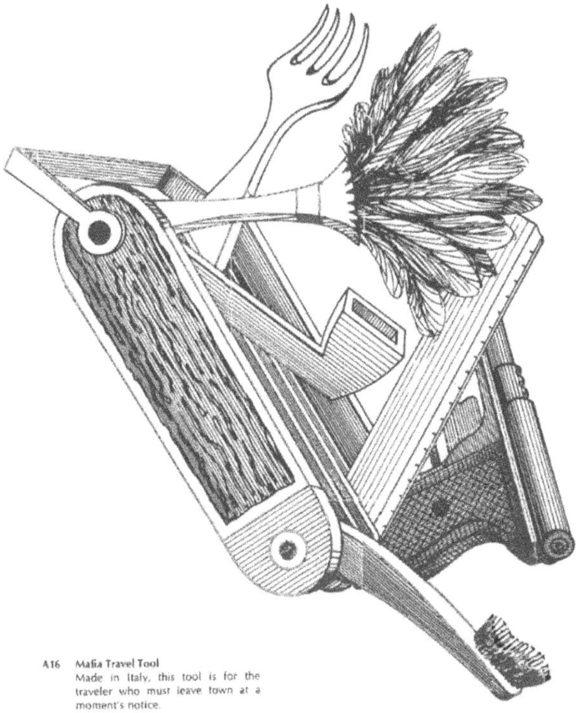

1. INTRODUCTION

The Swiss Army Knife is an interesting example to study the patent system, as it illustrates aspects of novelty and use. The inventiveness requirement may be at stake as well, notably when adaptations are made for particular user groups, leaving the principal design of the tool intact. The above Mafia Travel Tool may be considered a case in point. Does each small addition, which by itself may not be novel, warrant a new patent? This raises the question whether a parallel may be drawn with a situation in a very different field of innovation: plant varieties. In that area the general idea has always been that it is the combination of things (traits) that requires protection, since most components, on their own, might not always be new. This is a basis for Plant Breeder's Rights as the dominant IP-system which explicitly bypasses the complexities of the inventiveness requirement for protection.

Technological developments over the past 50 years have challenged the concepts of the protection of plant varieties and introduced the traditional practice of patent law into the arena of crop-related innovations. This has led to strong debates resulting in some 'repair actions' to the European patent practice, but debate is ongoing on how to maximise innovation in plant breeding. Such debates are not obvious on the protection of multitools. This makes a comparative analysis of the protection of multi-component tools such as the one depicted here, and multi-component crop plants relevant.

We conclude that specific wisdom is required to navigate the different interests and that such wisdom is hard to find when key academics who lived through the period in which the protection systems came to maturity, will no longer be available in academia.

2. HISTORY OF THE SWISS ARMY KNIFE

When Karl Eisener improved a multitool pocketknife and called it *Schweizer Offiziers und Sportmesser* in 1896, he obtained a design patent one year later. This was during a time when the Swiss patent system was not up to the international standard,[1] which benefited particularly its chemical industry. This design and the protection he obtained lifted him out of an almost certain bankruptcy since he was unable to manufacture an earlier design, the Model 1890, at a cost that was competitive with those produced in Solingen, Germany. Model 1890 was a multitool that could cut, open tins and service the standard Schmidt-Rubin rifle.

His workshop grew into the Victorinox company after stainless steel became available for producing the knives. Victorinox is still the 'Swiss army knife' brand, which comes in a wide variety of sizes and shapes, combining few or very many tools. The idea of a pocketknife that could safely be transported and that combined different tools, was not new. The Romans already had folding knives made of iron or bronze; the Vikings had types of their 'seax' that contained a knife and other tools as well. In the 18th century corkscrews had already been

---

1 Eric Schiff, *Industrialization without national patents: The Netherlands, 1869–1912; Switzerland, 1850–1907* (Princeton Univ. Press 1971) 87.

added by various manufacturers, including some Swiss blacksmiths. Different types were made for peasants, soldiers and craftsmen.

Therefore, Eisener did not get a patent on the foldable knife as such, nor for the multitool aspect. His design involved the new folding mechanism at both sides of the handle through which more different tools could be put to use. Over the years, Victorinox and Wenger, the two primary manufacturers, have secured numerous patents to protect various aspects of the knife's design, including its blade mechanisms, tools, and ergonomic features, and catering for a wider range of users. A long list of patents has been granted on these adaptations. In addition, the Victorinox brand has been protected with its iconic design of the Swiss federal flag.[2]

3. PATENTS ON POCKETKNIVES

In light of the foregoing, a brief – and utterly incomplete analysis of patents granted to Victorinox is relevant. We limit ourselves to the most recent ones and which are available on the 'Justia' platform.[3]

First, while the knife itself contains a portfolio of tools, it is interesting to note that some patents (mostly granted in the U.S.) relate more specifically to certain additional elements to the knife than to the knife itself, despite their similar (or identical) names. For example, two patents granted in 2006 refer to 'pocket tool' but claim, on the one hand, an additional 'memory and interface' element,[4] and the other, concerns the addition of a 'light'.[5] Another US application[6] claimed a complete media player set to the multitool, comprising 'a plurality of function keys, a monitor, a LED light, an identifier, a microphone, a camera lens, a speaker, a storage device, and an output/input device, and thereby the knife structure provides a knife tool and can be used as an entertaining object.'

A related patent, but differently framed, is a multitool aimed at a different or 'new' user group. This patent claims rights on a 'multiple purpose golf tool.'[7] Its abstract reads as follows:

> 'The invention relates to an especially handy and user-friendly multiple purpose tool for the sport of golf, which is light yet solidly built. Operation of the pitch fork is done with one hand, as well as the removal and insertion of the ball marker. The blade of a

---

2 See www.victorinox.com/en/Victorinox-Trademark-Protection-Policy/cms/trademark-protection/, accessed 04 March 2025.

3 See https://patents.justia.com/assignee/victorinox-ag, accessed 04 March 2025.

4 US7146667B2 – Pocket tool.

5 US7059741B2 – Pocket tool.

6 US20060087845A1 – Knife structure. Application abandoned. The applicant here was not Victorinox but an individual inventor.

7 US6413173B1 – Multiple purpose golf tool.

> new kind of tee hole puncher for hard or frozen ground also serves for cleaning the flutes of the golf club. It is also combined with additional functional elements like nail files, cap openers, and the like. The economically manufacturable tool can also include, for general use, a knife blade, a pair of scissors, a pincer, a toothpick, a ball point pen, and other tools as the case may be.'

Second, what may be striking regarding these various patents, is that the abstracts of a number of them are exactly the same. For example, US9517569B2 – 'Pocket tool, in particular a pocket knife', was granted in 2016 and includes the following abstract:

> 'The invention relates to a pocket tool with a housing, a compartment region, pins (11a, 11b) and an implement (13) interchangeably mounted on one of the pins (11a, 11b) by means of a coupling mechanism (22) and which can be moved by means of a pivot bearing (18) between an inwardly pivoted transport position and an outwardly pivoted functional position, which is mounted against a spring element and can be moved relative to the pin (11a, 11b) into an uncoupling position and removed from the pocket tool. The coupling mechanism (22) has a guide track guiding the implement (13) in the uncoupling position at an angle with respect to a longitudinal axis (68) of the housing (2) during its uncoupling movement along the compartment region.'

Surprisingly, US8528215B2 – "Pocket tool, in particular a pocket knife", had already been granted in 2013 with the same abstract. It is interesting to observe that the innovative aspects which may differ between these two patents do not feature in the abstract. Apparently, these innovative aspects were not important enough (??).

4. NOVELTY, INVENTIVENESS AND INDUSTRIAL USE

The concept of a foldable multitool pocketknife was not novel at the time of Eisener Sr., so like his followers, he had to resort to adaptations to the tool rather than the tool itself. Any alteration to the tool made it in principle comply with the novelty requirement even if the components that were included in the tool were not new, such as the LED-light – or earlier, a screwdriver or a pair of scissors. Their industrial use may be considered a sine qua non, as long as the additions such as the light would likely change the utility of the knife.

The main question I have relates to the inventive step requirement. Is it inventive to think of a little light connected to a pocket knife? It would in my view be pretty obvious to try to do that as soon as LED technology came along. Similarly, is it inventive to think about what golfers (or any other specific user group) might want from a pocketknife, or is that simple customer care to combine some features specifically for such users? It appears to me that the distinction between novelty and inventiveness is difficult to draw.

Victorinox is now thinking of making a pocketknife without a knife. Their argument is that carrying knives in public places is increasingly restricted in many countries. An interesting question would be whether subtracting a tool be worth a patent? It could be considered quite inventive to make a pocketknife without a knife. It would be a novelty for Victorinox, even though carpenters and plumbers carry multitools for their day-to-day work that do not include a common knife, but these are not called pocketknives. However, the fact that Victorinox publishes this idea probably indicates that they do not think removing the knife would is patentable just like adding a tool.

5. MAFIA TRAVEL TOOL

Given the above, let's turn to the multitool presented herewith. Can such a tool be patented? Comparing it with the patent on the multipurpose golf tool it would be certain that a patent application for this specific target group should be honoured. Similar to the golf tool, the 'industrial use' would need to be interpreted broadly. Similar to the golf tool, the inventiveness of the tool as such may be questionable, even though in this case there are certainly a number of technical challenges to be overcome. For example, one would be posed by the minimum width of the cartridge holder of the gun, which would likely challenge the pocket-size of the tool. Given that the individual components would not necessarily be novel as such, their combination in this multitool could convince patent examiners.

Further, such a mafia multitool may be in use already so absolute novelty can likely not be proven. However, but given that criminals are commonly not very transparent in the tools that they use, this design would likely not be published anywhere even when it has been widely used. This would mean that a patent application would bear a good chance of being approved on the novelty requirement. It would be wise though for the applicant to include broad descriptions of any tool, such as 'a pocket size multitool that can be used for menacing, distortion, forms of torture and other actions necessary for the trade of mafiosi.' It is likely that a person, skilled in the art and trade of that user group will be able to refine such formulation. Such broad formulation would reduce the risk of infringement on the concept – even though counterfeit is a common part of the business of some of these families. Using those terms in the application may cause concern though in relation to the '*ordre public*' and morality article (Article 53(a) EPC) but given that patents are available for guns and other dangerous equipment this article would unlikely block protection.

Finally, given that the multitool concept is two millennia old, described in Italy – which is the territory of the mafia multitool applicant – it is unlikely that the right on the fabrication of the tool would be dependent on earlier right holders. A member of the mafia who would obtain a patent on this tool interestingly bridges the underworld with the regulated society, which is however an increasingly common feature in several regions that the clans call home.

6. INVENTIVE OR NOT?

An invention should be non-obvious to someone skilled in the art. This word, used in the United States, is a bit clearer for an outsider to the patent world than 'inventiveness' as used in Europe. Is it obvious to include a revolver or a stiletto in such a mafia multitool, and tools to wipe surfaces at the crime scene? Or is it obvious to add a screwdriver or a led light to the Swiss knife designed for use by campers? If so, why are patents granted to such additions? The answer generally is that in hindsight a lot of things seem inventive, but that in inventor actually realised it and was the first one to make it work. However, it appears to me that quite some things that are new and useable are not necessarily non-obvious or inventive.

I consider it wise that the developers of the concept of Plant Breeder's Rights (PBRs) dropped the whole inventiveness requirement and simply used distinctness and stability as basic requirement for the protection of a new plant variety, and uniformity as a measure of stability. It released PBR-administrators from the impossible task that patent examiners are still charged with, i.e. to define inventiveness. Further, it is wise that they dropped the publication aspect in the novelty requirement for patent applications and replaced it by 'common knowledge' relating to the marketing of planting materials. And the most essential rule to stimulate innovation in plant breeding was of course that they opened up the research exemption to a full breeder's exemption covering not only research on, but also research with the protected subject matter with the aim of commercialisation of the varieties that result from the research.

That full breeder's exemption avoided the blocking aspect of patents as was experienced already in the early days of internationally coordinated patents following the Paris Convention. When Edison disallowed any research with his light bulb by competitors without his own involvement, it took the Dutch decision to cancel its patent laws in the late 19th century to speed up the development of a longer lasting lightbulb, with a wolfram rather than carbon filament and its mass production by Philips. Plant breeding is by definition a cumulative activity where the best plants need to be used as parents to create even better ones. A limited research exemption such as that in patents would stall crop improvement for lengthy amounts of time and would delay by decades the improvements that farmers and global food security so badly need.

7. ANALYSIS: A PLANT VARIETY AS A MULTITOOL

The distinctive feature of a multitool such as the Swiss Army Knife or the Mafia multitool described above is that it combines various functions in one tool. Similarly, we may consider a plant variety a multitool, combining many different traits in one plant or one variety. Plant Breeders' Rights consider the combination of (many) traits to constitute the protectable subject matter, a 'plant variety'. The strategy that any new combination of traits would be regarded a new product which requires an independent variety right worked without much debate as long as technologies were absent that could change any individual trait. Trouble started in the peaceful and profitable world of plant breeding when a biotechnologist could add 'his' new trait in all popular varieties through genetic modification. This could create independent rights over all commercially important varieties by adding the trait, leaving conventional breeders empty-handed. It even provides possibilities for renouncing breeders to use these plants as parent material for further breeding, following in the limited research exemption on their patent rights.

There was an attempt to 'repair' the fundamental aspects of PBR granting independent rights by introducing the concept of 'Essentially Derived Variety'. The implementation of this concept is still, 23 years after its introduction, heavily debated, notably whether it is the act of derivation or the genetic distance that should be leading in the determination whether a new variety is EDV. Similarly, the adopting of a repair mechanism in European patent practice in 2017, according to which natural traits cannot be patented (framed as 'products of essentially biological processes') has led to complex issues. First, it appears possible to 're-make with technical means' a trait that was found in the existing diversity, thus creating the opportunity to patenting it. A patent was granted on a trait that the inventor found in nature, described it at the DNA-level, and then identified it in a (man-made) mutant population. Secondly, even though a disclaimer to that rule reads that when the same trait of a man-made trait is observed in plants in nature, the use of that natural material does not fall within the scope of the patent. Cases have not come to a court but proving either or the other is bound to be complex, starting with the question who carries the burden of proof. Another repair attempt is the inclusion of a limited breeder's exemption in the Unitary Patent system, allowing breeders to freely use plants that contain patented components, but restrict the commercialisation of the newly bred variety when the patented component is still present. This provides breeders of a few crops with an important freedom to operate, but most breeders still lobby for a full exemption that includes independence of the new variety from earlier claims, just like in the Plant Breeder's Rights system.

8. DISCUSSION

The multitool aspect of plant varieties does not seem to shed light on the applicability of patent law on plant varieties. Patent law is not prefect and applying it to living plants and varieties creates a wide range of debates, including on the analysis whether such patenting would promote or frustrate the production of the diversity of new varieties. Such diversity is essential to provide sufficient choice of seeds for farmers in different locations, serving different markets. It also relates to the business models in which the different types of innovation are pursued. The investment levels in research and development in the breeding sector, based on breeder's rights, which reach up to 30% of turnover, does not seem to indicate that additional IP-protection through patents is needed even if such breeders need to invest in biotech-laboratories and -brains. Bottom line is that intellectual property protection creates a certain power in the market, and it is up to society how much power it considers optimal and what kinds of business models it wants to support. 'Repair mechanisms' likely introduce new grey areas and interpretation challenges; more radical choices may need to be pursued.

Whether this means that patenting plant traits (not just native ones) should be abolished, whether a full breeder's exemption in patent law is the answer to optimally sustaining innovation, we do not know. Alternatively, society could leave it to the private sector to remove the worst limitations of the patent system. There are already initiatives to increase transparency about which plants fall under patent claims, such as through the voluntary 'Pinto' database. This may allow breeders to analyse their risk of using particular plants as parent material in breeding. Another initiative relates to private licensing agreements, see for example, the 'International Licensing Platform Vegetable'[8] or the 'Agricultural Crop Licensing Platform'.[9] However, many breeders consider these stopgaps in a dis-functional (patent) system.

Turning to the comparison with the Mafia multitool. There may be additional considerations for market access of such 'inventions'. For plant varieties, this may be the 'contribution of the new variety to sustainability' (e.g. in production or the value chain), arguments that are creeping in, both at the discussion about market access (e.g. variety registration in the plant reproductive material PRM discussions[10]) and approvals under the GMO-rules in the 'new genomic techniques' debates in the European Union.[11] This is not yet the case for IP

---

8 Available at www.ilp-vegetable.org, accessed 04 March 2025.

9 Available at https://aclp.eu/, accessed 04 March 2025.

10 See European Commission, Future of EU rules on plant and forest reproductive material, https://food.ec.europa.eu/plants/plant-reproductive-material/legislation/future-eu-rules-plant-and-forest-reproductive-material_en, accessed 04 March 2025.

11 See European Commission, New techniques in biotechnology, https://food.ec.europa.eu/plants/genetically-modified-organisms/new-techniques-biotechnology_en, accessed 04 March 2025.

protection systems – just like the mafia-multitool, but pressure is rising on authorities to weigh other values than 'distinctness, uniformity and stability' or 'novelty, inventiveness and industrial use' in the granting of rights. Such added requirements are likely to make the system overly complex and reduce the number of varieties and thus biodiversity in farmers' fields.

9. CONCLUSION

Plant varieties have some similarities with multitools but also significant differences, mainly because of the biological nature of the subject matter that is to be protected. This requires wise, independent IP-specialists like Geertrui Van Overwalle, to have the interest and the time and before all, intelligence, to analyse challenges and creatively look for opportunities. This should lead to the necessary support to innovation in a pluralistic seed sector that is badly needed to secure the future of food and a healthy green environment and that can effectively fight counterfeiting, including by mafiosi organisations.

PART IV

UNLOCKING THE FUTURE: SCIENCE, KNOWLEDGE AND BIOLOGICAL MATERIALS

CHAPTER 13

SCIENCE IN THE GARDEN OF MIDNIGHT

Peter DRAHOS
Professor Emeritus, European University Institute
and Australian National University

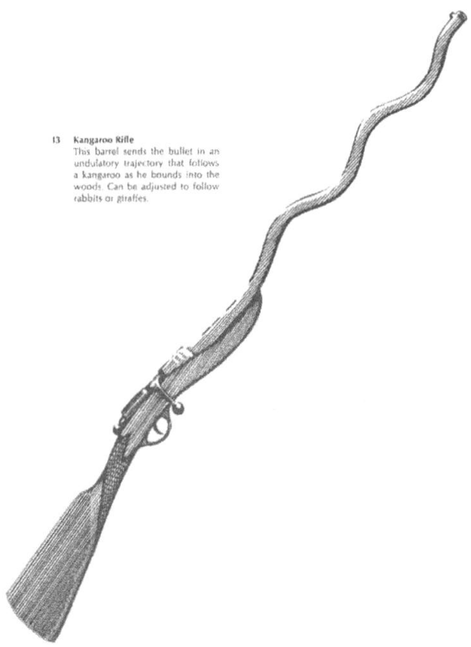

13 **Kangaroo Rifle**
This barrel sends the bullet in an undulatory trajectory that follows a kangaroo as he bounds into the woods. Can be adjusted to follow rabbits or giraffes.

1. INTRODUCTION

In 1969 the artist and designer Jacques Carelman published *Catalogue of Objets Introuvables* (translated in 1971 as the Catalog of Fantastic Things). Carelman's eye-catching drawings of his fantastic objects included a weapon, the Kangaroo Rifle. This rifle, runs the sales pitch, has a barrel designed to send the bullet in an undulating trajectory to follow the evasive manoeuvres of a bounding kangaroo. For purchasers of weapons by mail order in the United States the Kangaroo Rifle was probably more quaint than fantastic. By 1971 the Sidewinder missile had been in military service for 14 or so years. The missile's name came from the Sidewinder snake which tracks the body heat of its prey. Much like its reptilian namesake, the Sidewinder missile could generate the wave-like movement needed for lethal accuracy. For an arms lover if one really wanted to make quick work of a hapless bounding Australian marsupial the Sidewinder missile had to be the preferred purchase.

The Sidewinder had been used with astonishing success in a dogfight in 1958 between Taiwanese-piloted Sabres (sourced from the U.S.) and Chinese-piloted MiG-15s (sourced from the Soviet Union).[1] Despite being outnumbered the Taiwanese pilots were able to release the heat-seeking Sidewinders before the Chinese MIGs came close enough to be able to use their cannons. As the number of kills by the Taiwanese pilots mounted the Chinese pilots retreated. Not for the first time an innovation in weapons had changed the rules of engagement.

In what follows I outline why the link between intellectual property and weapons innovation deserves more attention. My purpose is not to trace the patenting of weapons. This use of the patent system has always been there. The Sidewinder missile is a case in point. After its invention in 1947 by William McLean, Director of a Naval Ordnance Test Station, it was kept a secret but then a series of patents were granted on the missile technology in the 1970s.[2] One can trace the links between patent privileges and weapons much further back; for example the grant of monopolies by the English Crown in the 16th century for the making of saltpetre and sulphur (important in the making of explosives).

In this paper I show how intellectual property and contract have been integral to the construction of an enframing paradigm of militarised science for the institution of science. I begin with a discussion of how the organisation of academic knowledge in Germany played a crucial role in the rise of the military industrial complex (section 2). The Manhattan project provided the U.S. with its first large-scale experience of using contracts and intellectual property to restrict the diffusion of sensitive military technology (section 3). The ties of private law, namely contract and intellectual property, were then used to bind the military, firms and universities into a system (sections 4 and 5). The cost of this comes in the form of an enframing paradigm for science that diminishes the capacity of science (section 6). University science finds itself in an iron cage. In the final section I ask whether private law tools can help science break out of the iron cage (see section 7).

Finally, a quick word about the metaphor in the title. In 1947 the scientists of the Bulletin of the Atomic Scientists (founded in 1945 by Einstein, Oppenheimer,

1 For a short history of the missile see Alex Hollings, 'The Almost-Unbelievable True Story of the Sidewinder Missile' 21 March 2021 Popular Mechanics www.popularmechanics.com/military/weapons/a35701747/sidewinder-missile-story/, accessed 4 May 2024.

2 See Stacy V. Jones, 'Patents' *New York Times* (New York, 8 March 1980) 29.

and other scientists) created the Doomsday Clock with midnight being the moment of a man-made apocalypse. I return to another version of the metaphor in my conclusion.

2. UNIVERSITIES IN THE MILITARY-INDUSTRIAL COMPLEX – ORIGINS

Whenever the political system of a state chooses war, the reaction from its citizens is manifold, ranging from passionate patriotism to conscientious objection. As the twentieth century showed, when it comes to killing on a large scale it is the reaction of inventors, especially scientifically trained ones, that really matters. During World War I the US patent office was flooded with suggestions for improving weapons, most of which did not show much promise.[3] Individual artisanal invention did not meet the industrial-scale needs of large armies. Science and, just as importantly, the organisation of science were needed to extract the gifts of Mars.

Fritz Haber was a German patriot, a chemist, a Nobel Prize winner and the first to have success with a large-scale gas attack in World War I.[4] Haber's leadership had been central to organising the provision of scientific solutions to be scaled by German industrial firms such as BASF and Bayer to satisfy the materiel needs of the German army. The stalemate in mud produced by armies dug deeply into networks of trenches had led France, Germany, and the United Kingdom to conduct small-scale experiments with the release of gas to drive the enemy out of their trenches. These experiments had suggested a gas attack was too difficult to control. Haber approached the problem by focussing on potentially deadly gases like chlorine rather than those designed for extreme discomfort, like tear gas. He also recruited as many scientists as he could find to refine poison gas into a usable weapon. By the time he finished his unit housed five future Nobel Laureates in chemistry and physics (including Haber who was awarded a Nobel in chemistry in 1918).[5] Haber brought his scientists together at the Kaiser Wilhelm Institute for Physical Chemistry and Electrochemistry to investigate the chemistry of poison gas, and to build a knowledge of meteorology. Staff rotated between the laboratory and frontlines, theory and practice entwining to deadly effect.

---

3 Karl Fenning, 'Patents and National Defense' (1941) 27 AB J 305.

4 For a detailed account of Haber's life see Daniel Charles, *Mastermind: The Rise and Fall of Fritz Haber, the Nobel Laureate Who Launched the Age of Chemical Warfare* (HarperCollins e-books 2005).

5 William Van der Kloot, 'April 1915: Five Future Nobel Prize-Winners Inaugurate Weapons of Mass Destruction and the Academic-Industrial-Military Complex' (2004) 58 Notes and Records of the Royal Society of London 149, 150.

On the 22nd of April 1915 Haber's science troops released 150 tons of chlorine gas on the frontlines near Ypres. Thousands of Allied infantry enveloped by a green cloud of gas experienced what the poet Wilfred Owen would later memorialise as 'guttering, choking, drowning.'

For the rest of the war Haber's institute became the centre of gas research, growing to some 1500 personnel and becoming part of the German military command. Out of its laboratories came other gases, phosgene, and then mustard gas. Van der Kloot is probably right to describe Haber's re-organisation of his Kaiser Wilhelm Institute as a forerunner of the 'Academic-Military-Industrial Complex' although perhaps the order should be military-industrial-university complex to reflect the real chain of command.[6]

In the U.S., some scientists, anticipating US involvement in World War I, pushed for the creation of an organisation that would bring system to science's service of the military-industrial needs of the U.S. Their wish was granted in the form of the US National Research Council in 1916.[7] Under an executive order signed by President Wilson in 1918 the functions of the Research Council included organising research on military and industrial problems raised by the war.[8] The first steps in creating what would become the world's largest planned defence economy had been taken.

3. THE (PATENTED) DESTROYER OF WORLDS

Some 36 years after the formation of the National Research Council, the Manhattan Project accelerated military-university cooperation. For scale and structure there had never been a military project to rival it. Over the life of the project some 500,000 people were employed across several hundred sites mostly scattered across the U.S., including more than two dozen universities.[9] The number of patents covering the atomic bomb, like everything else associated with the project, mushroomed. Within the Office of Scientific Research and Development (OSRD), which had been set up in 1941 to integrate processes of industrial innovation for military purposes, a patent group was established to manage the patent issues raised by the number of inventions coming out

6 *Ibid.* 149. For some historians the relational core of the US and British military-industrial complexes were forged at the end of the nineteenth century. See Katherine C. Epstein, *Torpedo: Inventing the Military-Industrial Complex in the United States and Great Britain* (Harvard University Press 2014).

7 For a brief history of the Council see www.nasonline.org/about-nas/history/archives/milestones-in-NAS-history/organization-of-the-nrc.html, accessed 14 May 2024.

8 Albert L. Barrows, 'A History of the National Research Council, 1919–1933: X. The Divisions of General Relations' (1933) 2021 Science 254.

9 See the facts reported in Alex Wellerstein, 'Manhattan Project,' October 2019 Encyclopedia of the History of Science https://doi.org/10.34758/9aaa-ne35, accessed 14 May 2024.

of the project. By the end of 1946, this group had approved some 2,100 patent applications for filing of which 1,250 were filed with the US Patent Office. As Wellerstein's detailed study makes clear, these numbers should be put in the context of their time.[10] In 1946 1,250 applications represented 1.5% of all patent filing applications.

The decision to use the patent system for atomic weapons invention was largely driven by Vannevar Bush, the scientist who had been appointed by President Roosevelt to head the OSRD.[11] In Bush's view the use of patents and contract by the US government represented the best path to inhibiting the spread of atomic weapons knowledge. Since under the patent social contract publishing the details of the invention is required, secrecy orders had to be applied to patents related to the bomb. The basic thinking was that a combination of exclusive government ownership and secrecy was the most effective way for the U.S. and the United Kingdom to control the future of nuclear power.

Ownership of the Manhattan Project's patent rights appears to have been a matter of intense negotiation. Vannevar Bush's plan for the government to own all the intellectual property had received Roosevelt's blessing.[12] However, industrial firms and universities saw that nuclear power would have important civil uses, most obviously in energy markets and so were reluctant to part with any intellectual property they either brought to the project or generated during its course. In the end four standardised contracts were used to settle the patent ownership and licence issues depending on whether it was a contract for research and development or whether, for example, it covered the construction of a plant.[13] In the case of research and development some contracts gave the government full ownership of the patent, but in others the contractor retained ownership, with the US government being provided with a licence to use the patented technology for defence purposes.

The diversity of contracting around patent ownership when the US government was involved in the funding and/or purchase of technology led President Roosevelt in 1943 to request the US Attorney General to report on the policies and practices followed by US government agencies when dealing with inventions made by employees or private contractors.[14] One bedrock principle animated the Attorney General's report in 1947 – the patent ownership of

---

10 For the numbers see Alex Wellerstein, 'Patenting the Bomb: Nuclear Weapons, Intellectual Property, and Technological Control' (2008) 1999 Isis 57, 78–79.

11 *Ibid.* 61.

12 *Ibid.* 66.

13 Richard G. Hewlett and Oscar E. Andersen, JR., *The New World, 1939–1946: A History of the United States Atomic Energy Commission* (Volume 1, Pennsylvania State University Press, 1962) 496-97.

14 U.S. Department of Justice, *Investigation of Government Patent Practices and Policies: Report and Recommendations of the Attorney General To The President* (Volume I, U.S. Printing Office 1947).

publicly funded inventions, whether produced by a public employee or a private contractor, should remain with the public. Among the dangers of allowing private contractors to acquire title to inventions financed by the public was 'undue concentration of economic power in the hands of a few large corporations.'[15]

However, the standardised patent clause for defence contracting that made it into federal regulations in the 1950s started from the position that the contractor could elect to own the patent with the government being granted an irrevocable and royalty free licence.[16] The principle of public ownership of publicly funded inventions became over time muted in other ways, one notable example being the passage of the University and Small Business Patent Procedure Act (commonly referred to as the Bayh-Dole Act) in 1980. This legislation created a starting position in which small businesses and non-profit organisations could be the first owners of inventions the research for which had been financed federally.[17]

4. HUB AND NODES

The early university involvement with the military was primarily a market in bilateral contracting in which individual universities or their faculty saw economic opportunities. So, for example, before World War I the US Navy and the Federal Telegraph Company entered into contracts for the development of radio technology for naval use, contracts which allowed the Federal Telegraph Company to build a patent portfolio. Stanford faculty were involved with and investing in this company.[18] World War II placed US defence on another plane altogether, one in which centralised planning and acquisition came to the fore. The U.S. transformed itself into the national security state.[19] The practical organisational expression of the national security state was the establishment of a defence bureaucracy administering defence acquisition contracts to support industrial innovation of new technologies by US firms in emerging areas of weapons technology such as atomic energy, computing and jet engines. As big as the spending on weapons innovation had been during World War II, what came afterwards dwarfed it. In 1957 approximately 50,000 companies had been included in Defence Department contracts to work on missile development (obviously only one area of weapons innovation) and by the end of the 1960

---

15 *Ibid.* 4.

16 Thomas F. Olson, 'Patent Rights in Department of Defense Research and Development Contracts' (1959) 47 California Law Review 721.

17 For a discussion on the effects on universities see Rebecca S. Eisenberg & Robert Cook-Deegan, 'Universities: The Fallen Angels of Bayh-Dole' (2018) 147 Daedalus 76.

18 Stephen B. Adams, 'Arc of Empire: The Federal Telegraph Company, the U.S. Navy and the Beginnings of Silicon Valley' (2017) 91 The Business History Review 329.

19 Daniel Yergin, *Shattered Peace: The Origins of the Cold War and the National Security State* (Andre Deutsch 1978).

fiscal year the Department projected a spend of US$3 billion on research and development, a sum that exceeded the spend by all the armed forces during World War II.[20] In approximately two decades a market in bilateral contracting had been replaced by a hub and spoke architecture in which the hub is a system and the spokes nodal actors such as individual universities or firms. The private law tools used to build this hub-and-spoke architecture have been, as we will see in the next section, contract and intellectual property.

5. CARROTS OF NODAL INTEGRATION

Tracing the web of relationships in US university militarised science is not especially easy. Lists of defence contractors are available, such as the list of the top 100 defence contractors to the Department of Defence, but the DoD is not the only government entity contracting for weapons innovation.[21] The large and small players in this paradigm are part of complex network relationships that can be housed in a variety of legal forms including research partnership agreements, resource-use agreements (e.g. allowing access to special testing facilities) and personnel exchange agreements.[22] A large prime contractor like Lockheed will typically have multiple relationships with the university sector. There are also fora in which universities participate that are cooperatively relational that may lead to contractual relations for specific projects.[23]

Universities can also enter the defence market using federal government programs aimed at helping high technology startups with research and commercialisation. For example, the DoD is a huge player in issuing grants

---

20 Thomas F. Olson, 'Patent Rights in Department of Defense Research and Development Contracts' (1959) 47 California Law Review 721.

21 Lists of top 100 vendors for many US government departments and agencies can be found at the following official US website https://sam.gov/reports/awards/static. For fiscal year 2022 the Department of Defense and DARPA have separate listings with 13 universities appearing in the DARPA list. John Hopkins is the first university appearing on the DARPA list, being ranked 5th. DoD has also published a list of vendors with contracts over $25,000. A search of this document turns up some 305 cases of university vendors (this includes different campuses of the same university). See https://dodsoco.ogc.osd.mil/Portals/102/Documents/Conflicts/2023%2025K%20covering%20FY2022.pdf?ver=f7CHvUlbGeU%3D, accessed 16 May 2024.

22 For a detailed discussion see Nayanee Gupta, Brian J Sergi, Emma D Tran, Rashida Nek, Susannah V Howieson, Research Collaborations Between Universities and Department of Defense Laboratories, IDA Science and Technology Policy Institute (2014) www.ida.org/research-and-publications/publications/all/r/re/research-collaborations-between-universities-and-department-of-defense-laboratories, accessed 04 March 2025.

23 E.g. the Universities Space Research Association appears on the DARPA list at number 91. The USRA was established in 1969 to facilitate collaboration between NASA and the university research community. According to USRA's website close to 500 universities were involved in its programs.

under programs such as the Small Business Innovation Research and Small Business Technology Transfer (SBTT) programs. In 2023 it made 3,140 awards to 1570 applicants totalling over USD 2.2 billion.[24] The SBTT program requires small businesses to partner with non-profit research institutions based in the U.S. Through this program universities can work on military projects such as improving the accuracy of hypersonic missiles using machine intelligence.[25] Keeping in mind that the SBTT program was established in 1992, it is likely that over more than 30 years thousands of defence contracts have drawn in thousands of US universities to work on inventing for the military.

Contract and the use of intellectual property rights combine to build the paradigm of militarised science with different forms of contract being used to incentivise actors to enter the paradigm. An important form of contract is the other transaction authority (OTA). The OTA has its origins in the creation of NASA in 1958 when Congress decided that the new agency had to have maximum flexibility to bring in the research resources it needed to overtake the Soviet Union in the space race.[26] The purpose of these contracts is to draw into the defence-contracting world the many smaller technology companies that are deterred by the compliance costs normally attached to government contracts.[27] On the issue of intellectual property an agency using an OTA can allow a contractor to keep the intellectual property in the technology even though the agency has paid for the research and development.[28] Integrating 'non-traditional commercial defence contractors' into the US defence system came to be seen as vital because from the 1980s onwards private research and development was driving so much of the innovation that mattered to the US national security state.[29]

For players like Lockheed another form of contractual enticement comes from the way in which independent research and development is treated in defence contracts. In that mythical place, the competitive market, the research and development costs underpinning a product are either recovered or not depending on the success of the product. Defence contracting is far less risky

24 See www.sbir.gov/awards, accessed 09 April 2025.

25 See e.g. the contract involving Ata Engineering and the University of Arkansas to work on 'Data-Driven Hypersonic Turbulence Modeling Toolset' www.sbir.gov/awards/207473, accessed 09 April 2025.

26 See Moshe Schwartz and Heidi M. Peters, Department of Defense Use of Other Transaction Authorization: Background, Analysis, and Issues for Congress, 2019 CRS Report, R45521.

27 On the issue of lower compliance costs see www.darpa.mil/work-with-us/contract-management#OtherTransactions, accessed 14 May 2024.

28 The DARPA website makes this point expressly. See https://acquisitioninnovation.darpa.mil/years-of-innovation, accessed 14 May 2024.

29 Jacques S. Gansier, William C. Greenwalt and William Lucyshyn, *Non-Traditional Commercial Defense Contractors*, University of Maryland, School of Public Policy, Center for Public Policy and Private Enterprise (2013) https://apps.dtic.mil/sti/tr/pdf/ADA613239.pdf, accessed 15 May 2024.

when it comes to such costs. Major contractors can recover their independent research and development costs in 'real time' through progress payments from the government, making such contracts a source of liquidity and profit for defence contractors.[30] In addition the contractor gains the benefits of intellectual property rights it developed through the expenditure of its independent (but reimbursable) research and development costs.[31] Allowing defence contractors to keep publicly-funded intellectual property rights is a practice that has been going on for decades in the U.S.[32]

In a world where weapons innovation increasingly depends on innovation with dual or multi-use characteristics (compare the atom bomb with semiconductor chips) the US defence system's monopsony power suffers some decline. Intellectual property rights have been a key tool to incentivise nodal suppliers of private goods to enter the defence system. Contracts allowing nodes to keep the intellectual property arising out of publicly funded research is part of the price of keeping the nodes integrated in the system. Contract in this particular case has a particular public ordering effect that moves beyond relational contracting and into an integrative function. The rents and the rights to rents delivered through contracts create incentives for the nodes to stay engaged with the system hub. Nodes have the best opportunity for earning the highest rents from being integrated into the US hub because it is willing to and does outspend the system hubs of all other nation states.

6. ENFRAMED – THE COSTS OF SYSTEM

Two big risks flow from the existence of a militarised system of science. One risk revolves around the failure to gain sufficient levels of knowledge to manage crises. A militarised paradigm of science carries an opportunity cost. It diminishes the capacity for grasping opportunities to build the knowledge we need for coping with the problems of our world.[33] Eisenhower warned of this opportunity cost in his famous 1961 address when he referred to the danger of 'domination of the nation's scholars by Federal employment, project allocations.'[34]

---

30 See *Contract Finance Study Report*, Department of Defense, Office of the Under Secretary of Defence for Acquisition and Sustainment Defence Pricing and Contracting April (2023) 154. www.acq.osd.mil/asda/dpc/pcf/docs/finance-study/FINAL%20-%20Defense%20Contract%20Finance%20Study%20Report%204.6.23.pdf, accessed 15 May 2024.

31 *Ibid.* 158.

32 Walter Adams, 'The Military-Industrial-Complex and the New Industrial State' (1968) 58 American Economic Review 652.

33 Stuart W. Leslie, *The Cold War and American Science: The Military-Industrial-Academic Complex at MIT and Stanford* (Columbia University Press, 1993) 9.

34 The text of Eisenhower's speech is available at www.archives.gov/milestone-documents/president-dwight-d-eisenhowers-farewell-address, accessed 15 May 2024.

The other risk flows from continuous cycles of weapons innovation races aimed at improving the power to destroy. Innovation in nuclear weapons has never stopped. Both the Trump and Biden administrations have pushed on with modernising the nuclear arsenal of the U.S.[35]

The problems here run deep. On Kuhn's account of change in scientific knowledge, one paradigm is replaced by another when the anomaly build-up in the paradigm is net of the puzzles it explains.[36] If we extend the paradigm concept to include the broader institutions within which the funding, practice and steering of science occurs, then the military-industrial-university system becomes part of the institutional reality within which successive paradigm changes in science have become and will continue to be nested. This institutional nesting is not just a point about the infrastructure of support for science. The system itself becomes epistemically directive. It operates as the enframing paradigm for successive paradigms of science. Each paradigm shift in science sets new puzzles for the young minds of science, but these new puzzles are nested within a large systems reality of a defence hub seeking to turn abstract puzzles into contextual problem-solving tasks. Quantum physics is an example of Kuhn's paradigm revolution in science if anything is. The enframing puzzles provided by militarised science for quantum physics appear to be many, one into which rival militarised systems will eventually pour trillions of dollars as they look to quantum scientists to use their knowledge to build war technologies, like better gyroscopes for nuclear submarines along with better devices for detecting them as they glide through our warming oceans.[37]

In a recent book John Braithwaite argues that independent universities are one important institutional idea for generating the knowledge we need to understand complex and interlinked crises such as war, pandemics and climate change.[38] The challenge, as he recognises, is to find ways to escape the integration of universities into the military-industrial complex. In the late 1960s students confronted MIT (sometimes referred to as Pentagon East because it was at the time the number one university defence contractor) and Stanford because of the research these universities were doing for the military.[39] At MIT the organisers were focussed

35 For a list of innovative bombs and war heads see Stephen Young, 'Why the Biden Administration's New Nuclear Gravity Bomb is a Tragedy' Bulletin of the Atomic Scientists February 13 2024 https://thebulletin.org/2024/02/why-the-biden-administrations-new-nuclear-gravity-bomb-is-tragic/#:~:text=In%20late%20October%202023%2C%20the,%2D13%2C%20a%20gravity%20bomb, accessed 15 May 2024.

36 Thomas S. Kuhn, *The Structure of Scientific Revolutions* (University of Chicago Press 1962).

37 For a review of this and many other possibilities see M. Krelina, 'Quantum technology for military applications' (2021) 8:24 EPJ Quantum Technology 1 https://doi.org/10.1140/epjqt/s40507-021-00113-y, accessed 15 May 2024.

38 John Braithwaite, *Simple Solutions to Complex Catastrophes: Dialectics of Peace, Climate, Finance and Health* (Palgrave Macmillan, 2024).

39 See Stuart W. Leslie, *The Cold War and American Science: The Military-Industrial-Academic Complex at MIT and Stanford* (Columbia University Press, 1993) chapter 9.

on creating a public discussion around the social costs of using science to build war machines rather than to tackle what today we call wicked problems. Two laboratories at MIT were heavily involved in classified work, the Instrumentation Laboratory and the Lincoln Laboratory. They became the focal point of rallies and confrontations. At Stanford the admission that for eight years the CIA had funded work at the university on electronic surveillance lit a blaze of revelation about the university's involvement in military work.[40] The Stanford Research Institute, which the university had incorporated as a non-profit entity, turned out to be holding defence contracts worth millions of dollars. For students it became the symbol of what had gone wrong with Stanford's values as a university. Eventually MIT divested itself of the Instrumentation Laboratory. Stanford followed the same legal path with the Stanford Research Institute. By the 1980s it was clear that this reshuffling of legal identities had done little to stop the building of war machines or the involvement of university staff with these new entities.[41]

As the evidence in the previous section suggests, since those protests in the 1960s many US universities remain contractually integrated into the militarised system of innovation. The dangers that come from cycles of intensifying arms races is why John Braithwaite argues for the adoption by universities of 'a simple rule that neither our brightest and best, nor our greediest and worst, should be permitted to deploy the knowledge-creation infrastructure of universities to invent weapons of war.'[42] In the next and final section I outline some of the obstacles facing the implementation of this rule and the possible use of private law to help meet the goal of the rule.

7. ESCAPING THE IRON CAGE?

Freeing the knowledge-creation infrastructure of universities from the military-industrial system is the right goal for which to fight. There are recursive globalising dangers in this US model of militarised knowledge development. As the model is seen to be more 'successful' in delivering innovative weapons of war, so other states will copy the institutional model so they also can be more 'successful', leading all states into the enframing paradigm of militarised science. An illustration of this modelling dynamic can be seen in the way the Bayh-Dole Act of 1980, which allowed US universities to file for patents on inventions supported by federal research funding, led some OECD countries to adopt similar rules.[43]

---

40 *Ibid.* 241.

41 *Ibid.* 250–251.

42 Braithwaite (n 38) 62.

43 David C. Mowery and Bhaven N. Sampat, 'The Bayh-Dole Act of 1980 and University-Industry Technology Transfer: A Model for Other OECD Governments?' (2005) 30 Journal of Technology Transfer 115.

Reversing the integration of US universities into the military industrial complex is, as the student protests of the 1960s showed, difficult. These days the starting point of most US universities is that they own the intellectual property produced by their employees.[44] Technology transfer offices now dot university campuses to manage transacting in intellectual property. Whatever knowledge-washing universities do for the benefit of their prospective students there is a reality that many of them are careful not to speak about – they chase money and intellectual property in weapons innovation. They do so in a more bureaucratically organised way and on a larger scale than in the past.[45] To borrow one of Max Weber's most famous metaphors, perhaps universities with their technology transfer offices have entered a military iron cage.

Acts of rebellion against the military industrial system, whether individual or through social movements, will always occur. Conscience will drive people to ask why their work is being utilised by military-industrial systems in ways that they see as breaching human rights standards. A recent example is Google and Amazon employees forming No Tech for Apartheid to protest the contracts that Google and Amazon have entered into for the provision of AI and cloud services to the government of Israel.[46] For these employees the contracts are 'part of a larger pattern of Big Tech fuelling state violence across the globe.'[47] Developing AI systems to kill human beings is easy with today's technology, 'a graduate student project.'[48] AI research leaders like Stuart Russell, who have been warning of the dangers for years, have been key to starting processes of UN scrutiny and possible multilateral regulation of lethal autonomous weapons.

Treaties are but one thread in a regulatory web for solutions to complex problems. To place the weight of hope on one thread is likely to see those hopes dashed. Acts of conscience have a role to play but conscience will direct individuals down very different paths of reasoning and action. Fritz Haber saw himself as being under a duty to invent a gas weapon of mass destruction. Over 150 scientists in the Manhattan Project did not want the U.S. to drop the bomb on cities in Japan and signed a petition to that effect.[49] The mathematician

---

44 For a survey showing this see Patricia E. Campbell, 'University Inventions Reconsidered: Debunking the Myth of University Ownership' (2019) 11 Wm. & Mary Bus. L. Rev. 77.

45 For the argument that the integration of the university into the military-industrial complex has deepened post 9/11 see Henry A. Giroux, *The University in Chains: Confronting the Military-Industrial-Academic Complex* (Routledge 2016).

46 Billy Perrigo, Google Workers Revolt Over $1.2 Billion Contract With Israel, April 8 2024 https://time.com/6964364/exclusive-no-tech-for-apartheid-google-workers-protest-project-nimbus-1-2-billion-contract-with-israel/, accessed 15 May 2024.

47 www.notechforapartheid.com/, accessed 15 May 2024.

48 AI researcher Stuart Russell quoted in David Adam, 'Lethal AI weapons are here: how can we control them?' Nature 23 April 2024 www.nature.com/articles/d41586-024-01029-0, accessed 15 May 2024.

49 Fred Jerome, *The Einstein File: The FBI's Secret War Against The World's Most Famous Scientist* (Baraka Books 2018) 88.

and game theorist Von Neumann, also part of the Manhattan Project, was very much in favour of dropping the bomb. He made the calculations around the explosive force needed to maximise the number of civilian deaths and was key in the selection of the Japanese cities to erase (although he did not get his first preference, Kyoto).[50]

If we want to draw universities out of servicing the weapons desires of military industrial systems, university employees should contest the claims of universities to own the intellectual property of their employees. My basic position here is that universities have demonstrated they are not to be trusted with that ownership. It is, I would argue, better to let those who generate intellectual property make choices about its future uses rather than letting university managers with the profit mentality of a Midas decide its licensing future. No doubt some researchers will happily take the military's money in exchange for delivering weapons. But if they wish to do so they will under John Braithwaite's simple rule of prohibition, have to leave the university. Other researchers, with a different view of what a university community should be doing, will choose differently. Everyone's decision should be made transparent, especially to students. Transparency is needed to expose dissembling by faculty about claims to be doing basic research. When Stanford students in 1969 managed to obtain around 100 contracts between faculty members and the US Defence Department, they saw large discrepancies between the claims of the faculty members to be doing basic research and the practical nature of what the military were expecting to be delivered under the contracts.[51] The enframing paradigm of militarised science allows academics to engage in a doublethink in which making a bigger better weapon counts as foundational research.

Tools of private law might also be employed to complicate the weapons acquisitions strategies of military industrial systems. Scientists interested in restricting the use of patented multi-use inventions for peaceful purposes could adopt the defensive patent licence. This licence mimics the copyleft style of licence in which, under a principle of reciprocity, free access by a party to patented inventions is conditional upon that party making their inventions freely available.[52] This type of licence could be used to support a community of scientists interested in patents for peace. Over time it might be possible to build a network across universities and firms (perhaps facilitated by disillusioned Google employees) that wished to see technology being used for peaceful purposes alone.

There are, of course, transaction costs in assembling, monitoring, and defending patent portfolios for peace. Perhaps some foundations could be

---

50 See Alan Bollard, *Economists at War: How a Handful of Economists Helped Win and Lose the World Wars* (Oxford 2019;online edn) chapter 7 https://doi.org/10.1093/oso/9780198846000.003.0007, accessed 15 May 2024.

51 Leslie (n 39) 248.

52 For details of the licence see https://defensivepatentlicense.org/, accessed 04 March 2025.

persuaded to help meet the cost. An interesting idea for reducing the costs of traditional patents for open innovation comes from Geertrui Van Overwalle's proposal for a new form of patent, the inclusive patent, a lower cost patent aimed at allowing a community to develop enforceable conditions of open sharing.[53] The problem with any patent reform proposal is, as Van Overwalle recognises, the potential for gaming behaviour to undermine it. The military-industrial system might respond by pulling on levers of state power such as compulsory licensing to acquire the technologies it wanted. Still, in a democratic society with a free press, a government would have to explain its actions to a wider public.

My own preferred position is for universities not to chase intellectual property rights at all. Rather they should stay focussed on generating propositional knowledge that, among other things, will increase the range of socially beneficial actions for dealing with crises such as pandemics and climate change.

8. CONCLUSION

US universities, through being enframed by a paradigm of militarised science, have become central to propagating two kinds of risks – the risk of things going wrong with ever larger arsenals of weapons and the risk of not producing the knowledge we need in times of crisis. Other countries in the name of innovation will likely follow the U.S. in building this enframing model. A simple rule for researchers not to work on the fruiting of knowledge in weapons of destruction should be a rallying point for those working in universities. Private law tools may be able to help researchers prevent the use of their knowledge for weapons innovation.

Decisions of conscience by scientists matter to our collective future. Scientists stand in the garden of midnight where there are a thousand different trees of knowledge, a thousand different futures to choose. Universities should be one of the places to help drive collective discussions of the effects of knowledge, not places where knowledge is used to facilitate a trade in military procurement contracts. Collectively we need to be open to the idea of not building some things from trees of knowledge. Fritz Haber's development of gas technology was refined and during World War II used in Germany's sealed gas chambers to murder millions of people, including Haber's close relatives. The Doomsday Clock does not have to chime in the garden of midnight. Midnight can arrive and pass peacefully. Everything depends on the wisdom we show in choosing trees of knowledge to develop.

---

[53] Geertrui Van Overwalle, 'Inventing Inclusive Patents: From Old to New Open Innovation' in Peter Drahos, Gustavo Ghidini and Hanns Ullrich (eds), *Kritika: Essays on Intellectual Property* (Vol. 1 Edward Elgar 2015) 206.

CHAPTER 14

REVERSE ENGINEERING AND ITS LIMITS

Lessons from the Nostalgia Clock

Rochelle C. Dreyfuss
Pauline Newman Professor of Law Emerita, New York University School of Law

1. INTRODUCTION

At first blush, it may seem odd to honour Geertrui Van Overwalle with a Nostalgia Clock, which moves in reverse to tell the time that was. She is, after all, such a forward-looking scholar. However, close examination reveals why it is an appropriate choice. As depicted in the *Catalog of Fantastic Things*, the clock has a statuesque stem and an extremely expressive face. Is that not reminiscent of someone we know?

The Nostalgia Clock also hints at how looking not only forward, but also backward, can stimulate creativity. Consider Albert Einstein, who served as a patent examiner before time was standardised. He examined railway clock assemblies. Each station had a clock system which was synchronised with the clock at the station ahead and with the clock at the station behind. That way passengers on trains moving in both directions could know the local time, as well as the time where they had been and where they were going. Is it not reasonable to think that Einstein's focus on trains hurling back and forth across time and space contributed to his development of the theory of special relativity?[1]

More prosaically, innovators often need to look back at what was in order to move forward to what can be. Indeed, looking at what was, can be necessary not only for technological progress but also for the accomplishment of other significant social goals, such as equal treatment, universal health care, competition, and sustainable development. Thus, another reason to start with a clock is because it comprises three types of knowledge: disclosed knowledge, trade secrets, and what I will call deep trade secrets. Since learning all three can be essential, examining the clock is a helpful way to think about how the law has treated efforts to acquire information from the past and what more is needed to insure we have the information we need to deal with emerging technologies and new problems.

2. CATEGORIES OF INFORMATION AND THE LIMITS OF LOOKING BACKWARDS

As noted, the Nostalgia Clock contains three types of information. While all three are important for multiple purposes, they are not all equally easy to acquire. Nor are they treated equivalently by current law.

2.1. DISCLOSED INFORMATION

Observing the Nostalgia Clock does more than allow us to tell the time that was. Observation also shows how the hands move, how the face is arranged to reflect time moving backward, and how the clock is mounted on its statuesque base. This disclosed information is enough to learn what the clock does, judge its value, and get a sense of how to put such a clock together. But looking at the clock does not reveal how it works. To be sure, if it is sufficiently inventive, the clock may be patented. If so, the patent will disclose the information that a person

1 Peter Galison, *Einstein's Clocks and Poincaré's Maps: Empires of Time* (W W Norton & Company 2004).

with ordinary skill in the art would need to make the clock and use it. That is, the patent specification will reveal the clock's gears, their relative size and the materials that connect them to one another and to the hands on the clock's face. It will also explain how the gears are arranged relative to one another.

2.2. TRADE SECRETS

But the clock may not be patented. If not, a person who wishes to learn how it works will have to take it apart to examine the gears and what connects them. Indeed, even if it is patented, taking the clock apart would probably be necessary to find out how to make it. If the patent is limited to the arrangement for telling time backwards, the winding mechanism may not be described. Nor would the patent reveal the absolute size of the gears and the connectors, or the way in which the pieces are packed into the clock's casing to create the exact figure depicted in the *Catalog*.

It would, of course, not be surprising if the originator of the clock objected to this practice – the effort to 'reverse engineer' the clock. The information, she would claim, is a trade secret. If rivals could copy that information for free, they could compete down the price and deprive her of the ability to recoup the costs of inventing the clock or make a profit on it. Future inventors would then be discouraged from wasting time, effort, or resources to make other fantastic things – or indeed, any subpatentable invention. That, she would say, is why both national and international law protect information that is not generally known and has commercial value by reason of being secret from disclosure through dishonest commercial practices, what the law calls 'misappropriation'.[2]

Unfortunately, however, for the discoverer of the Nostalgia Clock, neither national nor international law regards disassembling a lawfully acquired embodiment to learn how it works as dishonest or as a misappropriation. For example, the EU's Trade Secrets Directive specifically states that 'The acquisition of a trade secret shall be considered lawful when the trade secret is obtained by … observation, study, disassembly of a product that has been made available to the public …'[3]

Of course, the inventor of the Nostalgia Clock could take more forceful action to protect her secrets. She might lock the casing and refuse to distribute the key. The reverse engineer would literally have to engage in breaking and entering

[2] Article 2(1) Directive (EU) 2016/943 of the European Parliament and of the Council of 8 June 2016 on the protection of undisclosed know-how and business information (trade secrets) against their unlawful acquisition, use and disclosure [2016] OJ L157/1 ('Trade Secrets Directive'); 18 USC §1839 (3); Article 39.2 Agreement on Trade-Related Aspects of Intellectual Property Rights (TRIPS Agreement) (15 April 1994).

[3] Article 3(1)(b) Trade Secrets Directive.

to see the gears and how they are arranged. That certainly sounds dishonest. And if the inventor had created a modern Nostalgia Clock, one that relied on software, she could refuse to distribute the source code. The reverse engineer would then have to make copies of the object code – which may be protected by copyright – and work with it on a computer to learn its functionality. Those activities similarly do not sound above board.

But even in these contexts, reverse engineering is not actionable. For example, in *Chicago Lock v Fanberg*,[4] the plaintiff made locks for use on vending and bill-changing machines and provided keys only to purchasers. But locksmiths could pick the locks, observe the tumbler configurations, make their own keys, and associate the configurations with the serial numbers on the locks. The plaintiff sued when the defendant compiled a manual of these configurations and their associated serial numbers, which it then sold to locksmiths – and to anyone else wishing to obtain keys to open the plaintiff's locks. The court agreed with the plaintiff that the information inside the locks was a trade secret. Nonetheless, it held that 'so-called reverse engineering, that is, starting with the known product and working backward to divine the process' is fair and honest even when it involves picking the locks, except in situations (not present in the case) where the defendant owed a duty of confidentiality to the plaintiff.[5] To find otherwise, the court reasoned, would essentially give the plaintiff a monopoly without his having done the inventive work required to merit a patent. Similarly, the Software Directive provides that '[t]he person having a right to use a copy of a computer program shall be entitled, without the authorisation of the rightholder, to observe, study or test the functioning of the program in order to determine the ideas and principles which underlie any element of the program.'[6] Moreover, the Directive allows code to be reproduced to extract the information necessary to achieve interoperability.[7]

Several rationales underlie this approach. First, there is the matter of fairness. As the *Chicago Lock* court noted, trade secret holders typically will not have advanced a technology enough to merit the exclusivity associated with patent protection. Thus, they should not receive equivalent protection. Moreover, patent rights can be acquired only by revealing the information the public needs to make and use the invention after patent expiration. If trade secrets could not be reverse engineered, they would fail to give the public that knowledge. In other words, there would be no quid pro quo to justify exclusivity.[8]

---

4 676 F.2d 400 (9th Cir 1982).

5 *Ibid.*, 400.

6 Article 5(3) Directive 2009/24/EC of the European Parliament and of the Council of 23 April 2009 on the legal protection of computer programs [2009] OJ L111/16.

7 *Ibid.*, Article 6.1.

8 Pamela Samuelson and Suzanne Scotchmer, 'The Law and Economics of Reverse Engineering' (2002) 111 Yale Law Journal 1575, 1582–84.

Second, as an economic matter, it is not always the case that the reverse engineer is a free rider. When the cost of reverse engineering is high (such as when inventors take forceful action to protect against it), the reverse engineer will compete with the originator on a fairly level playing field. Indeed, where the costs of invention and reverse engineering are not comparable – when the first work is extremely inventive and much more expensive to create than to reverse engineer, or when the work is very cheaply copied – other law may step in to protect the creator. As the *Chicago Lock* court noted, there is patent law; there is also copyright law. In some circumstances, the originator may use technological protection measures, and these may themselves be protected from hacking, for example by the US Digital Millennium Copyright Act (DMCA) and the EU Software Directive.[9]

Third and perhaps most important, the reverse engineer's objective may not be competition. After all, splitting the market with the originator may not provide enough return to make the effort worthwhile. Rather, the reverse engineer may be intent on offering an entirely different product geared to a different market, as in *Chicago Lock*, or creating products that interoperate with the original, as contemplated by the Software Directive. Advancing the art and revising it for new uses is clearly in the public interest. Significantly, even the legal safeguards introduced to prevent hacking technological protect measures include exceptions designed to release the protected information for uses that are regarded as socially important, such as to engage in security research, to make materials accessible to the visually impaired, or for interoperability purposes.[10]

To put this another way, trade secrecy law recognises that knowledge is cumulative; that without the ability to look backwards – to build on what is already known – progress would be slowed if not impossible. In the absence of voluntary disclosure, reverse engineering promotes technological development. It can also serve other important social purposes. As Pamela Samuelson memorably put it:

> 'People tinker with technologies and other human-made artifacts for a variety of reasons: to have fun, to be playful, to learn how things work, to discern flaws or vulnerabilities, to build their skills, to become more actualized, to tailor the artifacts to serve one's specific needs or functions, to repair or make improvements to the artifacts, to adapt them to new purposes, and, occasionally, to be destructive.'[11]

---

9 17 UC §1201; Article 6 Directive 2001/29/EC of the European Parliament and of the Council of 22 May 2001 on the harmonisation of certain aspects of copyright and related rights in the information society [2001] OJ L167/10.

10 US Copyright Office, 'Exemption to Prohibition on Circumvention of Copyright Protection Systems for Access Control Technologies' (28 October 2021) 86 *Federal Register* 59627; 17 USC §1201 (f).

11 Pamela Samuelson, 'Freedom to Tinker' (2016) 17 Theoretical Inquiries in Law 563, 564.

As she also noted, reverse engineering and tinkering create 'intellectual freedom to imagine,' protect autonomy, and can build community around a norm of sharing.[12]

2.3. DEEP TRADE SECRETS

Observing the Nostalgia Clock. and even breaking into its casing, do not, however, reveal all the information the clock embodies. Even if the reverse engineer can identify the metal used in the gears, she will not be able to determine how the metal was cut or tempered, what lubricants were used to reduce friction between the various surfaces, or the method adopted to assemble the finished product.[13] These 'deep secrets' have always been considered beyond the reach of prying eyes. Those who would compete with the originator must therefore figure out their own ways to do these things. That, in turn, raises their costs and provides more assurance that if there is competition, it will be on a level playing field. It also prolongs the lead time the trade secrecy holder enjoys, allowing her a period of exclusivity in which to charge supra-competitive prices, recoup costs, and earn a return on investment.[14]

That view about deep secrets has, however, always rested on the assumption that if needed, this type of information can be independently re-invented or serviceable substitutes can be identified. But recent developments undermine that assumption. Artificial intelligence (AI) is increasingly used to guide cars; to make decisions about important issues, such as pre-trial detention, entitlement to public housing and medical benefits, and placement in schools and jobs;[15] and, more recently, to generate text.[16] The quality of this guidance, the validity of these decisions, and the accuracy of the generated output all depend on how the AI was trained. The training data is, however, not disclosed by the AI itself. Nor can it be reverse engineered. Similarly, search and marketing data now influence consumer spending and shape markets. Competition is more difficult without access to that information. However, firms like Google and Amazon, who hold vast amounts of such data, do not disclose it. And it cannot be reverse engineered.[17]

---

12 Samuelson and Scotchmer (n 8) 565–566.

13 For an example, see the facts of *Christianson v Colt Industries Operating Corp* 870 F.2d 1292 (7th Cir 1989).

14 *Ibid.*, 1582.

15 Kate Crawford and Jason Schultz, 'AI Systems as State Actors' (2019) 119 Columbia Law Review 1941.

16 Mehtab Khan and Alex Hanna, 'The Subjects and Stages of AI Dataset Development: A Framework for Dataset Accountability' (2023) 19 Ohio State Technology Law Journal 171.

17 Amy Kapczynski, 'The Law of Informational Capitalism' (2020) 129 Yale Law Journal 1460, discussing Shoshana Zuboff, *The Age of Surveillance Capitalism: The Fight for a Human Future*

This problem is particularly acute in the life sciences. The treatment of patients is now often geared to the patient's genotype and depends on empirical data about relationships between genotypes and phenotypes. While a genetic sequence, like source code, can be reverse engineered, its functionality cannot be determined in the way that the functionality of code can be discerned by experimenting with it on a computer.[18] Whether the information is available thus depends on the decisions of the laboratories that do the sequencing. However (and despite scientific norms favouring dissemination), firms like Myriad Genetics tend to consider the information to be trade secrets.[19] Successful treatment also requires medicine that is safe and effective. But data on safety and effectiveness cannot be reverse engineered. Even if that information is disclosed, treatment is possible only if the medicine is available. Yet as the COVID pandemic demonstrated, even the waiver of patent protection for COVID vaccines did not create enough supply to immunise the world's population. The manufacturing information needed to produce vaccines identical to the ones approved as safe and effective was not revealed and could not be reverse engineered.[20]

3. REVEALING DEEP TRADE SECRETS

In many ways, the law on trade secrets mirrors the law of patents and copyright. There are requirements for protection (inventiveness; originality; value by reason of being secret); acts that give rise to liability (making/using/selling/importing; copying; misappropriating), and a limit on the period of protection (20 years; life plus 50 or 70; until the information is generally known). However, there is one crucial difference: there are public-regarding exceptions to liability for certain unauthorised uses of patented and copyrighted material, but not for deep trade secrets.[21]

Now that it is evident that deep secrets can be needed to advance knowledge and to fulfil the other purposes Samuelson so eloquently described, it behoves the legal community to consider ways to force their disclosure and enable their

at the New Frontier of Power (Public Affairs 2019) and Julie E. Cohen, *Between Truth and Power: The Legal Constructions of Informational Capitalism* (OUP 2019).

18 Jacob S. Sherkow, 'The Myth of Genomic Trade Secrecy' (2024) 75 University of California Law Journal 1047.

19 Christi Guerrini, Amy L. McGuire and Mary A. Majumder, 'Myriad Take Two: Can Genomic Databases Remain Secret' (2017) 356 Science 586.

20 Tahir Amin and Aaron S. Kesselheim, 'A Global Intellectual Property Waiver is Still Needed to Address the Inequities of COVID-19 and Future Pandemic Preparedness' (20 September 2022) 59 Inquiry https://doi.org/10.1177/00469580221124821 (noting that the problem persists for vaccines addressing new variations of the virus).

21 The TRIPS Agreement illustrates the point: there is a general exception for patents (Article 30) and for copyright (Article 13), but only a very minor exception for trade secrets (Article 39.3 for data used to obtain market approval of pharmaceuticals and agricultural chemicals 'when necessary to protect the public.').

use. There is already some progress on this issue. For example, many US states are considering (or have enacted) legislation that requires manufacturers to make available to purchasers the information needed to repair their products, including diagnostics that are not otherwise publicly available.[22] Presumably, such laws also prohibit the use of new-fangled digital locks, which blow the product up if an attempt is made to see inside. And as Chris Morten and Amy Kapczynski have argued, the US Food and Drug Administration currently holds as confidential considerable amounts of information that it has the authority to publicly reveal and which would lead to improvements to the safety and efficacy of drugs, vaccines, and medical devices.[23] Likely, the same is true for the health authorities in other countries. Morten has also suggested that there are many more regulatory bodies that hold socially significant data that they could be encouraged to release.[24]

Other laws can and should be revised with an eye toward making deep secrets more available. For example, patent law's disclosure requirements could be expanded to include manufacturing information. In cases where data is used to distort the competitive marketplace, antitrust (competition) law remedies could include disclosure of the information needed to compete effectively.[25] Contract law could regard conditions on sales and licences that ban reverse engineering as unenforceable. Furthermore, governments (and private parties) could engage in self-help. For example, criminal justice systems that rely on AI to make bail, sentencing and probation decisions could condition purchase of the AI on the release of the algorithms and training data used. They could then make the information available for examination by parties who wish to challenge decisions as biased or as inaccurate in other ways.[26]

Admittedly, revealing deep secrets could sometimes harm incentives to innovate. Thus, in addition to finding new approaches to mandate disclosure, the legal system must develop ways to govern the information that is released. In an article on reverse engineering, Pamela Samuelson and Suzanne Scotchmer

---

22 National Conference of State Legislatures, Right to Repair 2023 Legislation, www.ncsl.org/technology-and-communication/right-to-repair-2023-legislation, accessed 18 May 2025.

23 Christopher J. Morten and Amy Kapczynski, 'The Big Data Regulator, Rebooted: Why and How the FDA Can and Should Disclose Confidential Data on Prescription Drugs' (2021) 109 California Law Review 493. As states consider regulating laboratory testing services, they could also require disclosure of other information such as genomic data, Guerrini, McGuire and Majumder (n 19).

24 Christopher J. Morten, 'Publicizing Corporate Secrets' (2023) 171 University of Pennsylvania Law Review 1319.

25 Michal S. Gal and Nicolas Petit, 'Radical Restorative Remedies for Digital Markets' (2021) 36 Berkeley Technology Law Journal 617.

26 Mirko Bagaric, Dan Hunter and Nigel Stobbs, 'Erasing the Bias Against Using Artificial Intelligence to Predict Future Criminality: Algorithms Are Color Blind and Never Tire' (2019) 88 University of Cincinnati Law Review 1037; Deirdre K. Mulligan and Kenneth A. Bamberger, 'Procurement as Policy: Administrative Process for Machine Learning' (2019) 34 Berkeley Technology Law Journal 773.

suggested several approaches to governing information revealed through that process.[27] All are equally relevant to deep secrets. First, they noted that not all disclosures destroy incentives to innovate. Thus, they argued that the first step is always to consider the economic impact of the disclosure requirement (they would put the burden on the party resisting disclosure to show a detrimental effect). For example, some of the deep secrets noted above were not invented by the firms that hold them. AI training data, for example, often involves the use of preexisting materials. Requiring disclosure will thus not affect incentives to develop that material. By the same token, marketing data is generated by consumers, not the businesses that collect it. Moreover, some of these businesses had access as a result of network effects and lock-in, and sometimes, their own anticompetitive conduct. Analogously, some firms' unique access to genetic information resulted from their exploitation of patents that were later held invalid.[28] Since these firms had no right to exclusive acquisition of such information in the first place, disclosure should not be viewed as destructive of their incentives to innovate in their principal businesses, be it search engines, marketing platforms, or genetic testing.

That said, there are surely situations where the disclosure of deep secrets would have an impact on incentives to invent or could have other market-destructive consequences. Samuelson and Scotchmer offered several suggestions for such cases. One is a breadth requirement. Rather than allow the parties to whom the secrets are revealed compete directly with the originator, the authors would permit use of the information only to exploit markets in which the originator was not active. For example, disclosure of the method for manufacturing COVID vaccines would not have been destructive of the originators' markets if lawful uses of the method were limited to supplying the low-income countries that the originator had not entered. Under the authors' approach, adaptation and follow-on innovation would also be allowable when directed at applications remote from those of the originator. Or as Jerry Reichman suggested, disclosure of deep secrets (in his case, clinical data) could be accompanied by a liability rule that would require that recipients of deep secrets to pay a proportionate share of the development costs.[29]

Other limits could be imposed on the uses that can be made with the data that is disclosed. In their paper, Samuelson and Scotchmer discussed interoperability, which, as we saw, is also mentioned in the Software Directive. Use of AI training data could similarly be limited to such uses as challenging the accuracy of

27 Samuelson and Scotchmer (n 8).
28 Guerrini, McGuire and Majumder (n 19).
29 Jerome H. Reichman, 'Rethinking the Role of Clinical Trial Data in International Intellectual Property Law: The Case for a Public Goods Approach' (2009) 13 Marquette Intellectual Property Law Review 1.

AI-based decisions or investigating the source of bias in generated texts.[30] Essentially, this is the approach taken in right-to-repair legislation: the material can be used only to repair embodiments the user purchased. As sustainability becomes an increasingly important goal, the same idea could be used for deep secrets needed to reuse, adapt, or recycle products.

The public-regarding exceptions in patent and copyright law follow a somewhat analogous approach. For example, many countries' patent laws include an exception to liability for those conducting scientific experiments.[31] It is based on the view that permitting researchers to make unauthorised use promotes technological development, fosters industrial growth, and can lead to significant improvements in social welfare. For much the same reason, some countries have exceptions in their copyright laws for researchers who mine data for scientific and scholarly research.[32] Deep secrets could be treated this way too: the disclosure requirement could be limited to people who need the information to engage in activities that advance the public interest. Interestingly, Samuelson and Scotchmer suggested that once a specific use or user is regarded as legitimate, those holding secrets may disclose them voluntarily to avoid the expense of litigation they are sure to lose.

To be sure, more than just a new approach to revealing secrets will be required: a regime for sharing this information must also be established. As noted above, some secrets may be revealed only for certain uses or only to certain users. Some might be revealed only to users who promise that whatever they create with the deep secrets will be made publicly available for free or at a reasonable price. At the same time, however, there may be cases where recipients will need the strong incentives available under patent and copyright law to further develop the information they acquire. Efforts are already underway (including by our honouree) to develop law that promotes open innovation, private-private partnerships, and other commons arrangements.[33] These regimes may be adaptable to this use or form a starting point for discussion. In addition, there are already attempts to build the infrastructures necessary to improve the efficiency

---

30 David S. Levine, 'Secrecy and Unaccountability: Trade Secrets in Our Public Infrastructure' (2007) 59 Florida Law Review 135.

31 WIPO Standing Committee on the Law of Patents, *Exceptions and Limitations to Patent Rights: Experimental Use and/or Scientific Research*, SCP/20/4 (18 November 2013).

32 Michael W. Carroll, 'Copyright and the Progress of Science: Why Text and Data Mining Is Lawful' (2019) 53 UC Davis Law Review 893.

33 Geertrui Van Overwalle, 'Inventing Inclusive Patents: From Old to New Open Innovation' in Peter Drahos, Gustavo Ghidini and Hanns Ullrich (eds) *Kritika: Essays on Intellectual Property* (vol. 1, Edward Elgar 2015) 206; Liza S Vertinsky, 'Patents, Partnerships, and the Pre-Competitive Collaboration Myth in Pharmaceutical Innovation' (2015) 48 UC Davis Law Review 1509; Robert Cook-Deegan, Mary A. Majumder and Amy L. McGuire, 'Sharing Data in a Medical Information Commons' (2019) 47 Journal of Law, Medicine & Ethics 7; Brett M. Frischmann, Michael J. Madison and Katherine J. Strandburg (eds) *Governing Knowledge Commons* (OUP 2014).

of storing and sharing large database and to monitor their use.[34] As these develop, it may also be possible to ensure data is formatted in ways that permit only certain types of uses. There is, in short, no scarcity of ideas on how to govern deep trade secrets once the challenge to require their disclosure is overcome.

4. CONCLUSION

The legal system has long understood the value of 'nostalgia' and the need to know the past in order to push forward the knowledge frontier. Trade secrecy law has relied on reverse engineering for that purpose. But emerging technology, such as AI, and emerging problems, such as pandemics, demonstrate that there are limits to that process. Some secrets – deep secrets – cannot be learned by breaking into casings and investigating what is inside. And yet deep secrets are inherent in many modern technologies and business methods. They can constitute substantial obstacles to progress and to other socially valuable activities. In particular, they can block advancement on issues dear to our honouree's heart: genetic research, public health, and nutrition. Exploring how deep secrets can be revealed, used, and shared is therefore of increasing public importance. A study of deep secrets is also deeply resonant with Professor Van Overwalle's influential contributions to the scholarship on open innovation.

---

[34] Benedict Kingsbury, 'Attributive Justice in International Law: The Global Law and Infrastructure of Pathogen Genomic Sequence Data-Sharing and Benefit-Sharing' (2023) 55 NYU Journal of International Law and Politics 627; W. Nicholson Price II, 'Risk and Resilience in Health Data Infrastructure' (2017) 16 Colorado Technology Law Journal 65.

CHAPTER 15
PATENTING HUMANS

Dianne Nicol
Distinguished Professor Emerita, University of Tasmania
Member, Centre for Law and Genetics

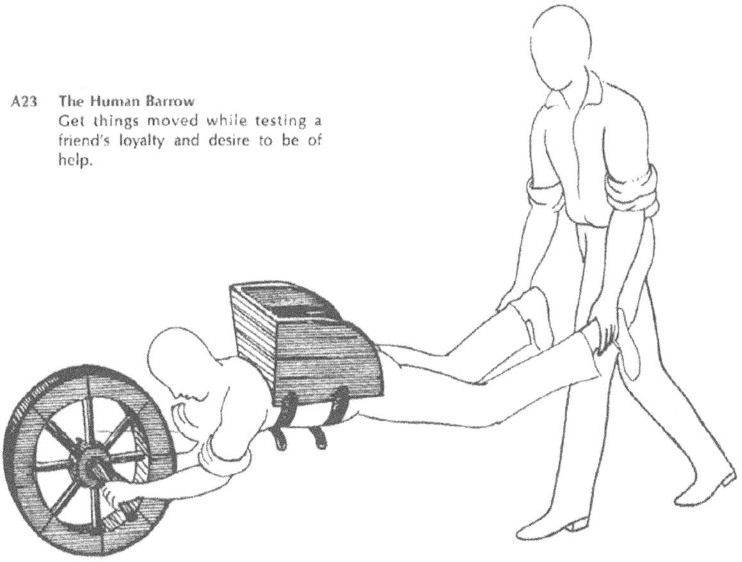

ACKNOWLEDGEMENTS

My work has been funded by the Australian Research Council (ARC) and the Australian Medical Research Futures Fund (MRFF) over many years. I particularly acknowledge my current ARC funding for *Reforming the Regulatory Environment for Innovative Health Technologies* (ARC DP180101262) and MRFF funding for *Developing an Evidence Based Model for Building Trust in Australian Stem Cell Research and Therapies* (MRFF Stem Cell Therapies Mission).

I also acknowledge my many colleagues and students (too many to list) who have given me great joy in my work on intellectual property and biotechnology.

1. INTRODUCTION

I am deeply honoured to be given the opportunity to write this chapter in the Festschrift in recognition of the incredible career of my dear colleague and contemporary, Professor Geertrui Van Overwalle, for whom I have the deepest respect. I am not at all surprised that she has chosen this intriguing challenge for us all: to base our chapters around images from the *Catalog of Fantastic Things*. Her innovative approach to intellectual property scholarship is exemplified in this choice of subject matter.

Over many years, our research interests have closely aligned. We have both sought to examine the ways in which the grant and use of patents can either directly or indirectly affect human health and welfare. Given these interests, it was immediately obvious to me that the only choice for me to base my chapter around was the Human Barrow. The theme of my chapter is patenting humans. I have taken on the challenge of writing on this theme via the vehicle of the Human Barrow with enthusiasm but also with some trepidation. At the outset, I must confess that mine is not the type of brain to engage in deep philosophical reflection on what it is to be human. Rather more prosaically, I start from the simple premise that human beings as such cannot be patentable because it would be immoral to allow such patents to issue. I examine the existence, origin, nature and scope of the exclusion of humans from patenting based on morality in three jurisdictions: the US, the European Union (and other member countries of the European Patent Convention[1]) and my own country, Australia. I have chosen these three jurisdictions not just because of my familiarity with them, but also because of the ways in which they differ in addressing this issue of patenting humans. The one common theme I highlight is that in each jurisdiction setting boundaries on the exclusion of humans from patenting based on morality has been extremely challenging.

Many intellectual property scholars have written on the topic of morality in patent law. It would be impossible for me to even try to summarise, let alone analyse the totality of this scholarly debate in this small contribution. Instead, I have chosen to rely on the works of a small number of academic commentators including some of the leading intellectual property scholars in Europe and the US, together with primary sources. One lingering question is why I would even try to add to this body of academic literature here. My reason for doing so is because of the broad array of new reproductive technologies that are currently emerging. Each has the potential to pose significant challenges around the

1 Convention on the Grant of European Patents (EPC) of 5 October 1973, as revised by the Act revising Art. 63 EPC of 17 December 1991 and the Act revising the EPC of 29 November 2000.

theme of patenting humans. Techniques such as germline genome editing, mitochondrial donation, creation of artificial gametes and creation of embryo models using reprogrammed embryonic and induced pluripotent stem cells are all relevant here.

Each of these innovative reproductive technologies has scientific value in that they can be utilised to help us better understand the mysterious process of human reproduction. Potentially, each technology can also be used to assist those of us who struggle to fulfil our reproductive aspirations. As such, each has high social value. Each of them also has significant commercial potential. But each also raises significant ethical and legal concerns.[2] Here, then, we have a confluence of issues about the role of patent law in encouraging innovation and the appropriate limits on patentability of subject matter relating to humans. Yet we will see from the commentary that follows that very little guidance is actually provided to patent offices, patent review boards and courts in determining how to analyse and respond to these issues.

To a large extent, the heart of the problem is the requirement for these institutions to examine and decide on the patentability of subject matter based on questions of morality, which is well outside their areas of expertise. This particularly problematic because they are provided with very little guidance on how to respond. I argue that because the immorality of patenting humans has already largely been decided, the immediate task for these institutions should be to evaluate the scientific evidence, interpret patent claims and governing legislation and engage in legal reasoning to determine whether or not the subject matter falls within the scope of the exclusion. This is a task that they have been trained to do, and that they are likely to have a much higher level of comfort with than engagement with questions of morality.

2. THE US: THE THIRTEENTH AMENDMENT, MORAL UTILITY AND APPROPRIATIONS

It will be well known to most readers that one of the significant contrasts between US and European patent law is that US patent legislation includes few exclusions from patenting,[3] whereas the EPC includes a raft of exclusions. These European

2 The Nuffield Council on Bioethics provides some of the leading commentary on these issues. See the Beginning of Life topics on its website www.nuffieldbioethics.org, accessed 10 June 2024.

3 For an explanation on the reasons for this lack of express exclusions in US patent law see Ana Nordberg and Timo Minssen, 'A "Ray of Hope" for European Stem Cell Patents or "Out of the Smog into the Fog"? An Analysis of Recent European Case Law and How it Compares to the US' (2016) 47 IIC 138, 169–170.

exclusions were incorporated into the global Agreement on Trade-related Aspects of Intellectual Property Rights (TRIPS) in the form of subject matter that member states *may* (not must) exclude.[4]

My analysis of the US situation begins with a reflection on the bold move by Stuart Newman, a developmental biologist, and Jeremy Rifkin, a well-known social activist, to lodge a patent application with the United States Patent and Trademarks Office (USPTO) in 1997, claiming human-animal chimeras. In 2002 Newman provided a frank account of his rationale for lodging this patent application.[5] As he explained, a chimera results from the aggregation of early embryonic cells from two different species, such that the resulting creature is a 'mosaic of the originating species, an unprecedented life form that could not be achieved without technological intervention.'[6] To be clear, no human-animal chimeras had yet been produced by Newman; nor was it his intention ever to make one. Rather, it appears that his and his co-applicant's intention was to engender deeper public debate on the topic. In this regard, it appears that Newman and Rifkin were successful. According to Ryan Hagglund, the application did indeed spark a debate about the morality of patenting such life forms.[7] Disappointingly, however, the political response to this debate was underwhelming.

As to the origins of morality conversations in US patent law, the story must begin with the US Supreme Court decision in *Diamond v Chakrabarty* which, in 1980, famously opened the door to patenting of life forms.[8] Although the decision was a narrow one, with five judges in favour and four opposed, it laid the foundation for the raft of biotechnology-specific patent applications, grants and USPTO and judicial decisions that were to follow.[9] Perhaps most famously, in the majority judgment of Burger CJ, he reminded us that: 'The Committee Reports accompanying the 1952 Act inform us that Congress intended statutory subject matter to "include anything under the sun that is made by man".'[10]

Despite the lack of limitations in this pronouncement by the Chief Justice (and in the original Committee Reports), the USPTO added some gloss, stating

---

4 Agreement on Trade-related Aspects of Intellectual Property Rights, Annex 1C in the Final Act Embodying the Results of the Uruguay Round of Multilateral Trade Negotiations (1994) 33 ILM 81.

5 Stuart A. Newman, 'My Attempt To Patent a Human-animal Chimera' (2002) L'Observatoire de la Génétique. www.nymc.edu/media/schools-and-colleges/nymc/pdf/newman/LObservatorie_Genetique_chimera.pdf, accessed 07 June 2024.

6 *Ibid.*

7 Ryan Hagglund, Patentability of Human-Animal Chimeras (2012) 25 Santa Clara High Technology Law Journal 51.

8 447 US 303 (1980) Supreme Court of the United States.

9 Baruch A. Brody, 'Intellectual Property and Biotechnology: The U.S. Internal Experience – Part I' (2006a) 16(1) Kennedy Institute of Ethics Journal 1; Baruch A. Brody, 'Intellectual Property and Biotechnology: The U.S. Internal Experience – Part2' (2006b) 16(2) Kennedy Institute of Ethics Journal 105.

10 447 US 303 (1980) Supreme Court of the United States, 309.

that: 'the Patent and Trademark Office now considers non-naturally occurring *non-human* multicellular living organisms, including animals, to be patentable subject matter within the scope of 35 U.S.C. 10.'[11] According to Dan Burk, the USPTO based the exclusion of humans on the Thirteenth Amendment to the US Constitution, which prohibits slavery and involuntary servitude. Burk strongly rejected the assertion that the Thirteenth Amendment reached into patent law, on the basis that patent rights are not the same as ownership rights, because 'the patent right is quite separate from any given embodiment of the invention.'[12] But he was willing to concede that: 'patenting humans may conflict with the right of reproductive freedom or autonomy found under the Fourteenth Amendment.'[13]

Later, in 2003 and again in 2006, following the rejection of Newman and Rifkin's patent application, Margot Bagley also cast doubt on the legitimacy of reliance on the Thirteenth Amendment as the source of any exclusion of humans from patenting, particularly in respect of pre-birth foetuses.[14] Citing *Roe v Wade*, 410 U.S. 113, 157 (1973), she noted that the Supreme Court had held in that case that the word 'person' as used in the Fourteenth Amendment, does not include the unborn. This led her to conclude that 'The Supreme Court has already interpreted the patent statute without reference to any limits based on moral considerations and the idea that the Thirteenth Amendment could support the denial of patents, on genetically modified previable foetuses for example, is doctrinally unsound.'[15] She also cast doubt on whether a patent on a genetically modified human being could actually 'force the patented human to "do" anything.'[16]

Bagley also made reference to the so called 'moral utility' doctrine which provided the USPTO and judiciary the opportunity to deny patents on morally controversial subject matter on the basis that they were not 'useful', in the sense of failing to produce a 'good' result. From Bagley's account, it appears that the doctrine originated with Justice Story in 1827 in *Lowell v Lewis*, in which his Honour stated that: 'the invention should not be frivolous or injurious to the well-being, good policy, or sound morals of society.'[17] It appears that the doctrine eventually fell into disuse following the introduction of a broader utility

11 Donald J. Quigg, U.S. Patent & Trademark Office, 'PTO Policy on Patenting of Animals' (1987), Reprinted In 5 U.S. Congress Office of Technology Assessment, New Developments In Biotechnology: Patenting Life 93; as cited In Dan L. Burk, 'Patenting Transgenic Human Embryos: a Nonuse Cost Perspective' (1993) 30 Houston Law Review 1597, 1597 (emphasis added).

12 Burk (n 11) 1648.

13 *Ibid.* 1649.

14 Margo A. Bagley, 'Patent First, Ask Questions Later' (2003) 45 William and Mary Law Review 469; Margo A. Bagley, 'A Global Controversy: The Role of Morality in Biotechnology Patent Law', in Peter K. Yu (ed) *Intellectual Property and Information Wealth: Issues and Practices in the Digital Age* (Praeger Press 2006).

15 Bagley 2003 (n 14) 477.

16 *Ibid.* 503.

17 15 F. Cas. 1018, 1019 (C.C.D. Mass. 1817) (No. 8,568); Cited in Bagley 2006 (n 14) 320.

requirement, but seemed to enjoy a 'revival' following the filing of Newman and Rifkin's chimera patent application.[18] A public statement by the USPTO hinted that inventions of this nature might 'fail to meet the public policy and morality aspects of the utility requirement.' However, prior to any decision on the chimera patent, the Federal Circuit decision in *Juicy Whip v Orange Bang* appeared to 'sound the death knell' for morality as a component of utility.[19]

Given the apparent lack of clear legal foundation for the exclusion of humans from patenting, whether in US patent legislation, the US Constitution or case law, the US Congress wrestled with ways to give legal force to such exclusion, particularly with regard to human-animal chimeras following the Newman-Rifkin application.[20] The only success was the so-called Weldon Amendment to appropriations legislation, which prevented funds appropriated to the USPTO in any given year from being used in relation to patent applications claiming human organisms.[21] This legislative instrument remains the only clear pathway to excluding human-related patent claims in the US. This has led scholars such as Bagley and Baruch Brody to call for inclusion of morality provisions in US patent law, along the lines of the European provisions.[22]

It may be that the US Congress would be more willing to provide a clear legislative foundation for excluding humans from patenting at the present time, should they choose to do so. However, even if this were to occur, the nature and scope of any such exclusion, whether based on restrictions in appropriations legislation, a clear legislative provision excluding humans from patenting, or a morality provision, is likely to remain uncertain until tested in the courts. And whether Congress is likely to rise to such a challenge in the present political climate, given that it raises issues associated with the right to innovate and commercialise, reproductive rights and the moral status of the human embryo, is questionable. Choosing appropriations legislation as a means of excluding humans from patenting is hardly desirable, given that it has to be renewed annually. But basing an exclusion on grounds of public order and morality is not without risk. As we will see in the next section, European provisions based on morality are not without their own flaws. Whether or not a provision specifically excluding humans from patenting would fare any better is explored later in the chapter.

---

18 Bagley 2006 (n 14) 320–321.

19 *Juicy Whip, Inc. v Orange Bang, Inc.*, 185 F.3d 1364, 1367 (Fed. Cir. 1999). Bagley 2006 (n 14) 321.

20 See Bagley 2006 (n 14) 327.

21 *Ibid.*

22 Baruch A. Brody, 'Intellectual Property and Biotechnology: The European Debate' (2007) 17(2) Kennedy Institute of Ethics Journal 69; Bagley 2006 (n 14) 330–336. See also more generally Shobita Parthasarasay, *Patent Politics: Life Forms, Markets, and the Public Interest in the United States and Europe* (University of Chicago Press 2017).

3. EUROPE: INTERPRETING THE EUROPEAN PATENT CONVENTION AND THE BIOTECH DIRECTIVE

The focus of this section is on patenting of human embryonic stem cells, with particular attention to the challenges faced by the European Patent Office (EPO) Boards and the Court of Justice of the European Union (CJEU) in setting boundaries around what is and is not contrary to *ordre public* and morality. Collectively, their jurisprudence demonstrates that morality can play a role in informing assessment of the limits of patent protection in controversial areas of technology. But it also shows that, even with explicit provisions, morality remains a concept which is difficult to apply in practice.

Readers will likely be familiar with Article 53(a) of the EPC, which specifically provides that patents shall not be granted for inventions where their commercial exploitation would be contrary to *ordre public* or morality.[23] Two key decisions of the Boards of Appeals of the EPO on the applicability of Article 53(a) to human-related subject matter are particularly relevant. The first, referred to hereafter as *WARF*, related to the experiments undertaken by James Thomson and colleagues at Wisconsin University in the US involving primate embryonic stem cells, which laid the groundwork for much modern human embryonic stem cell research.[24] The second, referred to as *Technion*, related to methods for maintaining undifferentiated human embryonic stem cells, as well as cell cultures including both human embryonic stem cells and human foreskin cells.[25]

The important aspects of the *WARF* and *Technion* decisions were explained in two articles published in 2015 by Aurelie Mahalatchimy and colleagues.[26] In essence, in *WARF*, the Enlarged Board rejected patent applications claiming human embryonic stem cells on the basis that this amounted to using human embryos for industrial or commercial purposes, contrary to Article 53(a). Crucially, the Board stated that this exclusion extended to products and processes prepared 'exclusively by a method which necessarily involved the destruction of human embryos.' On this basis, it could be argued that use of stem cells stored in biobanks was not caught by the exclusion.[27] Later, in *Technion*, the Technical Board concluded that it was irrelevant whether the stem cells were newly derived or stored – in both circumstances the applications should be rejected.

---

23 Article 53(a) EPC (n 1).

24 EPO Enlarged Board of Appeal, *WARF*, G02/06 (November 25, 2008).

25 EPO Boards of Appeal, *Technion Research and Development Foundation Ltd.*, T2221/10 (February 4, 2014).

26 Aurelie Mahalatchimy et al., 'Impact of European Courts' Decisions on Embryonic Stem Cells Patents: Toward New Research Strategies' (2015a) 33(1) Nature Biotechnology 41; Aurelie Mahalatchimy et al., 'Exclusion of Patentability of Embryonic Stem Cells In Europe: Another Restriction by the European Patent Office' (2015b) 37(1) EIPR 25.

27 *Ibid.*

In addition to Article 53(a) of the EPC, further specific guidance on the circumstances in which the commercial exploitation of biotechnological inventions would be contrary to *ordre public* or morality is provided in Article 6 of what has become known as the Biotech Directive.[28] Brody provided a detailed account of the tortuous history of the Biotech Directive in his 2007 account of the European debate on intellectual property and biotechnology.[29] Whilst it is not necessary to repeat this historical account here, it is worth mentioning that the original draft of the Directive in 1992 included a specific exclusion from patenting the human body or parts of the human body per se, based on the EPC *ordre public* or morality provision.[30] It is interesting to speculate on whether an exclusion of this nature might have provided greater clarity than the provisions that were ultimately agreed to. Brody appeared doubtful on this point.[31] What remains of this exclusion is included in Article 5 of the Directive, which distinguishes between the human body, at the various stages of its formation and development, and the simple discovery of one of its elements in paragraph 1, and elements isolated from the human body or otherwise produced by means of a technical process in paragraph 2 (with only the former being excluded).[32]

Whilst Article 5(1) of the Biotech Directive does seem to open the door to the types of legal analysis and reasoning suggested in the introduction to this chapter, almost all of the judicial and academic analysis has been directed towards Article 6. Beyond the general *ordre public* or morality exclusion in EPC Article 53(a) and repeated in Biotech Directive Article 6(1), Article 6(2) provides a list of subject matter which should be excluded including uses of human embryos for industrial or commercial purposes in sub-paragraph 6(2)(c):

> 'processes for modifying the genetic identity of animals which are likely to cause them suffering without any substantial medical benefit to man or animal, and also animals resulting from such processes.'

The CJEU decision in *Oliver Brüstle v Greenpeace e.V.* ('*Brustle*') related to a patent filed in Germany claiming, inter alia, neuronal precursor cells.[33] The Court held that this amounted to patenting embryonic stem cells and was contrary to Article 6(2)(c) of the Biotech Directive. The decision has been described by

28 Directive 98/44/EC of the European Parliament and of the Council of 6 July 1998 on the legal protection of biotechnological inventions, OJ EU L 213.

29 Brody (n 22) 70–83.

30 *Ibid.* 75.

31 *Ibid.* 75–76.

32 For helpful commentary on the impact of Article 5 on gene patents, see Geertrui Van Overwalle, 'Biotechnology and Patents: Global Standards, European Approaches and National Accents' in Daniel Wüger and Thomas Cottier (eds) *Genetic Engineering and the World Trade System* (Cambridge University Press 2008) 77, 91–94.

33 *Oliver Brüstle v Greenpeace e.V.* [2011] OJ 362/5, Judgment of the Court (Grand Chamber) of 18th October 2011 ('*Brüstle*').

Shawn Harmon and Graeme Laurie as casting a 'bewilderingly broad' definition of human embryos.[34] In particular, these authors were critical of the Court's lack of acknowledgement of the 'subtleties' of scientific evidence, in that it failed to make a clear distinction between totipotent and pluripotent embryonic stem cells.[35] Ana Nordberg and Timo Minssen further pointed to the breadth of the Court's holding that Article 6(2)(c) applies whenever 'the technical teaching of the patent application requires the prior destruction of human embryos ... even if the claims' description does not refer to the use of human embryos.'[36] Added to this, the Court considered that the definition of human embryos extended to entities created by fertilisation, entities created through a process of ovum enucleation and nucleus transfer from a mature human cell into the ovum (that is, embryos created by somatic cell nuclear transfer), and unfertilised ova stimulated to develop by parthenogenesis (parthenotes).[37] Nordberg and Minssen went on to note that in the *Technion* decision mentioned above, the EPO Technical Board of Appeal used the CJEU decision to justify its exclusion of stored stem cell lines as well as newly created lines.[38] The German Supreme Court, in contrast gave a quite different and much narrower interpretation of the CJEU decision in *Brustle*, resulting in different approaches to interpretation of the same provisions between jurisdictions.[39]

Subsequently, a referral was made from the UK courts to the CJEU in *International Stem Cell Corporation v Comptroller General of Patents* ('*ISCO*').[40] This case provided the CJEU with an opportunity to provide some nuance to their *Brüstle* definition of the human embryo and give appropriate acknowledgement to scientific advances and the accompanying changes in societal opinion regarding human embryonic stem cell research. The disputed patent claims were over methods for the production of stem cell lines and synthetic corneal tissue, both of which were derived from parthenotes. Both ISCO and the United Kingdom considered that a strict application of the *Brüstle* exclusion ignored the scientific reality that these cell types are incapable of developing into a *viable* human being (emphasis added) and, as such, should not be excluded from patent eligibility:

> 'to exclude parthenotes from patentability does not strike a balance at all between, on the one hand, research in the field of biotechnology which is to be encouraged by

34 Shawn Harmon and Graeme Laurie, 'Dignity, plurality and patentability: the unfinished story of *Brüstle v Greenpeace*' (2013) 38 European Law Review 92, 97.

35 *Ibid.* 97.

36 Nordberg and Minssen (n 3) 144.

37 *Ibid.* Alice Yuen-Ting Wong and Aurelie Mahalatchimy, 'Human Stem Cells Patents – Emerging Issues and Challenges in Europe, United States, China, and Japan' (2018) 21 Journal of World Intellectual Property 326, 329. See also Mahalatchimy et al. 2015a, 2015b (n 26).

38 *Technion* (n 25). Nordberg and Minssen (n 3) 145.

39 Nordberg and Minssen (n 3) 145.

40 *International Stem Cell Corporation v Comptroller General of Patents, Designs and Trade Marks* [2014] OJ C 65/7 judgment of the Court (Grand Chamber) of 18 December 2014 ('*ISCO*').

> means of patent law and, on the other hand, respect for the fundamental principles safeguarding the dignity and integrity of the person, objectives which are set out in particular in recitals 2 and 16 in the preamble to Directive 98/44.'[41]

The Court concluded that because advances in scientific knowledge had informed the *Brüstle* definition of the human embryo, it was appropriate to take into account scientific advances in considering the patentability of parthenotes. The Court thereby concluded that patenting of inventions which lacked the inherent capacity to develop into a viable human being did not offend *ordre public* or morality.[42]

These decisions show that patent boards and courts are cognisant of the critical need to take account of accepted scientific knowledge in making decisions on questions of patentability. However, given that the exclusion from patenting is based on *ordre public* or morality, it is also crucial that proper attention is given to moral arguments, what Harmon and Laurie have referred to as a 'patent law understanding of morality.'[43] Various European scholars have expressed deep concern about the lack of attention to such matters by these institutions. In particular, in a series of articles and book chapters Aisling McMahon has critiqued the continuing marginalisation of the morality provisions.[44] She has predicted that there will come a time in the future when decisions will need to be made about the morality of allowing patents for 'novel beings' that 'display characteristics of agency akin to human agency.'[45] Although that time is not yet upon us, I argue that the that time has already come for us to consider how new reproductive technologies are changing our views on the nature of the human embryo and how that affects our views on the nature and scope of the exclusion of humans from patenting.

Presciently, in 2007 Brody reflected that '[t]he European experience clearly demonstrates that it is possible to have a workable patent system that excludes many biotechnological inventions from patentability on the grounds that they are morally offensive.'[46] However, critiquing the lack of well-articulated criteria

---

41 *ISCO* (n 40) [19].

42 *Ibid.* [38].

43 Harmon and Laurie (n 34) 106.

44 See particularly Aisling McMahon, 'Patents, Governance and Control: Ethics and the Patentability of Novel Beings and Advanced Biotechnologies in Europe' (2021) 30(3) Cambridge Quarterly if Healthcare Ethics 529. Aisling McMahon, 'Institutions, Interpretive Communities, and Legacy in Decision-Making: A Case Study of Patents, Morality, and Biotechnological Inventions', in Edward S. Dove and Niamh Nic Shuibhne (eds), *Law and Legacy in Medical Jurisprudence: Essays in Honour of Graeme Laurie* (Cambridge University Press 2022). Aisling McMahon, 'The "Ethical" Regulation of Novel Being Technologies: The Potential Role for Patents as Drivers, Blockers and Ethical Guiders', in David R. Lawrence and Sarah Morley (eds) *Novel Beings: Regulatory Approaches for a Future of New Intelligent Life* (Edward Elgar 2022).

45 McMahon 2021 (n 44) 529.

46 Brody (n 22) 106.

for determining what should be excluded, he concluded that '[u]ntil the needed criteria are developed, the European experience is an incomplete experiment in incorporating moral considerations into patent law.'[47] The same criticism could well be made today. An alternative and perhaps more satisfying mechanism for excluding humans from patenting may be through the employment of more direct language in patent legislation. Article 5(1) in the Biotech Directive provides one example of such direct language, though it has received far led attention than the *ordre public* or morality exclusion in Article 6 (and Article 53(a) of the EPC). The viability of a direct exclusion is examined in the next section in this chapter.

4. AUSTRALIA: GENERAL INCONVENIENCE, HUMAN BEINGS AND THE BIOLOGICAL PROCESSES FOR THEIR GENERATION

One of the curiosities of Australian patent law is that it still uses the language of 'manner of manufacture' derived from the very first English patent law: section 6 of the *Statute of Monopolies 1623*. Despite its antiquity, reports considering reform of Australian patent law have consistently recognises that section 6 has served its purpose well over time and should remain as the touchstone of patentability.[48] Of particular relevance to the present discussion, this provision includes the particularly curious concept of general inconvenience. There have been hints by the judiciary that general inconvenience could allow the introduction of moral and public policy considerations in the patent process.[49] However, the judiciary has largely been reluctant to employ this tool, preferring to leave controversial exclusions to Parliament. The highest Australian court, the High Court of Australia, was given some opportunity to consider the role of general inconvenience in two recent cases, in respect of methods of medical treatment in *Apotex Pty Ltd v Sanofi-Aventis Australia Pty Ltd*,[50] and human gene

---

47 *Ibid.*

48 Industrial Property Advisory Committee, *Patents, Innovation and Competition in Australia* (Australian Government Printing Service, 1984). Intellectual Property and Competition Review Committee *Review of Intellectual Property Legislation under the Competition Principles Agreement Final Report* (Australian Government Printing Service, 2000).

49 In *Joos v Commissioner of Patents* (1972) 126 CLR 611, for instance, Barwick CJ referred to the method of medical treatment exclusion being based on public policy using the *Statute of Monopolies* language of being generally inconvenient, and Gummow J confirmed that the question should be framed in this way in *Rescare Ltd v Anaesthetic Supplies Pty Ltd* (1993) 25 IPR 119. See also Miranda Forsyth 'Biotechnology, Patents and Public Policy: A Proposal for Reform in Australia' (2000) 11 Australian Intellectual Property Journal 202. Oksana Mitnovetski and Dianne Nicol, 'Are Patents for Methods of Medical Treatment Contrary to the Ordre Public and Morality or 'Generally Inconvenient'' (2004) 30 Journal of Medical Ethics 470.

50 [2013] HCA 50.

sequences in *D'Arcy v Myriad Genetics Inc.*[51] In what will by now be a familiar story to readers, in neither case was the court prepared to elaborate on the role of morality via the vehicle of general inconvenience in Australian patent law.

The remainder of this section will focus on a different provision in the Australian *Patents Act 1990* (Cth), which may offer a more fruitful path through the weeds of the debate around the nature and scope of the exclusion of humans from patenting. I refer to this as an 'accidental' provision, as it was inserted into the Bill that was to become the *Patents Act 1990* at the 11th hour. This was because the leader of one of the minor parties in the Australian Parliament at the time the Bill was introduced sought to include a provision excluding gene patents.[52] History shows that this move was unsuccessful (after all, if it had been successful there would have been no *D'Arcy v Myriad Genetics Inc*). In the alternative, one of the independent members of Parliament at the time put forward what was to become Section 18(2) of the current Act, which excludes human beings and the biological processes for their generation.[53]

Although there have been no judicial decisions interpreting Section 18(2), the Australian Patents Office has had three opportunities to consider its applicability. The claimed subject matter under consideration in *Fertilitescentrum* was a method of growing pre-blastocyst human embryos.[54] The Deputy Commissioner of Patents pointed to the complexity of the task at [12]: 'This section, which superficially looks very simple, has the inherent difficulty of defining the exclusion by reference to "human beings", without any definition of what constitutes a "human being".' The Deputy Commissioner undertook an extensive analysis of the submissions, practical considerations, history of the provision, and options for interpretation. This led the Deputy Commissioner to conclude at [36] that human beings are in the process of generation: 'from the time of the processes that create a fertilised ovum (or other processes that give rise to an equivalent entity) up until the time of birth.' The Deputy Commissioner added further at [37] that:

> '[t]he prohibition of 'human beings' in my view is a prohibition of patenting of any entity that might reasonably claim the status of a human being. Clearly a person that has been born is covered by this exclusion. But to the extent that there is a process of generation of a human being that lasts from fertilisation to birth, I consider that a fertilised ovum and all its subsequent manifestations are covered by this exclusion.'

51 [2015] HCA 35.

52 Australian Senate Standing Committee on Industry, Science and Technology Report on the Consideration of the Patents Bill (1990).

53 Australian Senate, Hansard Parliamentary Debates 20 September 1990, 2653; Australian House of Representatives, Hansard Parliamentary Debates 16 October 1990, 2947. See the discussion by the Deputy Commissioner of Patents in *Fertilitescentrum AB and Luminis Pty Ltd.* (2004) (APO 19) (*Fertilitescentrum*), [13]–[25]. See also J. Petering and P. Cowin, 'The Patentability of Stem Cells in Australia' (2015) 5 *Cold Spring Harbor Perspectives in Medicine* a020966.

54 *Fertilitescentrum* (n 53) Abstract.

And finally, at [38]:

> 'the exclusion of biological processes includes the processes of generating the entity that can first claim a status of human being. For example, processes for fertilising an ovum; processes for cloning at the 4-cell stage by division; processes for cloning by replacing nuclear DNA.'

The same Deputy Commissioner decided that an application for a method of producing a hybrid embryo using inter-species nuclear transplantation techniques was also caught by the section 18(2) exclusion in *Woo-Suk Hwang*.[55] In contrast, in the later decision of *International Stem Cell Corporation*, which related to the same subject matter as the European *ISCO* case,[56] a different Deputy Commissioner concluded that section 18(2) does not extend to parthenotes because it is not possible for any subsequent entity to develop into a human being.[57] As such, the same outcome was reached in this case as in the CJEU decision, but through a very different process.

Irrespective of whether or not one agrees with the reasoning of the Deputy Commissioners, what these cases illustrate is that despite the complexity of the task, these officials clearly are able to utilise their skills in evaluating the scientific evidence, interpreting the patent claims and legislation and applying legal reasoning to reach their conclusions. Should the Australian courts ever be given the opportunity to decide matters relating to section 18(2) they may come to different conclusions but would need to exercise these same skills. Though the Deputy Commissioners did not address questions about the morality of allowing patents for the subject matter before them, nor were they required to do so. Arguably, the fact that section 18(2) excludes humans from patenting means that this question already has been fully addressed, without needing further elaboration. I do recognise, though, that this point will not find favour with some of my colleagues, who might argue, in the alternative, that questions of morality must always be addressed for human-related subject matter.

5. CONCLUSION

This chapter has presented a brief analysis of the approaches taken to excluding humans from patenting in the US, Europe and Australia. Although it probably goes without saying that it would be unthinkable and abhorrent to allow patents for humans as such, we have seen that putting these sentiments into practice is far from straightforward. As new reproductive technologies continue to

---

[55] [2004] APO 24.
[56] *ISCO* (n 40).
[57] [2016] APO 52 [31].

emerge, and patent applications continue to be made for them, patent offices, patent review boards and courts will inevitably have to confront these issues. Their tasks are unenviable ones, particularly when these institutions are not provides with the necessary legal tools to undertake them. The lack of a clear legal pathway to exclude humans from patenting in the US, and the requirement to address issues of *ordre public* and morality without adequate guidance in Europe are problematic. The situation in Australia, where these institutions are allowed to operate in their more traditional areas of expertise, may ultimately provide a better model for dealing with these complexities. It is only with more jurisprudence that we can properly assess which approach provides a more satisfying mechanism in achieving an appropriate balance between encouraging innovation in reproductive technologies and properly recognising the complex ethical and social concerns that patenting of subject matter of this nature raises.

CHAPTER 16

UNLOCKING OUR COMMON BODY?

Biological Materials, Data and Knowledge Commons for Research & Development

Enrique Santamaría Echeverría
Assistant professor in Law & Technology, Department Law & Markets,
Erasmus School of Law, Erasmus University Rotterdam
Affiliate researcher, Research Group Social Enterprises and
Institutions for Collective Action

Tine de Moor
Professor of Social Enterprise and Institutions for Collective Action,
Department of Business-Society Management,
Rotterdam School of Management (RSM), Erasmus University Rotterdam

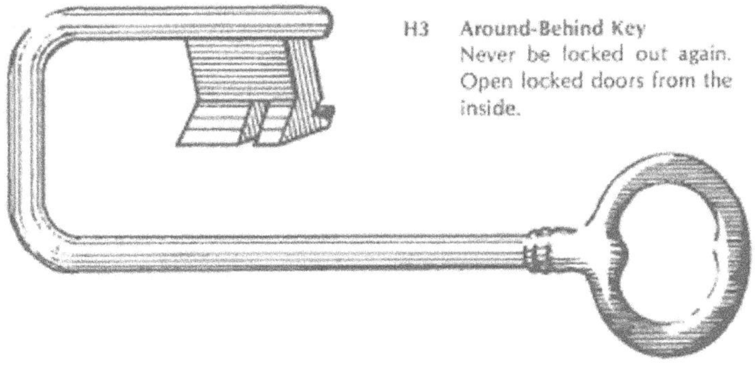

1. INTRODUCTION

'Never be locked out again. Open locked doors from the inside' reads the catalogue description of the 'Around-Behind Key'. This uniquely designed key allows you to open doors from the inside while being outside. As its name suggests, the key seemingly travels around and behind an imaginary door frame to access the lock from the inside, enabling entry from the outside.

The very existence of this key raises several intriguing questions and amusing paradoxes. First, the likelihood of losing or misplacing the 'normal' key and the 'Around-Behind Key' is identical. More importantly, the key's function would only make sense if there were no distinct inside or outside, but rather a self-standing framework. Interestingly, Belgian artist René Magritte captured a similar concept in his painting 'Found Child' (1967). The artwork depicts a door standing alone in a vast landscape of sand and clouds, through which one can see what appears to be a forest inside.

This chapter explores the concept of 'Around-Behind' keys to unlock the potential of the human body and access its resources for research. Traditionally, the human body is viewed as belonging solely to its 'owner', with exclusive rights to consent to its use. However, new paradigms propose models in which the human body and its resources are either 'opened' from the outside or, at the very least, collectively governed. These paradigms are often rooted in the idea of the 'commons'.

While the concept of the commons dates back many centuries,[1] Garrett Hardin significantly shaped the discourse with his 1968 article in *Science*. In this influential piece, he argued that individual self-interest leads to the overuse of and underinvestment in common resources. This article has since sparked two different but interconnected bodies of literature, fostering an ongoing, multidisciplinary discussion that includes contributions from legal scholars.[2]

The first set of responses to Hardin's argument disputed his characterisation of an open pasture as a common: an unfenced pasture is not equivalent to an ownerless field. According to this perspective, the commons, which rely heavily on collective use rights, may function better than other models for the governance of common-pool resources. Building on this premise, Elinor Ostrom expanded the types of resources that can be governed as commons beyond land, such as irrigation systems. She also developed the Institutional Analysis and Development (IAD) framework for governing common-pool resources (CPR).[3] Subsequently, Ostrom's framework underwent adaptations, developments, and

---

1 Tine de Moor, Paul Warde and Leigh Shaw-Taylor (eds.) *The management of common land in north west Europe, c. 1500–1850* (Brepols Publishers 2002).

2 One could also identify a third body of literature in the field of philosophy, which considers the commons as a means for radical political and economic change. See for example, Michael Hardt and Antonio Negri, *Commonwealth* (Harvard University Press 2009); Massimo De Angelis, *Omnia sunt communia: On the commons and the transformation to postcapitalism* (Bloomsbury Publishing 2017); Pierre Dardot and Christian Laval, *Commun: essai sur la révolution au XXIe siècle* (La découverte 2014); Peter Linebaugh, *The magna carta manifesto* (University of California Press 2008); Peter Linebaugh, *Stop, thief!: The commons, enclosures, and resistance* (pm Press 2014).

3 Elinor Ostrom, *Governing the commons: The evolution of institutions for collective action* (Cambridge University Press 1990); Elinor Ostrom, 'Background on the institutional analysis and development framework' (2011) 39 Policy Studies Journal 7.

refinements to accommodate diverse disciplines and types of commons.[4] Many colleagues applied the IAD-framework subsequently, on a variety of natural and manmade resources, and some of those applications also led to new forms of methodological approaches in commons-studies (such as the Institutional Grammar-approach).[5]

Another set of responses came from legal scholarly literature,[6] with Carol Rose's theories on inherent public property in the *Comedy of the commons* being particularly noteworthy.[7] Rose's rejoinder focused no longer on a critique of the notion of the commons, but on the alleged negative consequences of public or open access. Rose highlighted the positive externalities and benefits arising from open access. After her article, various theories within the same scholarly realm have been developed to understand the dynamics of these types of goods (also known in the specialised literature as 'open commons' or 'commons unmodified') and the public domain.[8] Notable legal scholars like Yochai Benkler,[9]

4 Tine de Moor, 'From common pastures to global commons: A historical perspective on interdisciplinary approaches to commons' (2011) 19 Natures Sciences Societes 422; Tine de Moor, 'What Do We Have in Common? A Comparative Framework for Old and New Literature on the Commons' (2012) 57 International Review of Social History 269.

5 See e.g. Fisheries: James M Acheson, *Capturing the commons: Devising institutions to manage the Maine lobster industry* (University Press of New England 2003); Forestry: Arun Agrawal and Elinor Ostrom, 'Collective action, property rights, and decentralization in resource use in India and Nepal' (2001) 29 Politics & Society 485; Urban Commons: Community Gardens in New York City: Sheila Foster, 'Collective action and the urban commons' (2011) 87 Notre Dame Law Review 57. Water Management: California Water Systems: William Andrew Blomquist, *Dividing the waters: Governing groundwater in southern California* (ICS Press 1992).

6 Italian scholarly literature has been extraordinarily prolific in the legal study of the commons. See e.g. Stefano Rodotà, 'The role of common goods in fostering shared responsibility, linking sustainable social cohesion to the reduction of inequalities' (International University College of Turin, 2–11, 2011); Ugo Mattei, Rocco Alessio Albanese and Ryan J Fisher, 'Commons as possessions: The path to protection of the commons in the ECHR system' (2019) 25 European Law Journal 230; Ugo Mattei, 'I beni comuni fra economia, diritto e filosofia' (2013) 7 Spazio filosofico 111; Ugo Mattei, 'The state, the market, and some preliminary question about the commons' (International University College of Turin, 2011), http://ideas.iuctorino.it/RePEc/iuc-rpaper/1-11_Mattei.pdf, accessed 9 May 2024; Ugo Mattei, 'First Thoughts for a Phenomenology of the Commons' (2012) 75 Socialisation and Commons in Europe; Antonio Gambaro, 'Note in tema di beni comuni' (2013) 1 Aedon 11; Maria Rosaria Marella,'Beni comuni: oltre l'opposizione natura/cultura' (2012) 113 Lettera Internacionales 9; Maria Rosaria Marella, 'Per un Diritto dei Beni Comuni' in Maria Rosaria Marella (ed), *Oltre il Pubblico e il Privato* (Ombre Corte 2013) 9.

7 Carol Rose, 'The Comedy of the Commons: Custom, Commerce, and Inherently Public Property' (1986) 53 The University of Chicago Law Review 711, www.jstor.org/stable/1599583?seq=1&cid=pdf-, accessed 25 June 2024.

8 James Boyle, *The Public Domain: Enclosing the Commons of the Mind* (Yale University Press 2008).

9 Yochai Benkler, *The Wealth of Networks. How Social Production Transforms Markets and Freedom* (Yale University Press 2006); Yochai Benkler, 'Between Spanish Huertas and the Open Road' In Brett M. Frischmann, Michael J. Madison and Katherine J. Strandburg (eds), *Governing Knowledge Commons* (Oxford University Press 2014) 69; Yochai Benkler, 'The

Lawrence Lessig,[10] James Boyle,[11] and Brett Frischmann[12] have contributed to this line of research.

These two bodies of scholarly literature on the commons have distinct foundations, genealogies, and interpretations of what 'the commons' entail. For the purposes of this chapter and to avoid terminological confusion, we will refer to the first type of commons as Common Pool Resources Commons (CPRC) and the second type as Open Access Goods (OAG).

OAG are conceptually situated outside the property regime, where all actors enjoy symmetrical freedom to operate – everyone has equitable rights regarding the resource, but also correlative duties. In contrast, CPRC are situated within the property regime, with rights and duties concerning the management and appropriation of resources being collectively agreed upon. Despite these differences, Elinor Ostrom herself recognised the potential connections between these strands of literature in the early 2000s. At the Duke Law School Conference on the Public Domain, Ostrom, alongside Charlotte Hesse, emphasised the importance of linking CPRC and the public domain, noting the significance of these connections in the following terms:

> 'There is an increasing concern about the implications of recent and impending legislation on the future of academic research, open science, traditional knowledge, and the intellectual public domain. The Duke Law School Conference on the Public Domain brought together, for the first time, an interdisciplinary group of leading scholars studying the increasing enclosure of the global information commons. [...] Information that used to be "free" is now increasingly being privatized, monitored, encrypted, and restricted. The enclosure is caused by the conflicts and contradictions between intellectual property laws and the expanded capacities of new technologies. It leads to speculation that the records of scholarly communication, the foundations of an informed, democratic society, may be at risk. This "intellectual land-grab" is an outcome of new technologies and global markets. [...] The goal of this article is to summarize the lessons learned from a large body of international, interdisciplinary research on common-pool resources in the past twenty-five years and consider its usefulness in the analysis of scholarly information as a resource. We will suggest ways

Political Economy of Commons' (2003) IV Upgrade: The European Journal for the Informatics Professional 6; Yochai Benkler,'Open access and information commons' (2017) In Francesco Parisi (ed), *The oxford handbook of law and economics: Volume 2: private and commercial law* (Oxford University Press 2017) 256.

10 Lawrence Lessig, 'Keynote Address' (Conference on Media Convergence, Fordham University Law School 1999), https://cyber.harvard.edu/works/lessig/Fordham.pdf, accessed 25 June 2024.

11 Boyle (n 8).

12 Brett M. Frischmann, *Infrastructure: The social value of shared resources* (Oxford University Press 2012).

in which the study of the governance and management of CPRs can be applied to the analysis of information and the "intellectual public domain".[13]

In the last two decades, the enclosure movement described above has extended into the realm of biomedical research. This shift has often been accompanied by the commodification and privatisation of three critical resources on which biomedical research heavily relies: human biological materials (HBM), health data, and existing scientific knowledge. At the EU level, this development is the result of the interplay of various sectoral legislations (e.g. CFREU, GDPR).

Against this background, this chapter has two main objectives. First, it will analyse how the interplay of different principles and rules in EU legislation facilitates the commodification of human biological materials, data, and knowledge. Second, by revisiting the connections between Open Access Goods (OAG) and Common Pool Resources Commons (CPRC), the chapter will propose an alternative commons-based model for the governance of these resources, with a particular focus on their application in research and development (R&D).[14]

For this purpose, Section 2 begins with a description of how the current regulatory landscape and the European Health Data Space (EHDS) enable the commodification of human biological materials and health data, leading to the enclosure of science. Section 3 analyses alternative commons-based approaches for the governance of these resources for research and development (R&D), such as knowledge commons,[15] medical knowledge commons,[16] medical information commons[17] and genomic commons.[18] Section 4, building on these accounts, and jumping from theory to practice, briefly describes the phenomenon of health data cooperatives as an example of existing institutions of collective action for the governance of human body commons for R&D. Section 5 concludes.

---

13 Charlotte Hess and Elinor Ostrom, 'Ideas, artifacts, and facilities: information as a common-pool resource' (2003) 66 Law and contemporary problems 111.

14 This article uses the term human body commons, instead of other similar terminology (e.g. medical knowledge commons) to stress the material dimension of knowledge creation and to include three different types of resources necessary for Research & Development (R&D). We are aware of the problem of designating a set of resources as a 'commons'. We have nonetheless chosen to so to demonstrate how different types of resources (human biological materials, data and knowledge) can successfully be governed under a commons model.

15 Frischmann et al. (n 9).

16 Katherine J. Strandburg, Brett M. Frischmann and Michael J. Madison (eds), *Governing Medical Knowledge Commons.* (Cambridge University Press 2017).

17 Robert Cook-Deegan and Amy L. McGuire, 'Moving beyond Bermuda: sharing data to build a medical information commons' (2017) 27 Genome Research 897; Robert Cook-Deegan, Rachel A. Ankeny and Kathryn Maxson Jones, 'Sharing data to build a medical information commons: from Bermuda to the Global Alliance' (2017) 18 Annual review of genomics and human genetics 389.

18 Jorge L. Contreras and Bartha M. Knoppers, 'The genomic commons' (2018) 19 Annual review of genomics and human genetics 429.

2. THE COMMODIFICATION OF HBM AND (HEALTH) DATA: THE ROLE OF THE EU

This section explores how various EU legal instruments work together to turn HBM and health data into commodities for research and development (R&D). Key instruments include the Charter of Fundamental Rights of the European Union (CFREU),[19] the Directive 98/44/EC on the legal protection of biotechnological inventions (known as the Biotechnology Directive),[20] and the General Data Protection Regulation (GDPR).[21]

In the CFREU, Article 3.2 prescribes that 'In the fields of medicine and biology, the following must be respected in particular: [...] (c) the prohibition of making the human body and its parts *as such* a source of financial gain' (emphasis added). As such, as it is widely understood, this precludes the onerous transfer of the human body and its parts as such (i.e. in their natural state) from the original donor (usually a natural person) to a first recipient (usually a legal person), which may derive financial gain from this. However, if the initial recipient modifies the separated human body part (such as human biological materials) through technical means, they may profit from its transfer. This provision does not prohibit the initial recipient, such as a hospital, from embedding a human biological sample in a paraffin block and transferring it to another party in exchange for financial compensation. Importantly, the donor (original transferor) of the sample is excluded from benefiting financially. In essence, the creator of the value is barred from commodifying their own resources.

This unbalanced construction is mirrored by the Biotechnology Directive. Article 5 of this Directive prescribes that: '1. The human body, at the various stages of its formation and development, and the simple discovery of one of its elements, including the sequence or partial sequence of a gene, cannot constitute patentable inventions. 2. An element isolated from the human body or otherwise produced by means of a technical process, including the sequence or partial sequence of a gene, may constitute a patentable invention, even if the structure of that element is identical to that of a natural element.' Here again, patentability of the human body and its parts in their natural state is precluded. However, an isolated element produced by means of a technical element, even if identical to the one in natural state, can be the object of patentable invention.[22]

---

19 Charter of Fundamental Rights of the European Union [2012] OJ C326/391.

20 Directive 98/44/EC of the European Parliament and of the Council of 6 July 1998 on the legal protection of biotechnological inventions [1998] OJ L213/13.

21 Regulation (EU) 2016/679 of the European Parliament and of the Council of 27 April 2016 on the protection of natural persons with regard to the processing of personal data and on the free movement of such data, and repealing Directive 95/46/EC (General Data Protection Regulation) [2016] OJ L119/1.

22 The Netherlands brought an action for the annulment of this Directive before the CJEU. In the fifth plea, the Netherlands submitted that '[...] the patentability of isolated parts of the human

The circle is completed by a potential interpretation of the GDPR provisions concerning the secondary use (uses other than those for which the data were originally collected) of sensitive data. Notably, there is no requirement for data subjects to consent to the use of their sensitive data, including health-related data, for 'scientific research'. Article 9(2)(i)-(j) of the GDPR covers grounds such as public interest, including public health, as well as scientific research and statistical purposes. These exemptions have sparked significant academic interest.[23] For example, considerable discussion has centred around whether 'research', as defined in the GDPR, is solely the domain of public institutions like universities and regulators, or if private enterprises such as pharmaceutical companies and insurers can also utilise this exemption. Unsurprisingly, the opinions on these matters differ starkly[24] – in research, as in many other walks of economic life, the public and the private are joined in an intricate nexus of, *inter alia*, capital and labour.[25] The complexity of this situation makes it exceedingly challenging to determine whether a specific activity is intended for private or public actors, particularly when this determination is made in a hypothetical or abstract context. If the secondary use of data by industry for research purposes without the consent of the data subject is allowed, the legal structure supporting the commodification of human biological materials, (health) data and knowledge would be complete. The consequence is an obvious imbalance whereby the original donor and data subject are excluded from the (financial) exploitation and their materials and data while the first and subsequent recipients can commercially exploit them, possibly without consent (see Figure 1). In other words, the legal basis for the transfer

---

body provided for by Article 5(2) of the Directive reduces living human matter to a means to an end, undermining human dignity'. See C-377/98 *Kingdom of the Netherlands v European Parliament and Council of the European Union* [2001] ECR-I 7079.

23 See generally, European Data Protection Supervisor, (2020) 'A Preliminary Opinion on data protection and scientific research'; European Data Protection Supervisor (2020) 'Preliminary Opinion 8/2020 on the European Health Data Space'; MLC Foundation, & Med Law consult, *GDPR and research. A basic overview* (2017); Giovanni Comandè & Giulia Schneider, 'Can the GDPR make data flow for research easier? Yes it can, by differentiating! A careful reading of the GDPR shows how EU data protection law leaves open some significant flexibilities for data protection-sound research activities' (2021) 41 Computer Law and Security Review; Mary Donnelly & Maeve McDonagh, 'Health research, consent and the GDPR exemption' (2019) 26 European Journal of Health Law 97; European Data Protection Supervisor. (2020). Opinion 3/2020 on the European Strategy for data. *EDPS*; Mark J. Taylor & Tess Whitton 'Public Interest, Health Research and Data Protection Law: Establishing a Legitimate Trade-Off between Individual Control and Research Access to Health Data' (2020) 9 Laws 6; Paul Quinn, 'Research under the GDPR – a level playing field for public and private sector research?' (2021) 17 Life Sciences, Society and Policy; Regina Becker and others, 'Secondary Use of Personal Health Data: When Is It "further Processing" under the GDPR, and What Are the Implications for Data Controllers?' (2022) European Journal of Health Law; Victoria Chico, 'The impact of the general data protection regulation on health research' (2018) 128 British Medical Bulletin 109.

24 Johan Hansen et al., 'Assessment of the EU Member States' rules on health data in the light of GDPR' (2021) 57; European Data Protection Supervisor (n 23) 3.

25 European Data Protection Supervisor (n 23) 8.

of data and HBM between the donor and first recipient is consent. As altruism constitutes the normative justification of the transfer, the donor (always the first transferor) is excluded from profiting economically from it. The first recipient and subsequent recipient can transfer both data and HBM in exchange of economic remuneration because, as a general rule, the prohibitions included in Article 3.2 CFREU and Article 5 of the Biotechnology Directive do not apply to them.

Figure 1. The commodification process of health data and HBM

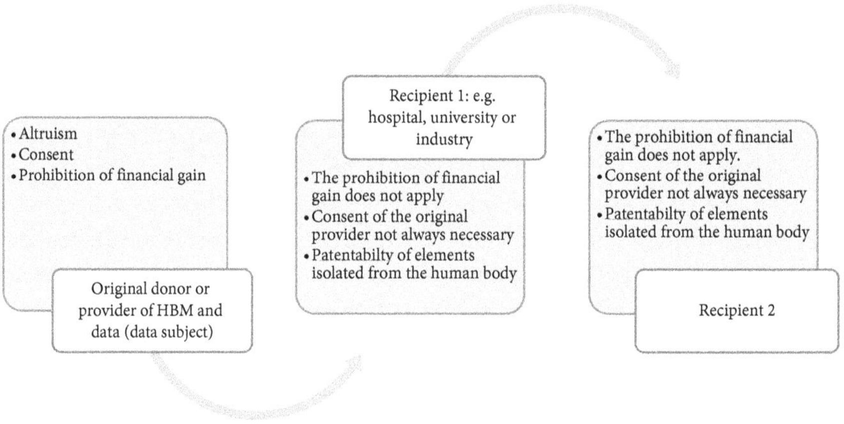

At least two possible responses arise to counter this unbalanced picture. The first possibility would be to allow total commodification from the very beginning of the chain by recognising property rights on the human body,[26] its parts and related (heath) data and by permitting the conclusion of onerous contracts[27] on these resources. A different response can be found in the commons (both as

[26] For an overview of the literature on property rights on the human body see: Harjeet Marway and others, 'Commodification of Human Tissue' in Henk ten Have and Bert Gordijn (eds) *Handbook of Global Bioethics* (Springer 2014) 581 with further references; D Dickenson, *Property in the body: feminist perspectives* (Cambridge University Press 2007); Leslie A. Sharp, 'The commodification of the body and its parts' (2000) Annuel Review of Anthropology with further references.

[27] For some scholarly proposals on contractual models for the use of human biological materials see Christian Lenk and Nils Hoppe, 'Using tissue and material from the human body for biomedical research: proposals for a normative model', in Michael Steimann, Peter Sykora and Urban Wiesing (eds) *Altruism recosidered, Exploring new approaches in property in human tissue* (Routledge 2016) 133; Christine Noiville, 'Preventing conflicts of interests in the fields of human biological materials: the 'contractual model' as an avant-garde', in Michael Steimann, Peter Sykora and Urban Wiesing (eds), *Altruism recosidered, Exploring new approaches in property in human tissue* (Routledge 2016) 143; Florence Bellivier and Christine Noiville, 'La circulation du vivant humain: modèle de la propriété ou modelèle du contrat?', in Thierry Revet (ed), *Code civil et modéles. Des modèles du Code au Code comme modèle* (Presses de la Sorbonne 2006) 101; Florence Bellivier and Christine Noiville, *Contrats et vivants. Le droit de la circulation des ressources biologiques* (LGDJ 2006); Radhika Rao, 'Genes and spleens: property, contract or privacy rights in the human body?' (2007) 35 Journal of Law Medicine and Ethics 371.

Open Access Goods or as Common Pool Resources Commons) as governance models that may create value for all stakeholders (donors, further recipients and potentially society as a whole) without relying on the recognition of property rights on the human body, its parts and data.

The establishment of an OAG can be the result of top-down regulation or can be carved out (individually or collectively) from the existing legal regime. The recent establishment of a European Health Data Space[28] (EHDS) constitutes a (failed) attempt to create an OAG[29] on health data. This Regulation, using a commons-based terminology, aims at regulating the secondary use of health data for, among other purposes, research, innovation, and development. However, the proposal has been criticised for creating power imbalances,[30] for creating an unbalanced panorama for the use of data which facilitates health data capture by powerful private actors, and for not properly addressing the so-called paradox of open,[31] i.e. opening data resources exposes them to the risk of enclosure and control by powerful actors within the data ecosystem.

Furthermore, the concept of scientific research plays a prominent role within the EHDS, serving at least two key functions: (a) as a determining factor for identifying data holders obligated to share health data for secondary use, and (b) as a legitimate purpose for the secondary use of electronic health data.[32] Regarding the first function (a), data holders must provide access to health data collected by various entities (both public and private) in the health and healthcare sectors for purposes such as healthcare provision, public health initiatives, research, innovation, and other related purposes.[33] Therefore, if an entity is conducting health research it should make health data available for a specific list of purposes, including (b) scientific research related to health or care sectors.[34] The scope of the concept of scientific research is set by Recital 61, according to which: '(t)he notion of scientific research purposes should be interpreted in a broad manner, including technological development and demonstration, fundamental research, applied research and privately funded research.'[35]

---

28 Regulation (EU) 2025/327 of the European Parliament and of the Council of 11 February 2025 on the European Health Data Space and amending Directive 2011/24/EU and Regulation (EU) 2024/2847.

29 On the notion of open commons see Benkler 2014 (n 9).

30 Petros Terzis, 'Compromises and Asymmetries in the European Health Data Space' (2022) 1 European Journal of Health Law 1.

31 Paul and Alex Tarkowski, 'The paradox of Open' (*Open future*, 5 March 2021), https://paradox.openfuture.eu/, accessed 26 June 2024.

32 For an analysis of secondary use of data under the EHDS see: Enrique Santamaría Echeverría, 'The European Health Data Space: A New Paradigm for Secondary Uses of Health Data for Scientific Research?' in *The European Health Data Space* (Routledge 2025) pp. 162–178.

33 Article 2(2)t and recital 59 EHDS.

34 Article 53 EHDS.

35 For a critique on the EHDS, the notion of scientific research and the commons see Petros Terzis and Enrique Santamaria Echeverria, 'Interoperability and governance in the European Health Data Space regulation' (2023) 23 Medical Law International 368.

The foregoing may be taken to imply that the EHDS, which is replete with references to the 'general interest of society'[36] and the 'benefit of society,'[37] establishes a health-data OAG.[38] The data users' duty to 'make public the results or output of the secondary use of electronic health data'[39] would also be consistent with such an inference. However, the existence of a European OAG on health data may, at this point, be just an illusion. On the one hand, to reseed the open access, it is uncertain what constitutes the research results that ought to be made public (open?). On the other hand, one may doubt the legitimacy of including private research as an activity in the general interests.

However, the effort to create an EHDS, incomplete though it may be at present, is in line with recent theorisations about data as a relational and collective good.[40] According to these novel theories, it is necessary to transcend the individualistic conceptualisation of privacy and to account for its relational dimensions, in such a way that that the socially beneficial use of the data subject's data is no longer subject to the requirement of consent.[41] In other words, OAG for the secondary use of health data could arise without the consent of the data subject as long as the purposes for the use of data contribute to the common good.[42] However, what constitutes 'the common good' in this sense remains a much-vexed issue in practice.[43] In contrast with top-down regulatory proposals like the EHDS, scholars have put forward CPRC based theories for the collective management of data, materials, and knowledge. The next section explores some of these proposals.

3. THEORIES ON HUMAN BODY COMMONS

At the turn of the 20th century, several voices raised concerns about practices and regulatory trends leading to the enclosure of science and technology and the shrinking of the public domain.[44] At the international level, the 2020 General

36 Recital 61 EHDS.

37 Recitals 1, 53, 59, 61 EHDS.

38 The EHDS conceptualisation of what constitutes 'health data' is surprisingly broad, see Article 51.

39 Article 61(4) EHDS.

40 Salome Viljoen, 'A relational theory of data governance' (2021) 131 Yale LJ 573: Elettra Bietti, 'Data is Infrastructure' in *Theoretical Inquiries in Law* (2024).

41 Barbara J. Evans, 'Genomic data commons' (2017) Governing medical knowledge commons 74, 97.

42 Recently, theories on the common good have been applied to health innovation. See for example, Mariana Mazzucato, 'A collective response to our global challenges: a common good and "market-shaping" approach' (2023) Working Paper Series IIPP WP 2023-01, www.ucl.ac.uk/bartlett/public-purpose/wp2023-01, accessed 25 June 2024; The WHO Council on the Economics of Health for All, 'Governing health innovation for the common good' (2021).

43 *Ibid.*

44 Boyle (n 8).

Comment of the UN Committee on Economic, Social and Cultural Rights on Article 15[45] of the ICESCR,[46] warned on how large-scale privatisation of scientific research and property rights may have negative effects on the enjoyment of the benefits of scientific progress and other human rights (e.g. right to health).[47]

With specific reference to biomedical research, Michael Heller and Rebecca Eisenberg – adding another layer to the metaphor of tragedy[48] – denounced how patents can deter innovation by creating 'anticommons'.[49] According to them, while the privatisation of biomedical research holds promise, it also carries the risk of hindering innovation by fostering the proliferation of concurrent, fragmented, and overlapping intellectual property rights.[50] Legal scholarship responded to Heller and Eisenberg's critique in various ways. On one hand, a strand of scholarship, prominently represented by Geertrui Van Overwalle, argued that despite the expansion of intellectual property (IP) rights in the life sciences, there was insufficient widespread and compelling evidence of patent thickets in biomedical research. Accordingly, a plea was made to abandon the 'tragedy of the anticommons' metaphor.[51] On the other hand, a second strand of scholarship leaned towards the necessity of overcoming the tragedy of the anticommons and reclaimed the commons,[52] by developing several proposals on commons-based governance of (health) data, HMB and scientific knowledge. This section explores both strands of scholarship by analysing the most prominent advancements on knowledge commons, medical knowledge commons, genomic commons, and medical information commons.

---

45 On the right to enjoy the benefits of scientific progress and its applications.

46 United Nations Human Rights Office of the High Commissioner 'General comment No. 25 (2020) on science and economic, social and cultural rights (Article 15 (1) (b), (2), (3) and (4) of the International Covenant on Economic, Social and Cultural Rights)' [2020] E/C.12/GC/25, https://tbinternet.ohchr.org/_layouts/15/treatybodyexternal/TBSearch.aspx?Lang=en&TreatyID=9&DocTypeID=11, accessed 25 June 2024.

47 For the multiple connections between the commons and the right to health see Stefano Rodotà, 'The role of common goods in fostering shared responsibility, linking sustainable social cohesion to the reduction of inequalities' IUC Research Commons 2-11 International University College of Turin 2011.

48 Mark A. Heller, 'The Tragedy of the Anticommons: Property in the Transition from Marx to Markets' (1998) 111 Harvard Law Review 621.

49 Mark A. Heller and Rebecca Eisenberg, 'Can Patents Deter Innovation? The Anticommons in Biomedical Research' (1998) 280 Science 698.

50 *Ibid.* 701.

51 See e.g. van Geertrui Van Overwalle, 'Patent pools and clearinghouses in the life sciences: back to the future' In Duncan Matthews & Herbert Zech (eds) *Research Handbook on intellectual property and the life sciences* (Edward Elgar 2016) 304. It remains to be seen whether the alleged absence of patent thickets can be equated to the absence of an 'anticommons' in biomedical research. Contreras, for example, has argued that although the existence of a patent thicket cannot be fully demonstrated, the anticommons in biomedical research may still constitute a problem derived from the use of trade secret law to protect data from patients and test subjects. Jorge L. Contreras, 'The anticommons at 20: Concerns for research continue' (2018) 361 Science 335. American Association for the Advancement of Science.

52 Donna Dickenson, *Property in the Body* (Cambridge University Press 2017).

As usual, Ostrom's Institutional Analysis and Development (IAD) framework constitutes the starting point of these theories. Initially, Hess and Ostrom posited that, just as with natural resources, one could apply the IAD-framework (see Figure 2) to data and information[53] which -together with other intelligible ideas and scientific knowledge- are covered under the umbrella term knowledge commons. It is beyond the scope of this chapter to delve deeply into the IAD framework. However, in simplified terms, it can be described as a framework that analyses: (a) the characteristics of the common resource (including the attributes of the community sharing the resource and the formal and informal rules in use); (b) the action arena where stakeholders interact; and (c) the resulting patterns of interaction and outcomes from these interactions. Examples of knowledge commons include digital collections of existing resources.

Figure 2. Institutional Analysis and Development Framework

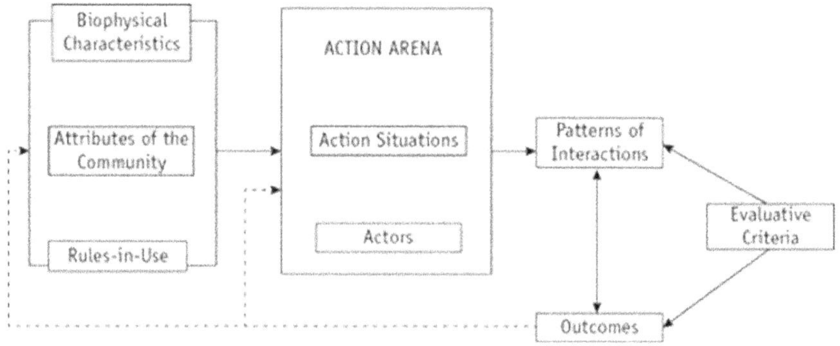

Source: Charlotte Hess and Elinor Ostrom, *Understanding knowledge as a commons: From theory to practice* (MIT press 2007).

After Hess and Ostrom laid the foundations for the analysis of knowledge commons, several scholars continued to modify and adapt the IAD-framework (see Figure 3) to account for a special trait which characterises knowledge: it is a resource that not only can be shared but also created within the commons. In this regard, the efforts of Katherine J. Strandburg, Brett M. Frischmann, and Michael J. Madison are remarkable.[54] According to these scholars, '[k]nowledge commons arrangements usually must create a governance structure within which participants not only share existing resources but also engage in producing those resources and, indeed, in determining their character. These characteristics of knowledge commons suggest that neatly separating the attributes of the managed

[53] Charlotte Hess and Elinor Ostrom, *Understanding knowledge as a commons: From theory to practice* (MIT press 2007) 7.

[54] Frischmann, et al. (n 11).

resources from the attributes and rules-in-use of the community that produces and uses them is impossible.'[55]

Moreover, four peculiar attributes of knowledge ought to be taken into consideration if it is to be governed as a common. First, if the generation of knowledge is taken as a process of economic transformation, then it must be acknowledged that the inputs into that process, such as time and money, are rivalrous. Second, the outputs of past transformative processes serve as inputs into future ones, which complicates the matter considerably. Third, since the processes in question are cumulative, there is no ironclad boundary between the creation and dissemination of knowledge. Fourth, knowledge *per se* is non-rivalrous and non-excludable; consequently, rivalry and excludability are either introduced by institutional means, say through the institution of intellectual property law, or emerge in consequence of the unique properties of some of the inputs into knowledge-generation, such as those of the biological materials from which data may be extracted. Examples of knowledge commons include the following: astronomical data commons, intellectual property pools, online creation communities, open-source software, medical knowledge commons and genomic data commons.[56]

Figure 3. Strandburg, Frischmann & Madison Knowledge Commons Framework

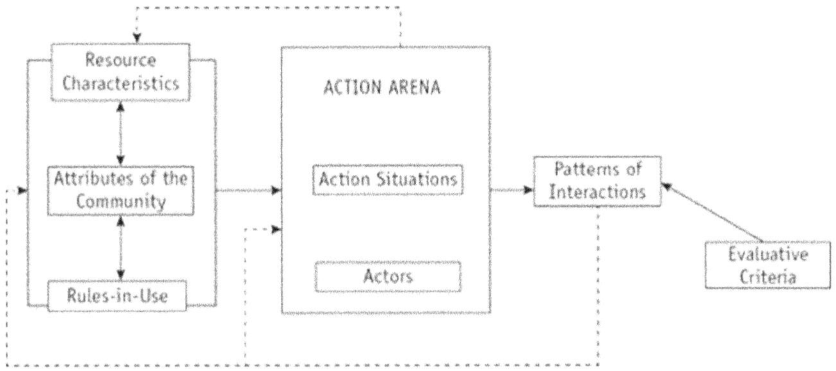

Source: Frischmann et al. (n 9).

Building on the knowledge commons framework, Strandburg, Frischmann & Madison further developed its application to a very special type of knowledge commons: the medical knowledge commons.[57] Here again, the central idea is that innovation and knowledge creation can happen beyond the intervention of

55 *Ibid.* 17.
56 Strandburg et al. (n 16) 11.
57 Strandburg et al. (n 16).

the state and market stimuli (e.g. intellectual property), through commons-based mechanisms.[58]

Particularly relevant for the purposes of this chapter are the genome commons, also called genomic commons.[59] According to Contreras and Knoppers' definition, genomic commons are 'the world-wide collection of publicly accessible repositories of human and nonhuman genomic data' including 'germline and somatic DNA and RNA sequences, haplotype and single-nucleotide polymorphism (SNP) data, allele frequencies, variant data, epigenetic data, genotype-phenotype associations, annotation, and related phenotypic, genealogical, and clinical data.'[60] These scholars applied the IAD framework to the analysis of the genomic commons' characteristics, stakeholders, rules-in-use for data sharing and access and, rules for regarding privacy and data protection, consent and proprietary rights. Their analysis revealed several necessary moves forward to maintain and grow (also beyond their scope) the genomic commons: (a) The need to integrate genomic data with other types of health data as well as with repositories of physical human biological samples; (b) An increase of interoperability and compatibility of different data sources for the sharing of data in areas outside the genomics; (c) Guided by the principle of proportionality the need to reconsider the balancing between sharing and privacy and; d) the construction of a framework firmly grounded on human rights (including the right to health) to benefit from the fruits of scientific research.[61]

In a very similar fashion, other scholars have proposed to move from genome commons to medical information commons.[62] The rationale behind this move answers to the need of researchers to link different types of data, from indeed, genomic data, to other types of health data, collected through the analysis of human biological samples or electronic body internal or external devices. In particular, the boldest proposals for the medical information commons is to merge the kingdoms of research and clinical care,[63] -which have been traditionally treated in legal scholarship as independent domains- and the development of a Global Alliance

58 *Ibid.* 3.

59 Jorge L. Contreras and Bartha M. Knoppers, 'The genomic commons' (2018) 19 Annual review of genomics and human genetics 429; Jorge L. Contreras, 'Constructing the genome commons' (2014) 99 Governing Knowledge Commons 112. Similar proposals for commons on the results on genetic tests have also been advanced. See e.g. B J Evans, 'Genomic Data Commons', In K J Strandburg, B M Frischmann & M Madison (eds), *Governing Medical Knowledge Commons* (Cambridge University Press 2017) 74.

60 Contreras and Knoppers (n 59) 431.

61 *Ibid.* 447.

62 Robert Cook-Deegan and Amy L. McGuire, 'Moving beyond Bermuda: sharing data to build a medical information commons' (2017) 27 Genome Research 897; Robert Cook-Deegan, Rachel A Ankeny and Kathryn Maxson Jones, 'Sharing data to build a medical information commons: from Bermuda to the Global Alliance', (2017) 18 Annual review of genomics and human genetics 389.

63 Patricia A Deverka and others, 'Creating a data resource: what will it take to build a medical information commons?' (2017) 9 Genome Medicine 1.

of Genomics and Health to develop new principles, beyond Bermuda and Fort Lauderdale,[64] to account for the new paradigms in sharing, privacy, and consent.[65] In other words, the question raised was again how to balance the need for sharing data and materials whilst at the same time safeguarding individual privacy.

It is now evident that the framework for (medical) knowledge and its applications are modified versions of the IAD framework, categorizable as variations of Common Pool Resources Commons (CPRC) types of commons. In this context, Benkler's interpretation of CPRC as 'institutional elements of an organisational layer built on top of either the public domain knowledge commons or its proprietary alternative' is particularly relevant.[66] In some cases, such as Contreras and Knoppers' description of genomic commons, one could argue that they represent a nod towards Common Pool Resources Commons (CPRC) within a larger network of Open Access Goods (OAG). In other words, genomic commons would be a network of different Common Pool Resources Commons.

Moreover, some other scholars have taken up the task of investigating ways of opening human body related commons. Amidst several proposals, Van Overwalle's plea for open commons (in our view the same as OAG) in genomic data is particularly interesting.[67] Building on Contreras' analysis of the genome commons and using Benkler's distinction between open commons and common pool resources type of commons, Van Overwalle proposes jumping from a limited research genome commons, a CPRC 'in which access and use of resources is restricted to researchers for research purpose'[68] to a full genome commons (which in reality would constitute an OAG) in which access and use is granted to all for all purposes, including not only research and clinical practice, but also commercialisation (see Figure 3).[69] In Van Overwalle's words full genome commons would be those 'in which access and use of the resources is offered to all (data holders/data generators and data users) for a variety of purposes (ranging from research through clinical practice to commercialisation).'[70] In this framework, commercial access to the commons would be permissible as long as data users pay a reasonable compensation for access and use of the genomic resources.

---

64 The Bermuda principles were designed for the rapid sharing (24 hours) during the publicly funded Human Research Project, which led to the mapping of the human genome. These principles have been identified as one of the keys for the success of the project and the victory over the commercial competition of the project by Celera. The Fort Lauderdale principles were designed in 2003 to develop rules for biological infrastructure projects.

65 Cook-Deegan, Ankeny and Jones.

66 Benkler 2014 (n 9) 74.

67 Geertrui Van Overwalle, 'Governing Genomic Data: Plea for an "Open Commons"' in Brett M. Frischmann, Michael J. Madison & Katherine J. Strandburg (eds) *Governing Knowledge Commons* (Oxford University Press 2014) 137.

68 *Ibid.* 150.

69 *Ibid.* 144.

70 *Ibid.*

Figure 4. Van Overwalle's provisioning and consumption of the genome commons

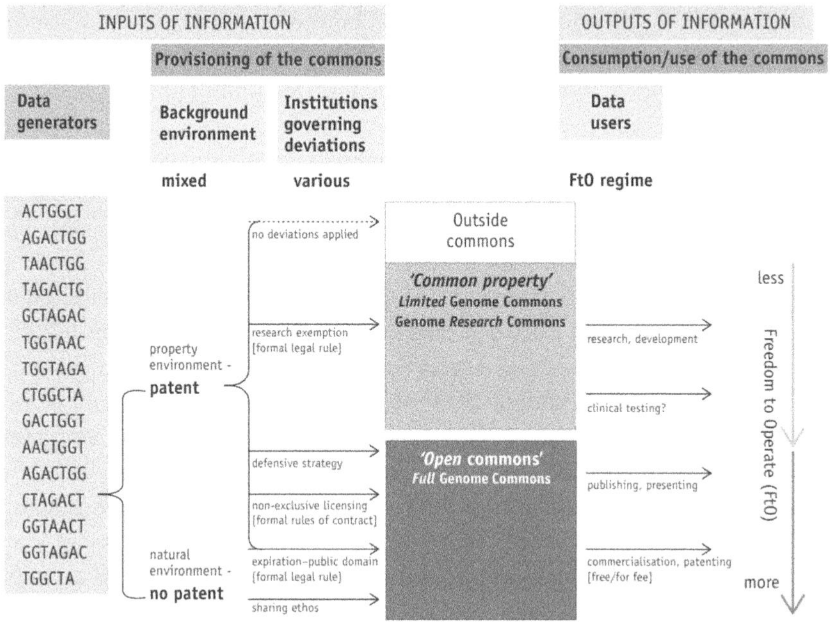

In our view, Van Overwalle's plea overlooks two critical issues. Firstly, common to many previous proposals concerning the human body commons, is the lack of detailed consideration for the embodiment of genomic data – specifically, human biological materials. These materials are crucial not only because they serve as the essential raw materials for certain types of research that cannot be conducted solely on disembodied data, but also because their legal status differs significantly from that of data.

Secondly, there is the issue of replenishing resources belonging to CPRC or OAG. As we have observed, knowledge accumulation requires building upon past innovations and creations. However, commercial use of the entire 'open genomic commons' in exchange for economic compensation (e.g. payment) does not contribute to replenishing the resource. Therefore, it is imperative to explore complementary or alternative mechanisms to the 'take now, pay later' – model for commercial access to the human body commons. Models on benefit sharing may contribute to addressing this challenge by for example making treatments developed freely available to donors and affordable to other citizens.[71]

[71] For an overview of the public perception of the different way of benefit-sharing stemming from the use of data and materials in commercial research see: Jarod Walsh, Brad Elphinstone, Dianne Nicol, & Mark Taylor (2024). A systematic literature review of the 'commercialisation effect' on public attitudes towards biobank and genomic data repositories. Public Understanding

Moving from theory to practice, next section examines health data cooperatives as an example of institutions of collective action for the governance of health data for R&D.

4. DATA COOPERATIVES FOR R&D

Cooperative models for the governance of health data are especially relevant. Data cooperatives, where data are controlled by citizens, have the potential to achieve an optimal balance between efficiently utilising data and safeguarding the personal rights of data subjects, provided those persons are members of the cooperative.[72] The institutional arrangement could involve the issuance and sale of membership certificates by a cooperative, which would offer data repository and management services. Decisions regarding the use of the data and the allocation of proceeds from their utilisation between the cooperative and its members would be subject to a vote. This model was initially theorised for genomic data,[73] but could retain much of its value if expanded to encompass all types of personal or health data, regardless of their origin (e.g., apps, wellness devices, medical devices). Under a cooperative model, industries such as pharmaceuticals or medical technology would pay a fee to access and utilise the shared data agreed upon by cooperative members. Depending on the agreed terms, they may also share research outcomes with the cooperative members. Crucially, members would have the autonomy to decide whether the benefits derived from their data should be reinvested into research or other public-interest initiatives. By consolidating diverse data sources for biomedical research, data cooperatives clearly serve as a mechanism of collective action for governing resources within the human body commons.

An example may be useful at this juncture. MIDATA is a Swiss health-data cooperative (MIDATA *Genossenschaft*). The secure MIDATA-platform is available to natural persons who wish to share their data with a view to contributing to research. Those natural persons retain a considerable degree of autonomy even after they have shared their data in this fashion. Thus, an individual member can accept or reject third-party requests for access. If access is granted, the

---

of Science, 33(5), 548–567. https://doi.org/10.1177/09636625241230864 (Original work published 2024).

72 See generally on Data Cooperatives: Ernst Hafen, Donald Kossmann & Angela Brand, 'Health data cooperatives – Citizen empowerment' (2014) 53 Methods of Information in Medicine 82; Alessandro Blasimme, Effy Vayena, & Ernst Hafen, 'Democratizing Health Research Through Data Cooperatives' (2018) 31 Philosophy and Technology 473;. I van Roessel, M Reumann, & A Brand, 'Potentials and Challenges of the Health Data Cooperative Model' (2018) 20 Public Health Genomics 321.

73 Ernst Hafen, Donald Kossmann & Angela Brand, 'Health data cooperatives – Citizen empowerment' (2014) 53 Methods of Information in Medicine 82.

proceeds accrue to the *Genossenschaft*[74] which manages the proceeds and results from the secondary usage of the data.[75] Specific rules regarding monitoring and enforcement of membership rules can be found in MIDATA's articles of association.[76] Although there is no publicly available information on the number of members, the success of this arrangement could have significant implications for managing privacy within the human body commons. Furthermore, it may suggest alternative legal pathways for processing and sharing health-related data.[77] At the same time, MIDATA also shows how a cooperative in which personal data are aggregated can reseed the commons in practice.

Health data cooperatives as commons constitute a great example of a governance model that: 1) Keeps the control over collective -but individually provided- resources, in the hands of the original providers; 2. Reseeds the commons by utilising the knowledge created by research on the pooled data and; 3. Integrates different sources of data through an interoperable system that facilitates the reading of different data formats.

However, data cooperatives do not take into account the material dimension of the human body commons, i.e. human biological materials. Intuitively, one potential solution, depending on its economic feasibility, could involve integrating the management of repositories or biobanks into the cooperatives. However, these ideas exceed the scope of this paper and remain topics for future research.

5. CONCLUSION

This paper demonstrated how current EU legislation and recent policy proposal underpin the commodification of three types of resources necessary for research and development: human biological materials, data and knowledge.

As an alternative model, we have explored various theories regarding the human body commons to derive a set of recommendations for governing resources in research and development (R&D). While data cooperatives represent an exceptional model for balancing the interests of various stakeholders in R&D – from patients and data subjects to industry – there is a need to develop new

---

74 Article 2, Subparagraph e MIDATA articles of association.

75 Article 2, Subparagraph h MIDATA articles of association.

76 Its articles of association are available at www.midata.coop/wp-content/uploads/2019/01/MIDATA_Statuten_20170905_English.pdf, accessed 12 May 2025.

77 For a detailed analysis of privacy and MIDATA see Felix Gille and Effy Vayena, 'How Private Individuals Maintain Privacy and Govern Their Own Health Data Cooperative' in Madelyne R. Sanfilippo, Brett M. Frischmann & Katherine J. Strandburg (eds) *Governing Privacy in Knowledge Commons* (Cambridge University Press 2021) 53. On privacy in the commons see generally Madelyn R. Sanfilippo, Brett M. Frischmann & Katherine J. Strandburg (eds), *Governing Privacy in Knowledge Commons* (Cambridge University Press 2021).

governance solutions that incorporate the integration of human biological materials into the governance of commons models.

Finally, this chapter aligns with contemporary calls to recognise human dignity and human rights as foundational principles in global bioethics and biolaw. Such principles serve as essential links between the protection of human subjects and the advancement of scientific progress.

CHAPTER 17

WHAT IF INVENTION ALREADY HAPPENED?

Reactionary vs Ingenuity Bike

Lodewijk VAN DYCKE
Assistant Professor, Centre for IT and IP Law, KU Leuven

Capitalism is for profit. Yet with bicycles you cannot make much profit. Accordingly, they are not supported by state and law as they should, although they are among the best inventions ever, on par with the laundry machine. Climate breakdown is urging us to reconsider the bicycle and, with it, innovation policy.

'Never forget, the electric car is here to save the car industry, not the planet.'

Brent Toderian (@BrentToderian) on Twitter/X, 18 June 2022

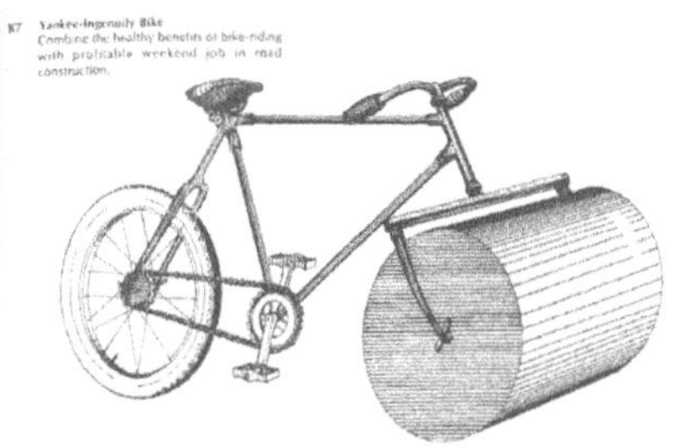

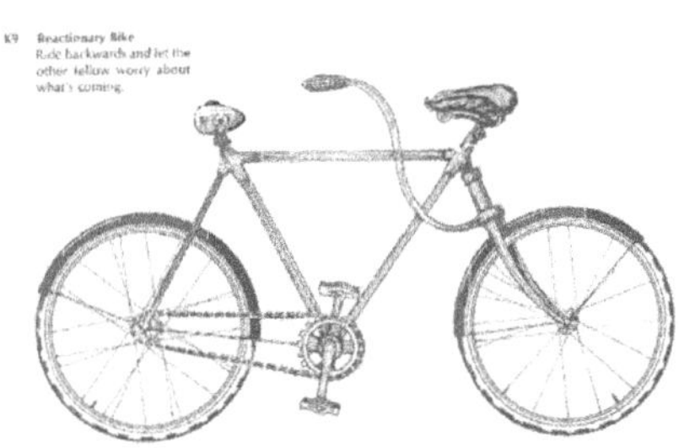

1. INTRODUCTION

We are told that we are living in a time of accelerating innovation.[1] Governments, captains of industry and finance tell us to buckle up and toughen up, so we can

[1] 'Why a Dawn of Technological Optimism Is Breaking' (*The Economist*, 16 January 2021) www.economist.com/leaders/2021/01/16/why-a-dawn-of-technological-optimism-is-breaking, accessed 05 March 2025.

reap the benefits of the digital and green transitions, including self-driving, electric cars and generative AI. These groundbreaking technologies promise far-off blue skies but require new regulation, infrastructure and legal incentives for investment. Companies and employees alike are told to reskill, reschool and adapt.[2]

At the same time, one solution to some of our most intricate problems – from urban air pollution over climate change to obesity – has been around for decades. Said solution would revolutionise society and empower ordinary citizens, decentralise economic power, make technology more transparent and, therefore, more democratic. Yet, this solution is not supported to the extent that one would hope. The technology I am talking about is the bicycle. I will argue, on the basis of the example of the bicycle as opposed to the electric car as a technology for urban personal transport, that innovations can be shunned by the state exactly *because* they are decentralised, democratic and transparent.

The choice for bikes is no coincidence. Geertrui likes bicycles. She has always cycled to work, up and down the 'Bergstraat' or 'Mountain Street'. She is the proud owner of a Brompton, an innovative foldable bike, and currently rides an electrical KU Leuven service bike. In line with Geertrui's research and values, bikes are inclusive, and their invention was wildly creative and stimulated by patent law. Hower, at this point in time, the concept of the bike is set, and patents can only play a role regarding additional improvements in infrastructure, clothing, and materials. Instead, the institution of patent law and current patent statistics point towards what is, in essence, the distraction of the electric car. Patent law builds on an innovation mantra that suggests that the solution to new problems will always be ever newer technology, even when invention already happened and we can take the best solution off the shelve.

This contribution was inspired by the contrasting images of the Yankee-Ingenuity Bike (K7) and the Reactionary Bike (K9) from Carelman's *Catalog of Fantastic Things* (1971). The Ingenuity Bike allows the cyclist to earn a little by paving the road while cycling with a front wheel steamroller. The Reactionary Bike paddles backwards in space and, so it seems, in time. Given the physics and history of the bike, the suggestion that bikes could plausibly be reactionary or need added features to be ingenious was implausible to the point that I knew I had to write this contribution.

This article elaborates a theoretical hypothesis about the deep political reasons for why the car lane remains in the middle of the road, and for why

---

2 E.g. the Commission's priority area; European Commission, 'A Europe fit for the digital age' https://commission.europa.eu/strategy-and-policy/priorities-2019–2024/europe-fit-digital-age_en, accessed 05 March 2025.

we keep perusing patent inventories hoping for electric car breakthroughs, even after thirty years of climate politics. The contribution provides an inductive, under-theorised analysis of innovation in the context of urban transport. This instigates a meditation on the works of Schumacher, Illich and Schumpeter.

In Section 2, I discuss the technical development of the bicycle. Section 3 chronicles the social history of the bike. Section 4 argues that bikes have become even more praiseworthy due to the climate emergency. Section 5 emphasises that, instead of supporting the bike, most policy efforts foster the electric car. This is true, too, in the field of invention as recorded via patent statistics. Meanwhile, bicycle transport could benefit from additional invention, too. Section 6 contains the core of the article. It sets out a policy vision for bike-centred public transport and proceeds to advance a deep political economy explanation for why this policy is not being implemented. Section 6 concludes by arguing that market-based innovation, profit-oriented entrepreneurs and growth-oriented states will never award the bicycle the priority it deserves.

2. INVENTION ALREADY HAPPENED

According to Rob Penn's *It's all about the bike*, bicycles are the result of a long, incremental process of innovation. Patenting played a key role in incentivising bike development. The first predecessor of the modern bike was the dandy horse, a 'running machine' without pedals or chain, invented by Baron von Drais in 1817. Drais duly applied for patent protection in France, among other places.[3,4] Building on the dandy horse, a steady sequence of improvements resulted in today's safe, reliable, and efficient bicycle design. The velocipede (1860s–1870s) put pedals directly at the front wheel.[5] The 'ordinary' (1880s) had the iconic high front-wheel.[6] The bicycle as we know it, with two equal wheels of reasonable height, was first called the 'safety', as it came straight after the dangerous high-wheeler. One feature of the safety was the familiar diamond-shaped two-triangle frame. The Rover Safety was first manufactured in 1885.[7]

3 Deutsches Patent- und Markenamt, '200 years ago: Patent for Drais' "Laufmachine", the ancestor of all bicycle' (*DPMA*, 12 January 2018) www.dpma.de/english/our_office/publications/news/milestones/200jahrepatentfuerdasur-fahrrad/index.html, accessed 05 March 2025.

4 Robert Penn, *It's All About the Bike: The Pursuit of Happiness on Two Wheels* (Bloomsbury USA 2012) 48–49.

5 *Ibid.*51–52.

6 *Ibid.*143–147.

7 *Ibid.* 26–29.

In parallel to the development of the bike, essential components were taking shape through complementary innovation processes. The rear-wheel drive-chain was patented in 1879.[8,9] The pneumatic tyre was invented and patented[10] in 1888.[11] The 'ball bearing', a connecting part designed to reduce friction between the moving and the immobile parts of the bike, was serially patented throughout the 1870s.[12]

The defining parts of the bike – frame shape, ball bearings, drive train, tyres etc. – were developed in parallel, mutually reinforcing innovation processes that led to separate strings of original patents between the 1860s and the 1890s. About *one third* of the patents in the US Patent Office in the 1890s were bicycle-related. This caused the Patent Office to house the 'bike department' in a separate building.[13] By the year 1890, the bicycle was complete. In contrast to an airplane or a car, the basic design of the bike – safe, reliable, efficient, comfortable – has barely changed since.[14]

To date, bikes have had two peak moments of deployment in the West: in the 1890s across the Atlantic and in the 1950s in Europe. In 1890, there were about 150,000 cyclists in the US and a bike cost half a worker's yearly salary. By 1895, however, the price was down to a few weeks' wages and the US were adding a million cyclists a year.[15] In the US, the release of Ford's model T in 1908 heralded the arrival of the car age. Europe remained poorer and, moreover, suffered heavily from the two world wars. Altogether, this caused the 1950s to be a new golden age for the European bicycle industry. In the early 1950s, '[t]here were 12 million regular cyclists in Britain alone.'[16] In the UK, 3.5 million bikes were sold in 1955, but this number dropped to 2 million by 1958 and, ominously, the Mini went on sale in 1959.[17] The bike's popularity would know a huge rebound in the early 1970s, as a response to the oil crises and environmental concerns.[18]

---

8 Google Patent Scholar, 'US345851A' (*USPTO*, 20 July 1886) https://patents.google.com/patent/US345851A/en, accessed 05 March 2025.

9 Penn (n 4) 91.

10 Deutsches Patent- und Markenamt, 'Re-inventing the wheel: 100 years ago John Dunlop, the (re)inventor of the pneumatic tire died' (*DPMA*, 23 November 2021) www.dpma.de/english/our_office/publications/milestones/inventionsthatmadehistory/dunlop/index.html, accessed 05 March 2025.

11 Penn (n 4) 116.

12 *Ibid.* 61–64.

13 *Ibid.* 3.

14 *Ibid.* 28.

15 *Ibid.* 2.

16 *Ibid.* 13.

17 *Ibid.* 13.

18 Carlton Reid, *Bike Boom: The Unexpected Resurgence of Cycling* (Island Press 2017).

Figure 1. Wilson's Graph

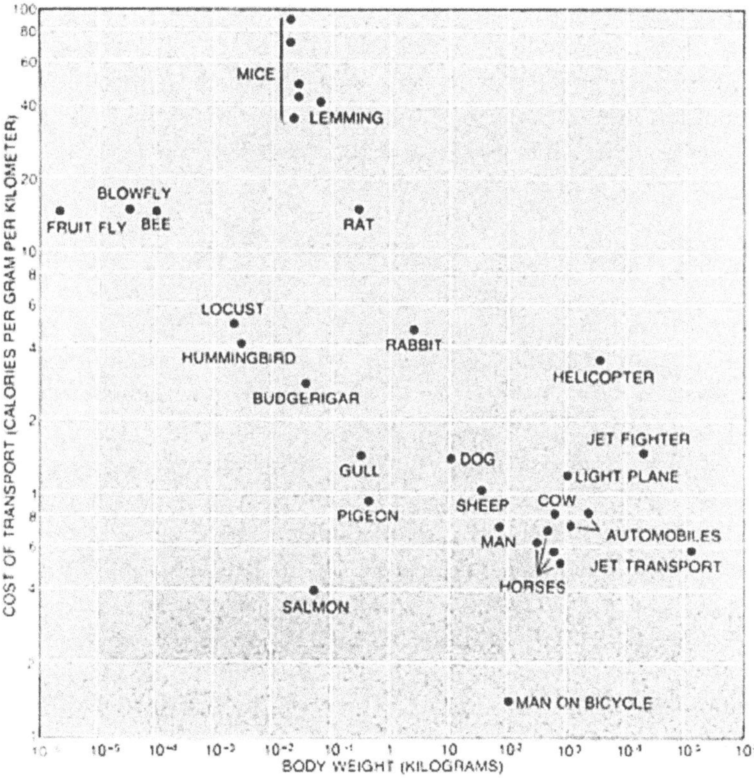

MAN ON A BICYCLE ranks first in efficiency among traveling animals and machines in terms of energy consumed in moving a certain distance as a function of body weight. The rate of energy consumption for a bicyclist (about .15 calorie per gram per kilometer) is approximately a fifth of that for an unaided walking man (about .75 calorie per gram per kilometer). With the exception of the black point representing the bicyclist (*lower right*), this graph is based on data originally compiled by Vance A. Tucker of Duke University.

In March 1973, Oxford Professor S.S. Wilson published a celebratory article about the bicycle titled 'Bicycle Technology' in the magazine Scientific American.[19] It was in this article that the ultimate, often reproduced,[20] graph on the miracle of the bicycle was published. The graph shows that of all known forms of biological

---

19 S.S. Wilson, 'Bicycle Technology' (1973) 228 Scientific American 81.

20 See, for instance, Thalia Verkade, 'Waarom de fiets veel sneller is dan je denkt (en de auto veel trager)' (*De Correspondent*, 26 July 2018) https://decorrespondent.nl/8416/waarom-de-fiets-veel-sneller-is-dan-je-denkt-en-de-auto-veel-trager/ce3997f0-b4d0-001a-1446-286b3ee9a89e, accessed 05 March 2025; and 'Bikes make humans better, just ask Steve Jobs' (*Bicycle Network*, 7 May 2020) https://bicyclenetwork.com.au/newsroom/2020/05/07/bikes-make-humans-better-just-ask-steve-jobs/, accessed 05 March 2025.

or human-made movement, the bike is the most energy-efficient way of moving a certain mass over a certain distance.[21] Cycling appears to be an extraordinarily efficient way of moving, far more economical than driving, flying or even walking. By biophysical standards, the bike may be perfect and has proven timeless. Naturally, a lot of bike-related inventions were – and are – still to follow, for instance, regarding gearing, materials, and clothing. However, the standard design of the bike dates back to 1885 and has not changed ever since: invention already happened.

3. A TECHNOLOGY OF EMANCIPATION

The bike is more than just a technological miracle. Its impact on society is surprisingly deep and wide-ranging. The bike was the first affordable means of mass transport. In the West, the working class became mobile, and people could move further away from their homes, to find employment. They could move out of the crammed, unhygienic late 19th-century inner cities to take up residence in dedicated living quarters in the suburbs. There, they could establish sports clubs, choirs, and libraries. Naturally, they could also cycle further to join meetings of labour unions, or to take up better employment in another factory.[22]

The bicycle also supported women's emancipation. Cycling required women to wear 'rational' clothing. Cycling women claimed the freedom of the road and the freedom to dress practically. In short, they claimed ownership over their movement and bodies.[23] Today, bicycles are still used and even reconsidered as enabling transportation technologies in many countries in the Majority World,[24] also and especially in rural environments. Farmers bring their produce to market on bicycles and children can get to far-away schools, courtesy of their bikes.[25]

These examples illustrate that the bike is a prime example of an 'appropriate technology', a concept developed by Ernst Fritz Schumacher (1973). Appropriate technology is technology with a human face. It does not use more energy, resources or capital than required for the job. Appropriate technologies are inclusive towards the poor by substituting labour for capital. Examples of appropriate technologies include self-contained solar lamps, hand-powered

---

21 Whereas many of the data embedded in Wilson's graph were compiled by researchers at Duke University, Wilson himself added the bike data. The graph does not specify the speed at which the energy efficiencies were measured, nor any assumptions about the biological or mechanical specifics of the modes of movement considered (i.e. what kind of mouse, what kind of cyclist). Nor have I found replications of the original study.

22 Penn (n 4) 3–5.

23 *Ibid.* 6–7.

24 Emmanuel Mogaji, 'Cycling Could Be a Boon for Lagos – but People Fear for Their Safety on Bikes' (*The Conversation*, 1 June 2023) http://theconversation.com/cycling-could-be-a-boon-for-lagos-but-people-fear-for-their-safety-on-bikes-196584, accessed 05 March 2025.

25 See, e.g., Qhubeka, a bike-based development project in Southern Africa; Qhubeka, 'About us' www.qhubeka.org/about-us, accessed 05 March 2025.

water pumps and natural building materials. Schumacher sang the virtues of appropriate technology in light of his humanistic, labour-centred vision of economics and his concerns about unsustainable resource use.

Recently, the appropriate technology movement has teamed up with the open software and open design movements.[26] As a consequence, the more common term is currently 'open source appropriate technology' (OSAT). The open source movement contributed that appropriate technology is only ever truly inclusive if it is transparent. People should not only be able to use the technology but also to cocreate it. The technology has to be readily understandable to consumers who take an interest. Only such technologies are truly emancipatory and democratic. The bike fully qualifies. Even today, the non-electric bike is a machine one can intuitively understand.

It was the Austrian priest and radical philosopher of technology, Ivan Illich, who first implied that bicycles are appropriate technologies.[27] In *Energy and Equity: The Industrialisation of Traffic*, originally published in 1974, he calculated how 'fast' cars actually drive when the hours spent in traffic (jams) are compounded by the hours car owners spend to finance the car, including vehicle purchase, petrol, insurance, servicing and taxes. 'The model American puts in 1,600 hours to get 7,500 miles: less than five miles per hour,' Illich maintained.[28] Bicycles, meanwhile, let people move at far greater speed than walking 'without taking up significant amounts of scarce space, energy, or time.'[29] Does that mean that cars are completely redundant to Illich? No, '[m]otors can be used to transport the sick, the lame, the old, and the just plain lazy.'[30]

4. BIKES IN TIMES OF CLIMATE CHANGE

In times of environmental crisis in general and climate change in particular, the argument in favour of the bike gains another dimension. It is one thing to compare the bike to the combustion-engine car. It is quite another to identify the environmental advantages of the bike over the electric car. The use of bicycles and electric cars alike reduces CO_2 emissions and exhaust fumes. I nevertheless maintain that biking has added advantages for the environment and

---

26 Joshua M. Pearce, 'The Case for Open Source Appropriate Technology' (2012) 14 Environment, Development and Sustainability 425; Kerstin Balka, Christina Raasch and Cornelius Herstatt, 'Open Source Enters the World of Atoms: A Statistical Analysis of Open Design' (2009) 14 First Monday https://firstmonday.org/ojs/index.php/fm/article/view/2670, accessed 05 March 2025.

27 Schumacher's *Small is Beautiful* does not mention the bicycle. Ernst F Schumacher, *Small Is Beautiful: A Study of Economics as If People Mattered* (Blond & Briggs 1973).

28 Ivan Illich, *Toward a History of Needs* (Pantheon 1978) ch 'Energy and Equity', 110ff.

29 *Ibid.*17–19.

30 *Ibid.*19.

for health over and above the advantages derived from driving an electric car. I quote from reports of the UN Intergovernmental Panel on Climate Change, which summarise the natural and social science of climate change and inform policy-making processes under the UN Framework Convention on Climate Change (UNFCCC).[31]

The Intergovernmental Panel on Climate Change (IPCC) has stated that about 8 percent of global CO_2 emissions are due to urban transport.[32] To reduce this carbon footprint, different options are on the table, including electric cars, public transport and cycling. The IPCC maintains that shifting towards 'active mobility' – i.e. cycling and walking – can 'reduce demand for transport services.' Meanwhile, '[e]lectric vehicles powered by low-emissions electricity offer the largest decarbonisation potential for landbased transport, on a life cycle basis.'[33] In other words, bicycles precede electric cars; the motorised transport that remains can afterwards be greened through electrification. How much CO_2 per passenger-kilometre a bicycle emits depends, in reality, on the diet of the cyclist. Although bikes are not fuel-powered, they are food-powered and certain (meat- and dairy-heavy) diets emit more CO_2 per kcal of cycling energy than others. It is, therefore, not easy to determine how much CO_2 cycling saves, compared to internal combustion cars and electric cars.[34] For maximum impact, though, cycle and become vegan.

When compared to electric cars, a definite advantage of bicycles is that the material, particularly steel, required for construction is reduced. If, moreover, the bicycle under scrutiny is analogue and not electric, then the need for rare earth materials, used in bike and car batteries alike, is reduced to zero. Rare earths will have to be sourced through mining, which has additional influences on local environments and politics.[35] Cycling most certainly has the edge over electric cars when the additional health-benefits are taken into account. The Summary for Policymakers of the IPCC's 2023 Synthesis Report claims that 'Accelerated climate action can also provide co-benefits [...]. Many mitigation actions would have benefits for health through lower air pollution, active mobility (e.g. walking,

---

31 Adopted at New York on 9 May 1992.

32 Priyadarshi R Shukla et al. (eds) Climate Change 2022: Mitigation of Climate Change. Contribution of Working Group III to the Sixth Assessment Report of the Intergovernmental Panel on Climate Change (CUP 2022) ch 'Transport', 1059.

33 Core Writing Team, Hoesung Lee and José Romero (eds) Climate Change 2023: Synthesis Report. Contribution of Working Groups I, II and III to the Sixth Assessment Report of the Intergovernmental Panel on Climate Change (Intergovernmental Panel on Climate Change 2023) 26–31, 105–106.

34 Hannah Ritchie, 'Which form of transport has the smallest carbon footprint? How can individuals reduce their emissions from transport?' (*Our World in Data*, 30 August 2023) https://ourworldindata.org/travel-carbon-footprint, accessed 05 March 2025.

35 Lukas Boer, Andrea Pescatori and Martin Stuermer, 'Energy Transition Metals: Bottleneck for Net-Zero Emissions?' (2023) Journal of the European Economic Association 39.

cycling), and shifts to sustainable healthy diets.'[36] Active commuting can substantially reduce overall mortality, as well as morbidity of lifestyle diseases like obesity and type-2 diabetes.[37]

5. INVENTIONS FOR LOW CARBON URBAN TRANSPORT

Not bikes but electric car are the talk of the town, despite some setbacks in early 2024 due to the continued popularity of cheap internal combustion cars.[38] Biden's Inflation Reduction Act has massively subsidised the sale of electric cars with final assembly in the US.[39] Chinese electric car manufacturers, meanwhile, are making big strides and export around the globe.[40] Torn between the desire to protect their domestic manufacturers and the desire to green their economies, European governments may end up supporting the sale of cheaper Chinese electric vehicles over more expensive European cars. The Flemish public bus company De Lijn, for instance, ordered 92 electric busses from Chinese company BYD instead of Belgian bus manufacturer Van Hool.[41] The Flemish Government, moreover, provides up to 5,000 euros in subsidies for the acquisition of a mid-range electric car, without local content requirements.[42]

It is clear that the electric car takes pride of place in the political mind as a strategy for reducing greenhouse gas emissions from urban transport. How does this translate into the domain of invention, as documented through patent statistics? It turns out that electric cars are, also there, star technologies. In

36 Core Writing Team (n 33) 26.

37 Pekka Oja et al., 'Health Benefits of Cycling: A Systematic Review' (2011) 21 Scandinavian Journal of Medicine & Science in Sports 496.

38 Steff Chavez and Peter Campbell, 'Stellantis warns of EV 'bloodbath' as Ford cuts F-150 Lightning output' (*Financial Times*, 19 January 2024) www.ft.com/content/a6b40484-7774-4aad-91a4-4e9115006b60, accessed 27 January 2024 and, Tabby Kinder, 'Tesla shares drop 12% after sales growth warning' (*Financial Times*, 25 January 2024) www.ft.com/content/b37912bf-6f01-4393-85cc-df064332b10f, accessed 27 January 2024.

39 Leo Banks, 'How Inflation Reduction Act Electric Vehicle Incentives Are Driving a U.S. Manufacturing Renaissance' (*Center for American Progress*, 22 November 2023) www.americanprogress.org/article/how-inflation-reduction-act-electric-vehicle-incentives-are-driving-a-u-s-manufacturing-renaissance/, accessed 05 March 2025.

40 Edward White and Peter Campbell, 'China's electric vehicle dominance presents a challenge to the west' (*Financial Times*, 5 January 2024) www.ft.com/content/de696ddb-2201-4830-848b-6301b64ad0e5, accessed 27 January 2024.

41 Igor Bulcke, 'De Lijn onder vuur vanwege aankoop elektrische bussen uit China: "Schande"' (*Het Laatste Nieuws*, 5 January 2024) www.hln.be/binnenland/de-lijn-onder-vuur-vanwege-aankoop-elektrische-bussen-uit-china-schande~a51b84a1/?referrer=https%3A%2F%2Fwww.google.com%2F, accessed 05 March 2025.

42 Departement Mobiliteit en Openbare Werken, 'Premie voor aankoop van een zero-emissievoertuig' www.vlaanderen.be/premie-voor-aankoop-van-een-elektrische-wagen, accessed 05 March 2025.

April 2021, the International Energy Agency (IEA) and the European Patent Office (EPO) jointly published a report titled *Patents and the Energy Transition: Global trends in clean energy technology innovation*.[43] The IEA contributed a roadmap for the energy transition, thus providing guidance as to what types of inventions are required for sustainable development around the globe while complying with the Paris Agreement.[44] The EPO, in turn, contributed a patent database and a classification of all patents that are of relevance to the energy transition. These patents on 'low carbon energy' inventions are divided into patents that relate to energy supply (solar, wind, efficient combustion etc.), enabling cross-cutting technologies (batteries, smart grids etc.) and end-use technologies (electric vehicles, insulation etc.). The report does not even mention bicycles, including electrical ones.

The EPO identified about 420,000 'international patent families' related to the energy transition that were filed between 2000 and 2019. These families represent patents that have been filed and published at more than one national patent office, at a regional patent office or via an international patent application. These patent families represent inventions that are sufficiently important in the eyes of their inventors as to warrant international protection.

The report is revealing. Since 2015, the single most important category of patents on low carbon energy inventions regards the duo of electric vehicles – among end use technologies – and batteries – among enabling technologies.[45] As a consequence, among the top-15 applicants for patents on low carbon energy inventions, there are six carmakers (Toyota, Ford, General Motors, Honda, Volkswagen and Hyundai) and six major battery providers (Samsung, Panasonic, LG, Robert Bosch, Hitachi, Toshiba).[46] Car batteries and electric vehicles represent the most pronounced cluster of patents in low carbon energy inventions. In total, about 100,000 of the 420,000 international patent families are related to road transportation. The vast majority of these patents are related to electric cars.[47]

In turn, a lot of the invention and subsequent innovation in *cycling* today targets high-profitability niches that are only partly conducive to putting the bike *as an appropriate technology* in the centre of the road. These include bike-renting services,[48] employer-based bike-leasing schemes for up-market

43 Yann Ménière et al., 'Patents and the Energy Transition' (European Patent Office and International Energy Agency 2021).

44 Paris Agreement under the United Nations Framework Convention on Climate Change (UNFCCC), adopted by the 21st Conference of the Parties (COP) on 12 December 2015.

45 Ménière et al. (n 43) 38–39.

46 *Ibid.*13.

47 *Ibid.*52.

48 For instance, Swapfiets, 'Welcome to Swapfiets' https://swapfiets.com/, accessed 05 March 2025.

bikes[49,50] bike insurance,[51] electric bike development,[52] spare-time bikes like gravel bikes[53] and further advances in off-the-charts racing bikes. Whether these schemes improve bike-centred urban mobility depends on who uses them in what circumstances and how technologies and legal schemes are translated into more down-to-earth, day-to-day applications. The fact that even young, fit people currently ride e-bikes that contain patented batteries with rare earths most certainly does not increase the standing of the bike as an inclusive, health-enhancing technology.[54]

What would be truly sustainable inventions that improve the bike as an appropriate technology? – Dynamos that work better in the rain, better mudguards and rain protection, materiel improvements to protect bike lanes more cheaply from sun of rain, better and faster drying rain gear, light but cheap bike materials, more distinctive bike bells, price reductions for cargo bikes and tandems, improvements in bike locking technologies. Generally, anything that makes the average city bike faster and the average race bike more comfortable is going in the right direction.

Arguing in favour of making urban transport bike-centred is not a Luddite argument. Many aspects of the bike can change, have changed and will change. Although the standard design is fixed, invention is not over, and intellectual property might be able to play a role in continuing improvements. Tullio Campagnolo (1901–1983) – founder of the eponymous company that provides the components on the bike that won Tadej Pogačar the 2020, 2021 and 2024 Tour de France – registered 135 patents on bike-related inventions is his life.[55]

One recent example of innovation in professional cycling that could be of use to commuting cyclists is the Gabba.[56] Around 2010, cycling gear manufacturer Castelli wanted to improve its rain gear. They tested several materials until

---

49 For instance, Lease a Bike, 'Ride your dreambike' www.lease-a-bike.nl/, accessed 05 March 2025.

50 See, for an overview of the trend, Lars Becker, 'Bike Sharing and Bike Leasing are Becoming Established' (*ISPO*, 16 October 2018) www.ispo.com/en/trends/bike-sharing-and-bike-leasin g-whats-behind-trend, accessed 05 March 2025.

51 For instance, 'Bike Insurance made easy' (*BikeInsurance.eu*) www.bikeinsurance.eu/en, accessed 05 March 2025.

52 See, for an overview of the trend, 'Electric Bike Market Size: Market Research Report' (*Fortune Business Insights*, 29 April 2024) www.fortunebusinessinsights.com/electric-e-bik e-market-102022, accessed 05 March 2025.

53 See, for an overview of the trend, Simon Usborne, 'Why gravel cycling is the next big biking trend' (*National Geographic UK*, 19 February 2023) www.nationalgeographic.com/travel/ article/gravel-cycling-biking-trend-uk, accessed 05 March 2025.

54 Rijksinstituut voor Volksgezondheid en Milieu, 'Vooral jongvolwassenen voldoen minder vaak aan beweegrichtlijnen' (13 November 2023) www.rivm.nl/nieuws/vooral-jongvolwassene n-voldoen-minder-vaak-aan-beweegrichtlijnen, accessed 05 March 2025.

55 Penn (n 4) 96–97.

56 Vern Pitt, 'A love letter to my Castelli Gabba jacket' (*Cycling Weekly*, 25 October 2023) www.cyclingweekly.com/news/a-love-letter-to-my-castelli-gabba-jacket, accessed 05 March 2025.

Norwegian professional bike racer Gabriel Rasch came up with a new assemblage using waterproof and windproof textile and other materials. The 'Gabba' (after Rasch's nickname) was born through a process of 'user innovation'.[57] Quickly, it was patented by Castelli. Several competitors started tinkering, trying to work around the Castelli patent. The original, however, remains most popular with the riders. The Gabba allows riders to peddle for hours in rain and wind while hardly getting wet or cold. The Gabba is moreover light, aerodynamic, and fashionable and, in that way, further reduces the resistance to cycling in the rain.

6. THE STATE HATES BICYCLES

Section 4 showed that patents are *de facto* used to invent better electric cars and batteries. Meanwhile, there is no comprehensive policy nor institutional framework to stimulate bike-focused inventions. These are aspects of a broader tendency. Given the marvels related to cycling, a deeply democratic state would be required to put walking and cycling central in any system of urban transport. Unfortunately, little of the sort is actually being implemented.

A bike-centred urban transport system would mean moving the bike to the centre of the road, providing impeccable infrastructure including smooth road surfaces and covered bike lanes where it is too hot or too wet to cycle otherwise. It means radically improving the safety conditions for cyclists by dismantling car-serving road designs. It means providing priority for bikes in all circumstances, providing parking space for bikes instead of cars, especially attached to residential or office buildings. It means incentivising people financially to cycle to work. It means encouraging employers to provide changing rooms and showers. It means banning car commercials, thus undermining 'car culture'.[58] It means acting far more aggressively against bike theft. It means fostering innovation in cycling clothing, materials, and infrastructure. It means encouraging supermarkets to facilitate shopping by cargo bike. Naturally, such a system has to be supplemented with effective alternatives for the less able, the young and the old. There will still be a need for a well-developed, flexible public transport system that allows passengers to take their bikes with them. Cars, naturally, will still be required for longer trips and for moving stuff and less able people when public transport is unavailable.

Still, despite the urgency of climate change, only the most partial version of this plan is turned into reality. After a spike in the popularity of cycling

57 Eric von Hippel, 'Democratizing Innovation: The Evolving Phenomenon of User Innovation' (2005) 55 Journal für Betriebswirtschaft 63.

58 Matthew Paterson, 'Car Culture and Global Environmental Politics' (2000) 26 Review of International Studies 253.

during the pandemic,[59] cycling has been caught in the general scepticism towards green politics. Certain established policies that facilitate cycling have come under increasing pressure in places like London and Berlin.[60] These are examples of the general phenomenon of the 'bikelash',[61] or organised opposition against biking policies and cycling lanes.[62] This bikelash has become part of the so-called 'culture wars'[63] and conservative political parties like Germany's Christian Democrats and the British Tories are leading the charge.[64] The question I want to address is, what factors of political economy provide a deep explanation for the phenomenon of 'bikelash'? What are the reasons, beyond conservative ideology and self-reinforcing community outcry, that cause the bike to be a threat?

My argument boils down to the idea that there is a 'car-industrial complex'[65] that has captured the state.[66] Many interests are vested in the car industry. These relate to both the industry (profits, wages) and the state (jobs, taxes, industrial capacity) sides of the equation. These interests together lock in the continuation of the car industry and point towards electric cars – stimulated by patent protection – rather than bikes – for which breakthrough invention happened long ago – as a solution to greenhouse gas emissions in urban transport. Even in liberal democracies like most European countries, and even if arguments for deep democracy scream 'bike', current car-addicted states are no good platforms to implement the overdue overhaul of the urban transport sector that would put the bike lane in the middle of the road.

In 'The political economy of car dependence: a systems of provision approach', Mattioli et al. discuss the political economy of car use in current industrial economies. Mattioli et al. point out the scale and the economic

---

59 Carlton Reid, 'Bicycling booms during lockdown – But there's a warning from history' (*Forbes*, 1 May 2020) www.forbes.com/sites/carltonreid/2020/05/01/bicycling-booms-during-lockdown-but-theres-a-warning-from-history/, accessed 05 March 2025.

60 Aitor Hernandez-Morales and Peter Wilke, 'Bikeless in Berlin: Europe's cycle backlash has begun' (*Politico*, 12 October 2023) www.politico.eu/article/europe-bikes-cycling-backlash-berlin-germany-cycling-cars-emissions/, accessed 05 March 2025.

61 Janette Sadik-Khan and Seth Solomonow, 'The bikelash paradox: how cycle lanes enrage some but win votes' (*The Guardian*, 29 October 2021) www.theguardian.com/environment/bike-blog/2021/oct/29/the-bikelash-paradox-how-cycle-lanes-enrage-some-but-win-votes, accessed 05 March 2025.

62 Kirsty Wild et al., 'Beyond "Bikelash": Engaging with Community Opposition to Cycle Lanes' (2018) 13 Mobilities 505.

63 Andrew John Hoffman, 'Climate Science as Culture War' (June 2012) Ross School of Business Paper No. 1361, Stanford Social Innovation Review, 10(4): 30–37 https://papers.ssrn.com/abstract=2944200, accessed 05 March 2025.

64 Hernandez-Morales and Wilke (n 60).

65 After the 'military-industrial complex', as first hinted at by President Eisenhower in his 17 January 1961 fairwell address, see William D Hartung, 'Eisenhower's Warning the Military-Industrial Complex Forty Years Later' (2001) 18 World Policy Journal 39.

66 Giulio Mattioli et al., 'The Political Economy of Car Dependence: A Systems of Provision Approach' (2020) 66 Energy Research & Social Science 101486; Paterson (n 58).

significance of the automotive industry. Based on data of 2005, Mattioli et al. assert that car manufacturing provides employment to 5 percent of the world's total manufacturing workforce and has a turnover that rivals the size of the entire Italian economy. The sector has, moreover, many systemic linkages to other crucial sectors, including steel, rubber, glass, oil, and construction. Due to the size of the sector, the state receives significant tax income from the automotive industry.[67]

The interests of the state in supporting the car industry play out in a specific way, according to Mattioli et al., because passenger car manufacturing is characterised by important economies of scale.[68] Consequently, there is a limited number of large companies with multiple brands and global reach. These companies make cars in large factories. Competition between global conglomerates is fierce and the break-even point in car manufacturing is only reached when car factories run at 85 percent capacity. The industry and the specific units of production are, in other words, badly positioned to cope with fluctuations in demand. If the industry fails to make a profit, then bankruptcies or relocations may follow that could destroy local and national economies, as car manufacturers and their suppliers tend to be concentrated in specific areas (Detroit, Lower Saxony etc.). Politicians, meanwhile, are often judged on their economic record, including the number of jobs they have managed to create. Labour unions, also desirous to save jobs, often cooperate with car manufacturers and form a front opposing the Government. Car manufacturers have, therefore, become are 'too big to fail' and thus have to be bailed out when, in an economic downturn, people postpone the sale of a new car.[69]

Mattioli et al. point towards the interests of car manufacturers in profits and the interests of the state in the directly connected jobs (politicians need to be re-elected), taxes (the state needs income) and industrial capability. Let me spell out the rationales of industrial capability and profit in more detail. I want to highlight the fact that there are significant links between the industrial capability and the geopolitical power of a state. For among others geopolitical reasons, states may want to maintain a domestic automobile industry.[70] During the Second World War, the US automobile industry shifted to wartime production of military vehicles and aircraft components. The industry contributed about a fifth towards the total US war production.[71] Today, major geopolitical powers – the US, China, Japan, Korea and the EU – retain the capacity to mass-produce

67 Mattioli et al. (n 66) 4.

68 A key cause of the important economies of scale is the fact that cars require all-steel bodies.

69 Mattioli et al. (n 66) 4–5.

70 Paterson (n 58) 268.

71 Charles K. Hyde, *Arsenal of Democracy: The American Automobile Industry in World War II* (Wayne State University Press 2013).

cars.[72] The US experience during World War Two has proven that in times of (World) war, this industrial capacity can make a difference towards the state's fighting power.

Bikes, meanwhile, certainly have military application. They were used as early as the Franco-Prussian War (1870–1871) and first became important in the Second Anglo-Boer War (1899–1902). They were used throughout the World Wars and remain salient for reconnaissance and in asymmetrical warfare.[73] Recently, the American Defense Advanced Research Project Agency (DARPA) funded the development of a foldable, optionally electric mountain bike that is used by US scouts jumping from aircraft.[74] Be that as it may, it is obvious that motorised vehicles – tanks, armoured vehicles, lorries, cars – and the vastly bigger manufacturing infrastructure they bring with them, have become more important than bicycles to large-scale, industrial, interstate warfare in the 21st Century. This constitutes another reason to maintain the car-industrial complex.

Finally, as regards the profit drive of the car industry, Mattioli et al. do not specifically assess the profitability trade-offs between car-based and bike-based transport. It is hard to find publications that have asked what would happen with absolute profitability (total profits) and relative profitability (profits in relation to turnover) if cars – whether electric or fossil fuel – would be replaced by bikes for urban transport. A back-of-the-envelope calculation shows, however, that there would be a sizeable loss of aggregate profits if urban transport shifted from cars to bikes. I am working here with publicly available Statista data on the yearly sales of new bicycles[75] and passenger cars[76] around the world.[77] Multiple informal internet sources report that the sale of a combustion engine passenger car, which is still dominant today in global new car sales, will provide a margin of profit of around 5 percent.[78] Bike manufacturers are actually said to have higher

---

72 Observatory of Economic Complexity, 'Cars' (OEC, 2022) https://oec.world/en/profile/hs/cars, accessed 23 January 2024.

73 John Norris, *The Military History of the Bicycle: The Forgotten War Machine* (Pen and Sword Military 2021).

74 Police Bike Store, 'Montague Paratrooper – Military Folding Mountain Bike' (*Police Bike Store*) www.policebikestore.com/montague-paratrooper.htm, accessed 05 March 2025, about the foldable electric military mountainbike 'Montague Paratrooper'.

75 Including electric bicycles but excluding second-hand bikes, motorbikes, scooters, mopeds, bike rentals etc.

76 Including SUVs and electric vehicles but excluding buses, trucks and motorcycles.

77 Statista, 'Passenger cars – Worldwide' (*Statista*, 2023) www.statista.com/outlook/mmo/passenger-cars/worldwide, accessed 24 January 2024 and Statista, 'Bicycles – Worldwide' (*Statista*, 2023) www.statista.com/outlook/mmo/bicycles/worldwide, accessed 24 January 2024.

78 Patricia Nilsson, 'BMW to stop raising car prices after years of increases' (*Financial Times*, 15 March 2023) www.ft.com/content/51b174c6-bf04-4cb7-870f-c4058210b7de, accessed 24 January 2024 and Markus Hagenmaier et al., 'How to Profit in Tomorrow's Automotive and Mobility Industry' (*Boston Consultancy Group*, 16 February 2023) www.bcg.com/publications/2023/profiting-in-the-future-of-automotive-industry, accessed 05 March 2025.

profit margins of 10 to 12 percent.[79] Bike manufacturing is thus on average relatively more profitable than internal combustion engine car manufacturing, given the current competition and economies of scale in both sectors.

However, the *absolute* profitability of car manufacturing appears to be an order of magnitude higher than the absolute profitability of bike manufacturing. In 2024, about 140 million new bikes are projected to be sold worldwide, alongside 70 million new cars. Still, the total turnover of the car industry is almost 2 *trillion* USD compared to only 70 billion USD for the bike industry. The car market size is thus about 25 times as big as the bike market size in dollar value. The underlying reason is, of course, that the average new bike sold is projected to cost only 500 dollars in 2024, whereas the average new car will be priced at 28,000 dollars. If one accounts with profit margins of 5 percent for cars and 15 percents for bikes, then the profits captured on a yearly basis are in the order of a 100 billion in the car industry and 10 billion in the bike industry.

If we assume that 50 million of said 70 million new cars are used predominantly for urban transport and that these cars could be replaced by bikes at a rate of two bikes for every car that goes off the road – also assuming that the economies of scale would not change – then we can calculate the shift in profits that would result from a shift towards a more bike-centred urban mobility. 50 million cars represent about 70 percent of the sales volume of cars worldwide. In a simple mathematical representation, their substitution would result in the evaporation of *70 billion USD* in car-related profits, or 70 percent of the total profits of 100 billion USD. The 100 million extra bikes at an average price of 500 USD per bike and a profit rate of 15 percent would represent an additional profit of only *7 billion USD* from the additional sales of new bikes. The net loss of profits to be captured in urban transport from the sale of new cars and bikes would thus be in the tune of 60–70 billion USD, every year. This is on par with the GDP of the DR Congo or Belarus.

In reality, the situation would be worse because second-hand cars are far more expensive than second-hand bikes, and car-related profits would be lost in this market, too. Profits would also be lost from the insurance industry, repair services, etc. Moreover, the economies of scale in car manufacturing imply that many car manufacturers would eventually not survive in the tighter market, as scaling down is not always an option. More companies and capital would go into bike manufacturing, potentially increasing competition, strengthening the economies of scale, and reducing the price of bikes further. All of these elements suggest that far *more* profits than 60 billion annually would be lost, providing

79 Neha Dewan, 'Profit margins on bicycle exports can range between 10-12%' (*Inthedollarbusiness*) https://in.thedollarbusiness.com/magazine/profit-margins-on-bicycle-exports-can-range-between-10-12-g-d-kapoor-ed-sm-hero-cycles/2318, accessed 10 April 2025.

even bigger incentives to car companies to lobby a receptive state against drastic reforms.

That a lack of private profitability can undermine the roll-out of proven, deeply democratic technologies has been on display regarding other environmental technologies, too. Renewable energy is a case in point. The sources of renewable power that have been taken up most broadly, notably solar photovoltaic (PV) energy and wind energy, have exhausted their growth potential under the current incentive system as prices are falling and, with them, profitability. Solar PV electricity is currently often cheaper than the cheapest electricity from coal-fired power plants. Selling electricity from solar and wind can thus no longer provide a healthy margin over the costs of producing and installing solar and wind capacity. Cut-throat competition has led to many bankruptcies and has caused surviving firms to seek rents through, among others, trademark and patent protection.[80]

In solar PV, there are few barriers to entry and, accordingly, competition is fierce. Solar PV works in a highly decentralised fashion – any household with roof solar capacity can make solar PV electricity – which makes it increasingly difficult to control energy production and capture profits. Fossil fuels, meanwhile, are scarce by design and found in specific locations that can be owned and controlled.[81] Whereas consumers may, upon careful reflection, prefer cheap renewable energy and cheap bikes over more expensive fossil fuel energy and cars, producers do not. As production precedes consumption, the supply-side of the economy matters. In effect, solar PV is eliminating electricity production as a sector of the economy in which profits can be made, and capital can be accumulated. That is an important reason why oil and gas companies do not invest.[82]

The parallel with biking and the urban transport sector is uncanny. Due to an impending erosion of total car-related profits that cannot be remedied by moving into less profitable bicycle manufacturing, car companies do not want urban transport to be built around cycling. States are dependent on the car industry for industrial capacity, jobs and taxes and are therefore disinclined to wholeheartedly embrace the bike, even if the bike is a far more democratic technology than the car and even if states are desperately looking for ways to comply with the Paris Agreement's climate change mitigation targets (Article 4.2).

---

80 Jack Copley, 'Decarbonizing the Downturn: Addressing Climate Change in an Age of Stagnation' (2023) 27 Competition & Change 429, 439–441.

81 Brett Christophers, 'Fossilised Capital: Price and Profit in the Energy Transition' (2022) 27 New Political Economy 146, 157.

82 Andreas Malm, *Fossil Capital: The Rise of Steam Power and the Roots of Global Warming* (Verso Books 2016).

7. THE LIMITS OF MARKET-DRIVEN INNOVATION

Invention is finding and developing a new technology. Innovation is spreading 'new combinations' around the economy. Innovation is what entrepreneurs do. The two are related but are not identical.[83] Innovation can relate to combinations of *new* technologies, products, or processes – i.e. it can involve inventions – but it can also relate to the adaptation of already existing technologies. Schumpeter made this distinction between inventions and innovations and claimed that entrepreneurs revolutionise the economic fabric of society through innovation, leading to 'creative destruction'.[84] In Schumpeter's vision for a dynamic capitalism, entrepreneurs move because they are motivated to revolutionise the market, build a private kingdom, conquer and find joy in the process of mainstreaming new ideas.[85] The determining factor is that the entrepreneur's move into the markets will create profits, i.e. surplus over costs, by virtue of the new combination.[86] In a capitalist system, even if entrepreneurs do not explicitly mean to get rich, they will finance their further expansion out of earlier profits or – at the very least – will need to capture some profit to repay the bank that extended the original capital as credit.

The bike surfaces as an ambiguous technology in light of Schumpeter's theory of creative destruction through entrepreneurial innovation. A genuine bike revolution that puts the bike lane in the middle of the road would, naturally, be a true example of creative destruction. It would free up trillions of capital from car manufacturing, insurance, health care and construction, which would all become obsolete to a certain extent. Many households would slice their transport budgets and households; companies and states alike would be able to avoid costs related to climate change mitigation and adaptation. These trillions, no longer required to fuel urban car drives or to fight air pollution and diabetes, could then be put to productive use in other sectors. We could spend more money on both welfare and blue-sky research programmes. The bike revolution would also free plenty of time, space, and labour to be deployed leisurely or gainfully in other parts of the economy.

Still, the bike revolution sits uneasily with the idea of Schumpeterian entrepreneurial innovation. That the bike is an existing technology and no

83 Karol Śledzik, 'Schumpeter's View on Innovation and Entrepreneurship' (29 April 2013) Management Trends in Theory and Practice, (ed.) Stefan Hittmar, Faculty of Management Science and Informatics, University of Zilina & Institute of Management by University of Zilina, 2013 https://papers.ssrn.com/abstract=2257783, accessed 05 March 2025.

84 Joseph A. Schumpeter, *Capitalism, Socialism and Democracy* (Routledge 2013).

85 John T. Dalton and Andrew Logan, 'Teaching and Learning Schumpeter: A Dialogue Between Professor and Student' (April 11, 2019) www.ssrn.com/abstract=3370486, accessed 05 March 2025; Śledzik (n 83) 5.

86 Joseph A Schumpeter, *The Theory of Economic Development: An Inquiry Into Profits, Capital, Credit, Interest, and the Business Cycle* (Transaction Publishers 1983) 128–156.

recent invention is not the real problem. The problem is that the bike cannot ever be mainstreamed throughout urban transportation via entrepreneurial activity because the bike revolution would *destroy* rather than *create* profits. It would save a lot of costs for its users – like some cooperative structures do – but the size of the economy would shrink, at least at first. No bank would extend credit to the entrepreneur who intends to make the bike the predominant means of urban transport, as their venture would, ultimately, lose money. Even if bike entrepreneurs succeed, they will never make more profit than the combined profits of the car industry. That is the central difference between the car entrepreneur who destroys the horse-drawn carriages industry and the bike entrepreneur who wants to destroy the car industry.

The fact that Schumpeter explicitly links creative destruction to profit-*generating* entrepreneurial activities, and the fact that a profit-*oriented* version of his theories has become commonplace in capitalist and – later – neoliberal economic policymaking, preclude the advent of the bike revolution by undermining the business case of the bike. Economic change, development and growth in our societies do not only generate profit, but they are also *incentivised by* profit and *conducted by* profit-seeking entrepreneurs *financed by* profit-seeking banks.[87] Accordingly, in our societies, innovation is embodied in 'new combinations' that allow and even facilitate the capture of additional profits. By linking innovation with private, profit-driven entrepreneurship, our economic system has in essence established a direct, solid link between creative destruction and capital-intensive technologies. Capital-intensive is relative here. It means *more* capital-intensive than the previous technologies: more expensive, less transparent, less democratic, less open and less inclusive than previous technologies and thus more capable of capturing profits for the few.

When one is looking for something more capable of capturing profits than the previous technologies that have been implemented by profit-seeking entrepreneurs, it is rather likely that, in the long run, one has to come up with something new and thus invent something. Other entrepreneurs will have combined all existing technologies already. As, moreover, most simple technologies will have been invented already, ever more profitable technologies will logically have to be less transparent, more complicated and thus less inclusive than the previous generation of technologies. Strong patent rights, as mandated by the World Trade Organisation's (WTO) 1995 Agreement on Trade-related aspects of Intellectual Property Rights (TRIPs Agreement),[88] play

[87] These dynamics were not as pronounced with Schumpeter, who was ambivalent about who would capture the profits generated by the entrepreneurial activity – the entrepreneur, the capitalist, the bank, the workers or society at large Schumpeter (n 86). – and who later started to recognise entrepreneurial systems or even entrepreneurial states Schumpeter (n 84).

[88] Annex 1C to the Marrakesh Agreement establishing the World Trade Organisation of 15 April 1994, as amended on 23 January 2017.

a central role in today's Schumpeter-derived view of innovation because they allow investments in complicated technologies by facilitating the postponement of imitation, so that the inventor-innovator can capture a larger share of the return on their ever expanding investment. The requirement of complexity is built right into the heart of patent law, which determines that only *new* and *non-obvious* technologies are worthy of protection (Article 27.1 TRIPs Agreement). Patents are not there to stimulate the use of valuable existing technologies. There is thus no way the simplifying and profit-destroying bike revolution can happen via market-driven innovation, private entrepreneurship and patent law. The bike actually needs state planning,[89] but unfortunately, the state is captured.[90]

Patent law and Schumpeter's theory of secular growth due to profit-seeking entrepreneurship primes our innovation system to assume that the technical solution to a technical problem always needs to be some new technology that will come about by the inventive-innovative activities of private enterprise. It is simply not on the cards that invention might already have happened. Bicycles emerge in this paradigm as 'reactionary technologies'. In some way, riding a bike, you seem to be peddling backwards. Ever dynamic capitalism always imagines progress to be more convenient, more enigmatic, more involved, more technologically complicated. It is never simpler, more basic, more direct, and intuitive. Or, to quote Schumacher: 'Any intelligent fool can make things bigger, more complex, and more violent. It takes a touch of genius – and a lot of courage to move in the opposite direction.'[91]

---

89 Mariana Mazzucato, *Entrepreneurial State: Debunking Public Vs. Private Sector Myths* (Anthem Press 2015).

90 Paterson (n 58) 265–268.

91 Schumacher (n 27) 22.

PART V

INTERPRETING THE FUTURE: PATENT LANGUAGE, POLICY AND PROCEDURE

CHAPTER 18

SEMIOTIC TRANSLATION IN PATENT CLAIMS

Dan L. Burk[†]
Chancellor's Professor and Distinguished Professor of Law, University of California, Irvine

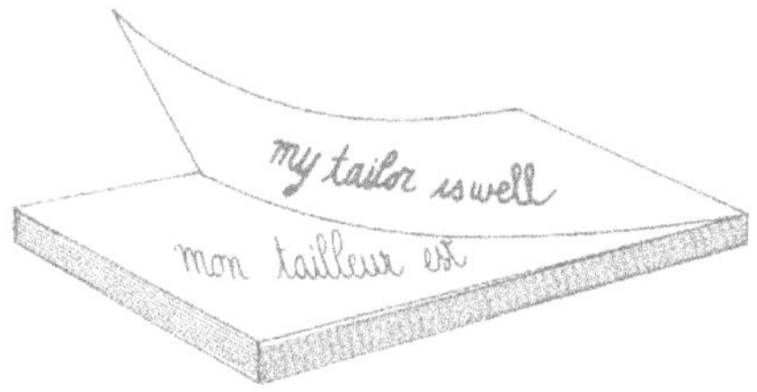

C1 UN Carbon Paper
Write in English and simultaneously the sentence appears in any language you select on the sheet underneath. Unexpurgated paper available at slightly higher cost.

1. INTRODUCTION

Item C1 of Jacques Carelman's *Catalog of Fantastic Things* is entitled 'UN Carbon Paper', and depicts a stack of paper sheets with an English phrase written on the top sheet. A corresponding French phrase appears on the second sheet, immediately below the writing on the first. The caption explains that the fantastical contrivance allows you to 'write in English and simultaneously the sentence appears in any language you select on the sheet underneath.' In addition to some presumably unintended amusement to the modern reader – that no one uses (or probably even remembers) conventional carbon paper, long since superseded by xerography and myriad other copying technologies – Item C1 suggests the conceit of a material device that instantaneously and effortlessly transliterates written language.

Beyond its entertainment value, the marvelous 'UN Carbon Paper' witticism points to a fundamental question in semiotics, or in the study of signs and their meaning.[1] In gesturing toward semiotics, Carelman also highlights – and

† 1962–2024.
1 *See* Umberto Eco, *A Theory of Semiotics* (Indiana University Press, 1976) 7.

perhaps illuminates – a fundamental problem in patent practice and patent doctrine. This is not a coincidence, as the text and drawings of every patent are quintessentially an exercise in signification. The semiotic nature of the patent document suggests that it may lend itself to the insights and methods developed to study signification more generally. This may be particularly apt in the circumstance of interpreting patent claims, which is a notoriously fraught exercise in determining meaning.

Consequently, with Carelman as my guide, in this chapter I pursue these questions in tandem, sketching out the beginnings of a semiotic approach to patent claim construction, to which 'UN Carbon Paper' contrivance provides an illustration. Surprisingly little has been previously said about patent semiotics.[2]

The overall project of exploring the details of patent semiotics would call for a much longer and more extensive exposition, but here it is possible to identify some fundamental parameters, offer an initial analysis and suggest where future inquiries might go. I begin by establishing some basic concepts and terminology, which I then consider in the context of claim construction. I conclude with brief observations as to the significance of this approach.

2. SIGNS AND WONDERS

We begin our consideration of patent semiotics, and of the 'UN Carbon Paper' contrivance, by observing that semiotics generally is the study of signs and the manner in which they convey meaning. Such signification occurs across a wide range of situations and domains. Certainly, language constitutes the paradigm system of signification, but signs and signification are found in myriad other circumstances. An animal, such as an eagle, may stand for or signify the United States of America; a geographic outcropping, such as a mountain, may stand for or signify the country of Switzerland. The reproductive organs of plants may signify different human emotions; a hammer or a wig or test tube may signify a particular profession. Signification of one type or another will occur in almost any situation or context to which human intellect turns its attention.

---

2 For rare exceptions, see Simone R.N. Reis et al., 'Semiotic Aspects in Patent Interpretation' (2019) 32 Int. J. Semiotic L. 359; Kevin Emerson Collins, Semiotics 101: Taking the Printed Matter Doctrine Seriously (2010) 83 Indiana L.J. 1379. Some of Collins' work also contains elements of semiology not always identified as such. See, e.g. Kevin Emerson Collins, The Reach of Literal Claim Scope into After-Arising Technology: On Thing Construction and the Meaning of Meaning (2008) 41 Conn. L. Rev. 493.

The simplest model of such signification, as developed by Ferdinand Saussure, postulates a material signifier that references an antecedent signified.[3] Together, these elements of signifier and signified constitute the sign. The signifier is typically some material symbol or object that may be conceptually associated with the signified. The signified may be any object or concept or feeling or other item that is subject to signification. The sign conveys meaning through the association of the perceptible signifier with the imperceptible signified. Exactly how this conveyance occurs, however, is the subject of some difference and dispute.

Two distinct approaches (at least) have coalesced around comprehending the operation of Saussure's model; we may designate these as modern and postmodern semiotics. Modernist semiotics has been characterized by what has been called a 'spiritual' approach to semiotics, drawing an analogy to widespread mystical or religious belief that the physical form of the body serves as a container for an immaterial animating spirit.[4] On a modernist view, the signifier channels or contains the signified; the material of the sign provides a type of pipe or conduit for the transmission of meaning. This conduit model is seen as connecting the sender and receiver of meaning in a sort of semiotic machine.[5] Generally, little attention is paid to the physical signifier; the focus in modernist semiotics is on the immaterial signified that lends meaning to the sign.

But this rather Platonist model of the sign as a conduit carries with it a variety of practical and philosophical, almost mystical troubles. In particular, it leaves the nature of the relationship of the two components of the sign as something of a mystery. What is the nature of the immaterial meaning or message contained within the physical signifier? How can a physical word or symbol contain something conceptual, that seems insubstantial or ethereal? By what mechanism or process is the ephemeral signified contained or conveyed by the signifier? Is the existence of a transcendent signified even rationally plausible?

An alternative approach, associated with postmodern semiotics, sidesteps such arcane questions by focusing instead on material or hyletic – from the Greek *hulê* – instantiation of the sign. Whereas modernist semiotics is largely

---

3 An alternative, related, but more complex 'triad' framework for the sign, advanced by Charles Sanders Pierce, has also been highly influential. See Daniel Chandler, *Semiotics: The Basics* (Routledge. 1st edn. 2002) 32–33. Kevin Collins has used the Piercean framework for a detailed and helpful examination of the patent 'printed matter' doctrine. See Collins, *supra* note 2. Reis et al. have also adopted the Piercean triad to describe a very elementary and analytically sparse concept of patent claims. See Reis et al., *supra* note 2.

4 George Aichele, Two Theories of Translation with Examples from the Gospel of Mark (1992) 47 J. Stud. New Testament 95, 102.

5 Gilles Deleuze & Félix Guattari, *Anti-Oedipus: Capitalism and Schizophrenia* (Univ of Minnesota Press, 3rd edn. 1983) 36.

concerned with the ethereal signified, postmodern semiotics rejects the model of the 'ghost in the sign' and gravitates instead toward the hyletic signifier. Postmodern analysis refuses to permit the separation of meaning and material instantiation.[6] Meaning is not considered an idea that dwells within the sign. Rather, on this view the sign constitutes the mechanism through which meaning is constructed, and the physical signifier is an irreducible element of such a construct. Thus, the structure and presence of the signifier is viewed as a focal point for social action.

Here we will be primarily concerned with signification in the context of *codes*, which constitute a set of conventions for understanding or meaning that is shared among a community. In particular, we will be concerned with the codes we call language, which is generally recognized to be the most powerful and pervasive system of human signification.

3. SEMIOTICS AND TRANSLATION

The marvelous 'UN Carbon Paper' directly raises the issue of linguistic translation, and the question of translation is intimately associated with semiotic analysis. However, semiotic analysis does not necessarily contemplate translation in the colloquial sense most common to the term and reveals that there is in fact more to Carelman's fantasy than initially meets the eye. The familiar kind of linguistic translation miraculously depicted in the 'UN Carbon Paper' contrivance constitutes a particular type of translation – an interlingual translation between different codes. This form of translation is certainly present in the 'UN Carbon Paper' depiction (shifting a phrase from English to French) but also entails translation in a broader semiotic sense. Linguistic translation only hints at the larger problem, toward which a careful scrutiny of Carelman's conceit points us.

Scholars in semiotics have identified at least three modes of translation that may be illuminated by semiotic analysis, all of which bear on patent translation. The first is *intralingual* translation, occurring within a particular code, such as the rewording of a text in the same language. A second type of translation is *interlingual*, between codes, such as the translation of signs between English and French. The third would be *intersemiotic*, or translation that occurs between different codes, such as the lingual description of a picture, or Mussorgsky's musical depiction of visual illustrations.[7]

Each of these modes implicates translation in the sense of transfer. The term 'translation' is taken from Latin, meaning a movement from place

6 Aichele, *supra* note 4 at 110.

7 See Alfred Frankenstein, Victor Hartmann and Modeste Musorgsky (1939) 25 Musical Q. 268 (discussing Mussorgsky's 'Pictures at an Exhibition').

to place (which is an alternate, less used definition of the term). This must metaphorically occur in linguistic translation, as the meaning of a sign is 'moved' between different systems of communication. Even where shifts between codes or 'languages' are not concerned, every communication requires multiple instances of translation. First the thoughts of the speaker must be translated into spoken or written language, then there must be a movement of such symbols across space and time to a recipient, who must finally translate the received language back once again into mental impressions.[8]

Such transfer is depicted in the 'UN Carbon Paper,' which intimates that the meaning or content of signifiers can be transferred to alternative signifiers, literally in a single stroke. The illustration in the Catalog does not show subsequent sheets in the stack below the second sheet, but one presumes that – if one only presses hard enough when writing – sheets further down will display the written phrase not only in French, but in Italian, Arabic, Swahili, Urdu, and other languages (so long, presumably, as the language is associated with some UN member nation).

But material signs resist inevitably such translation, making a seamless transfer from one code to another effectively impossible. This effect is well illustrated in the signs depicted by Carelman's translational whimsy. As the *Catalog's* 'UN Carbon Paper' entry depicts, 'tailleur' is the almost certainly the closest French cognate to the English 'tailor', in spelling, pronunciation, and denotation. The magic of the contrivance seems to have matched the initial English transcript to a proper French analog transferring the immaterial meaning of the signified concept from one paper to the other. Yet the two signifiers are clearly also different in spelling, length, and pronunciation, and so the material form of the signifier has changed when translating one to the other. If the next sheet down in the 'UN Carbon Paper' stack transfers the writing to the German cognate 'Schneider', the material construction of the signifier will change even more noticeably. It is precisely such resistance that in the irony of the 'UN Carbon Paper' is magically smoothed away.

4. MODERN AND POSTMODERN TRANSLATION

The modern and postmodern models of the sign sketched out above lead as well to two rather different views of translation. The first view regards the meaning of a text as an idealized reference that is to be found already extant in a text, and is generally selected by the text's originator or author by virtue of the sign recorded by the author.[9] Given that meaning is already embedded

---

8 George Aichele, *Sign, Text, Scripture: Semiotics and the Bible* (Sheffield Academic Press, 1st edn. 1997) 41.

9 See *ibid.* at 49.

in the sign, on this view, the process of translation involves transferring the content or meaning of the recorded signifier to a new and appropriate signifier. This view is associated with modernist schools of semiotics that bifurcate the material instantiation of the signifier from its reference content, an immaterial signified.

Thus, optimally under the modern approach, the translator is simply the vehicle by which the content of the sign is transmitted from one state to another.[10] The ineffable content of the signified is transferred to a different signifier in a different language or code, which then contains or embodies the signified. The signified should remain the same, or as nearly as possible identical, to that in the source language. Any alteration, bias, or influence introduced by the translator during transmission would constitute a distortion of the message. The amusement of the 'UN Carbon Paper' is of course that there is no translator, that the contrivance transmits the meaning of the sign to a subsequent instantiation seamlessly and mechanically.

The alternative postmodern approach rejects the assumption of an immaterial meaning carried by the signifier, highlighting the resistance of the text that we have already identified. Rather than allowing translation based upon the inchoate meaning of the text, postmodern or literal translation stays close to the physical dimension of the text. This approach focuses on matching the physical transcript of the initial text to its translation, on finding cognate signifiers for the translated text. The material instantiation or *hulé* of each signifier is paramount. What Walter Benjamin dubs a 'literal' translation of each word is preferred, because substitutions or re-phrasing of textual clauses or passages elevates global, contextual meanings at the expense of the characteristics of the physical signifier.[11] Broader attempts at conveying meaning are avoided.

As a result, such literal translation, word by cognate word, often yields awkward or infelicitous syntax at the level of the word or phrase. For postmodern semiotics, the advantage of such word-by-word, literal interpretation is that it juxtaposes different transcriptions of the signifier with one another, placing them in tension with one another.[12] Thus, meaning emerges across signifiers, from the comparison and contrast between the signifiers chosen for translation. This is a common experience for translators, or for any multilingual speaker – choosing between strict cognates of words in different languages, so as to maintain the sense of the initial term, and the alternative of adopting phrases or constructions that convey the sense of the initial text, because that sense would be lost in a string of literal cognates. Often neither approach is entirely

---

10 Willis Barnstone, *The Poetics of Translation: History, Theory, Practice* (Yale University Press, 1st edn. 1993) 230.

11 Walter Benjamin, *Illuminations* (Hannah Arendt, ed., Harry Zohn, tr., 1968) 82.

12 George Steiner, *After Babel* (OUP, 1st edn. 1975) 375.

satisfactory for capturing the sense of the initial text, and typically neither can be plausibly maintained as the sole translational technique for any text.

We can therefore see that in addition to its magical modernist translation, the translation illustrated by the Carelman *Catalog* item also signals a postmodern translational dimension. The juxtaposition of the first two sheets illustrated call to our attention the physical differences in signification between an English phrase and its cognate French. We have noted that 'tailleur' may be the cognate of 'tailor', but they are materially not the same word in spelling, length, and other physical signification. This in turn raises the question of which nuances, contexts, or understandings might have been lost in transliterating even the very short and simple phrase illustrated.

One way of understanding this distinction is to consider the translation question as an interplay of denotation and connotation. These semiotic functions operate at the level of the signifier, modulating the relationship between signifier and signified. Thus, every signified will have both a denotative and a connotative aspect. Denotative meaning of the sign is typically the most usual, common, or ordinary definition that may be assigned to a sign – for linguistic signs, the definition likely found in the dictionary.[13] In contrast to denotation, connotative meanings of the sign take into consideration the web of nuances and alternatives associated with the signified.[14] In our Carelman example above, the common or customary denotative meaning of 'tailor' is that of a clothes maker or fitter, and in this meaning maps readily onto the translation 'tailleur'. But other, more diffuse connotative associations may permeate the connotative meaning of the words in either English or French usage. These associations may escape the ready translation depicted in the 'UN Carbon paper'.

Each expansion in search of connotative meaning adds further connotative options beyond the most constrained denotative definition. Often connotative cultural and cognitive associations will be extensive and might stretch on infinitely if not cabined in some fashion. Clearly at some point connotative meaning does in fact run out. Connotation thus depends upon the codes, upon the shared cultural framework, that define contextually appropriate associations for the signified.[15] Such associations may include the other signs or words in physical proximity to the given sign in a text, or they may extend to the cognitive associations for the sign that are generated within social discourses. This broader set of associations makes signs more polysemic – more susceptible to multiple meanings – in their connotation than in their denotation.[16]

13 Aichele, *supra* note 8 at 90.
14 *Ibid.* at 91–92.
15 *Ibid.* at 93.
16 Chandler, *supra* note 3 at 140.

5. PATENT TRANSLATION

The principles illustrated in the Carelman example lead us directly to the question of patent translation. The translative activity that interests us here will generally not be translation in the typical or colloquial sense – that is, converting words in one language to their cognates in another, which is the most conventional, superficial takeaway from the miracle of the 'UN Carbon Paper'. Some translation between linguistic codes is of course inevitable for patents written and filed in a global environment – patents filed in the official language of one country's patent office may need to be linguistically translated into the official language of a different patent office when the application finds its way to another jurisdiction. Choices or mistakes in such linguistic translation can create impediments, for example where the term that should be 'nitrous' is translated into English as 'nitric' and the mistakenly translated description of the claimed invention becomes on its face inoperative.[17]

We are instead concerned with the translation of a claimed invention from an inventor to the world. This maps onto the doctrinal structure of American patent claiming. The act of invention is purely mental, a conception of the invention in the mind of an inventor. To claim patent rights in that conception, it must be translated into a written description in a patent application. Often this requires passage through the mind and understanding of an intermediary such as a patent agent or attorney, who translates the inventor's words, drawings, or texts into the jargon and format of the patent application. That document must then be understood by a patent examiner, or later in its existence by a judge or by competitors, who must again translate the patent text into their own comprehension.

An elaborate interpretive mechanism has grown up around such translation. American patent courts routinely begin their interpretive process by searching for the 'literal' meaning of the claims. I draw particular attention to the label of 'literal' interpretation because of the similar label postmodern understanding of the sign. These two uses of the term 'literal', in patent claim construction and in postmodern semiotic analysis, at first glance seem to share definitional commonalities – each is concerned with assigning the most common, unembellished, barebones meaning to a particular sign. Each favors word-by-word consideration of meaning, rather than readings at a more abstract conceptual level.

But there the commonalities end. Something rather different (and somewhat startling) seems to be going on in the case of literal claim interpretation, and while the similar terminology could be confusing, when framed properly

17 *In re* Oda, 443 F.2d 1200 (C.C.P.A. 1970) (considering the mistranslation of 'nitrous' to 'nitric' from a Japanese patent).

the differences between the uses of 'literal' are instructive. Juxtaposing the postmodern semiotic understanding of literal translation with the practice of patent courts is both disconcerting and enlightening. Thus, Benjamin's use of the term 'literal' and the use of the term by patent courts is neither identical nor harmonious, but the exploring tensions between these closely related uses reveal some of the hidden complications that plague patent doctrine.

Literal claim interpretation does not, oddly enough, involve literal semiotic meaning. Courts that are seeking the 'literal' meaning of claims do not appear to be thinking of literal meaning at the level of the signifier, where literal language may be distinguished from figurative language. Consider that figurative claim language, incorporating rhetorical tropes such as metaphor or synecdoche, would be highly unusual in patents, probably unheard of, and in any event would be statutorily dysfunctional. Claiming figuratively that the invention is 'like a butterfly' or that the invention 'is a raging storm,' or referring to a component of the invention such as 'the baffle' to represent the whole would almost certainly fail the statutory requirement of claim definiteness. Such linguistic forms are entirely foreign to the patent genre.[18] Claims incorporating these linguistic forms would never be allowed and would quickly be invalidated if there were to pass the scrutiny of some poetically minded examiner. (Additionally, the mind boggles at the prospect of drafting a disclosure that would support such figurative claims.)

Rather, it generally appears that 'literal' claim meaning, as the term is used by interpreting courts, is being sought at the level of the *signified*, in the sense that the interpretation is intended to be entirely modern and denotative. Denotative meaning is typically confined to the most common shared understandings associated with a signifier,[19] a definition that appears to track pretty closely the judicial quest for 'plain meaning' in patent claims (and other legal language). The use of dictionaries is particularly telling as a mechanism to try and fix a broad or universal consensus of denotative meaning;[20] courts resorting to dictionary are clearly attempting a denotative reading of claim terms.

6. THOROUGHLY MODERN CLAIM CONSTRUCTION

This hunt for defined meaning is in large measure a feature of 'peripheral claiming', which requires that the text of the claims specify the outermost boundary of the inventor's rights in the patented technology. The underlying assumption is

18 See Dan L. Burk & Jessica Reymann, 'Patents as Genre' (2014) 26 L. & Lit. 163. See also Dan L. Burk, 'Patents in Action' (2023) 63 Jurimetrics J. 221 (observing that patents adopt the form of scientific or technical literature).

19 Aichele, *supra* note 8 at 90.

20 Chandler, *supra* note 3 at 140.

that words – which is to say, signs – are capable of a firmly distinct meaning that can provide what the Supreme Court has dubbed 'reasonable certainty' as to the perimeter of the claimed patent rights. The rationale is that a rigid textual boundary will give patent readers notice as to what technology is exclusive to the patentholder and will also prevent the patent holder from expanding the patent's coverage to encroach on the public domain.

But note that the modernist, 'spiritual' formulation of the sign creates a closed system consisting of the signifier and whatever meaning of the signified is considered to be contained in that vessel. There is no explicit mechanism for external reference; the sign in this model 'erases the world.'[21] Considering this in the context of patent claims, the inventor may use the term 'baffle', and this term is deemed to reflect or embody the concept of 'baffle' envisioned by the inventor, not necessarily the concept of 'baffle' as used in other contexts.[22]

The inventor is, as the saying goes, her own lexicographer[23] and can use the term 'baffle' in some idiosyncratic way that is unrelated to any consensus or generally accepted meaning of the term. If she chooses to do so, she had best indicate this in some extra-terminological fashion to the interpreter – perhaps by providing her own definition in the patent specification, by going outside the channel of the sign. Otherwise, the interpreter may choose the 'plain meaning' denotation of the term as a likely first approximation of the sign's meaning and stop there.

At the same time, external reference is implicit in the formulation of the signified. In patenting, the imagined components of the inventive conception must reference particular items outside the mind of the inventor. If the sign in question is the term 'baffle', the 'baffle' as envisioned by the inventor must reference some form of baffle already at large in the world, or a novel form of baffle that is the inventor's own creation. Yet even in the latter case, some external reference must be present, as the inventive conception will necessarily be formed of elements drawn from the outside. As C.S. Lewis observed, the human mind is incapable of true creation *de novo* – we are incapable of, say, imagining a new primary color or 'even a monster which does not consist of bits of existing animals stuck together.'[24] Thus, the inventive signified always references objects external to the sign.

Resorting to the 'plain meaning' or literal interpretation of a claim is (perhaps paradoxically) an attempt to discern the external reference most likely drawn from the inventor's mental conception of the invention. Even when courts

---

21 Robert Scholes, 'Language, Narrative, and Anti-Narrative' (1980) 7 Critical Inquiry 204, 205.

22 *Cf. Philips v AWH Corp.*, 415 F.3d 1303 (Fed. Cir. 2005) (attempting to interpret the term 'baffle' in a patent claim).

23 See *Johnson Worldwide Assocs., Inc. v Zebco Corp.*, 175 F.3d 985, 990 (Fed. Cir. 1999).

24 *Clive Staples Lewis to Sister Penelope, February 20, 1943* in The Letters of C.S. Lewis 371 (W.H. Lewis & Walter Hooper, eds., rev. ed. 1993).

resort to 'extrinsic' evidence of meaning, drawn from the use and literature of the relevant technical field, any meaning derived lies at the outermost edge of the 'literal' claims interpretive exercise. A postmodern approach might look to such evidence intending to establish the meaning of the sign by looking to the usage of those having skill in the art. But to the contrary, even the resort to assessing extrinsic use of a term is not employed to adopt the meaning determined by the community, but rather to determine such usage as an indicator or clue as to the meaning which the inventor intended to invest the signifier.

7. CLAIM CONSTRUCTION, POSTMODERN STYLE

Literal translation carries with it the illusion that denotation is universally accepted meaning; this is evident, for example, in the judicial quest for 'plain meaning' that is somehow apparent on the face of the signifier. The assumption in this search is that the channel contains a meaning, and the court's job is to locate or determine that meaning, largely by paring down potential alternative readings of the sign. The premise is that the signifier could be associated with more than one potential signified, and the proper one must be determined. Locating the denotative meaning is intended to assure translation from the immaterial, mental concept of the inventor through an appropriately cabined signifier to the mind of the reader.

But semiotics teaches us that denotation is in fact a single facet of connotation,[25] a common meaning situated within the range of meanings that may be associated with the signified. This in turn means that denotation is a truncated or abridged version of the sign's broader array of connotation.[26] The search for 'literal' claim interpretation is therefore necessarily dependent on the range of acceptable connotations associated with a term. And we know that both denotation and connotation rely upon cultural codes, on a shared set of cultural codes that guides the winnowing of relevant associations associated with a given sign.

Neither should we assume that these modes of understanding the sign are exclusive, or discrete. No reading of the sign is ever entirely denotative nor fully connotative. Interpretation exists in a continuum between these poles, as can readily be seen in the ever-widening gyre of literal claim interpretation: beginning with the isolated 'plain meaning' of a term, perhaps augmented by a dictionary reference; moving to the meaning derived from context and conjunction with nearby claims; then to context provided by other references in the patent disclosure; perhaps adding the context drawn from prosecution

25 Chandler, *supra* note 3 at 141.

26 Aichele, *supra* note 8 at 91.

documents; and ultimately to the common practice and terminology of the art as reflected in relevant treatises and literature. Each extension of this search expands the potential universe of running from constrained denotative meaning to a range of connotative meanings.

Returning to Carelman's illustrative carbon papers, we have already seen that the denotative cannot be separated or confined from the connotative. The English sign 'tailor' might be associated with the German 'Der Schneider'. But this denotation is possible only due to a constellation of connotative meanings: The most literal English translation of the German term 'Der Schneider' might be 'the cutter' or 'the slicer' but it has generally taken on the connotation of a cloth cutter, 'the tailor', and the choice among each of these signifiers must be guided by the connotative context of both the initial and translated signifiers. The same process inevitably occurs in the search for 'literal' claims meaning in patents.

Moreover, the impossibility of separating connotative and denotative readings means that both will inevitably be value-laden, because the codes that shape either type of meaning are themselves deeply value-laden.[27] Denotative meaning may appear to be the 'natural' or 'common' or 'obvious' meaning, but this is due to processes of habituation and acclimation within the relevant ideological framework.[28] This type of naturalization creates the tendency to accept denotative meanings as manifest, incontrovertible, or self-evident truths.[29] Indeed, one expects that interpretive 'plain meaning' is a popular judicial trope for exactly this reason – the façade that assigning a consensus meaning will be uncontroversial, concealing no hidden dimensions.

But to the contrary, the denotative readings that are necessarily formed through evaluative codes are highly ideological.[30] Here we speak of ideology not so much in the political sense (although that may be present) as in the sense of shared communal frameworks for attributing meaning. Denotative meaning may therefore appear to be neutral or inevitable but is every bit as ideologically laden as any connotative reading.[31] Recognizing that denotative reading – the 'literal' interpretation of American claim constructions – is drawn from the range of connotations demonstrates that the meaning chosen is never inevitable and requires us to ask how that choice of meaning is made. Recognizing that all meanings of the sign, denotative or connotative, are socially situated shows us that the choice of meaning will be based on ideological influences and not on any fixed interpretation of the sign.

---

27 Valentin Voloshinov, *Marxism and the Philosophy of Language* (Seminar Press, Ladislav Matejka & I R Titunik tr., 1973) 105.

28 Chandler, *supra* note 3 at 141.

29 *Ibid.* at 144.

30 Kaja Silverman, *The Subject of Semiotics* (OUP, 1st edn. 1983) 30.

31 Chandler, *supra* note 3 at 141.

In the postmodern approach to semiotics, ideology is acknowledged as establishing the dominant reading of a text and so defines the community to which the text belongs.[32] In the case of the patent text, this is the specialized and insular community of patent practice – the lawyers, the judges, the bureaucrats that surround the crafting and usage of patents. I have shown elsewhere that this community shares a common language,[33] and they surely share a common ideology couched in terms of 'innovation', 'incentive', and 'progress'. Whatever one might think of such tropes, they surely provide a set of codes within which the patent text is infused with meaning.

8. CONCLUSION

Carelman's *Catalog*, exactly as it is captioned, surely falls within the genre of the fantastic. Todorov distinguished between the 'marvelous' and the 'uncanny' in literature, where the marvelous story depicts a world including the impossibly supernatural, whereas the uncanny story depicts a world of amazing coincidences and incredible, but not unbelievable events.[34] Fantasy, Todorov observed, blurs the boundary between these two, as Carelman surely does. Some items in the *Catalog* fall into the category of the merely improbable, but others like the 'UN Carbon Paper' seem firmly situated in the category of the supernatural.

Semiotic analysis reminds us that the patent itself straddles the border between the marvelous and the uncanny. The invention disclosed in the text of the patent is by definition required to be at least uncanny – improbable, perhaps; incredible, but not unbelievable. The invention must be 'non-obvious' to one of ordinary skill in the pertinent art, meaning that the majority of practitioners in that art could not imagine or envision it themselves – only one of extraordinary skill, which is to say an inventor, would be capable of doing so. That imagined innovation must then somehow be translated to conventional, comprehensible signification that allows its practice by those of ordinary skill who could never have imagined it. At the same time, if the innovative imaginary reaches the level of the impossible, the patent is forfeit.

Under the EPC, claims to such an invention might be deemed to be implausible, meaning that they either lack sufficient support in the specification, or that the specification fails to support the achievement of such an inventive step. Under USPTO practice, claims that reach a degree of implausibility dubbed 'fantastic utility' are deemed to lack proper utility. Thus, no matter how detailed,

---

32 Aichele, *supra* note 8 at 103.

33 See Burk & Reymann, *supra* note 18.

34 Tzvetvan Todorov, *The Fantastic*, (The Press of Case Western Reserve University, R. Howard, tr.; 1973) 41–47.

claims to faster than light warp drive or perpetual motion machines are what Todorov would call marvelous, not fantastic.

But even without reaching the level of supernatural implausibility, what we have seen here shows the patent to flirt with and embrace the uncanny. There is surely an element of the incredible in the mentalist view of invention, as well as in the patent practice of 'literal' claims interpretation. Such partake of the rather uncanny assumptions of modernist signification, attributing a discrete and ineffable meaning to the material text of the claims. As shown here, searching for the ghost in the claim is something of a fool's errand; as postmodern analysis indicates, the roots of meaning spill out of denotation of any given sign. The interpretation of patent claims is inevitably a connotative exercise.

CHAPTER 19
(IR)RATIONALITY IN PATENT LAW

Daria Kim
Senior Research Fellow, Max Planck Institute for Innovation and Competition

1. INTRODUCTION

Flipping through the pages of the *Catalog of Fantastic Things*, one is transported into a whimsical, amusing wonderland where everyday items take on extravagant appearances, defying logic and common sense. It feels like an escape from the framework of rationality through which we are accustomed to making sense of reality. Conceived as a parody,[1] the catalogue entertains through its frisky use of hyperbole, mocking marketing jargon and the obsession with efficiency. At times, this obsession is taken to absurdity: a dual-use fork can be used to sign five copies at once;[2] a rolling iron avoids scorching clothes by not touching them at all;[3] a sofa converts into 'a spacious, fully equipped bath-tub or waterbed,'[4] a sun-magnifying parasol saves time by speeding up tanning;[5] and a 'never-clean sink [hangs] neatly on any wall.'[6]

For a patent law researcher, the *Catalog of Fantastic Things* is an immersion into an upended world of objects and humorous ingenuity that contrasts with what one typically finds in a patent database.[7] Patent law aligns with instrumental rationality – a worldview where technology is a means to serve one's ends. Fantastic things are a playful and liberating departure from this type of rationality, practical reasoning, and logical constraints associated with patent law.

Drawing inspiration from Carelman's world of fantastic things, I reflect in this contribution on the manifestations of rationality and its limitations in patent law. The concept of rationality intersects with the patent system across various dimensions – from historical developments[8] to the notions of technological progress, technical problem-solving, and invention as an objective, reproducible technical teaching. In this essay, however, I am interested in mapping the aspects of rationality about how we – individually and collectively – make sense of, apply and decide to transform patent law. Part B outlines the rational actor premise underlying patent law and discusses five instances that illustrate contradictions

---

1 In particular, it parodies the catalogue of the mail-order company Manufrance. www.artandpopularculture.com/Jacques_Carelman, accessed 14 September 2024.

2 Carelman 18.

3 *Ibid.* 37.

4 *Ibid.* 24.

5 *Ibid.* 25.

6 *Ibid.* 41.

7 This is not to say that 'fantastic things' – once unthinkable, implausible, or impractical – cannot enter and transform our rational world. See Phil Edwards, '7 World-Changing Inventions People Thought Were Dumb Fads' (*Vox*, 29 June 2015), www.vox.com/2015/2/9/8004661/fads-inventions-changed-world, accessed 5 March 2025. One also finds outliers, for which at least an attempt has been made to patent them: James Cutmore, '15 of the World's Weirdest-ever Inventions' (*BBC Science Focus*, 19 May 2024) www.sciencefocus.com/science/the-weirdest-inventions-ever-in-pictures, accessed 5 March 2025.

8 For instance, the European Enlightenment – with its emphasis on the power of reason, the celebration of knowledge, increased literacy driven by the printing press, individualism, individual freedoms, and the notion of achievement as a source of entitlement – is reflected in both the spirit and the letter of patent law. See Carla Hesse, 'The Rise of Intellectual Property, 700 B.C.-A.D. 2000: An Idea in the Balance' (2002) 131 Daedalus 26-45; Sean M. O'Connor, 'The Overlooked French Influence on the Intellectual Property Clause' (2015) 82 U. Chi. L. Rev. 733.

or departures from it. Part C concludes by highlighting the value of rationality theories for the normative analysis of patents and considering how a rationality lens can teach holistic thinking about patent law. As a contribution to this *Festschrift*, this perspective aims to reflect what I see as Professor Van Overwalle's distinctive blend of razor-sharp logic and outside-the-box thinking – a signature of her contributions to patent law scholarship.

2. RATIONAL CHOICE THEORY APPLIED TO NORMATIVE ANALYSIS OF PATENT LAW

The mainstream justification of patent law is rooted in rational choice theory, an 'overarching meta-theoretical paradigm in the social sciences.'[9] Normative discourses on patent law draw from both key areas of application of rational choice theory: economics and sociology.[10] From the economic version patent theorising derives the premise that innovators are rational utility maximisers responding to incentives to adjust market behaviour and make decisions regarding resource allocation. The sociological version enhances legal analysis by factoring in social and cultural influences on rationality and focusing on social interactions, non-economic motivations, and collective action challenges.

The central notion of rational choice theory is the rational actor, a utility maximiser who makes decisions by weighing the costs and benefits of available alternatives to achieve their goals. The Chicago school of law and economics assumes that 'man is a rational maximizer of his ends in life'[11] – even 'a rational utility maximizer in *all* areas of life'[12] – and, therefore, that 'people respond to incentives.'[13] While limitations of the rational actor premise are acknowledged, including by its proponents,[14] the utility maximisation premise takes centre

---

9 Rafael Wittek, 'Rational Choice' (*Oxford Bibliographies* 2013), www.oxfordbibliographies.com/display/document/obo-9780199756384/obo-9780199756384–0070.xml, accessed 5 March 2025.

10 Peter Hedström and Charlotta Stern, 'Rational Choice and Sociology' in Steven N. Durlauf et al. (eds), *The New Palgrave Dictionary of Economics* (Palgrave Macmillan UK 2008) DOI: 10.1057/978-1-349-95121-5_2736-1.

11 Richard A. Posner, *Economic Analysis of Law* (9th edn, Wolters Kluwer Law & Business 2014) 3. See also Richard A. Posner, 'Rational Choice, Behavioral Economics, and the Law' (1997) 50 Stanford Law Review 1551, at 1551 (clarifying his use of the term 'rationality' as 'choosing the best means to the chooser's ends').

12 Posner (2014) (n 11) 4 (emphasised in the original).

13 *Ibid.*

14 Ibid. (noting that 'an assumption must not be confused with a finding. The assumption that people are rational choosers in all areas of life is just the starting point of economic analysis. It holds only as an approximation. Even perfectly normal people are not always

stage in patent law. By their exclusive nature, patents enable right holders to maximise their own gain, market conditions permitting, while limitations and exceptions to this premise are designed and interpreted narrowly. In the following, I show that the critique of the patent system failures – even if not appealing directly to rational choice theories – essentially comes down to the limitations of the rational actor premise in reaching the objectives of the patent system.

2.1. BOUNDED RATIONALITY OF INNOVATORS

While patents are rationalised as innovation incentives, they are one among many factors shaping the rate, direction, and qualitative dimensions of innovation. By improving appropriability conditions, patents create an economic opportunity, which is also determined by the market and demand size.[15] The fact that one would not typically find the subject matter akin to Carelman's 'fantastic things' – fanciful but impractical – in a patent database supports the conventional wisdom that innovation incentives stem from the market demand and size. Besides the economic opportunity, successful innovation depends on the state of technological opportunity, particularly the ripeness of the knowledge base and the presence of knowledge spillovers.[16]

Both technological and economic opportunities need to mature and align for innovation efforts to take place and succeed. Ideally, innovators would need to have perfect knowledge about such opportunities and the conditions under which they can be realised. In contrast, objective limitations – particularly uncertainty about the correlative factors of R&D productivity – often enter the utility maximisation function and deter the rational decision-maker from responding to patent incentives. Moreover, subjective factors such as cognitive biases can constrain the capacity to make rational decisions that maximise both individual and collective utility (assuming the innovator is equally motivated to serve both). A case in point is vaccines and treatments

---

rational. […] And there are situations in which rational choice is precluded by uncertainty, defined as noncalculable risk.'). See also Christine Jolls, Cass R. Sunstein and Richard Thaler, 'A Behavioral Approach to Law and Economics' 50 Stan. L. Rev. 1471 (1998); Posner (1997) (n 11) (responding to Jolls, Sunstein and Thaler's critique of the rational maximisation premise).

15 Relevant factors include 'the market value of the invention, the structure of the market involving the patented process or product, and the attributes of the patentee (such as marketing and production capacities) that determine its range of options within that market.' Louis Kaplow, 'The Patent-Antitrust Intersection: A Reappraisal' (1984) 97(8) Harv. L. Rev. 1813, 1823.

16 Rebecca Henderson and Iain Cockburn, 'Scale, Scope, and Spillovers: The determinants of research productivity in drug discovery' (1996) 27(1) RAND J Econ 32.

for rare diseases – textbook examples of the systematic failure of patents as a regulatory instrument to remedy a market failure of insufficient innovation incentives.[17] While small market size is often invoked as a key factor behind the lack of incentives, industrial R&D efforts are also hampered by gaps in basic scientific knowledge.[18] Even though allocating more resources can improve the knowledge base, research does not respond linearly to the amount of effort or money invested in it.[19]

What would be irrational is for policymakers to presume the sufficiency of patents in promoting innovation – or, even more so, that greater patent protection necessarily induces greater innovation. Imperfect knowledge and cognitive biases underscore the need to more extensively and systematically factor the limitations of rational decision-making into the design of innovation policy. This can take the form of making greater use of targeted 'push' incentives in critical domains – particularly measures aimed at improving technological opportunities by supporting basic research and promoting knowledge externalities.

2.2. THE MISSING LINK BETWEEN INDIVIDUAL AND COLLECTIVE VALUE MAXIMISATION

Rational choice theory embraces the collective outcome of individual choices as a theoretical assumption and an analytical focus. Assuming that actors 'act rationally in a broad sense, and focus on the aggregate outcomes that individual actors in interaction with one another are likely to bring about,'[20] the analysis focuses 'on explaining macro-level or aggregate outcomes such as [...] various forms of collective action [by examining] the actions and interactions that

---

17 European Commission, 'Better Regulation "Toolbox" 2023' (2023) 96, https://commission.europa.eu/document/download/c0561a9c-d112-4d20-b1ec-145748e2c61c_en?filename=BRT-2023-Chapter%202-How%20to%20carry%20out%20an%20impact%20assessment_0.pdf, accessed 5 March 2025 (defining a regulatory failure as a situation where '[i]ntervention by public authorities to resolve market failures can fail to achieve a socially efficient allocation of resources').

18 Alonso Ruiz A. et al., 'Pharmaceutical Policy and Innovation for Rare Diseases: A Narrative Review' (2023) 12 F1000Research 211; Bregtje Kamphuis, Thyra de Jongh and Veerle Bastiaanssen, 'Tackling Rare Diseases. Challenges, Opportunities and Gaps for Action on Rare Diseases in the European Union', www.europarl.europa.eu/RegData/etudes/STUD/2024/754210/IPOL_STU%282024%29754210_EN.pdf 26, accessed 5 March 2025.

19 WHO, IUPHAR and CIOMS, 'Clinical Pharmacology in Health Care, Teaching and Research' (CIOMS 2012) 33 (concluding that 'high expectations of innovation models that involve combinatorial chemistry, high-throughput screening, rational drug design, pharmacogenomics, bioinformatics and disease and pathway modelling have not been met despite the high level of investment').

20 *Ibid.*

brought them about,'[21] rather than seeking to explain the actions of single individuals. In other words, from a rational choice theoretical perspective, the question is whether and how maximisation of an individual gain can enhance the collective outcome.

Nothing in the design of the patent system conditions the maximisation of individual utility on the maximisation of collective utility. The exclusive nature of patents allows right holders to maximise the utility of their patents for their own benefit – profits – under restrained price competition and, in some cases, competition by substitution.[22] The very structure of the patent system prioritises the patent holder's utility maximisation. Exclusivity stands as the default rule, while provisions intended to balance – or 'tailor' – the scope of protection are cast as exceptions or limitations, canonically interpreted narrowly, even when rationalised based on the public interest. The very fact that the legislature sets statutory boundaries on patent protection suggests that individual utility maximisation cannot be trusted to maximise collective gain. However, existing exceptions and limitations typically concern extraordinary situations, while it remains uncertain and contestable whether the everyday exercise of patent rights – the allocation of use rights through voluntary licensing – happens on a societally optimal, collectively beneficial level.

One could argue that the collective benefit of patents subsists in the very act of bringing innovation into the market. However, as noted above, no straightforward causal relationship between patent protection and socially beneficial innovation can be presumed,[23] as evidenced by multiple examples of unmet societal needs in innovation, including vaccines, antibiotics, and green technology. Thus, the assumption that maximising individual gain leads to collective benefit is, at best, probabilistic and raises doubts about the reliance on economic incentives intended to improve appropriability conditions as a central pillar of innovation policy. Moreover, social returns on innovation are generally assumed to far exceed private returns,[24] making it practically unfeasible to fully

---

21 *Ibid.* (referring particularly to rational choice sociology).

22 E.g. brand drug sales can prevail despite the availability of generics due to brand loyalty, marketing campaigns, patient assistance programs, and physician preferences.

23 See Giovanni Dosi, Luigi Marengo and Corrado Pasquali, 'How Much Should Society Fuel the Greed of Innovators? On the Relations between Appropriability, Opportunities and Rates of Innovation' (2006) 35 Research Policy 1110, 1111 (noting that '[t]he rates of innovation [...] fundamentally depend on paradigm-specific opportunities rather than on mere appropriability conditions [...] and even less so on the specific subset of appropriability devices represented by legal IPR protection'). See also Arho Suominen, Matthias Deschryvere and Rumy Narayan, 'Uncovering Value Through Exploration of Barriers – A Perspective on Intellectual Property Rights in a National Innovation System' (2023) 123 Technovation 102719. For epistemological limitations regarding the linkage between patents and innovation, see also below at B.3.

24 Social returns to innovation include private returns (profits for innovating firm) and benefits to customers and other firms. The rate of social returns is considerably higher than the rate of private returns. See e.g. Bronwyn H. Hall, Jacques Mairesse and Pierre Mohnen P, 'Measuring

realise them through individual patent licensing.[25] In this respect, protection by liability-based rules – a much-discussed alternative to the exclusivity-based paradigm – appears to offer a more defensible solution to the public good problem in innovation, particularly in terms of balancing individual and social returns to innovation activity.

2.3. THE EPISTEMIC VALIDITY OF THE PATENTS-INNOVATION PREMISE

Justifying patents as innovation incentives requires both theoretical and empirical knowledge about the functional relationship between the goal and its means. The validity criteria for this knowledge are no different from the criteria for knowledge in general. In epistemology, knowledge is understood as justified true belief, where the justification of a belief implies rationality, and rationality is derived from the belief-forming process. For a belief to be justified and true – hence, to qualify as knowledge – it must be 'reliably formed'.[26] Thus, the robustness of both theoretical and empirical methods is key to qualifying the proposition that patents promote innovation as knowledge.

In theory, patents are rationalised as an instrument to remedy a market failure associated with public goods. To improve appropriability conditions in the market, patent rights transform a non-excludable good (knowledge) into an excludable one. In so doing, patents are meant to resolve the static-dynamic efficiency trade-off caused by unrestrained imitation – that is, the trade-off between the benefits of price competition (static efficiency) and the incentive for future innovation (dynamic efficiency). However, patent rights do not resolve this trade-off but swap its sides: The prospect of enhanced dynamic efficiency comes at the cost of static efficiency – i.e. restrained price competition and limited access to innovation. While this model is typically framed as a need to balance the costs and benefits of patents, there is a logical difficulty in balancing values that are being traded off.

However, the static-dynamic efficiency trade-off presents only a formal model of the innovation-appropriability relationship that does not account for the multiple factors that mediate the relationship between investment and R&D productivity and determine its nonlinear nature. While patents create an economic opportunity by improving appropriability conditions, they are not

the Returns to R&D' in Bronwyn H. Hall and Nathan Rosenberg (eds), *Handbook of the Economics of Innovation*, vol 2 (1st edn. Elsevier 2010) 1034.

25 Dominique Foray, *Economics of Knowledge* (The MIT Press 2006) 114.

26 Patrick Rysiew, 'Rationality' (*Oxford Bibliographies* 2012) DOI: 10.1093/obo/9780195396577-0175. See also Alvin I. Goldman, 'What Is Justified Belief?' in George Pappas (ed), *Justification and Knowledge. New Studies in Epistemology* (Springer 1979) 1.

the only or primary determinant of innovation activity,[27] which also explains why patents as innovation incentives perform differently across the economic sectors and technological domains. This is where a sociological perspective, with its broader contextual view on the rational actor premise and its focus on 'the human factor', can be particularly enriching for the normative analysis of patents.

Another significant limitation of the static-dynamic efficiency model is that it does not factor in the impact of patents on follow-on innovation – that is, the potential reduction in dynamic efficiency due to the suboptimal utilisation of patented technologies as inputs for further innovation.[28] While patents are, in part, justified as a means of optimally allocating use rights in technology through licensing, economic analyses posit a systematic failure in this regard.[29]

A further theoretical framework conventionally invoked to justify patents is the welfare cost-benefit function. However, this construct is widely acknowledged to be elusive.[30] Particularly in the case of patents, the dynamic and probabilistic nature of their effects makes it nearly unfeasible to ascertain their net impact on social welfare – a challenge known as the 'calculability' critique of patents.[31] The proponents of the utility maximisation premise acknowledge this difficulty too.[32] Even if we conceptualise the balancing exercise in terms of minimising the costs and maximising the benefits of protection, identifying the golden mean and the operative rules for transposing it remains challenging both theoretically and practically.[33]

---

27 Dosi, Marengo and Pasquali (n 23) 1111 (observing that 'appropriability conditions are just one of several factors (possibly a second order one) shaping the propensity to innovate' and that 'the relative importance of the various factors and their interaction is highly sector and technology specific').

28 See e.g. Suzanne Scotchmer, 'Standing on the Shoulders of Giants: Cumulative Research and the Patent Law' (1991) 5(1) J Econ Perspect 29, 30.

29 Yi Zhou, 'The Tragedy of the Anticommons in Knowledge' (2016) 48(1) Review of Radical Political Economics 158; Ronald King, Ivan Major and Cosmin Gabriel Marian, 'Confusions in the Anticommons' (2016) 9(7) Journal of Politics and Law 64.

30 Richard E. Just, Darrell L. Hueth and Andrew Schmitz, *The Welfare Economics of Public Policy: A Practical Approach to Project and Policy Evaluation* (Edward Elgar Publishing 2004) 41.

31 Robert P. Merges, 'Philosophical Foundations of IP Law: The Law and Economic Paradigm' in Peter S. Menell, Ben Depoorter and David Schwartz (eds), *Research Handbook on the Economics of Intellectual Property Law*, vol 1 (Edward Elgar Publishing 2019) 80 f.

32 See Richard A. Posner, 'Intellectual Property: The law and economics approach' (2005) 19(2) Journal of Economic Perspectives 57, 59; William M. Landes and Richard A. Posner, *The Economic Structure of Intellectual Property Law* (Harvard University Press 2003) 9.

33 US Senate, *Administered Prices. Drugs. Report of the Committee on the Judiciary, United States Senate, Made by Its Subcommittee on Antitrust and Monopoly. Hearings before the Subcommittee on Antitrust and Monopoly*, 87th Congress, 1st Session (U.S. Government Printing Office 1961) 114 (referring to an attempt 'to determine the proportion of the higher price under patents that would be offset by new discoveries made possible by the awarding of patents' as an 'impossible undertaking').

Empirical findings on the relationship between patents and innovation are fragmented, hardly generalisable and, at times, contradictory.[34] Tracing and ascertaining the causal effect of patents on innovation is methodologically challenging as this effect can hardly be isolated from other factors, which might also be difficult to observe, trace, or measure. Furthermore, patent protection would also need to be compared to other incentive mechanisms to confirm that patents are not only net-positive from a social welfare perspective but are also superior in terms of their cost-benefit ratio relative to the alternatives. Conducting this comparison is hardly possible, absent 'a true counterfactual'.[35]

In summary, both theoretical and empirical methods, as 'belief-forming' processes used to validate the relationship between patents and innovation, have considerable limitations. Not that the patent-innovation premise might be invalid per se, but rather the knowledge about the specific conditions under which it holds remains incomplete. These limitations weaken the epistemic validity of the assumption that patents are a suitable means for optimally allocating both resources to innovation and use rights in R&D results. This leaves us with the famous statement made by Fritz Machlup in 1960: 'If we did not have a patent system, it would be irresponsible, on the basis of our present knowledge of its economic consequences, to recommend instituting one. But since we have had a patent system for a long time, it would be irresponsible, on the basis of our present knowledge, to recommend abolishing it.'[36] Resolving this stalemate is not only a question of epistemological justification and political epistemology but also political will.

2.4. THE EXPLANATORY AND PREDICTIVE POWER OF RATIONALITY PARADOXES

The normative analysis of patent law applies legal and extra-legal concepts and theories testing their explanatory, justificatory, and predictive power. Not all legal researchers might be aware that building blocks of the law-and-economics analytical framework – such as the notions of collective goods, transaction costs, and free-riding – originate from rational choice theory.[37] Moreover, patent law discourse shares with rational choice theory a focus on incentives to explain individual actions entailing collective consequences.

---

[34] Daria Kim, 'Patents for Enabling Technologies: The Puzzle of the Normative Delineation of Protection' in Florent Thouvenin et al. (eds), *Kreation Innovation Märkte – Creation Innovation Markets* (Springer Berlin 2024) 551, 555.

[35] Bronwyn H. Hall and Dietmar Harhoff, 'Recent Research on the Economics of Patents' (2012) 4 Annu Rev Econ 541, 554.

[36] US Senate, *Administered Prices in the Drug Industry. Hearings before the Subcommittee on Antitrust and Monopoly* (86th Congress, 2nd Session, Washington, DC, 1960) 80.

[37] Hedström and Stern (n 10).

A mismatch between individual incentives and collective outcomes where 'the maximisation of short-term self-interest yields outcomes leaving all participants worse off than feasible alternatives'[38] has given rise to the anticommons critique of patents. Focusing on the role of patents in technology diffusion, the anticommons analysis posits a suboptimal allocation of use rights due to high transaction costs, strategic rent-seeking, and cognitive biases.[39] Practices such as stacking licenses and reach-through provisions, employed to maximise individual utility, can illustrate a rationality paradox where 'individually rational strategies lead to collectively irrational outcomes'[40] and a social dilemma of conflicting 'individual short-term incentives and overall group incentives.'[41] Not accidentally, anticommons concerns have been particularly articulate regarding patents for enabling technologies, given their role as inputs in knowledge creation – more precisely, intermediate non-rivalrous goods – that enable cumulative knowledge discovery and innovation. The anticommons research thus exposes limitations of the static-dynamic efficiency model, which does not factor in the restrictive effect of patents on follow-on research and innovation.[42]

The conflict underlying the anticommons critique of patents exemplifies rationality paradoxes – logical contradictions that challenge the rational actor premise applied in both sociological and economic accounts of rational choice theory.[43] Normative challenges in patent law, particularly those related to the utility maximisation premise, can be understood in terms of rationality paradoxes resulting in social dilemmas, such as public good market failure, often framed as a prisoner's dilemma,[44] failed cooperative initiatives to facilitate access and utilisation of aggregated innovation inputs,[45] and more broadly, tensions between private and public interests. The concept of anticommons demonstrates the significant analytical utility of a rationality paradox for understanding the incentives and decision-making of innovators, patent holders, and policymakers.

---

38 Elinor Ostrom, 'A Behavioral Approach to the Rational Choice Theory of Collective Action' in Filippo Sabetti and Paul Dragos Aligica (eds), *Choice, Rules and Collective Action: The Ostroms on the Study of Institutions and Governance* (ECPR Press 2014) 121, 122.

39 Michael A. Heller and Rebecca S. Eisenberg, 'Can Patents Deter Innovation? The Anticommons in Biomedical Research' (1998) 280 (5364) Science 698.

40 Elinor Ostrom, *Governing the Commons: The Evolution of Institutions for Collective Action* (CUP 2015) 5.

41 Jane Sell, 'Social Dilemmas' in George Ritzer (ed), *The Blackwell Encyclopedia of Sociology* (John Wiley & Sons, Ltd 2015), DOI: 10.1002/9781405165518.wbeoss143.pub2.

42 Above (n 30) and the accompanying text.

43 Roy A. Sorensen, 'Paradoxes of Rationality' in Alfred R. Mele and Pierre Rawling (eds), *The Oxford Handbook of Rationality* (1st edn, OUP 2009) 257.

44 James M. Buchanan, 'Cooperation and Conflict in Public-Goods Interaction' (1967) 5(2) Economic Inquiry 109; Steven Kuhn, 'Prisoner's Dilemma' in Edward N. Zalta and Uri Nodelman (eds), *The Stanford Encyclopedia of Philosophy* (2009), https://plato.stanford.edu/entries/prisoner-dilemma/, accessed 5 March 2025.

45 Daria Kim, 'Knowledge Sharing as a Social Dilemma in Pharmaceutical Innovation' (2016) 71(4) Food and Drug Law Journal 673.

This contribution can only hint at the potential utility of theoretical and practical rationality paradoxes for the normative analysis of patents. However, there may be value in a more systematic examination of their explanatory and predictive power when applied to patent-related phenomena, particularly those related to the premise of expected utility maximisation.[46] This value lies not necessarily in rendering accurate and generalisable predictions about the effects of patents but in generating hypotheses and setting directions for research that ultimately expands our understanding of patent law, even if the initial hypothesis cannot be supported or requires refinement.

2.5. BOUNDED RATIONALITY IN PATENT POLICYMAKING

In remedying the public goods market failure, patent policy should follow the general principles and methodology of designing a policy intervention by choosing the most effective and efficient measure to achieve a certain societal goal.[47] This choice should be based on a cost-benefit analysis of alternative measures relative to the status quo. Furthermore, adjusting incentives necessitates the assessment of short- and long-term costs and benefits of patents on innovation and society. The calculability and contestability critique of knowledge on the relationship between patents and innovation discussed above weaken the basis for rational policymaking. The capacity of policymakers for rational decision-making is bounded by imperfect theoretical and empirical knowledge regarding the determinants of socially beneficial innovation and the optimal point at which social costs and benefits of patents are in balance. Identifying this golden mean has long been recognised as an 'impossible undertaking'.[48]

An attempt to base policy decisions on cost-benefit calculations is in line with the constructivist type of rationality.[49] An acknowledgement of limitations of 'maximizing strategies' and the impossibility of determining the 'global optimum' calls for ecological, or evolutionary, rationality that adopts the 'bottom up' or 'home-grown' approach and 'domain-specific heuristics.'[50] It focuses on environmental adaptation rather than solution optimisation[51] and relies on the contextual, empirical understanding of the problem emerging from the collection

[46] For an overview, see Sorensen (n 43).

[47] European Commission (n 17).

[48] US Senate (n 33) 114.

[49] Vernon L. Smith, *Rationality in Economics: Constructivist and Ecological Forms* (CUP 2007) 25 (defining constructivist rationality as being associated 'with attempts to model, formally or informally, rational individual action and to invent or design social systems').

[50] Peter M. Todd and Gerd Gigerenzer, 'Précis of *Simple Heuristics That Make Us Smart*' (2000) 23(5) Behavioral and Brain Sciences 727.

[51] Gerd Gigerenzer, 'The Adaptive Toolbox' in Gerd Gigerenzer and Reinhard Selten (eds), *Bounded Rationality: The Adaptive Toolbox* (The MIT Press 2002) 37, 46.

and evaluation of the available evidence. In the context of IP law-making, this principle is in line with the idea of 'tailoring' national IP legislation according to the socio-economic development and policy objectives of a particular country. The guiding principle is that policymakers should adopt a strategy and make decisions that take into account idiosyncratic factors and make sense given the local circumstances.[52] Notably, the ecological type of rationality aligns closely with a less known passage from Fritz Machlup, where right after pointing out uncertainty about the net effect of patents,[53] he states: 'While economic analysis does not yet provide a basis for choosing between "all or nothing", it does provide a sufficiently firm basis for decisions about "a little more or a little less" of various ingredients of the patent system.'[54]

Yet national legislators rarely make robust use of the policy space, notwithstanding the flexibility of internationally harmonised IP protection standards. Despite the weak epistemic validity of the utility maximisation premise, patent policy and law-making have steered not towards tailoring but expansion of patent protection in breadth and length, remaining overly cautious about limitations.[55] Betting on maximising patent protection – or other exclusivity-based incentives for that matter – fails to account for the non-linearity of the relationship between appropriability mechanisms and innovation performance and the notion of the inverted-U relationship where increasing protection beyond a certain point is counterproductive.[56] The expansion of patent protection may also demonstrate the phenomenon of 'motivationally biased belief' – instances where 'practical considerations sometimes seem to influence beliefs in ways that violate epistemic norms.'[57] In the case of IP, such motivation might stem from the quid pro quo of the WTO membership or participation in regional or bilateral preferential trade agreements. Ignoring the limitations of both theoretical and empirical knowledge in the normative discourse on patents results in IP becoming 'faith-based' and 'a step backwards in a rational society.'[58]

---

52 On constructivist and ecological rationality in policymaking, see Daria Kim, 'Rationalizing Innovation Incentives under Drug Approval Regulation. National Policy Perspective' in Bryan Mercurio and Daria Kim (eds), *Contemporary Issues in Pharmaceutical Patent Law: Setting the framework and exploring policy options* (Routledge 2017) 203, 221 ff.

53 US Senate (n 36) 80.

54 *Ibid.*

55 See Matthias Lamping et al., 'Revisiting the Framework for Compulsory Licensing of Patents in the European Union – Reflections on the European Commission's Initiative' (2023) 72 GRUR International 471.

56 Dosi, Marengo and Pasquali (n 23) 1111. Yuichi Furukawa, 'Intellectual Property Protection and Innovation: An Inverted-U Relationship' (2010) 109(2) Economics Letters 99.

57 Alfred R. Mele and Piers Rawling, 'Introduction: Aspects of Rationality' in Alfred R. Mele and Piers Rawling (eds), *The Oxford Handbook of Rationality* (1st edn, OUP 2009) 3, 4.

58 Mark A. Lemley, 'Faith-Based Intellectual Property' (2015) 62 UCLA Law Review 1328, 1328.

3. CONCLUDING THOUGHTS

The rational choice theory perspective can enrich the normative analysis of patent law in several ways, particularly by placing a greater focus on the conditional linkage between individual and collective utility maximisation, the validity of knowledge about effects of patents, complementary analytical tools such as rationality paradoxes, and a greater awareness of methodological weaknesses and knowledge gaps regarding our understanding of the relationship between the social benefits and costs of patents – hence the inherent imperfection of rational decision making in patent and innovation policies.

As with many conceptual tools, (ir)rationality is not a binary dichotomy but a continuum reflecting varying degrees of certainty and knowledge of causative factors. Navigating this continuum can teach holistic thinking, which involves an understanding of the patent world in its complexity where opposites coexist, assessments are contextual and relational, and phenomena are understood as emerging from interactions of multiple variables and factors rather than straightforward causality. Moreover, (ir)rationality should be viewed as a dialectic continuum where evolving paradigms and modes of thinking can replace once rationalised dominant premises. This has not been reflective of patent law in books, which remains firmly rooted in the rational actor premise, despite the extensive criticism surveyed in this contribution. It requires the efforts of scholars like our honouree to engage in thought experiments, challenge established pathways, and expose the imperfections inherent in the efficiency-centric approach to patent rationalisation – on a par with Carelman's mockery of efficiency in terms of sharpness and ingenuity.

CHAPTER 20

DOUBLE PATENTING

A Sensible Approach or Abuse of Proceedings?

Liesbet Paemen
Partner and European patent attorney, De Clerq & partners
Guest professor, University of Antwerp and KULeuven

Geertrui and I have had many interesting discussions on how the patent system is used and perceived by different actors in society, particularly with regard to the patenting of plant material, medicines and diagnostics, which directly affects global wellbeing. While I was usually the one defending the patent system, I of course agree that the system must be fair and that the possibility of abuse should be prevented. This is just one small example thereof.

While generally one will argue that it is better to have too much protection than too little, for the patent system to be conceived as fair by those using it and the general public, it should avoid loopholes which allow patent owners to 'overprotect' their inventions. With the introduction of the UPC, the door to double patenting, which most offices had been closing, appears to be opening again.

The concept of 'double patenting' is sometimes broadly used to describe the existence of two or more patents owned by the same patent holder relating to the same subject matter for the same territory.

However, there is a difference between the development of a patent portfolio and actual double patenting. It is not uncommon that applicants aim to protect multiple aspects of their commercial product or process. This is often linked to further development efforts. Subsequent patent applications covering these follow up inventions may also be aimed at extending protection beyond the term of the basic patent (20y) (Figure 1), of which in some cases (such as for therapeutic products) a significant portion can have passed by the time the product can be placed on the market. This strategy has also been dismissed as 'evergreening',[1] i.e. an attempt to 'artificially' extend the life of the patent. However, as under the European Patent convention (EPC), the earlier patent filing will be considered as a prior art document relevant to the patentability of the later filed application, the new aspect will have to be novel (and depending on the filing date also inventive) over the original invention.[2,3] Provided the patent examiners apply the criteria of patentability appropriately, from a legal perspective, the extended protection appears justified.

Figure 1. Diagram illustrating the principle of extending patent protection for a given product by subsequently protecting different aspects thereof

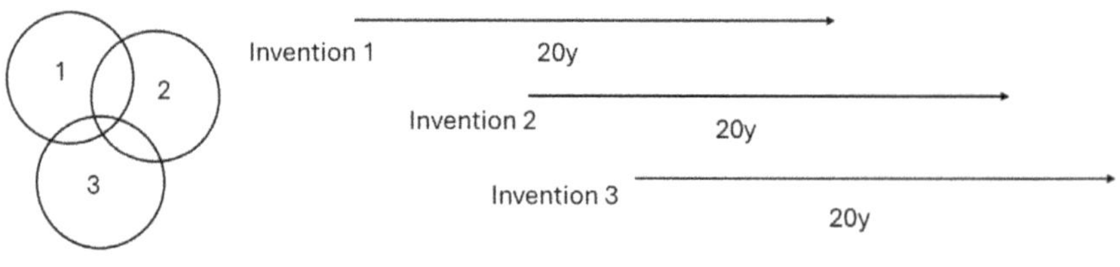

[1] Robin Feldman 'May your drug price be evergreen' (2018) 5(3) Journal of Law and Biosciences 590–647 https://academic.oup.com/jlb/article/5/3/590/5232981, accessed 5 March 2025.

[2] Under Article 54(3) EPC, the earlier application will only be relevant for the assessment of novelty if the later application was filed prior to the publication of the earlier application. If the later application is filed after the publication of the earlier application, the earlier application becomes prior art for the assessment of novelty and inventive step.

[3] This in contrast to the US system, where an application filed within 12 months in the name of the same inventor is not prior art, but the USPTO requires that if the inventions are not patentably distinct a terminal disclaimer is filed that ensures that the patent term of one patent is not extended over that of the other patent.

In a stricter sense, 'double patenting' refers to the coverage of the same subject matter for the same territory by different patents having the same filing date, i.e. such that they cannot be considered as prior art for each other.

In this respect, a difference should be made between claims to identical subject matter and claims to overlapping subject matter (Figure 2). Indeed, while there are no explicit provisions on double patenting in the EPC, this distinction between identical and overlapping subject matter is also made in the guidelines of the European Patent Office (EPO). While in the case of two European applications from the same applicant with identical claims, the applicant is requested to amend the claims of one of these applications, no such objection is made if the claims are merely overlapping.[4] Indeed, the EPO recognises that an applicant may have an interest in obtaining a first patent more quickly with narrower claims to the preferred embodiment and pursuing broader claims in a divisional application and that this should not be considered abusive behaviour.[5] For instance, in the case of a divisional application (a separate application but with the same description and filing date of the parent application), the patent term will be the same for both applications such that, while the divisional application may extend the scope of the claims compared to the parent patent, it will not extend the patent term.

Figure 2. Diagram illustrating the situation where claims with overlapping claim scope may be granted in divisional applications

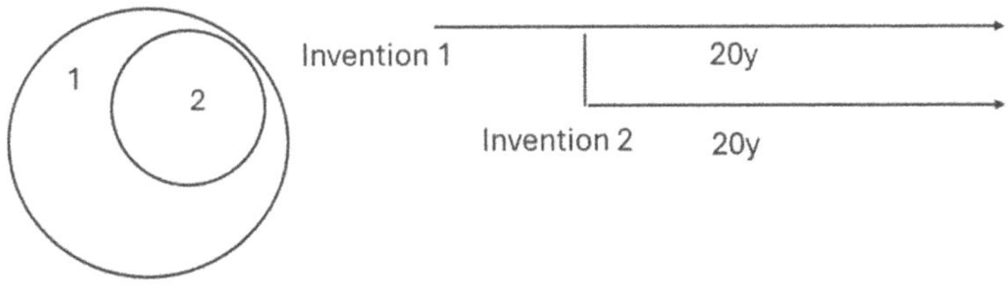

This further limits the actual concept of double patenting to granted patents with identical claims. As indicated above, Examiners of the European patent office will prevent applicants from getting two European patents granted with identical claims, thus effectively limiting the possibility of double patenting. However, other situations may result in identical claims being granted to the same applicant in the same jurisdiction within Europe.

[4] Guidelines for Examination of the EPO G-VI.5.4 Double patenting. Available at http://epo.org/en/legal/guidelines-epc/2024/g_iv_5_4.html, accessed 5 March 2025.

[5] EPO Enlarged Board of Appeal, *Disclaimer/SCRIPPS*, G2/10 (30 August 2011).

First, the priority system introduced by the Paris Convention foresees that an applicant can file a first application in one country, and within 12 months file an application relating to the same invention in one or more other countries, which will then enjoy, for purposes of determining the prior art, the filing date of the earlier application.[6] The priority system was developed to allow applicants to investigate the value of the invention prior to deciding on whether protection on the invention should be extended to other countries. In practice for applicants in Europe, the first application is often a national filing (which is less costly) which is extended at the end of the priority year to a filing with the EPO. Upon grant, this European filing can be validated in the European countries of interest (including that of the priority filing) (Figure 3). While the priority application is often abandoned in favour of the later filing (having a later filing date and thus a longer term), in case the priority application is maintained, two applications will exist for the same jurisdiction. Thus, it is possible that the national priority filing, and the European application, are granted with the same claims.

Figure 3. Use of the priority system can lead to co-pending applications/patents in the same country

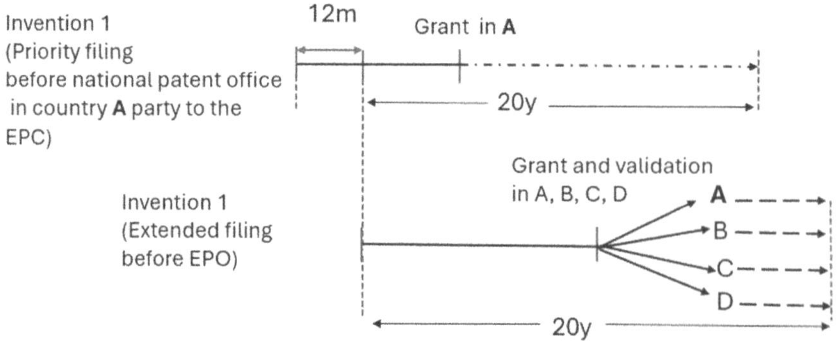

Secondly, the co-existence of the European patent system and national patent systems makes that, irrespective of the priority system the applicant may file simultaneously in Europe and with one or more of the national patent offices (Figure 4). A motivation to do so is in some cases the fact that the national patent systems do not examine the patent applications but allow for an automatic grant (without examination), thus providing a granted patent on a much shorter term.

---

6 Embedded in the European patent convention in Article 87–89 EPC.

Figure 4. Parallel national and European filings can lead to co-pending applications/ patents in the same country

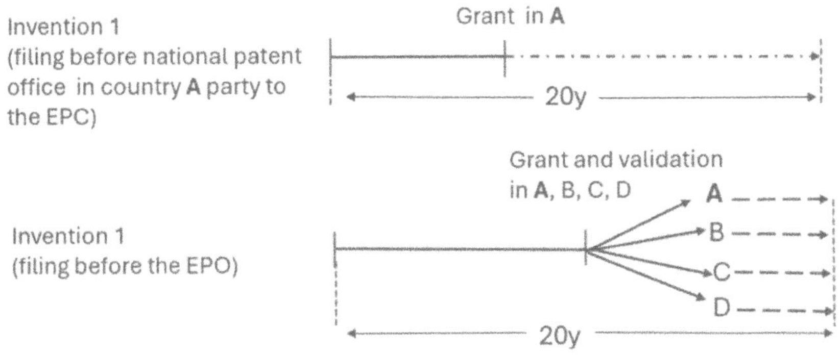

Article 139(3) of the EPC specifies that 'any Contracting State may prescribe whether and on what terms an invention disclosed in both a European patent application or patent and a national application or patent having the same date of filing or, where priority is claimed, the same date of priority, may be protected simultaneously by both applications or patents.' Most contracting states have specified in their national law that simultaneous protection by both a national patent and a national validation of a European patent is not possible, in that the national patent in such cases will cease to have effect.[7] Exceptions thereto are Austria, Denmark, Finland, Italy, Portugal, Slovenia (under certain conditions) and Sweden.

With the introduction of the Unitary Patent (UP) and the Unified Patent Court (UPC) on June 1st, 2023, a new jurisdiction was created which in fact overlaps with the national jurisdiction of each of the participating EU Member States. The UP provides a common validation and maintenance system in all signatory states[8] for patents granted by the EPO, as an alternative to the classical validation system. The UPC has been set up as a court which has jurisdiction over patent infringement and validity of unitary patents and classically validated granted European patents, provided that, for these latter patents, the patentees have not 'opted out'.[9]

---

7 The national laws relating to the EPC can be consulted under 'National measures relating to the Unitary Patent, III. Simultaneous Protection'. Available at www.epo.org/en/legal/national-measures-up/2022/iii/index.html, accessed 5 March 2025.

8 The 18 states in enhanced cooperation which participate in the Unitary Patent are: Austria, Belgium, Bulgaria, Denmark, Estonia, Finland, France, Germany, Italy, Latvia, Lithuania, Luxembourg, Malta, the Netherlands, Portugal, Romania, Slovenia, Sweden. For more information see www.epo.org/en/applying/european/unitary/unitary-patent, accessed 5 March 2025.

9 According to Article 83(3) of the Agreement on a Unified Patent Court (UPCA), applicants for and proprietors of a 'classic' European patent, as well as holders of a supplementary protection

Interestingly, a number of countries have decided to allow simultaneous protection by a national patent and a UP. These countries include France, Germany and Italy which have been at the forefront of the implementation of the UPC, with seats of the Central division of the Unified Patent Court being allocated to Munich, Paris and Milan.[10]

In practice this means that in these countries a UP and a national patent can coexist and in case of an infringement only in one or more of these countries, the patent holder can decide in which jurisdiction to start an action. More particularly, they can decide to file an action only before the national court(s), rather than before the UPC thereby risking only the invalidity of the national patent(s). While this option is also provided by opting out of the European patent of UPC, the ability to maintain both a UP and a national patent on the same invention allows for patentees to select a strategy based on the envisaged strength of their case.[11]

Given the cost of obtaining and maintaining patents, the patent system is already viewed by many to further mainly the interests of the large commercial entities. Most smaller companies will also not have the budget to maintain two patents on the same invention in the same jurisdiction. While the absence of a regulation against double patenting is in some countries justified by the argument that it would be too complicated to draft and apply a ban,[12] it appears that this type of double patenting on the level of overlapping jurisdictions does not further legal certainty and could be considered as abuse of proceedings. Despite what is suggested by the umbrella invention, one cannot use an umbrella and expect it not to get wet.

---

certificate (SPC) issued for a product protected by a 'classic; European patent, can opt out their application, patent or SPC from the exclusive competence of the Court. The opt-out is available until the end of the 'transitional period' which will expire at least seven years from the 01 June 2023 (and may be extended by a further seven years). For more information see http://unified-patent-court.org/en/faq/opt-out, accessed 5 March 2025.

10 Simultaneous protection between a Unitary Patent and a national patent is also allowed in Austria, Denmark, Estonia, Finland, Italy, Malta, Portugal, Slovenia and Sweden.

11 Note that the European principles of *lis pendens* apply, so that if both the national court and the UPC are seized for a related patent, the court seized second should stay the proceedings pending the outcome of the court seized first.

12 See comments on the reasons for allowing simultaneous protection at 'National measures relating to the Unitary Patent, III. Simultaneous Protection, Sweden'. Available at www.epo.org/en/legal/national-measures-up/2022/iii/se.html, accessed 5 March 2025.

CHAPTER 21
PROTECTIVE LETTERS
To Be or Not to Be?*

Carina GOMMERS
Partner, Wiggin LLP

* The author wishes to express her thanks to Joris Evenepoel, associate at Wiggin LLP, for his collaboration in drafting this article.

1. INTRODUCTION

I first met Prof. Geertrui Van Overwalle as a student in the KULeuven Master of Intellectual Property and ICT law program. Although she did not teach patent law in that programme at that point in time, she has of course for a very long time been the patent law expert of the KULeuven. I am therefore very honoured to contribute to this *Liber Amicorum* and dedicate this chapter to her.

Since the implementation of the Enforcement Directive,[1] protective letters have become part of the Belgian intellectual property practice, in particular in patent matters. Protective letters are letters filed with the court on behalf of parties who are concerned that a petition for a descriptive seizure will be filed against them. The holder of an intellectual property right can file such a petition when there are indications that its intellectual property right is being infringed.

A petition for a descriptive seizure is a request to the court to appoint an expert to describe the alleged infringement, but it can also contain a request for effective seizure measures. The petition is filed *ex parte* or unilaterally. The alleged infringer is thus not able to bring its arguments in defence to the court's attention. The proceedings are *ex parte* to be able to effectively gather the necessary evidence of the alleged intellectual property infringements when the seizure is granted. The main purpose of the descriptive seizure order is thus to provide the holder of an intellectual property right, through the surprise effect of the unilateral petition, with effective means to gather evidence to be able to adequately prosecute the potential intellectual property infringement at a later stage. The descriptive seizure order could also be combined with effective seizure measures.

As a pre-emptive step, parties who are concerned that an intellectual property right holder may proceed with filing a petition for a descriptive seizure order may file protective letters in an attempt to have such request for a descriptive seizure order dismissed or at least to be heard by the presiding judge prior to the grant of such order. Protective letters contain a statement of defence as to why the descriptive seizure order should not be issued and/or why the alleged infringer should be heard.

Protective letters have their origin in the German practice of '*Schutzschriften*'. In Germany, '*Schutzschriften*' have become widespread not only in the field of intellectual property law but also in disputes relating to company, press and labour laws.[2] In fact, any legal relationship that can be subject to an interim injunction or a seizure can fall within the scope of a protective letter. Turning

---

1 Directive 2004/48/EC of the European Parliament and of the Council of 29 April 2004 on the enforcement of intellectual property rights [2004] OJ L157/45 (Enforcement Directive).

2 Drescher, 'ZPO §945a Einreichung von Schutzschriften' in Wolfgang Krüger (ed), *Münchener Kommentar zur ZPO* (CH Beck 2020, Munich) (free translation of title: 'Submission of protective letters – Munich Commentary on the ZPO').

back to intellectual property matters, the practice has also more recently been codified under the Unified Patent Court (UPC). Apart from Germany, protective letters are also a practice in the Netherlands[3] and France.[4]

The practice of filing protective letters raises interesting questions as to whether or not this practice is necessary to allow for effectively exercising the rights of defence, including the right to be heard or whether this practice should not be allowed at all or at least most carefully scrutinised since it may hamper effective enforcement of intellectual property rights.

Is a protective letter like an umbrella protecting the alleged infringer from a descriptive seizure order so that it can continue to conduct the shady business of committing intellectual property infringements? Or is it a necessary tool to keep a correct balance between the rights of the holder of the intellectual property right on the one hand and those of the alleged infringer on the other hand? These questions will be further examined both from a Belgian practice point of view and from the point of view of the UPC.

2. BELGIAN PRACTICE

As already indicated above, in Belgium the practice of protective letters has its origins in the implementation of the Enforcement Directive. Article 7 thereof provides that EU Member States shall ensure that measures for preserving evidence are in place, even before the commencement of proceedings on the merits.

Such measures were already in place in Belgium, since descriptive seizure proceedings existed long before the Enforcement Directive was enacted. What was new for Belgium was the introduction of a right to be heard within the first stage of the proceedings. The Enforcement Directive indeed takes a more balanced approach and has also considered that descriptive seizure proceedings can potentially be misused. This could be harmful for the business of the alleged infringer. Firstly, trade secrets or confidential information and know-how of the alleged infringer could be disclosed to the petitioner. Secondly, the continuity of the operations of the business of an alleged infringer could be harmed when, in addition to the pure descriptive measures, also effective seizure measure is granted.[5]

---

3 In the Netherlands, the practice was abandoned in so-called soft IP (trade marks, copyright, designs) matters in 2017.

4 Protective letters may also be a practice in other EU Member States, but this goes beyond the remit of this article.

5 Explanatory Memorandum to the Bill on Civil Aspects of the Protection of Intellectual Property Rights, Parl St Kamer 2006–07, 2944/1.

Therefore, Article 7 of the Enforcement Directive specifically refers to confidential information and also introduces a right to be heard. This right to be heard is relevant in the framework of protective letters. The right to be heard is introduced in Article 7.1 stipulating:

> 'Those measures shall be taken, *if necessary* without the other party having been heard, in particular where any delay is likely to cause irreparable harm to the rightholder or where there is a demonstrable risk of evidence being destroyed' and 'Where measures to preserve evidence are adopted without the other party having been heard, the parties affected shall be given notice, without delay after the execution of the measures *at the latest*. A review, including *a right to be heard*, shall take place upon request of the parties affected with a view to deciding, within a reasonable period after the notification of the measures, whether the measures shall be modified, revoked or confirmed.' (emphasis added)

This provision, therefore, introduces a right to be heard, possibly even before the execution of the measures, since the notice given to the affected party could be given before the measures are granted.

In Belgium, the possible right to be heard prior to the execution of the measures was implemented in Article 1369*bis*/1 § 4 of the Belgian Judicial Code, but only in so far as the effective seizure measures are concerned, not with respect to the mere descriptive measures. In case effective seizure measures are requested, the alleged infringer may be heard in chambers. The petitioner will, however, first be notified thereof and can then withdraw the petition in full or partially, i.e. as far as it concerns the effective seizure measures and limit it to a mere descriptive exercise. In that case, there is no further right to be heard by the alleged infringer.

In practice, this right to be heard is exercised only exceptionally by the court.[6] This is considered a consequence of the court first needing to inform the petitioner about the court's intention to hear the alleged infringer. After receiving this information, most petitioners limit or withdraw their petition.

There is no further provision in the Belgian Judicial Code regarding the right to be heard and thus also no specific provision regarding protective letters. However, given the broader wording of the Enforcement Directive, the Belgian practice of protective letters was developed outside of the legislative framework.[7]

---

6 Ignace Vernimme, 'De pretoriaanse praktijk van het verzoek om gehoord te worden: een stand van zaken' (2022) 3 IRDI 293 (free translation: 'The Praetorian practice of the request to be heard: a state of affairs').

7 See Jan-Diederik Lindemans, 'Het verzoek om te worden gehoord van de partij die het voorwerp dreigt te worden van een beslag inzake namaak: voorkomen is steeds beter dan genezen' (2010) 4 Ing Cons 496 (free translation: 'The request to be heard of the party at risk of becoming the subject of a descriptive seizure order: to prevent is always better than to cure').

It is based on a customary practice developed by private practitioners who began filing such protective letters at the Belgian companies courts.

At a certain point, the Dutch-speaking Brussels Bar was confronted with the question whether the practice of filing protective letters was actually allowed.[8] Following this question, the Dutch-speaking Brussels Bar issued a communication specifying under which conditions protective letters were allowed.[9]

Based on the recommendation of the Dutch-speaking Brussels Bar, protective letters should consist of two parts. The first part of the protective letter is a short cover letter referring to the possibility of a petition for a descriptive seizure order and should also include the identification of the parties as well as the patent, trade mark or other intellectual property right concerned. This cover letter will allow the court's clerk's office to understand why they are addressed and to keep a registry of the protective letters so that these can be consulted once a petition for a descriptive seizure order based on that intellectual property right is received by the court. It is also good practice to refer in this cover letter to the Dutch-speaking Brussels Bar's recommendation, so there is no doubt about the nature of this letter by the court's administration and the letter can be kept in a proper registry and timely consulted when necessary.[10]

The second part of the protective letter should be an attachment in a closed envelope in which the argumentation is included against the descriptive seizure order. The argumentation can address not only why the alleged infringer should be heard but also why the descriptive seizure order should not be issued (e.g. because there is a lack of a valid intellectual property right or a lack of infringement). It could also be argued in subordinate order that a descriptive seizure order could only be granted under certain conditions (e.g. a need for a deposit to be made by the holder of the intellectual property right at stake, a need to prohibit the presence of the representatives of the holder of the intellectual property right when the descriptive seizure order is executed by the court-appointed expert, etc.).[11] In practice, the attachment in the closed envelope will also repeat the information of the cover letter (intellectual property rights at hand, identification of the parties).

To avoid a challenge of recusation by the President, the closed envelope should only be opened once a descriptive seizure order has been requested. The inclusion of the arguments in a closed envelope indeed avoids that the judge

8 See Bruno De Vuyst, 'Verzoek om gehoord te worden bij de behandeling van een eenzijdig verzoekschrift tot beslag inzake namaak door middel van een brief aan de rechtbank (Schutzschrift)' (2010) IRDI 28 (free translatione: 'Request to be heard by a letter to the court (Schutzschrift) when a unilateral petition for descriptive seizure order is issued').

9 Informatieblad Nederlandse Orde van Advocaten te Brussel (free translation: 'Informative communication Dutch speaking Brussels Bar'), 2008–2009, 1401, see also Vernimme (n 6) 298.

10 Vernimme (n 6) 298.

11 *Ibid.*

considering the descriptive seizure petition already would have knowledge of the arguments of the alleged infringer before the descriptive seizure petition is filed. Should the judge already know the arguments of the alleged infringer before assessing the petitioner's request, the judge would have to abstain since he would have prior knowledge of the case before the petition was submitted. The mere knowledge of the names of the possible parties and other identifying data regarding a possible future descriptive seizure order, which are contained in the cover letter, is not considered a ground to challenge the judge.[12]

It is also noteworthy that the Dutch Brussels Bar Association's publication is rather succinct and leaves a number of questions unanswered, causing legal uncertainty. Firstly, it is uncertain whether or not the court needs to inform the petitioner of a descriptive seizure that the judge decides to consider a protective letter. Also, it is not clear when the court should inform the petitioner of the protective letter. Should the court inform the petitioner of the protective letter only in case it informs the petitioner about the court's intention to hear the alleged infringer before granting the effective seizure measures? Or also in other circumstances before granting the order? Furthermore, it is also uncertain how and how long a protective letter should be kept, whether a protective letter should be added to a central registry and if court fees should be paid when filing a protective letter.[13]

As far as the author knows, all Belgian companies courts consider protective letters, apart from the Brussels French-speaking companies court and the companies court in Liège.[14] In addition, it is noteworthy that protective letters seem to be filed mostly in cases in which later no descriptive seizure orders are requested. Again, to the author's knowledge, not a single court in Belgium has taken a protective letter into account and there is therefore no case law on the matter.[15]

3. UPC PRACTICE

Whereas the practice in Belgium is not based on explicit regulation, this is on the contrary the case in the UPC. The practice of protective letters is explicitly regulated in the rules of procedure of the UPC, namely in Rules 194, 207 and 209.

---

12 Article 828(9) juncto Article 831 Belgian Judicial Code; Lindemans (n 7) 508.

13 Vernimme (n 6) 296–297.

14 In the Brussels French-speaking companies court, judges seem to not take note of protective letters in the absence of a legal provision. In the companies court in Liège the judges apparently do not always check if a protective letter has been filed for a case in which a descriptive seizure order has been requested; see also: Vernimme (n 6) 299.

15 Vernimme (n 6) 299.

In addition, in the context of the UPC, the protective letter practice exists in the framework of *ex parte* provisional measures. A provisional measure could be a seizure order or a preliminary injunction. Provisional measures could pose a serious risk to the alleged infringer's business since the UPC allows the enforcement of patent rights across all 18 participating UPC member states. Protective letters will, therefore, gain importance since through the UPC system protective letters become part of the legal system in all the 18 participating member states that have signed and ratified the UPC agreement.

3.1. RULES OF PROCEDURE UPC

Rule 207 Rules of Procedure UPC (hereinafter: 'RoP UPC') provides: 'if a person [...] considers it likely that an Application for provisional measures against him as a defendant may be lodged before the Court in the near future, he may file a protective letter.'

Different formal requirements must be met for the protective letter to be accepted in the registry. The second paragraph of Rule 207 RoP UPC contains the mandatory information a protective letter must contain:

- the name of the alleged infringer filing the protective letter and of its representative;
- the name of the presumed applicant for provisional measures;
- postal and electronic addresses for service on the alleged infringer filing the protective letter and the names of the persons authorised to accept service;
- postal and, where available, electronic addresses for service on the presumed petitioner for provisional measures and the names of the persons authorised to accept service if known;
- where available, the number of the patent concerned and, where applicable, information about any prior or pending proceedings referred to in Rule 13.1(h);[16] and
- the statement that the letter is a Protective letter.

Furthermore, a fee should be paid for filing the protective letter.[17]

If the letter does not meet the formal requirements, there is the possibility of regularisation within 14 days of a deficiency notification.[18] If the protective letter

16 This concerns information about any prior or pending proceedings relating to the patent concerned before the Court including any action for revocation or a declaration of non-infringement pending before the central division and the date of any such action, the European Patent Office or any other court or authority.

17 Rule 207(5) Rules of Procedure of the Unified Patent Court (RoP UPC).

18 Vernimme (n 7) 295.

meets the formal requirements, it is recorded in the register and communicated to all the divisions of the UPC.[19] It is important to note that protective letters are kept confidential until an application for provisional measures is filed. As a result, the patent holder will be unaware that a protective letter has been filed with the UPC.

Furthermore, the protective letter may contain the following:

- an indication of the facts relied on, which may include a challenge to the facts expected to be relied on by the presumed applicant and/or, where applicable, any assertion that the patent is invalid and the grounds for such assertion;
- any available written evidence relied on;
- the arguments of law, including the reasons why any application for provisional measures should be rejected.[20]

A protective letter may be filed with the UPC at any time. Upon an application for provisional measures, the registry shall forward a copy of the protective letter to the panel or judge appointed together with the application for provisional measures. The registry shall also send a copy of the protective letter to the applicant 'as soon as practicable.'[21] When a protective letter is filed after the application for provisional measures, the registry shall inform the panel or the judge appointed about the filing of the protective letter.[22]

Finally, a protective letter shall be removed from the register if no application for provisional measures has been lodged within six months after the receipt of the protective letter unless an extension is requested. An extension of 6 months can be requested upon further payment of the extension fee prior to the expiry.[23]

3.2. CASE LAW

With only one year of UPC practice, there is, nonetheless, already case law on protective letters before the UPC. Two cases can be mentioned in this respect.

3.2.1. *Mystromer/Revolt*[24]

In this first case, the protective letter was not successful in preventing the *ex parte* preliminary injunction. The preliminary injunction was granted by the UPC local division of Düsseldorf. MyStromer AG (hereinafter: 'myStromer') is

19 Rule 207(5) RoP UPC.
20 Rule 207(3) RoP UPC.
21 Rule 207(8) RoP UPC.
22 Rule 207(5)(d) RoP UPC.
23 Rule 207(9) RoP UPC.
24 UPC, Local Division Düsseldorf, 22 June 2023, *myStromer v Revolt*, UPC CFI 177/2023.

the co-owner of the European patent EP 2 546 134 B1 protecting a part of an electrical bike, i.e. a combination structure of bicycle frame and a motor hub characterised by several features claimed in the patent. myStromer applied for a preliminary injunction against an alleged infringer, Revolt Zycling AG (hereinafter: 'Revolt'), prohibiting Revolt from exhibiting one of its series of speed pedelecs at an international tradeshow in Germany because these allegedly infringed the aforementioned patent.

Revolt, on the other hand, had already previously filed a protective letter, requesting for dismissal of a potential request for provisional measures or, in the alternative, a right to be heard. In the protective letter, Revolt invoked exhaustion and, in addition, that its series of speed pedelecs did not infringe myStromer's patent.

The court took the protective letter into account in its judgment, and several references can be found thereto throughout the judgment. Firstly, the non-infringement argument was considered not persuading by the court. Secondly, regarding the exhaustion of rights, the court ruled that this argument had previously been heard and dismissed by a Swiss court and, therefore, was also not convincing. Finally, the court underlined that Revolt could not present relevant prior art that could challenge the validity of the patent at stake.

This case shows that the protective letter was, in this case, carefully reviewed and taken into account by the UPC. It also shows that filing a protective letter is not a blank cheque to prevent a preliminary injunction from being granted. On the contrary, in the case at hand, the court proceeded with granting the preliminary injunction, and this even without hearing the other side in view of the irreparable harm caused to myStromer by any further delay.

3.2.2. Ses-Imagotag/Hanshow et al.[25]

This second case is important in relation to reimbursement of the costs of the protective letter.

In this case, the preliminary measures requested by the patent holder were not awarded by the Munich UPC local division. The applicant SES-imagotag was the unsuccessful party and was, therefore, ordered to pay the legal costs. Per article 69.1 of the UPC Agreement, the unsuccessful party must bear the costs of the legal dispute and other costs of the proceedings incurred by the defendants, depending on the value of in dispute. The Munich UPC local division, in this respect, clarified that the defendants' costs for filing protective letters were to be included as other costs of the proceedings and thus to be paid to the successful party.

---

25 UPC, Local Division Munich, 4 September 2023, *SES-imagotag SA v Hanshow and others*, UPC CFI 292/2023.

4. WHAT CAN WE LEARN FROM THE UPC PRACTICE? CLOSING THE GAPS OF UNCERTAINTY

Notwithstanding the longer-standing practice of filing protective letters in Belgium, it does not really seem a useful practice in Belgian intellectual property litigation. As indicated above, no protective letters seem to have been taken into account previously in Belgian intellectual property litigation. The lack of regulation also leads to a dispersed practice among the courts as to how to file and keep the protective letters in a registry, let alone any clarity regarding how and when these are consulted.

It is still early days to draw conclusions on the practice of protective letters within the UPC, but it at least has the advantage of being a codified system. In addition, the UPC also has the advantage of having technically qualified judges who can carefully review and assess the merits of such letters. In a system where a preliminary injunction can be in force in no less than 18 Member States, such a system can be useful to prevent aggressive intellectual property rights' holders from misusing an effective enforcement tool at the detriment of a competitor that is perceived as an alleged infringer. I consider it, therefore, a useful tool within the UPC. It provides for a more balanced approach. But as said above, it is still in the early days, and we need more case law to draw any further conclusions.

To conclude, certainly, the practice of protective letters as codified within the UPC seems to be not an umbrella under which alleged infringers can hide to continue to conduct any shady business, but a way of providing a balance between effective enforcement tools and freedom of competition.

CHAPTER 22

REINVENTING PATENTS

Catalina MARTINEZ
Senior researcher, CSIC Institute of Public Goods and Policies, Madrid

'"In three months I'll be rich," replied the inventor with an inventor's certainty.'

– Honoré de Balzac, *Lost Illusions,* Part Three: The Torments of an Inventor, 1877

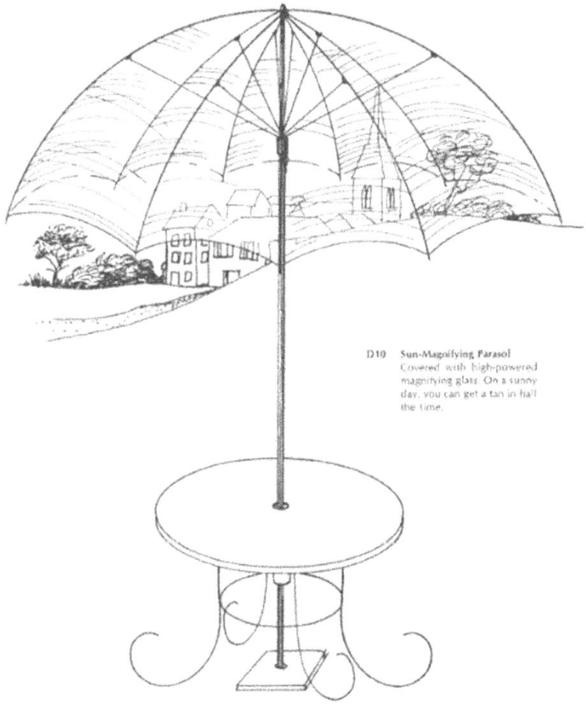

1. INTRODUCTION

Patents confer exclusive rights to inventors, but they also respond to a social contract whereby they need to disclose their inventions in exchange for protection. Patents provide the right *to decide* whether to exclude or include others in the use and exploitation of their inventions and are paradoxical in many respects. They can become *weapons* against others, but they can also be used to *share* access to knowledge.

These apparent contradictions have been the focus of a large number of studies by Professor Geertrui van Overwalle. The title of one of her most cited works is 'Inventing inclusive patents: from old to new open innovation' where she proposes to establish a new inclusive patents regime, which could coexist with the traditional patent system. 'Rather than offering a right to exclude, the "inclusive patent" encompasses the right to include: by empowering owners to include others, to control licensing conditions and to enforce alignment with the open source like commitments.'[1]

The title of my contribution to this *Liber Amicorum* is 'Reinventing patents' with the aim to reflect a shared vision of the patent system as a dynamic, ever-growing, evolving, and challengeable system. The status quo of patent systems can and should be challenged if there is room for improving its impact on social welfare. There is a large and growing interdisciplinary academic community advancing research to do so, in which the dialogue and collaboration between economists and legal scholars with policy makers, practitioners, patent attorneys, and business is essential.[2]

Patents are granted to preserve the ownership of an invention for a period of time, generally less than twenty years. Their existence serves as an incentive to bring into reality something that did not previously exist and opening doors to unexplored pathways. Innovation is the production of knowledge, but once shared, that knowledge can be used by those who have not invested in its creation. This leads to market failure and may result in insufficient incentives to innovate in the absence of legal mechanisms like patents. By granting

1 Geertrui Van Overwalle, 'Inventing inclusive patents. From old to new open innovation' in Peter Drahos, Gustavo Ghidini and Hanns Ullrich (eds.) *Kritika: Essays on Intellectual Property* in (vol. 1 Edward Elgar 2015) 208.

2 I met Geertrui at one of the conferences of the European Policy for Intellectual Property (EPIP, www.epip.eu). I attend almost every year since 2003, as researcher in economics of innovation and patents and discuss. I got to know her better when I joined the EPIP board in 2015 (to which she belonged since 2007) and I really liked her passion and determination to ensure the association was a forum to train and engage new generations of scholars in the field. The EPIP association was created in 2005, to continue the activities of a European research project led by Dominique Foray. Between 2005 and 2024, the association has had 19 presidents. The first president was Jacques Mairesse in 2005/2006, Geertrui van Overwalle was the 8th in 2012/2013, and I had the privilege to be 16th EPIP president for the academic year 2021/2022.

patents, the government entrusts the inventor with the decision to invest in the necessary research for innovation and allows them to recover their investment through market revenues. However, even though patents aim to bring about improvements, they do not always succeed if they are not utilized. And when they are, they can lead to abuse and divide the world between those with access to knowledge and those condemned to lag behind.

Yet, most patents have very low value, and for those that provide high returns, complementary assets and time to market tend to matter more than the patent itself to obtain revenues from the market. Patented inventions face competition from other patented and unpatented products and only a few cannot be invented around. Patents that are widely perceived as impossible to invent around are those protecting genes, an area that has also been extensively studied by Prof. van Overwalle. In particular in her *Science* paper '*Turning patent swords into shields and shares*' where she proposed changes in patent licensing modes following the Myriad case,[3] which involved genetic patents and issues of follow-on innovation, access to gene-based diagnostic tests and human rights.[4]

In what follows I will discuss briefly the evolution of patents in recent years and how challenging it is in view of current developments to maintain the social contract aspect of patents, when making proposals to continuously re-invent the patent system timelier than ever.

2. THE EXPANSION OF PATENTS ACROSS COUNTRIES

A growing number of international treaties and institutions aim to enable inventors to protect their inventions beyond the territory where they are generated and to simplify procedures with that aim. They are still far from providing global protection through a single procedure valid in all countries, but they aim to pave the way to considering patent protection as a sort of canopy covering all countries, as in the image that introduces this chapter. The question is whether such protection is a canopy producing shadows and blocking some parts of the world from using patentable inventions, or whether instead it should be pictured as a magnifying glass, amplifying the diffusion and sharing of inventions.

The first patent was published in Venice in 1474, and the privilege it granted was only valid in the Republic of Venice. The modern patent system derives from the Statute of Monopolies approved in 1623 by the English Parliament. The first patent laws for France and United States were enacted by the end of the 18th

3 US Supreme Court in the case of *Association for Molecular Pathology v Myriad* Genetics invalidating patents on human genes, see US Supreme Court (2012), Syllabus: *Association for Molecular Pathology et al. v Myriad Genetics, Inc., et al. Rep.*, US Supreme Court, Washington, DC.

4 Geertrui Van Overwalle, 'Turning patent swords into shields and shares' (2010) 330 Science, 6011, 1630–1631.

century. The international aspects of patent protection started to be introduced at the end of the 19th century and have gradually evolved since then.

The Paris Convention of 1883 was the first milestone enabling inventors to protect their inventions in other countries, while keeping priority rights from seeking patent protection less than 12 months before in their home country. The Convention now has more than 175 signatory countries worldwide. The last country to join was Afghanistan in 2017.

Almost a century later, the Patent Cooperation Treaty (PCT) of 1970 introduced a single procedure managed by the World International Intellectual Property Organisation (WIPO), created in 1967, whereby instead of applying separately in every country where protection is sought, inventors can file a single international PCT application which is then recognized in all member countries. Twenty-five years later, the World Trade Organisation (WTO) Agreement on Trade-Related Aspects of Intellectual Property Rights (TRIPS) of 1995 established minimum standards for intellectual property rights (IPRs) and required patents to be available in all fields of technology.

The geographic patent landscape has changed dramatically in recent decades. The number of patents per country is increasing every year, with some countries moving faster than others in what looks like a patenting race. Of the 3.55 million patent applications filed worldwide in 2023, more than 1.5 million correspond to domestic filings made by residents in China, and altogether patent offices located in Asian countries received around 69% of all the patent applications.[5]

As shown in Figure 1, the US Patent Office received the highest number of patents almost every year since 1883, until Japan took the lead in 1968 and retained its position until 2005. As shown in the chart below, China receives by far the largest number of patent applications, but as mentioned earlier most of them are domestic filings by residents. If instead of looking at patent applications independently, we consider patent families grouping together all patent applications protecting the same invention in different offices,[6] we observe that most families correspond to single offices: around 85% of patent families created worldwide between 2019 and 2021 were filed at a single office. Around 97% of patent families originated in China only include filings in China, whereas more than two-thirds of all patent families originating from the Netherlands, Sweden and Switzerland, much smaller countries, cover two or more offices.[7]

---

5 As regards distribution across technology fields, computer technology is the technology field with the largest number of applications worldwide, with 12% of the total in 2022 (the latest year for which information on fields is available), followed by electrical machinery (7%), measurement (6%), medical technology (5%) and digital communication (5%) WIPO, World Intellectual Property Indicators 2024 (World Intellectual Property Organisation, Geneva 2024).

6 Catalina Martínez, 'Patent families: when do different definitions really matter?' (2011) 86 Scientometrics, 39–63.

7 WIPO, World Intellectual Property Indicators 2024 (World Intellectual Property Organisation, Geneva 2024).

Figure 1. Number of patent applications received by top patent offices, filing years 1883–2020

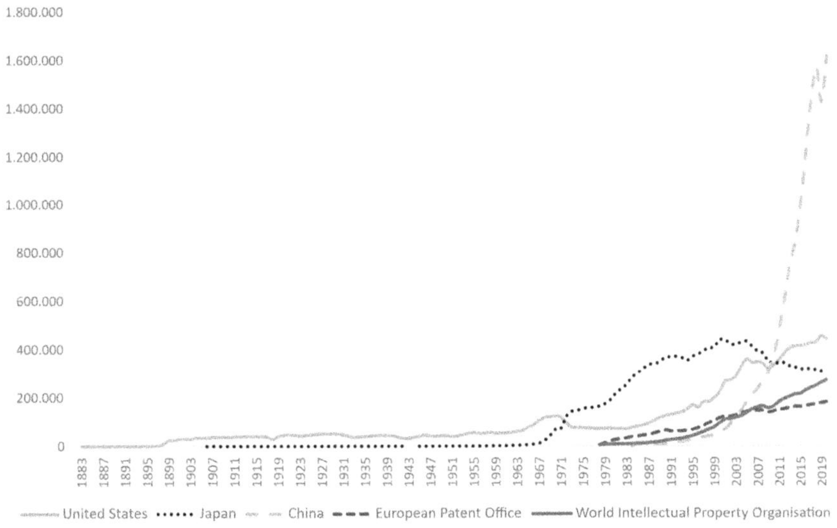

Source: Own elaboration, data from Patstat Spring 2024.

At the European level, the European Patent Convention (EPC) of 1977 created the European Patent Office and established a single procedure to apply for patent protection in all EPC member countries (currently 39) through a single application that is examined and eventually granted at EPO, but needs to be validated nationally afterwards.[8] Two important steps towards simplifying and unifying patent procedures in Europe, although limited to a number of countries within the European Union after decades of negotiation, are the Unitary Patent (UP) and the Unified Patent Court (UPC) that entered into force in June 2023. The global uptake rate, defined as the percentage of requests received with respect to European patents granted, has increased from 17.5% in 2023 to 25.2% in 2024. The EPO states' uptake, considering only applicants from EPO member states, is much higher and equal to 25.9% for 2023 and 35.7% for 2024. EPO receives around 2 500 UP requests every month since June 2023.[9] Most European Union (EU) countries have agreed to join the UP and UPC system by November 2024, and eighteen of them have already ratified the corresponding international

8 Other international treaties at the regional level, similar to the European Patent Convention (EPC) of 1977 include the African Intellectual Property Association (OAPI) of 1962; the African Regional Eurasian Patent Convention (ARIPO) of 1976; and the Eurasian Patent Convention (EAPO) of 1995.

9 www.epo.org/en/about-us/statistics/statistics-centre#/unitary-patent, accessed 18 May 2025.

agreements and are fully part of the system. Three EU countries have not joined yet: Spain, Poland, and Croatia.

Even though international negotiations to harmonize and simplify procedures to internationalize patent protection are lengthy and not always fully successful, the tendency seems to be to move towards a global patent system. Is a global patent system with patents available everywhere good for innovation and welfare? Economic literature has largely studied the impact of the introduction and strengthening of patent protection on patent filings and R&D investments globally over time, as well as on follow-on innovation in specific technology areas. One of the most well-known studies is that of Lerner who concluded that stronger patent laws do not lead to more patent filings based on data from patent policy changes in 60 countries over 150 years.[10] The conclusion is more nuanced when looking at specific technologies and impacts beyond patent filings. For instance, Kyle and Quian examine the effect of pharmaceutical patent protection on the speed of drug launch, price, and quantity in 60 countries from 2000–2013 and find that in the absence of a patent, launch is unlikely, even with generic entry, and conditional on launch, patented drugs have higher prices but higher sales as well.[11]

3. PATENTABLE SUBJECT MATTER AND THE CASE OF GENE PATENTS

Patentable subject matter evolves over time and is shaped by policy, patent law and court decisions as well as innovation, economic and social forces. The question of what is, and what is not, an invention made by human ingenuity and creativity has been central to the patent debate for decades, particularly since the emergence of bioinformatics and widespread use of IT tools in the 1970s and 1980s. Artificial intelligence (AI) is posing new challenges to patent law and practice, specifically since generative AI tools such as Large Language Models (LLMs) were made available to the public at large at the beginning of 2023 with ChatGPT by the company OpenAI.

In 1952, the US Congress Drafting Committee of the US Patent Law described patentable inventions as 'anything made by man under the sun.'[12] But what matters is how the scope of a patent is defined by its claims, as that is what

10 Josh Lerner, 'The Empirical Impact of Intellectual Property Rights on Innovation: Puzzles and Clues' (2009) 99(2) American Economic Review 343.

11 Margaret Kyle and Yi Qian, 'Intellectual Property Rights and Access to Innovation: Evidence from the TRIPS Agreement' (2017) 128(6) The Quarterly Journal of Economics 3219.

12 This quote was later used by Judge Burger in the famous *Diamond v Chakrabarty* decision of 1980, to argue that genetically modified living organisms were patentable.

makes it more or less difficult to invent around.[13] In the area of gene patents, which are arguably the most difficult ones to be invented around, a number of patents filed by Myriad Genetics Inc. in the 1990s became highly controversial and the object of several lawsuits. They covered both isolated gene sequences and methods for testing genetic mutations linked to breast and ovarian cancers and were invalidated partly in 2013 by the U.S. Supreme Court. The Court decision stated that naturally occurring DNA cannot be patented merely because it has been isolated from the human genome but allowed patents for synthetic or complementary DNA (cDNA), given that it is not naturally occurring.

The patents claimed by Myriad Genetics gave the company the exclusive right to isolate BRCA1 and BRCA2 genes, or any strand of 15 or more nucleotides within them, and the exclusive right to create BRCA cDNA. Supported by a strong assertive patenting strategy, Myriad was the only company at the time that could administer the BRCA1/2 test, for which it charged USD 3000–4000, yielding a profit of USD57 million through June 2013. As soon as the Supreme Court ruling invalidated some of Myriad's patents, other companies began offering lower-cost BRCA1/2 testing at less than half the price.[14]

Initiatives such as compulsory licenses for public health, diagnostic use exemptions, patent pools and clearinghouses have been proposed to ensure access to gene patents, in a context where genome sequencing and testing is increasingly available and less costly.[15]

As regards the impact on follow-on research, the empirical analysis of Sampat and Williams (2019)[16] suggests that published US patent applications claiming genes do not have important effects on follow-on scientific research and product development. Their conclusion contrasts with the common perception that gene patents hinder follow-on innovation and introduces a positive aspect of patents into the debate, their disclosure requirement. According to them, 'the patent system's disclosure requirement induced explicit reporting of the claimed DNA sequence in a way that enabled open access to the sequence data underlying both accepted and rejected applications for all prospective follow-on users.'

The EU Biotechnology Directive of 1998 (Directive 98/44/EC) established the legal basis for the patentability of biotechnological inventions within the EU, so that genes can only be patented in Europe if they are isolated and meet the requirements of novelty, inventiveness, and industrial applicability. It also stated that genes are not patentable in their natural form, but isolated genetic sequences

---

13 Paul Klemperer, 'How broad should the scope of patent protection be?' (1990) 21(1) The RAND Journal of Economics, 113–130.

14 Jacob S. Sherkow and Christopher Scott, 'CASE STUDY: Myriad stands alone' (2014) 32 Nature Biotechnology 620.

15 Van Overwalle (n 1); Geertrui Van Overwalle et al., 'Models for Facilitating Access to Patents on Genetic Inventions' (2006) 7(2) Nature Review Genetics, 143–148.

16 Bhaven Sampat and Heidi L. Williams, 'How Do Patents Affect Follow-On Innovation? Evidence from the Human Genome' (2019) 109(1) American Economic Review, 203–236.

that have an industrial function may be patented, provided their specific utility is clearly stated.

The number of gene-related patents granted by USPTO and EPO increased exponentially until the mid-2000s but decreased significantly in the EPO in the 2010s and has not recovered since, while at the USPTO it has recently grown again. Genetic patenting remains an area of continuous debate in most jurisdictions.

Figure 2. Gene-related patents granted by USPTO and EPO with grant years 1970–2022

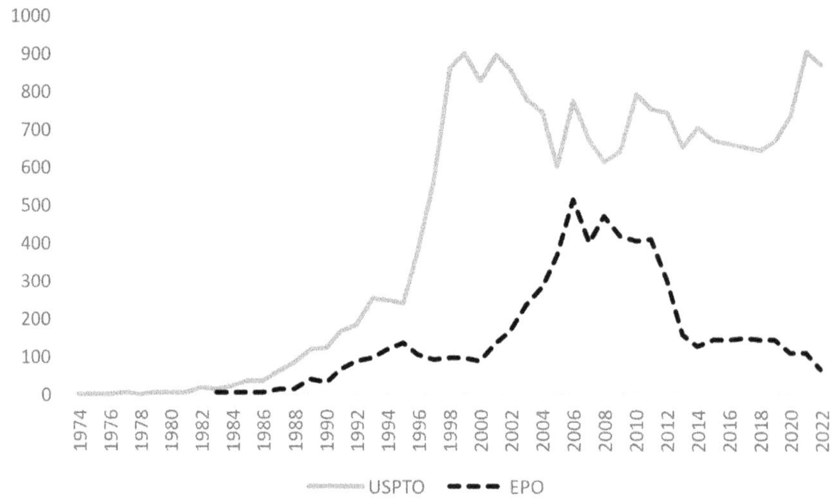

Source: Own elaboration, data from Google patents search of the word 'gene' in the title or abstract of USPTO and EPO granted patents simply for illustration purposes. Note that most empirical papers related to gene patents use more fine-grained data collection methods.

4. CONCLUSIONS

Patents are increasingly available worldwide and in areas where inventing around is more difficult, such as gene patents, and less costly, such as inventions assisted with AI tools. Patents also increasingly rely on public funding and are filed by public research sector institutions. In this context, and following Van Overwalle (2015), 'a patent can no longer be viewed as a title giving (almost) complete freedom of action, but rather as a temporary permit to exploit rights under fair and reasonable conditions investing technology owners with the authority to invent and share.'[17]

[17] Van Overwalle (n 1).

Reinventing patents requires a better understanding of patenting strategies and the costs and benefits of alternative strategies to protect innovative knowledge (secrecy, public domain, time to market, complementary assets, etc.) to be able to evaluate the welfare effects of patent policy changes.[18] It now becomes even more important to advocate for patents to be more inclusive, while preserving their role to incentivize investment in research and development and commercialization of new ideas, taking into account advances in economic and legal analysis.[19] The relevance of academic and policy reflections aiming to reinvent the patent system became evident during the COVID-19 pandemic and remain relevant in view of possible future crises.

The key is whether we can transform patent protection at the international level into an imaginary umbrella that looks like the one depicted in the *Catalog of Fantastic Things* set out at the beginning of this contribution, where patents enlighten inventions, and plays the role of a magnifying glass that amplifies inclusion and disclosure over exclusion and secrecy.

---

18 Sampat and Williams (n 16).

19 David Encaoua, Dominique Guellec, and Catalina Martinez, 'Patent systems for encouraging innovation: lessons from economic analysis' (2006) 35(9) Research Policy 1423–1440.

PART VI

DIGITISING THE FUTURE: COPYRIGHT, LABOR, AND DIGITAL TECHNOLOGIES

CHAPTER 23

FLEXIBILISATION AND DIGITALISATION OF WORK

Finding a New Income Paradigm for the Financing of Social Security*

Paul Schoukens
Full professor social security law, KU Leuven
Instituut Gak chair on International and European Social Security Law, Tilburg University

Eleni De Becker
Assistant professor of social security law, Vrije Universiteit Brussel
Substitute professor in European social security law, KU Leuven

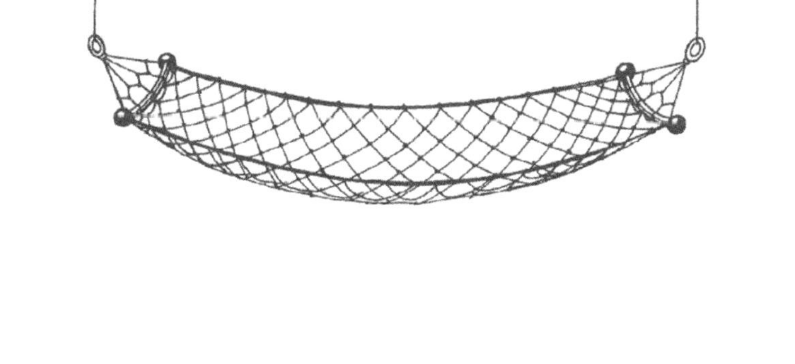

* This contribution was written and finalised in June 2024.

1. INTRODUCTION

A disclaimer (or a joke?) at the beginning of this contribution: 'ceci n'est pas a contribution on intellectual property' or is it? The main topic will be the flexibilisation and digitalisation of work: a further digitalisation of our society and in particular the role of artificial intelligence (AI) could (or will?) require a fundamental rethinking of the foundations of intellectual property law. Needless to say, other areas of law are facing similar challenges, including social security law. Labour markets in EU Member States have already become more flexible in recent decades, posing significant challenges to the sustainability and protection of social security systems; increasing digitalisation will only add to these challenges.[1] This brings us to some fundamental (and not necessarily new) questions: 'At what point does an activity become a professional activity?' and 'What sources of income can (still) be considered as wages or, more broadly, as professional income?'. These fundamental questions, which are crucial for social security as the collection of contributions and earmarked taxes depends heavily on them, are becoming more difficult to answer. However, a key to the strategy for meeting these challenges is likely to be found in the concept of income. We believe that this concept may need to be redefined to better reflect the current realities of income generation. Consequently, the concept of income may need to be broadened to help find new alternative ways of financing social security beyond the traditional contributions levied on wages.[2]

On the occasion of the retirement of our colleague Geertrui Van Overwalle, we would like to address this future challenge of reinventing the concept of income for social security law. Financing and its revenue sources are a crucial cornerstone to ensure the (financial) sustainability of our social security systems; reinventing the concept for future generations is urgently needed. This would help to find a new balance in social security systems: in social security systems it is necessary to find an eternal balance between finding resources (financing) on the stronger (income) shoulders and spending these resources to benefit people in need. This is why the hammock has been chosen in this contribution as a symbol of this balance. We thought it would be appropriate to celebrate a colleague whose core competence is the legal protection of inventions and who has taught and mentored future generations of lawyers specialising in legal

---

1 These challenges were also addressed in the report made by the High-Level Group on the future of social protection and of the welfare state in the EU: European Commission, *High Level Report on the Future of Social Protection. The Future of Social Protection and of the Welfare State in the EU* (2023).

2 Several experts in the field of social security also referred to this challenge as discussed further in Paul Schoukens, Eleni De Becker and Thijs Keersmaekers (eds), Living and Working Tomorrow (2035): Challenges for Social Security (Administrations) (European Institute of Social Security 2024); similarly see also: the High-Level Group on the future of social protection and of the welfare state in the EU: European Commission 2023 (n 2).

research. Looking into the future (developments) and outlining the challenges for future law-making was part of her professorship, and so we hope that with this contribution we can stay in line with her vision of law and society in teaching and research.

The structure of this paper is as follows. First, we briefly explain why the concept of income is so important for social security, both from a financing and a benefit perspective. Second, we outline some developments in the evolution of the labour market, characterised by further flexibilisation (increase in non-standard forms of work) and digitalisation of work organisation (i.e. increase in platform-based forms of work). In a third part, we develop some ways in which the concept of income could evolve alongside these developments in order to ensure that future generations (of workers) can continue to benefit from the social protection guaranteed by social security systems. We end with some concluding remarks.

2. RELEVANCE OF INCOME FOR SOCIAL SECURITY

Social security systems in Europe are still largely based on their traditional design, either adopting a more Bismarckian approach (protection of workers and professionally active at large) or tending towards a Beveridgeian approach (protection of residents).[3] The former explicitly emphasises the standard employment relationship, i.e. the worker who has a stable, open-ended, full-time arrangement with a single employer.[4] Although the latter tends to focus on uniform protection for all residents, the standard employment relationship is also seen as the starting point for the social risks associated with the exercise of a professional activity, such as unemployment or accidents at work.

The main objective of social security systems is to provide a set of arrangements to express solidarity with people who face (the threat of) a lack of sufficient resources or special costs due to a social risk.[5] The provision of an adequate level of social protection requires a method of financing that is capable of providing adequate benefits in the event of loss of income. Since the emergence of the first

---

3 More information on the different types of welfare models and their underlying principles can be found here: Gøsta Esping-Andersen, *The Three Worlds of Welfare Capitalism* (Princeton University Press 1990); see also Jos Berghman, 'Basic Concepts of Social Security' in Danny Pieters (ed) *Social Security in Europe* (Bruylant 1991) 16–17 and Bernd Von Maydell et al., *Social Policy in the 21st Century* (Springer 2001) 19–20.

4 See also the discussion in Paul Schoukens, Eleni De Becker and Charlotte Bruynseraede, 'The Evolution of Standard Work' in Mick Moore, Christoph Scherrer and Marcel Van der Linden (eds), *The Elgar Companion to Decent Work and the Sustainable Development Goals* (Elgar Publishing, forthcoming 2025), https://papers.ssrn.com/sol3/papers.cfm?abstract_id=4682600, accessed 18 June 2024.

5 Danny Pieters, *Social Security: An Introduction to the Basic Principles* (Kluwer Law International 2006) 3–4.

social protection schemes in the late nineteenth century, income or wages have played a key role in the financing of schemes, but also in the determination of social security benefits, in particular income-replacement benefits (e.g. when the amount is expressed as a percentage of the previous wage or when higher benefits are granted to persons/households with a lower income).

In almost all EU Member States, social contributions are still the main source of funding for income-replacement benefits.[6] The importance of social contributions has decreased over the years and the importance of general government resources has increased.[7] General government resources can be divided into direct taxes (e.g. personal income tax) and indirect taxes (e.g. VAT), although the latter plays only a minor role in the financing mix of social security schemes in the EU Member States.[8] As far as direct taxes are concerned, it is clear that income plays an important role as a source for the determination of taxes on income. Regardless of whether we are in a Bismarckian or a Beveridgeian system, a correct assessment of income is crucial.

3. LABOUR MARKET EVOLUTIONS: FLEXIBILISATION AND DIGITALISATION OF WORK AND THEIR IMPACT FOR THE DELINEATION OF THE CONCEPT OF INCOME

3.1. FLEXIBILISATION OF WORK

In recent decades, there has been a significant increase in flexible work arrangements, with around 40% of the European Union's workforce engaged in various forms of flexible work, including part-time work, fixed-term contracts and self-employment.[9] These non-standard forms of work are not only becoming more common,[10] but also more diverse, often occupying a grey area between employment and self-employment.[11] We refer to previous studies for a more

---

6 Arthur Van de Meerendonk, 'Financing Social Protection' in Esther Schüring and Markus Loewe (eds), *Handbook of Social Protection Systems* (Edward Elgar 2021) 137.

7 Slavina Spasova and Terry Ward, *Social Protection Expenditure and its Financing in Europe. A Study of National Policies* (ESPN Brussels 2019) 12.

8 *Ibid.* 44–45.

9 European Commission, 'Report from the Commission to the Council on the Implementation of the Council Recommendation on Access to Social Protection for Workers and the Self-Employed' COM (2023) 43 final 2.

10 ILO, *Conclusions of the Meeting of Experts on Non-Standard Forms of Employment. GB.323/POL/3* (International Labour Office 2015).

11 Adrian Goldin, 'Labour Subordination and the Subjective Weakening of Labour Law' in Guy Davidov and Brian Langille (eds) *Boundaries and Frontiers of Labour Law: Goals and Means in the Regulation of Work* (Hart Publishing 2006) 109–132.

detailed overview. What is clear, however, is that labour market relations have become more complex, exacerbated by new digital developments and work patterns that lead to less stable careers. In particular, the combination of different forms of flexible work increases the complexity of flexible work. For example, individuals work part-time while juggling multiple fixed-term contracts, and the number of workers combining self-employment with short-term wage employment may increase in the future. In particular, the emergence of platform work, characterised by the fragmentation of work tasks into micro-level tasks or 'gigs' outsourced to a variety of potential workers, represents a new dimension of flexibility in work arrangements.[12] These developments pose unique challenges for social security administrations.

Firstly, there is a need to define the minimalist nature of some activities carried out in the context of fixed-term contracts, especially when such activities are mediated through platforms. Can these activities be classified as work and, if so, at what point should they be considered as such for social security purposes? The rules and definitions for determining when an activity qualifies as work are often unclear. Similarly, setting the minimum threshold for work to be considered for social security purposes is challenging. There is a growing trend to set minimum income levels as a condition for the accrual of social security rights. At the European level, there are calls to include as many activities as possible for social security purposes, even if they are marginal, so that workers do not lose out on future entitlements.[13] This will require careful monitoring of activities by administrations.

Second, there is a growing group of individuals who have multiple (micro) jobs, sometimes simultaneously maintaining different employment statuses, such as self-employment and traditional employment.[14] There are concerns that individuals may lose their entitlement to social security benefits if too strict conditions are imposed on these so-called 'minor' or 'mini' jobs. The EU Council Recommendation on access to social protection underlines the need for implementing rules that aggregate different activities for social security purposes to prevent individuals from losing their potential benefits.[15] Instead of exempting

---

12 See also the discussion and the references cited in E. De Becker et al., 'Mapping the Social Protection Coverage for Platform Workers: A Comparative Analysis of Belgium, Italy and the Netherlands' (2024) European Journal of Social Security 3–26, https://doi.org/10.1177/13882627241236489, accessed 18 June 2024.

13 Recital 19 and Articles 7(h), 9 and 10 Council Recommendation of 8 November on Access to Social Protection for Workers and the Self-Employed [2019] OJ C 387.

14 See also the discussion in Iain Campbell, 'Platform Work and Precariousness: Low Earnings and Limited Control of Work' in V. De Stefano et al. (eds) *A Research Agenda for the Gig Economy and Society* (Edward Elgar Publishing 2021) 121–122 where platform work is mentioned as an example of a continuum of different kinds of casual on-call jobs people have to take up to make ends meet.

15 Article 10 Council Recommendation of 8 November on Access to Social Protection for Workers and the Self-Employed [2019] OJ C 387.

secondary activities from social security, internal coordination rules need to be established to combine insurance records from different activities. However, this places an additional burden on social security administrations, which have to carefully monitor insurance periods, especially considering that these activities do not always follow a stable schedule (often part-time and spread over different time intervals), which further complicates administrative tasks.

A third challenge relates to the increased difficulty in determining certain essential factors for social security, such as the presence of an employer, hours worked and place of work. For example, in the context of contributions and eligibility for incapacity for work and unemployment benefits, individuals may now be simultaneously engaged in several activities, each with a different employer. This complexity becomes apparent in the administration of incapacity for work and unemployment schemes. Questions arise as to which institution is responsible for paying sickness benefits or for assessing the involuntary nature of unemployment. In cases of part-time unemployment combined with other minor activities, determining the availability for work is a challenge. The problem is not only the multiplicity of employers, but also the difficulty of identifying the responsible employer, especially in situations involving temporary work, platform work and economically dependent self-employment.

3.2. DIGITALISATION OF WORK

It is difficult to predict the impact that further digitalisation, in particular the development of AI, might have on work and work performed. It could be expected that such new trends could further and more profoundly change the labour market in EU Member States and also reduce the hours worked by employees or self-employed persons.[16] Such changes in labour markets will require new responses from social security systems in order to provide adequate protection against the financial consequences of under- and unemployment.[17] As a result, existing schemes will have to reflect on what kind of protection can and should be offered in combination with training activities, for which a tailored programme adapted to the needs of different types of workers will be a major burden on such schemes.

Not only do these new labour market trends have an impact on the overall protection one can (not) receive from social security schemes, but they can also

16 Andres Viia et al. 'Futures of European Welfare Models and Policies: Seeking Actual Research Questions and New Problem-Solving Arsenal for European Welfare States' (2016) Eur J Futures Res 1.1; Marius Busemeyer et al., 'Digitalization and the Welfare State – Introduction' in Marius Busemeyer et al. (eds) *Digitalization and the Welfare State* (Oxford University Press 2022) 1.

17 Busemeyer et al. (n 17) 13.

have a negative impact on the financial equilibrium of the social security system, which is financed by social security contributions based on work done. Overall, employment rates in EU countries are (still) high. Despite high employment, the share of labour in national income appears to be declining worldwide, including in the EU.[18] If non-standard forms of work were to increase even further, combined with employees and self-employed persons working fewer hours, the necessary attention should also be paid to maintaining the financial sustainability of social security systems with a broad financing base.

The example of the recent strikes by screenwriters in the United States of America for better pay shows the complexity of an ongoing flexibilisation and digitalisation of labour markets for social security systems. The challenges that AI and streaming services pose for the organisation of the labour (market) have been addressed by many and have recently even led to a serious social conflict in the Hollywood film industry. In 2023, the Writers Guild of America (hereinafter: 'WGA') published a report[19] highlighting the fact that the working conditions and protection of screenwriters have been severely neglected by the companies that employ them. While screenwriters are struggling to make a living from an income that is characterised by a high degree of insecurity in terms of the duration of their work, the level of their pay and the often unpaid periods during which they work on their scripts, the profits of these companies and the costs associated with the production of films and TV series, particularly through streaming services, continue to rise.[20] As a result of the ongoing labour dispute between the WGA and the Alliance of Motion Picture and Television Producers, several strikes broke out in Hollywood before the WGA ratified the Minimum Basic Agreement (MBA) reached in October 2023.[21] It is interesting to note that while the agreement mainly deals with setting minimum wages and improving working conditions, a separate chapter is dedicated to the responsible use of AI.[22]

Similarly, the Screen Actors Guild – American Federation of Television and Radio Artists (hereinafter: 'SAG-AFTRA') also participated in collective action

18 Georgios Petropoulos et al., *Digitalisation and European Welfare States* (Bruegel 2019) 21.

19 WGA, 'Writers are not Keeping Up: Driven in Large Part by the Shift to Streaming, Writers are Finding their Work Devalued in Every Part of the Business' (14 March 2023), www.wgacontract2023.org/updates/bulletins/writers-are-not-keeping-up, accessed 18 June 2024.

20 WGA, 'State of the Industry: Despite Wall Street Noise, Entertainment Remains a Profitable Business' (10 March 2023), www.wgacontract2023.org/updates/state-of-the-industry, accessed 18 June 2024.

21 See: WGA, '2023 MBA Ratified: We Are Pleased to Announce that 99% of WGA Members Have Voted in Favor of Ratifying the 2023 MBA' (9 October 2023), www.wgacontract2023.org/announcements/2023-mba-ratified, accessed 18 June 2024.

22 See: Memorandum of Agreement for the 2023 WGA Theatrical and Television Basic Agreement of 25 September 2023, www.wga.org/uploadedfiles/contracts/2023_mba_moa.pdf, accessed 18 June 2024 and WGAW, 'Summary of the 2023 WGA MBA', www.wga.org/contracts/contracts/mba/summary-of-the-2023-wga-mba, accessed 18 June 2024.

before concluding a similar MBA.[23] This MBA addressed the issue of AI for work purposes in a more comprehensive way, distinguishing between the type of AI used and the consequences for social protection. It explicitly regulates and includes compensation in the case of the use of, for example, employment-based digital replicas of performers. In addition to compensation, social contributions will have to be paid.[24] The question is, what can be considered as an income base for this? If AI is used to complete or copy scripts, music or acting performances, to what extent will these artists still receive remuneration and what are the consequences for the social security contributions due?

Although research on the impact of digitalisation and AI on labour protection is widespread, new ways of working will inevitably have an impact on the financing of social security schemes. For example, while fiscal initiatives on the robotisation of work processes have already been explored,[25] the role of social security has been understudied or rather undervalued. For example, while AI has the potential to improve work processes and profits, does this automatically have a positive impact on the income of individual workers? Can and should we not therefore focus on rethinking the financing of social security for these workers by broadening the contribution base of self-employed persons who are responsible for their employment? While the example of the strikes from the Hollywood screenwriters has clearly shown the possibility of a lack of social protection in the case of the use of new digitalised technologies and automated work processes, it is to be expected that the companies making use of the digitalisation of work will continue to generate profits; at the same time, the wages on which the screenwriters have to live will become less important, which in turn reduces the financial basis for (future) social security (rights). In addition to the increased volatility of the labour market, it is also not always clear how people make a living: if individuals derive income from increasingly diverse (marginal or not) forms of work, but also to a greater extent from other forms such as real estate, stocks, etc., the question arises as to how this new trend should be incorporated into national social security systems.[26]

---

23 See: Summary of 2023 Tentative Successor Agreement to the 2020 Producer-SAG-AFTRA Codified Basic Agreement ('Codified Basic Agreement') and 2020 SAG-AFTRA Television Agreement ('Television Agreement') (16 November 2023), www.sagaftra.org/files/sa_documents/TV-Theatrical_23_Summary_Agreement_Final.pdf, accessed 18 June 2024 and 2023 Memorandum of Agreement between the Screen Actors Guild-American Federation of Television and Radio Artists and the Alliance of Motion Picture and Television Producers (10 November 2023), https://deadline.com/wp-content/uploads/2023/11/2023-SAG-AFTRA-TV-Theatrical-MOA_F.pdf, accessed 18 June 2024.

24 Article II, B.3.f) Summary of the SAG-AFTRA Agreements.

25 See e.g. Parthasarathi Shome, 'Taxation of Robots' (2022) The Governance Brief No. 44.

26 Paul Schoukens and Alberto Barrio, 'The Changing Concept of Work: When Does Typical Work Become Typical' (2017) European Labour Law Journal 328.

4. TOWARDS A NEW CALIBRATION OF THE INCOME CONCEPT?[27]

4.1. POSSIBLE PATHWAYS – A BROADER FINANCING MIX?

One of the proposals put forward in this paper is the need to review the revenue mix used to finance national social security systems. This is not an entirely new idea: it has been (re)introduced and discussed on several occasions in EU Member States, the EU and at international level (e.g. OECD and ILO). A review of the income mix seems much needed due to a possible erosion of the contribution base for social security due to non-standard forms of work and the increasing diversity of ways in which people earn an income, as well as an ageing population, the automation of work, etc.[28] However, agreeing on how this can be achieved is more difficult. Some proposals, put forward in literature, are discussed in more detail below. The first three proposals start from existing financing techniques based upon more traditional professional income sources such as wages; here suggestions are made to finetune the existing techniques to address in a more focused manner high(er) incomes. In a last proposal we go beyond the mere professional income and see how income from capital could be addressed better to co-finance social security schemes.

4.1.1. Extending the Reach of Social Protection to New Forms of Work

Often, social security systems exclude certain groups from social security coverage for one or more social risks, for instance, the exclusion of self-employed persons and/or marginal forms of employment in some EU Member States. Similarly, countries often have more favourable schemes (for certain social risks). Rethinking these (partial) exclusions and/or more advantageous schemes can lead to more social security contributions being available. However, extending social protection to new forms of work would likely require additional revenues, as social security benefits will also be due.[29]

---

27 This section builds further on an earlier contribution by Eleni De Becker, 'How Do People Make a Living in 2035? The Impact of Income on Social Security' in Paul Schoukens, Eleni De Becker and Thijs Keersmaekers (eds), *Living and Working Tomorrow (2035). Challenges for Social Security (Administrations)* (European Institute of Social Security 2024).

28 E.g. Christina Behrendt and Quynh Anh Nguyen, *Innovative Approaches for Ensuring Universal Social Protection for the Future of Work*, ILO Future of Work Research Paper Series (ILO 2018), 29; Pierce O'Reilly, 'Tax Policies for Inclusive Growth in a Changing World', OECD Taxation Working Papers, No 40 (2018) 33.

29 O'Reilly (n 29) 33.

4.1.2. *Review the Progressivity of the Current Social Security Framework*

Another pathway to increase revenue for social security would be to review the progressivity of the current social security framework. Some have argued that tax and social security systems in EU Member States are insufficiently progressive.[30] Revising such limits could be an (easier) possible course of action. However, this may not be enough: as income from other sources, especially capital, increases as labour income increases, this would mean that higher income groups would still contribute less.

4.1.3. *Higher Social Security Contributions for Certain Types of Work*

Another suggestion could be to make certain forms of non-standard work, which place a greater burden on the social security system, subject to more stringent rules.[31] We refer to the example of Belgium (2022), where users whose annual use of the special social security scheme for artists exceeds a certain threshold have to pay an additional social security contribution.[32] Similarly, employers who exceed the number of daily contracts for temporary agency workers as set in law (2022) have to pay an additional social security contribution as well.[33] However, such proposals could entail administrative difficulties and a possible discrimination between certain sectors. Moreover, such a rule is of a behavioural nature, i.e. less use of such contracts. It is therefore a rather unstable source of income for social security.

4.1.4. *Broadening the Financing Mix to Other Income Sources*

Broadening the financing mix for social security could mean using other (non-labour related) income sources to finance national social security systems. The increased importance of capital in the economy is one reason to broaden the income base.[34] As financial resources already available can be reinvested, this could potentially lead to even more wealth. Moreover, capital is unequally

---

30 Spasova and Ward (n 8) 15; European Commission 2023 (n 2) 72.

31 Spasova and Ward (n 8) 124.

32 Article 13, §1 Act of 16 December 2022, published in the official gazette on 27 December 2022.

33 Article 144 Act of 26 December 2022, published in the official gazette on 30 December 2022.

34 See Kevin Spiritus, 'Optimale belastingen op kapitaalinkomen: inzichten uit economisch onderzoek' in Matthias Somers (ed), *Fundamenten. Sociale Zekerheid in Onzekere Tijden* (2019) 215, https://static1.squarespace.com/static/580dffc9f7e0ab87773fc653/t/5cc1bce6e5e5f0f36f16cafe/1556200691503/Fundamenten_Matthias_Somers.pdf, accessed 18 June 2024; Wim Van Lancker, 'Hoe financieren we de sociale zekerheid in een onzekere toekomst?' in Paul Schoukens, Bert Demarsin, Eleni De Becker and Thijs Keersmaekers (eds), *Liber Amicorum Danny Pieters. Out of the box denken* (OWL Press 2022) 117.

distributed.[35] In most countries, the taxation of capital (e.g. residential property, dividends, bank deposits, etc.) is taxed to a lesser extent and not subject to social security contributions. Overall, there seems to be a lack of a clear and coherent framework. The increasing importance of capital at the expense of labour in national income means that those who earn their income mainly from capital contribute little or nothing to social protection.[36] As the importance of capital increases, it will become increasingly difficult to finance national social security systems through taxes and social security contributions that focus heavily (or only) on income from labour.[37] In addition, increasing digitalisation and automation of work may mean that capital becomes an even more important source of income for certain groups in society.

Although there is some agreement on the need to include capital in the financing mix of social security, how to do so is a more difficult puzzle to solve.

Some proposals have been made to increase taxation on consumption goods (e.g. tobacco, carbon emissions, etc.).[38] However, consumption taxes seem less suitable as a means of differentiating the financing mix of social security. Low-income earners (but also pensioners) consume a larger share of their income and pay proportionally higher taxes in relation to their income. Moreover, consumption taxes are not very stable and sometimes include a behavioural element, where the intention is to reduce the consumption of certain services or goods (e.g. alcohol).[39] Suggestions have also been made to introduce taxes on robots, machinery and other technologies; although the implementation of such measures seems less feasible.[40]

Other proposals are to tax the (fictitious or actual) income from capital,[41] with some also proposing that these additional sources should be explicitly earmarked for social security.[42] In practice, however, such a proposal could be difficult to implement, e.g. for administrative reasons as countries would need to keep a register of the different sources of capital, or due to a lack of political will or the fear for income instability. For this reason, Van Lancker pointed out that income from real estate could be a first step, as real estate assets are less volatile and lead to fewer behavioural effects.[43] Similar to other forms of capital, income from real estate is hardly taken into account from a tax and/or social security

35 See also Spiritus (n 35) 215 and the references cited.
36 Van Lancker (n 35).
37 Spasova Ward (n 8) 123.
38 See also Behrendt and Nguyen (n 29) 29.
39 Van Lancker (n 35).
40 Behrendt and Nguyen (n 29) 30.
41 Spiritus (n 35); Van Lancker (n 35) and Spasova and Ward (n 8) 123.
42 See the discussion in Spasova and Ward (n 8) 123.
43 Van Lancker (n 35) 118–119.

perspective.[44] Moreover, the highest incomes are associated with the ownership of property other than one's own home.[45]

Others have stressed the need for an equitable distribution, with both non-work income and other forms of income being taken into account equally in the financing mix; if this were not the case, there would be a shift towards sources of income subject to lower taxes and social security contributions.[46]

Another possibility is to better integrate the capital reserves of enterprises created by the (solo) self-employed persons into the income mix. This practice is problematic in some countries, as it fictitiously reduces the real income of the self-employed persons who organise their activities in a legal entity which they (co-)own and from which they receive a fixed income that is independent of the turnover or profit of the legal entity. In other words, the self-employment activities are carried out within the legal unit; the external contracting of the work is carried out by the entity (owned by the self-employed persons). The remuneration is split: the entity is paid for the contract, and the self-employed person receives a fixed remuneration for the work carried out on behalf of the entity. This remuneration is fictitious and can be kept low and/or disconnected from the tax results (profit; turnover) of the entity. Part of the income received remains in the reserves of the entity. Traditionally, when the legal entity pays out the profit in the form of dividends or (finally) liquidates the reserves to the (self-employed) shareholder, social security contributions are not levied on this return of profit in the form of dividends. Countries refrain from doing so because it is considered to be income from invested capital; social security contributions are traditionally levied on income from work. In some countries, the integration of self-employed activities into legal entities is common practice; it turns out that the income of the self-employed person working in these legal entities is kept fictitiously low, often for parafiscal reasons.[47]

However, this fictitious undervaluation of income by (solo) self-employed persons is legal and therefore not to be considered as a fraudulent practice. Nevertheless, it can undermine the sustainability of the social protection system. In essence, the practice touches on a key issue in the financing of (work-related) social protection: should the collection of contributions be limited to income from work or should it also extend to income from capital? In an era of growing importance of digital and platform work, where it is increasingly difficult to

44 See also Spasova and Ward (n 8); Alexander Leodolter, Savina Princen and Aleksander Rutkowski, 'Immovable Property Taxation for Sustainable & Inclusive Growth' in European Commission, *European Economy Discussion Papers* (Publications Office of the European Union 2022) 1; European Commission 2023 (n 2) 74.

45 See also European Commission 2022 (n 2) 74.

46 Spiritus (n 35).

47 See the discussion in Commissie Borstlap, *In wat voor land willen wij werken?* 48–55, www.rijksoverheid.nl/documenten/rapporten/2020/01/23/rapport-in-wat-voor-land-willen-wij-werken, accessed 18 June 2024.

distinguish professional activities from other activities, and where income is generated by different types of activities (whether professional or not), we tend to favour the second option. However, this is still very much under discussion. The case of the increasing integration of self-employment activities into legal entities shows that it is very difficult to maintain the distinction between income from professional activities and income from capital.

Social security systems are gradually beginning to incorporate these new income dynamics into their financing frameworks or are considering doing so in the future. This evolution will bring additional challenges to the determination of income for social security purposes, especially as income components continue to diversify. Enhanced cooperation with tax authorities will be essential to manage this complexity effectively. But even beyond the determination of income, the broadening of the concept of income may pose challenges for the calculation of social security benefits. What constitutes the income base for benefit calculations becomes a key issue, especially in traditional income-based social security schemes of the Bismarckian type. It is not easy to determine when a number of income components contribute to workers' earnings.

At the macroeconomic level, the diversification of income sources is expected to continue. Although this has been a topic of discussion for many years, the development of alternative sources of finance that are not dependent on income from work is likely to gain momentum in the coming years. This, in turn, will pose challenges for the collection of these alternative sources of financing when implemented by social security institutions, especially in the case of earmarked contributions. Past experience suggests that direct collection of alternative sources by social security administrations may not always be the most efficient option, as these administrations may lack the necessary infrastructure or expertise. Contributions have traditionally been collected through employers, but alternative financing levies often go beyond labour and employer-related income. Co-operation with tax administrations is becoming more likely, although it poses a different set of administrative challenges, as tax administrations are not always sympathetic to the social considerations that underpin social security initiatives for insured persons.[48]

4.2. POSSIBLE PATHWAYS – TOWARDS MORE UNIVERSALISATION?

A recurring idea in discussions on how to address the challenges of digitalisation and non-standard work is the universalisation of national social security systems. Although various authors have argued for the introduction of a basic income,[49]

48 See in that regard also the Dutch Toeslagen scandal.

49 See e.g. Philippe Van Parijs and Yannick Vanderborght, *Basic Income: A Radical Proposal for a Free Society and a Sane Economy* (Harvard University Press 2017).

this is generally not considered appropriate,[50] as it would imply the complete abolition of national social security systems or a profound change in them.[51] It seems more feasible in the short term to universalise the personal coverage of certain social risks. Such an exercise can also give impetus to the broader debate on taking into account the role of part-time work and non-paid care activities, mainly performed by women, in social security schemes.

In many countries, certain social risks have already been extended to all employees and self-employed persons or to all citizens, e.g. health care, long-term care or family benefits. In several EU Member States, pension systems are also based on citizenship rather than employment. Even in Bismarckian pension systems there is a tendency towards harmonisation, at least for the minimum protection provided (e.g. Belgium) or providing certain top ups or basic pensions.[52]

The broad financing mix discussed higher can be used to provide a more universal social security coverage (e.g. for all citizens or all workers). This would allow individuals to switch (regularly) between different schemes or to combine different schemes at the same time without losing social security rights. It can also lead to a simplification at the level of national administrations, who have to switch less between the different labour statuses and social protection schemes. In the case of short-term income replacement benefits, initiatives can be found in EU Member States to extend protection to all employees and the self-employed persons, for instance, for unemployment and sickness. However, with increasing digitalisation and automation, it will be more difficult to ensure a decent standard of living in the event of under- or unemployment for (certain groups of) employees and/or self-employed persons. In a situation where there is no longer sufficient work available, the question arises as to whether social security systems should provide support. Special care needs to be taken into account when designing such measures, as they could lead to an inactivity trap.

However, universalisation cannot answer all upcoming challenges. A universal system will only function optimally when the number of people with low earnings or income is restricted. A growing number of low earners will put pressure on these systems too, especially when the universal basic level of protection is higher than the average income on which low-income workers pay contributions/taxes. Even if there is no direct equivalence between what people pay in and what they ultimately receive from the system, universal protection schemes are only sustainable where the income base on which they are financed

---

50 See the discussion in Behrendt and Nguyen (n 29) 29.

51 See also the discussion in Yves Stevens and Jakob Werbrouck, 'Forum Text – Basic Income and Social Security: A Structural Problem' (2019) BTSZ 185–196.

52 Spasova and Ward (n 8) 118; see on those protection mechanisms also the book edited by S. Devetzi, *Minimum Income Protection in Old-Age: A Legal Comparison of Selected European Countries* (Sakkoulas Publishing 2023), www.hs-fulda.de/fileadmin/user_upload/1_Fotoware/devetzi_minimum_ebook.pdf, accessed 18 June 2024.

is broad enough. And even though these schemes are based upon residence, labour income remains an important factor in the eventual financing of them. Although it goes beyond the issue of formal access in a strict sense, financial sustainability can only be guaranteed if efforts are made to move low-income workers into decent work opportunities and/or solid businesses. By the same token, the need to broaden the income that serves as a financial base may even bigger here than in traditional Bismarckian social insurance systems. The need to explore new approaches (additional taxes) is even greater.

5. OUTLOOK

The landscape of income generation is undergoing profound change. This change affects both traditional sources of income, such as wages, and less standardised forms of income, such as income from self-employment linked to returns on capital. If we want to maintain the social security system as we know it today, we need to adapt it to these new developments. Broadening the income base towards more capital-based returns is definitely a strategy to consider. Making protection more universal is a way forward, but it has its limits and requires a strong financial base to guarantee access to adequate levels of protection. Here again, the need to define the income base broadly enough for any type of social protection (professional or universal) must be addressed. The fundamental question is whether the time has not come to move from social protection of professional income to income protection. This would mean that additional sources of income beyond professional income, such as income from rent, dividends and returns on capital, would have to be reflected in the contribution base.

In raising these questions, we are going beyond the scope of this paper, as it calls for a fundamental reflection on the kind of protection we ultimately want to guarantee to our (working) citizens; by the same token, it will fundamentally change the current financing systems, especially those systems that are now focused solely on professional income. However, confronting the limits of the current discussion on access to (work-related) social protection invites us to be creative in finding solutions that can cope with the ongoing changes in society. And this urge for creativity brings us back to our celebrated colleague, Geertrui Van Overwalle. We can only hope that our reflections are paired with her research legacy and address the issues raised in this *Liber Amicorum*.

CHAPTER 24

BE YOUR OWN STRING QUARTET?

A Plea for the Legal Revaluation of Musical Performances*

Jozefien VANHERPE
Assistant Professor, KU Leuven Centre for IT & IP Law (CiTiP)

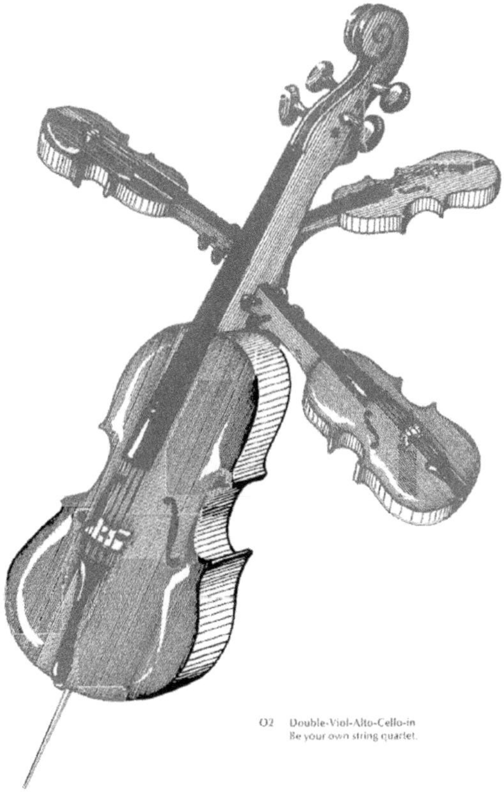

O2 Double-Viol-Alto-Cello-in
Be your own string quartet.

* This contribution was included in amended form in the book by the author entitled *Music Contracts in the Streaming Age. Law and Policy in the European Union and the United Kingdom* (Cambridge University Press 2025).

1. INTRODUCTION

Professor Dr. Geertrui Van Overwalle, the celebrated emerita of this *Festschrift*, is an excellent listener. She listens intently and emphatically, not only to those who expressly seek her advice – and over the years, there have been many, including myself – but also those who, simply, have something to say. If somebody speaks, Geertrui listens, always with sincere, profound interest and with a genuine will to contribute in a constructive way. She never fails to give astute, cross-cutting observations that provide her conversation partner(s) with new insights and inspire them to look further, to dig deeper, and, ultimately, to find something that may qualify as 'truth'. I am quite certain that we could all learn a lot from her.

Geertrui not only listens when people talk, but also when music plays. This brings us (seamlessly?) to the substantive topic of my contribution, which will undoubtedly not surprise readers who are familiar with my interests, namely the wondrous world of music. Music forms the soundtrack that accompanies and brightens our daily lives. It is one of the very few endeavours that unites us all.[1]

Music may appear in several forms. First, on an abstract level, there is a musical 'composition'. This is an intangible work that consists of a melody, chord progressions, a certain instrumentation, is structured in a certain way and is often accompanied by specific lyrics. Music, however, is more than notation alone. A 'performance' brings a composition to life. Musical performers are the driving force of this activity. They transform paper notes into real-life action on stage. The resulting sound waves may bring listeners to experience a wealth of emotions. As Leonard Bernstein said, 'music can name the unnameable and communicate the unknowable.' Finally, a performance may be recorded in one way or another, resulting in a sound recording or 'phonogram'. Such a phonogram allows a performance to transcend its ephemeral nature and be safeguarded for posterity.

This proverbial musical triumvirate provides the backdrop of this contribution, which centres around the research question whether the current allocation of rights between musicians may be considered as being conducive to creativity as well as inclusivity, and whether any changes may be envisaged in this context.

Following the present introduction, Section 2 provides a typology of musicians that serves as a backdrop for the legal analysis of the rights allocated to musicians as the law currently stands in Section 3. The jurisdictions selected for the purpose of this analysis are – in alphabetical order – Belgium, France, Germany, the Netherlands, and the United Kingdom (UK). Section 4 zooms out, providing a stakeholder analysis that looks behind the legal 'curtain', to the interests of those whom the legal framework seeks to protect. Before concluding, Section 5 brings the insights of the preceding sections together and suggests that opening up copyright in the strict sense to performing artists under certain circumstances may contribute to enhanced creativity as well as inclusivity in music copyright.

1 Alan B. Krueger, *Rockonomics* (John Murray 2019) 2.

2. TYPOLOGY OF MUSICIANS

While artistry is not susceptible to exhaustive categorisation, it is first useful to take a closer look at different 'types' of musicians. There are two main broad categories, namely composers/lyricists (jointly referred to as 'composers' below) and performers.[2]

In the category of *composers*, artists who write both music and lyrics are referred to as songwriters. Singer-songwriters are songwriters who also perform their music and are credited as such. Within the category of musical *performers*, there are two main types of musicians, namely *featured artists* and *session musicians*. Featured artists' work is credited on a phonogram, while session musicians are hired on either a freelance or more lasting contractual basis to perform in recording sessions or live performances without receiving express credit therefor.[3] Within these two types, an enormous variety exists, from singers to multi-instrumentalists.[4] Musicians who are featured on a certain phonogram may be session musicians on another, and vice versa. A final important subcategory of the broad range of session musicians includes orchestral musicians[5] and chamber music players, active in the genre of classical music. This typology may be schematically represented as follows:

Table 1. Typology of musicians

<table>
<tr><td colspan="4">musician</td></tr>
<tr><td colspan="2">composer (sensu lato)</td><td colspan="2">performer</td></tr>
<tr><td>composer (sensu stricto)</td><td>lyricist</td><td rowspan="2">featured artist</td><td rowspan="3">session musician</td></tr>
<tr><td colspan="2">songwriter</td></tr>
<tr><td colspan="3">singer-songwriter</td></tr>
</table>

2 *Cf.* Lorenz Haidinger, *Online-Musiklizenzierung in der Europäischen Union und in den USA* (Schriften zum europäischen Urheber-, Immaterialgüter- und Informationsrecht, De Gruyter 2021) 12–16.

3 Europe Economics and others, 'Remuneration of Authors and Performers for the Use of Their Works and the Fixations of Their Performances. Final Report' (Publications Office 2015) 63; Christian Castle and Claudio Feijóo, 'Study on the Artists in the Digital Music Marketplace: Economics and Legal Considerations' (2021) 17.

4 Ananay Aguilar, '"We Want Artists to Be Fully and Fairly Paid for Their Work". Discourses on Fairness in the Neoliberal European Copyright Reform' [2018] JIPITEC 160, 169.

5 Given the real time influence that orchestra conductors and/or choir directors exert on the tempo and the expression of the performers, their status as a performing artist is generally accepted, see Fabienne Brison, *Het Naburig Recht van de Uitvoerende Kunstenaar* (Creatie Informatie Communicatie 7, Larcier 2001) 43; Mathilde Pavis, 'The Author-Performer Divide in Intellectual Property Law: A Comparative Analysis of the American, Australian, British and French Legal Frameworks' (University of Exeter 2016) Vol I, 35.

The process of making music varies significantly across different genres. Classical musicians most often either perform or compose music and are thus easy to categorise on this basis.[6] Contemporary classical musicians are an exception, as they often create dedicated works and perform these works themselves. This seems especially true for creations with a significant conceptual aspect. Jazz musicians combine existing music structures with their own improvisations, thus continuously crossing the line between being a performer and a composer-performer.[7] In modern music, there is a large variety of artistic processes, ranging from singer-songwriters and indie folk bands who write their own music, to pop stars who perform melodies composed entirely by a team of collaborating songwriters. A final group is populated by DJs, whose status as creating and/or performing musicians is disputed.[8]

3. RIGHTS ALLOCATED TO MUSICIANS

3.1. INITIAL ALLOCATION OF RIGHTS

In their capacity as either composers (and thus authors) or performers, musicians are granted initial ownership of rights in music: copyright *sensu stricto* in the composition and a neighbouring right in (the fixation of) a performance.

Authorship leads to initial ownership of copyright *sensu stricto*. It may only be claimed in the event of a contribution that fulfils the conditions for copyright protection.[9] Copyright protection is available to 'literary and artistic works',[10]

6 Richard Arnold, 'Reflections on The Triumph of Music: Copyrights and Performers' Rights in Music' (Oxford Intellectual Property Invited Speaker Seminar, Oxford, UK, 20 October 2009) 14; Luc Gulinck, *Hier Tekenen! (en Let Niet op de Kleine Lettertjes ...) Wegwijs in het Juridische en Zakelijke Labyrint van de Muziekwereld* (Academia Press 2019) 158.

7 Original improvisations are protected by copyright *sensu stricto*. *Cf.* Arnold, 'Reflections on The Triumph of Music: Copyrights and Performers' Rights in Music' (n 6) 5; Stefan Skopelja, 'The Boundaries of "Authorship" and "Performance" in Musical Copyright' [2015] UNSWLJ Student Series No 15-04 9.

8 See e.g. Jan Pauly and Yannick H'Madoun, *Poppuntgids voor muzikant en dj* (Poppunt vzw no date) 62; Gulinck (n 6) 47, 411. See also the case between Dutch DJ and producer Martin Garrix and his primary corporate partners Spinnin Records and MusicAllstar Management, where the court found that Garrix qualified both as a performing artist and as a phonogram producer: *Gerechtshof* (hereinafter: 'Court of Appeal') Arnhem-Leeuwarden 24 December 2019, docket number 200.227.882/01, ECLI:NL:GHARL:2019:11117, paras 7.77–7.86. The further appeal before the Dutch Supreme Court on matters of law failed on this particular point, see *Hoge Raad der Nederlanden* 17 December 2021, docket numbers 20/01155, 20/01158, ECLI:NL:HR:2021:1923, paras 3.5.1–3.5.3.

9 See Daniela Simone, *Copyright and Collective Authorship: Locating the Authors of Collaborative Work* (Cambridge Intellectual Property and Information Law 50, Cambridge University Press 2019) 58–69; Kathy Bowrey, *Copyright, Creativity, Big Media and Cultural Value. Incorporating the Author* (Routledge 2020) 10–28; Lionel Bently and others, *Intellectual Property Law* (6th edn, Oxford University Press 2022) 135–46.

10 Article 2(1) Berne Convention.

including music.[11] It is not granted to mere abstract ideas and principles. These must be expressed in a concrete way, identifiable with sufficient precision and objectivity.[12] Copyright protection only arises if the condition of originality is fulfilled. In accordance with established case law of the European Court of Justice (ECJ),[13] this implies that the work must be an intellectual creation of the author(s) expressing free and creative choices and reflecting their personality.[14] The work must show the personal stamp of the author – i.e. their *authorship*. The determination of authorship in a specific case is a matter of national law. The concepts of 'joint', 'collective' or 'co-'authorship differ per country and are not harmonised at the EU level.[15]

A particular dimension arises in case a work or performance is created in an employment context. Under Belgian, French and German law, the employee is awarded initial ownership.[16] In the Netherlands and the UK, the opposite rule applies to works (not performances): copyright is deemed to vest in the employer, unless contrary contractual arrangements have been made.[17]

---

11 This refers to melody (successive sounds), harmony (simultaneous sounds) and rhythm (structure of sounds whereby the dominant sound recurs in periodical intervals), as well as the combination thereof. Arrangements of music (including variations) are also susceptible to copyright protection, see Article 2(3) Berne Convention. In the UK, 'musical works' are expressly listed as protectable subject matter, see Articles 1(1)(a) *jo.* 3 Copyright, Designs and Patents Act 1988, hereinafter: 'UK CDPA'; Bently and others, *Intellectual Property Law* (n 9) 76–77.

12 Article 9(2) TRIPS Agreement; Article 2 WIPO Copyright Treaty (hereinafter: 'WCT'); Case C-310/17 *Levola Hengelo* [2018] ECLI:EU:2018:899, paras 37, 40.

13 See as to the relevance of ECJ case law in the UK subsequent to Brexit *TuneIn v Warner Music UK* [2021] *EWCA Civ* 441, [2021] *EMLR* (18) 575; Paul Torremans, 'Transposition of the DSM Copyright Directive 2019/790 in the United Kingdom' [2021] AM 374, 377; Bently and others, *Intellectual Property Law* (n 9) 24–28.

14 See ia Case C-5/08, *Infopaq International A/S v Danske Dagblades Forening* [2009] ECLI:EU:C:2009:476; Case C-393/09 *Bezpečnostní softwarová asociace – Svaz softwarové ochrany v Ministerstvo kultury* [2010] ECLI:EU:C:2010:816; Case C-145/10, *Eva-Maria Painer v Standard VerlagsGmbH and Others* [2011] ECLI:EU:C:2011:798, para. 94; Case C-161/17 *Land Nordrhein-Westfalen v Dirk Renckhoff* [2018] ECLI:EU:C:2018:634, para. 14; Case C-310/17 *Levola Hengelo* [2018] ECLI:EU:2018:899, para. 36; Case C-469/17 *Funke Medien NRW v Bundesrepublik Deutschland* [2019] ECLI:EU:C:2019:623, para. 19.

15 See Simone (n 9) 201–72.

16 Jean-Christophe Lardinois, *Les Contrats Commentés de l'Industrie de La Musique 2.0: Cadre Général et Pratique Contractuelle* (Création Information Communication Pratique 1, 2nd edn, Larcier 2009) 70; Andreas Rahmatian, 'Dealing with Rights in Copyright-Protected Works: Assignments and Licences' in Estelle Derclaye (ed), *Research Handbook on the Future of EU Copyright* (Research Handbooks in Intellectual Property, Edward Elgar 2009) 294; Brigitte Lindner, 'European Union. Part A – Copyright and Contract Law Issues' in René Viljoen (ed), *Cross-Border Copyright Licensing Law and Practice* (Elgar Intellectual Property Law and Practice, Edward Elgar Publishing 2018) 75; Jeff Keustermans and Peter Blomme, *Auteursrecht. Capita Selecta* (2nd edn, Intersentia 2021) 35–36.

17 Article 7 Auteurswet (hereinafter: 'Dutch Copyright Act'); Article 11(2) UK CDPA. A company that publicly discloses a work without mentioning a physical person as its author is designated as its author, unless this disclosure is proven to be unlawful, see Article 8 Dutch Copyright Act.

This brief analysis of authorship and the person of the author(s) may be contrasted with the concepts of performance and performers.[18] Article 2(a) WPPT[19] defines 'performers' by enumeration as 'actors, singers, musicians,[20] dancers, and other persons who act, sing, deliver, declaim, play in, interpret or otherwise perform literary or artistic works,' i.e. works that are susceptible to – but not necessarily subject to – copyright protection. A certain degree of artistry is required. Mere technical contributions, such as those by sound engineers, are generally deemed insufficient.[21] Ancillary performers are excluded in some jurisdictions.[22] Finally, while a performance must not necessarily take place during a live concert, the performer's contribution must take place at the same time as the performance.[23] Thus, performers are persons who perform.[24] A clearer definition could conceptualise performers as artists whose contribution is not deemed sufficiently *original* to give rise to copyright, who merely interpret the work of somebody else and operate within the boundaries of such work. This would detract from the possibility of performers also being the composers of the works they perform. In any case, the legal consequence of a musician's categorisation as a performer is the acquisition of a neighbouring right relating to (the fixation of) the performance.

Finally, a specific place in the popular music-making process is occupied by music producers (also known as 'studio producers').[25] They are involved in the process of recording music but occupy a more artistic than commercial position. They oversee the recording process and seek to ensure that all parties involved contribute to the best of their abilities.[26] In other words, producers function as a kind of personified quality control.[27] Their task requires detailed knowledge of

---

18 See Brison (n 5) 42–52, 362–74, 531–48.

19 WIPO Performances and Phonograms Treaty, www.wipo.int/wipolex/en/treaties/textdetails/12743, (hereinafter: 'WPPT').

20 The concept of 'musicians' in this provision is narrower than the term used here.

21 Brison (n 5) 43–44; Bob Donnelly, 'Everything You Need to Know about Copyright Reversions' (2012) 1 St John's Entertainment, Arts and Sports Law Journal 1, 13–14; Gulinck (n 6) 55.

22 Both in Belgium and France, ancillary artists are expressly excluded from neighbouring rights protection (see Article XI.205(1) *Wetboek Economisch Recht*, the Belgian Code on Economic Law, hereinafter 'Belgian CEL'; Article L 212-1 *Code de la propriété intellectuelle*, hereinafter: 'French IP Code'). Neither German, Dutch nor UK law expressly excludes ancillary artists. However, it may be argued that auxiliary artists do not fulfil the substantive requirement of artistry.

23 Gulinck (n 6) 410.

24 See Pavis, 'The Author-Performer Divide in Intellectual Property Law' (n 5) Vol I, 31 et seq.

25 Well-known music producers include Brian Eno, Quincy Jones, George Martin, Nile Rodgers and Rick Rubin. See e.g. David Stopps, 'How to Make a Living from Music, Second Edition' (Creative Industries, WIPO 2014) 16–17, 104–05; Donald Passman, *All You Need to Know About the Music Business* (10th edn, Simon & Schuster 2019) 125–36; Chris Castle, 'Record Producer Agreements, a Practical Guide' (2023).

26 Lardinois (n 16) 107; Isabelle De Voldere and others, 'Mapping the Creative Value Chains. A Study on the Economy of Culture in the Digital Age. Final Report' (2017) 137.

27 Gulinck (n 6) 405.

recording techniques as well as a strong affinity with music. However, unless an original contribution to the composition may be proven, music producers have no right to copyright protection *sensu stricto*. The Court of Appeal of Amsterdam held that music producers are not entitled to claim neighbouring rights protection as either a performing artist or a phonogram producer.[28] Producers may only claim performing artist status if the sounds they produce with their voice and/or with an instrument are incorporated in the performance and, thus, the phonogram.[29] The intervention of a music producer is not a prerequisite in the music recording process – musicians may also perform the tasks of a music producer themselves. Music producers often make their intervention in the recording process dependent on receiving credit and/or part of the exploitation rights in the composition and/or the phonogram, independent of the nature of their intervention(s).[30]

As initial rights owners, musicians obtain the exclusive, negative right to either prohibit or authorise certain acts on the part of third parties.[31] Both copyright *sensu stricto* and the neighbouring right of performing musicians have an economic and a moral dimension.

On the one hand, the economic prerogatives allow musicians to extract (commercial) value from their work(s) / performance(s) by granting certain rights to other parties through exploitation contracts. The economic prerogatives assigned under copyright law *sensu lato* may be indicated as 'exploitation rights'. These exploitation rights are curtailed by certain exceptions and limitations.[32] On the other hand, moral rights protect the link between authors or performers and their output.

The first and primary exclusive exploitation right is the right to make reproductions of their protected work and/or the fixation(s) of their performance(s). This right is to be interpreted broadly and is largely harmonised at the EU level.[33] The music industry wields the term 'mechanical rights'.[34] The mechanical rights granted to composers differ from those enjoyed by performers.

---

28 Court of Appeal Amsterdam 4 May 2010, docket number 200.002.411/01, *Various artists (Koelewijn and others) v SENA* [2010] IEF 8821; IER 2010, 516–22.

29 Gulinck (n 6) 55, 410.

30 See on the role of music producers Virgil Moorefield, *The Producer as Composer. Shaping the Sounds of Popular Music* (MIT Press 2005). See also Lardinois (n 16) 108; DCMS Committee, 'Economics of Music Streaming. Second Report of Session 2021–22' (15 July 2021) 46.

31 Case C-301/15 *Soulier and Doke* [2016] ECLI:EU:C:2016:878, para. 33.

32 Nikita Malevanny, *Online Music Distribution – How Much Exclusivity Is Needed?: A Study of International, European, German and U.S. Copyright Systems and Their Objectives*, vol 12 (Munich Studies on Innovation and Competition, Springer Berlin Heidelberg 2019) 101–83; Stavroula Karapapa, *Defences to Copyright Infringement: Creativity, Innovation and Freedom on the Internet* (Oxford University Press 2020).

33 See (1) re authors: Case C-5/08 *Infopaq International* [2009] ECLI:EU:C:2009:465, para. 43; Case C-145/10, *Painer v Standard* [2011] ECLI:EU:C:2011:798, para. 96; Case C-301/15 *Soulier and Doke* [2016] ECLI:EU:C:2016:878, paras 30–31, and (2) re performers Case C-484/18 *Spedidam* [2019] ECLI:EU:C:2019:970, paras 36–37.

34 See e.g. Europe Economics and others (n 3) 27.

Composers have the exclusive right of authorising the reproduction of their work(s) in any matter or form (i.e. by making copies), such as by recording a phonogram or by digitally storing a protected work.[35] A copy subject to the author's consent exists when it takes over original elements of the initial work.[36] While coincidental resemblance is not actionable, no bad faith is required for an infringement to arise.[37] Illicit copying may take place subconsciously.[38] The reproduction right *sensu lato* further includes the right to adaptation (i.e. making musical arrangements[39]).[40] Authors also obtain a right of translation.[41] For music, this right only bears relevance for a composition's lyrics (e.g. an opera libretto).

Performing musicians first obtain a right to authorise or prevent the fixation of their performance(s).[42] Second, they are granted a right of reproduction relating to such fixations. This means that they may prevent a third party from making copies thereof, including digital storage of such copies.[43]

---

35 Article 2(a) Directive 2001/29/EC of the European Parliament and of the Council of 22 May 2001 on the harmonisation of certain aspects of copyright and related rights in the information society [2001] OJ L167/10 (hereinafter: 'InfoSoc Directive'); Article XI.165(1) paras 1–3 Belgian CEL; Articles L 122-1, L 122-2-2–L 122-4 French IP Code; Articles 15–18 *Urheberrechtsgesetz*, hereinafter: 'German Copyright Act'; Articles 13–14 Dutch Copyright Act; Articles 16–17 UK CDPA. See also Article 9 Berne Convention; Agreed Statement concerning Article 1(4) WIPO Copyright Treaty, https://bit.ly/3as9O0z.

36 See Joined Cases C-403/08 and C-429/08, *Football Association Premier League and others (FAPL)* [2011] ECLI:EU:C:2011:631, paras 153–159.

37 Jane Ginsburg, 'Copyright' in *The Oxford Handbook of Intellectual Property Law* (Oxford Handbooks, Oxford University Press 2018) 501.

38 *Ibid.*

39 Gulinck (n 6) 74.

40 Article 12 Berne Convention.

41 Article 8 Berne Convention.

42 Article 7(1) Directive 2006/115/EC of the European Parliament and of the Council of 12 December 2006 on rental right and lending right and on certain rights related to copyright in the field of intellectual property (codified version) [2006] OJ L376/28 (hereinafter: 'Rental and Lending Directive'); Article XI.205(1) Belgian CEL; Article L 212-3(I) French IP Code; Article 77 German Copyright Act; Article 2(1)(a) *Wet op de naburige rechten*, hereinafter: 'Dutch Neighbouring Rights Act'; Article 182 UK CDPA. See also Article 6(ii) WPPT. Article 2(c) WPPT defines a 'fixation' as 'the embodiment of sounds, or of the representations thereof, from which they can be perceived, reproduced or communicated through a device.' The fixation refers to 'the material object on which the sounds are fixed,' see Judica Krikke, 'Directive 2006/115/EC – on Rental Right and Lending Right and on Certain Rights Related to Copyright in the Field of Intellectual Property (Rental and Lending Right Directive)' in Thomas Dreier and P Bernt Hugenholtz (eds), *Concise European Copyright Law* (2nd edn, Kluwer Law International 2016) 287. See in detail as to the rights of performers AEPO-ARTIS, 'Performers' Rights Study 2022' (2022).

43 Article 2(b) InfoSoc Directive; Article XI.205(1) paras 1–2 Belgian CEL; Article L 212-3(I) French IP Code; Article 77 German Copyright Act; Article 2(1)(a)–(c) Dutch Neighbouring Rights Act; Article 182A–B UK CDPA. See also Article 3(e) Rome Convention; Article 14(1)

Performing musicians do not acquire an express right of adaptation or translation.[44]

The mechanical rights granted to both composers and performing musicians further include the rental and lending right as to works embodied in phonograms and fixations of performances.[45] Finally, composers and performers acquire the exclusive right to either authorise or prohibit the distribution to the public of the original or copies of their works and/or fixations of their performances, which is limited by the principle of exhaustion.[46]

Musicians also acquire certain performing rights. First, composers obtain the exclusive right to authorise the public performance of their works by any means or process.[47] This right of public performance implies the presence of a live audience at the place of the performance.[48] In addition, composers acquire exclusive rights relating to the communication to the public of their compositions by wire or wireless means.[49] This broad concept implies a transmission to a public that is not present in the same location.[50] The scope of this right includes music played in shops, restaurants and music venues, as well as broadcasts via radio and/or TV or by satellite[51] and cable retransmission[52]

TRIPS Agreement; Article 7 WPPT; Agreed Statement concerning Articles 7, 11 and 16 WPPT, https://bit.ly/3arTY5U.

44 Gulinck (n 6) 73.

45 Articles 2–3 Rental and Lending Directive. See also Article 7 WCT. See also Europe Economics and others (n 3) 31; Krikke (n 42) 275–95; Gulinck (n 6) 75–76; Sylvie Nérisson, 'The Rental and Lending Rights Directive' in Irini Stamatoudi and Paul Torremans (eds), *EU Copyright Law A Commentary* (Elgar Commentaries, Edward Elgar 2021) 118–50.

46 See re composers Article 4 InfoSoc Directive; Article 6 WCT. See re performers Article 9 Rental and Lending Directive; Article 8 WPPT. See also Ansgar Ohly, 'Economic Rights' in Estelle Derclaye (ed), *Research Handbook on the Future of EU Copyright* (Research Handbooks in Intellectual Property, Edward Elgar 2009) 219–23. See re exhaustion Simon Geiregat, *Supplying and Reselling Digital Content: Digital Exhaustion in EU Copyright and Neighbouring Rights Law* (Edward Elgar Publishing 2022); Péter Mezei, *Copyright Exhaustion: Law and Policy in the United States and the European Union* (2nd edn, Cambridge University Press 2022).

47 Article XI.165(1) para. 4 Belgian CEL; Articles L 122-1–L 122-2-2 French IP Code; Articles 15, 19–22 German Copyright Act; Article 12 Dutch Copyright Act.

48 Ginsburg, 'Copyright' (n 37) 504.

49 Article 3(1) InfoSoc Directive. See also Articles 11–11*bis* Berne Convention; Article 8 WCT. See Justin Koo, *The Right of Communication to the Public in EU Copyright Law* (Hart Publishing 2019); Branka Marušić, *The Autonomous Legal Concept of Communication to the Public Interpretation in EU Copyright Law* (Edward Elgar Publishing 2023).

50 Recs 23–24 InfoSoc Directive.

51 Article 4 Council Directive 93/83/EEC of 27 September 1993 on the coordination of certain rules concerning copyright and rights related to copyright applicable to satellite broadcasting and cable retransmission [1993] OJ L248/15, amended by Directive (EU) 2019/789 of the European Parliament and of the Council of 17 April 2019 laying down rules on the exercise of copyright and related rights applicable to certain online transmissions of broadcasting organisations and retransmissions of television and radio programmes, and amending Council Directive 93/83/EEC [2019] OJ L130/82 (hereinafter: 'Satellite and Cable Directive').

52 Article 8 Satellite and Cable Directive.

(as provided for under Member State law[53]).[54] A final subset of this right is the right to make their works available to the public in a way that allows individualised access by the public.[55]

Performers may authorise or prevent the broadcasting by wireless means[56] (including by satellite[57] and cable retransmission[58] as provided for under Member State law) and/or the communication to the public of their performance.[59] As is the case for composers, the right to communication to the public includes an exclusive right to making available.[60] Save this making available right, performers' right to communication to the public largely equates to an unwaivable remuneration right, subject to mandatory collective management.[61]

Following the no formalities rule, the rights granted under copyright law *sensu lato* are generated automatically, upon either the creation of the work, (the fixation of) the performance or the creation of the phonogram at issue.[62] The term of protection starts then.

Copyright *sensu stricto* in the EU as well as in the UK lasts for 70 years after the death of the (last surviving) author, subject to a limited number of exceptions.[63] The term of protection is different for anonymous or pseudonymous works. Unless the identity of the author becomes clear within 70 years after the work

---

53 See definition in Article 1(1) Satellite and Cable Directive. See Article 2 as to the exclusive broadcasting right granted to authors regarding the communication of works to the public via satellite and Article 8 regarding the cable retransmission right.

54 Ginsburg, 'Copyright' (n 37) 504.

55 Article 3(2) InfoSoc Directive; Cheryl Foong, *The Making Available Right. Realizing the Potential of Copyright's Dissemination Function in the Digital Age* (Elgar Law, Technology and Society series, Edward Elgar Publishing 2019).

56 'Broadcasting' is defined as 'the transmission by wireless means for public reception of sounds or of images and sounds', see Article 3(f) Rome Convention.

57 Article 4 Satellite and Cable Directive.

58 Article 8 Satellite and Cable Directive.

59 Article XI.205(1) para. 3 Belgian CEL; Article L 212-3(I) French IP Code; Article 78 German Copyright Act; Article 2(1)(d) Dutch Neighbouring Rights Act. Article 8 Rental and Lending Directive harmonises this right at the EU level as far as live performances are concerned. See also Article 7(1) Rome Convention; Article 14(1) TRIPS Agreement; Article 6(i) WPPT.

60 Article 3(2)(a) InfoSoc Directive. See also Article 10 WPPT.

61 Article 8(2) Rental and Lending Directive. See on the scope of the concept of 'relevant performers': Case C-265/19 *Recorded Artists Actors Performers v Phonographic Performance (Ireland)* [2020] ECLI:EU:C:2020:677. See also Article 11*bis*(2) Berne Convention; Article 15 WPPT. See also in more detail below, Section 3.2.

62 See Article 5(2) Berne Convention re copyright *sensu stricto* and Article 20 WPPT re the neighbouring right of performing artists.

63 Article 1 Directive 2006/116/EC of the European Parliament and of the Council of 12 December 2006 on the term of protection of copyright and certain related rights [2006] OJ L372/12, amended by Directive 2011/77/EU of the European Parliament and of the Council of 27 September 2011 amending Directive 2006/116/EC on the term of protection of copyright and certain related rights [2011] OJ L265/1 (hereinafter: 'Term Directive' and the amending directive in particular 'Term Extension Directive'), maintained in the UK following Brexit in Article 12 UK CDPA.

has been lawfully made available to the public (starting from the first of January following that event[64]), the protection lapses after that period.[65]

The term of the rights granted to performers is somewhat more complex and has also changed over the past decades: while these rights traditionally expire 50 years after the event giving rise to the protection (e.g. in case of unfixed performances),[66] a longer period of protection is granted in case of fixation on a phonogram, namely 70 years after its publication.[67] The relatively recent[68] term extension from 50 to 70 years was prompted by the EU legislator's wish to improve the social situation of (session) musicians in view of their increased life expectancy.[69] It was controversial in view of its perceived ineffectiveness and the intrusion on the public domain that it entailed.[70]

In addition to exploitation rights, musicians acquire certain moral rights.[71] First, in some jurisdictions, composers acquire a right of first disclosure, which

64 Article 7(5) Berne Convention.

65 Article 1(3)-(7) Term Directive. See also Article 12 TRIPS Agreement.

66 As required under Article 14(5) TRIPS Agreement and Article 17 WPPT.

67 Article 3 Term Directive, maintained in the UK following Brexit in Articles 13(b)-(c), 191 UK CDPA. For this extension to apply, the fixation of the performance in a phonogram must be lawfully published or communicated to the public within 50 years following the date of the performance at issue. See André Lucas and others, *Traité de la Propriété Littéraire et Artistique* (5th edn, LexisNexis 2017) 1119–26; Fabienne Brison, 'Art. XI.208' in Fabienne Brison and Hendrik Vanhees (eds), *Hommage à Jan Corbet Huldeboek* (3rd edn, Larcier 2018) 371–73; Gunda Dreyer and others, *Urheberrecht* (Heidelberger Kommentar, 4th edn, CF Müller 2018) 1361–66, 1371–73; Philipp Möhring and Käte Nicolini, *Urheberrecht* (4th edn, CH Beck 2018) 932–60, 968–71; JH Spoor and others, *Auteursrecht. Auteursrecht, portretrecht, naburige rechten en databankenrecht* (Recht en Praktijk, 4th edn, Wolters Kluwer 2019) 876–78; Richard Arnold, *Performers' Rights* (6th edn, Sweet & Maxwell 2021) 83–93.

68 It applies to phonograms and fixations that were still protected on 1 November 2013 (the implementation deadline of the Term Extension Directive) and later performances/ phonograms, see Article 10(5) Term Directive.

69 Recs 5–7 Term Extension Directive.

70 See e.g. P Bernt Hugenholtz and others, 'The Recasting of Copyright & Related Rights for the Knowledge Economy' (2006) 83–137; Natali Helberger and others, 'Never Forever: Why Extending the Term of Protection for Sound Recordings is a Bad Idea' (2008) 30 EIPR 174, 174–81; Lionel Bently and others, 'Creativity Stifled? A Joint Academic Statement on the Proposed Copyright Term Extension for Sound Recordings' (2008) 30 EIPR 341, 341–47; Reto M. Hilty and others, 'Comment by the Max-Planck Institute on the Commission's Proposal for a Directive to Amend Directive 2006/116 Concerning the Term of Protection for Copyright and Related Rights' (2009) 31 EIPR 59, 59–72; Mireille van Eechoud and others, *Harmonizing European Copyright Law: The Challenges of Better Lawmaking* (Information Law Series 19, Kluwer Law International 2009) 181–234; Agnieszka Vetulani-Cęgiel, 'EU Copyright Law, Lobbying and Transparency of Policy-Making' [2015] JIPITEC 146, 151–52; Christina Angelopoulos, 'Directive 2006/116/EC – on the Term of Protection of Copyright and Certain Related Rights (Term Directive), as Amended by Directive 2011/77/EU (Term Extension Directive)' in Thomas Dreier and P Bernt Hugenholtz (eds), *Concise European Copyright Law* (2nd edn, Kluwer Law International 2016) 336–37, 356.

71 See e.g. Elizabeth Adeney, *The Moral Rights of Authors and Performers: A International and Comparative Analysis* (Oxford University Press 2006); Fabienne Brison and others (eds), *Moral Rights in the 21st Century. The Changing Role of the Moral Rights in an Era of Information*

entails the right to divulge their work(s) to the public.[72] This right does not apply to performers, which is logical, given that the performance itself constitutes a disclosure thereof. Second, the right of paternity or attribution implies that both composers and performers may (dis)claim paternity of their work and/or performance.[73] Notably, performers' right to paternity is limited by honest trade practices. By way of example, not all members of a symphonic orchestra can claim acknowledgement on a CD cover or in the metadata of a digital music file. This privilege is reserved to the conductor, the concertmaster and possible soloists.[74] Even so, many instances of infringement of the paternity right arise, largely due to the poor quality of metadata.[75] The third moral right is referred to as the right to integrity. It implies that composers and performers may object to actions relating to their output that would bring them into disrepute.[76] In the music industry, cases regarding this moral right may, for example, relate to the combination of a pre-existing work or performance fixation with offensive lyrics.[77] Finally, German and French law provide for a express, albeit very limited, 'right to repent' for authors, as a result of which a composer may withdraw or retract their work subsequent to its initial disclosure – in other words, reverse the exercise of their moral right of disclosure.[78]

The term of moral rights varies. This term is usually linked to the duration of the exploitation rights. This is the case in Belgium, Germany, the Netherlands, as well as the UK, the latter with a caveat as to the right to false attribution.[79]

Overload (Larcier 2015). See re authors: Article 6bis(2) Berne Convention. See re performers: Article 5(3) Rome Convention.

72 See Article XI.165(2) Belgian CEL; Article L121-2 French IP Code; Article 12 German Copyright Act. See on Dutch law Spoor and others (n 67) 446–49. See on UK law Bently and others, *Intellectual Property Law* (n 9) 303.

73 See re authors: Articles XI.165(2) Belgian CEL; Article L 121-1 French IP Code; Article 13 German Copyright Act; Article 25(1)(a)–(b) Dutch Copyright Act; Articles 77–79, 84 UK CDPA; Article 6*bis*(1) Berne Convention. See re performers: Article XI.204 Belgian CEL; Article L 212-2 French IP Code; Article 74 German Copyright Act; Article 5(1)(a)–(b) Dutch Neighbouring Rights Act; Articles 205C–205E UK CDPA; Article 5(1) WPPT.

74 The right to prevent wrong acknowledgement is absolute.

75 See on the difficulty to enforce moral rights online: Gillian Davies, 'Moral Rights in the Borderless Online Environment' in Johan Axhamn (ed), *Copyright in a Borderless Online Environment* (Nordstedts Juridik 2012) 37–46.

76 See re authors: Articles XI.165(2) Belgian CEL; Article L 121-2 French IP Code; Article 14 German Copyright Act; Article 25(1)(b)–(d) Dutch Copyright Act; Articles 80–83 UK CDPA; Article 6*bis*(1) Berne Convention. See re performers: Article XI.204 Belgian CEL; Article L 212-2 French IP Code; Article 75 German Copyright Act; Article 5(1)(b)–(d) Dutch Neighbouring Rights Act; Articles 205F–205H UK CDPA; Article 5(1) WPPT.

77 See e.g. *Confetti Records & Others v Warner Music UK Ltd* [2003] *EWHC* 1274; [2003] *EMLR* 790, where it was held that no reputational prejudice had occurred as the lyrics were deemed incomprehensible.

78 Article 42 German Copyright Act; Article L 121-4 French IP Code.

79 Frank Gotzen, 'Art. XI.166' in Fabienne Brison and Hendrik Vanhees (eds), *Hommage à Jan Corbet Huldeboek* (3rd edn, Larcier 2018) 72–73; Möhring and Nicolini (n 67) 822; Spoor and

By contrast, moral rights have no limitation in time under French copyright law and thus apply in perpetuity, for composers as well as performers.[80]

3.2. EXPLOITATION OF RIGHTS

If third parties want to use a musical composition, (a fixation of) a performance and/or a phonogram, consent thereto must be acquired from the relevant right owner(s).[81] In this context, the distinction between exclusive rights and remuneration rights bears particular relevance.[82] This distinction applies to both copyright and neighbouring rights.

Exclusive rights may usually be transferred or licenced out. Consent is either granted on an individual basis or, optionally, through a collective management organisation (CMO). A CMO is an organisation tasked by their members-rightholders with the management of their copyright or neighbouring rights through the grant of licences to third parties.[83] There is a large number of active CMOs.[84]

---

others (n 67) 445–46; Bently and others, *Intellectual Property Law* (n 9) 206. See as to UK law in particular Articles 86, 205I UK CDPA.

80 Rahmatian (n 16) 296; Lucas and others (n 67) 545–47, 1126–28; Lindner (n 16) 85.

81 Case C-301/15 *Soulier and Doke* [2016] ECLI:EU:C:2016:878, paras 33–34; Case C-161/17 *Land Nordrhein-Westfalen v Dirk Renckhoff* [2018] ECLI:EU:C:2018:634, paras 16, 29; Case C-484/18 *Spedidam* [2019] ECLI:EU:C:2019:970, para. 38.

82 There is also an 'in-between model' that combines the transfer of an exclusive right with a residual remuneration right. See in more detail Jozefien Vanherpe, *Music Contracts in the Streaming Age. Law and Policy in the European Union and the United Kingdom* (Cambridge University Press 2024) Chapter 5, Section 5.

83 *Cf.* Article 3(a) Directive 2014/26/EU of the European Parliament and of the Council of 26 February 2014 on collective management of copyright and related rights and multi-territorial licensing of rights in musical works for online use in the internal market [2014] OJ L84/72 (hereinafter: 'CRM Directive'). See ia Mihály Ficsor, *Collective Management of Copyright and Related Rights* (WIPO 2002); KEA, 'The Collective Management of Rights in Europe. The Quest for Efficiency' (2006); Maria Mercedes Frabboni, 'Collective Management of Copyright and Related Rights: Achievements and Problems of Institutional Efforts Towards Harmonisation' in Estelle Derclaye (ed), *Research Handbook on the Future of EU Copyright* (Research Handbooks in Intellectual Property, Edward Elgar 2009) 373–400; Sylvie Nérisson, *La gestion collective des droits des auteurs en France et en Allemagne: quelle légitimité?* (Bibliothèque de l'Institut de recherche juridique de la Sorbonne-André Tunc 49, IRJS Editions 2013); Daniel Gervais (ed), *Collective Management of Copyright and Related Rights* (Third edition, Kluwer Law International 2016); Malevanny (n 32) 185–239.

84 The main CMOs for composers and performers in the chosen jurisdictions are: (1) in Belgium: SABAM (*Société d'Auteurs Belge – Belgische Auteurs Maatschappij*) and PlayRight; (2) in France: SACEM (*Société des Auteurs, Compositeurs et Éditeurs de Musique*) and ADAMI for featured artists (*Administration des Droits des Artistes et Musiciens Interprètes*)/ Spedidam for non-featured artists (*Société de Perception et de Distribution des Droits des Artistes-Interprètes*) / SAI for both (*Société des Artistes Interprètes*); (3) in Germany: GEMA (*Gesellschaft für musikalische Aufführungs- und mechanische Vervielfältigungsrechte*) and GVL (*Gesellschaft zur Verwertung von Leistungsschutzrechten*); (4) in the Netherlands: Buma/Stemra (*Bureau*

The exclusive rights of composers include almost all of the mechanical rights and the performing rights set out in Section 3.1 above. This explains why voluntary collective management is of particular importance in the music publishing industry.[85] Performers only (initially and thus subject to further transfer) acquire the exclusive right to reproduce fixations of their performances, distribute these and make them available to the public.

In the context of optional (or 'voluntary') collective management, prospective users approach the relevant CMO(s) to obtain a licence relating to the exploitation rights of protected content. The user pays the rate set by the CMO, which retains a commission-based compensation for administrative costs and transfers the remainder of the fee to the rightholder(s).

For the exploitation of remuneration rights, no express consent from the rightholder(s) is required. Consequently, the relevant rightholders do not have the opportunity to prevent the exploitation at issue. Instead, in such cases, a compulsory licensing system subject to mandatory collective management applies. An equitable remuneration is collected by CMOs and subsequently transferred to the rightholder(s) after deduction of the CMOs' administrative costs. Remuneration rights are unwaivable.[86] Rental and lending rights are in principle both exclusive rights, but the EU framework leaves room for a qualification of the lending right as a remuneration right under national law.[87] As to the rental right, in case a transfer of this right occurs, an equitable remuneration through a system of mandatory collective management is required.[88]

A larger proportion of performers' rights has the status of a remuneration right compared with the rights granted to authors. This explains the importance of mandatory collective management in the recorded music industry. Indeed, in addition to the above, performers' right to broadcasting and communication to the public of fixations of their performances in a phonogram are largely treated as

voor Muziek-Auteursrechten / Stichting tot Exploitatie van Mechanische Reproduktierechten voor Auteurs), SENA (*Stichting ter Exploitatie van Naburige Rechten*) / NORMA (*Naburige Rechtenorganisatie voor Musici en Acteurs*); and (5) in the UK: PRS for Music and PPL (Phonographic Performance Limited).

85 Chris Cooke, *Dissecting the Digital Dollar* (3rd edn, Music Managers Forum and CMU Insights 2020) 12–13; Raquel Xalabarder, 'The Principle of Appropriate and Proportionate Remuneration for Authors and Performers in Art.18 Copyright in the Digital Single Market Directive. Statutory Residual Remuneration Rights for Its Effective National Implementation' [2020] InDret 1, 4–5.

86 Case C-277/10 *Martin Luksan v Petrus van der Let* [2012] ECLI:EU:C:2012:65; Séverine Dusollier and others, 'Contractual Arrangements Applicable to Creators: Law and Practice of Selected Member States' (2014) 88–89.

87 See Article 6 Rental and Lending Directive. This is the case under Belgian law. In accordance with Articles XI.243–245 Belgian CEL, the remuneration relating to sheet music is divided 70 percent for composers and 30 percent for publishers, while composers, performers and producers each receive one third of the remuneration relating to phonograms.

88 Article 5 Rental and Lending Directive.

remuneration rights (except for the making available right, which is an exclusive right).[89] This is referred to as the compulsory licence for secondary use.

The cable retransmission right has a particular status as an exclusive right that is nevertheless subject to mandatory collective management.[90] The equitable remunerations for private copying and reprography also occupy a specific position, since they function as compensation to the rightholders for the harm inflicted through the application of private copying and reprography exceptions.[91] These two equitable remuneration regimes are also subject to mandatory collective management.

Musicians may transfer (or 'assign'[92]) their exclusive exploitation rights to third parties, be it a natural person or a legal entity.[93] Consequently, these rights have traditionally been divested to commercial players, with the copyright in musical works being assigned from composers to music publishers and the neighbouring right of performers to record companies for the entire term of protection.[94] In return, the initial rightholder(s) usually obtains a form of compensation, either by way of a flat fee or through recurring royalty payments.[95] As a result, most copyright is owned by corporations instead of artists.[96]

As an alternative to the full transfer of rights, it is possible to grant a licence. Hereby, the counterparty obtains the right to use the object of the licence within

---

89 *Cf.* Article 8(2) Rental and Lending Directive. See also Case C-265/19 *Recorded Artists Actors Performers v Phonographic Performance (Ireland)* [2020] ECLI:EU:C:2020:677; Case C-147/19 *Atresmedia Corporación de Medios de Comunicación SA v Asociación de Gestión de Derechos Intelectuales (AG.EDI), Artistas Intérpretes o Ejecutantes, Sociedad de Gestión de España (AIE)* [2020] ECLI:EU:C:2020:935.

90 Article 9 Satellite and Cable Directive.

91 *Cf.* Rec 35 InfoSoc Directive.

92 This term is primarily used under UK law, see e.g. Abbe EL Brown and others, *Contemporary Intellectual Property: Law and Policy* (Fifth edition, Oxford University Press 2019) 220; Arnold, *Performers' Rights* (n 67) 97–99; Bently and others, *Intellectual Property Law* (n 9) 323–26.

93 Rahmatian (n 16) 298–301; Sébastien Raimond, *La Qualification du Contrat d'Auteur* (Le Droit des Affaires. Propriété Intellectuelle 34, LexisNexis 2009) 33–56; Nathalie Blanc, *Les Contrats du Droit d'Auteur à l'Epreuve de la Distinction des Contrats Nommés et Innommés* (Nouvelle Bibliothèque de Thèses 93, Dalloz 2010) 244–61; Alain Strowel and Bernard Vanbrabant, 'Copyright Licensing: A European View' in Jacques de Werra (ed), *Research Handbook on Intellectual Property Licensing* (Research Handbooks in Intellectual Property, Edward Elgar Publishing 2013) 34–35; Bernard Vanbrabant, *La Propriété Intellectuelle. Tome 2. Régime Patrimonial* (Création Information Communication, Larcier 2018) 371–74, 401–15; Robert B Merges, 'What Kind of Rights Are Intellectual Property Rights?' in Rochelle Dreyfuss and Justine Pila (eds), *The Oxford Handbook of Intellectual Property Law* (Oxford Handbooks, Oxford University Press 2018) 62. Under German law, no full transfer of copyright *sensu stricto* is possible.

94 Séverine Dusollier, 'EU Contractual Protection of Creators: Blind Spots and Shortcomings' [2018] Colum J L & Arts, 451.

95 See in more detail Vanherpe (n 82) Chapter 2, Section 4.

96 Orly Lobel, *Talent Wants to Be Free. Why We Should Learn to Love Leaks, Raids, and Free Riding* (Yale University Press 2013) 165.

certain limits, again usually in return for monetary compensation to the initial rights owner(s) – but not always, as is proven by open licences.[97] As opposed to a transfer of rights, which is always of an exclusive nature, a licence may be either exclusive or non-exclusive. In the latter case, the licensor(s) retain(s) the right to exploit the object of the licence themselves and/or to grant other licences to third parties, who may then perform actions of exploitation in parallel with the initial licensee.

Contracts that establish a transfer of or a licence to the exploitation rights associated with works protected by copyright and/or fixations of performances protected by the neighbouring right of performing artists may be referred to by the umbrella terms 'copyright exploitation contracts' or 'exploitation contracts'. In order to counter the difference in relative bargaining power between artists and their commercial counterparties, the content of such contracts is limited on several fronts, including by the protective framework provided by copyright contract law.

The exploitation of a phonogram has an impact on both the neighbouring rights associated with said phonogram and the copyright in the underlying composition embodied in the phonogram. As a result, a single exploitation activity requires permission under both copyright and neighbouring rights law.[98]

Finally, the exploitation of the exclusive rights associated with a jointly owned work and/or performance in principle requires express consent from all parties, especially if the individual contributions are not discernible. In such a case, a single rightholder can stop others from exploiting the work and/or performance. To mitigate this, rules have been established that modulate the requirement of consent relating to live performances by large groups of performing musicians, such as orchestras or large chamber music ensembles.[99] These rules designate specific musicians as representative(s) of the group, allowing the possibility of efficient contracting in large live productions. The applicable regimes differ, from the appointment of soloists, directors and conductors (Belgium and the Netherlands), to group leaders (Belgium and Germany) or elected representatives (Germany).[100] While French and UK law do not appear to expressly regulate such situations, musicians may provide a mandate to another party for this purpose.

---

97 Rahmatian (n 16) 298, 301–09; Raimond (n 93) 56–91; Blanc (n 93) 261–82; Alexis Boisson, *La Licence de Droit d'Auteur* (Bibliothèque de Droit de l'Entreprise 86, LexisNexis 2013) 119–352; Stopps (n 25) 32–33; Vanbrabant (n 93) 643–58, 690–703, 747–48; Lindner (n 16) 79–81.

98 *Cf.* Jeff Price, 'The Definitive Guide to Spotify Royalties' [2020] 50, 3, 14.

99 These specific rules should not be applied to small ensembles, such as trios and quartets. In such cases, the permission of all musicians is required.

100 See (1) in Belgium: Article XI.207 Belgian CEL; (2) in Germany: Article 80(2) *jo.* 74(2) German Copyright Act; and (3) in the Netherlands: Article 13 Dutch Neighbouring Rights Act. See also Article 8 Rome Convention, which expressly allows diverging national regimes.

4. ANALYSIS OF MUSICIANS' INTERESTS

Following the above typology of musicians and the rights that the law allocates to them, the next step is to analyse their interests. Indeed, only after having established what drives musicians to do what they do, a grounded position can be taken as to the appropriate legal framework surrounding their activities.

Several internal and external factors incentivise musicians to create and/or perform music.[101] The intrinsic wish to make music for the sake of personal development[102] and/or participation in cultural life[103] is a significant and primary driver,[104] but only constitutes part of the equation.[105] Musicians are also driven by a number of external incentives. A first important motivating factor is remuneration. This is especially true for professional musicians, whose income depends on music-related revenues.[106] However, this incentive applies across the board. Indeed, all musicians seek a certain degree of valuation of their work and proper remuneration constitutes an important part thereof.[107] However, 'money isn't everything.'[108] Beyond the purely monetary self-interest, a number

101 See in detail Sarah Polcz, 'Loyalties v Royalties' (2021) 74 Hastings LJ 765.

102 *Cf.* Jessica Silbey, *The Eureka Myth: Creators, Innovators, and Everyday Intellectual Property* (Stanford University Press 2014) 40–41, 44, 274–75; Alan B. Krueger, *Rockonomics* (John Murray 2019) 52, 57–58.

103 See Article 27(1) UDHR and Article 15(1)(a) ICESCR.

104 Jostein Gripsrud, 'Creativity and the Sense of Collective Ownership in Theatre and Popular Music' in Mireille van Eechoud (ed), *The Work of Authorship* (Amsterdam University Press 2014) 228; Silbey (n 102) 1–2, 8, 13, 39; Gulinck (n 6) 9.

105 Jonathan M. Barnett, 'Copyright without Creators' (2014) 9 RLE 389, 432–33; Jane C. Ginsburg, 'Exceptional Authorship: The Role of Copyright Exceptions in Promoting Creativity' in Susy Frankel and Daniel Gervais (eds), *The Evolution and Equilibrium of Copyright in the Digital Age* (Cambridge University Press 2014) 25; Bruno S. Frey, *Economics of Art and Culture* (SpringerBriefs in Economics, Springer International Publishing 2019) 32; Krueger (n 102) 3–4; Ruth Towse, *A Textbook of Cultural Economics* (2nd edn, Cambridge University Press 2019) 374–76.

106 Gripsrud (n 104) 229.

107 Martin Kretschmer and others, 'The Relationship between Copyright and Contract Law' (2010) 67; Jane C Ginsburg, 'The Role of the Author in Copyright' in Ruth L. Okediji (ed), *Copyright Law in an Age of Limitations and Exceptions* (Cambridge University Press 2017) 81; Stephanie Plamondon, 'Rational Faith: The Utility of Fairness in Copyright' (2017) 97 BU L Rev 1487, 1512–14; Aguilar, 'We Want Artists to be Fully and Fairly Paid for their Work' (n 4) 169–70; Alexander Cuntz, 'Creators' Income Situation in the Digital Age' (Economic Research Working Paper, 2018) 6–7; Ole-Andreas Rognstad and Joost Poort, 'The Right to Reasonable Exploitation Concretized: An Incentive Based Approach' in P. Bernt Hugenholtz (ed), *Copyright Reconstructed Rethinking Copyright's Economic Rights in a Time of Highly Dynamic Technological and Economic Change* (Information Law Series 41, Kluwer Law International 2018) 127; Hayleigh Bosher, *Copyright in the Music Industry. A Practical Guide to Exploiting and Enforcing Rights* (Elgar Practical Guides, Edward Elgar Publishing 2021) 6–8.

108 Krueger (n 102) 9. See also Lobel (n 96) 192–95; Silbey (n 102) 1–2, 14; Rethink Music Initiative, 'Fair Music: Transparency and Payment Flows in the Music Industry. Recommendations to Increase Transparency, Reduce Friction, and Promote Fairness in the Music Industry' (2015) 5;

of non-economic external incentives play a role. Many of these incentives are covered by the broad concept of (self-)agency.[109] This includes, first and foremost, credit where credit is due.[110] Musicians want to receive acknowledgement for their work.[111] The value of music must not only translate into money, but also into attribution and ensuing personal recognition.[112] Second, musicians want their music to be heard. This implies access to audiences through exploitation of the work and the wish to build a relationship with their audience in order to nurture a fan base.[113] Third, agency may be associated with artistic integrity and reputation, as well as the wish to retain a certain degree of control over the exploitation of their work.[114]

Internal motives to make music and external incentives to achieve artistic and commercial success ensure a continuous stream of hopeful music market entrants, forming a supply that significantly outmatches demand.[115] The consequences of this mismatch between supply and demand on artist income are palpable.[116] Several authoritative research projects may be referred to, such

---

Nancy K. Baym, *Playing to the Crowd. Musicians, Audiences, and the Intimate Work of Connection* (New York University Press 2018) 108; Simone (n 9) 210–11; Bosher (n 107) 8–11.

109 Tom Phillips and John Street, 'Copyright and Musicians at the Digital Margins' (2015) 37 Media, Culture & Society 342, 346; Ginsburg, 'The Role of the Author in Copyright' (n 107) 63, 79, 84; Juliet Fraser, 'Sharing the Spoils of a Shared Practice' (2019) 73 Tempo 51, 52.

110 Plamondon (n 107) 1511–12; Krueger (n 102) 216.

111 Rick Carnes, 'Developing a Copyright System that Works for Songwriters' (2015) 38 Colum JL & Arts 309, 309; Baym (n 108) 198.

112 *Cf.* Lionel Bently and Laura Biron, 'Discontinuities between Legal Conceptions of Authorship and Social Practices: What, If Anything, is to Be Done?' in Mireille van Eechoud (ed), *The Work of Authorship* (Amsterdam University Press 2014) 267–70.

113 Stopps (n 25) 50–51; William Deresiewicz, *The Death of the Artist. How Creators Are Struggling to Survive in the Age of Billionaires and Big Tech* (Henry Holt and Company 2020) 122–23. See also Yannos Paramythiotis, 'Fairness in Copyright Contract Law: Remuneration for Authors and Performers Under the Copyright in the Digital Single Market Directive' in Tatiana-Eleni Synodinou and others (eds), *EU Internet Law in the Digital Single Market* (Springer International Publishing 2021) 78.

114 Séverine Dusollier, *Droit d'Auteur et Protection des Œuvres dans l'Univers Numérique. Droits et Exceptions à la Lumière des Dispositifs de Verrouillage des Oeuvres* (Création Information Communication 10, Larcier 2005) 289–90; Silbey (n 102) 7, 142; Stopps (n 25) 52, 102; Carnes (n 111) 309; Ginsburg, 'The Role of the Author in Copyright' (n 107) 79; Krueger (n 102) 216. See on the importance of reputation for creators in particular Silbey (n 102) 75–76, 149–83. Both credit and reputation may be linked with moral rights protection – the right to paternity and integrity respectively, see Silbey (n 102); Rebecca Tushnet, 'Intellectual Property as a Public Interest Mechanism' in Rochelle Dreyfuss and Justine Pila (eds), *The Oxford Handbook of Intellectual Property Law* (Oxford Handbooks, Oxford University Press 2018) 114. See also above, Section 3.

115 Kretschmer and others (n 107) 66; Mark Mulligan, *Awakening: The Music Industry In The Digital Age* (Createspace 2015) 174; Lionel Bently and others, 'Strengthening the Position of Press Publishers and Authors and Performers in the Copyright Directive' (2017) 54.

116 Krueger (n 102) 58; Bruno Racine, 'L'Auteur et l'Acte de Création' (January 2020) 17–27. See also Richard L Florida, *The Rise of the Creative Class* (Basic Books 2012) 53; Pierre-Michel Menger, 'The Market for Creative Labour: Talent and Inequalities' in Candace Jones and others

as a study conducted by the Dutch Institute for Information Law (IViR).[117] This study pointed towards an average net annual income of composers in the EU per country between approximately 15.000 and 45.000 EUR – the high end numbers being due to a number of significant outliers.[118] The corresponding figures for performers lay between approximately 4.000 and 16.000 EUR.[119] More recently, reference may be made to the 2023 Musicians' Census in the UK, which found the average annual income from music work to be around 24.000 EUR.[120] In many cases, the income of musicians appears to lie below the minimum wage level.[121]

The heterogeneity of the group of musicians implies a large variety of perspectives and interests, which appear to only partially overlap. The fault line runs along the boundaries of the concepts of authorship and performance and the ensuing distinction between copyright *sensu stricto* and the neighbouring rights of performing artists. The interests of composers and performers are not necessarily aligned. Since both categories receive a part of the same 'pie', there is a persisting belief that increased focus on one subset of the broad category of musicians will lead to the other subset losing out.[122] Moreover, the categories of authors and performers are themselves quite fragmented, given the large variety in the cultural and creative industries (CCIs), as well as cultural differences between different (national or regional) territories.[123] Finally, for performers, there is a significant divergence between the small number of well-known featured artists and the vast majority of relatively anonymous session musicians, orchestral musicians and self-releasing artists. More specifically, well-known featured artists appear to be inclined to align their views with the interests of commercial

(eds), *The Oxford Handbook of Creative Industries* (Oxford Handbooks, Oxford University Press 2015) 150; Cuntz (n 107).

117 Europe Economics and others (n 3). See also DCMS Committee (n 30) 29–30.

118 Europe Economics and others (n 3) 198–99.

119 *Ibid.* 193, 203. See also DCMS Committee (n 30) 26–27.

120 Help Musicians and Musicians' Union, 'Musicians' Census. Financial Insight Report' (September 2023). See also https://bit.ly/3Pz9ORr.

121 In 2024, the median net annual income amounted to 30.392 EUR in Belgium, 25.557 EUR in France, 27.619 EUR in Germany, 31.981 EUR in the Netherlands. See statistics at https://bit.ly/3J1VAIf. For the UK, Statista reports that the median annual earnings for full-time employees in the UK amounted to approximately 37.430 GBP in 2024, see https://bit.ly/4m5IxnN.

122 *Cf.* Pavis, 'The Author-Performer Divide in Intellectual Property Law' (n 5) Vol I, 28-30, 106; Richard Osborne, 'Is Equitable Remuneration Equitable? Performers' Rights in the UK' (2017) 40 Popular Music and Society 573, 582, 586–87. See also Aguilar, 'We Want Artists to be Fully and Fairly Paid for their Work' (n 4) 171–72; Ananay Aguilar, 'The Collective Management of Performers' Rights in the UK: A Story of Competing Interests' (2019) 16 SCRIPTed 4, 14.

123 Peter C. DiCola, 'Money from Music: Survey Evidence on Musicians' Revenue and Lessons About Copyright Incentives' (2013) 55 Ariz L. Rev 301, 336–37; Bently and others, 'Strengthening the Position' (n 115) 54; Deresiewicz (n 113) 310; Racine (n 116) 12, 37–39. See for an overview of the CCIs in the EU: EIF, 'Market Analysis of the Cultural and Creative Sectors in Europe: A Sector to Invest In' (2021).

entities that are active in the music industry, such as record companies and music publishers.[124] Musicians have therefore traditionally found it difficult to speak with a unified voice. This contributes to an underrepresentation of their interests in the music industry debate.

The primary objective of continental copyright *sensu lato* is to protect and stimulate creativity.[125] Artists are at the centre of copyright and neighbouring rights protection.[126] Only they are granted the initial right to exploit their work.[127] Moreover, the 'high level of protection' that serves as a guiding principle for EU copyright law refers to the rights of artists, whose 'independence and dignity' must be safeguarded.[128] While the importance of internal incentives should be acknowledged, the primary objective of copyright protection is to further the external incentives for musicians to make music. This implies due attention to monetary as well as non-monetary aspects, to both agency and remuneration.

5. TOWARDS A LEGAL REVALUATION OF MUSICAL PERFORMANCES

As shown in *Section 3* above, the legal qualification of a musician's contribution depends on the nature and the creative intensity thereof. If a particular contribution attains the threshold of originality, the musician surpasses the bounds of performance and may in theory claim (joint) authorship of the creative musical work.[129] Many musicians fulfil a wide array of roles that may be situated somewhere on the continuum between authorship and performance, somewhere along the sliding scale of creativity.[130] Consequently, the application of legal concepts to this composer-performer spectrum may prove to be problematic.

---

124 Aguilar, 'We Want Artists to be Fully and Fairly Paid for their Work' (n 4) 169–70; Aguilar, 'The Collective Management of Performers' Rights in the UK' (n 122) 16–17.

125 See e.g. Rochelle Cooper Dreyfuss, 'In Praise of an Incentive-Based Theory of Intellectual Property Protection' in Rochelle Cooper Dreyfuss and Elizabeth Siew-Kuan Ng (eds), *Framing Intellectual Property Law in the 21st Century* (1st edn, Cambridge University Press 2018) 1–31; Johanna Gibson, 'Basis of Protection' in JAL Sterling (ed), *Sterling on World Copyright Law* (5th edn, Sweet & Maxwell 2018) 39–111.

126 *Cf.* Zechariah Chafee, 'Reflections on the Law of Copyright: I' (1945) 45 Columbia Law Review 503, 506–07.

127 Case C-301/15 *Soulier and Doke* [2016] ECLI:EU:C:2016:878, para. 47; Case C-484/18 *Spedidam* [2019] ECLI:EU:C:2019:970, para. 39.

128 Recs 4, 9–11 InfoSoc Directive.

129 Luke McDonagh, 'Rearranging the Roles of the Performer and the Composer in the Music Industry: The Potential Significance of Fisher v Brooker' [2012] IPQ 64, 76.

130 Robert Brauneis, 'Musical Work Copyright for the Era of Digital Sound Technology: Looking Beyond Composition and Performance' [2014] GW Law Faculty Publications & Other Works 60, 2; Pavis, 'The Author-Performer Divide in Intellectual Property Law' (n 5) 144; De Voldere and others (n 26) 64; Ananay Aguilar, 'Distributed Ownership in Music: Between Authorship and Performance' (2018) 27 Social & Legal Studies 776; Malevanny (n 32) 271.

This rings all the more true in view of the differences in the scope and duration of the legal protection accorded under the regimes of copyright *sensu stricto* and neighbouring rights.

If we want to ensure a legal framework that enhances the agency of all musicians, as conceptualised in *Section 4* above – an inclusive framework that leaves no musician behind and bolsters the creativity of all musicians – maintaining an overly strict line in the sand between the legal regimes applicable to composing and performing musicians may be untenable in the long run.

When sheet music leaves sufficient leeway for the performer to make free and creative choices that express their personality in the context of the performance, it could be argued that the performer may fulfil the requirement of originality and thus legitimately claim copyright protection in the strict sense.[131] Even outside the realm of aleatoric music, the performance of a piece of music may legitimately influence the essence of a work itself, not only inspiring future performances, but also leaving a creative, lasting imprint on the score.[132] For example, over the last decades, cellists everywhere have been inspired by the specific choices made in performances of the Bach Suites by Pablo Casals, and (later) Anner Bijlsma, Pierre Fournier, Yo-Yo Ma, Pieter Wispelwey, and so forth. While the desirability of requalifying such ground-breaking performances to protected works may be disputed, a consistent application of the originality criterion may yet result in such a legal requalification.[133] In such a case, performance and authorship would essentially merge.[134] A valid counterargument could be that an increased (legal) valuation of musical performance and an ensuing increase in potential joint authors would lead to both an increase in disputes on copyright ownership and an undue extension of the scope of copyright protection.[135] Taking the Bach analogy one step further, it could legitimately be asked whether any sort of exclusivity may be claimed on innovative bowings, nuances, rubatoes and/or fingerings. Yet, the position set out above merely pleads for a consistent application of the law

131 Pavis, 'The Author-Performer Divide in Intellectual Property Law' (n 5) 125–29; Irina Eidsvold-Tøien and Are Stenvik, 'Copyright for Performers – an Obligation under International Law' (2023) 18 JIPLP 754, 754–67. *Cf.* Arnold, 'Reflections on The Triumph of Music: Copyrights and Performers' Rights in Music' (n 6) 4; McDonagh (n 129) 64; Flavia Marisi, 'Law and Music: Copyright and Neighboring Rights' [2013] Review of Artistic Education 25; Skopelja (n 7); Mathilde Pavis, 'Is There Any-Body on Stage? A Legal (Mis) Understanding of Performances' (2016) 19 The Journal of World Intellectual Property 99; Arnold, *Performers' Rights* (n 67) 295–309.

132 *Cf.* Pavis, 'The Author-Performer Divide in Intellectual Property Law' (n 5) Vol II, 83.

133 See regarding this 'performative turn' recognising the value of performance in the context of the interdisciplinary field of performance studies *ibid.* Vol I, 164-167. See also *ibid.* Vol II, 58-60, 67-76, 116-143.

134 *Cf.* Lionel Bently, 'Authorship of Popular Music in UK Copyright Law' (2009) 12 ICS 179, 179–204; Osborne (n 122) 579, 587.

135 *Cf.* McDonagh (n 129) 75; Gulinck (n 6) 53. See extensively on the relevant arguments and counterarguments in this regard Pavis, 'The Author-Performer Divide in Intellectual Property Law' (n 5) Vol I, 36-45 and Vol II, 186-197.

de lege lata, of the existing criterion of originality. Many performers make free and creative choices in the context of their performance(s). In a way, objections against a legal revaluation of musical performance may be seen to object against the criterion of originality as such.[136]

Independently of the legal (re)qualification thereof, the contribution of musical performers risks being accorded less artistic and/or commercial value than that made by a composer.[137] While the creative genius of a composer is often quite readily accepted, many performing musicians – especially session musicians – are considered to be mere craftsmen, as providers of a certain service.[138] On a contractual level, this perceived statute is usually accompanied by standard contracts, with a full assignment of rights in return for a flat fee.[139]

This apparent underprivileged nature of performance may be unmerited.[140] 'Music' in itself does not exist in a palpable way, only the score does. A composition consisting of melody, harmony and rhythm requires a performance to bring it to life.[141] Illustrative reference may be made to variations in timbre, rhythmic articulation and other sound elements that can often not be exhaustively recorded through musical notation.[142] The artistic value of the creative, interpretative work done by performing musicians should receive due recognition, thus increasing performer agency.[143] Because of the overarching importance attached to notation

---

136 See Pavis, 'The Author-Performer Divide in Intellectual Property Law' (n 5) Vol II, 144-208. Among other things, Pavis pleads in favour of deleting the divide between musical and audio-visual performers and offers a number of avenues open to legislators should they wish to wholly drop the author-performer divide. Possible (linked) options include introducing performers as a new sub-class of copyright holders, expressly acknowledging performances as copyrightable works and broadening the scope of the condition of originality.

137 Richard Arnold, 'Are Performers Authors?' [1999] EIPR 464, 468–69; McDonagh (n 129) 64; Skopelja (n 7); Pavis, 'The Author-Performer Divide in Intellectual Property Law' (n 5) Vol I, 27, 75-76, 117 and Vol II, 4, 84, 102-107; Aguilar, 'Distributed Ownership in Music' (n 130) 777, 793; Fraser (n 109) 52–53; Bently and others, *Intellectual Property Law* (n 9) 370.

138 Daniel Leech-Wilkinson, 'Classical Music as Enforced Utopia' (2016) 15 Arts and Humanities in Higher Education 325, 326; Pavis, 'The Author-Performer Divide in Intellectual Property Law' (n 5) Vol I, 76; Aguilar, 'Distributed Ownership in Music' (n 130) 785; Aguilar, 'The Collective Management of Performers' Rights in the UK' (n 122) 31; Fraser (n 109) 52.

139 See above, Chapter 2, Section 4.5.

140 See Pavis, 'The Author-Performer Divide in Intellectual Property Law' (n 5). See also Kanchana Kariyawasam and Rangika Palliyaarachchi, 'The Song Would Be Nothing Without Someone to Sing It: Copyright and Performers' Rights in Music' [2020] Int Rev Law Comput Technol 1; Mathilde Pavis, 'Sixty Years of International Performers' Rights: Time for a Performers' Copyright?' in Hayleigh Bosher and Eleonora Rosati (eds), *Developments and Directions in Intellectual Property Law* (Oxford University Press 2023).

141 Daniel Leech-Wilkinson, 'Classical music as enforced Utopia' [2016] Arts & Humanities in Higher Education, 330.

142 The influence of such variations is readily noticeable in pieces of (classical) music that have been around for centuries, with significant evolutions in performance styles throughout the years. As noted by Leech-Wilkinson: 'the same notes can make (and have made) substantially different music.' See Skopelja (n 7); Leech-Wilkinson (n 139) 327–28, 332.

143 *Cf.* Rec 4 Term Directive. See also Leech-Wilkinson (n 139) 326, 334–35; Osborne (n 122) 578–79, 587–88; Aguilar, 'Distributed Ownership in Music' (n 130) 777.

in music, to the musical score, such aspects risk remaining underexposed.[144] In a way, the emphasis put on a musical score in a certain genre is inversely proportionate to the valuation of musical performance in practice.[145] In the field of classical music in particular, the score determines and separates the roles of musicians: the composer writes and owns the score, while performers merely interpret it and work in its service.[146] In such a context, possibly (mis)guided by a lack of knowledge regarding the legal status of their activities, performers see themselves as 'mere' performers. In other musical genres, where emphasis on the score is more limited (e.g. pop music, R&B or EDM), performing musicians may value the nature of their contribution more highly.[147] Attention to the appropriate artistic and commercial valuation of performances is therefore necessary.

Legally speaking, this translates into the desirability of a legal framework that does not force performers to always 'play second fiddle'. Composers and performers are entitled to an analogue level of protection, unless the specifics of their situation dictate otherwise in specific situations.[148] Indeed, an argument may be made in favour of a largely uniform interpretation where analogue provisions apply.[149] Significantly, moreover, the minimum thresholds for copyright exploitation contracts set by the DSM Directive[150] apply equally to the broad category of 'authors and performers', which includes all types of musicians.

Independently of the above, in order to avoid unnecessary friction in the long run, it is advisable for collaborating musicians to make clear, prior written arrangements regarding the initial allocation of ownership of any rights that result from their collaboration, as well as the distribution of any ensuing

144 Brauneis (n 130) 8–10, 15–17. See, however, on the waning role of the score in popular music and the consequences thereof, albeit from the perspective of US law, Brauneis (n 130) *ibid.* 18 et seq.

145 *Cf.* Skopelja (n 7).

146 This clear distinction is moreover seemingly perpetuated through formal education channels such as music conservatoires. See Leech-Wilkinson (n 139) 325–36; Aguilar, 'Distributed Ownership in Music' (n 130) 783–85, 787–88, 794; Daniel Leech-Wilkinson, *Challenging Performance: Classical Music Performance Norms and How to Escape Them* (e-book, 2020). Full text at https://challengingperformance.com/the-book. See in particular Chapter 18.1. Even so, it is noted that scores of early music leave much leeway for the performer, see Richard Caves, *Creative Industries. Contracts Between Art and Commerce* (Harvard University Press 2002) 273.

147 Aguilar, 'Distributed Ownership in Music' (n 130) 794.

148 *Cf.* P Bernt Hugenholtz and Lucie Guibault, 'Auteurscontractenrecht: Naar Een Wettelijke Regeling?' (2004) 78; European Copyright Society, 'Comment of the European Copyright Society Addressing Selected Aspects of the Implementation of Articles 18 to 22 of the Directive (EU) 2019/790 on Copyright in the Digital Single Market' [2020] JIPITEC 132, 132, 134.

149 *Cf.* Case C-484/18 *Spedidam* [2019] ECLI:EU:C:2019:423, Opinion of AG Hogan, para. 34.

150 Directive (EU) 2019/790 of the European Parliament and of the Council of 17 April 2019 on copyright and related rights in the Digital Single Market and amending Directives 96/9/EC and 2001/29/EC [2019] OJ L130/92.

revenues.[151] Whether a theoretical claim to (joint) authorship translates into ownership of copyright largely depends on the socio-legal bargaining power of the performer.[152] Only musicians with sufficient soft power and ensuing leverage in a contractual negotiation context will be able to claim rights.[153] It appears that contributions made by performers in a collaborative music-making context, e.g. during a 'jam session', are traditionally undervalued in such situations, precisely as a result of such imbalance in negotiating power on the part of performers.[154] In case no arrangements on ownership are spelled out in advance – and in writing, given the difficulties of proving the existence and content of oral agreements[155] – and a dispute arises after the fact, the consequences of power relations may be even more pronounced.[156] This rings all the more true in case the music at issue ultimately achieves economic success.

6. CONCLUSION

Concrete and original musical compositions obtain copyright protection in the strict sense, while performing musicians (merely) acquire a neighbouring right. Therefore, even if you are 'your own string quartet', as depicted in the ingenious drawing depicted at the outset of this contribution, you would *still* not acquire that coveted copyright protection.

---

151 This is done by way of a so-called 'band agreement' or 'band partnership agreement'. By way of example, the songwriting partnership between John Lennon and Paul McCartney entailed a 50/50 ownership share in all of the music they wrote for the duration of the partnership, see Gripsrud (n 104) 229. Another option is the 'Nashville style', which entails equal ownership shares for all those present in the room during the creative process, see Aguilar, 'Distributed Ownership in Music' (n 130) 789. Written band agreements may also lead to objectionable situations, as is evidenced by the way Lou Pearlman added himself as a sixth member of boybands Backstreet Boys and *NSYNC in the 1990s (see documentary at https://bit.ly/3DnqXEY). Reference may also be made to blockchain-based tools such as Bernstein; www.bernstein.io, see Marie-Christine Janssens and Jozefien Vanherpe, 'Blockchain and Copyright Beyond the Buzzword?' [2018] IRDI 93; Jozefien Vanherpe and Marie-Christine Janssens, 'Toepassingen van smart contracts in het auteursrecht: Tussen droom en daad' in Pieter-Jan Aerts and others (eds), *Smart contracts: een overzicht vanuit juridisch perspectief* (KU Leuven Centre for IT & IP Law, Intersentia 2020).

152 Gripsrud (n 104) 235; Aguilar, 'Distributed Ownership in Music' (n 130) 777, 780, 788, 790–91.

153 *Cf.* Daniel McClean, 'Introduction' in Daniel McClean (ed), *Artist, Authorship & Legacy: A Reader* (Ridinghouse 2019) 14; Gulinck (n 6) 314.

154 Arnold, 'Are Performers Authors?' (n 138) 469.

155 The fact that prior verbal arrangements may still lead to disputes is illustrated by e.g. the dispute between the members of rock band The Smiths, whereby drummer Mike Joyce successfully claimed 25% ownership of The Smiths' music, despite assertions of a contrary verbal agreement by band members Morrissey and Johnny Marr (*Joyce v Morrissey* [1999] EMLR 233).

156 Pavis, 'The Author-Performer Divide in Intellectual Property Law' (n 5) Vol I, 119-122; Gulinck (n 6) 63.

When sheet music leaves sufficient leeway to the performer to make free and creative choices that express their personality in the context of a performance, it may be argued that a performer may yet fulfil the requirement of originality and thus legitimately claim copyright protection in the strict sense. Moreover, even if this position were to be rejected, it is submitted that composers and performers are entitled to an analogue level of protection, unless the specifics of their situation dictate otherwise. The application of the provisions on copyright exploitation contracts set by the DSM Directive to all types of musicians therefore deserves emulation, as does the uniform interpretation of analogue legal provisions where this is feasible. This would be in tune with contemporary musical creativity, which is characterised by increasingly blurred lines between composition and performance. Moreover, this would contribute to enhanced creativity as well as inclusivity in the sphere of music copyright in particular, in line with the ambitious objectives of this *Festschrift*.

However, can we qualify the end point of this short contribution to this *Festschrift* as the unqualified 'truth'? Personally, I do not believe so. As is the case in almost all legal discourse, there are still many avenues to explore and stones left unturned. May Geertrui's *emeritaat* provide her with the time needed to keep on turning such stones and exploring new avenues that pique her interest. I am sure that she will keep on listening, methodically and meticulously digging ever deeper.

CHAPTER 25

REGULATING IP EXCLUSION/INCLUSION ON A GLOBAL SCALE

The Example of Copyright vs. AI Training*

Alexander PEUKERT
Professor of Civil, Commercial and Information Law, Goethe University Frankfurt am Main

1. INTRODUCTION

Exclusivity is the key feature of intellectual property (IP) rights in general, and patents in particular. The rightsholder has the exclusive power to either authorise or prohibit the use of the protected subject matter by third parties, thereby excluding them from the benefits of the IP.

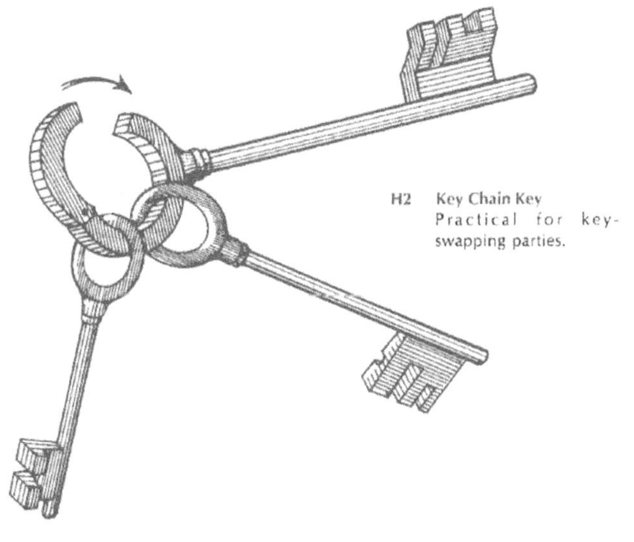

* This contribution is based in part on my article 'Copyright in the Artificial Intelligence Act – A Primer' (2024) GRUR International 497.

The concept of exclusivity in IP law has been a major theme in Geertrui Van Overwalle's oeuvre. In her 2012 article 'Individualism, Collectivism and Openness in Patent Law', she lays out how individual licensing schemes and collaborative/collective license structures such as patent pools and clearinghouses can 'moderate the effect of IP exclusivity and turn the [...] ownership regime into (semi-)open infrastructures.'[1] This observation points to the fact that patents are two-sided rights, which empower the patent holder, on the one hand, to exclude others and, on the other, to include others by authorising uses.[2] Thus, IP rights cannot be reduced to their exclusionary effect alone. They also form the basis for very flexible and granular modes of sharing, exchange, financing and risk-spreading.[3]

Contractual inclusion is not a panacea though. Rightsholders are generally free to deny authorisation of a requested use, and they can demand a royalty in an amount determined at will. In certain situations, the possibility of obtaining a license does not provide a sufficient solution to accommodate a legitimate interest to access and use protected IP.[4] Even if a rightsholder dedicates her invention to the public domain, problematic exclusionary effects may still return and prevent universal and sustainable access. In particular, follow-on innovations that build on the public domain can be re-commodified.[5]

These limits of voluntary inclusion have given rise to a rich and growing body of scholarship that looks for alternative ways to make IP law more 'inclusive'.[6] Geertrui Van Overwalle contributed a ground-breaking article to this strand of literature by inventing an 'inclusive patent', which would

1 Geertrui Van Overwalle, 'Individualism, Collectivism and Openness in Patent Law' in Jan Rosén (ed) *Individualism and Collectiveness in Intellectual Property Law* (Edward Elgar 2012), 71–116.

2 Geertrui Van Overwalle, 'Inventing Inclusive Patents. From Old to New Open Innovation' in Peter Drahos, Gustavo Ghidini and Hanns Ullrich (eds) *Kritika: Essays on Intellectual Property* (vol.1, Edward Elgar 2015), 206, 250.

3 See generally Daniel B. Kelly, 'The Right to Include' (2014) 63 Emory Law Journal 857, 922.

4 Regarding artistic sampling see German Federal Constitutional Court, Judgment of 31 May 2016, case 1 BvR 1585/13 – Metall auf Metall I, www.bverfg.de/e/rs20160531_1bvr158513en.html, accessed 20 June 2024, para. 98.

5 Van Overwalle (n 2) 232–233; Séverine Dusollier, 'The Commons as a Reverse Intellectual Property – From Exclusivity to Inclusivity' in Helena Howe and Jonathan Griffiths (eds), *Concepts of Property in Intellectual Property* (CUP 2013) 258, 273–4. For other shortcomings of voluntary inclusion through open source/access schemes see Séverine Dusollier, 'Sharing access to intellectual property through private ordering' (2007) 82 Chicago-Kent Law Review 1391, 1434; Séverine Dusollier, 'Ecologies of IP Openness' in Francois Thouvenin and others (eds), *Kreation Innovation Märkte – Creation Innovation Markets* (Springer 2024), 3–15.

6 Dusollier 2013 (n 5) 273; Séverine Dusollier, 'Inclusivity in intellectual property' in Graeme Dinwoodie (ed), *Intellectual Property and General Legal Principles* (Edward Elgar 2015), 101–118; Anna Rogler, *Inklusive Immaterialgüterrechte* (Duncker & Humblot 2020); Cristiana Sappa (ed), *Research Handbook on Intellectual Property Rights and Inclusivity* (Edward Elgar 2024).

empower its owner only to *in*clude others via open-source-type licenses, thereby establishing neutral and non-discriminatory, universal and perpetual access and use.[7]

It is accordingly important to distinguish between 'inclusion' and 'inclusivity'. While the former term describes an act of including someone or something, the latter denominates a quality of something being inclusive.[8] Studies on different modes of inclusion also tend to be descriptive, whereas the inclusivity literature expressly adopts a more forward-looking, normative perspective that criticises the exclusion of certain communities or individuals and instead favours a 'more open', inclusive regulatory framework for IP.[9]

This article builds upon the literature on inclusion/inclusivity in IP law by applying these concepts to the example of the scraping and mining of copyright-protected content for the purpose of training an artificial intelligence (AI) system or model.[10] Which mode of operation dominates in this technological area: exclusion, inclusion or even inclusivity? The example of data mining for AI training purposes is interesting because it tests the inclusion/inclusivity framework in an extreme context. First, general-purpose AI models (GPAIMs) such as Open AI's Generative Pre-Trained Transformers are typically developed and trained on 'vast amounts of text, images, videos, and other data.'[11] 'The larger a data set, the better even subtle relations in the data can be discovered' and represented in the model.[12] GPAIM providers therefore typically employ web robots to collect hundreds of millions or even billions of texts, pictures and other data by automated website scraping.[13] AI therefore represents a highly

7 Van Overwalle (n 2) 250. This proposal has been taken up and developed further by, e.g., Karen Walsh and others, 'Intellectual property rights and access in crisis' (2021) 52 International Review of Intellectual Property and Competition Law 379–416; Michael A Kock, 'Open intellectual property models for plant innovations in the context of new breeding technologies' (2021) 11(6) Agronomy 1218; Jaako Siltaloppi and Rosa Maria Ballardini, 'Promoting systemic collaboration for sustainable innovation through intellectual property rights' (2023) 11(1) Journal of Co-operative Organization and Management 100200.

8 *Cf.* www.oed.com/search/dictionary/?scope=Entries&q=inclusion; www.merriam-webster.com/dictionary/inclusivity, accessed 20 June 2024.

9 Van Overwalle (n 2) 225–226 ('"more open" is good for innovation'); Dusollier 2013 (n 5) 275 ('counter the empty promise of the public domain'); Dusollier 2015 (n 6) 118 (replace the foundational private/public dichotomy 'with a more complex and fertile mix of rights and privileges'); Cristiana Sappa, 'Introduction: Intellectual Property Rights and Inclusivity', in Sappa (n 6) 8.

10 For a definition of these terms see Regulation (EU) 2024/1689 of 13 June 2024 laying down harmonised rules on artificial intelligence and amending Regulations (Artificial Intelligence Act, in the following: EU AI Act), OJ L, 2024/1689, 12.7.2024, Article 3(1), (29) and (63).

11 Recital 105 2nd sentence EU AI Act.

12 European Commission, 'Artificial Intelligence for Europe' (Communication) COM (2018) 237 final, 15.

13 *Cf. HiQ Labs, Inc v LinkedIn Corp* 31 F.4th 1180, 1186–1187 (9th Cir 2022); Andres Guadamuz, 'A Scanner Darkly: Copyright Liability and Exceptions in Artificial Intelligence Inputs and Outputs' [2024] GRUR International 111, 115; Roman Konertz and Raoul

complex technology in the sense that its development regularly involves billions of potentially copyright-protected data, in contrast to a 'discrete' technology like an active pharmaceutical ingredient where separate technological opportunities or even final products are subject to only one or few IP rights.[14] Second, website scraping and consecutive AI training typically take place transnationally across many IP jurisdictions. Following the logic that much data is good, but more data is better, global data collections are preferable to data collections limited to a specific location or language. The territorial and cultural diversity of AI training sources also has a normative aspect. The World Economic Forum has emphasised that 'active inclusion of developing nations and diverse voices in generative AI development and governance is critical to ensure global inclusion in a future influenced by generative AI.'[15]

These features of AI training appear to call for universal and sustainable 'inclusivity' instead of a mere voluntary 'inclusion' of AI provider bots by copyright holders. As the following overview on the copyright status of AI training activities in different jurisdictions (*infra* Section 2) and emerging laws on AI safety (*infra* Section 3) demonstrates, the global regulatory landscape is, however, much too fragmented and dynamic to immediately jump to an inclusive global AI regime. For the time being, legally secure global AI training requires the voluntary cooperation between AI providers and copyright holders, and innovative techno-legal reasoning is needed on how to effectuate this inclusion (*infra* Section 4).

2. THE UNCERTAIN COPYRIGHT STATUS OF AI TRAINING

The question of whether and under what conditions copyrighted material may be reproduced for the training of commercial AI is currently a hot topic around the world and provides an example of the recurring conflict between IP exclusivity and access interests. Broadly speaking, there are three solutions

Schönhof, 'Vervielfältigungen und die Text- und Data-Mining-Schranke beim Training von (generativer) Künstlicher Intelligenz: Über die Codierung von Daten und Informationen in Künstlichen Neuronalen Netzen' [2024] Wettbewerb in Recht und Praxis 289, 290 (GPT-3 developed on the basis of 45 terabyte text, 159 gigabyte source code; Stable Diffusion on the basis of 160 million pictures).

14 Such a discrete technology is discussed in Van Overwalle (n 1) 71. On the difference between discrete and complex technologies see Alexander Peukert, 'Virtual Patent Networks and Their Network Effects' in Christine Godt and Matthias Lamping (eds) *A Critical Mind – Hanns Ullrich's Footprint in Internal Market Law, Antitrust and Intellectual Property* (Springer 2023), 303, 318–320 with further references.

15 World Economic Forum, 'Generative AI Governance: Shaping a Collective Global Future' (World Economic Forum 2024) 11. See also Maximiliano Marzetti, 'Towards a more inclusive global public domain' in Sappa (n 6) 212–228.

to solve the copyright vs. AI training conflict. At one extreme, scraping and mining of copyrighted content for AI training purposes could be considered an infringement if done without prior specific authorisation. At the other extreme, AI training could be deemed permissible without prior authorisation and payment, even if done for commercial purposes. Among the regulatory options in between these extremes, copyright law could permit reproductions for AI training under certain conditions, in particular only for non-commercial uses or on the condition of lawful access to the source or on the condition that the rightsholder has not vetoed the scraping of her content in a machine-readable manner. A brief comparative overview demonstrates that all of these solutions find support in different copyright jurisdictions.

Unauthorised reproductions for AI training purposes are likely to be found infringing under laws that do not provide a specific rule for this type of use, a text and data mining (TDM) exception, or a general 'fair use' clause.[16] A draft bill for an amendment of the Polish Copyright Act even explicitly states that the Polish TDM exception does not apply to 'the creation of generative artificial intelligence models, unless otherwise stipulated by the authorized party.'[17] The opposite outcome, namely the permissibility of commercial AI trainings, could be derived from the US 'fair use' clause,[18] and a provision in the Japanese Copyright Act legalising commercial uses of a work 'in a data analysis,' provided that this exploitation does not unreasonably prejudice the interests of the copyright owner.[19] An example for an intermediate solution can be found in Article 4 of the EU Directive 2019/790 on Copyright in the Digital Single Market (CDSMD),[20] which legalises reproductions and extractions of lawfully accessible works and other subject matter for the purposes of commercial TDM, subject to the condition that the use 'has not been expressly reserved by their

16 For Brazil see Florence G'sell, *Regulating under Uncertainty: Governance Options for Generative AI* (4 June 2024) 372–374.

17 Paul Keller, 'TDM: Poland challenges the rule of EU copyright law' (Kluwer Copyright Blog, 20 February 2024) https://copyrightblog.kluweriplaw.com/2024/02/20/tdm-poland-challenges-the-rule-of-eu-copyright-law/, accessed 8 April 2024. See also Haimo Schack, 'Auslesen von Webseiten zu KI-Trainingszwecken als Urheberrechtsverletzung de lege lata et ferenda' (2024) Neue Juristische Wochenschrift 113, 114 (Article 4 EU Directive 2019/790 does not apply to commercial AI training).

18 See 17 USC §107 and Matthew Sag, 'Fairness and Fair Use in Generative AI' (2024) 92 Fordham Law Review 1887.

19 *Cf.* Tatsuhiro Ueno, 'The Flexible Copyright Exception for "Non-Enjoyment" Purposes – Recent Amendment in Japan and Its Implication' [2021] GRUR International 145; but see Agency for Cultural Affairs, Government of Japan, 'AI and Copyright Concepts' (15 March 2024), www.bunka.go.jp/seisaku/bunkashingikai/chosakuken/hoseido/r05_07/pdf/94024201_01.pdf, www.bunka.go.jp/english/policy/copyright/pdf/94055801_01.pdf, accessed 20 June 2024 (the proviso should apply if the AI output competes with the works used for the training and if technical opt-outs are circumvented or ignored).

20 Directive (EU) 2019/790 on copyright in the digital single market (CDSMD) [2019] OJ L 130/92.

rightsholders in an appropriate manner, such as machine-readable means in the case of content made publicly available online.' It is, however, argued that this provision is not applicable to AI training activity in the first place,[21] and it is moreover unclear under which conditions 'reservations of rights' are in fact 'expressed pursuant to' paragraph 3 of this provision. Can an opt-out be expressed *ex post*[22] and with regard to a work as such and not only a particular digital representation/copy?[23] In which machine-readable manner must an Article 4(3) CDSMD reservation be articulated in order to be considered 'appropriate'?[24]

What these comparative remarks show is that the only thing certain on the global AI training market is that there is no legal certainty. A global consensus on how to regulate the conflict between copyright holders and AI providers does not exist. Solutions, including more inclusive, i.e. access-beneficial approaches, will only be worked out by the courts and national/regional legislators in the years to come.

3. EMERGING AI SAFETY LAWS

If AI training were subject only to conventional copyright laws, AI providers could still operate effectively, despite the uncertainties just described. The reason is that according to the universally accepted principle of territoriality and the corresponding rule of *lex loci protectionis*, reproductions in the course of AI model training are governed solely by the copyright law of the country in which

---

21 Schack (n 17); contra Alexander Peukert, 'Copyright in the Artificial Intelligence Act – A Primer' (2024) GRUR International 497, 503–4 with further references.

22 Péter Mezei, 'A saviour or a dead end? Reservation of rights in the age of generative AI' (2024) 46(7) European Intellectual Property Review 461, 465 ff (ex ante source-page opt-outs vs. ex post training-data opt-outs).

23 Paul Keller and Zuzanna Warso, 'Defining best practices for opting out of ML training' (Open Future, 28 September 2023), https://open-future.eu/publication/defining-best-practices-for-opting-out-of-ml-training/, accessed 27 March 2024, 12; compare also Thomas Margoni and Martin Kretschmer, 'A Deeper Look into the EU Text and Data Mining Exceptions: Harmonisation, Data Ownership, and the Future of Technology' (2022) GRUR International 685, 690 ('the content is not protected in its own right, the container is') with SACEM, 'Pour une intelligence artificielle vertueuse, transparente et équitable, la Sacem exerce son droit d'opt-out', https://societe.sacem.fr/actualites/notre-societe/pour-une-intelligence-artificielle-vertueuse-transparente-et-equitable-la-sacem-exerce-son-droit, accessed 7 April 2024 (public announcement of opt-out for the complete SACEM repertoire).

24 *Cf.* recital 18 2nd sentence CDSMD ('including metadata and terms and conditions of a website or a service'); Mezei (n 22) 465 ('doctrinal and practical minefield'); David Bomhard and Jonas Siglmüller, 'AI Act – das Trilogergebnis' (2024) Recht Digital 45, 50 with reference to the definition of 'machine-readable format' in Directive (EU) 2019/1024 on open data and the re-use of public sector information (recast) [2019] OJ L172/56, Article 2(13).

these reproductions take place.[25] Thus, if an AI provider trains a generative AI model exclusively on servers located in one country, the respective reproductions are governed solely by the copyright law of that country. As soon as courts in the country of training confirm that the reproductions are permissible, the respective models, which do not themselves contain copies of works used for the training, could be released worldwide in a copyright-compliant manner. Rightsholders could sue an AI provider only before the courts in the country where the training took place – with little prospect of success.[26] AI providers, in contrast, could select an AI-friendly copyright jurisdiction for their development activities and thereby trigger a regulatory race to the bottom.[27]

This scenario, however, already appears less likely in light of emerging AI safety laws, which will further complicate the copyright/AI issue. Numerous jurisdictions have adopted or are currently contemplating laws or regulations addressing the risks of AI for various individual and public interests.[28] China and the EU are at the forefront of these regulatory efforts. In August 2023, 'Interim Measures on the Management of Generative Artificial Intelligence Services' entered into force in China,[29] and on 1 August 2024, the EU Artificial Intelligence Act entered into force.[30]

The purpose these AI safety laws is to promote the uptake of generative and other AI while at the same time ensuring that only legally compliant and safe/trustworthy/healthy models and systems are released to the public.[31] The regulatory approach of these laws differs fundamentally from that of conventional copyright law. Like other private rights, copyrights empower each rightsholder to decide autonomously in individual cases who is permitted which use and under what conditions. In contrast, the Chinese AI Interim Measures and the EU AI Act do not follow this property logic, but rather the public law logic of legal obligations. AI safety laws are intended to protect various public interests and individual rights of AI users by imposing preventive, general and abstract

25 Regarding search engines see German Federal Court of Justice, judgment of 29 April 2010, Case I ZR 69/08 – Vorschaubilder I.

26 See generally Alexander Peukert, *Urheberrecht und verwandte Schutzrechte* (CH Beck 2023), §49 paras 15 ff; Franz Hofmann, 'Zehn Thesen zu Künstlicher Intelligenz (KI) und Urheberrecht' (2024) Wettbewerb in Recht und Praxis 11, 14; contra Schack (n 17) 113, 114, 115 (law of the country where the AI developer is domiciled).

27 Claims that AI output infringes copyright would, however, still be subject to the laws of each country in which the model is distributed.

28 For an overview of approaches see World Economic Forum (n 15).

29 生成式人工智能管理暂行办法www.cac.gov.cn/2023-07/13/c_1690898327029107.htm, accessed 20 June 2024 (hereinafter: 'Chinese AI Interim Measures"); Sara Migliorini, 'China's Interim Measures on generative AI: Origin, content and significance' (2024) 53 Computer Law & Security Review 105985, https://doi.org/10.1016/j.clsr.2024.105985, accessed 21 June 2024.

30 Article 113 EU AI Act.

31 Chinese AI Interim Measures, Article 1; Article 1(1) EU AI Act.

obligations on actors in the AI value chain.[32] They can thus be described as horizontal meta-regulation in the public interest.[33]

Nonetheless, IP rights and copyrights in particular feature prominently in the AI safety laws of China and the EU. According to Article 4(3) of the Chinese AI Interim Measures, the provision and use of generative AI shall respect IP rights. In a similarly broad manner, the EU AI Act obliges providers of GPAIMs to put in place a policy to comply with Union copyright law.[34] In addition, both laws establish copyright-related obligations for the AI training phase. Under Article 7(1) and (2) of the Chinese AI Interim Measures, training data processing activities shall only use lawful sources and not infringe IP rights.[35] The EU AI Act establishes a more concrete obligation by stipulating that providers of GPAIMs shall 'identify and comply with, including through state of the art technologies, a reservation of rights expressed pursuant to Article 4(3) of Directive (EU) 2019/790.'[36] In other words, the EU AI Act obliges AI model providers to respect (and not circumvent or otherwise ignore) machine-readable TDM opt-outs, i.e. the decision of copyright holders to not have their protected subject matter used for the training of AI models.

One of the questions raised by these meta-regulations of copyright interests concerns their territorial scope of application. For example: if an AI provider based in Japan trains a model on servers in Japan using content scraped exclusively from websites hosted in Japan, will she still have to prove that the training complies with EU copyright law when she places her model on the EU market? The answer to this question is far from clear.

On the one hand, the EU AI Act applies to all providers 'placing on the market general-purpose AI models in the Union, irrespective of whether those providers are established or located within the Union or in a third country.'[37] The universal application of EU law in the case that the internal market or legitimate interests of persons established or located in the Union are affected is already known, in particular, from competition law and from the Digital Services Act.[38] This solution corresponds to the general purpose of the AI

32 Article 4 Chinese AI Interim Measures; Article 2(1)(a) and (e) EU AI Act.

33 Alexander Peukert, 'Copyright and the meta-regulation of intermediary services and artificial intelligence' (Kluwer Copyright Blog, 13 June 2024), https://copyrightblog.kluweriplaw.com/2024/06/13/copyright-and-the-meta-regulation-of-intermediary-services-and-artificial-intelligence/, accessed 21 June 2024.

34 Article 53(1)(c) EU AI Act.

35 Migliorini (n 29).

36 Article 53(1)(c) EU AI Act; see Peukert (n 21) 503-6.

37 Article 2(1)(a) EU AI Act; similarly, see Article 2(1) Chinese AI Interim Measures ('provide the public in the People's Republic of China' with generative AI services); Migliorini (n 29).

38 *Cf.* Article 6(1) Regulation (EC) No 864/2007 on the law applicable to non-contractual obligations (Rome II) [2007] OJ L199/40; Article 2(1) Regulation (EU) 2022/2065 on a Single Market For Digital Services and amending Directive 2000/31/EC (Digital Services Act) [2022] OJ L 277/1.

Act to 'ensure a level playing field and an effective protection of rights and freedoms of individuals across the Union.'[39] It also follows logically from the fact that the AI Act does not apply during model development, as long as the model is not placed on the Union market.[40] Recital 106 EU AI Act confirms the universal scope of application of Article 53(1)(c) EU AI Act by stating that 'any' provider placing a GPAIM on the Union market should comply with the TDM opt-out obligation

> 'regardless of the jurisdiction in which the copyright-relevant acts underpinning the training of those general-purpose AI models take place. This is necessary to ensure a level playing field among providers of general-purpose AI models where no provider should be able to gain a competitive advantage in the Union market by applying lower copyright standards than those provided in the Union.'[41]

According to this maximalist interpretation, Article 53(1)(c) EU AI Act applies extraterritorially to model trainings that take place in a third country.[42] Meta-regulation overcomes the territorial limits of copyright law. The resulting rule is simple but far-reaching: if a GPAIM has not been developed in accordance with the AI Act, it may not be placed on the EU market.[43]

On the other hand, if the model training is not governed by Article 4 CDSMD in the first place (because it took place in another country), there is also no 'reservation of rights expressed pursuant to' Article 4(3) CDSMD that the GPAIM provider can identify and comply with. Even if websites hosted, for instance, in Japan use access restrictions like the robots.txt protocol, these opt-outs are not expressed 'pursuant to' Article 4(3) CDSMD because this provision is – according to the universally accepted territoriality principle – inapplicable on Japanese territory. The same conclusion follows from the fact that 'Union copyright law' only protects against uses, in particular acts of reproduction, that occur in the EU.[44] Thus, the obligation to 'put in place a policy to comply with Union copyright law' can logically only extend to actions in the EU that are subject to Union copyright law. According to this minimalist

---

[39] *Cf.* recital 21 and Article 1(1) EU AI Act.

[40] Similarly, see Article 2(3) Chinese AI Interim Measures.

[41] Recital 106 3rd and 4th sentence EU AI Act. See also European Parliament, 'Report on cultural diversity and the conditions for authors in the European music streaming market' 2023/2054(INI), para. 27; Bomhard and Siglmüller (n 24) 51.

[42] Martin Senftleben, 'AI Act and Author Remuneration – A Model for Other Regions?', http://dx.doi.org/10.2139/ssrn.4740268, accessed 5 April 2024, 13.

[43] Bomhard and Siglmüller (n 24) 46. It is beyond the scope of this article to consider whether this outcome is 'consistent with the rules applicable at international level'; *cf.* Case C-18/18 *Eva Glawischnig-Piesczek v Facebook Ireland Limited* ECLI:EU:C:2019:821, para. 51.

[44] Case C-523/10 *Wintersteiger AG v Products 4U Sondermaschinenbau GmBH* [2024] ECLI:EU:C:2012:220, para. 25; see also Viktoria Kraetzig, 'KI-Kunst als schöpferische Zerstörung' [2024] Neue Juristische Wochenschrift 697, para. 11.

reading of Article 53(1)(c) EU AI Act, copyright law defines the territorial limits of the EU AI Act.

As an intermediate solution, one could also consider making the application of Article 53(1)(c) EU AI Act dependent on whether the model provider scraped websites hosted on servers located in the EU. This approach has the benefit that it corresponds to the specific acts referred to in Article 53(1)(c) EU AI Act, namely the automatic scraping of websites by bots and the exclusion of those bots by machine-readable rights reservations.[45] It would also reflect the fact that Article 4(3) CDSMD grants rightsholders a de facto right to control access to protected content. If this content is hosted and access-controlled in the EU, it seems justified to oblige a GPAIM provider to identify and comply with the respective access controls and complementary EU laws, even if the consecutive training takes place in a third country. The problem with the *lex scraping* approach is that the location of a server hosting protected content is a more or less random point of attachment. One can imagine, however, that rightsholders who are particularly concerned about their content being used for AI training purposes (think about press publishers) will ensure that it is stored only on access-controlled servers located in the EU. AI model providers would have to comply with these machine-readable rules or risk that the European Commission restricts the availability of the model in the EU.[46]

In summary, the AI safety laws of the EU (and China) arguably extend the EU's and China's copyright laws to AI training activities taking place in a foreign country. AI providers therefore need to consider the possibility that access to the EU and/or Chinese markets may be conditional on the prior training of the AI model being in compliance with EU and/or Chinese copyright laws. In other words, AI providers can no longer be certain that training activities will not expose them to further copyright liability if the training complied with the copyright laws of the country in which the training took place. Instead, they have to align their training activities with the copyright laws of all countries in which the model will be released. Thus, AI safety laws reverse the trend that would follow from international copyright law: instead of a potential regulatory race to the bottom to attract AI development activity, AI safety laws trigger a race to the top. AI providers targeting the global market need to ensure that their training activities comply with the strictest copyright rules. Otherwise, they run the risk of being excluded from high protection markets. This effect also explains how a jurisdiction like the EU, which may not be a leader on the

---

45 *Cf. HiQ Labs, Inc v LinkedIn Corp* 31 F.4th 1180, 1187 n.3 (9th Cir 2022).

46 Article 93(1)(c) EU AI Act. Similarly, see Articles 20 and 21 Chinese AI Interim Measures. Critical regarding the effects of this policy: Margoni and Kretschmer (n 23) 700; Senftleben (n 42) 6 ff.

global AI development market,[47] can still leverage its power as an important market for the provision of AI applications to enforce and even export its normative vision of safe and trustworthy AI.

4. CONCLUSION

In summary, the global AI training market operates on the conventional IP logic of exclusion and voluntary inclusion, whereas specific regulatory measures to foster access to AI training data on inclusive terms could not be observed. Copyright holders defend their interest in the exclusion of AI training bots on the basis of conventional copyright law and emerging AI safety laws. The global public interest to train AI models on an inclusive range of data from different territorial and cultural sources so as to reflect the diversity of the source data in the AI output has not yet found its way into the copyright or AI safety laws analysed herein. Instead, copyright holders can employ technical measures to prohibit AI bots from scraping their content, and some laws, such as EU law, protect these voluntary exclusions against circumvention. And even if a jurisdiction would permit unauthorised reproductions of copyright-protected content for AI training purposes, this limitation of exclusivity would not automatically prohibit rightsholders from implementing technical measures to nevertheless exclude AI bots. No wonder we are seeing more and more partnerships announced between AI providers and copyright holders such as news publishers, allowing AI companies to access and use high-quality content for training purposes for a fee.[48]

Regarding the conceptual debate about IP inclusion/inclusivity, the example of copyright vs. AI teaches the two things. First, inherently global activities like the training and provision of AI models are subject to the traditional logic of exclusion/inclusion because this is the basic framework established by international copyright treaties such as the Berne Convention and the WIPO Copyright Treaty. In order to make this de facto global legal system more inclusive, contracting parties to the international copyright *acquis* would have to agree to replace the exclusion/inclusion dichotomy 'with a more complex and fertile mix of rights and privileges.'[49] In the case of copyright vs. AI, such a consensus does not exist. The more global the use, the harder it is to implement universal IP inclusivity through codification because one state can veto any respective change. Thus, the idea to make IP more inclusive through legislative change faces

47 *Cf.* European Commission, 'Communication from the European Commission on boosting startups and innovation in trustworthy artificial intelligence' COM (2024) 28 final.

48 See G'sell (n 16) 105 with further references.

49 Dusollier 2015 (n 6) 118.

a serious systemic problem in a global network society. More research is needed to address this issue.[50]

The second related conclusion is that efforts to improve the inclusiveness of AI training should instead focus on appropriate means to effectively express and operationalise the will of copyright holders to allow, disallow or allow only under certain conditions the training of their content. To achieve these goals in a digital world where code is law and AI training authorisations have to be fully automated,[51] conventional contract law doctrines need to be revised and possibly refined. For example, bot requests and replies expressed in robots.txt and other machine-readable files have to be translated into legally binding declarations of intent to enter into a contract.[52] In this context, the principle that exclusive rights should come with a flexible menu of options to execute the right proves true once again. The more options the rightsholder has, the more likely it is that win-win cooperation and inclusion occur.[53] And the interpretation of these transactions in view of customary online practices[54] can consider legitimate interests of users to be included in the cross-border use of the resource.[55] Accordingly, this article reconfirms the great value of contracts as a flexible 'golden oldie' of resource allocation and inclusion.[56]

---

50 The literature on IP inclusivity has not discussed cross-border uses and conflict of laws questions in detail; see also, regarding the examination of the inclusive patent, Van Overwalle (n 2) 261–2 ('Further research should look into the possible details of arbitration and mediation within the WIPO context').

51 *Cf.* Alexander Peukert, 'Copyright and the Two Cultures of Online Communication' in Paul L.C. Torremans (ed) *Intellectual Property Law and Human Rights* (4th edn, Kluwer Law International 2020) 387, 401.

52 Regarding TDM opt-outs see *supra* n 22–24. Regarding search engine and news aggregator bots see Alexander Peukert, 'Schutzbereich und Fungibilität des Presseleistungsschutzrechts' (2023) Zeitschrift für Urheber- und Medienrecht 233–247.

53 Van Overwalle (n 2) 249–50 (inclusive patent 'an additional, complementary type of patent', which expands the options of an inventor); Kelly (n 3) 922; Alexander Peukert, 'Immaterialgüterrecht, Privatautonomie und Innovation' in Stefan Grundmann and Florian Möslein (eds), *Vertragsrecht und Innovation* (Mohr Siebeck 2020) 69–98.

54 *Cf.* s 157 German Civil Code, English translation available at www.gesetze-im-internet.de/englisch_bgb/, accessed 21 June 2024.

55 Peukert (n 51) 401; German Federal Court of Justice, judgment of 29 April 2010, Case I ZR 69/08, paras 28 ff – Vorschaubilder I.

56 Robert Merges, 'Compulsory Licensing vs. the Three "Golden Oldies". Property Rights, Contracts, and Markets' [2004] Policy Analysis No 508.

KU Leuven Centre for IT & IP Law

The KU Leuven Centre for IT & IP Law Series brings together the results of research activities of the Centre for IT & IP Law. The central research themes of the series concern the legal and ethical aspects of information technology, innovation and intellectual property.

Each book in the series focuses on the essential developments in the current legal framework, necessitated by the rapid evolution of technology in various fields, such as government, media, health care, informatics, digital economy, banking, transport and culture. The research is characterised by an interdisciplinary approach, constantly cross-fertilising legal, technical, economic, ethical and socio-cultural perspectives.

Books are published in English, Dutch and/or French.

Recently published in this series:

10. Valerie VERDOODT, *Children's Rights and Commercial Communication in the Digital Era*, 2020.
11. Pieter-Jan AERTS, Frank HOOGENDIJK, Niels VANDEZANDE, *Smart contracts. Een overzicht vanuit juridisch perspectief*, 2020.
12. Griet VERHENNEMAN, *The Patient, Data Protection and Changing Healthcare Models. The impact of e-health on informed consent, anonymisation and purpose limitation*, 2021.
13. Jan DE BRUYNE and Cedric VANLEENHOVE, *AI and the Law*, second edition, 2022.
14. Ana Maria CORRÊA, *Discrimination in online platforms. A Comparative Law. Approach to Design, Intermediation and Data Challenges*, 2022.
15. Maja NIŠEVIĆ, *Profiling Through Big Data Analytics. The Interplay between the General Data Protection Regulation and Unfair Commercial Practices Directive*, 2023.
16. Niels VANDEZANDE, *Crypto-assets. The European Legal Framework*, 2023.
17. Giovana PELUSO LOPES, *Enhancing Decisions in the Courtroom. Exploring a Duty to Enhance Judicial Cognition*, 2025.
18. Charlotte DUCUING, *Data Commodification and the Law. Navigating Data Markets and Data Protection*, 2025.
19. Erik KAMENJAŠEVIĆ, *Mood Enhancement Technology. Ethical and Legal Challenges*, 2025.

www.ingramcontent.com/pod-product-compliance
Ingram Content Group UK Ltd.
Pitfield, Milton Keynes, MK11 3LW, UK
UKHW051430041026
8980IPUK00027B/918

9 781839 705953